Tudors & Stewarts: 2015

A Tudor Times Insight

By Tudor Times

Published by Tudor Times Ltd

Copyright © 2015 Tudor Times Ltd

The right of Tudor Times Ltd to be identified as the author of the work has been asserted in accordance with the Copyright, Designs and Patents Act 1988.

This ebook is copyright material and must not be copied, reproduced, transferred, distributed, leased, licensed or publicly performed or used in any way except as specifically permitted in writing by the publishers, as allowed under the terms and conditions under which it was purchased or as strictly permitted by applicable copyright law. Any unauthorised distribution or use of this text may be a direct infringement of the author's and publisher's rights, and those responsible may be liable in law accordingly.

www.tudortimes.co.uk

Tudor Times Insights

Tudor Times Insights are ebooks collating articles from our website www.tudortimes.co.uk which is a repository for a wide variety of information about the Tudor and Stewart period 1485 – 1625. There you can find material on People, Places, Daily Life, Military & Warfare, Politics & Economics and Religion. The site has a Book Review section, with author interviews and a book club. It also features comprehensive family trees, and a 'What's On' event list with information about forthcoming activities relevant to the Tudors and Stewarts.

Titles in the Series

Profiles

Katherine Parr: Henry VIII's Sixth Queen
James IV: King of Scots
Lady Margaret Pole: Countess of Salisbury
Thomas Wolsey: Henry VIII's Cardinal
Marie of Guise: Regent of Scotland
Thomas Cromwell: Henry VIII's Chief Minister
Lady Penelope Devereux: Sir Philip Sidney's Muse
James V: Scotland's Renaissance King
Lady Katherine Grey: Tudor Prisoner
Sir William Cecil: Elizabeth I's Chief Minister
Lady Margaret Douglas: Countess of Lennox
Sir James Melville: Scottish Ambassador

People

Who's Who in Wolf Hall

Politics & Economy

Field of Cloth of Gold
Succession: The Tudor Problem
The Pilgrimage of Grace and Exeter Conspiracy

Contents

Preface 8

Part 1: Katherine Parr: Henry VIII's Sixth Wife 11

    Introduction 11

    Family Tree 13

    Katherine Parr's Life Story 14

    Aspects of Katherine Parr's Life 33

Part 2: James IV: King of Scots 64

    Introduction 64

    Family Tree 65

    James IV's Life Story 66

    Aspects of James IV's Life 88

Part 3: Lady Margaret Pole: Countess of Salisbury 121

    Introduction 121

    Family Tree 122

    Lady Margaret Pole's Life Story 123

    Aspects of Lady Margaret Pole's Life 148

Part 4: Thomas Wolsey: Henry VIII's Cardinal 166

    Introduction 166

    Thomas Wolsey's Life Story 167

    Aspects of Cardinal Wolsey's Life 198

Part 5: Marie of Guise: Regent of Scotland 212

    Introduction 212

    Family Tree 213

Marie of Guise's Life Story 214

Aspects of Marie of Guise's Life 239

Part 6: Thomas Cromwell: Henry VIII's Chief Minister 256

Introduction 256

Family Tree 257

Thomas Cromwell's Life Story 258

Aspects of Thomas Cromwell's Life 292

Part 7: Lady Penelope Devereux: Sir Philip Sidney's Muse 305

Introduction 305

Family Tree 306

Lady Penelope Devereux' Life Story 307

Aspects of Lady Penelope Devereux' Life 322

Part 8: James V: Scotland's Renaissance King 337

Introduction 337

Family Tree 338

James V's Life Story 339

Aspects of James V's Life 363

Part 9: Lady Katherine Grey: Tudor Prisoner 386

Introduction 386

Family Tree 387

Lady Katherine Grey's Life Story 388

Aspects of Lady Katherine Grey's Life 421

Part 10: Sir William Cecil: Elizabeth I's Chief Minister 432

Introduction 432

Family Tree 433

Sir William Cecil's Life Story 434

Aspects of the life of Sir William Cecil, Lord Burghley 477

Part 11: Lady Margaret Douglas: Countess of Lennox 510

Introduction 510

Family Tree 511

Lady Margaret Douglas' Life Story 512

Aspects of Lady Margaret Douglas' Life 569

Part 12: Sir James Melville: Scottish Ambassador 590

Introduction 590

Family Tree 591

Sir James Melville's Life Story 592

Aspects of Sir James Melville's Life 644

General Bibliography 659

Preface

We are delighted to present Tudor Times' first collection of Tudor and Stewart profiles.

Over the course of the year we have focused on twelve personalities of the Tudor and Stewart courts. When choosing our personalities, we sought to create a balance between men and women; English and Scots; and different time periods. Our overarching aim is to give us as wide a view as possible of the political, economic and social life of the era.

During our research, we have identified several interesting themes. First, it soon becomes apparent that our perception of characters and personalities from the period is very heavily influenced by subsequent historiographical interpretations.

Occasionally, there is a glimpse of character traits that make the individual come alive: Wolsey's injunctions for his grammar school, that the boys should not be beaten too severely, and should be sent to school with warm clothes; Katherine Parr, so angry she says she could have '*bitten*' her brother-in-law; James IV showing off to his new bride by leaping into the saddle of his moving horse; Katherine Grey remembering being '*merry*' in bed with her husband.

Nevertheless, for most individuals involved there is very little first-hand written information from their own mouths or pens. So, whilst there are contemporary records, most of these have been written by somebody with their own beliefs, concerns and loyalties. These records are then interpreted by historians perhaps with the same, or perhaps with a different, perspective. Our aim throughout has been to be as factual as possible, avoiding the partisanship of particular viewpoints.

Second, we have identified that key to understanding the period is an awareness of the interrelationships of all of the ruling class, in England, Scotland and across Europe. The prevalence of second, third and even fourth marriages and the large families that people tended to have, together with the frequency with which step-siblings married each other, mean that everybody is somebody's cousin or in-law. Kinships that we would consider irrelevant – second and third cousinships, for example, were considered important. Sir William Cecil's brother-in-law was married to Katherine Grey's cousin, and the families socialised; Cromwell's son married the sister of Queen Jane Seymour; and an obscure record in the Cecil Papers suggests that Cecil's brother-in-law might also have been Sir James Melville's.

Once you become aware of these familial and network links, it becomes both harder and easier to interpret what might be going on. Easier, in that when you understand how people may have been related or connected in a family context, it comes as no surprise to discover that they remain political allies; harder in that with so many interrelationships, we cannot know why one particular loyalty was selected over another. After the Reformation, religious allegiance may have played a part, but that does not seem always to have been the case. Lady Margaret Douglas is always viewed as a committed Catholic, but her plan to marry her son, Charles, to Bess of Hardwick's daughter was hatched with her militant Puritan friend, Katherine Willoughby, Duchess of Suffolk, a life-long intimate of Cecil's and once Katherine Parr's closest friend.

A third interesting aspect of Tudor life, particularly in the latter half century, is the prevalence of spies and informers. Nearly every figure with any political influence at all seems to have had paid informers in other houses. This wasn't just the famous spy work of Cecil and Walsingham, it was also prevalent at the courts of Henry VIII and James VI. Lady Penelope Devereux and her brother, the Earl of Essex, kept themselves well-informed of James VI's movements, and entered into secret, and treasonable, correspondence with him; the Earl of Leicester probably had paid informants in Lady Margaret Douglas' home, and it was the reports of informers that brought Margaret, Countess of Salisbury and her family to their bloody ends.

We have thoroughly enjoyed putting Tudors & Stewarts 2015 together, and hope you will enjoy it too.

December 2015

The material was first published on www.tudortimes.co.uk

Part 1: Katherine Parr: Henry VIII's Sixth Wife

Introduction

Katherine Parr is often characterised as the least-well known of Henry VIII's six wives, a nurse to him in old age, and an affectionate step-mother to his children. However, that description is far from a complete portrait of a woman who married four times (once even for love), was an intellectual, a published author and Regent of England. Her influence on her step-daughter Elizabeth I was profound, and she left Elizabeth with a vigorous, and successful example of feminine strength and power in a male-dominated age.

Katherine was the first Queen of England to also be Queen of Ireland, and the first to be buried as a Protestant. She was one of the few members of the Tudor royal family to have lived and travelled outside the south-east of England and was thus a first-hand witness of the Pilgrimage of Grace, and the widening gap between the old, conservative north, and the new, radical south.

Katherine Parr seems to have been a woman of much charm and with a lovable nature. Her step-children were all very fond of her, and she had close relationships with her siblings and cousins. Henry clearly respected her intellect, and she was the first Queen to have her own works published. Her love of shoes and dancing and the pleasure she took in fine clothes and shoes endear her to a modern generation, even while her religious writings that she set so much store by, pass us by.

Part 1 contains Katherine's Life Story and additional articles about her, looking at different aspects of her life, including her relationships with her step-children, the places she lived and the religious writings that were such an important aspect of her life.

Family Tree

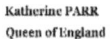

Katherine PARR
Queen of England

Sir William PARR
Born: 1434
Died: 1483

Elizabeth FITZHUGH
Lady Parr
Born: 1460 (app) in Ravensworth, Yorkshire
Died: bef 10 Jan 1507

Sir Thomas PARR
Born: 1478
Died: 11 Nov 1517 in Blackfriars, London

Sir Thomas GREEN
Born: 1461 (app)
Died: 9 Nov 1506

Joan FOGGE
Born: 1466 (app)

Maud GREEN
Lady Parr
Born: 6 Apr 1492
Marr: 1508
Died: 1 Dec 1531

Katherine PARR
Queen of England
Born: 1512 in Blackfriars, London
Died: 5 Sep 1548 in Sudeley Castle, Gloucestershire

Edward BURGH
Born: 1510 (app)
Marr: 1529 (app)
Died: bef Apr 1533

John NEVILLE
3rd Baron Latimer
Born: 17 Nov 1493
Marr: 1534 (app)
Died: 2 Mar 1543 in Charterhouse, London

Henry VIII
King of England
Born: 28 Jun 1491
Marr: 12 Jul 1543 in Hampton Court, London
Died: 28 Jan 1547 in Hampton Court, London

Sir Thomas SEYMOUR
Baron Seymour of Sudeley
Born: 1807 (app) in Wolf Hall, Wiltshire
Marr: May 1547 in Chelsea

Mary SEYMOUR
Born: 2 Sep 1548
Died: 1550 (app)

William PARR
Marquess of Northampton
Born: 14 Aug 1513

Lady Anne BOURCHIER
7th Baroness Bourchier
Born: 1517
Marr: 9 Feb 1527 in Stansted Hall, Halstead, Essex
Died: 28 Jan 1571

Elizabeth BROOKE
Marchioness of Northampton
Born: 23 Jun 1526
Died: 2 Apr 1565

Helena SNAKENBORG
Marchioness of Northampton
Born: 1549 in Sweden
Marr: 1571
Died: 10 Apr 1635 in Redlynch, Somerset

Anne PARR
Countess of Pembroke
Born: Jun 1515
Died: 20 Feb 1552

William HERBERT
1st Earl of Pembroke
Born: 1501 (app)
Marr: Feb 1536
Died: 17 Mar 1570 in Hampton Court, London

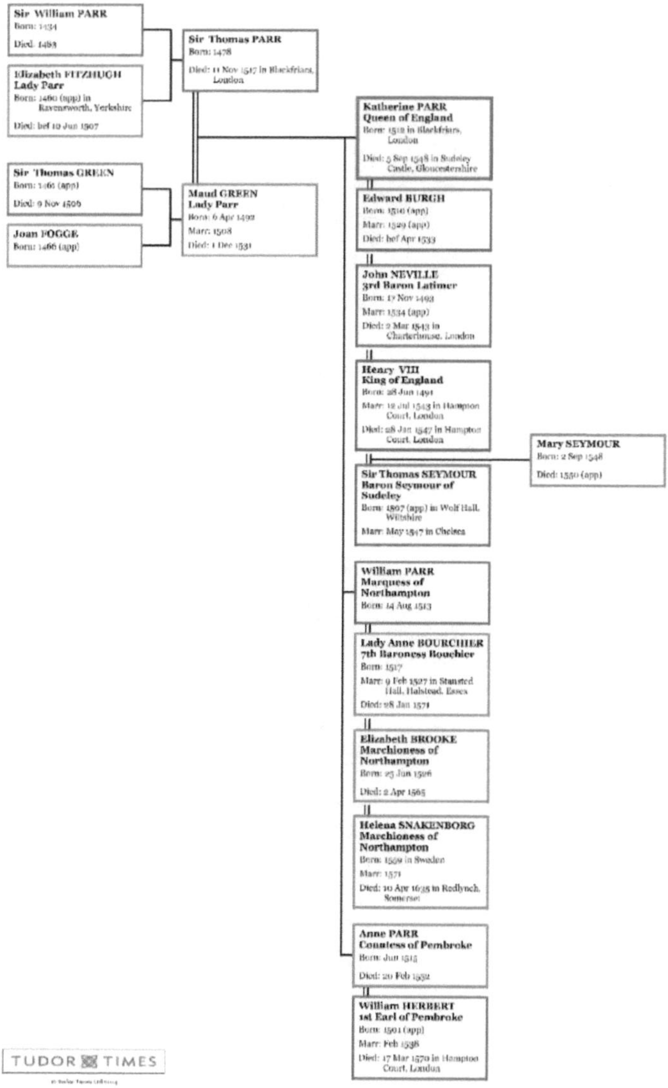

Katherine Parr's Life Story

Chapter 1: Birth and Childhood (1512 to 1529)

Katherine was born sometime in the summer of 1512 to Sir Thomas Parr and his wife Maud. At that time no-one could have foretold the child's regal destiny, for the Parrs were of that rank of Tudor courtiers known as the 'new men' - well connected, but not rich or powerful, and totally dependent on the will of the sovereign for advancement and wealth. Both Sir Thomas and Lady Parr were loyal servants of the king and queen, he as an ambassador and trusted emissary of Henry VIII, and she as one of Queen Katharine of Aragon's most favoured ladies in waiting. The baby was named Katherine, and, since it was customary to seek a godparent of the highest possible rank amongst the family's circle of acquaintance and to name the child after her, it seems likely that the Queen herself stood as young Katherine Parr's godmother.

Tradition has it that Katherine was born in the Parr family seat of Kendal Castle, but modern scholarship suggests this is unlikely - the castle had been a semi-ruin for 30 years and Sir Thomas and his wife were settled in the south in a variety of houses around the capital and court.

The most likely place for Katherine's birth was near Blackfriars in London where her father had a house and where Sir Thomas and Lady Parr were later buried at St Ann's Church.

Ladies in waiting worked on a roster, and were not always on duty, but once such a prestigious and influential position had been gained, a woman would be most unlikely to give up the chance of advancing her family by retiring. Maud would have returned to her duties as soon as possible, leaving Katherine in the care of nurses. The Parrs went on to have two further children who survived childhood, William, later Marquess of Northampton, and Anne, later Countess of Pembroke. The three Parr children were brought up together and remained close all their lives.

The chance to expand the family further was denied when Sir Thomas, who was some fourteen years older than his wife, died in 1517, leaving Maud a widow at the age of twenty-eight. Unusually, Lady Parr did not remarry but managed both her own estates (she had inherited a very handsome holding from her grandfather, Thomas Green of Green's Norton), and those of her children. Maud was supported in the upbringing of her children by her brother-in-law, Sir William Parr of Horton, and a distant Parr cousin, the influential Bishop of Durham, Cuthbert Tunstall. Katherine, only five on her father's death, clearly looked to both of these men for fatherly guidance throughout her life.

The young Parrs lived for a time with their uncle's family at Rye House in Hertfordshire, together with Sir William's daughter, Maud, later Lady Lane and another cousin Elizabeth Cheyney, later Lady Vaux. They were joined, as was customary at the time, by other young men and Lady Parr arranged the education of all of her young charges. Her establishment received high praise for educating young men in French and other languages.

There has been some dissension over the level of education Katherine received in her childhood. It was becoming fashionable amongst the upper classes to educate girls to a much higher degree than in earlier times, as Humanism began to sweep through the elite of Europe. Katherine certainly learned the standard curriculum of a well-born girl: reading, writing, French (her parents were both reputed to be particularly skilled speakers), needlework and housewifely skills. She may have learnt Latin at this period, she definitely studied it in more detail, together with Spanish and Italian, in later life. There is a charming anecdote, with no factual support whatsoever, that she objected to learning to sew after being told by a fortune teller that she was destined for greater things. She told her mother that, as her hands had been made for sceptres, she had no need for needle and thread. No doubt, if the story is true, Lady Parr soon put her straight – after all, Queen Katharine of Aragon was not too exalted to sew her husband's shirts.

Chapter 2: Mistress Burgh (1512 – 1533)

The primary secular duty of everyone in the late Middle Ages and early Tudor period was to advance the family unit, which generally meant the family as represented by the oldest son. The part of a daughter was to marry well, to increase the influence of her family. Although compatibility of age and tastes might be considered, as love following marriage was considered desirable, her parents made the choice and obedience was expected to be absolute.

Lady Parr took her duty of arranging a match for her eldest daughter seriously. She began negotiations with the Scrope family, via Lord Dacre, grandfather of the intended groom, Henry. Unfortunately, despite Lord Dacre's enthusiasm for the match, his son-in-law, Lord Scrope, seems to have been unimpressed with the notion of Katherine as a match for his son and made unreasonable demands. In particular, he demanded that he would be able to retain Katherine's dowry, should the marriage not take place because of an early death on the part of his son. Clearly Maud could not accept this, as Katherine would then have been unmarried and unprovided for, so negotiations were broken off. Perhaps Lord Scrope had had a premonition, or knew that his son was in poor health, as he did indeed die young, although the draft marriage contract had provided for Katherine to marry any surviving younger brother in such a case.

Lady Parr's next matrimonial scheme was more successful, and Katherine was married in 1529 to Edward Burgh, son of Sir Thomas Burgh of Gainsborough Hall, in Lincolnshire.

Traditional stories that she was married to an old man have their roots in a confusion between young Edward and his grandfather, Sir Edward Burgh. Katherine travelled to north Lincolnshire to live with her new in-laws, in a family that appears to have had what we might nowadays called dysfunctional elements. Old Sir Edward had been mentally disturbed, as had his younger son. The wife of young Edward's brother fell out with Sir Thomas and was thrown out of the house with her children on a charge of adultery. Sir Thomas himself appears to have dominated his family entirely. Katherine was probably glad to form her own household at Kirton-in-Lindsey after a couple of years.

The picture of Katherine as stuck in the country, far from London life and penned up with recluses and lunatics, although an appealing story, is not true. Sir Thomas was at the forefront of radical thought and a strong supporter of Henry VIII's divorce. His religious views were distinctly reformist and he became Chamberlain to Anne Boleyn and a stout resister of the Pilgrimage of Grace.

Katherine's biographers differ on whether this was the time in her life when she became influenced by religious reformers. Her father had died before religious reformation was more than a talking point at the dinner parties of intellectuals such as Sir Thomas More, and her mother remained a faithful servant of Queen Katharine up until her own death on 1531, so it is unlikely that Katherine would have picked up any evangelical ideas from her. It is difficult to believe that Katharine, only seventeen and in the home of a domineering man would not have been influenced by him, especially if he favoured her over his other daughter-in-law. Whatever Sir Thomas Burgh's influence over Katherine was, it proved short-lived, as Edward Burgh died in the spring of 1533 in his early twenties, leaving Katherine widowed before she was twenty-one.

There is more on Katherine's religious views in Chapter 10.

Chapter 3: First Widowhood (1533 to 1534)

In accordance with her marriage articles, once widowed, Katherine had a small dower to live on, drawn from three manors in the south of England. However, the idea of living alone as a 20 year old woman with no children was unthinkable. With her mother dead, her brother in the household of Henry VIII's illegitimate son, Henry Fitzroy, Duke of Richmond, and her sister in the service of Queen Anne Boleyn, there was no family home for Katherine to retreat to. Tradition has it that she went to live with her cousin, Sir Walter Strickland's, widow at Sizergh Castle in Kendal.

This lady was Katherine Neville. Her first marriage to Sir Walter Strickland had produced a son, Sir Thomas, but on widowhood, Katherine Neville married Henry Burgh, the brother of Sir Thomas Burgh of Gainsborough, and thus became the aunt-by-marriage of Katherine Parr's husband. On being widowed a second time, a year or so after Katherine Parr married into the Burgh family, Katherine Neville returned to Sizergh to live with her son. This dual connection with Katherine Parr, make a sojourn at Sizergh very plausible. Such a living arrangement for Katherine Parr would not have been seen as more than a short period of reflection following the loss of her husband. Remarriage was inevitable.

As a widow, with no living parents and a younger brother who had only just reached his majority, Katherine would have had considerable control over the choice of a second husband, though she probably took counsel from Sir William Parr and Bishop Tunstall. However it was made, the choice fell on John Neville, 3rd Baron Latimer.

Chapter 4: Lady Latimer (1534 to 1542)

If he was Katherine's own choice, Lord Latimer was perhaps a rather surprising selection. He was another of the vast Neville family (which seems to have been the most prolific family in all of English history!) and Katherine's second cousin, once removed. At the time of his marriage to Katherine, he was about 40, and had spent most of his life in the north, taking part in Henry VIII's various military jaunts against the Scots, and only visiting London to attend Parliament from time to time, which he seems to have disliked, preferring to stay on his own estates. If this reluctance to travel was known to Katherine, she must have resigned herself to the improbability of seeing much of her own family, all based in the south.

Latimer had been married twice previously and was the father of a son, John, at thirteen, some eight years younger than his new step-mother, and Margaret, aged about eleven. It is apparent that young John had all of the attributes of a sulky teenager, before the term had even been invented. Katherine's later writings about young people as *"...offended at small trifles, taking everything in evil part, grudging and murmuring against their neighbour"* sound heartfelt. Margaret, on the other hand, became devoted to her step mother, was strongly influenced by her, and stayed with Katherine until her own early death aged twenty.

Katherine settled down with her new family, mainly at Lord Latimer's seat of Snape Castle in Yorkshire. There were no children, but the couple seem to have been fond of each other, and Latimer trusted her enough to leave her well provided for in his will, and as the guardian of his daughter.

Latimer is generally described by Katherine's biographers as a man of conservative religious outlook, unlikely to have encouraged any interest in reformist thought and sympathetic to the cause of the Pilgrimage of Grace. However, Dr David Starkey points out that Latimer's daughter, Margaret, was betrothed to the son of Sir Francis Bigod, a radical reformer who was strongly influenced by Bishop Hugh Latimer, (later burned for heresy). Perhaps Lord Latimer was more torn between the old and the new than has been supposed. He had been a member of the Council in the North since 1530, and thus part of the regional government.

Katherine no doubt believed that she would live the quiet life of a country lady, perhaps occasionally visiting the court when her husband travelled south to attend Parliament, perhaps she also hoped for children of her own. But her tranquil country life was soon to be rudely shattered: not long after her marriage, the whole of the north of England was engulfed in the most wide ranging and serious rebellion of the whole Tudor period. Only the canny (not to say deceitful and treacherous) skill of Henry VIII, his chief minister, Thomas Cromwell, and the leader of the army sent against the rebels, Thomas Howard, 3rd Duke of Norfolk, prevented full scale civil war.

The Yorkshire contingent of the Pilgrimage laid siege to Snape Castle and forced Latimer to join its ranks. He took the Pilgrims' oath, later protesting to Henry that it had been under duress and that his purpose was to try to bring the rebels to a more obedient frame of mind. Nevertheless, it is certainly likely that his personal sympathies lay with the Pilgrims and his protestations of coercion do not ring entirely true. Following the disbanding of the Pilgrims, in early December 1536, Latimer returned home, but then left Katherine and his children again in the following January to plead for forgiveness in person at Court.

Unfortunately, however, this act was seen by unreconciled rebels as a betrayal, and a group of them again laid siege to Snape Castle with Katherine and her step-children inside, to try to coerce Latimer to remain true to their cause. There is no record of Katherine or young Margaret suffering any personal attack or violation during this siege, although they must have been terrified, and of course, the fate of many women in war is only too well-known. Hopefully, in the spirit of the Pilgrimage of Grace, they were not ill-treated, and nothing in Katherine's writings suggests any specific violence to her person although Snape Castle was ransacked. Latimer was at his wits' end – not knowing whether to return to Snape, or continue his journey to Doncaster in fulfilment of the King's orders. He elected to return to Snape, where he persuaded the rebels to leave, before racing, post-haste, to Pontefract to rendezvous with Norfolk.

Katherine's views on the Pilgrimage were, presumably, mixed. If she were already leaning toward religious reform, the aims of the Pilgrims would probably have seemed wrong (although Latimer's reformist friend, Sir Francis Bigod was one of the ring-leaders of the second wave of revolt). Additionally, her parents had been loyal servants of the Crown and her brother William was in the King's army, sent to overcome the rebellion. On the other hand, she had spent eight years in the more conservative counties of Lincolnshire, Westmoreland and Yorkshire, in the shadow of the great abbey of Jervaulx which was less than ten miles from Snape and with little opportunity to extend any evangelical leanings. She may also have been influenced by her husband's traditional outlook.

When the rebellion was finally vanquished, with great brutality, Latimer was lucky to escape with his life. He sent ingratiating letters to Cromwell with various presents and fortunately, a good word was put in for him by Norfolk who wrote to Cromwell that there was no evidence against Latimer and that he had acted under duress.

A plea of duress had not saved others, but Latimer was spared. He settled his family in the south, firstly at Wick in Worcestershire, then at a new manor he purchased in Stowe, Northamptonshire. This house was within a few miles of the homes of Katherine's uncle, Sir William Parr of Horton, his daughter, Lady Lane's home at Oldingbury, and the Harrowden estate, presided over by Katherine's cousin Elizabeth Cheyney, now married to Thomas, Lord Vaux. However, Latimer did not spend a lot of time with Katherine in their new home. He was called upon to continue service for the King on the Scottish border and on the numerous commissions that were set up to try and to hang the rebels from the Pilgrimage of Grace.

Following Cromwell's fall in 1542, Latimer recovered his London home near the Charterhouse (which Cromwell had taken a fancy to), and was there during the winter of 1541 - 2 to attend Parliament, accompanied by Katherine. Whether Latimer was worn out by stress, or caught an illness during his frequent journeys is unknown, but he lapsed into ill health at this point, and left Katherine a widow for the second time in March 1543.

Chapter 5: Second Widowhood

Latimer died on 2nd March 1543 at the Latimers' Charterhouse home. It is not clear whether Katherine was with him throughout his illness, or whether she had begun to spend time at Court with the Lady Mary (as Henry's elder daughter was now known, having been demoted from the rank of Princess).

Katherine's biographers differ as to whether Katherine was actually a paid, permanent member of the Princess's Privy Chamber, an 'extraordinary' member who attended the Princess from time to time, but did not need to be paid, or just a guest. There are certainly no records of payment of any salary to her, and Porter contends that this means she could not have been an official Lady in Waiting. James, on the other hand, cites a note in Henry's accounts, for clothes and material for Mary, with Katherine's request that the Henry's accounts department pay the bill as evidence that she was employed by the Princess.

Whatever her official role, Katherine was in a position to catch the eye of new suitors and she soon had two men courting her.

Katherine was very much taken, as was proven in later life, with the charms of the dashing Sir Thomas Seymour, brother of the late Queen Jane Seymour. Seymour was described as handsome with a magnificent voice, but *'somewhat empty of matter'*. The contrast with the old-fashioned Latimer, twenty years her senior and a nervous wreck following the Pilgrimage of Grace, could hardly have been greater.

However, Katherine was unable to accept Seymour's proposals, as the eye of the King had fallen upon her. Before long, he was sending gifts and visiting her daily. By summer 1543 her fate was sealed and she married Henry as his sixth wife.

It is impossible to accurately gauge Katherine's emotions – she must have been terrified, remembering the recent fates of Anne Boleyn and Katheryn Howard, yet the opportunity to be Queen, to raise her family to undreamed of heights, and perhaps, to lead Henry towards further reform of the Church cannot have failed to allure.

In any event, she had little choice. Even if her family did not press her into such an advantageous match, Henry would not take no for an answer. On 12th July, 1543, Katherine was married in the Queen's Closet at Hampton Court, and became Queen of England. At her marriage, she was attended by her sister, Anne, Lady Herbert, her step-daughter, Margaret Neville, and her two new step-daughters, the Ladies Mary and

Elizabeth, as well as Lady Margaret Douglas, Henry's niece and a great favourite at court.

Chapter 6: Queen of England (1543 to 1547)

Katherine set about the business of being Queen with great aplomb. During the first year or two, it was clear that Henry doted on her, lavishing her with gifts of clothes and jewels, (many of which had belonged to Katheryn Howard) as well as settling an impressive jointure on her. She ordered clothes and shoes (some 43 pairs in a variety of sumptuous materials), perfumes, beautiful furnishings and jewels. She had her greyhounds fed on milk and her parrot on hempseed. Porter interprets this creation of a materially beautiful setting as Katherine striving to keep Henry's physical interest in her strong, particularly the orders for herbs and flowers. James' view inclines more to the idea that the herbs and flowers were to hide the stench from Henry's diseased leg, and that the dresses and jewels were rather in the way of a consolation prize. On a more domestic note, Katherine had a spaniel, named Rig, which sported a crimson velvet collar, studded with gold.

For the first eighteen months of her marriage, Katherine rode high. She was praised on all sides, and described by a Spanish visitor to court in 1544:

'The Queen has a lively and pleasing appearance and is praised as a virtuous woman.'

Foreign ambassadors also noted her gracious behaviour towards the Lady Mary, who now lived at Court with her, and her pious and well-regulated household. They reported that the Queen loved to dance and enjoyed music and that the King continued to dote on her.

The culmination of this period of marital bliss came in 1544 when Henry appointed Katherine as Regent whilst he embarked on another of his fantastical forays into France, hoping to emulate Henry V. Katherine was to rule, aided by a Regency Council – this mark of respect shows clearly that Henry cherished and respected Katherine and relied on her loyalty and sense, as he had on that of his first Queen, thirty years before, when sallying into France.

Katherine lived up to his expectations and showed herself a competent and sensible manager – overriding the Council where she felt it was required, but carefully deferring decisions that were too contentious to Henry.

Perhaps this brief period of power went to her head a little, as, after Henry's return, she began to become more involved in questions of religion in a time when to contradict the King's views (which seem to have veered back and forth between Catholicism without the Pope, and a mildly Lutheran interpretation of Humanism) could quickly send a man to the gibbet as a Catholic traitor, or the fire as a heretic.

Henry had always enjoyed religious disputation, even before the divorce proceedings of the 1520s and he and Katherine obviously discussed religion frequently. Perhaps it was these conversations that led her to ponder matters more deeply, or perhaps the seeds of reform had been sown in her mind long before, in Lincolnshire. Whatever the basis for her interest, Katherine became more and more drawn to reform, seeming to move beyond the Lutheran position of most of the reformers at Henry's court, towards Calvinism. She wrote various prayers, including one for '*men to say on entering into battle*' that was probably created for Henry's French campaign in 1544. She also probably undertook the translation of Bishop Fisher of Rochester's *Psalms and Prayers taken out of Holy Scripture*, which translation was published in

1544 by the King's Printer. The first publication of her own creation was *Prayers or Meditations* in 1545.

Not content with translation and writing, Katherine began to involve herself more directly in religious matters, intervening in a case brought to the Court of Alderman in London, in which the widower of one of her servants was charged with voicing heretical opinions and printing radical books. Unfortunately, however, Katherine had enemies – perhaps not so much of her personally, as of her increasingly well-known move towards radical religion. The conservative faction at court, led by Stephen Gardiner, Bishop of Winchester, was determined to keep Henry from the clutches of the Protestants, and, as the king grew older, more paranoid and more irascible, the conservatives plotted to remove his dangerously reformist Queen.

The conservatives had a turn in their luck when Katherine played into their hands by arguing too vigorously with Henry in early 1546. He had obviously become tired of her growing inclination to preach to him, and, when she left the room he allegedly complained to Gardiner that '*It was a good hearing when women become such clerks and a thing much to my comfort to come in mine old days to be taught by my wife.*' Gardiner leapt at the opening and received Henry's permission to investigate Katherine for heresy. Investigations were made into some of the young men at Court who were accused of '*disputing indiscreetly of scripture*' during discussions in the Queen's household. The crux of the investigation, however, soon centred around Katherine's supposed relationship with a young Lincolnshire woman, named Anne Askew.

Anne Askew, a young woman of around twenty-five years old, and a native of Lincolnshire, was one of the most radical, and bravest, religious martyrs of the age. By 1546, she was becoming notorious for her evangelical faith, and her inability to keep quiet about it. She was interrogated in front of the Lord Mayor about her beliefs, and arraigned for heresy. Owing to lack of witnesses she was released, but, failing to be warned, Askew, would not, or could not keep her views to herself. She was again arraigned for heresy in June 1546, and now, the conservative councillors saw their chance.

The ladies of Queen Katherine's household, including Anne, Countess of Hertford, Katherine Willoughby, Duchess of Suffolk and Joan Champernowne, Lady Denny were suspected of supporting Askew, not just with money for her maintenance in gaol, which Anne admitted, but in her opinions. Gardiner and his cohorts were determined to find a link between Askew and the Queen which would send Katherine to the flames.

Shocking even to the hardened courtiers of Henry VIII, Anne was tortured on the rack, with the Lord Chancellor, Wriothesley and Sir Richard Rich personally turning the wheel to try to force her to confess to support from the Queen. Askew defied them all. She refused to incriminate anyone else and was burnt, maintaining her religion to the end.

Undaunted, Gardiner told Henry that the king was *'cherish(ing) a viper in his bosom,'* and that he would provide proof of Katherine's heresy. Henry agreed that the Queen could be arrested and investigated.

Somehow, Katherine got wind of what was in store, probably through her doctor. It seems likely that Henry himself had told the doctor, presumably with the intent that Katherine should hear about it. It was not the first time Henry had allowed action to be taken against one his favourites, only for the accusers to find themselves foiled at the last minute. Katherine reacted with predictable terror. She fell into a serious state of panic and grief. Henry, hearing of this, visited her and, having heard that she was worried that she had displeased him, comforted her. All was not complete, however. The next day, speedily recovered,

Katherine visited Henry. He began to draw her into controversial topics, but Katherine had rapidly learnt her lesson. She declined to dispute, saying that she was only a *'silly woman'* who desired to learn from her husband. On him taxing her with the suggestion that *'she was become a Doctor to instruct us and not...to be instructed or directed by us'* she immediately was all contrition and claimed that he had misunderstood. She only argued to take his thoughts off his recent illness, and so that she might learn from him.

Henry was clearly fond of Katherine, and perhaps was mindful of the idea that disposing of yet another wife would make him a laughing-stock. Perhaps too, he wanted the domestic peace and harmony that she had given to his family to continue. Whether he was really convinced that she had no heretical leanings must be a moot point. He was no fool, and had heard enough flattery in his life to recognise it. Nevertheless, he affected to believe her, declaring that they were *'perfect friends again.'*

From this time on, Katherine's political influence seems to have diminished. Henry continued to cosset her, but she was careful to play the part of the obedient wife. The change in their relationship can perhaps be seen in the contents of Henry's final Will. In his Will of 1544, Katherine was named as Regent for the Prince Edward, should Henry not return from France, but by late 1546 he had drawn up a new Will, with no mention of Katherine as Regent, but provision for a Regency Council.

During the last months of 1546 Katherine spent some time with Henry, but at Christmas of that year they parted, she to spend Christmas at Greenwich with her step-daughter Mary, and he at Hampton Court with only a few of his closest Councillors. She had never been parted from him at Christmas before, and perhaps knew that this heralded the end.

On 28th January 1547, Henry died. It is unlikely that Katherine was present during his final days.

Chapter 7: Queen Dowager (1547 to 1548)

Henry, even though he had dropped Katherine from any involvement in a Regency government, treated her well in his Will. He left her several houses, a substantial amount of money and her jewels, and ordered that she be treated as Queen for the rest of her life. Katherine retired to her home at Chelsea, accompanied by her younger step-daughter Elizabeth, and, to outward appearance, began an appropriate period of mourning. In secret, however, she was already receiving the attentions of Sir Thomas Seymour and at some time in spring of 1547, she secretly married him.

Katherine and Seymour's marriage has always been presented as a love match, that turned sour following his attentions to her step-daughter, but Porter contends that the match was not altogether without political motivation. Seymour was disgruntled at the speedy advance of his older brother, Edward Seymour, Earl of Hertford, who was now rapidly promoted to Duke of Somerset and Lord Protector by a coterie of his allies, who overthrew Henry's plans for a balanced Regency Council and arrogated the power (and a handsome round of titles and treasure) to themselves.

Sir Thomas Seymour received only the Baronetcy of Sudeley, and the continuation of his position as Lord High Admiral. Katherine, too, had her nose put out of joint by the loss of the position of Regent that she had probably expected. A marriage between the two of them, both of whom were loved by the young King, might enable them to regain influence.

The secret marriage shocked the court when it emerged – Katherine had married during a period when any pregnancy could (however unlikely) be the result of her marriage to Henry – this would throw a spanner into the succession. In particular, Lady Mary was hurt at the apparent disrespect to her father. However, Somerset and the rest of the Council had to accept a fait accompli, especially as Seymour had cleverly put the idea into young Edward VI's head that the marriage was his own idea. Edward, though, was as intelligent as all the rest of the Tudors and spotted that he had been manipulated, which did not endear the new couple to him further.

The early days of the marriage were overshadowed by an unseemly quarrel between Queen Katherine (as she was still addressed) and her new-sister-in-law, Anne Stanhope, Duchess of Somerset. Anne had been one of Katherine's inner, evangelical circle and one of her chief Ladies-in-waiting and there is no record of why they quarrelled, but now the fur really flew. The Duchess refused to carry the train of the former Queen, as she was now the wife of her husband's younger brother and wrote to her husband:

'If my Lord Admiral will teach his wife no better manners, I am she that will'.

Katherine was entitled to precedence as Queen on the strict instructions laid down in Henry's will, but was no match for the Duchess who jostled her in doorways. Katherine relieved her feelings by referring to the Duchess as *'that hell'*, (the word being the Tudor equivalent of c***) and saying she was so exasperated with the Duke that she could have *'bitten him'* when he refused to hand over her jewels.

Despite this family bickering, Katherine and Seymour were happily settled at Chelsea and Hanworth, Katherine's dower properties. The Lady Elizabeth formed part of her household, and Seymour purchased the wardship of Lady Jane Grey, on the promise to her father, Henry,

Duke of Suffolk, that he would arrange a match between Lady Jane and her cousin, the King.

Sadly, Katherine's bubble was burst. Sir Thomas began to flirt, to use no stronger term, with Lady Elizabeth, visiting her in her bedchamber whilst she was still in bed, slapping and tickling her, to the horror of her governess, Mrs Ashley. Mrs Ashley remonstrated with him, but to no avail and eventually told the Queen. Katherine dealt with the matter by joining in, but the damage was done, and eventually, in the spring of 1548 Katherine felt compelled to send Lady Elizabeth away, to protect the girl's reputation. Katherine was now pregnant for the first time (so far as is known). She and Sir Thomas were thrilled beyond measure, and the level of affection in their letters suggests that the tricky incident with Lady Elizabeth was forgiven and forgotten.

Seymour spent vast sums on refurbishing his new castle of Sudeley for the birth of his heir (obviously a boy – all Tudor men thought their children would be male) and the couple moved there in June of 1548, accompanied by the young Jane Grey. Katherine spent the sunny days in her garden, with Jane by her side, further pleased by being reconciled with Lady Mary and on good terms with Lady Elizabeth again. There are no reports of any illness and when she went into labour in late August of 1548 there was no reason to expect anything but a happy outcome. Unfortunately, however, after the birth of a girl, named Mary, she contracted puerperal fever, and died on 5th September 1548. In her delirium she accused Seymour of mistreating her, but when she regained lucidity she bequeathed him all her possessions *wishing them a thousand times more*.

As was the custom, Seymour did not attend the funeral. The chief mourner was Lady Jane Grey, who followed the sad procession the 100 yards or so from the Queen's privy chamber to the Church. The service was the first Protestant burial of an English Queen – no prayers for the dead, the candles and offerings only for the honour of the late Queen, and with no other significance, the psalms and Te Deum in English.

She lies still under the stones of the church, with an alabaster monument placed over her in the nineteenth century.

Her little daughter, Mary, was orphaned in 1549 when Sir Thomas was executed. She was last heard of in the household of Katherine's friend, Katherine Willoughby, Duchess of Suffolk in 1550 and it seems probable that she died not long after.

Aspects of Katherine Parr's Life

Chapter 8: What did Katherine look like?

There are no detailed descriptions of Katherine in terms of height, hair, figure, eye colour and so on, but we are lucky that she was the most frequently painted of Henry's queens and there are various references to her in sources that, whilst they don't describe her in detail, give an impression of her looks and personality.

It seems reasonable to suppose that Katherine was attractive – Henry VIII was very susceptible to physical appearance, as his rejection of Anne of Cleves because he didn't fancy her, shows. However, she is not referred to as beautiful by any of the ambassadors sending reports, and, in fact, Anne of Cleves is reputed to have complained that Katherine was less good-looking that herself.

Perhaps her attraction lay in her vivacity and joie de vivre. She seems to have a been a lively woman, fond of dancing, music and general merrymaking with a taste for the sensual pleasures in life – fine clothes, magnificent jewellery and numerous pairs of shoes. Her favourite colours for clothes were crimson, black and violet. All royal colours, designed to impress onlookers as well as frame her own charms.

Her height has been variously described by her biographers as 5 foot 4 inches, or 5 foot 10 inches, based on the length of her coffin. The shorter height seems more likely, as 5 foot 10 inches would be exceptional for a woman at that time. Tall women, such as Marie de Guise and her daughter, Mary Queen of Scots, were remarked on. Katherine's hair, a lock of which is preserved at Sudeley Castle, appears to be of a dark blonde hue, and so far as can be told from the paintings, her eyes were hazel or brown.

The best-known, authenticated portrait is the one by Master William Scrots, now in the National Portrait Gallery. It was probably painted in 1546 and shows the Queen wearing a very fashionable bonnet, rather than the traditional, stiff hood headdress and a dress with one of the new upstanding medici collars that were coming into fashion in the late 1540s. It also shows Katherine in her favourite crimson. Another portrait, probably by Master John, which used to be named as Lady Jane Grey, has now been shown definitively to be of Katherine. It is full length, and shows the Queen in a square-cut, embroidered gown with long, furred sleeves and a beautiful crown brooch. A similar portrait, by Lucas Herenbout, now at Melton Constable, shows another equally ornate dress with a similar brooch.

Katherine was described in 1544 by de Gante, the Secretary to the Duke of Najera:

'She is of a lively and pleasing appearance and is praised as a virtuous woman. She was dressed in a robe of cloth of gold and a petticoat of brocade with sleeves lined with crimson satin and trimmed with three-piled crimson velvet. Her train was more than two yards long. Suspended from her neck were two crosses, and a jewel of very rich diamonds and in her head-dress were many and beautiful ones. Her girdle was of gold with large pendants.'

Chapter 9: Katherine Parr as Step-mother

Katherine Parr's role as a step-mother has always been seen as central to her life and her success as Queen. It seems clear from the records and extant correspondence that she had a warm relationship with all of her five step-children, with the possible exception of Lord Latimer's son, John. Novels occasionally assert that she had step-children older than herself, but this is presumably based on the now discredited theory that her first husband was Sir Edward Burgh the elder, rather than his grandson of the same name.

Katherine's first experience of a maternal role would have been in 1534 when she travelled to Snape Castle as the wife of John Neville, 3rd Baron Latimer. Latimer had two children from his first marriage, John, later 4th Baron, and Margaret Neville. John was around 14 at the time of his father's third marriage and Margaret perhaps five years younger. They had already had a short experience of a step-mother, but Latimer's second wife died within two years of marriage, leaving no children of her own.

In an era when the vast majority of people were married at least twice, their father's remarriage cannot have surprised the Neville children. Katherine Parr, as a member of an important gentry family in the north, and a kinswoman, was an unexceptionable choice, and it appears that she took an immediate and active interest in the education of Margaret, winning a love and respect from the young girl that would last all of Margaret's short life.

It seems to have been rather different with John. His later history suggests that he was a violent man, and Katherine later wrote 'Younglings...are offended at small trifles, taking everything in evil part, grudging and murmuring against their neighbour...' which strongly suggests experience of a sulky teenager.

Nevertheless, whatever the difficulties of his adolescence, young John's wife, Lucy Somerset, was later appointed as one of Katherine's ladies-in-waiting.

The most terrifying incident in the lives of Katherine, Margaret and young John would have been the attack on Snape by the rebels in 1537.

The three of them were alone and unprotected by Lord Latimer who had been commanded to London to explain himself to the King and Council and beg for pardon for his part in the Pilgrimage of Grace. Latimer wrote to his friend Norfolk, lamenting his inability to protect his family as he was ordered to Doncaster. In the event, he ignored his immediate orders and raced towards Snape to effect a rescue. By the time of his arrival, however, the rebels had left. Latimer departed again, to head for Pontefract, leaving Katherine and the children behind.

As was common at the time, Margaret had been betrothed young, to Ralph Bigod, a son of Sir Francis Bigod. Unfortunately, Sir Francis, although a reformer, was one of the ring leaders of a second wave of revolt after which it was unthinkable that Latimer, who was desperately trying to shore up relations with the King, would let the match go forward. We cannot know what Margaret's reactions were - she may have been sorry that her match to a man she knew had been broken off, perhaps to be replaced by a wedding to a complete stranger. Whatever her feelings, we can safely assume that Katherine was her support.

During the first years of queenship, Katherine was attended by Margaret Neville, but sadly the girl died in 1545, probably aged no more than twenty. In her will, she speaks her regard of Katherine, and the will itself, which strongly reflects the reformed religion, suggests that Katherine had influenced her religious views markedly.

Katherine's role as stepmother to Henry VIII's children was one of the most important of her life, and her relationship with Elizabeth, in particular, had a lasting effect on England.

There is no evidence as to whether Katherine and the Lady Mary were childhood friends, as is often stated in novels. Maud Parr had remained in Queen Katharine's household until 1531 and it is probably safe to assume that the two girls had at least met, but the extent of their acquaintanceship was likely to have been slight, especially give the four year age gap. Lady Mary had spent the years 1525-8 in Ludlow as *de facto*, if not *de jure*, Princess of Wales, and Katherine left the south in 1528 to be married. Nevertheless from early 1542 Lady Latimer appears to have been closely connected with the Lady Mary's household. Dr James states that Katherine was a member of the Princess' privy chamber, but Porter points out that there is no evidence of payment to Katherine in the princess' accounts.

Lady Mary was, of course, well acquainted with Katherine's siblings. Anne Parr had received gifts from her, and was mentioned as in attendance on her in 1543 and this may be how the women became reacquainted. Whenever it happened, it is clear that a warm friendship sprang up between the two women.

Mary was present at the marriage of her father to Katherine and appears to have spent a good deal of time with the new queen. In particular, they shared intellectual interests. Katherine promoted the translation of Erasmus' *Paraphrases of the Gospels* from Latin in to English, and persuaded Mary, as a very accomplished Latinist, to undertake the translation of St John. In a letter to Mary, regarding the work's publication, she encouraged the Princess to let the work go forward under her own name:

'You will, in my opinion, do a real injury, if you refuse to let it go down to posterity under the auspices of your own name, since you have undertaken so much labour in accurately translating it...'

These intellectual interests were also the basis of relationships with her other two new stepchildren. Prince Edward was not yet six when Katherine became his stepmother. Up until this point his elder sister had been the closest to a mother he had known, but even allowing for the epistolary style that seems ludicrously overblown to modern readers, it appears from the letters between Katherine and Edward that a genuine love sprang up. She wrote to him (when he was aged 8!)

'I affectionately and thoughtfully consider with what great love you attend both me, your mother, and scholarship, at the same time.'

He wrote to her in similar style.

'Most honourable and entirely beloved mother, I have me most humbly recommended to your grace with like thanks both that your grace did accept so gently my simple and rude letters, ...[and that you] give me so much comfort and encouragement to go forward..'

The level of influence Katherine had over the selection of tutors for the young Prince is uncertain. Certainly, all his tutors were men who reflected her religious views (which were decidedly more progressive than Henry's) but it is difficult to imagine that the King would have left the choice to her entirely. It may be, of course, that the tutors kept their more radical views under wraps during Henry's reign, and that we are looking at them with the benefit of hindsight.

Elizabeth too, was charmed by her new step-mother, and, it appears, strongly influenced by her (although it is interesting to note that later, when choosing a new tutor, she rejected Katherine's choice). Her letters are also deeply humble and flattering, and the effort she put in to translating her step-mother's writings into several languages, and embroidering a beautiful book cover for a presentation copy of her work, suggest genuine admiration.

But following Henry's death, Katherine's relationships with her royal step-children began to go awry. She and Seymour undoubtedly traded on young Edward's affection for them to manipulate him into supporting their marriage. Of course, no-one is perfect and it is understandable that

Katherine would use every weapon she had to secure personal happiness following years of doing her duty, but it seems to have wounded Edward.

Mary, too, was hurt and offended by Katherine's hasty remarriage, feeling it showed a distinct lack of respect for her late father. So far as is known, the ladies did not meet again, although that they were reconciled is demonstrated by a letter written in summer of 1548 when Mary asks about Katherine's *'great belly'* and hopes to see her soon.

It is interesting to speculate on whether, had Katherine lived, she might have tempered Mary's zeal for reinstatement of the religious world of her childhood. It seems unlikely - many of Mary's friends and intimates were reformers but although they were never persecuted themselves, there is nothing to indicate they influenced her.

Katherine's relationship with Elizabeth, too, was irrevocably altered by her remarriage. Prior to Henry's death, Elizabeth spent time with her siblings at Hertford Castle or Hatfield; following it, she moved into the household of her step-mother. It is not clear why this was felt necessary: if the girl did not need supervision directly by her step-mother before Henry's death, then why after? One can only assume that it was the choice of both of them. For Elizabeth, the pleasure of a maternal relationship must have been great. And so, Elizabeth joined the Dowager Queen at Chelsea Manor, and then Hanworth, and all seemed set fair for a happy family life with her step-mother and new step-father, Sir Thomas Seymour, who secretly married the Dowager Queen in Spring of 1547.

However, into this paradise crept the serpent of temptation. Seymour, who should have known better, took to flirting, and, in its kindest light, indulging in excessively physical horse-play with the young princess. She was obviously thrilled, and, not the first adolescent girl to have a crush on an older man, responded, to the point where her governess, Katherine Ashley, felt obliged to remonstrate both with her and Seymour, and eventually, felt bound to inform the Queen.

Katherine must have been shattered. The match with Seymour had undoubtedly been based on sincere affection and the revelation that he was not only flirting behind her back, but that he was endangering the reputation of the King's sister – potentially a treasonable offence - must have hit her hard.

Initially, Katherine seems to have concluded that, by joining in the fun and games, it would take the heat and the sexual element out of the relationship between Seymour and Elizabeth, but it was too late. In due course, Katherine felt constrained to send Elizabeth to the house of Sir Anthony and Lady Denny, at Cheshunt, whilst she, herself, retired to Sudeley to await the birth of her child. Elizabeth, obviously shaken by events, quickly understood that her step-mother had done what was best, and wrote her a genuine letter of thanks.

During the last summer of her life, Katherine corresponded with both Mary and Elizabeth, and perhaps also with Edward, although no letters remain.

Despite the upheavals caused by her final marriage, the step-daughters who had loved and respected her, both wished her well and spoke of their affection for her.

There is no record of the responses of her step-children to Katherine's death. One can imagine Edward, only eleven, bravely bearing the demise of his dear '*mother*', and eliminating all public show of feeling, as he was later to do for the executions of his uncles.

For Mary, who had lost so many people she had loved, it was the passing of a dear friend, but for Elizabeth it was the loss of the only maternal affection she had ever known (although her governess, Katherine Ashley was very dear to her as well).

There is no evidence as to Elizabeth's immediate reactions, but surely her own success as Queen must owe something to the example set by Katherine and is Katherine Parr's greatest legacy.

Chapter 10: Katherine Parr's Spiritual Development and Religious Writings

Katherine Parr was the first Queen of England to publish a book. She was not the first royal woman to appear in print – her grandmother-in-law, Lady Margaret Beaufort, had translated and published *'The Mirror of Gold to the Sinful Soul'* in 1507. Queen Marguerite of Navarre, whose reforming influence on the young Anne Boleyn was so profound, had published a second translation of the same work into French, from its original Latin, in 1531.

Religious self-examination was all the rage amongst the educated women of the early sixteenth century, and Katherine was a worthy heir to the fashion. Nevertheless, it is apparent from her writings that her faith was a truly heart-felt matter. She seems to have undergone some sort of personal conversion experience which she wrote about - at great length and in language that to modern ears is excruciatingly self-abasing.

In her childhood, Katherine would have been brought up to practise the Catholic faith, as it had been understood for over fifteen hundred years in England. Emphasis was on obedience to the Church's teachings, the need for personal effort to achieve salvation and, at the heart of it all, the miracle of the Mass, where the bread and wine were actually (although not visibly) transmuted into the body and blood of Christ. However, with the growth of printing, and the increasing availability of ancient texts to scholars, many of the Church's teachings were being questioned. In particular, the great minds of the late fifteenth and early sixteenth century were exercised by the competing doctrines of Free Will and Justification by Faith Alone and their place in salvation. It is very likely that during Katherine's education, she would have heard discussion and debate on the topic – many people who continued to see themselves as good Catholics held opposing views.

Tangled up in the theological debate, were the more political issues of the power and corruption of the Church, which was also being questioned in the 1520s. No intelligent person could fail to be aware of the issues and, when Katherine was first married and went to live in Lincolnshire, she came under the influence of her father-in-law, Sir Thomas Burgh, who was a vocal supporter of Church reform. Whether she had any more than an intellectual interest in the issues at this point is unknown but it seems unlikely. She later wrote that *'[God] called me diversely, but, through frorwardness* [deliberate contrariness] *I would not answer.'*

Katherine's second marriage was to Lord Latimer, who was considered to be a religious conservative, and maintained a highly decorated chapel at Snape Castle, full of the images and relics that the reformers disliked. During this period, Katherine attended Mass several times a day. Nevertheless, the picture of the religious views surrounding her is not straightforward – Latimer betrothed his daughter to the son of Sir Francis Bigod, a well-known reformer. Katherine's uncle, Sir William Parr of Horton, her brother, William Parr, later Marquis of Northampton, and her sister, Anne, later Countess of Pembroke, all seem to have embraced reform – although the level of genuine religious conviction is hard to gauge.

By the early 1540s an unbridgeable gulf had opened up between the evangelicals of the early years who wanted reform of abuses within the Church, and the new Protestants, as they were increasingly called, who questioned the very foundation of Catholic faith. The Protestants could not accept that that the bread and wine actually changed into the body and blood of Christ during the Mass. This was not something that anyone was interested in compromising over, in a time when people believed there was one truth (their own). The increasing acrimony between the sides created two parties at Henry's court. What Katherine's exact position on this point of doctrine was in 1543 when she became Queen is uncertain, but she was certainly known as a follower of the reforming group. A member of her Privy Chamber wrote:

'Her piety cherishes the religion....introduced, not without great labour, into the palace.'

Henry VIII had always enjoyed theological discussion and research, even writing his own book, back in 1519 – '*Assertio Septem Sacrementorum Adversus Martinem Lutherum*'. It may be that a desire to develop an intellectual relationship with Henry and be good company was, as she implied later when he complained of her trying to lecture him, her initial reason for getting involved in theological study. It is realistic to suppose that she wanted to develop a bond with him that was not primarily physical. To begin with, Henry seems to have encouraged Katherine's interest in theology - until she began to contradict him too freely.

For by delving into these areas, her own emotional response to religion had been stimulated and was leading her to embrace the more personal relationship with God espoused by the Protestants.

One of the fundamental desires of the reformers, from the early evangelicals to the radical Protestants, had been for the Word of God to be available in English, and it is apparent from all of Katherine's activities, both as writer and patron, that this was a mission dear to her heart.

In April 1544, an English translation of Bishop Fisher of Rochester's Latin '*Prayers or Psalms taken out of Holy Scripture*' appeared. Despite appearing anonymously, this translation is attributed to Katherine by one of her biographers, Dr. Susan James, on three grounds in particular – the similarity of some of the wording to that used in Katherine's own later work; its regular publication with works she definitely wrote; and the bills for copies of books that might be this one. Another biographer, Dr Linda Porter, is a little more equivocal in attribution, but adduces a convincing reason for why it might have been done anonymously: Fisher had been executed by Henry VIII, causing shockwaves at home and abroad, so he was probably not a man to talk about too frequently or be seen emulating. Fisher was, of course, a martyr for the supremacy of the Catholic Church, and, if Katherine were his translator, that would tend to suggest a moderate theological position during the translation period.

From, perhaps, a personal translation, Katherine went on to be the moving spirit behind the publication of the English translation of Erasmus' *Paraphrases upon the New Testament*. The editor was Nicholas Udall – famous alike for his scholarship and his brutal sexual abuse of his pupils at Eton College. The translators were various – Katherine may have worked on the St Matthew personally, but her main contribution was in persuading well-known Latinists to take a share, including her step-daughter, the Lady Mary. The book went through numerous editions in the sixteenth century, from its initial publication in January 1548.

Katherine's first publication under her own name was on 6th November 1545 when a work entitled *'Prayers and Meditations'* appeared, a fairly anodyne collection of snippets from 'holy works'. It included the fifteenth century *'Imitation of Christ'* by Thomas a Kempis which had been a standard work of piety for the secular reader since the 1420s. The collection also included a prayer written for men to say before battle – directed at the army accompanying Henry VIII into France.

This work was then translated by Katherine's step-daughter, the Lady Elizabeth, aged thirteen, into Latin, French and Italian, and, encased in a beautifully embroidered cover of her own work, presented as a New Year gift to Elizabeth's father, Henry VIII.

Katherine's next and most ambitious personal project was the *'Lamentations of a Sinner'*. In the course of twelve prolix chapters with titles such as *'A Christian bewailing the miserable ignorance and blindness of men'*, we follow a sincere retelling of her journey from being mired in *'foul, wicked, perverse and crooked ways'* via utter rejection of *'the Bishop of Rome [as] a persecutor of the gospel, and grace, a setter forth of all superstition and counterfeit holiness'* to the sunlit uplands of the doctrine of Justification by Faith *'...we be justified by the faith in Christ, and not by the deeds of the law.'*

These, and later passages that seem to go beyond Lutheranism and dabble with the even more radical Calvinism that was emanating from Geneva, were well beyond anything that Henry VIII would have countenanced, although he would have loved the paragraphs hailing him as a new Moses and praising his role in *'[delivering] us out of captivity and bondage...'*. The book was not published in Henry's lifetime, instead emerging in late 1547.

By that time, Katherine's enthusiasm for writing seems to have waned. Her biographers imply that her religious enthusiasm emanated from repressed sexuality that needed a channel for expression during her first three marriages, but that could blossom happily in her final marriage to Sir Thomas Seymour. However, even if such a Freudian analysis is correct, it cannot detract from the genuine faith of the Queen that appears in her work and her dedication to the cause of setting forth religion in the vernacular for all people to read.

Chapter 11: Following the Footsteps of Katherine Parr

Alone amongst Henry's wives, Katherine Parr had an experience of life that was not completely submerged in Court circles. Her upbringing and life before her marriage to Henry, at the age of about thirty-one, was spent in the manors and castles of the gentry families of the Midlands and North of England. Whilst one could never say she knew what "ordinary" life was like, she was very much closer to it than any of Henry's other Queens, having been mistress of a country household, as well as of a great castle. She would have practised the housewifely skills of domestic economy, management of servants, preparation and administration of medicine and supervision of an estate that were the province of the wives and daughters of the gentry class. Thus, when we look at the places in which she lived, we can feel a faint breathe of daily life, which is denied us when we only look at palaces.

It is likely that Katherine was born at her parents' home in Blackfriars, although there is a slight possibility that the event took place at Fenel's Grove, near Great Kimble in Aylesbury, which her parents had possession of during the year of her birth. Blackfriars certainly seems to have been the place her parents considered as home, as they both chose to be buried in the Church of the Dominicans there. When the monasteries were dissolved the church, too, disappeared, to be replaced by St Ann's Blackfriars which, in turn, burnt down during the Great Fire. The Churchyard of St Ann's Blackfriars is now a garden, and is as close as we can get to the Parrs' tomb.

It is possible, although not likely, that Katherine visited the Court whilst her mother was in attendance on the Queen. In the early years of Henry's reign, he and Katharine of Aragon spent the majority of their time at Greenwich, Westminster, and the new palace built at Beaulieu. Hampton Court, of course, was not yet a royal residence.

After the death of Katherine's father, Sir Thomas Parr, in 1517 the young Parrs moved to live at Rye House, near Hoddesdon in Hertfordshire, in the household of their uncle, Sir William Parr of Horton, and his wife, Mary Salisbury. The Gatehouse, giving a clue to the red brick construction, remains and can be visited on a few days each year. The Parrs of Horton had four daughters of a similar age to the Parr siblings, and there were a number of other cousins and young men in the household, under the supervision of Katherine's mother, Maud, Lady Parr.

At the age of about sixteen, Katherine set out on a long journey to the northern part of Lincolnshire, to marry Edward Burgh. The journey, of some 135 miles would probably have taken around 10 days to two weeks, depending on the route taken, and the time of year. The obvious route, which we can follow today is up the Great North Road (the A1). A detour may have been made into Northamptonshire to visit other family members. There was a whole cluster of cousins, the Vaux, the Cheyneys and the Throckmortons, settled in that county, not far from the road north.

On reaching Newark, the party would have had the choice of turning off the Great North Road to visit Lincoln, which, with its Cathedral and Castle was a major town. Given that the itinerary followed by Henry VIII on his Northern Progress in the 1540s stopped at Lincoln, before proceeding to Gainsborough, we may infer that that is the route used at the time. Otherwise, Katherine's party would have continued north, turning off the Great North Road, as the modern traveller does, onto what is now the A1133 to Gainsborough.

When Katherine arrived in Gainsborough she is likely to have felt quite at home in the delightful modern manor house, Gainsborough Hall, that had been built by her new husband's great-grandfather, some sixty years earlier. For the modern visitor, the area is quite built up, but in the 1520s the whole area was still heavily forested.

Katherine lived for some time with her in-laws, but then her husband, Edward, was granted the Stewardship of the Manor of the Soke of Kirton-in-Lindsey. It was granted in survivorship (ie both parties retained the position until the death of the second) with his father Sir Thomas Burgh. Katherine and Edward would have travelled the twenty or so miles to the north-east of Gainsborough to take up residence. Today, there is a direct road between Gainsborough and Kirton, but even now it winds and twists, and five hundred years ago it was probably a difficult journey. Katherine may have been relieved that her in-laws could not visit too easily.

Kirton, set on an escarpment, overlooks the Lincolnshire Wolds. There is no trace of the house she would have lived in, the only current building of the time being the Church of St Andrew, where, no doubt, she and Edward would have worshipped.

On her widowhood in 1533, after four years in Lincolnshire, it is likely that Katherine journeyed across the Pennines to Sizergh Castle, Kendal to stay with her relative, Katherine Neville, Lady Strickland.

This would have been an arduous journey – further up the Great North Road, then either west to the south of the Pennines on what is now the A65, or north to Richmond, and then across on the route that is now the A66, or possibly even over the fells on what is now the A684. If she took this latter route (which is highly recommended as the views are fabulous) then she might have broken her journey at Snape Castle, home of her distant cousin, Sir John Neville, 3rd Baron Latimer.

Katherine's time at Sizergh would have been her first sojourn in a castle – dating from the 1300s it is significantly older than her previous homes. Her life there is likely to have encompassed visits to Kendal, the ancestral home of her father, although falling into disrepair by the 1530s. She may well have worshipped in the Church of the Holy Trinity in Kendal, where her grandfather's tomb can still be seen.

Whether Katherine was already acquainted with Lord Latimer is unknown, however at some point in 1533 she agreed to marry him and travelled the 50 miles back across the Pennines to Snape Castle.

Leaving Kendal for Snape nowadays, your Sat Nav will try to take you via the motorway, but overrule it and take the A684 (assuming that the weather is not icey in which case the road should be avoided as it is narrow and steep.) The route is a marvellous trek up and down the Lakeland fells and into the North York moors. If Lord Latimer came courting the widowed Mistress Burgh in 1533, this is the route he would have taken, and this is the route his bride would have ridden as she said goodbye to Lady Strickland and headed east to her new home.

Around 10 miles West of the Great North road, now the A1, but following the old Roman route and the main artery between York and London, Katherine would have turned off towards Snape, and just as it does today, the road passed Jervaulx Abbey, the lordship of which had passed to her father when he inherited his mother's moiety of the Barony of FitzHugh of Ravensworth. Whether Katherine would have wanted to visit the Abbey may depend on how advanced her religious views had become. In 1533, although some of the smaller houses had been closed by Cardinal Wolsey because of lack of numbers, there was no breath of the massive programme of dissolution that would overwhelm the country, changing it more in the following five years than in the previous five hundred.

Arriving at Snape, she would have found a new home very much grander than her old manor at Kirton-in-Lindsey, or even Gainsborough Hall. The fifteenth century castle had been built as one of the great Neville strongholds and commanded a large area of countryside.

Nowadays, Snape, and its attendant villages of Snape and Wells, seem very isolated, but in Katherine's day the route between Ripon and Jervaulx was well travelled, and there were many castles and manors in the surrounding area lived in by her various cousins – the Scrope castle of Bolton (which might have been her home had her mother's original marriage plans for her to the Scrope heir been fulfilled), and the royal castles of Sheriff Hutton and Middleham are all within a day's ride.

The church associated with the Latimers - St Michael and All Angels, Well - is less than three miles away, and would have been patronised by Katherine and her new Neville family.

However, her country life was rudely interrupted by the Pilgrimage of Grace. Following the suppression of the rebellion, and the reluctant pardoning of her husband for his part in it, according to her biographer, Katherine and Latimer moved south, first to Wick Manor in Worcestershire, and then to the bosom of her family in Northamptonshire.

From Snape to Wick is not an easy journey, even now. The easiest route is to rejoin the A1 at Kirklingon and then follow it south to Doncaster where you turn west onto the M18 to link up with the M1 southbound. The M1 will take you to the A42, and thence to the M42 and M5 south to Worcestershire. Exiting the M5 onto the A449, follow the road through the lovely market town of Pershore (famous for its plums!).

Pershore and its environs grew up around the great Abbey Church of the Holy Cross, which, when the Latimers arrived had not yet been dissolved.

Wick is on the eastern edge of Pershore, down a signposted side road. In fact, the manor of Wick belonged to Latimer's brother, William, in right of his wife, so the trip may have been more in the nature of a family visit, and perhaps a welcome oasis of tranquillity, as Worcestershire had played no part in the Pilgrimage of Grace.

There are many traces of mediaeval and Tudor buildings incorporated into current houses in the village, but the masterpiece is the one known as Wick Manor, which at first glance is the quintessence of a Tudor Manor House, but in fact it was almost completely rebuilt in the early twentieth century.

The Latimers did not remain long in Wick. According to his biographers, Lord Latimer then purchased a property called Stowe Manor in Northamptonshire, in the village of Church Stowe (also known as Stowe IX Churches). However, this property had previously belonged to his great-grandmother, Eleanor Beauchamp, and passed to his great-aunt, Katherine Neville, Lady Dudley. It seems likely that the reversion of the estate had fallen to Lord Latimer, rather than him needing to buy it. The remains of the Tudor Manor are incorporated in a more modern building. Katherine was granted a life interest in Stowe Manor on Latimer's death. Church Stowe is located on the A5, about 10 miles west of Northampton.

In addition, on consulting maps, and the History of Northamptonshire, it appears that Latimer had another manor at Burton Latimer, just south of Kettering, which is within 5 miles of the manors of Orlingbury and Harrowden, inhabited by Katherine's cousins, Maud Parr, Lady Lane, and Elizabeth Cheyney, Lady Vaux, where they may have spent time, although there is no trace of a house there of the right size or age.

The Church at Burton Latimer, however, remains as does that of Harrowden. The Orlingbury Hall Katherine would have known was demolished and rebuilt in 1709 and Orlingbury Church was also rebuilt in the nineteenth century. The Vaux Manor of Harrowden was completely rebuilt in the 18th Century. It now houses the Wellingborough

Golf Club. From Burton Latimer, take the A509 towards Wellingborough, from which Harrowden and Orlingbury are signposted, Harrowden is actually on the main road, and Orlingbury a mile off it.

Katherine's uncle, Sir William Parr of Horton, lived about 15 miles from this cluster of family. No traces of his home remain, although he and his wife are commemorated in the Church of St Mary Magdalene – not open other than on Sundays. Horton may be reached from Orlingbury by rejoining the A509 South, then turning onto the A428, then following the signposts onto the B526 Newport Pagnell Road.

Katherine would not, however, have remained at home all of the time. Latimer was called to various commissions for the suppression of the recent rebels, and she is likely to have accompanied him to York.

Finally, the Latimers moved to their house in Charterhouse Yard, London, presumably a house near the great Carthusian Monastery that had been one of the most resistant to the Dissolution. Latimer died here, and Katherine moved to Court, visiting or employed by the Lady Mary.

When Katherine married Henry in 1543 she would have found herself in previously unparalleled luxury and opulence, Hampton Court, Greenwich Palace, Oatlands and Nonsuch would all have been visited regularly. In addition, there were the smaller palaces and castles, such as Hertford Castle, where she visited the young Prince of Wales or the various hunting lodges that Henry favoured.

There was the Tower of London, still officially a Palace, although not much used as such by the end of Henry's reign and the mediaeval Westminster Palace, of which the 14th century hall (Westminster Hall) is the only remaining part.

Henry's new palace of Whitehall, the redbrick St James Palace and the mighty Windsor Castle were also Katherine's homes during her time as Queen.

On Henry's death, Katherine received the Manors of Chelsea and Hanworth. Neither of these exists any longer. Chelsea Place (as it was properly known) was built in the early 1500s, facing the riverside, under the current 19-26 Cheyne Walk. It was updated in the 1600s, then demolished in the late 1750s.

In the summer of 1548, Katherine travelled to what was to be her last home, Sudeley Castle in Gloucestershire, which had been granted to her fourth husband, the new King's uncle, Thomas Seymour. Seymour spent significant sums on renovating it and laying out gardens for the Queen's pleasure and we may imagine her, enjoying her beautiful surroundings as she awaited the birth of her first child. Unfortunately, Katherine died in childbirth and was laid to rest in the church at Sudeley.

Key to Map

1. Jervaulx Abbey
2. Hertford
3. Kendal
4. Sizergh Castle
5. Snape Castle
6. Sudeley Castle
7. Tower of London
8. Windsor Castle
9. St Paul's Cathedral
10. Holy Trinity, Kendal
11. St Andrews, Kirton-in-Lindsey
12. St Ann, Blackfriars
13. St Mary Magdalene, Horton
14. Chelsea Manor

15. Gainsborough Old Hall
16. Greens Norton Manor
17. Hanworth Manor
18. Harrowden Hall
19. Kirton-in-Lindsey
20. Rye House
21. Stansted Hall
22. Greenwich
23. Hampton Court
24. Nonsuch Palace
25. Oatlands Palace
26. Richmond Palace
27. Westminster Palace
28. Whitehall Palace

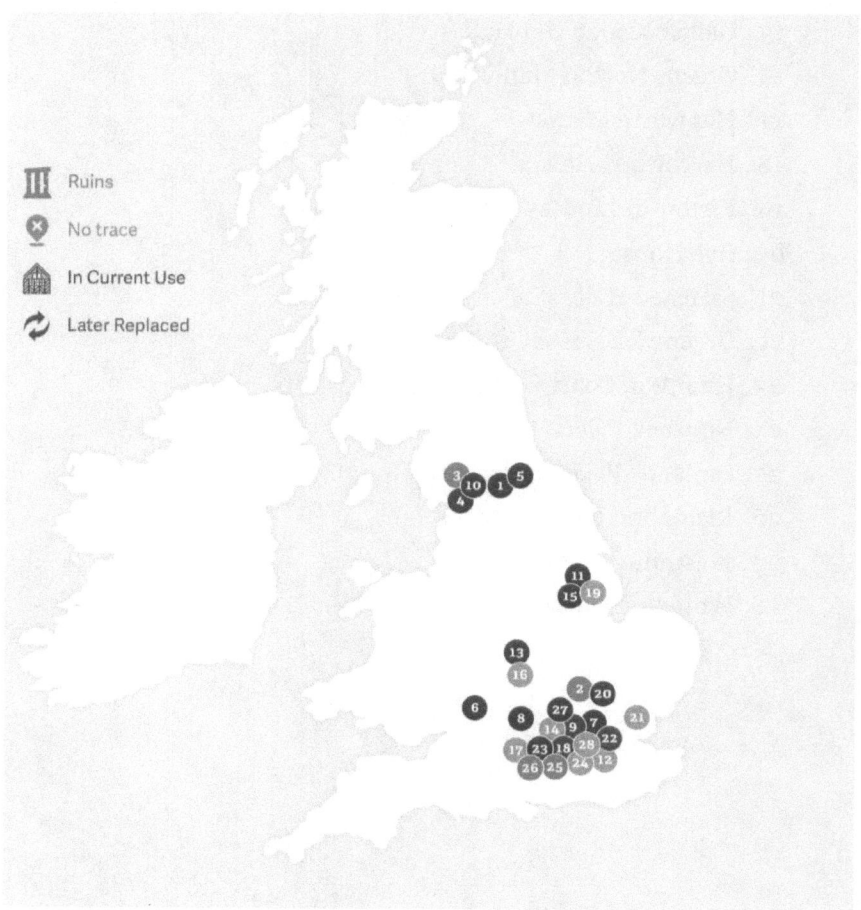

Chapter 12: Katherine Parr in Fact and Fiction

If, as is sometimes claimed, Katherine Parr was once Henry's least well known Queen, she has certainly emerged in the last few years from the obscurity in which she has been languishing.

To mark the centenary of her birth in 1512, three detailed, full-length biographies were published and detailed reviews of these are in Chapter 13.

To summarise, we would suggest:

Catherine Parr, Henry VIII's Last Love by Dr Susan James, if you are interested in very detailed, scholarly analysis and additional information about Katherine's siblings.

Katherine the Queen, the Remarkable Life of Katherine Parr by Dr Linda Porter, if you would like to form a balanced picture of Katherine in the context of her time, seeing both light and shade.

Catherine Parr by Elizabeth Norton. This is aimed at the general reader, and forms an excellent introduction to Katherine, and her relationship with Henry VIII.

In addition, Katherine plays her part in earlier joint biographies by, of course, Agnes Strickland, and, in modern times David Loades, Antonia Fraser, Alison Weir and David Starkey. The joint biographies are all very different in tone.

Lives of the Queens of England, Vol V by Agnes Strickland. This classic work in thirteen volumes was first published in the 1840s and has been referred to by every biographer of queens thereafter. Miss

Strickland, who moved in very exalted circles, had access to huge quantities of original papers and letters. She is a sympathetic portraitist of all of the queens, and is particularly attached to Katherine Parr, because of the relationship of the Parrs to her own Strickland ancestors. Although superseded in many ways, it is still worth reading for atmosphere and the human touch.

The Six Wives of Henry VIII by Alison Weir. Weir's book was published back in 1991, before the extensive research undertaken by Dr James was available. It is therefore reliant upon earlier research, particularly Strickland's rather romantic stories and perpetuates the myth of the nurse. Interestingly, however, Weir correctly identifies the portrait once labelled Lady Jane Grey, but now proved conclusively by James to be of Katherine Parr. Weir has not received (so far as we aware) any credit for this early identification.

The Six Wives of Henry VIII by Dr David Starkey. Dr Starkey's work is as challenging to received opinion as most of his books. As a worshipper of Henry VIII, he sees Henry's wives only as adjuncts to the great man, rather than having much of an interest in the ladies themselves. He does, however, raise a very interesting point around the possibility that Katherine's religious views were influenced by Sir Francis Bigod, which has been taken up vigorously by Elizabeth Norton.

The Six Wives of Henry VIII by Antonia Fraser. Although published more than twenty years ago, this has stood the test of time well. Fraser manages to convey a wealth of information in a very readable format. All of the key information about Katherine is here, and some interesting comparisons with Henry's other wives.

The Tudor Queens of England by Dr David Loades. Dr Loades' slim volume covers thirteen queens in a mere 220 or so pages, so cannot be expected to be a detailed account. In fact, the only details Dr Loades seems much interested in relate to Katherine's sex life. In the four pages devoted to her, he manages to mention that she was sexually frustrated on each one (although how he knows this is a mystery.) He is dismissive of her role as Regent, and scathing about her writings.

The Six Wives and Many Mistresses of Henry VIII by Amy Licence. This work concentrates solely on the personal relationships between the King and his various love interests. By the time he was married to Katherine Parr, the fires of passion were somewhat dimmed, although there is no question that he consummated the marriage. There were rumours that she would be replaced by her friend, Katherine Willoughby, Duchess of Suffolk, but Katherine Parr continued to please him enough to keep her place.

Katherine appears fairly frequently in fictional accounts. She is the main protagonist in:

The Queen's Gambit by Elizabeth Freemantle. This is well written fiction with the facts and interpretation largely drawn from the James biography.

The Taming of the Queen by Philippa Gregory. This is the latest in the best-selling author's series on the Tudor Court

The Sixth Wife by Suzanne Dunn. The very modern idiom takes a bit of getting used to, but it is well done. The novel centres, in fact on Katherine's friend, the Duchess of Suffolk, but, without giving too much away, Katherine Parr is an equally important character.

The Sixth Wife by Jean Plaidy – a bit out of date now, but always readable. It is also available in Audio.

Katherine also makes an appearance in the following books.

Heartstone and its sequel *Lamentation* by C J Sansom. Sansom has done a truly exceptional job of bringing the later years of Henry VIII alive. Katherine is an important and sympathetic character.

The Dark Rose by Cynthia Harrod-Eagles

The classic *Young Bess* by Margaret Irwin

The sadly out of print *I am Mary Tudor* by Hilda Lewis

Chapter 13: Katherine Parr: Three Book Reviews

Katherine the Queen: The Remarkable Life of Katherine Parr

Author: Dr Linda Porter

Publisher: MacMillan 19 March 2010

In a nutshell: A beautifully written account, with interesting new interpretations for the expert as well as a wealth of information for the generalist.

This is a very well balanced and informative book. Porter clearly admires Katherine, her intellect, her passion for learning, her ability to adapt to circumstances, but she does not allow Katherine's strong points to completely overshadow the less attractive elements of her character – her reluctance to pay her bills and her rather cynical manipulation of her step-son, Edward VI's, affections in her and Seymour's bid to have their marriage recognised, are noted. She also reads Katherine's very unkind letter to Lady Wriothesley, on the death of the lady's child, at face value and does not try to soften it.

Porter's underlying theme seems to be that Katherine, like all good daughters of a Tudor family was aiming for familial power: if possible, through a child of her own, and if not, through her influence over her step-children and the promotion of her relatives and servants.

Porter gives a new interpretation of Katherine's relationship with her fourth husband, Thomas Seymour. Acknowledging it to be a love match, she also speculates on it as a considered and deliberate route for both to achieve their joint ambitions of control of the minority government of Edward VI. Katherine, disappointed of the Regency by Henry VIII's final Will, wanted to retain influence in the new regime, and a marriage to the new King's uncle would improve her ability to stay close to the King. Unfortunately, she appears to have reckoned without Seymour's poor judgement and the sibling rivalry between the Seymour brothers.

As well as the wider issue of power politics and factionalism in the Tudor court, Porter concentrates on Katherine's journey from traditional faith to evangelism, and her strong influence over her step daughter, Elizabeth.

Porter never goes beyond the facts. In the debate about whether Katherine served in the household of Mary Tudor in the period around and after the death of Lord Latimer, she clearly identifies that there is no record of Katherine in Mary's accounts as an official member of the Princess' household. The evidence of an order for dresses and jewellery for the Princess issued by Katherine to be paid for by the King's accounts department she accounts for as an activity that any of Mary's friends or subordinates might have carried out for her, especially as Mary and Katherine were both lovers of fine clothes and jewels. However, this faithfulness to what can be proven does not make for a dull book, because Porter uses her facts to draw interesting inferences and interpretations that are new.

For example, the reconsideration of Katherine's physical relationship with Henry: the old Victorian idea that Katherine was merely his nurse has long been dismissed, but Porter argues for a determined effort by Katherine to keep the King sexually satisfied, citing the frequent purchases of perfumes, body lotions, flowers for her bedchamber and beautiful and sensual clothes as her efforts to keep him motivated.

*

Catherine Parr: Henry VIII's Last Love

Author: Dr Susan James

Publisher: The History Press

In a nutshell: For a reader who is interested in details and academic analysis, but also wants to gain an insight into Katherine's own tastes and habits.

Dr James has undertaken a vast amount of research and probably wins the title of 'scholarly biography' for this work.

There is no factual detail about Queen Katherine that she has not investigated. She has looked into her clothes, her jewels, her books, her clocks and her pets, and we emerge with a very definite feeling for Katherine's tastes and pastimes. James has effectively established the true identity of Katherine's first husband and dispelled the myths of him being an old man, although she perhaps draws stronger conclusions from the evidence on some matters than Porter does.

James clearly admires Katherine hugely and seems to identify with her emotionally – balancing on the point where any further empathy would tip her over into emotional invention. For example, with reference to a letter to Lady Wriothesley, purporting to be one of condolence on the loss of her child, when Katherine's injunctions to the lady to accept God's Will seem hard-hearted, even allowing for the religious views of the age, James defends Katherine's unkindness by referring to the lady's grief as hysterical.

James has also done extremely detailed work in investigating Katherine's religious writings, undertaking minute analysis of the structure and style of the works to establish likely authorship of previously uncertain attributions.

Also interesting and informative is the picture that emerges of Katherine's siblings, in particular William Parr, Marquis of Northampton. Again, meticulous research has paid dividends.

There are one or two bizarre mistakes of fact in relation to people other than Katherine herself. James refers on two occasions to Sir Edward Baynton, Anne Boleyn's Chamberlain, as Anne's brother-in-law – apparently married to her half-sister. If Anne Boleyn had a half-sister, only Dr James has ever heard of her. Anne Boleyn's brothers-in-law were the two husbands of her sister Mary, William Carey and William Stafford. James also quotes a description of Matthew, Earl of Lennox, as a 'lusty, lady-faced boy', a description that was, in fact, made of Lennox's son, Lord Darnley, some twenty years later.

But these oddities and a few editing quibbles (the constant confusion of the word tenet with tenant, giving us tenants of religion, was particularly irritating) do not detract from a really thorough and detailed account of Katherine Parr's life from cradle to grave.

*

Catherine Parr: Wife, Widow, Mother, Survivor. The Story of the Last Wife of Henry VIII

Author: Elizabeth Norton

Publisher: Amberley Publishing 4 January 2010

In a nutshell: A good introduction to the topic, covering the main aspects of Katherine Parr's life, with plenty of interpretation.

Norton has produced a series of works on the wives of Henry VIII, in which she concentrates on the Queens' own perspectives on life, with plenty of biographical detail, rather than the wider historical context.

Her work on Katherine Parr covers all of the events of her life, and attempts to draw conclusions about the Queen's own emotional or practical response to the turmoil that surrounded the Tudor gentry and nobility.

Whilst Norton has clearly benefited from Dr James' research, she draws her own conclusions from the information – for example, her views on Katherine's level of education and skill in languages differ from those of James, but are certainly very credible, and perhaps more likely.

More than any other of Katherine's biographers, Norton concludes quite definitely that Katherine's evangelical religion dated from her first marriage to Edward Burgh, when she came under the influence of Edward's father, a noted reformer. Whereas Dr Starkey infers that exposure to Lord Latimer's reformist friend, Sir Francis Bigod, may have influenced Katherine, Norton implies that it was Katherine who encouraged the friendship between the men, and the proposed match between Bigod's son and Latimer's daughter.

Norton explores the relationships Katherine had with Latimer's wider family – identifying the risks the couple were exposed to by the potentially treasonous activities of Latimer's brothers, William and Marmaduke. She notes, however, that Katherine must have had a soft spot for Marmaduke (*Ed - if only for his name!*) appointing him to a place in her household, once Queen.

Norton quite rightly identifies when an event is possible, but not proven. However, she sometimes then goes on to draw very definite conclusions from that event. An example is her use of the *Legend of Sir Nicholas Throckmorton* to demonstrate Katherine's reputation for helping her friends and family. She gives convincing reasons why the *Legend* may be accurate, whilst pointing out that it was written after Katherine had become Queen, so composed with the benefit of hindsight. In one paragraph she writes 'It is therefore not impossible that Catherine (sic) could have secured an audience with the king...' then on the next page says 'This is the first recorded meeting between Catherine and Henry.'

Katherine's reformist religious views are explored at length, and Norton gives her a very proactive role in shaping the religious position of her step-daughter, later Elizabeth I.

This is a very readable work (although it might benefit from more rigorous editing) and would be a welcome addition to a reader seeking a wide range of interpretations of Katherine's life.

Part 2: James IV: King of Scots

Introduction

James IV was the very ideal of a Renaissance Prince. Patron of learning, but skilled on the jousting ground, chivalrous lover of many ladies, yet a maker of pilgrimages, mighty in war and a dispenser of rapid justice.

He brought Scotland from a land of almost constant internecine warfare to a united country, able to raise an army equipped with the most advanced technology of the age, yet it was all lost, thrown away in a muddy field in Northern England by a man who was a great warrior, but an impulsive and foolhardy general.

James was one of Scotland's most successful kings. He united his country, enforced the rule of law, and showed that Scotland could take its place with pride on the European stage. The tragedy of Flodden and the chaos that the country was plunged into after his death have overshadowed his achievements. A charismatic, courageous and intelligent man, he deserves to be better remembered.

Part 2 contains James IV's Life Story and additional articles about him, looking at different aspects of his life. He was a man with a wide range of interests, taking part in intellectual and practical pastimes as well as the traditional jousting and military pursuits. He was also well-known for his colourful private life.

JAMES IV

Family Tree

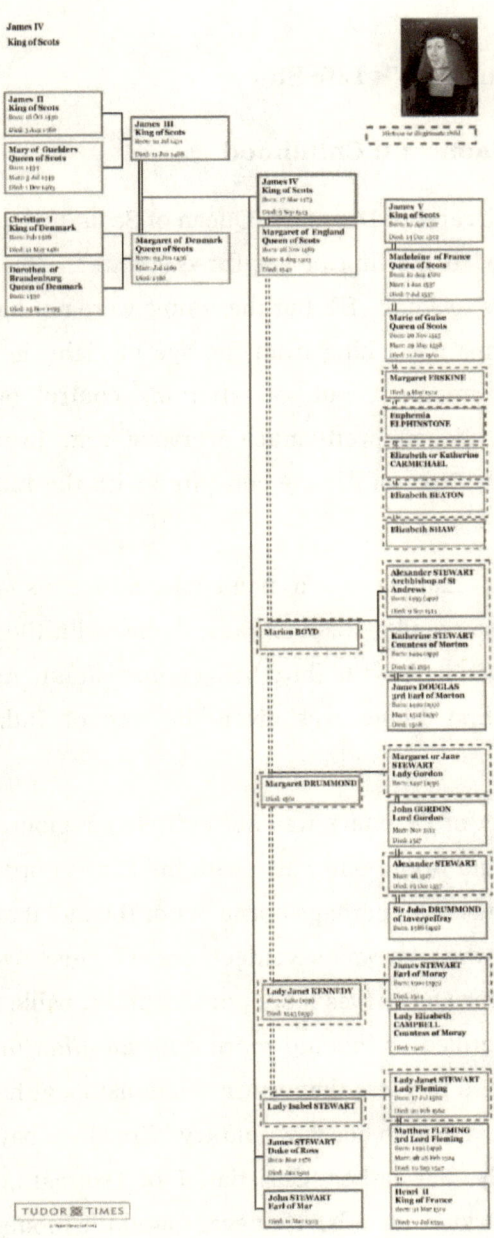

James IV's Life Story

Chapter 14: Childhood

On 17th March 1473, Margaret of Denmark, Queen of Scots gave birth, probably at Stirling Castle, to the first of her three children. She had been married for four years to James III, but the couple were not happy. James III was a difficult man – a king from the age of eight, he had survived a long, factious minority, but, on attaining control of his kingdom had proceeded to alienate pretty much everyone in it. Even his brother, Alexander Stewart, Duke of Albany conspired with the English to depose him.

The young couple's first child was a son, named James for his father and grandfather. In fact, so popular was the name James with the king that the second son was given it, too, the third being named John. As the heir to the throne, this first James was given the title of Duke of Rothesay.

It appears that Margaret of Denmark was not entirely enamoured of the duties of married life, and would only sleep with the King in order to become pregnant. This reluctance, perhaps borne out of the fact that the wedding had taken place when he was seventeen and she just twelve, together with the fact that the Queen was more popular and capable than her husband (she was described as *'having more aptitude than he for ruling the Kingdom'*) resulted in a less than warm relationship, although Margaret had brought a great deal to her new country. Unable to pay her dowry in cash immediately, her father, Christian I of Denmark, had pledged the Shetland and Orkney Islands. He never found the money, so the islands were ceded to Scotland.

Regardless of the state of their personal relationship, Queen Margaret stood loyally by James III when his brother, Alexander, Duke of Albany, who had escaped to France after being besieged by the King in Dunbar Castle, made an arrangement with Edward IV of England. England was to provide him with support in a bid for the Scottish throne and the price Albany was prepared to pay was the surrender of Berwick and other disputed border lands and an agreement to do homage to the English King.

In 1482, James III marched out to face Albany, who was backed by 20,000 English troops led by Richard, Duke of Gloucester (later Richard III). En route to Lauder in Berwickshire, which he had appointed as the meeting place for the feudal levies, the King was abducted in the '*Lauder Lynching*' by his own half-uncle, the Earl of Buchan and the Earl of Angus. Various of James III's supporters, who were looked down upon by the nobility for their lowly birth, were summarily hanged from the Lauder Bridge, and James III was taken back to imprisonment in Edinburgh Castle, under the wardenship of Lord Darnley, a known supporter of Queen Margaret.

This left Queen Margaret to negotiate with Albany. She was at Stirling with the nine-year old James, Duke of Rothesay, for whose education and upbringing she was responsible, as was traditional for Scottish queens. It can be inferred from the holding of James III in Edinburgh Castle, of which she was custodian, that Queen Margaret, if not actively involved in the abduction, was aware of the intention to rein him in. She was not, however, prepared to support his deposition. Queen Margaret and Prince James met Albany and negotiated around his desire to at least be nominated as Lieutenant General of the kingdom – effectively Regent. It appears that Hume and his colleagues were soon even less enamoured of the thought of Albany as king than James. Albany was just as rapacious as the king, and willing to submit Scotland to English overlordship, which James III, although he had pursued a pro-English policy, was not. That being so, Albany, to save face, besieged Edinburgh Castle, which quickly surrendered, allowing James to be set free.

James III therefore kept his Crown.

Soon, however, James and the lords were at loggerheads again. James had made a bitter enemy of Lord Hume - one of the most powerful Border lords, who commanded a significant portion of the eastern border with England. He and Hume had been in dispute about Church revenues and James decided to settle the matter by accusing Hume of treason, giving the latter the impression that his whole family was at risk of the King's vengeance. Hume's allies, including the Hepburns, began to fear for their own positions.

King James became suspicious of the motives of his son, despite the fact that Prince James had only been nine years old at the time of the abduction.

Prince James appears to have had a very close relationship with his mother who wished to inculcate in him the highest standards of princely behaviour. Allegedly, she taught him to wait upon her at the table, and bring her water to wash her hands, even though she had plenty of servants. This was to teach him the right way to command – mindful of his position, but not too proud. Nothing is known of his general education, other than that it must have been thorough and well-delivered, given James' later intellectual interests.

In 1486, Queen Margaret died, aged just 30, allegedly exhorting her thirteen year old son to the highest standards of kingship:

'When you succeed to your father's throne, above all else, love the people as yourself, with justice, mercy, generosity and affection...preserve the kingdom in peace and tranquillity...See that justice is not violated by greed...'

The Queen was buried at Cambuskenneth Abbey and Prince James remained at Stirling Castle, continuing his education.

Chapter 15: Rebellion and Coronation

Over the next two years, there was talk of a new marriage for James III, with Elizabeth Woodville – widow of Edward IV, and mother-in-law of Henry VII, the new English king. At the same time, the second Prince James, Duke of Ross, was mooted as a spouse for Katherine of York, daughter of Edward IV. The elder Prince James, previously considered for Katherine's older sister, Cicely, during the reign of her father, was not mentioned in these negotiations.

It may be that this promotion of his younger brother worried Prince James, or perhaps there was another cause, but on 2nd February 1488, Prince James left Stirling in secrecy to join a band of rebels, the chief leaders of which were Archibald Douglas, 5th Earl of Angus (known as Bell-the-Cat, although it is not a contemporary nickname), the Earl of Argyll and Lord Hume. James was probably aided and abetted by the Constable of the Castle, who was Hume's brother-in-law. King James, uncertain of his heir's whereabouts, realised that trouble was brewing and began to raise money for an army. Edinburgh and the south of Scotland were largely in the control of the nobles most dissatisfied with King James, so, on 24th March 1488, he marched north, to more loyal areas, to raise troops. He set up his base at Aberdeen and sent out requests for help to both England and France - it generally being politic for kings to help each other against disobedient subjects - but no help was forthcoming.

James III faced a growing group of rebels which encompassed the Humes, the Hepburns, the Earls of Angus and Argyll, the latter of whom had previously been a supporter of James, and even the Bishop of Glasgow. With the recruitment of Prince James to their ranks, they now presented a formidable opposition. The rebels also appealed to England for support, claiming, without any evidence so far as is now known, that James III, amongst other crimes and misdemeanours, had poisoned his wife.

King James still had a number of senior supporters, including his half-uncle, the Earl of Buchan, who although he had been involved in the *Lauder Lynching*, had returned to the King's side, and the chief prelate of the realm, the Archbishop of St Andrew's. The Archbishop, in particular, wanted to bring about a peaceful solution if at all possible.

Mindful that rebellion against the King was considered a sin, and should only be considered as a last resort, the rebels put forward a proposal for a negotiated settlement. Called the Articles of Aberdeen, the thirteen clauses, proposed some changes in behaviour on James III's part, including better maintenance and training of Prince James – he should be given mentors of *'wisdom and discretion...for the good governance of his person in his tender age.'*

The Articles were signed in May 1488, yet by early June the rebels were accusing the King of flouting them, although as they are rather vague, it is difficult to understand exactly what the King was expected to achieve in three short weeks. James began to march south, in part to reunite himself with his treasure – he was considered something of a miser, and, whilst debasing the coinage with cheap metals, stored gold in great chests for himself. Regardless of his personal affection for his gold, he would need it to pay any mercenaries sent by France or England.

James III headed for Blackness Castle on the Firth of Forth, in expectation of foreign troops who never arrived. The rebels appeared on his doorstep, and, leaving Buchan in charge, James slipped out the back door, crossed the Firth to the Port of Leith and re-entered Edinburgh

Castle by mid-May. Now in possession of his chests of money and able to pay his troops, James emerged from the Castle and marched towards Stirling where Prince James and the rebels lay.

There were also rebels at Linlithgow, so James crossed again to the north side of the Firth of Forth to approach Stirling from the north-east. In a brisk skirmish, the King captured the town of Stirling and its Castle, but Prince James evaded his clutches. Fortunately for the Prince, the main part of the rebel army was approaching, and he joined up with it. The two forces now joined in battle – Prince James apparently issuing orders that his father was not to be harmed.

The forces met on 11th June. There is no contemporary account of the battle.

It is believed that King James had more men, and the sword of Robert the Bruce girded at his side, but neither of these factors could give him the victory. The loyalty of his men was questionable and what exactly occurred, either before, during or immediately after the battle is unclear. Neither side used artillery - it was a traditional man-to-man encounter, on ground that was surrounded by marsh. It seems to have been over very quickly, with the young Prince James being pronounced King James IV within hours.

What had happened to James III? There is no certainty as to whether he died on the battlefield or off it. One story is that the James III left the fray, either voluntarily, or because his horse ran amok. He then tumbled off the animal crossing the Bannockburn (rather a symbolic note to the tale.) On being carried to the nearby Beaton's Mill, he asked for priest. One of the rebels, in disguise, entered the room and stabbed him to death.

On leaving the battlefield, James headed for Scone, where he was crowned on 24th June 1488. There was nothing hole-and-corner about the coronation, but it was conducted by the Bishops of Glasgow and Dunkeld, rather than the senior churchman, the Archbishop of St Andrews who had been a strong supporter of James III. Once James IV was crowned, the next step was to have his father buried. Two weeks after the battle, James III was interred at Cambuskenneth Abbey, not far from Stirling at the side of his wife, Margaret of Denmark.

The official enquiry into the King's death, held by James IV's first Parliament in October (almost the only indication that the battle actually took place) merely commented that James III *'happinit to be slayn'* and that

> *'oure soverane lord that now is and the trew lordis and barouns that wes withe him in the samyne feild war innocent, quhyt and fre of the saidis slauchteris feilde and all persute of the occasioune and cause of the samyne'.*

A reward for information on the identity of his killers, of 90 marks' worth of land, lies unclaimed to this day.

Whatever James IV's immediate feelings, he felt continuing guilt for his father's death, and, as penance, wore an iron belt around his waist for the rest of his life, adding a link each year – though whether that was to increase the penance, or the result of good living, who can tell? An entry in the accounts for six quarters of worsted to pad the belt suggests it was not as uncomfortable as all that.

James was still only fifteen, and thus, to some degree, controlled by the men who had rebelled against his father. The influence of the chief rebels, the Earl of Bothwell (who had custody of the minor king and his brothers) and Lord Hume was initially strong, and they gathered lands and offices as quickly as they could.

This was distasteful to the other nobles, such as the Earl of Lennox in south-west Scotland, and the Earl of Huntly in the north-east. Before long, Lennox and Huntly were in open rebellion. The plan was to abduct James, who was at Stirling.

James, always in the forefront of any action, rode out to meet the rebels and defeated them at the Battle of Gartloaning which took place just west of Stirling. Nevertheless, there was still concern about the stranglehold that Bothwell and Hume had over the Government. A new Parliament was called in early 1490, and the representation on the King's Privy Council was extended to a wider group.

Still disgruntled, however, was the Earl of Angus. He was cheered by two events – his appointment as Chancellor at the end of 1492, and his wife's niece, Marion Boyd, becoming the first of James' many mistresses.

In these early days, James began the journeyings around his kingdom that would come to characterise his reign. This was partly to make him seem as different as possible from his father, who had been disapproved of, in part, for his inclination to stay in Stirling or Edinburgh, surrounded by his particular favourites, rather than showing himself to his people and building relationships with his nobles.

However James IV was, by nature, an extraordinarily active man, and seldom stayed more than a week or two in any location, often moving on after a day or two.

He also soon showed an interest in naval affairs. The difficult terrain of Scotland necessitated frequent sea-travel and James became fascinated by ships and their potential as military weapons.

Another of James' trademarks was the frequency and thoroughness with which he carried out his role as giver of Justice. South of the Border, kings had stopped presiding over the courts some centuries previously, but this was still a key component of Scottish kingship.

James was well-thought of for the thoroughness with which he would listen to the cases, and the generally wise decisions he made.

Chapter 16: Extending Scottish Influence

The Western portion of the landmass of Scotland and the islands off its coast had never been fully under the control of the Kings of Scots. Instead, they were the last remnants of the old Gaelic-Scandinavian kingdoms, ruled by their own Clan chiefs, and claimed variously by Norway, Scotland and Orkney. The Lordship was essentially a sea-kingdom, and its rulers depended on sea-travel in the galleys that were descendants of the Viking long ships.

By the early 1480s, the chief clan, Clan Donald, had weakened its position. It had accepted a Parliamentary forfeiture of some of its lands and a Royal Charter as the basis of holding the remaining territory. In addition, the clan chief, John Donald II, Lord of the Isles, had clashed with his illegitimate son, Angus Og. In 1488 and 1491, Angus Og and his cousin began raiding into lands outside the lordship, attracting the enmity of the Earls of Argyll, Angus and Huntly, and drawing Crown attention.

In 1493, Parliament declared the Lord of the Isles lands forfeit to the Crown, and James undertook an extensive tour in the region to emphasise royal authority. He arrived by sea in August 1493 at the royal stronghold of Dunstaffnage in Lorn. John Donald II submitted and was granted a pension. The following year, James visited again, and refurbished Tarbert, Loch Fyne and Dunvarty Castles. However, although John Donald II had accepted the Scottish King's overlordship, not everyone else in the Isles was equally happy.

The following years saw internecine feuding amongst Donald's family and clan, with no overall leader arising who could challenge James IV.

From this time onward, the Lordship of the Isles never escaped its subjection to the Scottish Crown, despite later revolts in 1506-7.

One of the objections the Scottish nobles had had to James III was his inclination to a pro-English policy, rather the traditional alliance with France. James IV's councillors were not going to let him make the same mistake. In September 1491, the Auld Alliance with France was renewed. James' embassy, led by the Earl of Bothwell, was received at the French court in very honourable fashion by Charles VIII and his Chancellor, flanked by Bernard Stewart, Lord d'Aubigny, a distant cousin of James and Charles VIII's senior commander.

The delegation was treating with Charles about a possible marriage between James IV and Bianca Maria Sforza, sister of the Duke of Milan, but nothing came of it, and the Lady Bianca married the Emperor Maximilian as his second wife.

At the same time, James wanted to preserve the relationship with his mother's family, and throughout his reign he corresponded frequently with first his uncle, John of Denmark, and then his cousin, Christian II of Denmark. Relations with his grandmother, Mary of Guelders' family were also maintained.

Chapter 17: Hostility towards England

One of the most complex issues for Scottish kings to deal with was relationships with England. English kings frequently claimed overlordship of Scotland, and contenders for the Scottish throne were usually willing to grant it, in theory, at any rate, in return for English troops. Scottish kings had to resist this, often indulging in low level incursions across the Border that were designed to annoy, whilst not provoking their larger neighbour into outright war.

There was also the constant lawlessness in the Border territory. *"Reivers"* was the term used for the wild Border clans of both sides, living in the *"Debatable Land"*, ie in areas with no fixed border between the countries and minimal royal authority. *"Reiving"* is basically cattle-rustling but they did not confine themselves to cattle and murdered, raped and robbed each other, or any passer-by who fell into their hands, of any animals or goods quite cheerfully. This state of anarchy was often winked at, if not actively encouraged, by the nobles who were supposed to control it.

By and large, the Scots population was strongly opposed to cordial relations with England, but some of the nobles, in receipt of pensions and bribes from England, were willing to challenge this attitude. In particular, the Douglas Earls of Angus were often pro-English in their policy.

James IV began with the popular pro-French stance. His overarching ambition was for Scotland to be recognised as an independent state, definitely not subject to English suzerainty. To do this, he needed to build links with other countries, persuading them to see him as a powerful ruler. The major concern in 1490s Europe was the growing power of France, and its attempts to dominate the Italian peninsula, and, in exchange for detaching Scotland from its alliance with France, other European rulers were prepared to indulge James in his ambitions.

Ferdinand and Isabella, sovereigns of Spain, wrote to their ambassador in Scotland:

> *The Scots have such a very good opinion of themselves as to pretend that they can induce the King of France to restore the counties of Roussillon and Cerdaña to Spain. Puebla can therefore say that they shall have an Infanta of Spain as soon as they effect the restoration of the said counties. They will not be able to do it, and will lose much time in unpleasant negotiations, which perhaps might end in a*

quarrel with France. At all events, pending the negotiations, they would not assist France against Spain.'

For James, as for all mediaeval and renaissance kings, warfare and increasing his military might was a part of the job, and he took to it with gusto. A seven year truce had been signed with England in 1493, reflecting the pro-English stance of Angus and Bishop Elphinstone, but, his confidence boosted by success in the Isles, James grabbed the chance presented by trouble south of the Border in the 1490s to raise his profile on the European stage.

Henry VII was plagued by a young man claiming to be Richard, Duke of York, son of Edward IV. The man, whose real name was probably Perkin Warbeck, had been received with all honour in France, Burgundy and other parts of the Empire. He had failed, however, in his first attempt to invade England, and was now looking for more support.

Scotland in the early days of James' reign had been cautious about getting involved, and was actively discouraged from doing so by the Spanish sovereigns who wanted to maintain peace between England and Scotland. Now, James decided to welcome Warbeck with open arms. The young man was treated as a prince and married to Lady Katherine Gordon, daughter of one of James' chief earls.

Over the following eighteen months, Warbeck received Scottish support, culminating in an invasion, led by James and Warbeck in late summer of 1496. Warbeck, appalled by the reality of war, left after a day's campaigning, but James pressed on. His aim was the re-capture of Berwick.

For a few weeks, James and his well-equipped troops made trouble for England, destroying castles between the Rivers Tweed and Till and giving Norham Castle a severe battering. In late September, the English army, under Thomas Howard, Earl of Surrey, left Newcastle. James, retired back over the Tweed, pleased with his summer's work, especially as he had taken enough plunder to pay for the campaign.

Henry VII was by no means an aggressive king, but he would not tolerate incursions into his territory. With an enormous sum in taxation voted by Parliament, Henry set about raising an army to teach James a lesson. James stayed close to the Border over-wintering at Melrose Abbey and readying his artillery for war.

James owned the massive gun, *Mons Meg*, by far the largest artillery piece in the British Isles. *Mons Meg* was capable of doing spectacular damage with its eighteen-inch diameter 330lb cannon balls that could travel well over a mile and a half. *Mons Meg* was brought up from Edinburgh Castle and fitted with new wheels, ready to trundle into battle. The host was summoned for June 1497. There were efforts from both Spain and France to make peace between the countries, but, at this stage, neither King was prepared to back down.

In May however, Henry hit a snag as the £120,000 in taxes voted by Parliament came to be collected. Cornwall rebelled. The threat was so serious that Henry quickly looked to make peace with Scotland, even though the Cornish revolt was defeated by mid-June.

In July, Warbeck was provisioned by James with a ship to sail to Ireland or the West of England, where he failed to make any headway and was captured. James, meanwhile, with his army now arrayed, was showing his strength. Henry had sent three ambassadors to treat with his Scottish counterpart, including Bishop Richard Fox, one of his chief Councillors. James, with his levies arriving for the previously agreed June meet, declined to treat. He besieged Norham Castle with Bishop Fox inside and did significant damage to the fabric.

Before the Castle could be forced to surrender, Henry's army, under the Earl of Surrey advanced, so James, deciding to quit while he was ahead, retired to Edinburgh. Surrey did not pause at the border, but marched on to besiege Ayton Castle, the property of Lord Hume.

The majority of James' army had now finished its service and dispersed. However, he marched out again with as many troops as he could find. Surrey, although with more men, was not well provisioned. The two armies drew up, some twelve miles apart and their leaders sent aggravating messages to each other, with no real intent of coming to a pitched fight. Rather provokingly, James challenged Surrey to single combat, the winner to take Berwick.

The Earl, who was in his late fifties, compared with James' twenty-four, wisely declined, saying that although he was honoured that a king would fight a mere earl, Berwick belonged to his master and he could not pledge it.

Both armies retired, but James had shown himself as a successful leader with the resources and skill to cause Henry VII annoyance and unpleasant expenditure. He was thus in a position to make peace on good terms. A seven year truce, the Truce of Ayton, was signed on 5th September, pending a more comprehensive treaty.

Chapter 18: Peace & Prosperity

As part of James' plans to bring Scotland to centre-stage in Europe, he had negotiated throughout the late 1480s and 1490s for a suitable Queen. Bianca Sforza, sister of the Duke of Milan had been one possibility, and he even went so far as to ask for the hand of Marguerite of Austria, widowed daughter of the Emperor Maximilian. He tried for a Spanish princess, but was offered only an illegitimate daughter of Ferdinand, the pill of illegitimacy to be sweetened with a fat dowry.

The peace with England, however, led to a different choice – James was to marry Henry VII's eldest daughter, Margaret. Princess Margaret was a mere eight years old at the time of the Truce of Ayton, but the eventual agreement, known as the Treaty of Perpetual Peace and signed on 24th November 1502, agreed the union and assigned a very impressive dowry of £10,000 English for Margaret. In return, she received a jointure from James of land and rents of £2,000 Scots per annum, plus a further £1,000 Scots as a spending allowance.

With his mark made on the European stage, and the Treaty with England in place, James, in the opening years of the sixteenth century, was free to spend his time on other things.

He busied himself with architectural projects. James spent significant sums of money on turning the old hunting lodge at Falkland into a Palace fit for a renaissance monarch, adding the great hall at Stirling Castle and largely renovating Linlithgow.

He began the transformation of Holyrood Abbey into a Palace, surrounded by fruit orchards and pleasure gardens, the site for which was created by draining the adjacent loch in 1507. Architecture was not just an indulgence; it was a statement of power and wealth. Henry VII had recently constructed the new palace of Richmond, and James could not afford to fall too far behind in the magnificence stakes.

James also pursued his other interests, which were as varied as dentistry, embroidery and alchemy. Most exciting of all for the King, the Queen and his courtiers was the great tournament of 1507.

During this period, however, domestic tensions mounted as James, who was extravagant, began to outrun his income. His demands for taxation weighed heavy on his nobles, although there was no outright defiance. Part of the money he raised was devoted to the development of Scotland's naval power.

Chapter 19: Scottish Navy

The discoveries in the New World by Spain and Portugal in the latter quarter of the fifteenth century gave rise across Europe to an increased interest in ships and naval affairs. James was no exception to the rule, and he became fascinated by ships from the start of his reign, frequently visiting the dockyards at Leith, the port of Edinburgh.

Ships were also important for the protection of trade. James was descended from Mary of Guelders, and trade with the Low Countries had always been an important aspect of the Scottish economy. Unfortunately, Scottish merchant shipping often suffered from the depredations of English piracy.

In 1489, five English ships had sailed up the Firth of Forth and ravaged Leith and Fife. James and his councillors could not overlook this and issued Letters of Marque (effectively a commission to a private ship's captain to act on behalf of the Government) to Sir Andrew Wood, who confronted and trounced the English ships off Dunbar, with his two merchant vessels. Henry VII sent three men-of-war, but Wood saw those off, too.

This success encouraged James in his liking for ships, and all sea-towns were commanded to build ships of twenty tons, with *"vagrants"* to be pressed as crew. This sudden increase in ship-building required more timber than was available. Supplies were purchased from Norway and France and in 1503 an Act of Parliament was passed commanding every laird to plant an acre of woodland. Additional timber was procured from France in 1506, on the understanding that the Scottish navy would be at King Louis XII's disposal.

The two most important vessels for this nascent navy were the *Michael,* and the *Margaret.* The *Michael* was the largest ship afloat in the first quarter of the sixteenth century. At a length of up to 240 feet (c. 70 metres) and breadth of 56 feet (c. 17 metres) she was an impressive sight. Her crew consisted of 300 gunners and she could carry upwards of 1,000 fighting men, as well as 27 bronze guns and 300 smaller pieces of artillery. At a cost of some £30,000 Scots, she cost James about a year's income.

As well as the aforementioned Sir Andrew Wood, James had another seaman (or pirate) on whom he could rely to create tension. Andrew Barton and his brothers had been granted Letters of Reprisal against Portuguese shipping, by James III. A Letter of Reprisal was a licence to take measures against any shipping carrying the flag of a country that had offended the recipient. Barton sailed up and down the English Channel, and on more than one occasion captured shipping of countries trading with Portugal.

In 1507, James gave Barton another Letter of Reprisal as well as Letters of Marque, but it was clear Barton was soon overstepping his authority. In 1508, Barton was captured by the Emperor's men, and only personal intervention by James in 1509 secured his release. Undaunted, Barton captured an English ship heading for Portugal. James, embarrassed, revoked the Letter of Marque, but Barton ignored him and proceeded to take an Antwerp vessel. James ordered him to pay compensation, but there is no record of him doing so.

Barton was then lent to James' uncle, John, King of Denmark, in his bid to control Sweden, in return for timber. He continued to be a liability, leaving King John's service without permission, taking the ship James had lent with him.

By 1511, almost everyone was fed up with Barton. The Englishmen, Sir Thomas Howard and Sir Edmund Howard, sons of James IV's old antagonist, the Earl of Surrey, took to the seas to capture a man who was now bordering on piracy. The Howards were successful, killing Barton and taking possession of the *Lion* and the *Jenny,* the former of which went into the English navy.

James demanded redress, in accordance with the Treaty of Perpetual Peace, but was put off. He continued to pursue the matter, although not with any great vigour, but the incident damaged the relationship between Scotland and England. Henry VIII loftily informed James that kings did not involve themselves in discussions about pirates.

Chapter 20: Road to Flodden

The Treaty of Perpetual Peace also aimed to deal with the constant low-level lawlessness of the Borders. There were supplementary treaties that dealt with the Border courts (long in place to deal with the day to day issues), and the redress that each king could expect if the behaviour of the Reivers became too outrageous.

Murders were to be dealt with by courts with juries manned from both sides. It was agreed that, provided the relevant king handed over any miscreant for proper punishment, incursion into the other realm would not be considered an act of aggression.

Throughout the remainder of Henry VII's reign, the terms worked reasonably well, and peace between the countries enabled even the Borders to know some level of proper government.

This changed with the accession of Queen Margaret's brother as Henry VIII. Henry VIII was a man most unlike his father – fed on tales of chivalry, he dreamed of military victory in France and English overlordship of Scotland. Although the Treaty of Perpetual Peace was renewed in 1509, it soon became evident that Henry was not interested in maintaining good relations with his sister's husband.

In both the Andrew Barton affair, mentioned above, and other border matters, he failed to give the redress required by the treaty. He also withheld the legacy left to Queen Margaret by either her father, or late brother, Arthur. Most worrying of all, he encouraged insulting statements in the English Parliament about James being his vassal.

In 1511 James asked Pope Julius II to release him from the Treaty of Perpetual Peace, claiming that England had broken its terms on several occasions. The Pope refused as Anglo-Scottish affairs did not occur in a vacuum and wider issues were at stake. The perpetual Italian Wars that ravaged Europe throughout the first half of the sixteenth century affected everyone as alliances came and went.

By 1511, the line-up was Pope Julius II, allied with Spain, the Empire and England against France, supported by Florence. Julius wanted to do everything he could to minimise France's allies. He made it clear that James risked excommunication if he broke the Treaty himself and attacked England. Julius may have hoped that James, as a particularly devout son of the Church, would be reluctant to defy him in the matter.

James IV had made concerted efforts to broker peace between France and the Papacy. He had many times declared his desire to go on Crusade and believed that war in Europe should be avoided in order for Christians to unite against the Infidel. Such an idea tends to make modern people smirk rather cynically, but there is no real reason to doubt the sincerity of the religious feeling of the time. In particular, the fall of Constantinople in 1453, and the incursions being made by the Ottoman Turks in Hungary, had caused concern in Christian Europe.

James was notably superstitious in his religious practice, even by the standards of the time and, as aforementioned, continued to feel guilt over the death of his father. Creating a peace settlement that would enable

Christians to repel the Turks would surely have earned him heavenly forgiveness. Unfortunately, no-one else was interested in peace and when the French declared a Council of the Church at Pisa in 1512 which appeared to threaten the Papacy's spiritual leadership, the die was cast for European war.

James was in a cleft stick. He had a long term obligation to France, renewed in 1507, but he also had a treaty with England and risked excommunication if he broke it. In retrospect, it is simple to say that he should have kept quiet and not allowed himself to be drawn into the war, but that was not easy. Unfortunately, he could not please both Henry VIII and Louis XII of France. Both kings demanded support, specifically they both wanted to charter James' ship the *Michael*.

Henry was delighted to be offered the ostensibly legitimate excuse of protecting the Pope's spiritual leadership to lead an invasion into France. In June 1513, he set sail. Meanwhile, the French were pressing James to attack England. Louis tried a two-pronged approach. His Queen, Anne (herself the victim of French depredations in her own duchy of Brittany) sent James a turquoise ring from her own hand and pleaded with the chivalrous James to be her knight. Louis offered a rather more tangible incentive, sending 50,000 French Crowns to fund an invasion.

James was probably not sorry to take the opportunity, as he thought, of teaching a lesson to the twenty-two year old Henry, whom he doubtless felt to be a young whipper-snapper. It seems likely he thought he could repeat his successful raids of 1496-7 and return to Scotland unscathed. Despite the misgivings of some of his nobles and according to later stories, Queen Margaret begging him to desist, James invaded England in support of his obligations to France under the Auld Alliance.

For the third time James was heading over the border – this time with an army reckoned at some 42,000 men, the largest ever raised in Scotland. Norham Castle fell in 6 days, followed by Wark, Etal and Ford.

James' opponent on the final battlefield was not Henry himself, who was still campaigning in France, but the Earl of Surrey, whom he had faced back in the late 1490s. In a combination of skilled generalship by Surrey, who used his knowledge of James' brave and impetuous character well, and James' determination to press his early victory home, rather than quitting whilst ahead, the enormous Scots army, well equipped and with the odds strongly in its favour, was decimated. James and many of his leading nobles were slaughtered on the field.

It was sometime before James' body was identified amongst the thousands dead. In the end it was recognised by Lord Dacre, English Warden of the West March and taken to Berwick. From there, it travelled to Surrey, to Sheen Priory in a lead-lined coffin.

James had been excommunicated in the summer of 1513, as threatened by Pope Julius II, the sentence being carried out by Cardinal Bainbridge, Archbishop of York – hardly a neutral figure! This excommunication caused some difficulty in burying James, as, in theory, an excommunicate could not be buried in sacred ground.

Henry VIII, showing a modicum of Christian charity to his brother-in-law, wrote to the Pope, requesting permission to bury James IV:

'As it is to be presumed the King gave some signs of repentance in his extremities, the Pope allows him to be buried with funeral honours, trusting the oversight thereof to Richard [Fox] bishop of London, or some prelate chosen by the King.'

It was planned that James would be buried as befitted a king, at St Paul's Cathedral, however, that never happened and his body was left in a store-room at Sheen. There it remained for over fifty years, until it was opened and the body desecrated in Elizabeth's time. The head was, apparently, rescued by the Queen's Glazier, who arranged for it to be buried at the Church of St Michael at Wood Street, central London - a site now graced by the Red Herring Pub.

Aspects of James IV's Life

Chapter 21: James IV's Personality & Appearance

The most obvious characteristic about James IV that shines through every mention of him in Ambassadors' correspondence, his own actions, and the records of his reign, is his boundless energy. James was constantly on the move, seldom staying in one place for more than a few days, racing around his country, by both horse and ship, popping up unexpectedly in far-flung corners of the realm and dispensing largesse liberally.

Although not an especially tall man, his physical prowess was remarkable – his favourite party trick being the ability to leap into the saddle of a running horse. This vigour was reflected in his enjoyment of the traditional pastimes of gambling, hunting, hawking and jousting.

James' energy was not just physical, it was mental as well. He was widely read, fluent in several languages (including Gaelic) and encouraged both poetry and music at his court, playing and listening to musical instruments, such as harps, clasarchs, shawms and lutes. He rewarded the foremost poet of the age, William Dunbar, extensively, paying him an annual pension of some £80 Scots.

Literacy and education generally seem to have interested James. In 1496 the first act for compulsory education in the British Isles was passed, when all landowners were required to educate their sons in grammar (Latin) and law. His own illegitimate son, Alexander Stewart, was tutored by the most famous Humanist of all, Erasmus. The new printing press, too, was patronised by the King and during his reign myriad books on a wide range of topics were published.

A pastime that James apparently enjoyed, that would be unusual in the twenty-first century for a man who seems so masculine in his tastes, was embroidery and fine needlework. Perhaps he was so energetic that it was impossible for him to sit without doing something with his hands.

James took a keen interest in medical matters. According to Pitscottie he was:

'weill learned in the art of medicine, and was ane singular gud chirurgiane [surgeon]; and there was none of that profession, if they had any dangerous cure in hand, but would have craved his advyse'

Not content with giving surgical advice he actually got personally involved in dentistry - paying people to allow him to extract their teeth!

As James' power and influence grew, he became determined to create a suitable setting for his majesty. The old hunting lodge of Falkland was transformed into a Renaissance Palace, complete with gardens and tennis courts, and liberal sprinklings of James' thistle badge, which was coming to be synonymous not only with him personally, but with Scotland. Linlithgow, too, received a modern makeover and Stirling a new Great Hall.

Technology fascinated James, particularly military advances. The army he took across the Border in 1513 was equipped with the very latest in weaponry and tactical developments. Naval matters, too, were extremely important to him. Henry VIII has often been referred to as the father of the British Navy, but, in reality, James IV was there before him with his two enormous ships, the *Great Michael* and the *Margaret*, and he frequently visited the dockyards at Leith.

James may have been a modern king in many respects, but he was extremely traditional in the practice of his religion. As well as his penance of the iron belt mentioned earlier, he went on numerous pilgrimages to the various holy sites and shrines in the realm. When his Queen, Margaret Tudor, was ill following the birth of their first child, he undertook a pilgrimage on foot, to the shrine of Saint Ninian, some 120 miles from Edinburgh, to pray for her recovery; giving alms at the outer kirk, the rood, the altar, the high altar, the altar of Our Lady and the relics. The walk was sufficiently hard for him to need his shoes re-soling, at a cost of 16d.

An important aspect of kingly behaviour that obviously came naturally to James was the giving of extravagant '*drinksilver*', charity, and monetary presents for the little tributes that his people brought to him. The records show frequent payments such as the 14s given to a '*poor maiden*', another 14s to a woman who brought him butter at Stirling and 9s to a child who brought apples.

The most delightfully profligate expenditure of all was the 4s paid for wine to bathe the hooves of the horse owned by the tournament champion, Sir Anthony D'Arcy.

In 1498, James was described by the Spanish Ambassador, Pedro de Ayala:

'The King is 25 years and some months old. He is of noble stature, neither tall nor short, and as handsome in complexion and shape as a man can be. His address is very agreeable. He speaks the following foreign languages; Latin, very well; French, German, Flemish, Italian, and Spanish; ... He likes, very much, to receive Spanish letters. His own Scots language is as different from English as Aragonese from Castilian. The King speaks, besides, the language of the savages who live in some parts of Scotland and on the islands. It is as different from Scots as Biscayan is from Castilian. His knowledge of languages is wonderful. He is well read in the Bible and in some other devout books. He is a good historian. He has read many Latin and French histories, and profited by them, as he has a very good memory. He never cuts his

hair or his beard. It becomes him very well. He fears God and observes all the precepts of the Church.'

He may not have cut his hair or his beard in 1498, but that soon changed when he married! His young wife objected to the hirsute look and so, the morning after his wedding he was ceremoniously shaved by Queen Margaret's chief lady-in-waiting, Agnes Tilney, Countess of Surrey, and her daughter. The ladies received sumptuous presents in return for their labours.

The very few images available of James show him clean-shaven, so either date from after his marriage or are stylised.

Whilst James' enthusiasm and eagerness to be first in everything was an attractive trait, it was one that, in the end cost him his life. By the late fifteenth century, it was becoming unusual for a king to stand in the forefront of battle, instead they acted as generals at the rear, but James insisted on showing leadership in the traditional way.

'He is courageous, even more so than a king should be. I [Ambassador Pedro de Ayala again] am a good witness of it. I have seen him often undertake most dangerous things in the last wars. On such occasions he does not take the least care of himself. He is not a good captain, because he begins to fight before he has given his orders. He said to me that his subjects serve him with their persons and goods, in just and unjust quarrels, exactly as he likes, and that therefore he does not think it right to begin any warlike undertaking without being himself the first in danger. His deeds are as good as his words.'

Had James taken a more circumspect position at Flodden, rather than throwing himself into the thick of the battle, he might have lived to fight another day. But he died as he had lived – extravagantly, bravely and whole-heartedly.

Chapter 22: James IV's Wife & Four Mistresses

James IV took delight in the physical pleasures of life – music, poetry, rich foods, gambling, tournaments and food. This enjoyment of the physical included a love of women. He was well-known for having a string of mistresses. These women were not, however, just passing fancies (although there were some of those) but were also political statements. A mistress could rise and fall with her family and a change in the King's companion could signal a change in his policy. It seems that unmarried Scottish ladies of good birth were prepared to enter into relationships with the king, or other nobles – which was rather different from England, where such affairs would be considered disgraceful.

James' first 'official' mistress was Marion Boyd. Marion was the niece-by-marriage of Archibald "Bell-the-Cat" Douglas, 5th Earl of Angus. Angus had been involved in the rebellion that overthrew James III, but, suspect for his pro-English stance, had been side-lined by Bothwell and Hume in their initial control of James IV's government. Angus, one of the richest and most powerful nobles in Scotland, found a way around his exclusion by keeping James company at the dice and card tables. It would have been easy for him to introduce Marion to the King. The affair lasted for about three years, from 1492 to 1495, during which period Marion bore two children, Alexander Stewart and Katherine Stewart.

James acknowledged the children and Alexander was given the education of a prince, although a prince destined for the Church, not the throne. Following the grant of the dispensation necessary to overcome his illegitimacy, he became a sub-deacon, and at the early age of eleven was nominated as Archbishop of St Andrews.

This was a most inappropriate appointment and was an example of the blatant abuse of the Church for political ends, but there was minimal protest and James found the revenues from the appointment came in useful for replenishing the royal coffers. Alexander's early education took place in Scotland, but when he was about fourteen, he travelled to France, the Low Countries and Italy. It was in Padua that he studied under Desiderius Erasmus, who wrote:

> '..how quick, how attentive, how eager he was!...though he was a youth scarcely eighteen years old, he excelled as much in every kind of learning as in all those qualities that we admire in a man.'

Alexander perished at Flodden, with his father.

Marion Boyd's daughter, Katherine, was married to James Douglas, 3rd Earl of Morton, and bore several children.

In 1495 Marion fell from favour. She was found a husband, John Muir of Rowallan, and James found a new mistress.

Margaret Drummond, James' new love, was the daughter of John, Lord Drummond, and the sister-in-law of the Earl of Angus' son, George. Margaret took up residence in Stirling Castle and later at Linlithgow. It is unclear how long the relationship lasted and it was even suggested later that James and Margaret Drummond had been secretly married, although there is no contemporary evidence for this.

By 1501, Margaret was back at her father's house, where she died shortly after, together with two of her sisters. It seems the sisters were poisoned, whether accidentally or deliberately, is unknown. Cases of poisoning could, of course be natural, in a time with no refrigeration. Rumour at the time was divided between accusing the King's Councillors who wished to get Margaret Drummond out of the way to encourage James to marry Margaret Tudor, or accusing the husband of one of the sisters of wanting to get rid of her, and the deaths of the other siblings merely being fall out.

James IV's wife, Margaret Tudor, believed (or purported to believe – the man in question being her enemy) that the sisters were poisoned by Lord Fleming. Writing in 1523, she said

'For the Lord Fleming, for the evil will that he had to his wife, caused to poison three sister, and one of them his wife, and this is known of truth in all Scotland.'

Whatever the truth of the matter, King James paid for masses for Margaret Drummond's soul.

In 1496, a daughter had been born to Margaret Drummond, Margaret Stewart, whom James clearly doted on. The little girl had quarters at Edinburgh Castle with a nobly born governor and governess, a good sum for her board and attendance, and costly clothes. The only aspect of her education of which there is any evidence, is a payment for dancing lessons. In 1510 the thirteen year old Margaret was married to Lord Gordon, heir of the Earl of Huntly.

Widowed in 1517, with three children, she made two subsequent marriages, and had a further six children.

After Margaret Drummond's dispatch, whether by fair means or foul, James seems to have had a short relationship with Lady Isabel Stewart, daughter of the Earl of Buchan and thus a distant cousin. Lady Isabel had a daughter, Janet Stewart, who had a colourful career as governess to Mary, Queen of Scots, and mistress of Henri II of France.

The timing of this relationship with Isabel Stewart is difficult to understand – Janet Stewart's birth date is given as 1502, yet she definitely had the affair with Henri II in the late 1540s, giving birth in 1551 to Henri d'Angouleme. It is not impossible for a woman to have a child at the age of 49, but it is extremely unusual. This, together with the fact that her Christian name was Janet, rather than Isabel, might mean that she was, in fact, the child of James' final relationship of note, outside marriage.

This last liaison was with Janet Kennedy, daughter of Lord Kennedy. Janet Kennedy was married young, to Alexander Gordon, a distant relative. Janet and Alexander seem to have separated not long after the marriage and she began a connection with Bell-the-Cat Earl of Angus (yes – him again, he pops up everywhere!) The status of the relationship is unclear, as she is not referred to as his Countess, but he made grants of land to her, for her life, and for the benefit of any children they might have together. Some 30 years later, Janet referred to Bell-the-Cat as her husband when founding a charitable position, for the welfare of his soul. Since Angus was, at the time, married to Elizabeth Boyd, it is all rather confusing.

Whatever Janet's relationship with Angus, she certainly became James IV's mistress sometime in the late 1490s. The relationship lasted for several years, and she lived with him throughout the period of his marriage negotiations. On the arrival of his bride, Janet was granted Darnaway Castle, near Inverness, for her life, provided that she remained '*without husband or other man*'. James continued to visit Janet at least until 1505, when she married again, although she was divorced by 1508. Janet bore two or three children to James: their son was James Stewart, 1st Earl of Moray, and they probably had two daughters, one of whom at least is presumed to have died young.

However much James loved his various mistresses, there was no question of his marrying any of them. A king's marriage was a valuable commodity, and James intended to make the very best use of a card he could only play once.

During the 1490s negotiations for various foreign princesses were undertaken. One possible bride was Bianca Sforza, sister of the Duke of Milan. Another contender was the daughter of Frederick of Aragon, King of Naples, but as she was a baby in the 1490s, this was not a practical suggestion.

More serious negotiations took place with Spain. James would have been delighted to marry a Spanish Princess, both for the prestige, and also to strengthen ties with England, where Katharine, the youngest Spanish Princess was promised. Ferdinand and Isabella were willing to offer Ferdinand's illegitimate daughter, with a good dowry, but were less keen for a marriage with one of their legitimate girls. Nevertheless, they strung James along for a while to keep him out of the arms of France.

'Doña Juana is a natural daughter born before marriage. If the King of Scots know this, and nevertheless likes to marry her, her marriage portion might be doubled…If the Scots wish to have one of the Infantas of Spain they must be put off with false hopes, because if a plain refusal were given them they might be induced to reconcile themselves with the King of France.'

Eventually, however, it was settled that James should marry Margaret, eldest daughter of King Henry VII of England. The marriage would be the living symbol of the new Treaty of Perpetual Peace – the first peace treaty between the countries since the late fourteenth century. The only slight fly in the ointment was Margaret's youth. When the treaty was agreed she was well under the minimum marriageable age of twelve.

Polydore Vergil, historian of Henry's reign, recorded that Henry's Council raised a concern that marrying his daughter into Scotland would risk a later King of Scots becoming King of England. Apparently Henry replied equably:

'What then? Should anything of the kind happen (and God avert the omen), I foresee that our realm would suffer no harm, since England would not be absorbed by Scotland, but rather Scotland by England, being the noblest head of the entire island, since there is always glory and honour in the less being joined to that which is far the greater, just as Normandy once came under the rule and power of our ancestors the English." And so the king's wisdom was praised and they unanimously approved the measure. Margaret was betrothed to King James.'

A dispensation for the marriage was granted by the Pope on 28th July 1500. This was required as James and Margaret were both descended from John of Gaunt. The Treaty was signed on 24th January 1502 with Margaret taking part in a proxy marriage at Richmond the next day, where James was represented by the Earl of Bothwell.

It was agreed that the full marriage would not take place immediately but would be delayed until the bride was at least 13, which would be 28th November 1502. The reason for the delay was Margaret's youth. Her grandmother, Margaret Beaufort, matriarch of the Tudor dynasty, had been married at about the age of twelve and given birth to Henry VII at about thirteen. She described this early child-birth as having *'spoyled'* her, rendering her incapable of further child-bearing. She was adamant that her young grand-daughter should not suffer the same damage, particularly as the girl was described as very slight and small, clearly taking more after her father's family than her tall, robust, golden-haired Yorkist mother. Henry explained the reason for the delay to Don Pedro de Ayala, the Spanish Ambassador,

'The Queen and my mother are very much against the marriage. They say if the marriage were concluded we should be obliged to send the princess directly to Scotland, in which case they fear the

King of Scotland would not wait, but would injure her and endanger her health'

Eventually, Princess Margaret left Richmond Palace with her father on 27th June 1503 to be married to the 30 year old King James IV.

On her progress to her new kingdom, Margaret lacked nothing in the way of material comfort and splendour. Her father had fitted her out with a huge wardrobe, jewellery and horses. More personally, in a rare survival of evidence of personal affection from the time, he gave her a Book of Hours, inscribed in his own handwriting in two places:

'Remember yr kynde and loving fader in yr prayers – Henry R'

and

'Pray for yr lowving fader that gave you this boke and I gyve you at alle tymes godd's blessyng and myne. Henry R'

Henry accompanied Margaret as far as Collyweston in Northamptonshire, then on 8th July she parted from her family to head north, accompanied by a great train of ladies and gentlemen, including her grandmother's husband, the Earl of Derby. The leader of her entourage was Thomas Howard, Earl of Surrey, but his was a short term role, just to take her to Scotland and see her safely married. Her permanent household was to be led by Sir Ralph Verney, her Chamberlain, and his wife Eleanor Pole.

Despite all of this splendour one can imagine the fear and trepidation in Margaret's heart as she processed grandly through all of the cities on the Great North Road, greeting dignitaries and being royally entertained. She had just lost her mother in childbirth, an ordeal that could not be too far away for her, and she was to be married to a man she had never seen, much older and more experienced than herself. She is likely to have known that James, unlike her faithful father, was a womaniser.

Margaret finally arrived at the border at Berwick on 30th July 1503. She was met by the Archbishop of Glasgow and a host of her new subjects, including a clutch of trumpeters to blow her a fanfare. At Dalkeith, two days before her official entrance to Edinburgh, in keeping with tales of chivalry, James 'accidentally' met Margaret whilst purporting to be on a hunting trip. Fortunately, he was wearing a smart crimson velvet jacket, rather than anything more workaday.

James greeted his bride warmly and spent the two days putting her at her ease, quickly discovering a shared interest in, and aptitude for, music. On departing from her, he could not resist the opportunity to impress her with his favourite party trick – the ability to take a running leap onto his horse

Feeling safe in his masterful horseman-ship, on the 7th August Margaret made her official entry into her new city riding pillion behind James, to the delight of the crowds. He had first tried his own horse with a pillion on which was mounted a servant, to check whether it was safe for Margaret. The horse objected, so the saddle and pillion were put on her gentler palfrey.

James and Margaret were married at Holyrood Abbey, Edinburgh, on 8th August 1503 and Margaret was crowned following the nuptial mass, James holding her around the waist for much of the ceremony.

As a wedding present for Margaret, a Book of Hours was created, perhaps commissioned by James himself. It was the work of several hands, probably made in Ghent, with the most famous contributor likely to have been Gerard Horenbout, court painter to Margaret of Austria, Regent of the Low Countries. There is a portrait of James, perhaps taken from a known likeness, but Margaret is a more stylised figure.

James treated his young wife both courteously and kindly, granting her Kilmarnock as her morning gift and buying her clothes and jewels.

However he did not feel the need to break off his relationship with Lady Janet Kennedy. He may have continued the relationship partly because he seems to have been considerate enough to spare Margaret immediate consummation (although the accounts of their wedding state that they retired to bed together.) Her first pregnancy was not until 1506, resulting in the birth of a son, named James, on 21st January 1507 and christened on the 23rd of that month at Holyrood.

James was generous in his joy, giving £90 to the '*Lady Maistres*' who had given him the news, £7 to Margaret's mid-wife and £14 to the baby's nurse. The rapid christening may suggest that the baby was not strong and after the birth both Margaret and baby James were dangerously ill. King James was genuinely fond of his wife and her dangerous illness

> '*grevit him sa sair that he wald not be comforted: nouther of man wald receive ony consolatione.*'

This was the occasion on which he took the pilgrimage to St Ninian's shrine, mentioned above. Perhaps through divine intercession or perhaps on account of her own youth and strength, Queen Margaret recovered, but, after initial improvement, the baby died within a year. She went on to have four more pregnancies by James; two prior to the birth of James V on 15th April 1512 ended in still birth, with her final child by James being Alexander, Duke of Ross.

During his marriage, although James does not seem to have replaced Lady Janet Kennedy with an official mistress, there are quite a few payments to a woman named as Jane '*bare-arse*' in his accounts – we can probably guess what services were being provided!

After the succession of Queen Margaret's brother as Henry VIII of England, relations between the two royal families deteriorated. Henry withheld money due to Margaret under her father's will, and generally behaved in a way calculated to annoy James. Margaret supported her husband throughout the dispute, but she must have suffered when it became apparent that the nation of her birth and the country of which she was queen were heading for war. There were stories later that Margaret begged James not to fight, and that she retired to the tower of Linlithgow Palace, to watch and wait for the husband who never returned from the battlefield of Flodden.

Chapter 23: James IV and Tournaments

Tournaments, in which men competed both individually and in teams, were the late mediaeval sporting equivalent of modern motor racing – so expensive that only the richest could take part, adrenaline fuelled, dangerous, and guaranteed to impress the ladies.

The sport had developed in the Middle Ages as a genuine preparation for battle, with severe injury and death amongst the protagonists not uncommon when the bouts were held '*a l'outrance*' – that is, to the uttermost. By the end of the fifteenth century the activities were more stylised, with concentration on skill as much as strength, and proceedings were usually stopped before the death blow.

The great tournaments held in the Courts of Europe during this period were occasions for pageantry and display, as well as sporting prowess. Frequently, skilled combatants from across Europe would take part. It was not unusual for kings to take part personally, if they were sufficiently talented. The Emperor Maximilian I was a noted combatant.

James IV was as keen on tournaments as any king of his time, and spent considerable sums on armour. He had his own armourer, Alan Cochrane, but he also sent his armour to France for repairs and brought specialist armourers from France to supplement his own craftsmen.

Tournament armour was phenomenally expensive – made to measure, it was often elaborately decorated – unlike the more workaday models worn in battle. No pictures exist of James' armour exists but there are several extant suits belonging to Henry VIII, showing the different fashions over the first half of the century. A suit of jousting armour could weigh as much as 100lb (about 45 kg).

In accordance with custom James would announce a tournament to be held and invite

'all and sindrie his lordis, earleis, and barrouns (quhilk was abill for justing or tornament to come to Edinburgh to him, and thair to exerceis themselffis for his plesour as they war best accustomit, sum to rin with speir, sum to fight with the battell axe and harnis, sum to feight with the tuo-handit suord, sum to shut the hand bow, corsebow, and collverine [an early type of hand-gun].'

Valuable prizes were given, reflecting the specific sport – thus the winner of the spear-throwing would receive a golden, ceremonial spear. Even more pleasing in an age when reputation for physical courage was important, the King's heralds would proclaim the winner as the best in the realm.

One of the jousting heroes of the age was a Frenchman, Sir Antoine D'Arcy, later Sieur de la Bastie, and known as the *'White Knight'* – possibly from the colour of his armour, or perhaps because he wore a white scarf in honour of Anne of Brittany, Queen of France. Sir Antoine appears to have been reading the recently printed Arthurian romances, as he wandered round Europe, in the fashion of a knight from Camelot, challenging all comers.

Sir Antoine arrived in Scotland in September 1506 for a stay of four months. James extended lavish hospitality to the knight, who was lodged with one James Aikmen, paid 21s per week from the King's coffers. Not only was Sir Antoine's accommodation paid for, various small expenses charged by Aikman to a total of 42s were covered. There was also payment for food, for himself and his retinue, and a very large present of £112 before Christmas of 1506. Even more extravagantly, James paid for wine to bathe the hooves of Sir Antoine's tournament horse.

The White Knight's challenge was taken up by Lord Hamilton. The honours appear to have been even, although in rather sore-loser fashion, D'Arcy claimed to have been suffering from an *'indisposition of body'* on the day when Hamilton won a clear victory at Falkland Palace.

In the New Year of 1507, a further round of tournaments was held at Stirling, with the King, the Queen and the Court in attendance. It would appear that Sir Antoine was again the victor as he received £280 in cash. In an early episode of "re-gifting", the King also presented him with ten silver goblets which had been given to James by the Bishop of Moray, and a gold salt-cellar that Queen Margaret had given to her husband. These precious items were accompanied by a silver service from Flanders, costing £150 and a silver bowl and flask. Sir Antoine, no doubt well pleased with his rewards, was overtaken on his way home by further gifts from the King, including seven French saddles.

The tournament of the Black Knight and Lady, one of the great set-piece pageants of James' reign, took place in the summer of 1507. The tournament was announced by Marchmont Herald, to take place in the lists (the tournament ground) at Edinburgh Castle. The event was to last five weeks and the idea was that the Black Knight and his supporters would prove his Lady to be the fairest in the land, at the point of a sword.

A large silk pavilion was set up, with a couple of smaller canvas ones. From the top fluttered various standards of taffeta. In the grounds was set the Tree of Esperance (hope), planted in the garden of Patience and bearing the leaves of Pleasure, the flower of Nobleness and the fruit of Honour. Over the five week duration of the event, each week the shield of a new challenger was hung on the tree. This again suggests familiarity with the Arthurian romances – illustrations in the 12th century manuscripts by Chretien de Troyes show just such an arrangement. The pavilions had fringes of silk and painting the shields and blazons required six books of fine gold leaf.

James himself was to be the defending Black Knight. Parts of his sumptuous costume were delivered from London in a couple of locked trunks. His outfit included a gold clasp for the gorget that encircled his throat and an arming jacket (presumably worn under the armour) of black satin. His squires were dressed in cloth-of-gold and black velvet with matching bonnets (caps) and hose. Payments for silver horns suggest that his armour might have looked something like the helmet presented by the Emperor Maximilian to Henry VIII in 1514.

The Black Lady (who was probably black in fact, as well as name) was dressed in a gown of damask with flowers of gold. The dress was decorated with yellow and green taffeta and the Lady sported leather gloves. She was carried in some sort of litter, imported from Flanders, which was draped with around 160 yards (160 metres) of Flemish taffeta in various colours. The Lady had four attendants – two squires, dressed in white damask, and two girls, clad in more yellow taffeta. The horses, too, were sumptuously decked out.

As well as the contests between the King's defending party and the challengers, there were pageants and shows involving painted canvas dragons, which had saddles and reins, suggesting they were to be ridden in some way, and men dressed in goat skins.

Although there are no details of exactly how the tournament played out, the King was, (not altogether surprisingly!), the winner and claimed the Lady's hand as his prize.

So successful was the event, that it was repeated the following year, on an even grander scale. By staging spectacles of this sort, James was showing, not just that he was sufficiently master of his country to spend time on leisure, but that Scotland's court and nobles were the equivalent in skill and sophistication of Burgundy or France.

Chapter 24: Following the Footsteps of James IV

James IV lived the life of a peripatetic mediaeval monarch. He hardly ever remained in one place for more than a few days, or weeks at most.

There was a pattern to James' year, which reflected the passing of the seasons, the timing of the sessions of Justice in Ayre, the important religious celebrations, and the location of his current mistress. A typical year in James' life would have had an itinerary something like that below which is based on his activities in the year 1505. The numbers in the brackets show the locations on the maps which follow.

The year opened with the King in Edinburgh Castle (Residences 2). He made a trip to the Chapel at Restalrig, (Abbeys 19) where he bought some honey. He left the capital in February, to travel to Stirling Castle (Residences 1), which was the most centrally located of his Palaces, and the probable location of his birth. It is certainly where he spent his youth, prior to defeating his father at the Battle of Sauchieburn (Military 34).

En route to Stirling, he stopped at Linlithgow, (Residences 3) which he had spent considerable time and effort on renovating, and which was the favourite palace of his wife, Margaret of England.

In March James returned to Edinburgh, then left for Lochmaben (Military 47) to see the building works at his new castle. He travelled on to Dumfries, where he relaxed by listening to a local singer, *'the crukit vicar'*. He then moved on to Peebles, where he must have stayed in a very grand inn as it cost him 42s. Whilst there, he bought a mule – although for what purpose is unrecorded.

A quick return was made to Edinburgh Castle, followed by visits to various shrines, including Whitekirk (Abbeys 33), near Dunbar Castle (Residences 5) and the Ladykirk of Steill (Abbeys 24) which he had founded following his successful Border campaign in 1495.

He was back in Edinburgh for Maundy Thursday (or Skyre Thursday as it was known), where he performed the usual charitable activities. He also gave 28s to a poor woman from the north, who was trapped in Edinburgh, pending a decision in a legal case. The law was not much swifter then, than now!

Off he went again, to Stirling, where he paid an extravagant tip for the delivery of butter, and bought some gloves from a '*maiden*', most likely the daughter of his usual glove-supplier. A flying visit was paid to Falkland Palace (Residences 6) around the 7th May, but he soon returned to Stirling, having visited the shrine at Tillicoultry (Military 45). From Stirling he went to Dunblane, and returned to Edinburgh by 23rd May to hear High Mass at Holyrood (Residences 7) on the feast of Corpus Christi.

James then visited one of his favourite places – the Port of Leith (Military 35), where he inspected his shipping, dining on board a boat on 27th May – his silver plate having been sent for him to eat off.

The next location was Dumbarton Castle (Residences 8), where he was involved in preparations for a siege against a rebellious Walter Stewart, taking refuge in Lord Hamilton's house. Other than a two day trip to Glasgow and Paisley, the court remained at Dumbarton until 15th June. The return to Stirling was via Ayr, Auchinleck and Craigbernard.

By the end of June, the King was back in Edinburgh, again giving alms to the unfortunate, before returning to Dumbarton by mid-July. He followed this up with a visit to Lord Sempill's new chapel (Residences 16), where he made a donation of 14s before returning to Ayr and then visiting the Abbey of Crosraguel (Abbeys 27) and the Abbey of Glenluce (Abbeys 31). James was interested in gardening and we find him giving 14s to the gardener at Mytoun, home of Sir Alexander MacCulloch.

On the last day of July, the King was at the shrine of St Ninian, Whithorn (Abbeys 22). This shrine was dear to James' heart. When his Queen was very ill, following the birth of their first child, this was the shrine he walked to, barefoot, to pray for her recovery.

The night of 2nd August was spent at the monastery of Dundrennan, in return for an offering of 20s. He went on from there to Dumfries and Lochmaben again.

Travelling around the country with the number of attendants usual for a king could create problems, especially if the Court hunted or hawked as they travelled. During this August, compensation had to be paid for damage done to growing corn. Given the difficulty of growing sufficient grain in Scotland, it is unlikely that a cash payment would have cheered the farmer much.

To enhance his hunting pleasure, the King received a present of a couple of dogs: payment had to be made for someone to lead the animals back to Edinburgh. Hunting also required the purchase of copious arrows. An eye-watering gift of £4 was given to Richard Grey, Earl of Kent (Queen Margaret's first cousin, once removed) who gave James a present of bows and arrows.

James was at Stirling by mid-August, where he received the news that the final instalment of the Queen's dowry had been delivered – no doubt welcome news, as the King's expenses continued to out-run his income.

A late August hunting trip then took place – it was probably men only as the party slept in tents. Food supplies included presents of butter and curds from two country women, pike and eels from the Prior of Inchmaholme and pears from the Laird of Buchanan. James was not a gluttonous man, so simple food would have sufficed him. A quick visit to Dumbarton was squeezed in before returning to Stirling where the Court was entertained by a Spanish riding display.

The King returned to Edinburgh where the High Kirk (Abbeys 20) was celebrating the feast day of its patron, St Giles on 1st September. He would have attended the High Mass and watched the celebratory procession through the streets, the effigy of the saint being carried high on men's shoulders.

Hunting again occupied his time from 3 – 5th of the month.

Later in September, James was travelling in the south east, visiting the border town of Ayton, where the Truce of Ayton had been signed in 1497, and inspecting the works at Ladykirk again, giving '*drinksilver*' to the various workmen. He also found time to visit Whitekirk (Abbeys 33), where he played cards.

The final weeks of September were divided between Edinburgh and Stirling, before James travelled to the great Abbey and Palace at Dunfermline (Residences 12), followed by Falkland, Perth (Residences 14), Methven (Residences 9) and Dundee. Whilst he rested at Dundee for a day or so, his hawks and dogs continued north, to meet him at Arbroath before moving on to Montrose and Brechin. He continued north to Strathbogie and then went for a day or so to Darnaway Castle (Residences 10), which he had given to his mistress, Lady Janet Kennedy.

James moved on to Inverness, before crossing into the Highlands to visit the shrine of St Duthus at Tain. His journey south included another brief stop at Darnaway, before a visit to Aberdeen. Progress had slowed somewhat, and the dogs and hawks were again sent on ahead.

James was back in Stirling on 31st October, before travelling to Edinburgh where almost all of November was passed, perhaps in contemplation of the wolf that had been sent to the King as a gift!

Christmas was passed at Holyrood, before the whole cycle began again.

Key to Map 1: Royal and Noble Residences

1. Stirling Castle
2. Edinburgh Castle
3. Linlithgow
4. Scone
5. Dunbar Castle
6. Falkland Palace
7. Holyrood Palace
8. Dumbarton
9. Methven
10. Darnaway Castle
11. Jedburgh
12. Dunfermline
13. Dunbar Castle
14. Perth
15 Inchinnan Palace
16. Castle Semple

The main royal palaces were concentrated along the River Forth, between Stirling and Edinburgh, but James spent a good deal of time visiting the castles of his nobles, or other Royal Burghs, such as Perth and Ayr.

Map 1: Royal and Noble Residences

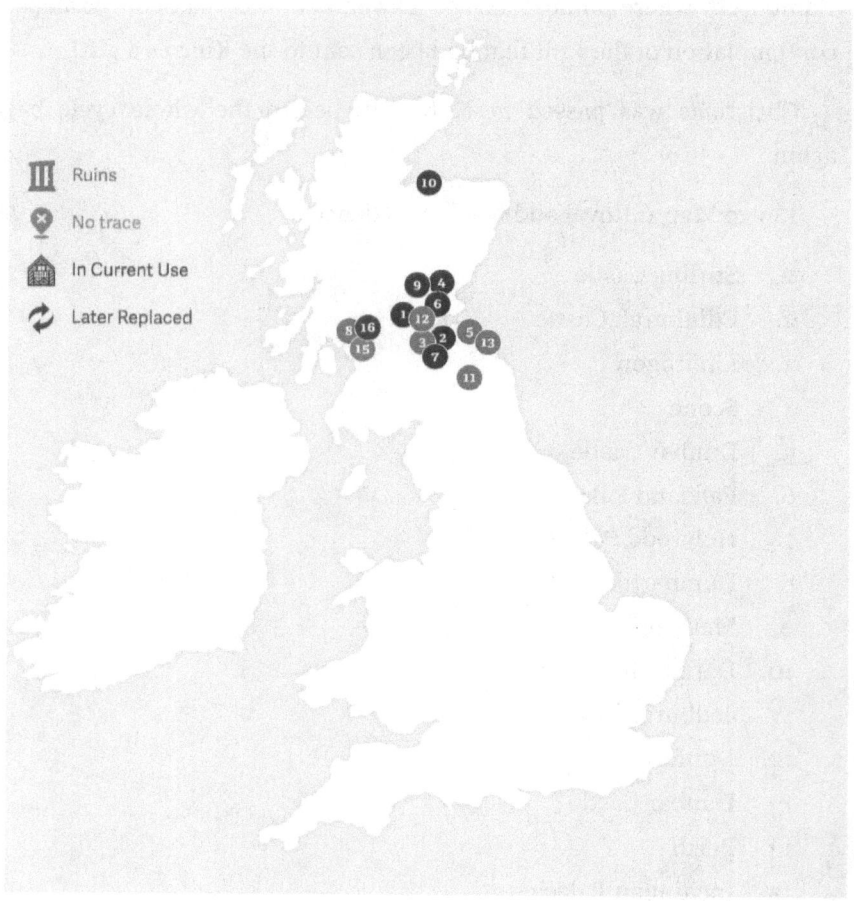

Key to Map 2: Abbeys, Priories and Places of Pilgrimage

James was an indefatigable pilgrim, visiting Abbeys, Priories and holy places the length and breadth of his realm.

1. Cambuskenneth Abbey
2. Scone
3. St Triduana's Chapel, Restalrig Edinburgh
4. St Giles Kirk, Edinburgh
5. Glasgow Cathedral
6. Shrine of St Ninian, Whithorn
7. Jedburgh
8. Ladykirk of Steill (Upsettlington)
9. Sheen Priory
10. Dunglas (Collegiate Church)
11. Crossraguel Abbey
12. St Michael, Wood Street
13. Whitehaven Priory
14. St John's Church Tower Ayr
15. Glenluce Abbey
16. Kilwinning
17. Whitekirk, Dunbar

Map 2: Abbeys, Priories and Places of Pilgrimage

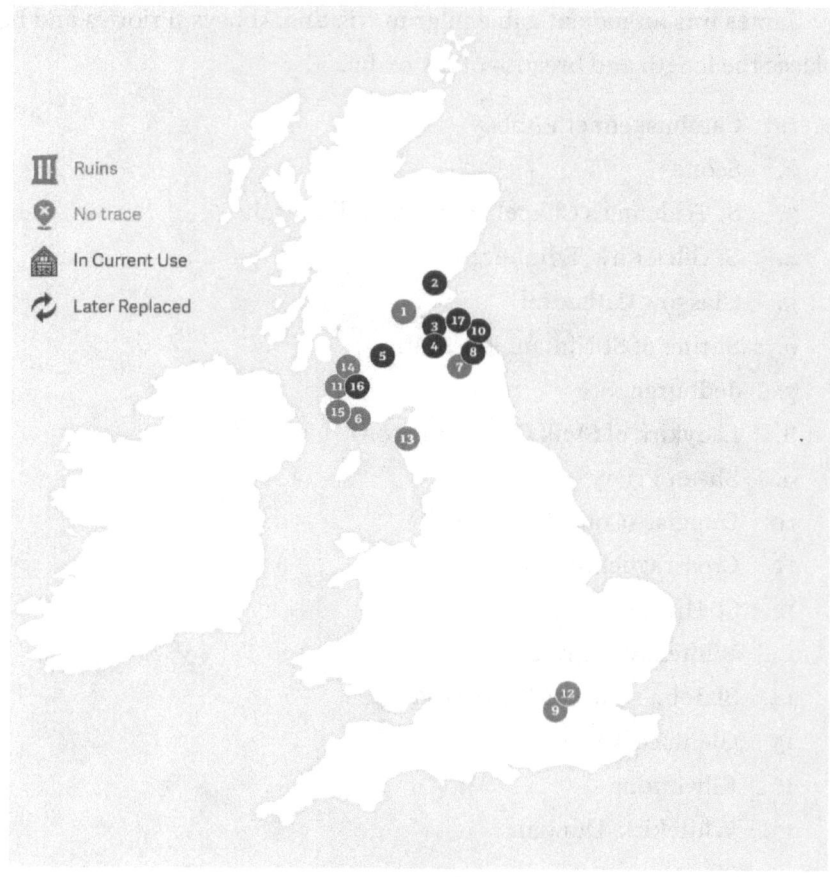

Key to Map 3: Military

James was a soldier and a man fascinated by ships. He campaigned both in the Western Isles and on the Anglo-Scottish Borders, capturing and losing castles and towns.

1. Sauchieburn
2. Port of Leith
3. Dunstaffnage Castle
4. Norham Castle
7. Etal Castle
8 Ford Castle
9. Flodden
10. Twizellhaugh
11. Coldstream
13. Burgh Muir, Edinburgh
14. Ellemford
15. Tillicoultry
16. Dunblane
17. Lochmaben
19. Isle of May

Map 3: Military

Chapter 25: James IV: Two Book Reviews

The last biography published of James IV was Norman Macdougall's James IV in 1997. The anniversary of Flodden in 1513 brought several books about the battle to the market, and there has also been a study of the whole Tudor and Stewart relationship. All of the writers bring James IV to life in different ways, looking at how his strong character shaped events.

Fatal Rivalry: Flodden 1513

Author: George Goodwin

Publisher: Weidenfeld & Nicolson (4 July 2013)

In a nutshell: An excellent retelling of this seminal battle in the Anglo-Scottish wars which will interest a far wider audience than just those interested in military history.

Books about military campaigns are often hard to follow as armies march hither and thither in terrain that may have changed out of all recognition since the event. Goodwin's writing style, however, is so fluid and fluent that the reader has no trouble at all finding out what happened at this most traumatic of battles. The book is not just a dry account of a battle, but describes in detail the personalities of the men (and women) involved, giving details of their courts, and their parallel approaches to displaying their wealth and power.

One of the best aspects of Goodwin's work is the firm placing of the battle of Flodden in its European context. Usually, the battle is only considered as another round in the endless Anglo-Scottish wars, but, in fact, it can be seen as one of the components of the War of the League of Cambrai.

The account opens with the succession of James VI to the English throne, some ninety years after the battle itself. It then backtracks to the early years of the reign of the Scottish King James IV, and examines the relationships between him, and, first, Henry VII, then Henry VIII of England.

Both James IV and Henry VII won their crowns in battle. Unlike the majority of renaissance princes, Henry was not naturally warlike, although he proved himself competent in war as in everything else. James, on the other hand, was keen to unite his factious nobles in the time-honoured way of annoying his southern neighbours. He therefore began the first of his three Border campaigns through support of the imposter, Perkin Warbeck, who claimed to have a better right to the English throne than Henry VII. Goodwin covers the wider diplomatic ambitions of James to be recognised as a player on the European stage by such illustrious monarchs as the Holy Roman Emperor, Maximilian I, and the Catholic Kings of Spain.

Having dealt with the diplomatic aspects, James followed up with a quick and very successful campaign in Northumberland, that, handily for a monarch who was not overburdened with wealth, paid for itself.

Henry VII, seriously alarmed by James' success, overreacted to a degree that almost cost him his throne. He raised such a huge army to counteract the Scottish threat that the necessary taxation led to rebellion in Cornwall. The peril was so great the Henry was obliged to send his family to the Tower of London and was quite unable to lead an army north.

Always quick to learn, Henry decided on a different strategy to deal with his northern neighbours and sent a senior member of his council,

Bishop Richard Fox of Durham, to negotiate. Keen to prove that he had the upper hand, James promptly besieged Fox in Norham Castle! Backup arrived for Fox in the shape of the Earl of Surrey, but after a little skirmishing, James emerged the victor.

James could now negotiate from a position of strength, and Goodwin describes the various complexities surrounding agreeing a peace between two countries that each had factions opposing a settlement. Also in the mix was a third group in the shape of the Border Reivers who had no interest in the rule of law being imposed by either King.

The long term treaty eventually signed was the Treaty of Perpetual Peace which was to be cemented by the marriage of Henry VII's daughter, Margaret, to James IV in 1503. Again, Goodwin explains all of the ramifications of the treaty in depth, whilst retaining the reader's interest.

Despite some minor incursions into both countries by the other, the Treaty of Perpetual Peace held for the rest of Henry VII's life. Matters changed, however in 1511. By that time, Henry VII had been succeeded by Henry VIII, brother of James' wife. Henry VIII was a whole different kettle of fish from his father. Impetuous where his father had been prudent, warlike where his father had been peace-loving, and, most of all, extravagant where his father had been parsimonious, the young Henry VIII was eager to prove his military mettle.

This leads us into the meat of the book – the early sea skirmishes, the arguments over Henry VII's bequest to his daughter, Margaret, Queen of Scots that was withheld, the blandishments of the French King in his quest to encourage James to remember the older treaty with France rather than the Treaty of Perpetual Peace, and finally, the desire of both Kings to prove themselves in war.

Goodwin describes the preparations for military action, the increasingly belligerent war of words in 1511-1513, and finally, the campaign itself. Despite knowing the outcome of the battle, its depiction is nail-bitingly suspenseful as the moves and countermoves of James and his opponent across Northumberland are retold, the relative strengths of the two armies measured, and the final result explained.

Highly recommended!

*

Flodden: A Scottish Tragedy

Author: Peter Reese

Publisher: Birlinn Ltd (4th July 2013)

In a nutshell: A really thorough examination of the military position of Scotland both before and during the reign of James IV, and a detailed description of the Flodden campaign.

This book sets the campaign of Flodden in its military context, as much as its political one. The first section of the book outlines the progress of the endless border campaigns fought between Scotland and England and the military issues that decided the outcome of each. Essentially, England could command more money, more arms and more men, but Scottish resistance was fierce, and, provided the Scots could wait a long invasion out, they could eventually repel the English. England, although richer, had neither the resources, nor the sustained will to permanently conquer and settle its northern neighbour.

The Scottish Kings played a dangerous game. As well as repelling English invasions, they often had an eye to extending the border south, claiming the ancient kingdom of Northumbria was subject to the Scots Crown. The prize most bitterly fought over was Berwick, which, although originally Scots, changed hands some thirteen times in all. In the 1460s it was ceded to Scotland by Marguerite of Anjou, the Lancastrian Queen, in return for troops, but was grabbed back a final time by Richard, Duke of Gloucester (later Richard III).

Reese then moves on to the events of James IV's reign and his relationship with Henry VII, the final victor in the Wars of the Roses and his flamboyant son, James' brother-in-law, Henry VIII.

James IV's development of artillery and the effective use of cannon in suppressing the early rebellions of his realm are touched on, then the very effective campaign of 1497. This provoked a more aggressive response than James had, perhaps, anticipated and it was lucky for James that Henry was diverted by the Cornish rising.

Following the 1497 campaign, and the eventual Truce of Ayton, war between the countries ceased, in principle at least, although low level border incursions continued. This period of peace was seized on by James to increase Scottish naval capability, and Reese looks at this in some depth.

Reese asks the interesting question of whether James' success in the early part of his reign led him to believe that his military strength was greater than was actually the case. He also points out that some of James' expenditure on his trophy ships might have been better spent on a fund for paying soldiers' wages, or mercenaries, to allow him to raise an army that was both larger, and longer-lasting than reliance on the feudal levies. James was, however, a mediaeval king and thought in terms of military service, rather than a paid army.

We then come to the deterioration of relations between the two countries in the period 1509 – 1513. Reese explores the sometimes similar, sometimes competing, characters of James IV and Henry VIII, and the effect their outlook and personalities had on political and military matters. He also looks at the Battle of Flodden in the context of wider European issues.

In his concentration on military matters, Reese does not always examine some of the political nuances that other writers consider in more detail, but he does look at the importance of military success to both kings, but particularly James, in preserving their positions in a society that fundamentally considered success in battle as the most important element of kingship.

Reese's real contribution is the detailed analysis of the battle preparations, the different methods raising of troops and how they were supplied and paid, the relative merits of the various weapons that the two armies deployed, the skill and experience of the commanders, and finally, the battle itself.

In all, a very thorough and readable account of a battle that had a major effect on the history of the British Isles.

Part 3: Lady Margaret Pole: Countess of Salisbury

Introduction

In the Middle Ages, the Wheel of Fortune was a popular motif, showing the transience of everything – no matter how high you might be today, soon, the Wheel would turn and you too would be brought low, whilst another took your place. The history of Margaret, Countess of Salisbury can be seen as a perfect example of this mediaeval narrative, as her life moved from wealth and magnificence, to poverty and obscurity, then back to power and influence, before descending into a pit of dishonour and death.

Part 3 contains Lady Margaret Pole's Life Story and additional articles about her, looking at different aspects of her life. Margaret wielded power and influence more commonly in the hands of men, and this made her a political figure, in a way unusual for women of the sixteenth century. This position affected both the way she lived, and the reasons for her death.

Family Tree

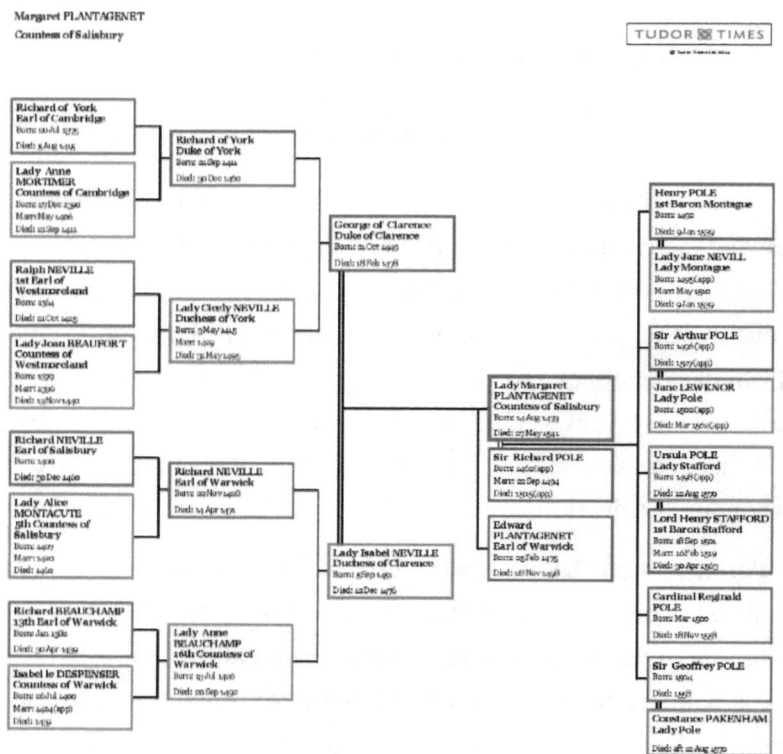

Lady Margaret Pole's Life Story

Chapter 26: Daughter of Clarence (1473 – 1487)

Margaret was born at the top of Fortune's Wheel, at the castle of Farleigh in Somerset. Her father, George, Duke of Clarence, was the brother of Edward IV, and her mother, Isabel Neville, was the daughter of that hero (or villain) of the Wars of the Roses, Warwick the Kingmaker. Isabel Neville, and her sister Anne, married to Clarence's brother, Richard, Duke of Gloucester, were co-heiresses to two of the greatest earldoms in England – Salisbury and Warwick, both of which were earldoms that could be inherited by women.

Clarence and Gloucester had quarrelled bitterly over the division of the spoils when Warwick the Kingmaker had been killed at Barnet. His widow, Anne, who was Countess of Warwick in her own right, was despoiled by her sons-in-law and treated as though she were naturally dead with the brothers sharing out her lands which covered great swathes of the south-west, the midlands and the north of England.

The household into which Margaret was born was the apogee of mediaeval power, wealth and 'good lordship', as the ties binding great peers to their supporters was known. The Clarence household was waited on by some 350 servants of all ranks, as they divided their time between Farleigh Castle, the mighty Warwick Castle, and their other numerous estates, transported by their 133 horses.

For the first eighteen months of Margaret's life, she was the Clarences' only child, until, in 1475, Duchess Isabel gave birth to a son, Edward. But Fortune's Wheel was turning and Isabel died in a third childbed, a year later, and was buried at the great Benedictine Abbey of Tewkesbury, which had been patronised by her Despenser and Beauchamp ancestors. Young Edward was confirmed by his uncle, the King, as Earl of Warwick, but the Salisbury inheritance, confiscated from Warwick the Kingmaker, remained vested in the Crown.

Soon after the loss of her mother, Margaret's father, a foolish, indiscreet, impulsive and injudicious man, for all his charm and good looks, fell foul, not for the first time, of his brother, Edward IV. Among his various misdeeds had been an alliance with Lancaster, in the years before Margaret's birth, and an attempt to upstage Edward IV by seeking to marry the great heiress, Mary, Duchess of Burgundy, against his brother's strict commands. Clarence receive a show-trial in Parliament, where the only accuser and prosecutor was the King himself, and the only defender was Clarence in person, no others being allowed to speak. Parliament found him guilty and he was executed in the Tower of London. According to legend, he was dispatched by being drowned in a butt of malmsey wine.

Clarence was not only condemned to death, he was also *'attainted'* which meant his lands, goods and titles were forfeit to the Crown. As Margaret's brother had already been confirmed as Earl of Warwick, his father's death did not affect his status, but she had no inheritance, and was dependent entirely on King Edward for her maintenance. Edward took his duty seriously, and Margaret, referred to in the accounts as his *'dear and well-beloved niece'*, was clothed, educated and served at his expense, although her precise whereabouts during the remainder of Edward IV's reign are unknown.

It seems probable that she was brought into the household of the queen, Elizabeth Woodville, and her cousins, the King's children, who varied in age between Elizabeth, seven years older than Margaret, and Bridget, seven years younger. Margaret's education would have been typical of that of a member of the royal family – reading, writing, keeping accounts, music (she played the virginals) sewing, both plain and fine, and, probably, French.

In 1483, political events changed Margaret's life again. Edward IV died, but his young son, proclaimed Edward V, never saw his coronation, his place being taken by his uncle Gloucester, now crowned as Richard III. As Clarence had been the older brother of the two, there were grounds for suggesting that Warwick was the legitimate heir if there were problem with the inheritance of Edward IV's children, but that idea was not likely to take root.

Again, Margaret's exact location during the next two years is uncertain, but by the time of the Battle of Bosworth in August 1485, when Richard III was defeated by Henry Tudor, Earl of Richmond, Margaret, her brother, and her female cousins, were all at the impressive Castle of Sheriff Hutton in Yorkshire. The new king, Henry VII, had vowed to marry Elizabeth of York should he be victorious, and the York princesses and Margaret were placed in the household of his mother, Lady Margaret Beaufort, Countess of Richmond and Derby. Initially, Warwick was there, too.

Lady Margaret Beaufort was a clever, intelligent and well-connected woman, devoted to her son's interests, and, although Henry VII was not a man to rely on anyone, he was close to his mother, and trusted her completely. By placing the Yorkist heirs in her care, he could be sure that they would be both safe, and kept away from anyone plotting on their behalf. In February 1486, Henry married Elizabeth, and Margaret became an important member of their court. She was listed, under the title '*My Lady Margaret of Clarence*', as the first of the great ladies attending the baptism of the royal heir, Arthur, in September of 1486. Fortune's Wheel was beginning to turn again in Margaret's favour.

Edward, Earl of Warwick, however, was not so fortunate as his sister. In 1487, whispers of a rebellion were abroad, with a young man, Lambert Simnel, claiming to be him. Warwick, no more than eleven years old, was paraded through the streets of London, to prove that Simnel was an imposter, then incarcerated in the Tower. Simnel's backers, Margaret's paternal aunt, Margaret, Duchess of Burgundy and her cousin, John de la Pole, Earl of Lincoln, raised an army greater than that brought by Henry VII to Bosworth, but were heavily defeated at the Battle of Stoke in November 1487.

Immediately following the battle, Elizabeth of York was crowned, reminding everyone of her status as the senior York heir. Margaret was present, watching the ceremony from a private viewing stage she shared with the King and Lady Margaret Beaufort. Margaret remained at court, but Warwick's estates were confiscated on 30 November 1487. Eventually, in 1490, the lands were returned to Margaret and Edward's grandmother, Anne, Countess of Warwick, who had been defrauded by her sons-in-law, twenty years before. Countess Anne was obliged to disinherit her grandson and leave her lands to the King. Edward, still referred to as Earl of Warwick, retained some of the Salisbury lands, for the time being, at least, although they were little use to him in the Tower.

Chapter 27: Tudor Matron (1487 – 1504)

In the aftermath of the Battle of Stoke, Henry VII was keener than ever to prevent any risk of Yorkist heirs popping up. His sister-in-law, Cicely of York, was married to the Tudor stalwart John, Viscount Welles, Henry's half-uncle, and Margaret was given in marriage to Sir Richard Pole. The marriage date of Margaret and Richard is usually given as 1491, but her biographer, Hazel Pierce, has made an excellent case for it being 1487, as a result of the Simnel rebellion.

It was later suggested that Margaret was '*disparaged*' by the marriage – that is, her royal blood was sullied by a match to such a low-born man, however, that is not entirely fair. Sir Richard, knighted after the Battle of Stoke, was Henry VII's half-cousin, and though not of royal blood, he was much favoured by the King and given many honourable positions.

Sir Richard was around fifteen or sixteen years older than Margaret. His father, Geoffrey, had been a trusted councillor of Jasper Tudor, Earl of Pembroke, and his mother, Edith St John, was Margaret Beaufort's much-cherished half-sister. Nevertheless, Margaret, whose father's income had been £6,000 per annum, might have been a little disgruntled at a husband whose landed wealth amounted to no more than £50. Margaret had no dowry, however, so this was a slight improvement over dependence on Henry and Elizabeth. In order to maintain his royally-connected bride, Sir Richard was given two more manors, bringing his income up to the pleasant, but hardly princely, sum of £170 per annum, supplemented by the income from his various offices.

Initially, Margaret lived on her husband's manor of Bockmer, Buckinghamshire, but was still present at court from time to time, in attendance on both Queen Elizabeth and Lady Margaret Beaufort at the Feast of St George in April 1488, and at Christmas that year. Her name appeared after the Queen's sisters and the other peeresses. In 1493, Margaret received the uncharacteristically generous present of £20 from Henry VII, perhaps as an adjunct to Richard's appointment to the prestigious office of Chamberlain to Arthur, Prince of Wales.

It is likely (although the exact timings are disputed) that it was at this time that Arthur's independent household was set up at Ludlow. Margaret and Richard moved to Staffordshire, being granted the use of Stourton Castle, near Kinver. Richard had a number of offices in Wales, in addition to the position as Chamberlain: Sheriff of Merioneth,

Constable of Harlech Castle and later Constable of North Wales, and Constable of Chester, and this location would enable him to be on hand to perform his duties.

Throughout the 1490s Richard was busy on royal business, travelling around the kingdom, and taking part in Henry VII's few foreign forays to Brittany and France. He was also honoured in 1499 by being appointed as a Knight of the Garter. Membership of the Order of the Garter was a most prestigious accolade, and Richard, a few years later, was noted as *'rychly arayed in his Coller'* at the proxy wedding of Henry VII's daughter (yet another Margaret) to James IV of Scotland.

Margaret's first son had been born in 1492, and named, not surprisingly, Henry. Her next three children, Arthur, Reginald and Ursula, were born at intervals up to 1500 and her last son, Geoffrey in 1504. There may have been another daughter who died young.

These tranquil years, spent between the Welsh Marches, the Court and the Pole manor at Bockmer were rudely interrupted in 1499 when, as a result of the long-drawn out Perkin Warbeck affair, her brother, Warwick, was executed.

The treatment of Warwick is a dark stain on Henry VII's reign, and something he apparently felt guilty about later. The Earl, confined to the Tower since 1486, had not been properly educated or attended, and it is almost certain that the attempted escape with Warbeck, for which he was charged with treason, was a put-up job. Henry VII at least had the grace to have Warwick properly interred at Bisham Priory, resting place of the Earls of Salisbury, and paid for the funeral.

Another person who claimed later to feel guilt over Warwick's death was Katharine of Aragon, whose parents, Ferdinand and Isabella, had insinuated that the marriage between Katharine and Prince Arthur could not take place whilst there was the least risk to Henry's throne.

There is no record of Margaret's reaction, but it seems reasonable to suppose that she was deeply upset by the loss of her brother in such tragic circumstances. Her later petition to Henry VIII for the restoration of the Earldom of Salisbury proclaims her belief that, if he had been drawn into treason, it was through innocence and ignorance. Warwick's attainder for treason meant that his inheritance was confiscated, so Margaret, although she was his heir, received nothing.

Whatever her inner feelings, Margaret had her duty to perform, and soon she would have a more pleasing one. Prince Arthur was married to the Spanish Princess in 1501, and the young couple took up residence at Ludlow, with Margaret almost certainly amongst the English ladies appointed to attend the Princess, whilst her husband continued in his role as Prince Arthur's Lord Chamberlain.

Whether Katharine favoured Margaret initially because of the circumstances of Warwick's death, or whether it was genuine regard, the two women struck up a close friendship, despite Margaret being some twelve years the elder.

Shockingly, within five months of his marriage, Arthur was dead, and the royal household broken up. Katharine returned to London, and Margaret and Richard continued to divide their time between Stourton and Bockmer.

But Fortune's Wheel turned again - in October 1504, either just before, or just after Margaret bore her last child, Geoffrey, Sir Richard Pole died, and Margaret was left a widow of small means and dangerous royal blood.

Chapter 28: Widows & Orphans (1504 – 1509)

Sir Richard's salary for the various offices he held would have ceased upon his death, and Margaret's dower rights would have been no more than her common-law entitlement of one-third of the £170 landed income from his manors in Buckinghamshire – as she had brought no dowry to the marriage, she is unlikely to have had a more generous jointure. The lands themselves were held by the King, as was customary, during the minority of the heir, Margaret's eldest son, Henry.

There was no family to whom Margaret could turn – her cousin, Elizabeth of York, who had frequently made presents of money to her sisters when they were in straitened circumstances, had died in 1503. The other York princesses, if they had any ready cash (Cicely had been banished and her lands confiscated in 1503 for making a disgraceful marriage and Bridget was a nun) may not have wished to draw attention to themselves by supporting Warwick's sister.

Margaret did receive some support from Richard's friend, Charles Somerset, a distant cousin of the King, who stood surety with her for a loan of £40 for the funeral, and two rather grudging bits of support from King Henry, who permitted the funeral loan to be repaid out of the income from the Pole lands and gave her just over £55 for food and clothes.

It does not seem a huge amount, given the years of loyalty Sir Richard had shown Henry, and the fact that the King was sitting on the vast Salisbury and Warwick estates that were Margaret's hereditary portion. Margaret and her children remained in the country, with her third son, Reginald, being sent to the Carthusian Monastery at Sheen when he was around seven, to be trained to the scholarly life.

Meanwhile, Margaret's friend, Katharine of Aragon, dowager Princess of Wales, was also hard up, and dependent on the unenthusiastic charity of her father-in-law. This joint experience of widowhood and poverty proved another link between the two women. But, just as things seemed at their lowest ebb, the Wheel of Fortune turned again, and Margaret moved into the limelight.

Chapter 29: Countess of Salisbury (1509 – 1521)

Henry VII died in 1509, and within weeks, Margaret had been whisked to court as the Lady-in-Waiting of the new Queen, Katharine of Aragon. Forty marks were shelled out by the new King for Margaret's board after her arrival in London for the coronation. Henry VIII, who may have remembered Margaret from his early childhood, showed himself willing, initially, to favour the remaining members of his mother's family of York, and was also pleased to accede to any requests Katharine made for her friends to be promoted. Margaret's son, Henry, now 17, was immediately given a place in the King's household.

Margaret was still only the widow of a knight, but, for the coronation, she received the cloth allowance given to countesses – perhaps an early indication that the royal couple were contemplating the restoration of her family. She also received an annuity of £100.

Over the next couple of years, more marks of favour were granted – Henry Pole was promoted in the King's household and given fine clothes, and Reginald's education was paid for by the King.

During these early years of Henry VIII's reign, Margaret remained close to Queen Katharine, no doubt comforting the Queen after her 1510 miscarriage, and again after the devastating loss of Henry, Duke of Cornwall in 1511. In 1512, Margaret finally returned to the top of Fortune's Wheel: her petition for restoration to the Earldom of Salisbury (see Margaret's family tree for her descent) was granted.

Salisbury was one of the oldest earldoms in the kingdom, and heritable by women – Margaret's great-grandmother had been Countess in her own right. Warwick was also heritable by women, but, for whatever reason, perhaps because it did not seem politic to ask too much, and because, legally, Henry VII had received the lands from Countess Anne by gift, rather than by confiscation, Margaret did not petition for that earldom to be restored.

Henry VIII's reasons for restoring the earldom were probably mixed – there was a general feeling that the execution of Warwick had been unjust and Henry wanted to contrast his generosity and open-handedness with Henry VII's niggardly later years. Katharine's support was probably helpful as well.

In the early years of his reign, with hopes of a male heir, Henry tried to weave the members of the wider royal family into a tight-knit unit, and promoted many of his Yorkist cousins, including restoring the son of his aunt, Katherine of York, to the Earldom of Devon, and later, promoting him to Marquess of Exeter. Not all Yorkist cousins were so fortunate – Edmund de la Pole (a different family from the Poles) was dragged out of the Tower and executed before Henry felt it safe to embark for France in 1512.

Of course, restoration of an earldom with an income of £2,000 per annum (some forty times the income Margaret had enjoyed as a widow) did not come free. Margaret paid the King 5,000 marks (c. £3,330 or eighteen months' income) as her entry fine. Margaret would not have had the cash to pay up front, so she must have borrowed the initial £1,000 she paid, and then she and her eldest son and heir, Henry, referred to thereafter as Henry, Baron Montague, were bound in a recognisance to pay the remainder.

Margaret, from being a poor widow, was now catapulted to the position of fifth or sixth richest noble in the land, after the King. It must have been a dizzying experience, and perhaps brought back traces of memory of her very early childhood.

Margaret, now Countess of Salisbury, took to her new-found wealth with delight, and recreated the lavish feudal household of her parents, with her arms plastered, painted, embroidered, and engraved on anything that stayed still long enough – clothes, tableware, window-glass, tapestries and horse-blankets. She had a London home, Le Herber (now under Cannon Street Station) as well as country seats at Clavering, Essex; Bisham, Buckinghamshire and Warblington in Hampshire, not forgetting the dozens of smaller manor houses she owned.

Despite such a choice of accommodation, Margaret continued her attendance at Court, and, in 1516 received the prestigious honour of standing as godmother at the Confirmation of the only child of Henry and Katharine to live more than a few weeks – Mary, born 18th February 1516.

It seems, too, that Henry and Katharine probably visited her at Warblington during their summer progresses and she received presents as generous, or more than as generous, at New Year, as the Dukes of Norfolk and Suffolk. The ultimate accolade of the King and Queen's affection and trust was her appointment as Lady Governess to Princess Mary in 1520.

Fortune could give no more, and inevitably, things began to go wrong.

Chapter 30: Suspicion (1521 – 1525)

Once Margaret had been restored to her inheritance, part of her duty was to arrange the best marriages she could afford for her children. In 1518 she arranged her son, Henry Pole's, marriage to Jane Neville, the daughter of Lord Bergavenny, and her daughter, Ursula's, marriage with the eldest son of Edward Stafford, 3rd Duke of Buckingham.

Buckingham was a descendant of Edward III, and the senior Duke in the kingdom. This was a splendid match for Ursula, who would, in due course, be the highest-ranking peeress in England, after the Queen, the Princess and the King's sisters. Margaret must have danced at the wedding with an exultant heart.

Unfortunately, Buckingham was not just a distant relative of the King, he had all the arrogance, pride in his royal blood and disdain for lesser ranks that had characterised his father, the Duke who had rebelled against Richard III, and also Margaret's own father, Clarence. Henry VIII was no more tolerant of over-mighty nobles than his great-uncle and grandfather had been and Buckingham had made the additional mistake of treating Henry VIII's chief minister, Cardinal Wolsey, with contempt.

In 1521, Buckingham was charged with treason. It does not appear that he was really involved in any plot to overthrow Henry VIII, but he had grumbled about upstarts, speculated on the succession (the King had no male heir, and Buckingham was a possible contender for the throne) and, prone to violent rages, talked wildly about killing the King. Regardless of the meat of the charge, Henry VIII believed there was a genuine threat to himself and the House of Tudor.

Buckingham and his servants were arrested and interrogated, and so was Henry Pole, Lord Montague. Montague was connected, both through being the brother-in-law of Buckingham's son, and the son-in-law of Buckingham's own son-in-law, Lord Bergavenny. Buckingham was executed on 17th May 1521 and a cloud of suspicion hung over the whole Pole family. Margaret was removed from her office of Lady Governess to the Princess.

After some months in the wilderness, the Poles began to come back into favour. Montague was released and chosen to attend the King at his meeting with Charles V in 1522, and Margaret again received New Year presents from the Queen. Ursula, of course, was now deprived of the prospect of becoming a Duchess, and never ranked higher than wife of Baron, with twelve children and a rather more limited income than expected.

Chapter 31: My Lady Governess (1525 – 1533)

By 1525, Margaret was reappointed to the role of Lady Governess to Princess Mary. By this point, it was clear that Mary would have no brothers, and Henry was obviously considering her as his heir, although he would never definitely commit to the idea. In 1525, Mary was sent to Ludlow in the Welsh Marches to hold Court as the de facto Princess of Wales, as her Uncle Arthur had been in 1501, and her great-uncle Edward V had in 1473. Mary was never officially invested with the title, but was referred to by it from time to time. Margaret went with her to supervise the household as she and Sir Richard Pole had done in 1501.

Margaret's duties were carefully documented. She had charge of the Princess' education (although the teaching was delivered by masters), her health, exercise, diet and recreation. Margaret, like the King and Queen, patronised the Humanist scholars of Oxford and Cambridge, but her religion was as orthodox as theirs, and she would have ensured that Mary continued to worship in the time-honoured Catholic fashion. There would have been little concession to the evangelical thought spreading its way across Europe and, with the emergence of Anne Boleyn as a rival to Katharine, into the Court.

During the period 1525-1528, Margaret and Mary were based in the Marches, but travelled in the region, and returned to London in 1527 for Mary's betrothal (her third, by the tender age of 11) to Henri, Duc d'Orleans, second son of François I of France. It was around this time that Margaret's son, Arthur, died.

By 1528, Katharine's position as Queen, and Mary's as Princess of Wales, was beginning to look decidedly precarious. Henry was attempting to have their marriage annulled, so that he could secure the succession with a male heir. Margaret was, presumably, deeply concerned for her friend and for her charge, but Mary's household, although reduced in size and recalled from Ludlow, continued much as before, with Margaret remaining in post.

Margaret and Mary spent the Christmases of 1529 and 1530 at Court, and Henry continued to treat his daughter with affection. Margaret's job must have become increasingly difficult – she would have wanted to shield Mary from the worst of the pain of the breakdown of her parents' marriage, but by the time Henry finally left Katharine in the summer of 1531, it would have been impossible for Mary, by then fifteen and a half, and so considered adult, not to know the full situation.

Until 1533, Margaret was not called upon actively to support Henry's actions against Katharine and the potential disinheriting of Mary, but in 1533, she was obliged to nail her colours to the mast when an order arrived from Thomas Cromwell to Mary's Lord Chamberlain, Lord Hussey. He was to hand over Mary's jewels, with an inventory, to a Mistress Frances Elmer. Margaret impeded the dispatch of the jewels so far as she could, delaying the production of an inventory, then slowly writing one herself which she ordered Hussey and the other household officials to sign. Still she delayed the handover, refusing to act until she received an order direct from the King.

Hussey excused his failure to obey orders by telling Cromwell that:

> 'In no wyse she (Margaret) wyll as yete deliyver to Mistress Frances the jewells for anything that I can say or doo onlesse that yt may please you to obteyne the kings letters unto hyr in that behalf.'

Follow up commands to Hussey from Cromwell to sell the Princess' silver plate were answered with the news that he couldn't do so, as the plate was in the hands of *'my lady Governesse.'* It was impossible, Margaret said, that the plate should be sold, as it was used frequently, and could not be disposed of unless replaced. Of course, Margaret added, if the King commanded directly, *'she will at all tymes be redy upon her discharge to make thereof delivery.'*

Henry was beset on all sides by stubborn women. Anne Boleyn was demanding Katharine of Aragon should hand over the christening robes used for her children, which tasteless request Katharine rejected indignantly; Mary was refusing to accept the validity of Henry's new marriage and the demotion from Princess of Wales, which occurred in September 1533; and Margaret was making heavy weather of carrying out any orders. One could almost pity the man.

Angry and frustrated, but still fond of his daughter, Henry reacted to Mary's disobedience by removing those about her, whom he could blame for her obstinacy. Margaret was dismissed from her post, and Mary was sent with only a few attendants to a humiliating position in the household of the recently born Elizabeth.

Margaret was clearly willing to take risks on Mary's behalf, and offered to serve her with a suitable household, at her own expense. Henry was taking no chances, and rejected the offer out of hand. The Imperial Ambassador, Eustace Chapuys, opined that Margaret had been removed to make it easier *'to cause (Mary) to die of grief or in some other way, or else compel her to renounce her rights'*. Mary, however, did not need Margaret's stiffening to remain resolved.

Chapter 32: Darkening Days (1533 – 1536)

Henry continued to harbour resentment of Margaret, and, in 1535, when Chapuys suggested she be re-appointed as Lady Governess, spoke of her contemptuously, saying *'the countess is a fool, of no experience.'* Margaret had annoyed Henry not only in relation to her support of Mary and Katharine, but also by ill-advisedly persisting in an argument over land rights.

Margaret's world was disintegrating – her dear friend, Katharine, had been banished to the draughty castle of Kimbolton, well away from London; her charge, Mary, to whom she had been *'a second mother'* had been taken from her and sent, aged seventeen, to live amongst her enemies; and the King was attacking the Church which had seemed eternal. He was also rounding on anyone who had had dealings with Elizabeth Barton, the Nun of Kent.

Barton had made a number of prophecies over the years, and, having been examined by William Warham, Archbishop of Canterbury, found to be a woman of purity. In earlier times, Henry had met the Nun himself and listened to her, but now she was beginning to criticise him and his policies. There was a hunt for all those who appeared to have given credence to her loud proclamations against Henry's second marriage.

Katharine had refused to have anything to do with Barton, and had instructed Margaret to keep the Nun well away from Mary, but it was alleged that Margaret had had the Nun's prophecies concerning the King's imminent death repeated to her. In such turbulent times, it is not surprising that Margaret, now sixty, fell ill, and lay for several months on a sickbed at Bisham. The Nun's prognostications were particularly sensitive because they touched on the succession, a matter over which Henry was increasingly touchy, especially where his blood relatives were concerned.

Margaret lay low for the next three years, but not low enough. In 1535, she became involved in a dispute with Cromwell over the appointment of one William Barlow as Prior of Bisham. Bisham Priory was the ancestral mausoleum of the Earls of Salisbury and Margaret would normally expect a say in the appointment – she had certainly complained about the previous prior, although she now lobbied to have him retained. Barlow was not favoured by Margaret as he was a strong supporter of Henry's marriage to Anne Boleyn. Not surprisingly, Barlow was appointed despite Margaret's opposition.

Chapter 33: Mother of the King's Enemy (1536 – 1538)

In 1536, the Wheel of Fortune seemed to begin to turn again in Margaret's favour. Anne Boleyn was disgraced and executed, and Henry's third wife was a strong sympathiser with his elder daughter, now degraded from 'Princess' Mary, to mere 'Lady' Mary. Margaret reappeared at Court in June 1536, but the price of Mary's rehabilitation and forgiveness was the acceptance that her parents' marriage had been invalid. She was finally forced to accept the Act of Supremacy, and swallowed the bitter pill on 22nd June 1536.

It was believed that, with this change of Queen, and the return of Mary to Court, Margaret's influence would increase, and she began to be supplicated for favours as before, but Fortune had smiled, only to dash Margaret to the ground.

Reginald Pole, her son, had been studying in Europe, at Henry's expense, for many years. He was extremely well-thought of in Church circles, as a scholar, a man of sober life, and, of course, as a cousin of the King of England. He was a very influential figure in Rome and having studied the matter of Henry and Katharine's marriage, appeared, initially, to be in favour of annulment. He did not make any definitive statements in the early 1530s, despite being offered the Archbishopric of York, but then, in October 1535, he had written to Cromwell asking the latter:

' *to assure His Highness of my readiness to do him service at all times'*.

Henry obviously took this as a sign that Reginald was about to declare in his favour, so the arrival of a second, open letter, entitled *De Unitate*, in June 1536, was the Tudor equivalent of a bombshell. Reginald referred to Henry as:

'*a robber, murderer and greater enemy to Christianity than the Turk.*'

Not only that, he actively called upon Charles V and François I to invade the kingdom and depose Henry.

The first news Margaret had of this incendiary missive was when she was summoned to the King's presence and he told her in person of the outrageous, treasonable, ungrateful, perverse, ignorant etc etc behaviour of her son. There is no record, of course, of the actual conversation, but we can imagine Henry's fury. He was beside himself with rage - and the wrath of a Prince is death.

Margaret immediately consulted with her eldest son, Henry, Lord Montague, as to the best course of action for the family to take. Margaret and Montague were no doubt genuinely horrified that Reginald had uttered such appalling insults against the King. Even if, in their hearts, they opposed the divorce, and perhaps, the Royal Supremacy (although there is no indication they had made any difficulties in the matter on religious grounds), the King was still an almost sacred being. Insulting him was a shocking act of disobedience.

Montague and Margaret were both well aware that treason was a miasma that could envelope a whole family. They decided to inform all of their servants that Reginald was a traitor, and that he was to be reported to the authorities if he arrived in England. Margaret *'took her son for a traitor and for no son, and that she would never take him otherwise.'*

The King wanted more, and so Margaret wrote directly to Reginald, saying she could not bear the King's wrath. He should

'...take another way and serve our master as thy bounden duty is to do unless thou wilt be the confusion of thy mother'.

If he did not remember what was due to the King he could *'trust never in (her).'*

Henry continued to fume, and sent for Montague whom he harangued with quotes from Reginald's letter. Montague wrote to Reginald in anger and frustration, telling him not to visit the Pope, as he had heard Reginald planned, and pointing out that *'Learning you may well have but doubtless no prudence nor pity.'* If Reginald were to continue in his foolish course, Montague would disown him.

Margaret now retired from Court. Although Mary had been returned to the King's good graces, and had been allowed to select members of her new household, there was no place for Margaret in it. Having capitulated and accepted the annulment, Mary had more sense than to provoke her father again. Margaret and her god-daughter exchanged gifts at New Year (although, significantly, there were no gifts from the King) but did not meet again.

The Countess was in her sixties, and perhaps was content with a more retired life although she still took a very active part in managing her estates, and was kept occupied with the business of educating her granddaughters and training them up to be great ladies in their turn.

Sadly, this quiet retirement did not last long.

Chapter 34: The Wrath of a Prince (1538 – 1541)

Throughout the early 1530s, Margaret's sons (other than Reginald) had supported Henry VIII's government, accepting the Act of Supremacy, and the Act of Succession.

Even after the nightmare of Reginald's 1536 letter, Montague was retained at Henry's side and when, in October 1536, the major uprising, known as the Pilgrimage of Grace, broke out, Montague and Geoffrey acted in accordance with their duty, bringing 200 men and 20 respectively to the King's forces.

Montague was in high enough favour to attend the Earl of Sussex at the christening of Prince Edward at Hampton Court in 1537 and he also supported Lady Mary in her role as Chief Mourner at the funeral of Jane Seymour.

In early 1537, the immediate danger of rebellion was averted but the political mood remained tense and there were still worries over the succession, and very real concern about a foreign invasion. It was during this period that Henry began strengthening England's coastal defences with structures such as Deal, Dover and Portchester Castles.

By 1538, Geoffrey was blotting the family copy book almost as badly as Reginald, although in Geoffrey's case it was not principle that he was defending. Geoffrey was notoriously feckless, quarrelsome and debt-ridden, although these faults were, for many, redeemed by his charm. Nevertheless, a mounting series of ill-judged incidents led to him being refused entrance to Court on the day of Prince Edward's christening.

Meanwhile, Henry VIII was still determined to have revenge on Reginald, whom the Pope had provokingly named as a Cardinal in 1537, despite Reginald not actually being a priest, and assassins were sent to seek Reginald out in Europe, although without success. In fairness to Henry, it should be noted that he was not a great advocate of secret assassination.

The fear of foreign invasion was given further impetus by the signing of the Treaty of Nice in July 1538 between Francois I of France and Emperor Charles V. Reginald Pole was involved in the negotiations, and the Treaty was seen, in part, as preparation for an invasion of England.

Sometime in June 1538, one Gervase Tyndall, an informer reporting to Thomas Cromwell, was staying, whether by accident or design is not certain, in an infirmary maintained by Margaret. The surgeon in charge, a man named Richard Ayer, passed away the hours with his inmate gossiping about his employer, Lady Salisbury and her family.

What he had to say made Tyndall's ears prick up, and he was soon reporting back to Cromwell that the Pole brothers in England were communicating with their brother, Reginald. It also came to light that Lady Salisbury and her Council had forbidden the reading of the Bible in English, in contravention of the new law.

Despite Montague's best efforts to conform, and Margaret's quiet retirement, events were closing in on the family. On 29th August 1538, Geoffrey was arrested and taken to the Tower of London, where he languished for two months before being questioned: presumably the delay was planned to give him plenty of time to reflect on the wisdom of pleasing the King with his answers to his interrogators.

He was joined in early November by Montague and the Marquess of Exeter, Henry's first cousin, as well as various others. All were charged with treason.

On 12th November, the Earl of Southampton and the Bishop of Ely arrived at Margaret's home at Warblington Castle. She was questioned, then taken to confinement at Cowdray Castle, Southampton's seat.

The evidence against Montague and the others relates to letters and other communication between Geoffrey and Montague at home, and Reginald, still blasting the King from the safety of Europe. The content of the letters was the usual litany of complaints about the world being turned upside down, and warnings that Reginald was under threat from assassins. Geoffrey, being loose-tongued, had talked foolishly, and there was a fair case against him.

Unfortunately, whilst trying to limit the damage he had done, Geoffrey mentioned other names, including Montague's, and the more he tried to say to show they were innocent, the worse it sounded. Terrified (as would we all be) by the threat of torture and the fear that he would implicate his family, Geoffrey tried to commit suicide. Prevented, he was interrogated again.

Meanwhile, Margaret was being questioned at length at Cowdray. In the answers, copied at the time and signed in her own hand, she disclaimed the slightest involvement of either herself or Montague with any sort of treason.

'..If ever it be found and proved in her, that she is culpable in any of those things, that she hath denied, that she is content to be blamed in the rest of all the articles laid against her.'

She denied absolutely that she had received any letters from Reginald (there is one he apparently wrote to her, but it was sent to Montague, so she may well not have received it.) She also denied that she had heard of the destruction of other letters, or that she had heard her sons make any comments about the world being turned upside down. Nor had she ever heard Geoffrey or Montague say that they wanted to join Reginald, although she admitted she knew Reginald had escaped the assassins, at which *'for motherly pietie...she [rejoiced].'*

Her interrogators marvelled at her tenacity and probably believed her. The Earl of Southampton wrote to Cromwell:

'..[either] her sons have not made her privy ne participant of the bottom and pit [of] their stomachs, or else is she the [most] arrant traitoress that ever [lived].'

He also described her as *'rather a strong and constant man, than a woman'*. A kind of compliment, to Tudor minds!

Despite the best efforts of Geoffrey and Margaret to show that Montague was in no way involved in treason, on 2nd December 1538 he was tried and convicted and on the 9th he was beheaded on Tower Hill. On 2nd January 1539, Geoffrey was excused the death penalty, but was to remain in the Tower. He again attempted suicide.

The question then became, what to do with Margaret? There was no evidence against her, but as a powerful magnate she controlled huge swathes of land on the south coast. With the very real fears of an invasion by France or the Empire, it would have been foolhardy to leave her free.

An Act of Attainder was passed against her in May 1539, confiscating her Earldom and demoting her once again to Lady Margaret Pole. Southampton and his wife were fed up with holding her in their home at Cowdray. Margaret clearly knew how to make herself unpleasant and difficult and Lady Southampton refused to be left alone with her *'in nowise would she tarry behind me, the said Lady being in my house.'*

By 20th November 1540 Margaret had been dispatched to the Tower, and she and Montague's young son were not included in the general pardon issued in 1540. Exeter's wife (who had more involvement in the matter than Margaret) had been pardoned and given an income, so it is not unreasonable to assume that part of the reason for Margaret's continued incarceration was personal dislike of Margaret, and the desire for revenge on Reginald Pole, by Henry.

Nevertheless, whilst in the Tower, Henry paid reasonable sums for Margaret's maintenance, and the wages of her waiting woman. Now elderly, Margaret was suffering from the cold and asked for warmer clothes. In March 1541, perhaps beginning to relent, the King ordered furred gowns and warm footwear for her – maybe Fortune's Wheel was moving in the right direction at last?

But no, Margaret's star was about to be extinguished once and for all. Whilst the warm clothes were being ordered, a new investigation into correspondence between Reginald and two of the King's Ambassadors, Sir John Wallop (a relative of the Poles) and Sir Thomas Wyatt was ordered. Margaret's former steward was also questioned. Then came news of an uprising in the North.

On 27th May, 1541, Margaret was beheaded in the Tower. Few details are known, but it appears to have been a spur of the moment decision. No scaffold had been built, and a small block was improvised. Margaret was informed that she was about to die on the very morning itself. She protested that '*she found the thing very strange, not knowing of what crime she was accused, nor how she had been sentenced.*'

She must have been woken early, as at 7am she was led out onto Tower Green. As was customary, she was allowed to speak. She commended her soul to God and asked the bystanders to pray for the King, the Prince and for Princess Mary. Remembering the god-daughter who had been so dear to her, she sent her blessing, and asked Mary's in return. The guards were becoming fidgety, so she was told to '*make haste and place her neck on the block*'.

The hastiness of the execution and the absence of the usual executioner, who had been sent north to deal with the rumoured uprising, meant that Margaret was left to suffer at the hands of '*a wretched and blundering youth...who...hacked her head and shoulders to pieces.*' Her butchered remains were buried in the Chapel of St Peter ad Vincula in the Tower, where they were discovered in 1876.

The reaction of Reginald to her death was to declare her a martyr who had died for her faith. This view was taken up by the Roman Catholic Church, and in 1886, Margaret was beatified, consequently being known in the Roman Catholic Calendar as the Blessed Margaret Pole, who had not hesitated to '*lay down [her] life by the shedding of [her] blood ...for the truth of the orthodox Faith*'.

This was her son's belief at the time, but, whilst one hesitates to question the received opinion of Margaret as dying for her faith, there is no evidence at all that she ever seriously challenged Henry VIII's religious changes. Unlike More or Fisher, she did not refuse to conform, and, although she may have made her private distaste more obvious than was wise, there was no occasion when she was faced with a stark choice of conformity or death.

The injustice of her death lies in the very fact that she was obviously innocent of all of the charges of treason that ensnared her sons.

Aspects of Lady Margaret Pole's Life

Chapter 35: Margaret Pole: Feudal Magnate

In 1512, Margaret petitioned for the return of the Salisbury inheritance. The Earldom of Salisbury had first been granted to William de Montacute (the name is variously rendered as Montacute, Montague and Montagu), a close friend of Edward III, on 16th March 1337

It then descended over the next hundred years through sons and brothers until, in 1428, it was vested in Alice Montacute. Alice was married to Richard Neville, son of Ralph Neville, Earl of Westmorland and Lady Joan Beaufort. Neville, who had an older half-brother who preceded him in the Westmorland inheritance, was recognised as Earl of Salisbury in his wife's right.

The lands of the Earldom were vast, concentrated mainly in the counties of Hampshire and Wiltshire, although the family mausoleum was at Bisham Priory in Buckinghamshire. Countess Alice had ten children, who married into the various noble families of the kingdom, some becoming supporters of York, and others of Lancaster.

Alice's own husband, and her eldest son, another Richard Neville (known as Earl of Warwick in the right of his wife, Anne Beauchamp), were initially York's strongest supporters. Her husband was killed with his brother-in-law, Richard, Duke of York, at the Battle of Wakefield on 30th December 1460, and Anne died within two years.

However, by 1462, the House of York had been victorious, and Anne's son succeeded to her inheritance, although he continued to be known as Earl of Warwick – and, in later years as Warwick the Kingmaker. For, in 1470, Warwick reconciled with Lancaster, and replaced Edward IV of

York with Henry VI. In due course, Edward IV was triumphant, and Warwick was killed at the Battle of Barnet in 1471.

Warwick's wife, Countess Anne was still alive, and, in strict law, should have retained her Earldom, but Warwick's daughters (the couple had no sons) were married to King Edward's brothers, George, Duke of Clarence, and Richard, Duke of Gloucester and so all her lands were distributed between the brothers and their wives, as well as the lands of the Salisbury Earldom. Poor Countess Anne was to be treated as though she were 'naturally dead', according to the grants to Clarence and Gloucester.

The older sister, Isabel Neville, Duchess of Clarence, had two children, Edward, who was named as Earl of Warwick, and granted his mother's share of the Warwick lands on his birth, and Margaret. On Clarence's execution for treason, young Warwick, aged only five, inherited his mother's share of the Salisbury lands. His cousin, Edward of Middleham, son of Anne Neville, Duchess of Gloucester, stood to inherit the remainder, on Anne's death. Sadly, Edward of Middleham, by then styled Prince of Wales, as the son of Richard III, died young, followed, shortly thereafter by his mother. All of the Salisbury and Warwick lands therefore vested in Edward, Earl of Warwick, whose natural heir, until he married, was his sister Margaret.

There was no chance of the Earl of Warwick marrying. Kept under close watch first by his uncle Richard III, then by the new king, Henry VII, by 1487 he was in the Tower of London, never to emerge.

Henry VII, who liked to have a legal cloak to cover his financial exactions, suddenly remembered the plight of poor Countess Anne, defrauded twenty years before by her sons-in-law, and restored the Warwick lands to her. There was a catch – she was to disinherit her grandson, and will the lands to Henry himself.

Thus, when Warwick was executed, allegedly for attempting to escape from the Tower, in 1499, he had rights only to the Salisbury earldom, which rights devolved to his sister, Margaret, now married to Sir Richard Pole.

Lady Margaret and Sir Richard did not breathe a word about the loss of Margaret's inheritance whilst Henry VII was alive, but in 1512, with Henry VIII on the throne, and Margaret's friend, Katharine of Aragon as Queen, Margaret (now widowed) made a claim to have the Earldom of Salisbury restored to her.

She carefully worded her petition so that no word of blame fell on Henry VII, and did not try to unpick the will of Countess Anne of Warwick. Her request was to be restored to *the estate, name, degree, style and title of Countess of Salisbury* for herself and her heirs. The petition was granted, and was to take place on Ladyday 1513, from which point Margaret would take the income – although, in the event, it was 1st January 1514 before she took possession.

Excluded from the restoration were any lands the King could claim as the heir of Margaret Beaufort, or any rights he might have to the lands other than their confiscation from Margaret's brother. These were important reservations, and led to some trouble for Margaret later when she persisted in a suit for certain manors that the King claimed (with some justification) belonged to him.

As was usual when an heir took possession, Margaret had to pay an entry fine – in this case, 5,000 marks, (£3,333). This equated to about eighteen months income. The first instalment of 1,000 marks was receipted by Cardinal Wolsey in May 1513, and Margaret and her eldest son, referred to from that point as Henry, Lord Montague, gave a bond for payment of the remainder.

The Salisbury lands were vast, extending into seventeen counties of England, from Lincolnshire to the Isle of Wight, and even Calais. The main concentration of lands was in Devon, Somerset, Hampshire and Buckinghamshire, with major baronial seats at Clavering in Essex and Bisham in Buckinghamshire, as well as the grand palace of Le Herber in London which, in 1458 could accommodate the Earl and 500 men.

Le Herber, later remodelled and owned by Sir Francis Drake, is now under Cannon Street Station. Margaret's annual income by the late 1530s was some £2,300, rather more than the Dukes of Norfolk and Suffolk.

The first of her houses that Margaret spent time and money renovating was Bisham, in Buckinghamshire. It was a large property, with a mediaeval great hall, and several other chambers. It was also conveniently close to her married home of Bockmer, which was now passed to her son Montague. Bisham's Priory, which had been founded by William Montacute, 1st Earl of Salisbury, was the resting place of Warwick the Kingmaker, Margaret's brother, Edward, Earl of Warwick, and her son, Sir Arthur Pole, after his death in the late 1520s. On Margaret's death, Henry reserved Bisham for himself.

Despite Bisham being the resting place of many of the Salisbury Earls, Margaret commissioned one of the most fabulous chantry chapels in England, at Christchurch Priory, where she intended to rest for ever by the side of her husband, Sir Richard. The fan vaulted ceilings are of the most prestigious Caen stone, and the Countess' arms were originally carved into the ceiling bosses, but were defaced by the King's Commissioners in 1539, when the Priory was dissolved.

Clavering was a castle, surrounded by a moat, and the chapel there was the focus of work in 1523, with new wall paintings of saints commissioned. At Le Herber, too, Margaret's chapel was not neglected – a new tabernacle (a kind of enclosure for a statue) was commissioned for an image of the Virgin.

Margaret was not content, however, with these three grand homes and constructed a new castle at Warblington in Hampshire, about a mile inland of the coast. The castle was constructed in the newly fashionable (and very expensive) brick. It was also given a traditional air with a gatehouse, complete with arrow-slits and a moat.

Inside, there were multifarious chambers, including a great chamber, a dining chamber, parlours and a long gallery. It also had a chapel and some six or so acres of gardens and pleasure grounds.

Every element of furnishing, both hard and soft, proclaimed Margaret's rank – her arms were engraved on her silver, painted on her windows, embroidered on her hangings and even bedecked her horses' harness. She did not forget her husband, although he had died long before she came into her inheritance – some of her silver included his arms impaled with hers.

Margaret's clothes, too, proclaimed her rank – black velvet and satin, ermine and sable, tawny damask and embroidered gowns were all in her wardrobe.

Margaret kept an enormous household, in the great feudal tradition. There were nineteen chambers for her servants at Warblington – and, since lower servants slept in heaps on the floor, these must have been for the higher-ranking members of the household. The bill for wages was over £700 – which, when you realise that the total landed income she and Sir Richard Pole had enjoyed from his five manors was £170 gives an idea of the scale of the household.

In total, there were seventy-three indoor servants at Warblington, presided over by the Steward of her Household. Under the Steward were the Comptroller (accountant), the Marshal and Usher of the Hall (who seated everyone according to rank, and ensured everyone behaved in a seemly fashion – brawling was a not uncommon occurrence!)

Guests were waited on by six gentleman waiters – these would have been the sons of gentlemen, sent to her household to learn to be mannerly and to understand how things were done in a great house. She was also attended by five ladies who were her daily companions. Lady attendant to a Countess was a much coveted role – it was seen as a sort of finishing school and lesser ranking members of the nobility would have petitioned for a place for their daughters.

Central to the role of the feudal magnate was the concept of "*good lordship*". This was a system in which you promoted the virtues of your friends, relatives and dependents to other lords and accepted their protégées into your household, in the hope of spreading your influence, and, in due course, receiving some sort of reward. To the modern mind, it seems almost corrupt – the giving of a job because your mother's cousin's son's brother-in-law's friend has asked for it, but that was the way it worked. You showed your influence by arranging jobs for people, then, they would owe you a favour.

A vast estate of this sort was managed by a Council, which would have acted on her behalf in the day to day running of the estates, and there are receipts for painting '*my lady's council's*' chamber at Clavering. The members of the Council were drawn from across her lands, and would have moved around, sometimes with Margaret, sometimes separately. It was particularly important for Margaret to have a Council she could trust, as she had court duties to perform for Queen Katharine, and also as Lady Governess to Princess Mary – in the years 1525-1533 she was attached to Mary's household and would not have been able to attend to all her business herself.

Margaret's paramount duty was to ensure that her wealth and status could be passed on to her children – for her eldest son, Henry, Lord Montague, that was no problem, but the others had to be considered, too.

It was not, however, considered at all a good idea to sell lands for younger sons – no, they had to be found heiresses of their own. Her son Reginald was a scholar, and although he was not ordained as a priest during Margaret's lifetime, there does not seem to have been any thought of him marrying. He was well provided for, in that the King himself was paying for his education and maintenance abroad. Henry was a very generous patron of scholars.

The second son, Arthur, was found a young widow of around 17, when he was about 20. Jane Lewknor was the only daughter of Sir Roger Lewknor, by his first wife. As both he and his second wife were approaching sixty it seemed likely that Jane would inherit his entire fortune, which included the castle of Bodiam. Margaret's younger son was also found an heiress, Constance Pakenham, although she had to share her inheritance with her sister. Just in case Montague didn't have enough with Salisbury lands, he was married to Jane Nevill, daughter of Lord Bergavenny, another gentleman of advanced age and no other children.

The most splendid match of all, however, was reserved for Ursula, Margaret's only daughter. She was married in around 1520 to Lord Henry Stafford, oldest son of Edward Stafford, 3rd Duke of Buckingham, the richest, highest ranking man in the land, after the King. The 124 manors and 12 castles (plus a couple of hundred other properties) that Buckingham owned, dwarfed Margaret's Earldom.

Unfortunately, although all of these marriages seem to have been successful on a personal level (even if Arthur was often at logger-heads with his father-in-law) not one of them turned out to be the financial success Margaret had hoped for – and paid for, in complex negotiations that are the Tudor equivalent of a merger and acquisition strategy.

Buckingham was almost as royal as the King, and obviously thought he was actually more royal. He lost his head, and all his lands in 1521, leaving Ursula married to a man who never ranked higher than baron, although some of the poorer lands were restored in the 1550s. Montague's father-in-law married again and produced a son and several more daughters, thus disinheriting Jane Nevill completely. Arthur's widow remarried (despite Margaret and Montague trying to force her into a convent in disgraceful fashion) and his children had to share their inheritance with a number of half-siblings. Finally, Geoffrey's relationship with his father-in-law was not good, and Pakenham favoured his other daughter's husband in his will.

It is apparent that Margaret saw herself as the equal of any Earl of Salisbury before her, and of any noble in the kingdom. The confiscation of her earldom in 1540 must have been the most crushing blow, after the loss of her husband and sons, which she could have suffered. She had brought the family to the pinnacle of power, and had it all taken away. The Wheel of Fortune had turned.

Chapter 36: Following the Footsteps of Margaret Pole

Margaret's birthplace, the castle of Farleigh, near Farleigh Hungerford, on the border between Wiltshire and Somerset is now a ruin, in the care of English Heritage. At the time of her birth it was a splendid, modern residence, that had been seized from the Lancastrian Hungerford family and granted to Edward IV's brother, Richard, Duke of Gloucester. Why Margaret was born there, rather than in one of her parents' many houses, is unknown.

Margaret's home until she was around five years old was probably the enormous Warwick Castle – still one of the most impressive castles in all of England. It had been part of the inheritance of her mother, Isabel Neville, daughter of the Earl of Warwick and was the main seat of her parents, the Duke and Duchess of Clarence. Warwick Castle was the birthplace of Margaret's brother, Edward, and was also the place where her mother, Duchess Isabel, died in late 1477, when Margaret was only four.

It is highly unlikely that she attended the burial of her mother, whose body was taken to Tewkesbury Abbey, where it had not lain long before it was joined by that of Margaret's father, George, Duke of Clarence, executed in the Tower of London in 1478.

Margaret's whereabouts for the next seven years is uncertain, although it is likely that she was a member of the Court, and thus would have moved between the Palaces of Westminster and perhaps Sheen and Eltham.

By 1485, she, together with her brother and her cousins, the sisters of the deposed Edward V, were in Sheriff Hutton Castle, another of the great Neville Castles that had been part of the Warwick patrimony, but granted in this instance to Margaret's aunt Anne, and her husband, the Duke of Gloucester who was now Richard III. Sheriff Hutton, today a ruin, is cared for by English Heritage – but it is still possible to get a sense of its huge scale and grandeur.

So far as is known, this was the only time Margaret spent in the north of England. In 1485, she returned to London, and was put into the care of Lady Margaret Beaufort, but where exactly they lived is unknown. Soon, she was in attendance at Court, and was present at the christening, in Winchester Cathedral, of Prince Arthur, and at Westminster Abbey for the coronation of Elizabeth of York in 1487.

Following her marriage, probably in 1487, Margaret, now Lady Margaret Pole, moved to her new husband, Sir Richard Pole's home at Bockmer, in Buckinghamshire, of which there is now no trace.

In the late 1490s Sir Richard and Lady Margaret were given the use of the King's castle at Stourton in Staffordshire, to enable Sir Richard to perform his duties in the Welsh Marches. It is here that Margaret's most famous son, Reginald, Cardinal Pole was born in 1500. Stourton, which had at one time been owned by Margaret's father, dated from the 1100s. Much changed over the intervening centuries and it is now in private hands.

Sir Richard and Lady Margaret then moved to the impressive Ludlow Castle, where Sir Richard acted as Lord Chamberlain to Arthur, Prince of Wales, and Margaret was almost certainly there as well, as Lady-in-Waiting to Arthur's wife Katharine of Aragon. To mark the marriage of Arthur and Katharine, Sir Richard commissioned a carved screen for Aberconwy Abbey, on the north coast of Wales.

After the Prince's death in 1502, and burial at Worcester Cathedral, which Margaret may have attended, she probably spent most of her time between Stourton and Bockmer, until Sir Richard's death in 1504. In later years, Margaret built a tomb for herself and Sir Richard at Christchurch Priory, in what must be one of the most stunning examples of late mediaeval English gothic. It was finished in 1529, but the couple were never interred there.

Left as a widow with four children and a very small income, Margaret retired to Bockmer, but the management of the estate was in the King's hands, as the heir, her son Henry Pole, was a minor.

In 1509, Margaret returned to Court as one of the chief ladies of the court of the new King Henry VIII and his wife, her old friend, Katharine of Aragon. Margaret was in attendance on the Queen, and would have divided her time between the new palace at Richmond, and the King and Queen's favourite haunt, the Palace of Placentia, at Greenwich.

In 1512, Margaret was restored to the Earldom of Salisbury, held by her great-grandmother. It was a fabulously rich Earldom, and as Countess in her own right, she was now possessed of several castles and literally dozens of manor houses. Her four main residences were Le Herber, in London (only the very wealthiest nobles had London houses); Clavering, in Essex; Bisham in Buckinghamshire, close to Bisham Priory, the mausoleum of the Montacute Earls of Salisbury, and the new castle she built for herself at Warblington in Hampshire.

Bisham Abbey is now a sports centre, and nothing remains of Clavering or Le Herber (buried under Cannon St station). A single Tudor tower remains at Warblington, but it is on private ground.

In the mid-1520s, Lady Margaret returned to the Welsh Marches, now as Lady Governess to a new heir to the throne, Henry and Katharine's daughter, Mary. Mary was not officially invested as Princess of Wales, but she went to Ludlow Castle, and the surrounding royal residences of Tickenhill and Hartlebury Castle, as well as the mighty Thornbury, confiscated from the Duke of Buckingham in 1521.

Both Tickenhill and Hartlebury were remodelled in the eighteenth century. Tickenhill is in private hands, but Hartlebury is open to the public. Thornbury can also be visited, as it is a luxury hotel!

Following the marriage of Henry VIII to Anne Boleyn, Princess Mary's household was dissolved and Lady Salisbury retired to her estates, spending most of her time at Warblington.

She was at Warblington in November 1538 when the King's men came to question her about alleged treasonable activities. She was taken under guard to Cowdray Castle, home of the Earl of Southampton, where she was held until December of 1539 when she was removed to the Tower of London. The Tower was to be her last resting place – she was clumsily executed in 1541, and her mangled corpse was hastily buried in the Chapel of St Peter ad Vincula, within the Tower walls.

Key to Map

1. Farleigh Castle, Somerset
2. Tewkesbury Abbey
3. Warwick Castle
4. Tower of London
5. Sheriff Hutton, Yorkshire
6. Westminster Abbey
7. Stourton Castle, Stourbridge, Staffordshire
8. Christchurch Priory
9. Bockmer House, Buckinghamshire
10. Sheen Palace
11. Ludlow Castle
12. Aberconwy Church
13. Bisham Priory
14. Palace of Placentia, Greenwich
15. Le Herber
16. Clavering Castle, Essex
17. Warblington Castle
18. Thornbury Castle
19. Tickenhill Manor
20. Hartlebury Castle, Worcestershire
21. Cowdray Castle, Sussex

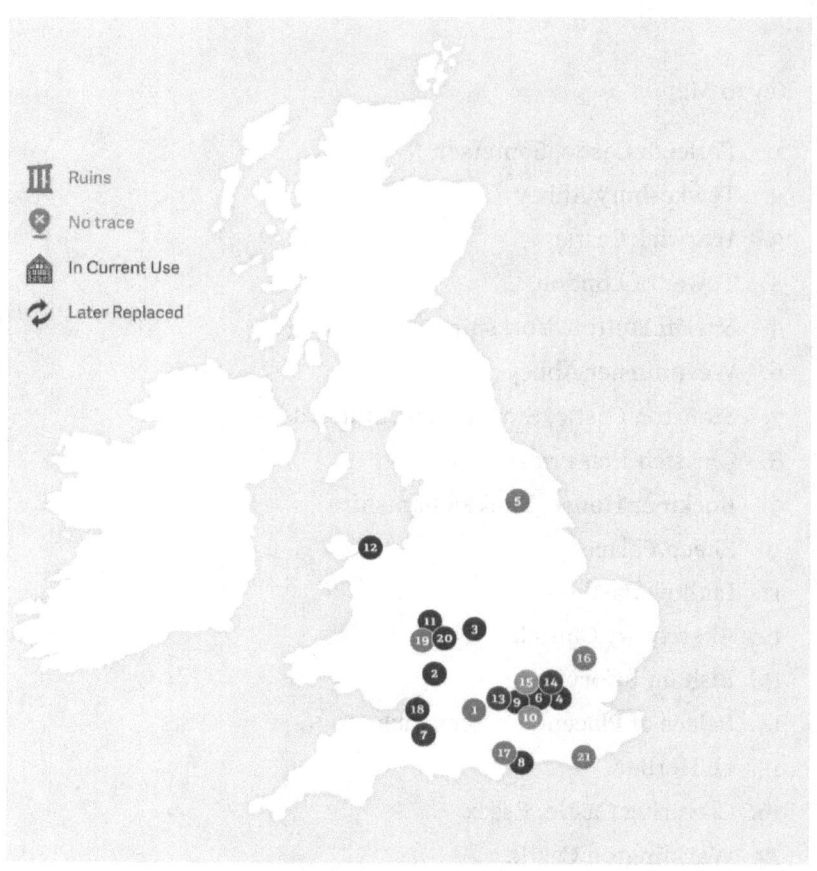

Chapter 37: Margaret Pole: Two Book Reviews

There is only one modern biography of Margaret, Countess of Salisbury that we have come across. Her life is mentioned in a plethora of works on the Wars of the Roses, the life of Mary I, and, in passing, in the biographies of her son, Reginald. We have reviewed two of the most important works here.

Margaret Pole, Countess of Salisbury (1473 – 1541)

Author: Hazel Pierce

Publisher: University of Wales Press (1 February 2009)

In a nutshell: This is an excellent, well-researched, academic study of the life of Margaret, Countess of Salisbury. Particularly suitable for readers who have good knowledge of the wider events of the period and want detailed information about Margaret.

Pierce's work concentrates on putting Margaret into the context of her time, first in her traditional role of daughter, niece and wife, but then in the very unusual context of Margaret as a great landowner, wielding the level of power and patronage normally reserved for men.

The author's great skill is in exploring the contemporary records to create a portrait of Margaret that shows her as an essentially mediaeval figure – believing, first in her duty to God, then to the King, but, only just behind her allegiance to the monarch, her duty to promote her family's wealth and position to the utmost extent of her ability.

Pierce has delved extensively into Margaret's management of her estates, and demonstrates that, whilst her situation as a Countess in her own right was unusual, Margaret had no hesitation in behaving in exactly the same way as her male counterparts - often ruthless and even unscrupulous in her determination to wring the last drop from every bargain. The treatment of her widowed daughter-in-law is shown to be particularly unsavoury - Jane Lewknor was strong armed by Margaret and Margaret's eldest son, Lord Montague, into taking a vow of chastity within weeks of her husband, Arthur Pole's death, to protect the inheritance of Arthur's children.

Margaret's determination is not specifically used to advance any issues of gender politics, however it is apparent that, regardless of any convention of the time about the weakness and inferiority of women, Margaret was not going to tolerate a position as a mild and dutiful ornament. She knew her rights, and she demanded them, whilst still conforming to a mediaeval pattern of feminine chastity and conventional piety.

The relationship between Margaret and her god-daughter, Princess Mary, and her efforts to shield Mary from the worst effects of Henry VIII's annulment suit are given a very human touch, without the author making any claims that can't be substantiated by records.

Margaret's terrible death at the hands of an unskilled headsman have added to the picture of her as a martyr for her faith, but Pierce's forensic analysis of the Exeter conspiracy shows quite clearly that Margaret was innocent of any plot (no matter how vague or insubstantial it might have been) to overthrow Henry and the Royal Supremacy. Whilst it may not quite accord with the picture of her as halfway to sainthood (Margaret was beatified by the Roman Catholic Church in 1886) it makes the injustice of her execution even more outrageous.

I would love to meet the Margaret that Hazel Pierce has revealed – but I wouldn't want to try to cheat her of her rights!

*

The Hollow Crown

Author: Dan Jones

Publisher: Faber & Faber (2nd September 2014)

In a nutshell: A panoramic sweep through English History from the marriage of Henry V in 1420, to the death of Margaret Plantagenet, Countess of Salisbury in 1541. A really thorough analysis, for experts and newcomers alike – fast-moving but with enormous amounts of detail packed into every paragraph.

It is generally not hard to tell whether a writer's sympathies lie with Lancaster or York, but in the case of *'The Hollow Crown'*, Jones is even-handed and judicious throughout. His devastating critique of Henry VI as entirely unfit for the inheritance left him by that Plantagenet hero, Henry V, is matched by his incisive portrait of Richard, Duke of York, as self-important, partisan and as lacking in political finesse as Queen Marguerite of Anjou.

The political theory that underlies the whole work is that, in the late middle ages, having a king of legitimate royal descent was not enough for the realm to function effectively. If the character of the man wearing the Crown were not sufficiently robust, and he failed to wield his power effectively, there was no way of filling the vacuum.

During the minority of Henry VI, his uncles and the other magnates held the realm together reasonably successfully, but there was no prescription for the ills that followed from an adult king who could not step up his responsibilities. Yet, the lords were hamstrung in reacting to the situation. Henry was not a tyrant – rather he was a gentle and kindly man, so there was no excuse for his overthrow. Attempts by others to manage the kingdom on Henry's behalf, were resented and feared by both the nobles excluded from the King's inner circle, and the public at large. Jones rehabilitates William de la Pole, Earl of Suffolk, who is often vilified, but, initially, at least, tried to keep Henry's rule on track.

As royal authority disintegrated in the 1440s and 1450s, there was growing discontent, and personal feuds between members of the nobility began to get out of hand – a situation not helped by Henry's wife, Marguerite of Anjou. It is hard not to admire some aspects of Marguerite's character as Jones presents her – she was phenomenally brave, determined and resolute in her attempts to protect the throne for her husband and son, but she was violently partisan, and, rather than rising above Court rivalries, she made the situation far worse.

Jones moves smoothly through the numerous battles that took place up and down the land, and keeps the reader on top of the dizzying changes of loyalties that characterised the period as the Crown became a plaything of the man with the biggest army. It is with a sense of relief, that must echo that of the population of 1471, that we read of the triumph of Edward IV at Tewkesbury, bringing a King to the throne who had something of the skill, tenacity and strategic brilliance of Henry V: a man whom the vast majority of Lancastrians were willing to accept as King, with Edward of Lancaster dead. The murder of Henry VI was skated over by most people as a little local difficulty.

But knocking an old and incompetent man on the head was one thing – usurping the throne of a twelve year old boy was quite another. Jones shows clearly how the usurpation of Richard III undermined all of the good work done by Edward IV. Richard may have had good instincts in how he wanted to rule, but nothing could undo the damage of his grab for the throne. Jones is no revisionist – it is perfectly plain to him that Richard had his nephews murdered. This one act, against all odds, united the remnants of Lancaster with the supporters of Edward IV, and brought the obscure Henry Tudor, Earl of Richmond, to the throne.

Unlike most historians, Jones does not bring the Wars to a close in 1485, or 1487 with Henry VII's victory at Stoke. He goes on to show how the lingering suspicion, the fear that any plausible rogue with an army could emulate the success of Henry in overthrowing an anointed monarch, slowly poisoned Henry's reign and led to the imprisonment and execution of almost anyone with a vague claim to the throne.

A new era appeared to dawn in 1509, with the accession of Henry VIII, heir to both Lancaster and York, but still the old fears ran deep. After an early attempt to bring the extended royal family together to turn the nobility's minds towards that perennial delight, war with France, dissensions from Henry's policies began to emerge. Nevertheless, Jones contends, the main focus was no longer the old one of York v. Lancaster, but, increasingly, families were divided between Catholic and Protestant. The final purge of possible claimants to the throne in 1538 – 41 when Montague, Exeter and the aged Countess of Salisbury were executed, was the last effusion of Plantagenet blood.

'*The Hollow Crown*' demands concentration – a huge amount of ground is covered – but it is well worth it. I can promise you will not be bored for a moment!

Part 4: Thomas Wolsey: Henry VIII's Cardinal

Introduction

Thomas Wolsey was the last, and probably the greatest, of the mediaeval ecclesiastics who wielded power in England. He rose from being the son of an Ipswich butcher, to being called the Arbiter of Europe and a credible candidate for the Papacy. Whilst he was not the first man to climb to power through the Church, he was one of the most talented, ambitious and controversial figures ever to hold a position of supreme authority under the king.

Wolsey was a byword in his own time for magnificence and extravagance. He understood the importance of spectacle and outward appearance as a tool of power and brought this to bear in his building programmes and his diplomatic triumphs.

He was a figure much hated by the king's other councillors, although his servants and colleagues seem to have been very attached to him, and there is no doubt that Henry VIII felt more personal affection for him than for the majority of his other ministers. It was not until the nineteenth century that his reputation was rehabilitated, and he was seen as a great statesman.

Henry VIII's right hand man for fifteen years, Wolsey's eventual fall was as precipitous as his rise.

Thomas Wolsey's Life Story

Chapter 38: Obscurity (1470 – 1501)

Ipswich, Suffolk, in the late 1470s was one of the most prosperous towns in England. East Anglia was an important centre of the wool trade, with English fleeces being sent from its ports to the Low Countries and goods imported in return. Within Ipswich there was a school, probably attached to one of the monasteries, where the sons of local traders and farmers could learn to read and write in English and Latin, and study enough mathematics to run a business. To this school, went a young boy by the name of Thomas Wolsey.

Thomas Wolsey's birth and parentage is not absolutely proven, but the generally accepted view is that he was born in the early 1470s to Robert Wolsey (or Wulcy) a butcher and grazier of Ipswich, and his wife Joan Daundy. It seems likely that he had an older brother, both from his name (most first sons were named for their father) and from the fact that his father was keen for him to become a priest, as evidenced by Robert Wolsey's Will. Had Thomas been the older son, he would have been expected to carry on the prosperous family business.

Thomas did so well at school that he was given one of the four scholarships in the gift of the Bishop of Norwich to Magdalen College, Oxford. His exceptional intellect enabled him to complete his BA by the age of fifteen – even in a time when many scholars completed their BA earlier than is done now, this was considered remarkable.

As with most scholars, the next step was a Fellowship of his College, followed by ordination as a priest on 10th March 1498. Later that year,

Wolsey was appointed as Master of Magdalen School, Oxford and then College Bursar in 1499. It has been alleged that whilst in his position of Bursar, he misappropriated funds - not for his own use, but for building works on the College tower. This story is plausible, given Wolsey's later penchant for building, but, according to his chief biographer, Peter Gwyn in *"The King's Cardinal"*, there is no record of it in the documents of Magdalen, and he was not deprived of his Fellowship.

Among the schoolmaster's pupils were the three sons of Thomas Grey, 2nd Marquess of Dorset, half-brother to Queen Elizabeth of York. At Christmas 1499, Wolsey was called upon to accompany the young Grey boys to their home at Bradgate in Leicestershire. He obviously impressed his host, the Marquess, and was granted a living at Limington in Somerset. Receipt of a living of the scale of Limington (£21 per annum) obliged him to resign his Fellowship. Priests were also supposed to live in their parishes, unless they had a licence to be absent.

According to his earliest biographer, his gentleman-usher, George Cavendish, Wolsey went to Limington and carried out his functions as parish priest and schoolmaster, and whilst there fell out with the local landowner, Sir Amyas Paulet, who had him set in the stocks for some misdemeanour. Later biographers have cast doubt on this, not only as it would be most unusual to shame a priest in such a manner, but also because there is some doubt as to whether Wolsey went to Limington at all. However, if the rumour were current during Wolsey's lifetime, or just after, it no doubt gave rise to a good deal of sniggering.

Chapter 39: Early Career (1501 – 1509)

There was never any possibility of a man so talented and ambitious as Wolsey living in the country and ministering to his flock. He was obviously expecting promotion, as he applied on 3 November 1500 for a Papal Licence to hold more than one living.

In 1501, presumably through the good offices of Dorset, he became Chaplain to Henry Deane, Archbishop of Canterbury, who was also Lord Keeper of The Great Seal – a crucial position in English Government, as without the Great Seal, no official business could be implemented.

Whilst in the Archbishop's household, Wolsey would have spent most of his time at Lambeth Palace, and was probably there when Katharine of Aragon stayed there in 1501, prior to being married by Archbishop Deane to Prince Arthur on 14th November 1501. The pageants for the wedding were magnificent, and this is when Wolsey may first have witnessed the power of spectacle as propaganda.

Wolsey was also in Archbishop Deane's train when he visited Scotland in negotiations related to the Treaty of Perpetual Peace that resulted in the marriage of Henry VII's daughter, Margaret, to James IV of Scotland. Wolsey presumably enjoyed this taste of foreign diplomacy, as, later in life, foreign affairs seem to have been his over-riding political interest.

On Deane's death in 1503, Wolsey became part of the household of Sir Richard Nanfan, Deputy Lieutenant of Calais. Peter Gwyn sees this as rather a come-down, but John Matusiak, Wolsey's most current biographer, in *"The Life of King Henry VIII's Cardinal"*, describes the opportunity quite differently.

Matusiak sees this as the period in Wolsey's career when he became thoroughly conversant with day-to-day administration of commercial, diplomatic and military affairs. Calais, the last English toe-hold in France, was the place where the majority of English exports were landed for transport into Europe. It was also a border town that had to be kept in a constant state of readiness, lest the French try to wrest it back.

The Deputy Lieutenant was answerable for everything that happened in Calais and its surrounding Pale. It was thus a position of great responsibility, and the elderly Nanfan entrusted much of the work to Wolsey. Wolsey probably spent the four years from 1503 to 1507 in Calais, returning to England on Nanfan's death.

Back in London, Wolsey obtained a post as Chaplain to the King himself. Henry VII's later years were overshadowed by gloom and a sense of repression – not altogether surprising when Henry's personal losses are considered. He lost a fifteen-month old son, a fifteen-year-old son, his wife and a new born baby all within the space of two years, as well as seeing his thirteen-year-old daughter depart for a new country. It would hardly be remarkable if he were depressed.

In true mediaeval fashion, the King, always religiously inclined, dealt with his sorrows by increasing his devotions, hearing several Masses daily and spending more time and money on his charitable projects. He would thus have had frequent contact with his Chaplains.

Wolsey is always seen as being Henry VIII's creation, but it is apparent that Henry VII recognised his talents almost immediately. Both Tudor kings were more than willing to promote men of ability, regardless of their background – partly because they recognised the importance of skill, and partly, no doubt to have servants who were dependent wholly on themselves for favour, without their own resources.

During this period, Wolsey also became close to Sir Thomas Lovell, and Richard Foxe, Bishop of Winchester, two of Henry VII's most trusted advisors. Lovell was President of the King's Council, Chancellor of the Exchequer (not the important role it is today, but not insignificant), Speaker of the House of Commons and Master of the King's Wards. Richard Foxe, although he had not been translated from his bishopric of Winchester to Canterbury on Deane's death, was Lord Privy Seal, and was closely involved in all matters of government, particularly foreign affairs. Wolsey became Foxe's Secretary and their relationship became one of personal trust and even affection, as evidenced by their letters in later times.

In 1508 Wolsey was sent by Henry VII to both Scotland, to negotiate over Border matters with James IV, and the Low Countries, on an embassy to the Emperor.

The trip to the Low Countries is one of the most famous episodes in Wolsey's early career. Apparently, he received the commission from the King at Richmond before noon, arrived in London by 4pm, took a barge to Gravesend and was there by 7pm, rode post to Dover, where he slept and took ship to Calais first thing in the morning, arriving by 10am. He then raced to the feet of the Emperor, whose court was not far across the border in Flanders, dispatched his business, returned to Calais that night, sailed in the morning, headed for London and was back at his post in Richmond early the next day. Henry, on seeing him, rebuked him for not having left, and was amazed to hear that Wolsey had been and returned.

The trip to Scotland was not quite so successful. James IV kept the delegation waiting in Berwick for five days. Even after he arrived, James was too busy to see him – he sent word that he was inspecting a gunpowder factory. Eventually, an audience was granted, and repeated over eight days. James, however, was not inclined to return the hostages that he was holding. Wolsey admitted to the King that there was some excuse for this as *'the offences of the Englishmen were to those of the Scotsmen as four to one'*.

Wolsey was back in the Low Countries in the autumn of 1508, negotiating a second marriage for Henry VII with Marguerite of Austria, the Emperor's daughter, and Regent of the Low Countries. Nothing came of the negotiations but Wolsey was rewarded with the post of Almoner in

November 1508, and then, on 2nd February 1509, the position of Dean of Lincoln.

This was the last office that Henry VII granted Wolsey, as the King died on 21st April 1509. Wolsey was one of the clergy who followed the solemn procession behind Henry VII's coffin, as it was finally laid to rest in his new-built Chapel at Westminster Abbey on 8th May 1509.

Chapter 40: A New Reign (1509 – 1513)

There is some debate amongst historians as to whether Wolsey was passed over in the first few months of Henry VIII's reign, because of the dislike of that doyenne of the Tudor house, Lady Margaret Beaufort, Countess of Richmond and Derby, who was nominally regent for the remaining few weeks of Henry VIII's minority (he was not 18 until 28th June).

It is not clear whether Wolsey was not reappointed as Royal Chaplain, or whether he is just not mentioned in the various household lists. Biographers Williams and Matusiak contend the former, whilst Gwyn believes the latter. His post of Almoner initially went to Dr John Edenham, but Edenham died in September 1509 and Wolsey resumed the post.

Whether or not Wolsey was passed over in the spring and summer of 1509, he was certainly back in favour by the autumn and a string of offices came his way in the next four years: among others, Privy Councillor (by November 1509); Registrar of the Order of the Garter (April 1510); Prebend of St George, Windsor (February 1511) and Dean of York (February 1513).

So why was Wolsey so popular with the new king? There is, on this, as on so many things, two schools of thought. The first is that the young

Henry VIII had no interest in conducting government business, and wanted only to enjoy himself and spend his father's money. In this scenario, Henry is presented as easily led and strongly influenced by Wolsey, who was a witty and eloquent man. This idea is borne out by some of the later Ambassadors' reports about Wolsey really wielding the power, and Henry as a figurehead.

If one looks more closely, however, it is apparent from the internal government papers that Henry and Wolsey had a worked out what might nowadays be called a *'good cop-bad cop'* routine with one feigning anger or disgust at a foreign request whilst the other expressed regret that it couldn't be fulfilled and promised to look into it.

The other school of thought, is that Henry was always a clever man at choosing others to do the "grunt" work, but that he was always the ultimate arbiter, and that, as soon as Wolsey failed to deliver what the King wanted, he went.

It seems likely that in the early days of his reign, Henry, eighteen, handsome, gifted, athletic and energetic may have found the day-to-day details of administration dull and left them to his able Councillor, but, to quote Cavendish, he gave power to Wolsey because

'he was most earnest and readiest of all the King's Council to advance the King's only will and pleasure, without respect to the case.'

The King's Council, comprising about a dozen men, met regularly in the Star Chamber at Westminster. If Henry were not present, and it seems that during his early reign he was more frequently out hunting, then he needed a reliable go-between, and this seems to be the role that Wolsey took. It was not until the other Councillors found that this gave Wolsey a unique position of influence that they realised they had been side-lined.

Henry and Wolsey also got on well personally. Wolsey was described by the Venetian ambassador as *'handsome'* and even by his enemy Polydore Vergil (the historian of Henry VII's reign) as a man of distinction. He also had many tastes in common with Henry. He was musical (he played the lute and had a well-trained choir at a later date) was interested in building, and was a great patron of the Humanists.

Chapter 41: Wars & Alliances (1513 – 1515)

Wolsey really came to the fore in 1513. In that year, Henry embarked on a huge campaign in France, in alliance with his father-in-law, Ferdinand of Aragon, and the Holy Roman Emperor, Maximilian. A previous campaign in 1512, led by Wolsey's erstwhile pupil, Thomas Grey, now 2nd Marquess of Dorset, had ended in abject failure, blamed by Ferdinand on English incompetence.

Whilst there had been major problems with supplies, equipment and dysentery in the English army, part of the blame should lie with Ferdinand, who cared as much about Henry's claim to be King of France as he would have cared about a claim to be Emperor of China. He had used the English attack to divert the French, whilst scooping up his ultimate goal of the Kingdom of Navarre and then independently making peace with Louis XII.

In 1513, however, there was to a multi-pronged attack. Wolsey was in charge of the organisation of men and supplies. This was his chance to shine, and he took it, although he still consulted with Richard Foxe, Lord Privy Seal, and his earlier mentor.

The previous French campaign had been ill-armed, so thousands of suits of armour were ordered from Italy, heavy artillery was bought from Flanders and gun-powder was made in quantity and stored at the Tower of London, Southampton and Calais. At this point, Wolsey's previous knowledge of Calais must have proved enormously useful – the materiel was collected there in preparation for invasion. The pièces de resistance were twelve enormous cannon, known as the Twelve Apostles.

In anticipation of that later great general, Napoleon, Wolsey was aware that *'soldiers march on their stomachs'* and ordered the purchase and slaughter of 25,000 oxen (not forgetting to have money knocked off the deal for the return of the non-meat products). Even Englishmen could not march on beef alone, so malt, beans, oats and lamb were also procured.

Remembering that Ferdinand and Maximilian both had a long history of double-crossing their allies, Wolsey kept up a spy network to remain abreast of their doings, whilst still finding time to organise medical services for the troops, and most important of all, a constant supply of beer.

With such a finely provisioned army, there was no room for indiscipline, and Wolsey drew up the *Statutes of War* – a list of dos and don'ts for soldiers, including strict injunctions against robbery, sacrilege, molestation of civilians (in particular, no soldier was to enter a house where a woman was in childbed), arson and gambling. In an article that has a very modern resonance, soldiers were forbidden from making jibes about each other's place of origin.

The cost of all of this preparation was enormous, and further increased by the English agreement to pay 100,000 crowns to maintain Maximilian's army. Parliament had voted supplies, but there were murmurings when the tax collectors came to the door.

Whilst Henry and Wolsey were surpassing themselves in preparations for war, Ferdinand was surpassing himself in treachery, signing another secret deal with France. On the Anglo-Scottish border, too, pressure was mounting, as James IV, Henry's brother-in-law, declined to break off his alliance with France. James was in a difficult position, as he was in alliance with both countries, and at some point had to choose.

To deal with the Scottish threat, it was agreed, presumably by Henry, but with advice from Wolsey and Foxe, that Thomas Howard, Earl of Surrey, and his son, Lord Thomas Howard, would be left behind to repel any invasion from the north. It is apparent that the Howards wished to be involved in the main French campaign (another of Surrey's sons had been killed in a naval action off Brest, and they were keen for revenge).

It is perhaps from this banishment from the greatest force to head to France for a hundred years that the Howard antipathy to Wolsey can be dated – an antipathy that would play a significant part in his eventual downfall.

The campaign in France was successful, so far as it went. A couple of towns were captured, Therouanne and Tornai - the first territory won by an English army for sixty years. At the Battle of the Spurs the French cavalry were put to flight and some valuable prisoners, including the Duc de Longueville (1480-1516), were captured for ransom. Strategically, however, the towns were of far more benefit to Maximilian than they were to England, whilst the cost of the war had been huge.

Throughout the campaign, Wolsey had been busy organising, directing, planning and enabling his master to make a splendid show with brightly caparisoned horses, chests of treasure and silver plate. His closeness to the King can be gauged by the fact that Queen Katharine, left as Regent in England, wrote to Wolsey frequently, as well as to her husband. She even went so far as to ask Wolsey to ensure the King had dry shirts as she thought him susceptible to colds.

These wifely concerns were not the only thing on Katharine's mind. James IV had decided in favour of his old ally, France, and had invaded England. Surrey and his son, Lord Thomas Howard, were sent north whilst Katharine raised troops, got together what cash hadn't already been spent on the French adventure and headed north to meet her army. Before the Queen had passed Bedford, news of an overwhelming victory over the Scots king at Flodden reached her. James and a significant portion of his nobility had been killed.

Chapter 42: Diplomacy (1514 – 1518)

When Henry and Wolsey returned from France, it was to a seriously depleted treasury. Henry's ambition to emulate Henry V and conquer France could not realistically be supported.

A hundred years before, England had territory in France that it could use as a base, far larger than the Calais Pale and the new towns won. France itself had been riven with civil war and led by a king who suffered from severe mental disturbances. Things were very different by 1514. France was rich, united and led by a competent king, even though he was old by contemporary standards. The very idea that England, smaller, poorer and with a comparatively tiny population, could conquer France was a pipe-dream.

Henry may have wanted glory but he was not stupid, and he and Wolsey now looked to other means of making England a powerful force in Europe, which did not rely on war supported by unreliable allies. Both Maximilian and Ferdinand had taken Henry for a fool, and he would not forget the injury.

It had been agreed that Maximilian and Ferdinand's joint grand-son, Charles of Castile, would marry Henry's sister, Mary, on 15th May 1514, but Maximilian delayed and came up with excuses. His daughter, Marguerite, Regent of the Low Countries, urged her father to carry out the match as promised, but he continued to procrastinate.

Whether Henry and Wolsey had always intended to serve Maximilian a dose of his own medicine and double-cross him, or whether the preparations for Mary's wedding, which involved vast expense and complex preparation, were just a bluff, must remain unknown. Nevertheless, as soon as it was apparent that the wedding, (which would have made Mary of England Empress in due course), was off, Henry and Wolsey were ready with another plan.

England would ally with France, pleasing the new Pope, Leo X, who was considerably less bellicose than his predecessor, and driving a wedge between Maximilian to the north of France, and Ferdinand to the south.

The price was the marriage of Mary to Louis XII whose Queen, Anne of Brittany, had just died. Wolsey was a tough negotiator on the dowry and jointure, and Mary received some extraordinarily valuable jewels from her betrothed, who had no doubt heard her described as *'the most attractive woman ever seen.'* In addition, Henry was to be allowed to keep Tournai and receive the back payments of the pension due to the English Crown from France.

If Louis had lived long enough to give Mary a son, the English would have been cock-a-hoop. A regency presided over by the English King's sister would have been a splendid opportunity. As it was, Louis wore himself out undertaking his conjugal duties and was dead by New Year's Day 1515. During her marriage, Mary felt she was not well treated, and said to her brother that, had Wolsey accompanied her to France, rather than Norfolk, she would have been better handled.

The heir to the French throne, if Mary were not expecting a son, would be François d'Angouleme, married to Louis' daughter, Claude (French law did not permit the Crown to pass to a woman). Whilst Mary withdrew for the customary mourning period, François made strenuous efforts to seduce her, partly no doubt for personal pleasure, as he was a notorious womaniser, but partly to muddy any claim to the throne of a child she bore.

In the event, Mary was not pregnant, but she did cause a scandal by hastily marrying Charles Brandon, Duke of Suffolk, who had been sent to fetch her, after expressly swearing an oath in front of Wolsey and Henry that he would not entertain such a marriage.

The young couple, once they had realised the enormity of their actions, wrote to Wolsey, begging his intercession with the King, which Wolsey, after telling them what a dangerous situation they were in, promised. He intimated that hard cash would soften the King's anger considerably, and eventually they were forgiven on promise of paying a huge fine.

This personal intervention with the King at the request of Mary, who was a Dowager Queen and Henry's own sister, shows the extent of Wolsey's influence. It was now becoming the object of resentment by the King's nobles, and also by the Queen.

For the first five years of their marriage, Katharine was probably the single greatest influence on Henry, but she could never be completely happy with a French alliance, even though she had been horrified by her father's betrayal of her husband and had firmly sided with Henry. It is likely that she felt jealous at a personal level too. Most wives would resent being supplanted in their husband's confidence by a third party. Her dislike of Wolsey would only increase over the next ten years.

The treaty with France was renewed with François but the balance of power was about to shift dramatically again. François, much to Henry's chagrin, achieved a victory over the Emperor at Marignano in 1515 that was stunning in its magnitude, and assured François of the disputed Duchy of Milan.

France was now riding too high. Men were dispatched from England to offer large sums of money to the Emperor to pay Swiss mercenaries, whilst a show of amity with France continued. Simultaneously, overtures were made to Charles, Maximilian's grandson, now King of Spain. Maximilian wrote gleefully to Charles that Charles could dupe the English, whilst he duped the French. True to form, Maximilian took the English gold, raised an army, then failed to fight.

Another solution had to be thought of to keep the balance of power, and Wolsey came up with a plan that would, he hoped, satisfy everyone and redound to his credit for all ages to come. Pope Leo was preaching a crusade, and whilst that might sound as though it were an old fashioned concept by the sixteenth century, it should not be forgotten that the Turks were advancing on Hungary, which they were to conquer in 1526.

The plan was for all the Christian Princes of Europe to swear eternal brotherhood and then concentrate on defending Christendom. The Treaty of London was signed in 1518. Intended as a non-aggression pact, some twenty-five European states were involved. All were to come to the aid of any of their number, if attacked. Wolsey received much of the credit for the treaty:

'Undoubtedly, My Lord, God continuing it (the Treaty) shall be the best that ever was done for the realm of England and after the King's Highness the laud and praise shall be to you a perpetual memory.' – Bishop Foxe

Nevertheless, whilst the ink was still wet, most of the signatories were busy doing side deals. As part of a bilateral Anglo-French agreement, Henry VIII's daughter, Mary, was betrothed to the Dauphin.

Chapter 43: Archbishop & Cardinal

Late in 1514, Wolsey was promoted to the Archbishopric of York, second only to Canterbury in seniority, although a very distant second in terms of wealth and influence. William Warham, who had succeeded Wolsey's own master, Henry Deane, as Archbishop of Canterbury in 1503, showed no signs of dropping off his perch.

The receipt of the Archbishopric of York did not come without scandal. The previous incumbent, Cardinal Bainbridge, had spent much of his archiepiscopate as English Ambassador in Rome, and in July 1514 he died there. It was almost immediately discovered that he had been poisoned and eventually confirmed (by means of torture) that it had been at the hands of a servant of his rival, Silvestri, the Italian Bishop of Worcester, although Silvestri's involvement was never proven.

There were dark rumours that Wolsey had been concerned, although there was never any accusation or evidence brought, and, as Wolsey had stayed well away from the cesspit of politics that was the Roman Curia, it seems unlikely.

Wolsey then received the highest ecclesiastical office of all. After much badgering and even more bribing, Pope Leo X appointed him Cardinal on 10th September 1515. In due course, the red hat that Wolsey coveted so much was dispatched and treated with extraordinary ceremonial '*as though it were the greatest prince in Christendom come into the realm.*' It was conveyed to London and placed on the High Altar at Westminster to be viewed reverently by the great and good of the realm.

A Mass was celebrated by Archbishop Warham, flanked by the Bishops of Armagh and Dublin. The sermon was preached by the Humanist John Colet, who observed, no doubt somewhat to Wolsey's chagrin, that his role was, like that of his ultimate master, Christ, to minister rather than being ministered to.

Leo refused, however, to give Wolsey the overriding power of *Legate a Latere* which would have given him overall control of English ecclesiastical matters. These were still in the hands of Warham.

This lack of jurisdiction was a disappointment to both Henry and Wolsey, as trouble was brewing between Church and State and, had Wolsey had a free hand, he would have bent the Church to Henry's will.

In 1512 Parliament had passed an Act limiting the right of Clergy to be tried only by Ecclesiastical Courts (the controversy that had raged in Henry II's time, resulting in the death of Thomas Becket). Not surprisingly, conservative churchmen were against this encroachment on the rights of the Church, and a conference was held at Blackfriars where Henry himself listened to arguments on both sides. In the end, he gave judgement, and, prefiguring a later controversy, announced:

> '*Kings of England in time past have never had any superior but God only...we will maintain the right of our crown and temporal jurisdiction...*'

Archbishop Warham requested that the matter be adjudicated by Rome, but Henry did not grant this the dignity of an answer. Wolsey's exact position on the primacy of Church versus state cannot be stated with certainty, but it seems likely he agreed with Henry.

The 1510s were a period of increasing anti-clerical feeling, particularly in London, and this was compounded after 1517, by the spread of what the Church considered to be heresy. In previous ages the Church had responded to heresy by trying to persuade the heretic to abjure, or recant his heresies, in which case, he would be given a penance and brought back into the fold of the Church.

As the temperature on religious matters rose, and as more and more people began to espouse the new teachings, the Church took a more hard-line position. It is difficult for us to accept that burning people for their beliefs was considered the right response, but for the people of the time, a heretic was a dangerous criminal who could lead others into sin and imperil their souls. Tough measures were absolutely necessary to protect the innocent. The only variation was on the definition of heretic.

Wolsey, however, seems to have been disinclined to severe punishments for heretics. Whilst he was active in the searching out and burning of heretical works, primarily those coming in from Europe containing Lutheran ideas, he seems to have confined his punishments of heretics to either penance and forgiveness, or a whipping. Wolsey was, of course, for many, the embodiment of clerical sin. He was an absentee priest, he held numerous livings, he lived in a level of unimaginable luxury, and he was not as celibate as he ought to have been - he had a single, long-term relationship with Joan Larke, by whom he had two children.

Nevertheless, he seldom exerted himself to punish his severest critics. Even Robert Barnes (burnt in the 1530s, long after Wolsey's time, for heresy) who had written scathing attacks on the Cardinal, was admired for his skill in argument and encouraged to make a general submission in front of Wolsey rather than face the more stringent Episcopal court. Despite being well aware of the need for reform in Church matters and undertaking some mild improvements in his own Archdiocese, it was never a matter of urgency for Wolsey.

It has been claimed that Wolsey was desperate to be elected Pope, and he was put forward on two occasions – 1522 and 1523. Henry VIII pressed his candidacy and he was promised the support of the Emperor Charles, which extended as far as writing a letter that was deliberately delayed. However it is apparent from Wolsey's correspondence that he did not anticipate any likelihood of victory, and that he had no interest in being Pope. He made no effort to cultivate friends in Rome, never visited, and largely ignored the Roman politics surrounding Papal elections. It may be that in 1528 he regretted his failure to attend to his ecclesiastic career, but it was too late by then.

Where he did use his influence at Rome was to promote Henry VIII's book against Luther, *'Assertio Septem Sacramentorum'*. Wolsey wrote a dedication, and also made it very clear to Pope Leo that a suitable honorific would be a welcome gift to the King. Leo took the hint and bestowed the title of Defender of the Faith on Henry, which title has been proudly displayed on English, and British, coins ever since.

Chapter 44: Lord Chancellor

In 1514, Archbishop Warham resigned the Chancellorship in Wolsey's favour. Wolsey was not trained in either Civil or Canon Law and this was both a blessing and a curse in his role as Lord Chancellor. In those times the Lord Chancellor still acted as a judge, and it is apparent that Wolsey took this very seriously. Whilst he was gaining a terrible reputation for pride, arrogance and avarice, he was also winning plaudits as a man who dispensed swift, impartial justice.

'He has the reputation of being extremely just; he favours the people exceedingly, and especially the poor, hearing their suits and seeking to dispatch them instantly.' – Venetian Ambassador

He was not interested in the niceties of the law, and would move suits from Common Law courts to Chancery which inevitably drew the enmity of Common Law lawyers, but it gave the principle of Equity in law a new lease of life. It soon became obvious that he would not tolerate law breaking by even the highest in the land. Nobles and gentlemen who were used to having their own way in the local Assize Courts were swiftly disabused of their belief that they were above the law. This may sound admirable to us, but it made Wolsey no friends at the time.

This lack of deference to his 'betters', and the ostentation and magnificence of his general demeanour (his Cardinal's hat was treated as though it were a holy relic), was creating a huge groundswell of resentment amongst the other men who surrounded the King.

A fine example of this is the imprisonment in the Fleet prison of no less a personage than the Earl of Northumberland for retaining ie having men at arms in his pay, wearing his livery instead of the King's. Another aspect of Wolsey's impartial law enforcement that earned him many enemies at court, was the rigorous enforcement of the laws against enclosure of land that had been passed by Parliament in 1517-18, but were frequently ignored by high-ranking men.

Chapter 45: Arbiter of Europe (1518 – 1522)

Not long after the Treaty of London was signed, Emperor Maximilian died, upsetting the balance of power again. The most likely successor was Charles of Castile, but, as the office of Emperor was elected, not inherited, other men could put their name forward, and François I immediately did so.

Henry VIII was also, for a time, mesmerised by the thought of an Imperial crown, but despite some mild efforts and sweeteners by England and some enormous bribes from François, Charles emerged, at the age of 19, as the secular leader of Christendom. Wolsey seems to have been half-hearted in supporting Henry's claims, no doubt aware that Charles' election was a racing certainty.

The election of Charles V meant that the power previously divided between the Empire and Spain was now concentrated in a single man. To countervail this, relations with France needed to be improved again. It was agreed that Henry and François would meet, and both Kings gave Wolsey the task of organising what turned out to be one of the costliest (and most pointless) junkets in history, the Field of Cloth of Gold. Taking place in June of 1520 at the Val d'Or, near Calais, it was an opportunity for Henry and François to meet, and hopefully, forge a personal bond.

Wolsey was, perhaps, naïve, or had forgotten his own youth. There was never any possibility that two young men (30 and 26 years old) both bursting with testosterone and each keen to prove himself as the most chivalrous, brave and successful king in Europe, would ever be anything but rivals. The two Queens, Katharine and Claude, seem to have got on well, but Henry and François, despite Wolsey's best efforts to keep them from direct rivalry, insisted on an endless game of one-up-man-ship.

Even before the meeting, France was aggrieved because Henry had received a visit from the Emperor Charles in May 1520. François assumed, not without reason, that they were plotting against him. His fears were further exacerbated when Henry and Katharine left, not to return home as anticipated, but to cross the border into Flanders to meet Charles and his aunt, Regent Marguerite, at Gravelines.

Although Katharine's influence with Henry had waned by 1520, they were still on good terms, and Katharine was always going to favour an alliance with her nephew. To be fair to Henry and Wolsey, they resisted Charles' immediate blandishments and did not enter into his latest scheme against France at this time.

As François and Charles moved inevitably towards war again (Charles could not stomach France's supremacy in Milan), Wolsey offered himself as arbiter. Whilst Wolsey had many faults, it seems unfair not to accept that he was a man more inclined to peace and compromise than war and waste. His own self-satisfaction (the son of a butcher to play mediator to an Emperor) was no doubt was one of his motives, but a true desire for stability and peace in Europe was there as well.

In Wolsey's own words mediation avoided war and '*the consuming of treasure, subversion of realms, depopulation and desolation of countries*'. Only if arbitration failed would England support the country attacked, in accordance with the Treaty of London.

Wolsey journeyed to Calais in 1521 to attempt to reconcile François and Charles. Charles refused to attend negotiations at Calais, and would only receive Wolsey if he went to the Emperor at Bruges. His biographers differ on his motivations for events that occurred. Neville Williams, in "*The Cardinal and the Secretary*", takes this at face value, and believes that Wolsey's summons by Charles was genuine. Matusiak, on the other hand, suggests that this was a ruse to allow Wolsey to meet with Charles away from the French delegation and negotiate a separate treaty. It was undoubtedly Henry's policy to form an alliance with Charles, but whether Wolsey was deliberately disingenuous at Calais is debatable.

Regardless of Wolsey's inner feelings, an Anglo-Imperial treaty was signed that stipulated that, should France and the Empire fail to make peace by May 1522, England would send an army in support of Charles. The betrothal between Henry's five year old daughter, Mary, and François' son was to be broken off, and she was to marry Charles, when she reached the age of 12.

Once the agreement with England was made, Charles showed himself utterly intransigent on the negotiations with France.

'The more towardly disposition I find in the French party, the more sticking and difficulty be found in (Charles' delegates)'" Wolsey wrote in despair.

Whilst acting in his capacity as arbiter, Wolsey surpassed himself with display – dressed in red taffeta, attended by scores of men and surrounded with the costliest plate and jewels. Any glory accorded to his minister reflected well on Henry and this is one of the reasons given by Wolsey for his excessive pomp and magnificence.

He did not seem to understand that embracing the Emperor or the King of France from his mule, as was the prerogative of fellow-monarchs, was not likely to endear him either to them, or to Henry's nobles who would not have dreamed of taking such liberties.

Chapter 46: Difficult Times (1522 – 1525)

The failure of the peace talks at Calais, whether or not Wolsey had been sincere, and the Treaty of Bruges made with Charles, meant that England was now, once more, committed to war to the tune of 40,000 men and horse, plus a fleet. Henry was delighted with Wolsey, sending letters in which he

'thanked God [he had] such a chaplain by whose wisdom fidelity and labour [he] could obtain greater acquisitions than all [his] progenitors were able to accomplish with all their numerous wars and battles.'

The talks with Charles were followed up by a state visit by the Emperor, which, again, Wolsey was responsible for arranging. Whilst not on the scale of the Field of Cloth of Gold, it was still impressive. It was agreed between the monarchs that any disagreement would be arbitrated by Wolsey. Charles must have been grinding his teeth, but the prospect of obtaining England through marriage, and achieving his ancestors' goal of completely encircling France, presumably made it worth his while to accept the dominance of Henry's cardinal.

Henry might have been excited at the prospect of renewed war, but Parliament was not. There was no alternative to calling Parliament – the anticipated costs of the campaign were nearly £400,000. A Commission had been sent out in March 1522 to assess the taxable worth of land, houses and valuables, and the City of London had been 'persuaded' to offer a loan of £20,000, but this was nowhere near adequate.

Parliament was called in April 1523. Wolsey, as Lord Chancellor, explained Henry's need for money, emphasising the treachery of the old enemy, France. He then asked for the unbelievable sum of £800,000, equivalent to a 20% tax across the board.

The Speaker of the Commons, Sir Thomas More, urged obedience to the King, but the Commons could not accept the demand. They asked Wolsey to request the King to take less, but Wolsey treated them roughly and refused to countenance such an idea. He then went to Parliament in his full glory, robed in red, with his Cardinal's hat and his Lord Chancellor's Seal, to intimidate the Commons. The House sat in silence, neither refusing, agreeing nor debating. Eventually, humiliated, the Cardinal left.

At last, a subsidy of 10% was voted, but there were murmurings across the country. Wolsey augmented the grant with a massive levy of 50% of a year's income on the Church, which he forced through as Legate, overriding Warham.

Despite the pain involved in raising the funds, the campaign of 1522-23 was a shambles. Unlike in 1513 when the English army had been considered a model of good behaviour, the campaign was largely about desecrating and laying waste the French countryside. Eventually, bogged down by the rain and mud of northern France, as every army in

European history has been, the commander, the Earl of Surrey, withdrew to Calais, to await a further advance in 1523 under the Duke of Suffolk.

Suffolk too, after initial promising gains, failed to make any serious progress. The appalling conditions '*which caused the soldiers daily to die*' led him to advocate a retreat, but Henry was adamant. Wolsey had interfered in military matters and should have borne some of the responsibility for the fiasco, but Henry appears to have heaped all the blame on Suffolk. Suffolk may have owed Wolsey a favour for helping him when in disgrace over his marriage, but this reverse wiped out all gratitude and pushed Suffolk firmly into the growing camp of Wolsey's enemies.

By 1524, the failure of Charles to keep his side of the bargain, and the exhortations of the new Pope, Clement VII, for peace, inclined England to begin making overtures towards France again. François was not particularly interested in coming to terms – his sights were firmly on Italy. He crossed the Alps, heading for his Duchy of Milan, secured nine years earlier at Marignano. This time, however, it was the Emperor's turn for glory. On Charles V's birthday, 24th February 1525, the Spanish-Imperial army won a crushing victory at Pavia, taking François prisoner and annihilating his army.

Back in England, Henry was initially delighted, jumping out of bed to run to his wife and share the good news. Now would be the time for Charles and him to dismember France. Soon enough, though, it became apparent that Charles had no more interest in helping Henry to the French Crown than his grandfathers, Ferdinand and Maximilian, had had. Moreover, he no longer needed the English alliance to be cemented by his marriage to Henry's daughter.

Henry, still keen to press the advantage of a France in turmoil, proposed to lead yet another invasion. The question was how to fund it. There was no hope of Parliament voting another subsidy, so Wolsey hit on the idea of a loan, the '*Amicable Grant*', based on the feudal prerogative of the King being '*aided*' with money if he led an army abroad in person. The idea was no doubt taken up with glee by the King and Council, but the result was a miserable failure. Despite bullying in person by Wolsey, London refused to cough up. In the provinces, the Commissioners sent to collect it (including Sir Thomas Boleyn) were manhandled. East Anglia was close to open rebellion.

Henry, seriously worried, cancelled the grant. He was not pleased with Wolsey. Not pleased at all.

Troubles came thick and fast as the Emperor came to terms with France, and, in the Treaty of Madrid, allowed François to return home, with a new wife (Charles' sister) but minus a huge sum of cash, and his two sons, who were sent to Spain as sureties. Charles also calmly announced that he would not be marrying Princess Mary after all, but would seek a bride from wealthy Portugal. The rest of Europe was now horrified at Charles' overwhelming strength, and united in the Treaty of The More, negotiated again by Wolsey and signed on 30th August 1525 at his home.

Chapter 47: The King's Secret Matter (1525 – 1529)

By 1525, Wolsey's only friend was the King. The nobles hated and were envious of him; Queen Katharine believed he was favouring the French over her Spanish connection; the Church at home resented his financial exactions, and the Pope was not impressed by his lack of interest in keeping Rome informed of events. Emperor Charles and King François had been thoroughly offended by his pride, and the only person to have a good word for him was Charles' aunt, Marguerite, Regent of the Low Countries, whose power was limited.

But these were all known enemies – Wolsey had also crossed someone who would be far more dangerous to him than all the rest put together – Anne Boleyn.

Cavendish's *"Life of Cardinal Wolsey"* is the source for the story that Wolsey had incurred Anne's enmity in the early 1520s by breaking off her romance with Henry Percy, heir to the Earl of Northumberland. According to Cavendish, this had been instigated by the King himself, but Anne vowed revenge on the Cardinal. If she did, he no doubt dismissed it as angry talk by a mere girl. If the Queen could not influence her husband against him, what chance did Anne have?

However, by 1525, Henry VIII had fallen in love with Anne, and, before long, was planning to marry her. It would do a real disservice to Henry to believe that infatuation with Anne was his only reason for seeking an annulment of his marriage. Katharine had not had a pregnancy for seven years, and it seemed her child-bearing days were done. Henry thus had no legitimate male heir, and there were concerns about female succession. In addition, the betrayal of England by Charles and his rejection of Princess Mary meant that the Anglo-Spanish alliance that Katharine represented was now outworn.

Whether Anne was a suitable choice for a second match is a different matter, and, probably at the start of the annulment proceedings, not a definite decision.

Wolsey was blamed then, and subsequently, for Henry's decision to seek an annulment, however, Henry himself stated that Wolsey had, instead, tried to dissuade him. Wolsey was all too aware of the difficulties that would need to be overcome for Henry to gain his freedom. First, the Pope would have to admit that his predecessor had been wrong to grant a dispensation for the marriage, and, second, the Emperor would have to accept the Pope's decision and see his aunt and cousin humiliated.

In May 1527 Henry's campaign opened when Wolsey constituted a secret court, presided over by himself and Archbishop Warham, that cited Henry to appear to answer a charge of living in sin with his brother's widow. Henry therefore was a defendant, and appointed a proxy to act for him, brandishing the dispensation granted by Pope Julius II in 1503.

It was open to Wolsey and Warham to state that the dispensation was insufficient, and perhaps, had they done so, the matter might have passed quickly into the realms of the *fait accompli*. However, they could not bring themselves to take the hazardous and potentially sinful step of ruling that a Papal dispensation was invalid. They therefore ruled that the matter was open to doubt, and would have to be adjudicated in Rome.

Henry was not, of course, the first king or noble to seek an annulment, and generally, matters proceeded fairly smoothly. Some technical fault was found and the deed was done, with general face-saving all round. In some cases the discarded wives (it was usually, but not always, a wife who was discarded) were persuaded to enter a convent, which allowed the husband to remarry.

In the mid-1520s however, the situation was clouded by two factors – first, the spread of Lutheran ideas challenging the supremacy of the Pope. Clement VII would not be eager to add fuel to these notions by suggesting his predecessor had been wrong to grant the dispensation under which Henry and Katharine were originally married. The second obstacle was the sack of Rome by Emperor Charles' forces in May 1527, which resulted in the Pope becoming his prisoner.

Wolsey tried to turn this situation to advantage, by travelling to Avignon, France, in a bid to be recognised as the Pope's regent, able to act for him whilst he was in bondage. However, he was circumvented, first by Katharine smuggling a letter out to Charles V, and by the immediate efforts of his enemies at home to undermine him as soon as he was out of the country. The King was persuaded by Anne's faction, which combined Anne's relatives with Wolsey's enemies (her uncle, the Duke of Norfolk, her father, Sir Thomas Boleyn and Charles Brandon, Duke of Suffolk being the ringleaders) to send messengers directly to Rome.

Wolsey failed in his trip to Avignon, the other Cardinals not showing any enthusiasm for Wolsey as the Pope's deputy, and returned to England in September 1527. Henry's messengers had met with no more success than Wolsey's move, so Wolsey was once more expected to come up with a solution. He persuaded Clement to grant a commission to Wolsey, and a fellow Cardinal, Lorenzo Campeggio (who was also Bishop of Salisbury) to hear the case and pronounce on it. Whilst Clement would not openly agree to accept the verdict, he gave a private letter, assuring them he would, whilst, at the same time telling Campeggio the letter was not to be used, and could only be shown to Henry and Wolsey.

In 1529, the famous Legatine Court opened at Blackfriars to try the case of matrimony between Henry VIII and Katharine of Aragon. After some opening legal business, Katharine famously appealed to her husband in person, then refused to accept the authority of the Court, appealing directly to Rome. Clement was horrified, but unable to resist the pressure of the Emperor, who now controlled Italy, removed the authority of the Blackfriars Court. On 31st July 1529 Wolsey was obliged to stand up in Court and tell the King that his case was not concluded, but must be heard in Rome.

Chapter 48: The End (1529 – 1530)

Henry had suspected for some time, owing to the seeds of doubt planted by Anne and her supporters, that Wolsey was not as diligent in pursuing the annulment as Henry required, and the failure of the Legatine Court seemed to support that fear. He was not, however, certain that he could, or should, try to manage without Wolsey. He also remained personally attached to the Cardinal.

Wolsey was in disgrace, but Campeggio asked that he be permitted to accompany him on Campeggio's visit to Grafton in Northamptonshire to take his leave of Henry. Henry agreed, much to the chagrin of Anne. When Wolsey arrived, it was to find there was no room for him at the house, but Sir Henry Norris, one of the King's gentlemen, took pity on him and let him use his own room.

On being allowed into the King's presence, the Cardinal was unusually deferential to his assembled enemies, but he was soon chatting familiarly to the King again, tucked in a window embrasure, exchanging confidences.

Overnight, however, Anne hatched a plan to take the King hunting on the following day, leaving Wolsey to accompany Campeggio back to London. The knives were now out for Wolsey. He was indicted for *'praemunire'* (the useful expedient that was brought out from time to time to keep the Church in its place and which consisted of a charge of putting the Church above the King), which he admitted, beseeching the King to forgive him.

> *'I, your poor, heavy and wretched priest do daily pursue, cry and call upon Your Royal Majesty for grace, mercy, remission and pardon...'*

In October 1529, Wolsey was stripped of his position of Lord Chancellor and told to remove from York House to Esher. En route, he was met by Sir Henry Norris, with a ring from the King. Grateful beyond words, Wolsey sank to his knees in the road, thanking the King for his kindness, which he reciprocated by sending his fool, Patch to the King's service – much to Patch's displeasure - he had to be taken by force.

Henry again sent positive messages in November, before Parliament opened, but Wolsey's enemies were baying for his blood, and the Lords introduced a bill to prevent Henry ever employing him in public office again. The bill contained an enormous list of, mainly ludicrous, charges, including embezzlement, putting the Cardinal's hat on the coinage, referring to himself in the same sentence as the King, and endangering the King's health by breathing infection on him. Wolsey was ably defended in the Commons by his secretary, Thomas Cromwell, and the bill was dropped. The King, meanwhile, agreed to make such provision as he thought fit, bearing in mind the articles in the original bill. He did not wish to commit himself to never employing Wolsey again.

In the new year of 1530, Norfolk continued his assault, but, when Wolsey fell seriously ill, Henry exclaimed that he would not lose him for £20,000 and sent his own doctors, as well as another ring. He also persuaded Anne to send a token of esteem. Nevertheless, the pressure from Norfolk, Suffolk, Boleyn and the rest was unrelenting – it was now a fight to the death. If Henry re-established Wolsey in his favour, they could not hope to survive.

The Council, unable to persuade Henry to completely abandon him, went along with a full pardon on 12th February, together with banishment to reside in his Archbishopric of York. Wolsey pleaded poverty and attempted to persuade the French and Imperial courts to send the arrears of pensions promised many years before. Henry, too, sent him £1,000. In April, he began his journey north. He remained at the Archbishopric's house at Southwell for some months, living more ostentatiously than was wise, in direct contravention of Cromwell's advice.

Wolsey, who had been so aware of the shifts of power, and had used his knowledge of men to attain the heights he had, now seemed to lose his head completely. He had obviously not grasped the level of Henry's attachment to Anne Boleyn, and he sought to undermine Norfolk, and the process of the annulment by writing to the Imperial Ambassador and taking an interest in Katharine's case.

Always busy, Wolsey occupied his time in his diocese acting more in conformity with his vows as a priest than ever before – dispensing charity, Confirming children and saying Mass. He had never actually been enthroned as Archbishop, so, despite needing the King's consent, which he neglected to ask for, he sent out summons to the northern convocation of clergy to attend his enthronement on 7th November 1530.

This, together with information that a Papal Bull, threatening excommunication had been published, was enough to allow Henry to be persuaded that Wolsey was guilty of *'presumptuous, sinister practices'*. On 1st November, a warrant was issued for his arrest. On 4th November Wolsey was arrested and carried towards London. By Saturday, 26th November, he was at the Greyfriars Abbey, Leicester. He had been sickening all the while, and, tumbling from his mule, told the Abbot that he was '*come hither to leave (his) bones amongst (them)*'.

He died on the following Tuesday, uttering the famous words:

'If I had served my God as diligently as I have served my King, He would not have given me over in my grey hairs.'

He was buried in the Abbey church, close to the grave of Richard III.

Wolsey was, without doubt, one of the proudest, vainest and most arrogant men to wield power in England, yet he was also devoted to his king, a promoter of peace where that was practicable, and determined to give England an important place in foreign affairs. He was a patron of the arts and of education, and upheld the law impartially against the rich as well as the poor, whilst avoiding the harsh religious punishments so popular with his contemporaries. He worked indefatigably for the advancement of his country, and deserves a better reputation than he has.

Aspects of Cardinal Wolsey's Life

Chapter 49: Patron of Education

Wolsey was nothing if not grand in his vision. As a man who had risen high in the world, through his education, he determined to emulate some of his great ecclesiastical predecessors, such as William Wykeham, Bishop of Winchester, founder of Wolsey's own alma mater, Magdalen College, Oxford and found both a school and university college.

The college came first, with preparations beginning in 1524, and then the school in 1528. Even Wolsey's wealth was not sufficient for his ambitions, so he planned to fund the building work and endow the colleges through the suppression of some smaller monasteries, and the diversion of their wealth.

Cardinal College, Oxford – now Christ Church

The site chosen was the Augustinian St Frideswide's Priory and a Bull was received in 1524 from Pope Clement VII, permitting its suppression. The site was extended to include surrounding houses, the Oxford Jewish quarter, various inns and also Canterbury College.

Works began almost immediately, with the centrepiece being the Gothic quadrangle known as *'Tom Quad'* which, measuring 264 by 261 feet, is still the largest in Oxford. By the time of Wolsey's fall in 1529, the building work was incomplete, with only three sides of the quadrangle finished, and the fourth, the Chapel location, still at foundation level. The Hall was finished, worked on by the mason Thomas Redman and the glazier James Nicholson, as were the kitchens.

The College was to be staffed by a Dean (the first being John Higdon, formerly a Fellow at Magdalen with Wolsey) and sixty Canons, as well as a schoolmaster, priests, clerks and choir boys, honest paupers (!) and undergraduates.

Work stopped in 1529, then, in 1532, Cardinal College was re-founded as King Henry VIII's College, on a reduced scale, with only twelve canons.

On 20th May 1545, the College was surrendered to the Crown, as one of the last monasteries in England, and combined with the see of Oxford to create the new Christ Church, Oxford, which remains the Cathedral Church of the Diocese of Oxford.

Cardinal College, Ipswich

The plan was for a college of secular canons – that is, ordained priests who live in community as monks do, but go into the world to practise their ministry – together with a school for boys to act as a feeder for Cardinal College at Oxford.

The site selected was originally the priory of St Peter and St Paul, but Wolsey received a Bull from Pope Clement VII on 28th May, 1528 allowing the suppression of the monastery, confirmed by Henry VIII. In addition to the closure of St Peter and Paul (whose inmates were to be moved to other priories of the same order), a further ten monasteries (Snape, Dodnash, Wikes, Tiptree, Horkesley, Rumburgh, Felixstowe, Bromhill, Blythburgh, and Mountjoy) were also closed, and the land and funds diverted to the new College. Funds from the Church of St Nicholas, where Wolsey's father had been a Church Warden, and also from St. Peter, St.-Mary-at-Quay, St. Clement, and St. Matthew were diverted to the College.

The foundation stone was laid on 20th June 1528 by John Longland, Bishop of Lincoln, another ex-colleague of Wolsey's at Magdalen, and a couple of weeks later the formal royal licence for the Cardinal's College of St Mary, Ipswich, was granted by the King at Hampton Court.

The licence gave details of how the College would be manned. There were to be a Dean, twelve priests, eight clerks, eight singing boys and poor scholars, and thirteen poor men. Their role was to pray for the health and well-being of the King and the Cardinal, and for the souls of the Cardinal's parents. There was also to be one schoolmaster, learned in (Latin) grammar to teach the scholars and any others who came to the college, from any part of the country. The first Dean was Dr William Capon, Master of Jesus College, Cambridge and the school master was William Goldwin. The College was to be free from the normal supervision of the local Bishop.

As well as the organisation of the religious side, Wolsey took a keen personal interest in the scholars. He selected the Latin grammar book that was to be used, and wrote a special preface for it – rather pompous in tone, but his motives were good, and he was clear that competent school masters were necessary. The instructions for the school cast a light on an under-appreciated, but attractive aspect of Wolsey's character – his fundamental dislike of physical punishment. In an age that believed that to *spare the rod was to spoil the child*', he wrote

'We admonish particularly, that tender youth be not effected by severe stripes or threatening countenance or by any species of tyranny.'

He also enjoined the parents of his boys to send them to Ipswich with sufficient warm clothes for chilly East Anglian winters.

A great inaugural dinner was held in early September 1528, for which Anne Howard, Countess of Oxford sent two fine bucks, and her brother, the Duke of Norfolk, other supplies. At the same time, vast quantities of plate and vestments were brought by Wolsey's staff, including Thomas

Cromwell and Rowland Lee. Cromwell apparently took *'great pains'* to arrange everything.

On 7th September, there was a solemn procession in St Peter's Church (which was to continue as the College Church) for the service of Evensong. This was followed by a procession to the Lady Chapel, where Evensong was performed again. The following day, the planned procession, at which the Dean, Subdean, six priests, eight clerks, nine choristers, and all their servants who had attended on 7th, were to be joined by the Bailiffs and dignitaries of the town, was cancelled, owing to incessant rain.

A damp service was held in Holy Trinity, with the Bishop of Norwich in attendance. Dean Capon was pleased with the singers, but they complained that they had received better wages in their previous positions. There were also the usual complaints that everyone had too much to do, and that more staff were needed, as the five priests already in post were not enough to keep three Masses a day. The Sub-dean, Mr Ellis, was too busy to take a hand as he was managing the building works.

The choir master, Mr Lentall, took to his work with delight, promising 'there shall be no better children in any place in England than we shall have here shortly.'

Building works began with 120 tons of white Caen stone being delivered in early September 1528, with a further 100 to arrive by Michaelmas (29th September) and a thousand to be supplied before Easter 1529. Works continued apace in 1529, and on 24th July Cromwell received a letter informing him that the works were now above the ground and that the site was busy night and day.

Wolsey fell from power before the College was finished. On 14th November 1530 Commissioners arrived from the King to value everything on site. All the plate and valuables were seized, and Dr Capon accused of hiding £1,000 worth of goods. On 21st November, the Duke of

Norfolk's men took possession of the site and in 1531, the site of the College, and its Ipswich possessions were granted to Thomas Alvard, one of Henry's gentleman ushers. Some of the other property was granted to Eton College and some to the Abbey of Waltham. The site itself fell into disrepair and was used as a rubbish dump.

Chapter 50: Following the Footsteps of Thomas Wolsey

Wolsey travelled largely in the south-east of England, with a number of visits to Calais, the Low Countries, France, and Scotland during his life. The numbers in brackets refer to the key to the map below.

Born in Ipswich (1), he first left it in around 1485 to travel to Oxford where he studied at Magdalen College (2) and later founded Cardinal's College (now Christ Church College). Whilst acting as schoolmaster to the sons of the Marquess of Dorset, he went with the young men to their home at Bradgate, Leicestershire (3). This is likely to have been his first taste of the delights of wealth. His first modest living, however, as a priest, was at St Mary's Limington (4), Somerset, although whether he ever actually lived there is a moot point.

He was certainly back in London by 1501, in residence at Lambeth Palace (5). His next port of call was a stint in Calais, as assistant to the Deputy Lieutenant, Sir Richard Nanfan. On returning home in 1507, he joined the royal household, which was mainly centred on Henry VII's new palace at Richmond (6). Whilst in Henry's employ, he visited both Scotland and the Low Countries on diplomatic missions.

Wolsey's first great step forward in the Church was his preferment as Dean, then Bishop of Lincoln (7), although, if he went to the cathedral at all, it would have been a fleeting visit. He certainly did not take up residence.

Promoted to the Archbishopric of York in 1514, Wolsey took possession of York Place (8), the Archbishops' palace in London, which is now the location of Whitehall. York Place had been largely ignored by the previous incumbent, Cardinal Bainbridge, and Wolsey set about renovating the palace on a grand scale. The chief architect was Henry Redmayne, who was the master mason of Westminster Abbey. Overall, the renovations cost in excess of £1,250 in a time when a soldier earned 4d a day.

But York Place belonged to the Church – Wolsey wanted a place of his own. In 1514 he acquired Hampton Court (9), which he transformed into the most glittering renaissance palace in Britain, outstripping Henry VII's great construction at Richmond, and the King's favourite palace at Greenwich. Henry looked on Hampton Court with covetous eyes, and, in 1528, when times were becoming difficult for Wolsey, he gave it to the King, although with the proviso that he could stay there whenever he liked.

Not content with Hampton Court, Wolsey also acquired and spent considerable amounts of time during the 1520s at The More (10), near Rickmansworth. After his fall, this was the house to which Katharine of Aragon was banished.

During the period 1520 – 22, Wolsey travelled to Calais, in charge of the preparations for the Field of Cloth of Gold, and then for the negotiations of 1522, first in Calais, then in Bruges. In 1527 he was abroad again, heading for Avignon in the south of France, to persuade the College of Cardinals to accept him as deputy for the imprisoned pope, Clement VII.

One of the most significant scenes of Wolsey's life was played out at Blackfriars (11) – this was a Dominican monastery, but was frequently used for Parliament meetings or for other state occasions. It is now buried beneath Blackfriars station. In May 1529, Blackfriars was the location of the Legatine Court presided over by Wolsey and Cardinal Campeggio, to try the matrimonial cause between Henry VIII and Katharine of Aragon.

Wolsey's failure to obtain the annulment led to his fall from favour. He was given hope of reinstatement in Henry's good graces when he was graciously received by the King at Grafton Regis (12), but he was disappointed.

Sent to reside in his diocese of York, Wolsey took up residence, first at Southwell in Nottinghamshire, then at the Archbishops' Palace at Cawood Castle (13). Here too, he could not resist his desire to build and improve, and began spending money on renovations. Here too, he planned his enthronement at York Minster (14), but he was arrested, and died at Greyfriars Abbey, Leicester (15) before it could take place.

The most interesting thing about Wolsey's journeys, is not the actual locations, but the ceremony and pageantry that followed him as he went. Wherever he was, Wolsey would make the most of his appearance to strike awe and wonder into the watching crowds. As became a Prince of the Church, he rode a mule, but the mule would be trapped with gold, and his retinue in red satin.

Whilst he was residing at York Place in the period after 1514, he would visit the King at Greenwich each Sunday. Setting out early in the morning, he would descend the new water steps he had had built, into his painted and gilded barge, attended by a liveried retinue. He would be rowed downstream as far as either Queenhithe (now Cannon Street) or St Paul's.

Once arrived, he would leave the barge and be met by horses which would carry him past the treacherous rapids at London Bridge, then some 100 ft (30 meters) further downstream than now. *Shooting the bridge*, as it was called, when a vessel passed downstream under it, was a dangerous undertaking and avoided if at all possible. Past London Bridge, he would enter another barge to continue to Greenwich.

All the other days of the week, when he was in London, Wolsey would travel to Westminster to undertake his duties in the Star Chamber and in Chancery. Leaving York Place at 8am he would be preceded by two great silver crosses, one each for his roles as Papal Legate and Archbishop. These would be followed by two pillars of state, the Lord Chancellor's Sergeant-at-arms and a page, bearing the Great Seal in a silk bag. Wolsey would come next on his mule, his four footmen bearing silver poleaxes and a peer or a gentleman usher bearing his red cardinal's hat. To clear the crowds, ushers marched ahead, crying *'On, my Lords and Masters. Make way for my Lord's Grace, The Cardinal Legate of York, Lord High Chancellor of this realm.'*

The most magnificent trip of all was Wolsey's foray toward the French camp at the Field of Cloth of Gold, when he left the English camp to arrange the details of the two Kings' meeting.

He set forth on his mule, with fifty mounted gentlemen preceding him, gowned in red velvet and a further fifty ushers bearing gold maces as *'large as a man's head'*. In front of him was borne his great gold cross, with a jewelled crucifix. Behind the Cardinal rode a phalanx of bishops and other clergy, including the Grand Prior of the Knights of St John of Jerusalem. Bringing up the rear, were 100 mounted archers of the King's Guard.

It is not hard to see why Henry's nobles considered Wolsey an arrogant upstart.

Key to Map

1. Ipswich
2. Magdalen and Christ Church, Oxford
3. Bradgate Park, Leicestershire

4. St Mary's Church, Limington, Somerset
5. Lambeth Palace, London
6. Richmond Palace, London
7. Lincoln Cathedral
8. York Place, London
9. Hampton Court Palace, Surrey
10. The More, near Rickmansworth, Hertfordshire
11. Blackfriars Monastery, London
12. Grafton Regis , Northamptonshire
13. Cawood Castle near Selby, Yorkshire
14. York Minster, Yorkshire
15. Church of the Greyfriars, Leicester

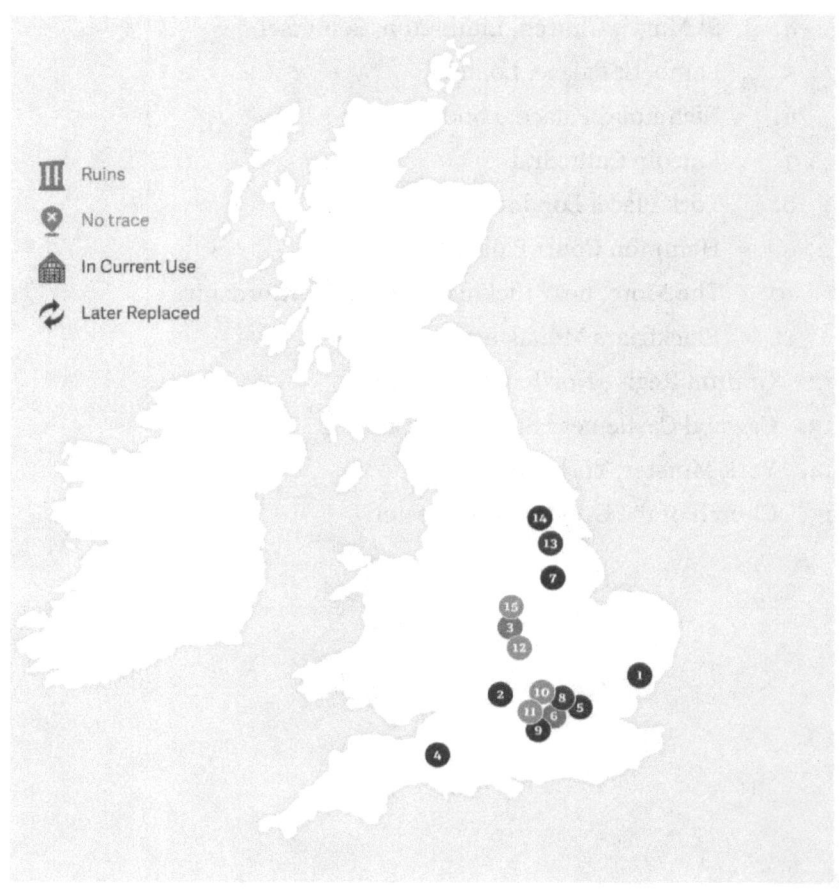

Chapter 51: Thomas Wolsey: In History & Literature

History

Wolsey was one of the first politicians and statesmen in England to be the subject of a biography. His early biographer was George Cavendish (brother of the Sir William Cavendish whose descendants are now Dukes of Devonshire). Cavendish was Wolsey's Gentleman-Usher in the last few years of his life. Thus, he was not only close to Wolsey in his triumph, but his position gave him access when Wolsey had less to do, and was therefore more inclined to talk to his attendants at length about the past.

Cavendish's biography, which is still in print, is a very positive portrait of his master.

Far less complimentary were Polydore Vergil and Edward Hall. Vergil, who is generally a balanced reporter, had a personal grudge against Wolsey, whom he believed had blocked him from promotion, and Edward Hall was a reformer who saw Wolsey as the exemplification of every ill of the old Church.

Throughout the following centuries Wolsey was seen as a villain – an early attempt by Richard Fiddes in 1724 to rescue his reputation was roundly condemned for casting aspersions on the glory of the Reformation. It was not until the late nineteenth century that he was rehabilitated by historians such as Creighton, who saw in his efforts to make England centre stage in European politics a foreshadowing of Empire.

In the twentieth century he was the subject of a major biography in the 1920s by that colossus of Tudor History, A F Pollard. Pollard is definitely of the school that believes Wolsey wanted to be Pope, and that he dominated Henry VIII.

Much of Pollard's basic thesis is overturned by Dr Peter Gwyn, in which several hundred pages of densely printed text give a complete picture of the political ins and outs in England between the years 1509 and 1530. Gwyn convincingly shows that Henry was in charge all along, but, the work, though a superlatively detailed political biography, tells us very little about Wolsey as a man.

The Cardinal is a joint subject with Thomas More and Thomas Cromwell respectively in Jasper Ridley's *'The Statesman and the Fanatic'*, and *'The Cardinal and the Secretary'*.

Any student of Henry VIII will, of course, meet Wolsey in J J Scarisbrick's work of 1968 which still retains its primacy as an account of Henry's reign. For a more modern take, there is Dr David Starkey.

Literature

Wolsey's earliest appearance in literature was in Shakespeare's Henry VIII (believed to be a collaboration between Shakespeare and Fletcher), in which he is shown as scheming to dispatch the Duke of Buckingham and then against Queen Katharine.

Katharine of Aragon disliked Wolsey and Anne Boleyn was his bitterest enemy so, since most of the fiction relating to the period has one or other of them as heroine, Wolsey comes off badly. However that has all changed with Hilary Mantel's novels *'Wolf Hall'* and *'Bring Up the Bodies'*, where her hero, Thomas Cromwell, is shown as being motivated by revenge as he tries to punish those whose ill-treatment of Wolsey, his first master, he resents.

Chapter 52: Thomas Wolsey: Book Review

Wolsey is the subject of one of the earliest biographies ever written, and then a couple of works in the 1970s, including the best academic reference, *'The King's Cardinal'* by Peter Gwyn. The most recent biography of Wolsey is *'Wolsey: The King's Cardinal'*, which we have reviewed here.

Wolsey: The King's Cardinal

Author: John Matusiak

Publisher: The History Press (30 Sept. 2014)

In a nutshell Informative, and makes a clear narrative of complex happenings. Likely to be enjoyed by general readers, rather than academics.

I was looking forward to reading this, as I enjoyed Matusiak's previous work on Henry VIII. One of the things I had liked was his writing style, a little more colourful and individual than just the bald recital of facts that some historians use. However, as time went on, the careful alliterations and the well-chosen adjectives began to pall, and seem over-written and contrived – *'the icy flood of events began to reach the Cardinal's nostrils'*. Maybe simplicity is not such a bad thing!

Matusiak has made much more of an effort than most of Wolsey's biographers to think about Wolsey's internal self. He is shown not just as the proud and vainglorious *'peacock'* but an incredibly hard working perfectionist – unable to delegate, prone to stress-induced illness and bursts of anger when under pressure. Matusiak shows how, the more Wolsey achieved, the more was expected of him – he could never rest.

He had given Henry VIII to think he was invincible and he had to keep delivering.

The author's general style leans towards the sceptical, if not the cynical. Most of the characters presented are shown with all their flaws, and if there is a choice between motives, the less virtuous one tends to be presented. Henry, in particular, is shown as not much more than a conceited buffoon, entirely led by his vanity. There is, of course, some truth in this, but it is only one strand in a multi-layered personality.

Where Matusiak really adds to our knowledge of the Cardinal, is in his early days – the relationship with Henry VII, that so many writers mention only in passing, is filled out, and the development of his working partnership with Richard Foxe, Bishop of Winchester. He also disagrees, with excellent reasoning, with Peter Gwyn whose biography of Wolsey is the standard work of reference, on the importance of Wolsey's time working for the Deputy Lieutenant of Calais, Sir Richard Nanfan. Matusiak shows how this experience equipped Wolsey for his later administrative roles.

He also demonstrates that the idea that Wolsey aspired to be Pope is quite unsupported by the evidence, and that much of our view of Wolsey comes from his enemies, writing after his fall – and that certainly part of his unpopularity with the nobles was based on Wolsey's determination that they should obey the law like lesser men.

It is clear that the author admires Wolsey's cleverness, what contemporaries called his *'angel wit'* and his enterprise. No sooner had one scheme failed, than Wolsey would have another in hand. Matusiak also lays out very clearly that in the last great matter, that of the annulment, Henry's actions completely undermined Wolsey, and could well have prevented the grant he so desperately sought.

Overall, Matusiak creates a very clear narrative from a mass of events, and the book is a good guide to Wolsey, although he is much less penetrating when considering the other people of the period, being inclined to repeat old generalisations.

Part 5: Marie of Guise: Regent of Scotland

Introduction

Marie of Guise was a French noblewoman who became Queen Consort of Scotland. Through her determination and political skill she managed to protect her daughter, Queen of Scots at eight days old, from the aggressive policy of the Queen's great-uncle, Henry VIII, who sought to annex Scotland. Finally achieving the position of Regent, she tried to steer a moderate course through the increasingly polarised religious factions, but died in the middle of a rebellion by the Protestant Lords.

Part 5 contains Marie of Guise's Life Story and additional articles about her, looking at different aspects of her life. Marie of Guise protected the inheritance of her daughter, Mary, Queen of Scots, and promoted the Auld Alliance between Scotland and France. She spent her youth in France, before arriving in Scotland aged about twenty-three, to be the second wife of James V. Marie travelled extensively in Lowland Scotland to carry out her functions, first as Queen Consort, then as Regent.

MARIE OF GUISE

Family Tree

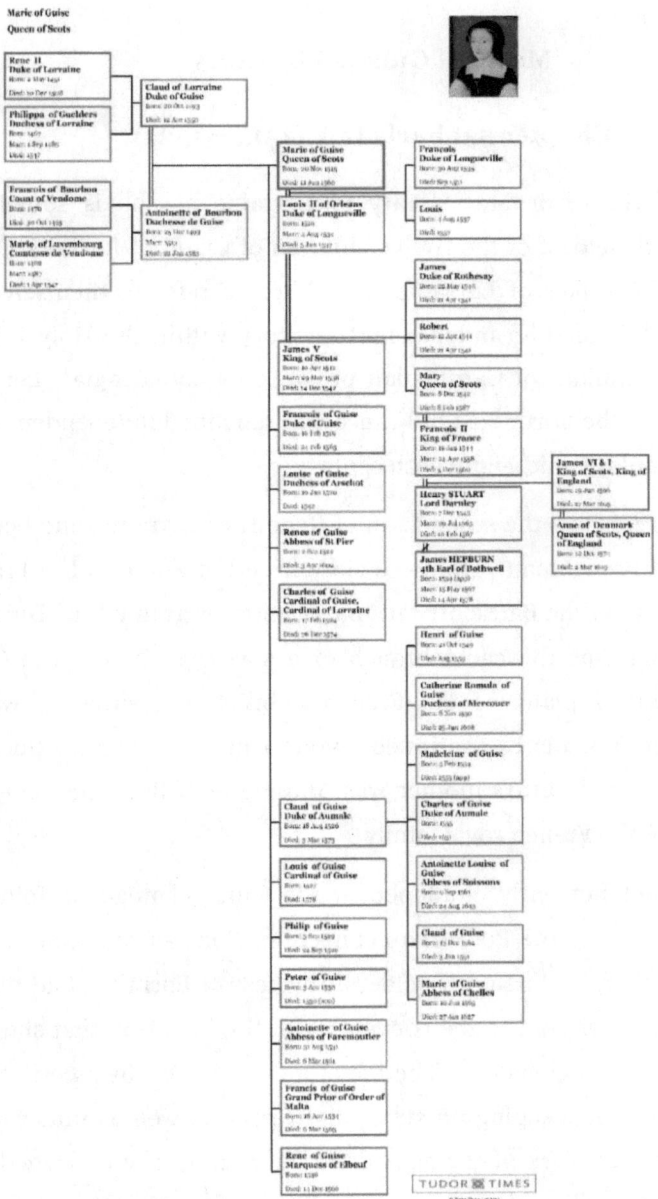

Marie of Guise's Life Story

Chapter 53: Early Life (1515 – 1531)

Marie of Guise, or Marie/Mary of Lorraine as she is sometimes known, was the eldest of the twelve children of Claud of Lorraine, Duke of Guise. The Dukes of Lorraine (who liked to refer to themselves as Kings of Sicily) ruled an independent territory within the Holy Roman Empire, the remnant of Carolingian province of Lotharingia. Lorraine was situated to the north-east of France and remained independent of its neighbour until the mid-eighteenth century.

Marie's father was the second son of Rene II of Lorraine, and became a naturalised Frenchman. He was a close friend of Francois I of France, fighting for him at the Battle of Marignano, and was granted the Duchy of Guise, although, as the cadet branch of a sovereign house, the Guise family outranked many of the French nobility – a situation which, together with Francois I's continued favour, caused some resentment at the French court. Marie's mother was Antoinette of Bourbon, daughter of a branch of the French royal family.

Marie spent her early childhood at the Guise chateau of Joinville, before being sent to the Poor Clare convent of Pont-au-Mousson, where her grandmother, Philippa of Guelders, Duchess of Lorraine, had retired in 1519. Marie was sent to the convent, with the intention that she, too, would enter the religious life. The life of a Poor Clare was ascetic in the extreme, including sleeping on straw mattresses as well as undertaking all of the manual work of the convent. The nuns cooked, cleaned and managed their gardens themselves as well as undertaking their religious duties. Marie is presumed to have done likewise.

Marie's education at the convent was designed to fit her for the role of Abbess, however in 1529, her uncle, Antoine II, Duke of Lorraine, decided there was a better use for his attractive and witty niece than being a nun. Following the Peasant Risings in Germany, precipitated by the early Lutheran movement, Lorraine, too faced internal insurrection.

The family needed to increase its strength and influence and a marriage for his niece to a peer of France (or even, if Antoine were lucky, one of the King's sons) would be valuable. Marie was taken to the Lorraine court at Nancy where the Duchess, Renee of Bourbon, taught her more worldly skills than those that had been deemed suitable for a contemplative nun. On 5 March 1531, Marie was presented to King François, and his new Queen, Eleanor of Austria. Marie was naturally charming and attractive, and won the approval of François I (not hard for a pretty girl to do, as he was a notorious lecher). She also developed friendships with his daughters, Madeleine and Marguerite.

Chapter 54: First Marriage (1531 – 1537)

It is likely that Marie spent the period 1531 – 1534 at the French Court. In 1534, François I personally involved himself in arranging her marriage to Louis d'Orleans, Duke of Longueville and Hereditary Grand Chamberlain of France. Marie's father, who seems to have been rather close-fisted as far as his daughters were concerned, refused to give Marie a sufficient dowry. François stepped in to make up the 80,000 livres offered by Claud, to the required 120,000.

The Longueville estates were in the north and west of France, centred round Normandy and the Loire, and Marie received the chateau of Chateaudun as her jointure. The whole of the French Court was present for the ceremony at the Louvre on 4th August 1534. The bride was 18, and the groom some five years older.

Marie and Louis' first son, Francois, was born 30th October 1535 at Amiens. Later letters from Marie's own mother, Antoinette of Bourbon, hint at some discord between Marie and her mother-in-law, Jeanne de Hochberg, who was Countess of Neuchatel in her own right, but whether there was anything more substantial than the not-unusual mother-in-law difficulties, cannot be ascertained.

On 1st January 1537 Marie attended the French court for the wedding of the Princess Madeleine to James V of Scotland. Madeleine's father had been reluctant to agree to the match as the princess was consumptive and the damp climate of Scotland was unlikely to suit her. James strongly desired the match to boost his ability to resist his menacing uncle, Henry VIII of England, and also seems to have become fond of Madeleine herself. Madeleine, too, wanted the match – apparently saying she wished to be a queen before she died. The match was celebrated at Notre Dame with Marie in attendance.

In the spring of 1537, Marie returned to Chateaudun, her husband being due to follow her. Unfortunately, Louis fell ill, perhaps with chicken pox, and died at Rouen on 9th June 1537. His last letter to his wife closes with the words

'I shall say no more...praying God to give you always whatever you desire, your good husband and friend, Louis.'

Marie was pregnant and on 4th August 1537 (her third wedding anniversary) gave birth to a second son, Louis, who died within months.

Chapter 55: Marriage Negotiations

1537 was a year of bad news for Marie. She heard in July that her friend, Madeleine, Queen of Scots, had died. Her first reaction is likely to have been sorrow, followed by dismay when she heard that James, still without a legitimate heir, was looking for a replacement bride, preferably of equal prestige to Madeleine. King François had other plans for his daughter Marguerite (who became Duchess of Savoy), and decided that Marie would make a suitable Queen of Scots. Marie did not want to leave her home and her son and initially refused. François pressed her and James wrote, pleading his suit, personally.

If Marie really did not want to be Queen of Scots, an alternative was soon available. Henry VIII of England, widowed by the death of his third wife Jane Seymour in childbed, was in the market for a fourth. He was eager for a match with either France or the Empire to re-establish himself as a member of the European royal circle after the rift caused by his casting-off of the Emperor's aunt. Henry was also happy to disrupt any plans James V might have and seized the idea that Marie might be just the wife for him - a widowed mother of sons, who was good looking, and exceptionally tall, seemed ideal.

Marie resisted this idea even more strenuously, apparently saying that although she was tall, her neck was very small. Suddenly, marriage to James looked more appealing. Her father again showed reluctance to provide the dowry expected – the Scots were demanding some 150,000 livres, and initially, Claud suggested that it should be paid from the Longueville estates. This would have defrauded her son, François, of part of his inheritance and Marie refused. Eventually, King François offered 70,000 livres and gouged the remainder from Claud.

The marriage contract was drawn up by Cardinal David Beaton, acting for James, and Marie's father. In return for the dowry, Marie's grant as

Queen of Scots was the palace of Falkland; Stirling, Dingwall and Threave castles; the revenues of the Earldoms of Orkney, Fife, Strathearn and Ross, and the lordships of Galloway, Ardmeneach and The Isles. In the event of James pre-deceasing her, if they had children, she would have one third of the amount of her dowry, or half if there were no children. Marie was also indemnified against responsibility for any of his debts. She would be able to retain this dower, even if she returned to France.

Chapter 56: Queen of Scots

The wedding took place at Chateaudun on 9th May 1538, following the necessary dispensation from the Pope, as the couple were third cousins. The link was the familial connection through the Duchy of Guelders. Marie's grandmother, Philippa of Guelders was niece to Marie of Guelders, wife of James II of Scotland.

For his second marriage, James was represented by his proxy, Robert, Lord Maxwell. The bride's wedding ring contained a single diamond and cost James 300 crowns. Marie was now Queen of Scots.

She set sail in June for her new country, arriving at Balcomie in Fife towards the end of the month, pleasingly free from sea-sickness. Marie and James went through a further marriage ceremony at St Andrew's, before taking a trip, both to show Marie the country, and to let the Scots see their new queen. A formal entry into Edinburgh took place on 16th November 1538, followed by her coronation on 22nd February 1540 at Holyrood Abbey.

Marie and James do not seem to have been very compatible personally. He continued his flagrant womanising, and there are letters from him in which he seems to be brushing aside her requests for him to return home and her fears that he has forgotten her. Whatever they felt about each other, they knew their duty and produced two sons in quick succession – James in May 1540 and Robert in April 1541. Heartbreakingly, both boys died on the same day, 21st April 1541. They were buried in the same tomb as Queen Madeleine.

Whilst Queen, Marie spent much of her time in architectural projects. This was one area of interest that she and James had in common, and significant sums were expended on the refurbishing and updating of Falkland Palace, Linlithgow and Stirling. Marie's knowledge of the beautiful palaces of the Loire must have influenced the design.

There was also frequent correspondence with her mother, in which Antoinette relays family news and reassures Marie as the health of her son, the Duke of Longueville. She tells her daughter that little François was so happy in the company of his grandfather, that he has '*lost some of his naughtiness*', and that the two could only part in tears.

In other letters from her son's governess, Mlle Jeanne, François sends messages to his mother typical of any little boy

'*I have a pony, now I want a big horse, it is to be black. Madame Grandmere takes me often round her garden.*'

Marie also managed to build a relationship with James' difficult mother, Margaret Tudor, the Dowager Queen. Henry VIII's Ambassador recorded Margaret's statement that '*she was well treated and made much of, of the new Queen (Marie)*'

Queen Margaret had spent most of her life trying to reconcile the country of her birth with the country of her adoption. Throughout the late 1530s both countries had carried out raids and low level acts of aggression, but Margaret had continued to press for a meeting between James and his uncle, Henry VIII.

Various plans had been drafted but it was not until 1541 that it looked as though years of negotiation might finally bear fruit. Henry believed that James had agreed to meet him at York, whither he was travelling as part of a wider progress to demonstrate royal power following the Pilgrimage of Grace. The Abbey of St Mary at York was refurbished for James and his entourage, and arrangements made for safe-conduct through the north of England. James however, had never made any specific promise and the upshot was that he remained at home. Henry was beyond furious. He felt he had been humiliated by James and he would have his revenge.

Talks continued, but there was no real will on either side for peace. In October 1542 Thomas Howard, 3rd Duke of Norfolk, marched in excess of 10,000 men into Scotland on a spree of burning and looting between Berwick and Kelso, before retiring back into England. Henry also repeated his inflammatory claim that he was Scotland's overlord.

James raised some 15,000 troops and made a counter-attack, although, learning the lesson of his father's death at Flodden, he did not lead his troops personally, but remained close by. Whether through ill-luck or incompetence, the Scots force was annihilated between the rivers Esk and Lyne and well over a thousand Scots were taken prisoner, including the Earls of Cassilis, Glencairn and Lord Maxwell who were sent south to Henry.

To compound the loss, James fell ill, probably with dysentery, and, retreating to Falkland Palace, died on the 14th December 1542. The news of his wife's safe delivery of a child failed to comfort his last hours, as the baby was a girl, named Mary. This week old child was now Queen of Scots.

Chapter 57: Appointment of the Earl of Arran

The politics of the following twenty years in Scotland, and its relationship with England, should be looked at through the prism of the long struggle for dominance in Europe between France and the Hapsburg empire (including Spain from 1519), which began in the 1490s and was not resolved for another two hundred years. Religion became a complicating factor in the 1560s but, although growing in importance, was not the paramount issue (other than for individual fanatics on both sides) in the period up until Marie's death.

Once Scotland was left with a sovereign Queen, the choice of her future husband became a serious matter. If Scotland were forced into a union with England, then this would tend to favour the Hapsburgs as the old Burgundian and Spanish alliances with England were still preferred. If France could retain its Scottish ally, that would continue its traditional strategy of diverting English troops to the Border, and making incursions into France by England, either unilaterally or in support of the Empire, more difficult.

On the death of James V, two factions began to form amongst the Scottish nobles, although the strength and make up of each ebbed and flowed, and the situation was never straightforward. By and large, there was a faction that was pro-English and, in the case of some of the nobles, there was a desire to bring in a measure of Protestant Reformation, which James had firmly rejected. The second group preferred the traditional Auld Alliance with France, and were generally committed to maintaining the Catholic faith. However affiliations were not black and white, and there were Protestants who looked towards France, and Catholics who believed an accord with England was appropriate.

Marie's own allegiance was always primarily to the advancement of her dynasty, through her daughter, the Queen of Scots, and the Guise family in France. There is no reason to suppose that she did not genuinely feel that Scotland would be better protected in alliance with France, but Scottish welfare was not necessarily her primary concern.

On James V's death, the twenty-four year old James Hamilton, Earl of Arran and heir to the throne after the baby Queen Mary, came forward as the likely Regent. He was the great-grandson of James II. This immediately caused a dispute, as Cardinal Beaton claimed that James V had appointed a Regency Council consisting of Cardinal Beaton himself, the Earls of Huntly, Murray, Argyll and Arran, perhaps with Marie included. Arran denounced Beaton's document as a forgery, but agreed to Beaton being named as Chancellor.

The rapprochement was short-lived and Beaton was arrested and sent to Blackness Castle at the end of January 1543. Arran was formally appointed Governor by the Estates of Scotland on 3rd March 1543 and Marie confirmed her allegiance to him on the following day.

One of Arran's first acts, rather surprisingly, was to write to the English general, Lord Lisle, that he hoped '*to put some reformation in the state of the kirk in the realm.*' The Catholic Church in Scotland was in no better state than anywhere else in Europe, with many of its clergy leading blatantly immoral lives and using church lands and benefices to line their own pockets. In a country poorer than most, the scale of corruption was even more distasteful. One of Arran's early reforms was to allow the reading of the Bible in the vernacular from March 1543. He did not go so far down the road of Protestantism as to reject the Pope entirely, and by May was requesting papal protection and aid against England, whilst still treating with Henry for an alliance.

Chapter 58: Rivals for the Regency

Within weeks of James' death, Henry VIII had come up with the splendid notion (in his own view, at any rate) that the little Queen should be married to his son, Edward, and the kingdoms united under their children. Marie received letters from Charles Brandon, Duke of Suffolk, one of Henry's chief councillors, promoting the scheme of the marriage and saying *'I cannot therefore bot rejoyse and be moste glad to heare tell of your good towardness and conformytie in that bihaulfe'.*

Henry was also working on the lords who had been captured at Solway, and extracting oaths from them that they would support the union. Once they had done so, they were permitted to return to Scotland to add weight to the pro-English faction and were referred to by their new English masters as *'the Assured Lords'.* Arran signed the Treaties of Greenwich, which would give effect to the marriage of Mary, Queen of Scots to Prince Edward. The Treasurer of Scotland, James Kirkcaldy of Grange, ratified the Treaties on Scotland's behalf on 25th August 1543, but by this time the political landscape had changed.

Arran had a rival for the regency in the shape of Matthew Stuart (he had adopted the French spelling), Earl of Lennox. Lennox was the grandson of James III. He had spent much of his life at the French Court and as soldier in Francois I's army and believed that he, rather than Arran, was the heir and ought thus to be Regent. His claim was based on Arran's possible illegitimacy. Lennox hotfooted it to Scotland, arriving at Linlithgow in April of 1543, ostensibly to act in the French interest.

Regardless of who held the regency, Marie was determined to hold on to her daughter physically, whereas the Scots nobles wished her to be delivered up to guardians, who would rotate quarterly in pairs between the Earl Marischal, the Earl of Montrose, Lords Erskine, Ruthven, Livingston, Lindsay, Seton and Calder. In late March or early April of

1543 she received a letter from George Gordon, 4th Earl of Huntley, saying she could not go to Stirling without handing over the Queen. Rather than comply, Marie remained at Linlithgow.

As the summer of 1543 progressed, the Scottish Estates and those opposed to Arran and the pro-English policy grew stronger. Lennox was hoping to improve his cause by marrying Marie and thus securing both the Regency and the guardianship of the Queen.

Marie, whose primary concern was her daughter's safety, sought to play all of the parties off against each other. She made gracious noises to the English Ambassador, Sir Ralph Sadler, and gave him reason to believe she approved of the proposed marriage of Mary and Edward. Sadler was invited to see the baby and told by Marie that

> 'she knew not throughout the world any marriage could be found so proper, so beneficial and so honourable as this.'

She added, to muddy the waters, that Arran was probably false in his protestations of desiring the match, as, in reality, he wanted the baby queen to marry his own son.

Meanwhile, Marie was giving encouragement to Lennox, allowing him to think that matrimony was a possibility and backed by his men, managed to make the journey from the difficult-to-defend palace of Linlithgow to Stirling, the most formidable fortress in Scotland. Marie and Mary spent the next few years there. Once there, Marie arranged for the coronation of the little girl, which took place on 9th September in the Chapel Royal – a significant date in Scottish history: thirty years to the day from the battle of Flodden.

Even Arran and his supporters, including the Assured Lords, were growing restive under Henry VIII's bullying tactics, and the overwhelming feeling in Scotland was pushing for a renewal of the

French alliance. The Estates of Scotland rejected the Treaty of Greenwich on 11th December 1543.

Lennox, too, was playing a double game. François I had finally realised the threat to French interests in Scotland and sent 10,000 crowns, munitions and ships to support Carinal Beaton and Lennox as the leaders of the pro-French party. By the end of October 1543, Lennox was at Dumbarton Castle, whence the French money, together with munitions, the Legate from the Pope, and the French Ambassador had been sent. Lennox, however, refused to hand it over.

Beaton and Marie were appalled at this betrayal and asked Francois to recall Lennox as a *'troubler of the state'*. Queen Marie told the Venetian envoy that she would have preferred the gold to be at *'the bottom of the sea'* rather than that it should fall into Lennox' hands.

In a last ditch attempt to bring the two factions together, a new agreement was arranged between Arran and Lennox, under which Lennox would accept Arran as Governor, but Lennox failed to observe its terms. Arran now moved decisively towards France, and Lennox defected completely to England, marrying Henry VIII's niece, Lady Margaret Douglas, who was also half-aunt to the Queen of Scots.

Chapter 59: War of the Rough Wooing

Henry VIII was beside himself at the rejection of the Treaty of Greenwich and thus began the *'War of the Rough Wooing'*. He would spare neither money nor men to bring Scotland to heel, and sent his brother-in-law, Edward Seymour, Earl of Hertford, to

'Put all to fire and sword, burn Edinburgh town...putting man, woman and child to fire and sword, without exception where any resistance shall be made.'

Hertford did his best to follow orders and wreaked destruction in the lands around Edinburgh, although he could not capture the Castle. Despite this, the Queen of Scots remained safe from her great-uncle, with Marie at Stirling.

By June of 1544, the Scots nobles were sufficiently unimpressed by the performance of Arran for them to consider giving Marie a place in government – presumably counting on her relationship with France as a factor in her suitability. A Convention held at Stirling agreed that she would head a sixteen-man advisory council for Arran.

Beaton, however, remained as the strongest adversary to Arran, although both were now, in theory, committed to resisting England.

Beaton, although not by any means a fanatical man of religion, despite his Cardinalate, had the radical, but popular, Protestant preacher, George Wishart, burnt for heresy. This was probably the single act that would bear most fruit for the Protestant Reformers in Scotland. Wishart's supporters, together with Beaton's political enemies, assassinated Beaton on 28th May 1546 and barricaded themselves in to his castle at St Andrew's, holding Arran's son hostage to prevent reprisals.

In 1547 both Henry VIII of England and François I of France died. This did not, as might have been expected, reduce tensions, rather it increased problems for Scotland as Lord Protector Somerset (Hertford's new title) upped the pressure, and François' heir, Henri II, began to take a serious interest in Scotland.

Before Marie married James V, there had been a rumour that Henri would divorce his wife, Catherine de Medici, to marry Marie – perhaps a warm personal relationship between Henri and Marie is one of the factors in his support of her. One of Henri's first moves was to send a force to relieve Beaton's castle of St Andrew's, which was achieved in six hours by bombardment from French shipping. One of the men captured and sent to the French galleys was John Knox, who was to prove a thorn in Marie's side.

In September 1547, Somerset led a huge force into Scotland. He had received assurances from the pro-English faction, including Lennox, that there would be local support for him, but it did not materialise. Even without this, despite some initial early Scottish success, the Scots were massacred on Saturday, 10th September; thousands cut down as they fled the carnage. The Battle of Pinkie Cleugh was the last, terrible conflict between England and Scotland as independent nations.

Somerset burnt Leith, but did not follow up his victory in any meaningful military way although he occupied land and fortified castles at Roxburghe, Home, Inchcolm, Broughty, Lauder, Haddington, Inchkeith and Dunglass with a view to having a base for further incursion. Simultaneously, he continued to promote the idea of a union between the two countries, designed to appeal to the growing Protestant faction.

Nevertheless, the vast majority of Scots, perhaps encouraged by French pensions, remained resolutely opposed to union, (or as they saw it, subjection), with England. On 16th October a Convention at Edinburgh agreed to ask for French help. In January 1548, Arran and Henri II agreed a new arrangement. Queen Mary would be sent to France to marry the Dauphin, and, in the long term, Mary's children would be kings of both France and Scotland. In the meanwhile, Henri would extend French protection, in the shape of money and men, to Scotland. For this he would also receive the two castles of Dunbar and Blackness.

Arran (who had hoped to marry his own son to the Queen) was mollified by 12,000 livres, a French Duchy (Chatelherault) and promises of the daughter of the Duke of Montpensier for his son. He was to remain Regent until Mary was of age. In addition, the French were to agree that

> 'the realm, laws and liberties thereof (were to be kept) as has been in all kings' times of Scotland bypast and to marry her (Mary) upon no other person but upon the said Dauphin.'

On 16th June 1548, 6,000 French troops arrived to reinforce Scottish strength and try to wrest the fortresses Somerset had grabbed from English control. Marie, together with the Court, travelled to Haddington, where the castle, held by the English, was under siege. The Estates were called to meet in the Abbey. The Earl of Angus carried the crown, the Earl of Argyll, the sceptre and Lord Rothes the sword of Honour. On 7th July 1548, Arran and the Estates consented to the marriage of Mary to the Dauphin, with the details enshrined in the Treaty of Haddington.

Politically, Marie was delighted with the outcome. Her daughter would be Queen of France as well as of Scots, and the Guise family would be able to increase its influential position in both countries. Personally, it must have been a terrible blow to send her little girl, only five years old, to France without her.

Chapter 60: Diplomatic Visits

During the following years Marie corresponded regularly with her daughter, whilst carefully drawing towards her goal of being declared Regent. Henri II of France, who now declared that he considered '[Scotland as a] Kingdom in my protection I consider mine' consulted Marie on everything before presenting any policies to Arran, who was, in effect, rubber-stamping Henri and Marie's plans. As yet, there was no religious discrimination in the policies pursued by France, with both Catholics and Protestants receiving offices and rewards.

England continued to make war-like noises, but Somerset's hands were tied, first by the Western Rebellion of 1549 which absorbed money and men originally destined for Scotland, and then by the outbreak of hostilities with France over the town of Boulogne, captured by Henry VIII in 1546. A peace between France and England was eventually brokered in 1549, with Scotland represented by the French envoys. There was still contention over the fate of the fortresses controlled by the English, but, eventually a final treaty was agreed between Scotland and England at Norham in June 1551.

In 1550, Marie decided to pay a visit to France. Henri II made a personal request for a safe-conduct for herself and her entourage, and any French galley sent to fetch her, to land in an English port, if necessary, and be treated as a friend. An additional request for her horses to travel overland was also requested. Edward VI's council granted the safe-conducts, for Marie and her train, and up to 100 horses, and 140 men to '*convey*' the animals.

Accompanied by numerous Scottish Lords, Marie embarked at Newhaven on 7th September. The journey took some twelve days in total and was beset by storms. Arriving in Normandy on 19th September, she was reunited with her son, Francois, Duke of Longueville, who was now fourteen. Six days later, she was greeted by Henri II and the French court at Rouen. Her daughter, Mary, Queen of Scots, aged seven, had prepared a solemn speech of welcome, but Marie brushed aside ceremony and ran towards her daughter to hug and kiss her before any speeches could be delivered.

The next few months were a combination of ceremony and politicking, as well as family reunion. According to Sir John Mason,

English Ambassador at the French court, the Scots nobles spent a good deal of time arguing amongst themselves, and generally comporting themselves in such a way as to embarrass Marie. However, his reports are not necessarily entirely impartial.

Marie was reunited with her son, only to lose him. He died at Amiens in April 1551.

Giving an insight into domestic life, and demonstrating that human emotions remain much the same through the ages, there is a letter from Joan, Queen of Navarre to Marie, saying that she has heard of the alarming state of health of Marie's son, and sends to know the truth and also of Marie's health. She adds that she and her husband (Marie's cousin) will do whatever they can to help Marie. Queen Joan was one of the strongest adherents of the Huguenots in France, although they were not quite yet a faction, but family ties still mattered.

According to the aforementioned Mason, Marie outwore her welcome 'The Dowager of Scotland maketh all this court weary from the high to the low, such a beggar she is for herself. The King (Henri II) would fain be rid of her.' Mason believed the delay was caused by Marie's desire to have the arrears of the pension due to her from France under the terms of her marriage treaty paid over, whilst Henri, short of cash, was promising to send her the funds later.

There was no obvious reason for Marie to return to Scotland at all. She was not Regent, and her family were all in France. However, the Scottish Lords requested her to return to *'for the execution of justice and the ordouring of the cuntrye'*. Putting her duty to her daughter, her dynasty and her adopted country before her own pleasure, Marie agreed to return.

In October 1551, therefore, Marie embarked at Dieppe to return to Scotland. Her initial intent had been to return directly by sea, but, driven off course by storms, she took refuge at Portsmouth and sent word to

Edward VI that she would take advantage of the safe-conduct that had been renewed to travel overland. A reception was organised for her at Hampton Court. A message was dispatched to the King's sisters, the Ladies Mary and Elizabeth, as well as other members of the court to invite them to meet Marie.

Marie was treated as an honoured guest by Edward VI, and the Lord President of the Council, who, now promoted to the title of Duke of Northumberland, was the same Lord Lisle who had refrained from pressing military advantage against the Scots after the death of James V. The chief hostess was Lady Margaret Douglas, Countess of Lennox, half-sister of James V and the woman Lennox had married when disappointed of Marie herself. The Lennoxes were not in good odour at Edward's court, as they failed to embrace the Protestant revolution he was embracing but Court etiquette demanded a suitable show, and for some unknown reason, despite the invitation, the Lady Mary was not present.

Whilst Marie was in England she heard that John Knox, the follower of Wishart, had served his term in the French galleys and been freed. Scenting danger, although she cannot have imagined how great a threat he eventually was to become, she sent an urgent message to her brother, Rene, the Duke of Elbouef, to capture Knox. Elbouef failed and Knox headed for Switzerland where he became even more radical in his views after coming under the influence of John Calvin. By the end of November, Marie was back in Scotland.

On her return to Scotland, Marie appears to have acted in concert with Arran, travelling with him to administer justice throughout the realm. During 1552, Arran and Marie worked together to agree the Anglo-Scots border with the English government. In August of that year, a French adjudicator confirmed his decision, which was illustrated on a map prepared by Marie and Arran.

When Mary I acceded to the throne of England, Marie corresponded with the new Queen in regard to *'disorders'* and *'slaughters'* on the Border, committed by the English and not redressed. Mary I, whilst pointing out that the reports she had received *'declared [the situation] to be otherwise'*, but that to show her *'plain affection to amity'* she would appoint councillors to meet with Marie's own to resolve matters.

Chapter 61: Regent of Scotland

Following Mary's eleventh birthday on 8th December, 1553, Henri II declared that she was of age – probably rather before the Regent Arran was anticipating such a move. The age of majority for a monarch usually being somewhere above fourteen, although there was no fixed rule. In accordance with the Treaty of Haddington, therefore Arran was no longer to be Regent on the former basis of being Mary's heir and the *'second person in the kingdom'*.

There would, of course, need to be someone exercising authority and as Mary was now considered of age, she was free to appoint whomever she liked – or rather, whomever Henri II liked. Queen Mary's choice, unsurprisingly, was Marie of Guise. The decision was accepted with mixed feelings, although by no means general hostility. The Scots could be sure that Marie would not have any designs on the throne herself, as Arran and Lennox were suspected of harbouring, and she had proven herself a capable member of the council prior to this date. The rub, of course, was the very thing that made her Henri's nominee – her strong allegiance to France. Her continued Catholicism did not pose an immediate problem. The majority of the Lords were still Catholic, although the Protestant group was gaining momentum.

The Court processed to Edinburgh where Arran, now Duke of Chatelherault, formally gave up his powers as Regent, and Marie was installed. In a gesture of supreme tactlessness, Marie had the crown of Scotland placed on her head by the French Ambassador d'Oisel, in theory representing her daughter, Mary, Queen of Scots, but looking very much to the entire country that the Scottish crown was in the hands of the French. Had they resisted England only to fall prey to the French?

Now Queen Mary was declared to be of age, Marie was pressed by her brother Charles, Cardinal of Lorraine, to send money for her to have her own household as Queen of Scots, rather than sharing that of the French princesses. Marie, always strapped for cash, managed this by assigning the pension of 20,000 livres she received from the French king herself, and sending some 25,000 livres from her dower estates in Scotland, as well as a further contribution from her Longueville dower.

This was despite Marie's own money troubles. There are several letters to the steward of her Ross lands, the Countess of Moray, asking the Countess to '*mak gud and haiste payment*'. She was also constrained to borrow small sums, including 200 crowns from the Countess of Montrose.

The Scottish economy still largely operated in kind and there was little actual coinage, which inhibited trade. Problems were exacerbated by the circulation of debased foreign coins. Thus, although monarchs and nobles could live well off the produce of their lands, finding large amounts of cash was difficult and made cash pensions (for which the modern mind, although not the contemporary one, might read bribes) from France and England was always an important factor in allegiance.

In part to remedy the lack of money for running the Government, in 1556 Marie requested the Estates to grant a perpetual yearly tax. This would have necessitated an inventory to be taken of every man's '*estate* and substance'. However, the Lords rejected the demand, stating that they *'meant not to putt their goodes in inventory, as if they were to make their last willes and testamentes.'*

Marie's regency saw the stepping up of hostilities between France and the empire again. South of the border, Mary I, who became queen in July 1553, immediately made moves to bring England and the Empire back into alliance, through her marriage to the Emperor's son, later Philip II of Spain. This put pressure on France, Henri II believing, not without reason, that England would join in any conflict on the Imperial side. Scotland too, would be threatened by an Anglo-Imperial alliance and a strong French presence in Scotland seemed more important than ever.

Henri's fears were confirmed when England followed Spain into war with France in June 1557. To strengthen his position, the marriage between Mary, Queen of Scots and his son Francois, took place on 24th April 1558. With the agreement of the Scottish Estates, Francois was granted the *'Crown Matrimonial'*, that is, he was joint sovereign with Mary and in the event of her death would remain King. As evidence that Scotland was under the *'protection'* of France, and not in any way a vassal state, following the wedding, the two governments granted mutual citizenship to all French and Scots.

Chapter 62: Rebellion (1557 – 1560)

Despite the marriage between Mary, Queen of Scots and the Dauphin having been planned since 1548, there was a group of Scots nobles who, by the end of December 1557, no longer wanted it to take place. The Earls of Argyll, Glencairn and Morton, with other lords signed a *'Covenant'* to bring Scotland to Protestantism. They, together with Lord James Stewart (James V's illegitimate son) invited John Knox to return from Geneva, although they then seem to have thought better of it – he received a letter when he was about to embark at Normandy, withdrawing the invitation. Knox saw their *'inconstancy'* as an affront to God, and set sail anyway.

Up until this point there had been a tacit acceptance of private Protestant preaching and some services being held in Scots. However, this was not enough for the radicals.

Marie, temperamentally inclined to tolerance, strove to preserve a balance between the Reformers and the Catholics but this became harder as the battle lines between Catholics and Huguenots became increasingly demarcated in France, and a new Protestant regime was in place in England, the Catholic Mary I having been replaced by Protestant (although not Calvinist) Elizabeth. Forced to choose, Marie issued orders for the proper Catholic observance of Easter 1559 and for all Scots to return to the old faith.

John Knox's return made compromise impossible. Knox was undoubtedly a hugely talented and charismatic preacher and writer, and although his style of preaching fire and brimstone seems excessive to modern readers, he was soon winning converts both at Court and elsewhere. His brand of Biblical fundamentalism led him to believe, and preach, that for women to *'bear rule'* was an *'abomination'* and an affront to God. He shared these views in his *'First Blast of the Trumpet against the Monstruous Regiment of Women'*, published in 1558 in Geneva, which inveighed in most intemperate language against both Marie and Mary of England.

On 11th May, 1559, in direct contravention of the law, Knox preached at Perth. His sermon was so inflammatory that a member of the congregation threw a stone at a priest, and whole-scale rioting followed. Such disobedience could not be tolerated and Marie headed for Perth with troops to restore order. The Lords of the Congregation, however, supported Knox, and faced with a larger force, Marie retreated to Dunbar.

The Lords advanced on Edinburgh, arriving early in the morning of 30th June 1559. Their plan, according to Kirkcaldy of Grange, a Protestant chronicler, was to *'maintain true religion, and resist the King of France.'*

The people of Edinburgh were not notably enthusiastic at the arrival of the Lords, and in July Marie was able to drive them out and begin fortifying Leith. Of necessity, she called on French troops and their brutal behaviour alienated the Scots further.

On 21st October 1559 the Act of Suspension passed by the Lords of the Congregation to remove Marie from the Regency because, according to Knox, of her

> *'Interprysed destruction of thair said commounweall and overthrow of the libertie of thair native countrie.'*

Marie maintained that the rebellion was against lawful authority and was not religiously motivated. The Protestants, however, did not necessarily see it the same way and they requested help from Protestant England, against Catholic domination in the same way that, nearly twenty years earlier they had requested French help against English domination.

In November 1559, the Lords of the Congregation wrote instructions to William Maitland of Lethington to carry messages to Elizabeth. He was to inform her of the *'cruelty and tyranny of the French captains and soldiers'* and the indifference of Marie to their *'frequent complaints'* and her obvious desire to conquer Scotland for France.

He was also to draw attention to the risk to Elizabeth herself of the marriage between Mary and Francois and their provocation of the English monarch by promoting Queen Mary's claim to the English throne. In support of the claim they had had a seal made quartering their arms with those of England and had sent Marie a *'staffe for hir to rest upon, having graven in the toppe the said usurped armes'*.

Lethington was then to *'beseech'* Elizabeth to *'afford them her gracious protection against the French intended conquest'*. Such a step, they continued, would allow Elizabeth to please the Almighty and procure *'perpetual love'* between England and Scotland, which love was, apparently, a thing *'much desired of all Christians, saving the French only'*.

Elizabeth hesitated. She was extremely reluctant to get involved. Although events did not always allow her free reign in her decisions, her preference was nearly always to put solidarity amongst monarchs and obedience to lawful authority above religious differences. Eventually, she was persuaded – her chief minister, William Cecil, was a determined Protestant and urged the importance of defending the Lords strongly. On 26th January, 1560, English ships arrived at Leith, and, following the February Treaty of Berwick with England, English troops arrived and by March were besieging Edinburgh Castle, with Marie in inside.

In the midst of this turmoil, Marie's health broke down completely. She referred to her ailment as *'dropsy'*, and it was probably some sort of congestive heart failure that caused her to retain water. By 1st June 1560 she could neither eat nor lie down, and knowing the end was near, she sent for Moray and Arran. After begging their forgiveness for any wrong she might have done them, she died on 11th June 1560 at Edinburgh Castle with them at her side.

Her remains were embalmed and left in the Chapel of St Margaret within the Castle precincts. The Protestant Lords refused to allow a burial in Holyrood Abbey by the Catholic rites. Eventually, in March 1561, her body was taken at night and embarked at Leith for France. She was buried at the Convent of St Pierre Les Dames, where her sister, Renee, was abbess. Her monument was destroyed during the French Revolution.

*

Marie was in many ways a successful Regent. She was clever, diplomatic and shrewd, and she achieved her immediate aims of preserving her daughter's person and crown. She was described as '*a woman with a man's courage.*' Nevertheless, Marie did no, see, or, if she saw, did not accept, that times were changing. Her ambitions, as a member of a family that strove to dominate Europe, were essentially dynastic, built on the mediaeval concept of a country as the personal fiefdom of its rulers. A move towards a more nationalist concept was growing, reinforced by the increasing rhetoric of religion as a defining characteristic of a country. The perception of Marie as the tool of a foreign state whose religion had been rejected by a large proportion of the ruling class condemned her to ultimate failure.

Aspects of Marie of Guise's Life

Chapter 63: Life of a Queen Consort

Marie was married to James V of Scotland, by proxy, at her home of Chateaudun on 29th May 1538. Her *'spousing ring'* consisted of a single diamond of the value of 300 crowns. Hopefully, no-one told her that James' first wife had had a ring to the value of 1,100 crowns! The tip paid to the notary who drew up her marriage contract was also less than he had received for the king's first marriage. Whether the difference in these sums is owing to the fact that James' first wife was a king's daughter, whilst Marie was only the daughter of a duke, or whether they reflect the lower level of enthusiasm James felt for his second marriage, is unknown.

The other important pre-nuptial expense was the collection of the Papal dispensation required because James and Marie were third cousins - both being descended from Arnold, Duke of Guelders (1410 – 1473). The expense of fetching the necessary document from Rome was 200 crowns.

Once married, Marie set out almost immediately for the coast, probably embarking from Rouen, in Normandy. Her dowry had been provided jointly by the King of France, and her father, Claud, Duke of Guise, but she does not seem to have been given any cash in hand, as, whilst at Rouen, she was obliged to borrow 450 francs against her expected income as Queen of Scots.

The new Queen's trip to Scotland was an opportunity for James to have wine shipped from France, and, together with her baggage, the flotilla, consisting of three galleys, carried 18 tuns of white wine and claret. Marie's ship was named the '*Riall*' and had a specially fitted glass window for her cabin.

Used to the splendour of the court of France, Scotland probably seemed somewhat less luxurious to Marie. However, James, with the dowries he had received both for Marie and her predecessor was, for the only time in his life, flush with money. He was a generous, not to say extravagant man, and spent lavishly on jewellery, plate and cloth.

Marie was crowned as Queen of Scots on 22nd February, 1540. The peeresses were summoned to attend her, and a completely new crown and sceptre were made for her. Fashioned of thirty-five ounces of gold, the crown was set with stones. Her sceptre was made of 31 ounces of silver-gilt. The work, carried out by the King's goldsmith, John Mosman, cost £45 Scots. The crown was further aggrandised in 1541 with the addition of another 35 ounces of gold.

Some of the gold used for the royal ornaments (including a basin of an astonishing 10lb weight) was obtained from the King's own gold-mines. Expert miners had been sent by Marie's father, Claud, Duke of Guise, in the summer of 1539 to give advice on operation of the mine. They had been given an interpreter

'*ane Scottis boy that spekis Frenche to serve them quhill thai gett the langage.*'

He received fifty shillings (£2 2s) for his service of a couple of months.

Marie benefited from the gold-mine, not just for her crown, but also in receiving a gold belt of 19 ounce weight, set with a sapphire, which cost the King £20 for making.

The King and Queen had court musicians, who received liveries twice a year. There were five Italian minstrels and four players of the viols, three of them dressed in parti-coloured red and gold, and one in head-to-foot red, with a red bonnet. They were paid the princely sum of £40 Scots. The trumpeters received about half as much. The *'tabourer'* (a tabor is a type of drum), an older man called Anthony, objected to wearing livery, and received cash to buy his own outfit instead.

As well as the household officers, Marie had her own attendants, including her French pantryman (the officer in charge of bread), M. Beglatt. She also had a French Master of Horse – an important role as he would have attended the Queen whenever she rode, and helped her mount. The Queen's geldings were looked after by an army of stable-hands, led by one William Gib.

Marie herself was attended by at least seven ladies, a mixture of French and Scots women. On the marriage of any of her attendants, it was customary to give clothes and money. Joanna Gresoner (or Gresmoir), who married Robert Beaton of Creich, received a red velvet gown to the value of £108 Scots to mark her marriage. This lady's daughter, Mary, was later one of the Four Marys who were the attendants of Marie's own daughter.

To entertain the ladies there was a female fool, called Serat, who was dressed in the usual livery colours of red and yellow, with a green kirtle. There was also a jester and a Frenchwoman, Jeanne, who was a dwarf. She was dressed in a gown of light blue velvet, with a green kirtle. Rather disturbingly to modern sensibilities, sixteenth century ladies often had dwarfs in their entourages and would send them to each other as presents.

Marie herself was sumptuously dressed. On one occasion £67 10s was spent on Venetian crimson damask for fifteen ells (about 18 yards or metres) for a gown.

During the three and a half years of her married life, Marie was pregnant three times, and she had nurses, rockers and other attendants, not only for her own children, but also for her husband's illegitimate offspring, who were brought up in the royal nurseries.

Marie's life as Queen Consort came to an abrupt end when her thirty-year old husband died, probably of dysentery, following a disastrous campaign against the English. For mourning wear, the Queen and her attendants received 246 ells (nearly 310 yards or metres) of *'Paris'* black cloth at 70s the ell, as well as Holland cloth (a type of fine linen), black velvet and white satin. She also had long black cloth saddle cloths for her horses, and the chair of her *'chariot'* was lined with black.

Chapter 64: A Family Visit

In 1548, Marie waved goodbye to her five-year-old daughter, Mary, Queen of Scots, when the little girl sailed from Dumbarton for France. She was now without any family in Scotland. It is apparent from Marie's extensive correspondence with her mother and her siblings that she was very close to her family, and missed them, as well as her son by her first marriage, François, Duke of Longueville.

In the Spring of 1550, Marie's father, Claud of Lorraine, Duke of Guise died. She wrote to her brother, now Duke of Guise, that she had lost the best father that any child had ever lost and this bereavement may have contributed to her desire to see the land of her birth and her family again.

On 23rd July 1550, Henri II of France wrote to Edward VI of England, requesting a safe-conduct for Marie to travel through King Edward's dominions, if necessary. It was unlikely that Marie planned to travel overland, but a safe-conduct was necessary in case she should be blown off-course and land at an English port, as indeed occurred on her return trip. Whether the English King and Council would have been quite so accommodating had they known that Henri was planning a grand fete to celebrate the *'liberation'* of Scotland from English forces is questionable!

On receipt of the safe-conduct, Henri sent six galleys under the command of Pietro Strozzi, Prior of Capua, to fetch Marie. When she heard the *'joyueuse nouvelles'* of her impending visit, Marie's daughter, Mary Queen of Scots was overjoyed, writing to her grand-mother, Antoinette de Bourbon, that to see her mother would be *'the greatest happiness that [she] could desire in the world'.'*

Marie embarked on the 6th or 7th September, at Newhaven, together with a large proportion of the Scottish court, no doubt to keep as many of them close to her as possible, and also as an opportunity for Henri II to meet them and *'reward'* the supporters of the Franco-Scots alliance personally. They landed in Normandy some twelve days later, either at Dieppe or at Havre-de-Grace – the sources conflict. It is likely that Marie spent the first few days at her son's home in Normandy before travelling on to Rouen by 25th September.

The entire French Court was assembled to meet the Scottish entourage – Henri II, his wife, Catherine di Medici and their children, his influential mistress, Diane de Poitiers, and, of course, the seven year old Mary, Queen of Scots. The little Queen of Scots had been taught a formal speech to deliver to her mother, but, unusually, Marie abandoned all protocol and ran towards her little girl, scooping her up in her arms.

The court remained at Rouen for some days. A procession had been arranged, reminiscent of the triumphs of Roman generals, with the court watching from pavilions erected by the bridge over the Seine. An endless stream of officials, courtiers and actors dressed in green, blue, and white velvet and satin passed by, enacting tableaux of ancient heroes. Even a mock sea-battle was staged, although it ended badly, with some of the actors being killed when the cannon went off. According to the English envoy, Sir John Mason, there was a good deal of squabbling amongst the Scots nobles in regard to lodgings.

Marie stayed in France for over a year – travelling to her childhood home at Joinville and around the north of France. According to the English envoy, she was treated *'like a goddess'*. Henri II also feted and lavishly rewarded her Scottish nobles – tying them to the Franco-Scottish alliance with chains of gold.

Whilst Marie was in France she was deeply distressed by the discovery of an assassination plot against Mary, Queen of Scots. Following the murder of Cardinal Beaton in 1548, the holders of the fortress of St Andrew's, referred to as the *'castilians'* remained under siege for months before the castle was captured and the castilians sent to the galleys. One of these castilians, after being released, changed his name and talked his way into the Scottish Guard at the court of France. From this position, he plotted the assassination of Queen Mary in April of 1551. The plan was to poison her favourite pudding of pears. Fortunately, the plot was discovered, but Marie was so distraught she became ill.

She was sufficiently recovered by June to attend the ceremony surrounding the investiture of Henri II with the Order of the Garter. The Marquess of Northampton (William Parr, brother of Queen Katherine Parr) led the embassy at the event which took place at Chateaubriand on 20th June 1551. The English embassy made a final request for the hand of the Queen of Scots for King Edward VI, but it was refused, as she was contracted to marry the Dauphin. In recompense, a marriage was agreed between King Edward and the Princess Elisabeth, Henri II's daughter.

Henri then took Northampton and the other English envoys to the chamber of Queen Catherine, where Marie and the Queen of Scots were also present. The whole company passed the evening in dancing. The following day, the King played tennis and then the court, including Marie, watched wrestling matches between English and Breton wrestlers. Once the treaty relating to the marriage of Edward VI and the Princess

Elisabeth was agreed, Henri entertained the court with a midnight picnic and deer hunt by torch-light.

Soon after, preparations began for Marie's departure, although, in the event, she remained another two months. According to the English envoy, this was because she and Henri II were wrangling about money matters. In the last month of her stay, she lost her son, the 15 year old Duke of Longueville, who died at Amiens, with Marie at his bedside. Grief-stricken, she contemplated remaining in France, but duty called her back to Scotland. She still was not named as Regent, but was requested to return to assist with the '*execution of justice*'.

Delayed by the loss of her son, Marie did not embark for Scotland until October, although she had received a second safe-conduct from England in September. Marie set out in a flotilla of ten ships, under the leadership of Baron de la Garde. Her plan was to travel directly home but the ships were blown by storms onto the English coast, and Marie took refuge in Portsmouth. The Captain of Portsmouth, Sir Richard Wingfield, immediately went to meet her to ask whether she wished to re-embark for Scotland, or travel through England. No doubt having had enough of an autumn sea-journey, Marie elected to travel overland. The local nobles went to pay their respects, and orders were received from the King's Council to the grandees of the counties between Portsmouth and London to give her appropriate hospitality.

It took Marie several days to reach London, staying at Sir Richard Wingfield's house at Southwick for two days, then at Warblington (the castle confiscated from Margaret Plantagenet, Countess of Salisbury following the Exeter Conspiracy) with dinner at the house of the Earl of Arundel, followed by a stop at Cowdray Castle in Sussex, and then Guilford where she was met by Lord William Howard, who accompanied her to Hampton Court.

A mile or so from the Palace, the Marquess of Northampton and his wife met her. She stayed at Hampton Court until the 2nd November, and spent the evening *'in dancing and pastime'* then travelled into London by barge to stay at the Bishop of London's Palace, Baynard's Castle. The Lord Mayor sent presents of veal, mutton, swine, beer, wine coals, and even a sturgeon to make her stay more pleasant.

On the 5th November, the Duke of Suffolk (Henry Grey) and the Earl of Huntingdon (Francis Hastings, the great-great-nephew of Edward IV) waited upon her. On 6th November, the ladies of the Court, led by Marie's half-sister-in-law, Lady Margaret Douglas, Countess of Lennox, and the Duchesses of Northumberland and Suffolk and the Countess of Pembroke (Anne Parr), together with some hundred noble and gentlewomen, accompanied her to court.

The sight of Lady Margaret might have been somewhat embarrassing as Lady Margaret's husband, Matthew Stuart, Earl of Lennox, had hoped to be named Regent of Scotland in place of Arran and had been a suitor to Marie when she was first widowed. Disappointed, he had changed allegiance to support the English faction against Marie's preferred French alliance.

Despite having received invitations, the King's sisters, the Ladies Mary and Elizabeth did not attend, although their reasons for absence are not recorded. The King met Marie in the entrance at Whitehall, and she was conducted to the Queen's Side of the Palace where she dined in state on the left of the King, under the Cloth of State. The room was decorated with the King's best plate – a sideboard with four shelves of gold utensils and one of six shelves of *'massy silver'*. Having recently met the young man her daughter was contracted to marry, the Dauphin François, Marie now had the opportunity to compare him with the alternative suitor – a boy of similar age.

According to the Protestant John Knox, who was one of Edward VI's chaplains and treated him as a Protestant hero, Marie said that *'she found more wisdom and solid judgement in the young King of England than she should have looked for in any three princes of full age then in Europe.'* After dinner, which finished at around 4pm, Marie returned to the Bishop's Palace, where she rested for another day, before departing for the North. Before she left, Northumberland, Winchester and other lords paid her a final visit to present her with two horses (or nags, as they were referred to) and a ring with a diamond, presents from the King.

Messages were sent to all of the Sheriffs in the counties she would pass through to meet her and pay her the appropriate honours. She was accompanied on her journey by Edward Dudley, son of the Duke of Northumberland, and a Mr Shelley, to make sure she was *'conveniently and honourably served'*. Marie was back in Scotland before the end of November. She would not leave the country again.

Chapter 65: Following the Footsteps of Marie of Guise

The numbers against the places correspond to those on the map at the end of this article.

Marie spent her youth in France, before arriving in Scotland aged about twenty-three. During her time as Queen Consort and later Queen Dowager and Regent of Scotland, she spent the majority of her time in the central belt of Scotland, in the castles and palaces within a few days' ride of Edinburgh.

*

Marie was born in Bar (now Bar-le-Duc) a town now in the north-east of France, in the department of Meuse, but at the time of Marie's birth in

1515 in the Imperial Duchy of Lorraine. Her early childhood was spent in the Guise chateau at Joinville, which her father extended after Marie's first marriage, with the construction of the recently restored Chateau du Grand Jardin.

Marie then spent some years at the convent of the Poor Clares in Pont-a-Mousson, before returning to Bar to the household of her uncle, Antoine, Duke of Lorraine, and his wife, Renee of Bourbon-Montpensier, in about 1529.

In 1534, she joined the French Court and would have spent time at the Louvre, and in Francois I's superb chateaux, including Fontainebleu, Amboise and Chambord.

After her first marriage, which took place at the Louvre, Marie moved to her husband's lands which were centred on Amiens, where her first son was born. Her favourite home seems to have been the Chateau of Chateaudun, at the northern end of the Loire, which had been largely rebuilt by her husband's father. Marie was again in Paris, at Notre-Dame on 1st January 1537, for the marriage of the Princess Madeleine to James V of Scotland, but returned to Chateaudun to await the birth of her second child.

Marie was at Chateaudun when she heard of the death of her husband, Louis, Duke of Longueville, at Rouen and it was there that she married James V of Scotland by proxy on 29th May 1538.

Marie was more fortunate than many royal brides in that she had at least met her husband previously, and also that he was only three years older than herself, and considered to be good looking. Nevertheless, it must have been with some trepidation that she embarked from Normandy to take the rough passage through the Channel and the North Sea to Scotland. Her passage was quick and she sailed into the Firth of Forth, arriving on 10th June 1538 at Balcomie Castle, property of the

Learmonth family. (1) The current building is a later replacement, dating from the second half of the sixteenth century.

On the 20th of the month, Marie and James were married at the cathedral of St Andrew's (2), the seat of the Archbishop of St Andrew's, primate of Scotland. Ancient St Andrew's, too, is gone, with only the ruins of the once vast cathedral visible.

After some months, Marie and James arrived in Edinburgh. When in the capital they divided their time between the ancient fortress of Edinburgh Castle (3) which still towers over the city from the rocky eminence of The Mound, and the new palace at Holyrood (4). Holyrood was largely created by James V and his predecessor, James IV. It was in the renaissance style, heavily influenced by French chateaux and likely to have been far more comfortable for the new Queen than the mediaeval castle. Holyrood Palace is still the official residence of HM The Queen when she is in Scotland, and is well worth a visit. The Castle is also open to tourists and displays the Honours of Scotland, as the Crown Jewels of the country are called. The crown on display is the one remodelled for James V that he wore for the coronation of Marie on 22nd February 1539.

Marie's dower included several palaces and castles. One of her personal favourites was Falkland Palace (5). Originally a hunting box, Falkland was turned into a renaissance palace by James IV and James V, with all of the most modern improvements seen in France, including a court for real tennis. During her married life, significant building works were undertaken in which Marie took a keen interest, apparently climbing a ladder to inspect works personally before authorising payment.

Another of Marie's dower castles was Linlithgow (6) and it was here that she gave birth to her third child, the only one to survive. Apparently, when asked what she thought about Linlithgow, she said she *'had never seen a more princely palace.'*

Stirling Castle (7), situated in the heart of Lowland Scotland, was probably the place where Marie spent most time. She retreated there with her daughter, the young Mary, Queen of Scots, after the death of James V, when it was feared that the little Queen would be kidnapped by the English who wanted to arrange a marriage between her and Edward, son of Henry VIII. James V had begun a new palace block within the castle walls, in the renaissance style. This has now been restored to look as it did during Marie's regency. The colours are surprisingly bright!

The Scottish Estates, having declined the offer of a match with Prince Edward of England, agreed the Treaty of Haddington. This was signed in Haddington Priory (8) on 7th July 1548, with Marie in attendance.

There were still fears for the young Queen, so Marie took her further inland from Stirling, to Inchmahome Priory (9) and then to Dumbarton Castle (10), the oldest and probably the most impregnable fortress in the whole of Scotland. There is little left of the sixteenth century structure, most of the extant building dating from some 200 years later.

As part of the Treaty of Haddington, Dunbar Castle (11) was handed over to the French. Marie was later forced to retreat there when the Lords of the Congregation rose against her in the summer of 1559.

During the War of the Rough Wooing (1543 – 1551) the English built or fortified a number of strongholds, including Broughty Castle (12). Marie and the Scottish nobles held a conference at Stirling at which they agreed that French troops would be requested to recapture Broughty. Marie watched the successful attack from the opposite bank of the River Tay, following which the English garrison surrendered the castle on 12th February 1550.

One of the duties of a Scottish monarch that Marie fulfilled as Regent for her daughter was the personal dispensing of justice. She and her court would travel to towns outside the capital where '*justices ayre*' were held. Jedburgh (13), a border town which had suffered badly during the Wars of the Rough Wooing, was one of the places where Marie carried out this function.

In 1559, Marie came into conflict with the increasingly Protestant nobility. Religious tensions in Perth (15) spilled over into violence, and Marie did not have sufficient troops to impose order. Her opponents, the Lords of the Congregation, were increasingly disaffected by the French domination of Marie's government. The rebels took control of Edinburgh, but Marie had enough support for them to have to withdraw. A truce was agreed in the Articles of Leith (14), signed on 25th August 1559, which granted freedom to worship in private, according to conscience.

Marie's health was deteriorating. She took to her bed in Edinburgh Castle in early June, and died there on 11th June. Her body lay in St Margaret's Chapel, within the Castle precincts before being shipped back to France in 1561, to be buried in the Convent of St Pierre-les-Dames, in Rheims, where her sister, Renee, was abbess.

Key to Map

1. Balcomie Castle, Fife
2. St Andrew's Cathedral
3. Edinburgh Castle
4. Holyrood Palace, Edinburgh
5. Falkland Palace, Fife
6. Linlithgow Palace, West Lothian
7. Stirling Castle
8. Haddington Priory

9. Inchmahome Priory
10. Dumbarton Castle
11. Dunbar Castle
12. Broughty Castle
13. Jedburgh Abbey
14. Leith, Edinburgh
15. Perth

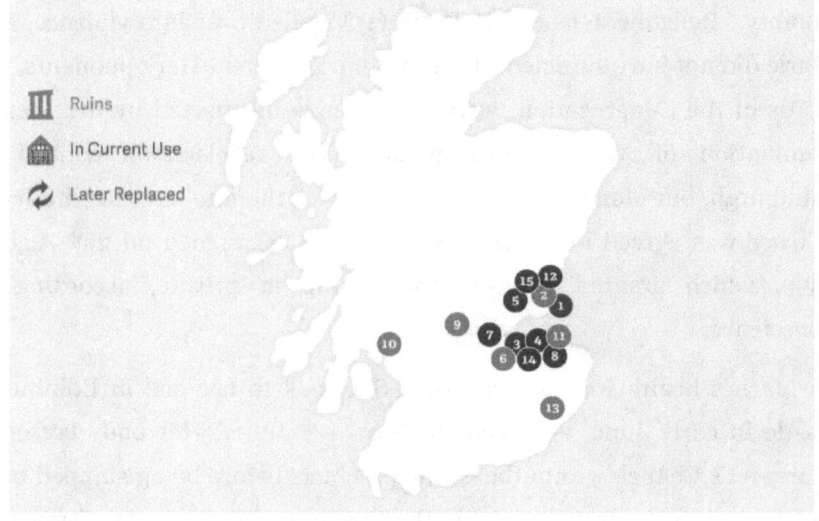

Chapter 66: Two Book Reviews

The best known biographies of Marie of Guise are by Rosalind Miles and Pamela Ritchie. Unfortunately, neither of these is easy to come by, so our reviews are of books relating to her daughter Mary Queen of Scots' life and reign, in which Marie played an important part as Regent.

My Heart is My Own

Author: John Guy

Publisher: Harper Perennial UK

In a nutshell A compelling interpretation of Mary, Queen of Scots' character and motivations. Guy has put the central drama of Mary's life – the murder of Darnley – into its political context and gives a very credible theory as to the truth of events.

John Guy is an experienced and well-respected historian who has written on topics as diverse as Thomas Becket and Henry VIII's children. His academic credentials, however, have not damaged his ability to write a clear narrative of events – something that is very necessary in the extremely complex political world that surrounded Mary, Queen of Scots.

Mary has been a controversial figure from the time of her second marriage, and given her obvious intelligence and charisma, it has always been hard to understand how she could have acted in ways that, in retrospect, appear to be completely lacking in the most basic common sense, let alone political skill. By using, wherever possible, the contemporary letters and papers Guy demonstrates that most (if not all) of Mary's actions were logical and understandable within the context of the information she had available. For what comes across very clearly, is that Mary did not always have the facts in her possession that would have enabled her to make different choices.

In so far as history books have villains, then William Cecil, Secretary of State to Queen Elizabeth I of England, is, in this book, a villain of the deepest hue. In Guy's interpretation, his constant interference in Scottish politics and his unshakeable enmity towards the Catholic Queen whom he saw as a threat to a Protestant succession in England destabilised an already unstable Scottish court. Guy is also very scathing of the part that Queen Mary's Guise relatives played. Her devotion to them, and her trust in their advice are shown to be misplaced – they cared far more for their own aggrandisement in France than for their niece in faraway Scotland, although they never hesitated to use her for their own ends.

Guy is clearly sympathetic to Mary, but he cannot avoid the judgement that she threw her crown away when she became entangled with Bothwell. His interpretation is that, although her abduction was forced, she was not raped, and that she married Bothwell willingly. This is a different interpretation from that of Porter, in '*Crown of Thistles*' (see page 384) and a comparison of both books is valuable.

Guy's review of the investigation into the murder of Darnley, and the Casket Letters is extremely detailed and gives a very welcome analysis of the actual evidence against the Queen – he also shows how and why it may have been fabricated.

Similarly, he gives a coherent and structured narrative of the various political imperatives that Mary was subjected to once she was imprisoned in England, and how, eventually, Mary had no choice but to support plots against Elizabeth, if she were to have any hope of regaining her freedom.

All in all, this is an excellent retelling of a well-known, but complex, story that has invited blind partisanship from many authors. Guy is clearly a supporter of Mary, and inevitably gives a positive interpretation of events where motivations are in question, but where Mary's actions were obviously wrong or foolish, he does not hesitate to say so.

Part 6: Thomas Cromwell: Henry VIII's Chief Minister

Introduction

Thomas Cromwell, son of a Putney blacksmith, rose to be the most powerful man in England after the King. A soldier, merchant, lawyer, politician and reformer, Cromwell cut a swathe through tradition to begin the transformation of England from a mediaeval country within Catholic Christendom, to a Protestant Nation State. His exceptional administrative ability made him indispensable to Henry VIII, and his political acumen helped him out-manoeuvre his many rivals. Like others before and after him, he eventually fell from power through entanglement with Henry's matrimonial problems.

In his youth, Cromwell travelled widely in Europe. After joining Wolsey's household, he spent much of his time in and around the south-east of England, attending to Wolsey's property matters. As Minister to Henry, he seldom went far from the King's side.

Cromwell has been a controversial figure for 500 years: ruthless schemer; visionary statesman; committed Protestant; destroyer of Queens and royal blood; saint and sinner. He was all of these and more; generous and supportive to friends, he made an implacable enemy.

Part 6 contains Thomas Cromwell's Life Story and additional articles about him, looking at different aspects of his life.

THOMAS CROMWELL

Family Tree

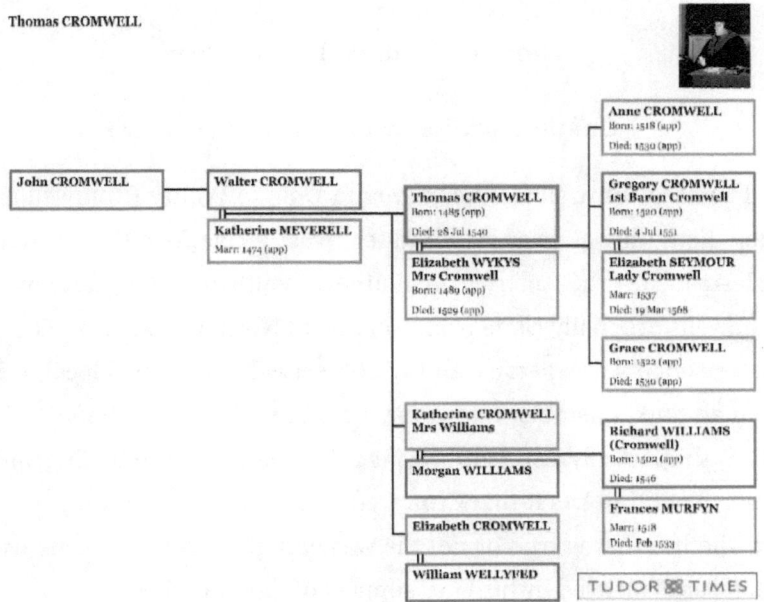

Thomas Cromwell's Life Story

Chapter 67: Early Life (c. 1485 – 1512)

Thomas Cromwell was born around 1485 to Walter Cromwell and his wife, Katherine Meverell. Walter was a blacksmith, brewer and tradesman in the district of Putney, south London, although the Cromwells originally came from Norwell in Nottinghamshire. The family was reasonably prosperous, and Walter served in the usual local offices of juryman and constable. However, he often fell foul of the law himself, and was repeatedly fined for breaking the assize of ale, brawling and even fraud. Tradition has it that Cromwell and his father were on poor terms, but whether that is true or not, he was certainly on good terms with his sisters, as evidenced by his later support of their families.

The level of education Cromwell received formally is unknown – given his class and background it is likely he would have been sent to school to read, write and pick up some Latin, as well, of course, as being taught the practice of his religion. At some time, perhaps around the turn of the century, he left England for Europe. The Imperial Ambassador, Chapuys, claimed this was following a brief spell of imprisonment, and Cromwell himself told Archbishop Cranmer that he had been a *'ruffyan...in his younger days'*. Other sources say it was owing to falling out with his father. Maybe both, or neither, are true.

Over the following years Cromwell became, first, a mercenary in the French army, involved in the terrible defeat the French suffered at Garigliano in December 1503, and second, the servant of an Italian merchant. A near-contemporary account says that the merchant found Cromwell begging in the street, and, recognising an Englishman far from home, took pity on him and helped him. The merchant in question was Frescobaldo Frescobaldi, head of the eponymous Florentine banking house. The Frescobaldis had been bankers to English and other European kings since the twelfth century, and had an office and wide network in London. Cromwell's master, in fact, spent most of his time in London, although Cromwell entered his service in Florence. Whilst in the service of the banker, Cromwell not only picked up his phenomenal business acumen, but also developed tastes and interests that influenced him for the rest of his life. Exposed to the art and literature of Renaissance Italy, and particularly of Michelangelo, who traded works for wine with Frescobaldi, he acquired an interest in the new artistic styles in painting and production of high-quality, beautiful items. He continued to be a lover of Italian culture for the rest of his life. The same chronicler (Bardello) who told the story of his meeting with Frescobaldi describes Cromwell as

'quick-witted and prompt of resolution, knowing excellent well to accommodate himself to the wishes of others, and could...dissemble his purpose better than any man in the world.'

Nothing in his later life gives the lie to this description!

Cromwell is next heard of working with a cloth-merchant in Antwerp, perhaps in connection with Frescobaldi's business, or perhaps for the chance to learn about a trade that was extremely important to England and thus might give opportunities for the future. Once he had learnt enough, he began to trade on his own account.

Chapter 68: Developing a Career (1512 – 1522)

On his return to England, probably around the end of 1512, Cromwell began to practise law, his speciality being conveyancing. Again, where, or even if, he received formal training is unknown. However, he still maintained his connection with the cloth trade, making several trips to Antwerp and the other Burgundian cities. He also travelled to Rome in 1514, staying in the English hostel and appearing before the Papal Court on 29th May, giving evidence in a dispute between two English clergy. It has been speculated that Cromwell was undertaking this in the course of employment by Cardinal Bainbridge, Archbishop of York, but he is not formally recorded as in the Archbishop's household.

Not long after settling back in England, Cromwell married Elizabeth Wykys, a widow with a comfortable inheritance, and connections to the court, her father having been a Gentleman Usher to Henry VII. Whilst marriage for love alone was completely foreign to the sixteenth century mind, it was expected that married couples should love and care for each other. As she was widowed, Elizabeth Wykys might have been guided in the choice of a second husband by her father, but would have had a high degree of freedom in selection. Cromwell, too, was a free agent. We can therefore infer that they were happy to marry. The Cromwells had a son, and two, or possibly three, daughters. All of the daughters died young, but the son, Gregory, survived, and had an interesting career of his own.

In the 1500s and 1510s a strong wave of *'anticlericalism'* was spreading through London – a feeling of antagonism towards some of the more corrupt and questionable practices of the priests and other officials of the Catholic Church. It was not, initially, a question of disputes around doctrine, more of the way in which the clergy conducted themselves. This resentment was particularly prevalent amongst the mercantile and trading classes – the butchers, brewers, blacksmiths and tailors, amongst whom Cromwell had spent his youth, and with which he had ties, and the more prosperous cloth-merchants, importers and exporters who were his clients. It seems likely, from his later actions, that Cromwell, too, subscribed to the view that corruption and venality were widespread. Nevertheless, his private religious views, whatever they might have been at this stage, did not prevent him from taking a commission in 1517 from the Guild of the Church of Our Lady in St Botolph, Boston (now known as the Boston Stump).

Cromwell obviously had an aptitude for languages. Following his years in Europe, he spoke French and Italian fluently as well as Spanish (although how he picked that up is a mystery) and some German. Presumably he also had Flemish in his repertoire. His Latin and Greek, too, were commendable – Greek being a very rare accomplishment, and usually confined to academic circles. This fluency in other languages may have been a factor in obtaining commissions outside England.

The Guild sent Cromwell to Rome as a support and guide for their representative, Geoffrey Chambers, on a mission to the Pope. The mission was successful and the story of how Cromwell achieved his aims gives an insight into his methods that illustrates his way of working throughout his life. He spent some time discovering the Pope, Leo X's, tastes and interests. Accordingly, whilst most petitioners had to wait months to be heard, Cromwell arranged to waylay the Pope early one morning, with a trio of singers and a plate of marmalade and other delicacies prepared in the English fashion. The pope whose '*holy tooth greatly delighted in new-fangled strange delicacies and dainty dishes*' munched through the sweets, and granted the Guild's petition to renew the Indulgences that brought in income to maintain their church. Cromwell had learnt a valuable lesson – finding the right route to pleasing the powerful gets results.

It is not clear how Cromwell came to the notice of Cardinal Wolsey, perhaps through work done for Cardinal Bainbridge, Wolsey's predecessor as Archbishop of York, or it may have been from legal business he was involved in, although there is no firm, dateable evidence showing when Cromwell began practising law. His biographers differ widely in dating the beginning of the connection, from as early as 1516, by Elton, to as late as 1524 which Everett demonstrates is the earliest provable date. Looking at all the different arguments, a date of around 1519 would seem not unlikely. Working for Wolsey, did not, however, preclude him from other employment, and he is referred to in 1522 as a servant of Thomas Grey, Marquess of Dorset, a former pupil of Wolsey's and later, as Dorset's attorney.

Chapter 69: Councillor to My Lord Legate (1523 – 1530)

In 1523 Cromwell was returned as a Member of Parliament, probably owing to Wolsey's influence. Although the constituency for which he sat is not recorded, it is thought to be Bath. This was Cromwell's first appearance on the public stage, and the draft of the speech he prepared makes interesting reading, although we cannot know whether it was actually delivered. The purpose of the Parliament was to raise a subsidy for yet another French campaign and Cromwell's speech argues vigorously against it, citing the difficulties of war in a foreign land; the cost; the danger of a king with no son, and only an eight-year-old daughter as heir, adventuring himself in warfare; and most of all, the pointlessness of the exercise. He refers to Henry VIII's previous conquests as having '*cost His Highness more than twenty such ungracious dogholes could be worth to him*'

Everett argues that Cromwell preparing a speech so antithetical to government policy demonstrates that he could not have been working for Wolsey. The counter-argument is that, as Wolsey was himself against further hostilities with France, he used Cromwell to point out the shortcomings of the policy.

Cromwell's later achievements relied heavily on Parliamentary process, however he was aware of its flaws, writing in amused tones to a friend that:

'we communed of war, peace, strife, contentation, debate, murmur, grudge, riches, poverty, perjury, truth, falsehood, justice, equity, deceit, oppression, magnanimity, activity, force, attemperance, treason, murder, felony, conciliation and also how a commonwealth might be edified. However, in conclusion we have done as our predecessors have been wont to do, that is to say, as well as we might and left where we began.'

In 1524, Cromwell was sufficiently respected in the legal profession to be nominated as a member of Gray's Inn, one of the Inns of Court, despite his lack of formal training. No doubt his position as *'Councillor to my Lord Legate* (Wolsey)' helped his acceptance into a profession as conservative then as it is now.

By 1525, Wolsey was relying on Cromwell to a considerable extent. Not the least of his responsibilities was the suppression of some thirty monasteries (with Papal consent), the incomes of which were to found Wolsey's colleges at Ipswich and Oxford.

In undertaking his master's orders, Cromwell made himself hugely unpopular. He approached the task with a zeal for destruction of shrines that foreshadowed the events of the 1530s. The actual scope of his task was to survey the property, value it, prepare detailed inventories of the moveable goods and arrange for them to be taken away and sold. The inmates had to be either given pensions, or have arrangements made for them to be transferred to other religious houses. Cromwell, together with his two assistants, Sir William Gascoigne and Dr Allen, carried out the work efficiently and with dispatch – indeed a sense of urgency and decisiveness characterises all his activity.

The thirty foundations dissolved, it was time to move on to the construction of the two colleges, and Cromwell was again in charge. By April 1528, he could write to Wolsey that

'the buildings of your noble college most prosperously doth arise...the like thereof was never seen nor imagined, having consideration to the largeness, beauty, sumptuous, curious and most substantial building of the same.'

It was customary in the Tudor age for people to conduct business in a way we could consider corrupt. Gifts and sweeteners that we might call bribes, were commonplace. Thus, it was expected that Cromwell would line his own pocket whilst working for Wolsey, through such matters as granting a tenancy to the bidder who gave him the highest fee, or not accounting for all of the sales. Nevertheless the scale of embezzlement seems to have provoked an outcry and *'incredible things'* were reported to the King.

Despite the amount of work Cromwell was doing for Wolsey, he continued to practise law, and gave advice in a case for Lady Clere, the aunt of Anne Boleyn, regarding an action for debt, as well as being involved in numerous other petitions, arbitrations and daily legal matters.

During the 1520s, Cromwell developed an ever-widening circle of friends. He hosted dinners at his home in Austin Friars, in London, and later at Stepney, and his hospitality and generosity to his friends was widely praised. His guests, the lawyers and merchants of London, not only talked business, but also of church reform. In particular, they talked of the desire to have the Gospel in English.

Cromwell lost his wife, Elizabeth Wykys, in 1527 or 1528, probably to the sweating sickness. Unusually, Cromwell did not remarry, and there is no record of any long-term relationship with another woman. His daughters, Anne and Elizabeth, also died at some point between 1529, when he made a Will, and 1532 when he updated it. His son, Gregory, however, flourished, although there are hints in Cromwell's correspondence that Gregory, although a diligent scholar, did not have his father's quickness of intellect.

Throughout Cromwell's service with Wolsey, he was concerned only with the Cardinal's private business and legal affairs, and was not employed on any state business although he can hardly have been unaware of the *'King's Secret Matter'* – the quest for annulment of the marriage of Henry VIII and Katharine of Aragon. The first task Cromwell performed in any way connected with the case was not until 1529, and even then it was a matter of looking for the paperwork relating to Wolsey's position as Legate, to show to the King's attorney.

As the King's favour towards Wolsey waned, his enemies (of whom the chief were the Dukes of Norfolk and Suffolk) began to circle. Nevertheless, although the writing was on the wall for Wolsey, Cromwell continued to serve him faithfully, giving the best advice he could and staying with him longer than many of his other servants. Wolsey's Gentleman Usher and biographer, George Cavendish, records a scene at the Cardinal's home at Esher, whence he had been sent into a sort of exile. Cavendish greeted Cromwell who was

'...leaning in the great window...saying Our Lady Matins (which had since been a very strange sight). He prayed not more earnestly than the tears distilled from his eyes...."Why Master Cromwell, what meaneth all this your sorrow? Is my lord in any danger for whom you lament thus? Or is it for any loss that ye have sustained...?" "Nay", quoth he. "...I am like to lose all that I have travailed for all the days of my life, for doing of my master true and diligent service....and this I understand right well, that I am in disdain with most men for my master's sake and surely without first cause...I intend, God willing, this afternoon when

my Lord has dined to ride to London an so to the Court where I will either make or marr.'"

Accordingly, Cromwell, with his personal clerk, Ralph Sadler, set off for London. A Parliament had been called, but up until this point, it does not appear that Cromwell had looked for a seat. Via a chain of connections, the Duke of Norfolk, the Lord Treasurer, was persuaded to ask the King if he would be happy for Cromwell to be in the House. (Although the King did not nominate members, it was certainly the practice of the chief nobles of the realm to present their own candidates for election by their tenants, so Parliament was not a widely democratic body).

On this occasion, Henry was happy that Cromwell should take a seat as a *'burgess"*. There was a general scurrying around to find a suitable place, and Cromwell was returned for Taunton, a seat within the influence of the Bishopric of Winchester, which had been one of Wolsey's clerical offices.

Chapter 70: The End of Cardinal Wolsey (1529 – 1530)

The Parliament called in 1529, that sat until 1536, is known as the *'Reformation Parliament'* and it would prove to be one of the most important ever assembled in England. During it, Henry VIII, ably assisted, if not led by Cromwell, changed the face of the nation for ever.

One of the first debates was in regard to a *'Book of Articles'* brought forward by Thomas Howard, 2nd Duke of Norfolk and Wolsey's inveterate enemy. Norfolk sought to have Wolsey condemned by an Act of Attainder, obviating the need for trial. Cromwell argued passionately, and successfully, against the Book. The charges were dropped, and in February of 1530, Wolsey was granted a general pardon by the King.

During this whole period, Wolsey wrote long, trusting letters to Cromwell and George Cavendish recorded that

'There could nothing be spoken of against my Lord in the Parliament House, but he (Cromwell) would answer it incontinent ...at length, for his (Cromwell's) honest behaviour in his Master's cause, he grew into such an estimation in every man's opinion, that he was esteemed to be the most faithful servant of his master...wherein he was of all men greatly commended.'

Despite this positive assessment by Cavendish, Cromwell's biographers differ in their treatment of his actions during 1529 and 1530 in regard to his support of Wolsey. Borman and Williams take his continued support of Wolsey at face value, but Robert Hutchinson gives a very much more cynical view, citing numerous letters where Wolsey begs for Cromwell to visit him, and points out that many of Cromwell's actions can be seen as advancing his own cause – for example, Wolsey, realising that Anne Boleyn's influence was growing ever stronger, wanted advice on what to do about it. Cromwell suggested that presents for her and her family would not come amiss, and, accordingly, Wolsey granted several pensions to the Boleyn family out of his estates as Bishop of Winchester. Hutchinson suggests that Cromwell was eager to take the credit with the Boleyns for these favours.

Elton's view is that, as soon as was compatible with decency, Cromwell sought out the King's service. Everett makes the interesting point that we are looking at the matter with hindsight – in the period 1529 - 1530 people could not know that Wolsey was doomed – Henry's behaviour was certainly ambivalent, and, given the King's genuine affection for Wolsey, and their long history together, it was certainly not impossible that the Cardinal could stage a come-back. Although Henry had shown himself ruthless in dispatching one or two of his nobles, the wholesale executions of wives and former favourites was yet to come. Cromwell may therefore have simply been continuing business as usual, until the time came when he had to choose between staying with the Cardinal when he was sent to live in his archdiocese of York, and remaining in London, perhaps to plead for Wolsey, or, by that time, to try to advance his own career.

The next stage of Cromwell's career is rooted in the work he did for Wolsey. As the man who arranged the founding and building of Wolsey's Colleges, and managed the Cardinal's financial and property business, he was the individual with the most knowledge and understanding of the complex legal issues surrounding the lands of the Colleges, and also Wolsey's other property, most notably York Place.

Strictly speaking, York Place belonged to the Archdiocese of York, not to the Cardinal. Henry, however, had taken a distinct fancy to it, and decided to appropriate it to build a new palace. He also wanted to use some of the revenues and lands belonging to York Place and other church lands to make grants to courtiers he wished to reward. The Tudor age was extremely legalistic and litigious. It was important that land grants were correctly made (and this involved a great deal of copying, stamping, signing, witnessing, sealing and use of correct terminology) or disputes would arise. As it was ecclesiastic land, there was some uncertainty as to the long term validity of any grants made by the King out of York Place's revenues. At the very least, it was thought that Wolsey needed to endorse some of the grants.

Cromwell was able to use of his legal skills and intimate knowledge of the Cardinal's lands to smooth the way for recipients. These activities brought him into regular contact with the King, as for example, when Henry wanted to grant Lord Scales an office in Wolsey's gift. Cromwell was requested to draft a letter for the King to send to Wolsey. In these legal matters, there was much profit to be made as suitors promised fees and pensions to Cromwell to have their matter treated expeditiously. The King was impressed, and, as Sir John Russell wrote to Cromwell, 'the King's Grace had very good commendation of you.'

At some point between February and April of 1530 this good impression was translated into a concrete reward, as Cromwell was officially retained as a servant of the King. Nevertheless he was still acting for Wolsey, and gave the Cardinal excellent advice, as, comforted by merely being banished to York, Wolsey could not help himself becoming embroiled in levels of display and extravagance that were bound to cause questions to be asked. The deal, whether or not explicitly stated to Wolsey, was that he would be allowed to retire quietly, provided no-one ever heard of him again. Cromwell told Wolsey to restrain his passion for building and content himself with a quiet life, advice Wolsey spectacularly failed to follow. In the last letter between them, Cromwell takes Wolsey firmly to task for having said or written something injurious to Cromwell – perhaps Wolsey believed he had been betrayed by his old servant. Cromwell was offended

'Truly your Grace in some things over shooteth yourself. There is a regard to be given what things you utter and to whom...'

Hutchinson believes that Cromwell had, in fact, betrayed the Cardinal and that his indignation was feigned.

Whatever the truth of the matter, Wolsey's death on 29th November 1530 released Cromwell from any lingering bonds of service and within a few weeks he was appointed to the King's Privy Council. According to Cavendish, on his promotion to the Council, Sir Thomas More, Lord Chancellor, advised him

'...in your counsel giving unto His Grace, ever tell him what he ought to do, but never what he is able to do. So shall you shew yourself a true

faithful servant and a right worthy councillor. For if a lion knew his own strength, hard were it for any man to rule him.'

Chapter 71: In the King's Service

As well as spending more time with the King and his ministers, during 1531 Cromwell continued to immerse himself in legal activities, acting for the King in property matters, but not yet fully involved in policy making. He was not, in 1530, involved in the annulment, and without the Cardinal, it appeared that Henry did not know quite how to progress the case. One action the King set in motion was to send Thomas Cranmer, a Fellow of Cambridge, to collect the opinions of the theologians at the various European universities.

He also made a personal appeal to Charles V, but, with a lack of tact that is quite extraordinary, sent George Boleyn, Viscount Rochford, Anne's brother to make the plea. If Charles V were going to be persuaded to turn a blind eye to his aunt's humiliation, sending the brother of the *'other woman'* was not likely to be the most successful method.

By mid-1530, however, the King had a new idea – perhaps he did not need the Pope's ruling at all. After all, had not English Kings always been supreme in their own realm? Fifteen of the senior clergy were indicted for the crime of *'praemunire'* (obeying a foreign power, rather than the King). To avoid conviction, the Convocation of Clergy (the Church's governing body, subject in spiritual matters only to the Pope) on 24th January 1531 offered Henry the enormous sum of £100,000 in token of its penance.

They acknowledged that he was the Supreme Head of the Church in England, although the caveat *'as far as the law of God allows'* was hastily tacked on. Cromwell has been credited with putting the notion into Henry's head, but there is no evidence at all supporting that – no letters and no memoranda, which is not, of course, proof in itself, but given the amount of correspondence and paperwork that exist relating to Cromwell it is likely some note would be there.

Nevertheless, Cromwell's influence was growing and by the middle of 1531 he appears to have been involved in drafting bills to be placed before the Parliamentary session that opened in January 1532. The bills ranged from procedural matters about the import of bow-staves to further measures to curb the power of the Church. Following the payment of the aforementioned fine by Convocation, an act was introduced *'forgiving'* both clergy and laity. Cromwell seems to have worked with another of Henry's advisers, the lawyer, Thomas Audley, Speaker of the House in the Reformation Parliament, on drafting bills.

An early scheme for solving the annulment issue was suggested – the supremacy of the Archbishop of Canterbury over the English bishops would be invested in Convocation instead, thus enabling Convocation to grant the annulment that Archbishop Warham would not. Henry himself felt this was too controversial, and, instead, decided that a threat to the Pope's purse would be more effective.

A bill to stop the payment of *'first fruits and annates'* (the first year's income for a new bishop, customarily paid to the Pope) was introduced, although Cromwell seems to have been somewhat dubious about its efficacy. A clause was added, to keep the Act in abeyance until the King implemented it by letters patent, which demonstrates that even as late as Spring 1532, Henry still hoped that the Pope would grant his annulment. Despite the anti-clerical stance of the Commons, only Henry's personal intervention, through a visit to the Lords, got the bill through the Upper House.

The House of Lords may have had misgivings about attacks on Rome and the Church, but the Commons had the bit between their teeth. In

1529, Cromwell had drafted a series of complaints against the Clergy on behalf of the Commons that was now developed further into the *'Supplycacion against the Ordinaries (Ecclesiastic supervisors)'* of 1532.

This *'Supplycacion'* was a petition from the Commons to the King to control the powers of the Church. There is debate over whether the petition was spontaneous and truly represented the feeling of the Commons, or whether it was set up by the King, using Cromwell as his tool. As noted before, London, in particular, had a strong anti-clerical feeling so it may be that the King, whose intelligence and political acumen is often underrated, saw an opportunity to put further pressure on the Pope by listening to the *Supplycacion*.

After a lengthy preamble in which the Commons alleged that dissension was being sown, not only by the growth of *'heretical opinions'*, but, more substantially by the *'uncharitable behaviour of the Ordinaries'* the *Supplycacion* puts forward various complaints that Parliament wished the King remedy. These included, conveniently for the King, a complaint against the authority of Convocation. Convocation was too powerful, and used its authority in arbitrary fashion.

In support of the view that the *Supplycacion* did really emerge from the Commons, Henry did not immediately act, but requested a reply from Convocation. In April 1532, when Convocation reconvened it had prepared an answer against the *Supplycacion*. The meat of Convocation's reply was that scripture upheld its position as a law-making body. Individual failings of clergy did not negate the laws of the Church. Regardless of whether he had been behind the *Supplycacion* or had just decided to use this new tool that had fallen into his hands, Henry was not satisfied.

On 10th May 1532, Convocation was required to assent to three articles that effectively established royal authority over them. In essence, Convocation could only make and enforce canon law with royal assent.

The following day, the King made a speech in Parliament saying that he now saw that the clergy were but *'half his subjects'* and that their allegiance to Rome was contrary to their allegiance to him, but that he was sure the Commons, being *'a great sort of wise men'* would know how to act. Cromwell and Audley drew up a plan for Convocation, acceptance of which would require it to submit all of the existing Canon law to the King for approval, after it had been vetted by a committee of Clergy and Commons, and any items repugnant to the law of England deleted.

Warham's compromise suggestion was refused and on 16th May 1532, the Convocation of Clergy submitted itself to Crown jurisdiction. As the Imperial Ambassador, Chapuys noted, Convocation was now less than the guild of cobblers, as the cobblers could at least manage their own guild and make rules for it. On 17th May, Sir Thomas More resigned the Chancellorship, and was replaced by Audley.

Chapter 72: Increasing Influence (1532 – 1534)

Although from January 1532 Cromwell seems to have had the role of managing the King's business in the Commons, he was still busy with other work, including overseeing building works at the Palace of Westminster and the Tower of London, for both of which he had comprehensive responsibilities in managing construction, and auditing the accounts.

He also acted as Receiver General for what had previously been Cardinal College, Oxford, but was now to be re-founded as King Henry VIII's College. During this period, Cromwell was closely involved in financial and administrative matters relating to the King's revenues from vacant bishoprics or other ecclesiastical payments due to the Crown.

It was in April 1532 that Cromwell received his first official position, as Master of the King's Jewels, and shortly afterwards the low-key, but useful, Clerkship of the Hanaper – this brought in a fee every time a patent was sealed. His third office, nowhere near as important as it is today, was as Chancellor of the Exchequer. This trio of offices, although none was particularly significant in itself, gave him a spread of influence across the King's Household, the legal department of Chancery and the Exchequer. One of his early tasks as Master of the King's Jewels was to call in the plate that had Katharine of Aragon's arms as queen on it, for melting down.

Cromwell's next three appointments, as Principal Secretary in 1534, Master of the Rolls in 1534 and Lord Privy Seal in 1536, gave him oversight of the departments that executed government business. Although the Principal Secretaryship was not officially his until 1534, he began acting in that capacity in 1532, when the Secretary, Gardiner, was abroad on various diplomatic missions. Gardiner and Cromwell, from an early career together in Wolsey's household were, by now, at daggers drawn. Whether this was personal dislike, resentment by Cromwell at how easily Gardiner had abandoned Wolsey for the King, increasing distance on religious matters or mutual envy of the other's proximity to the King, can only be guessed at, but their rivalry continued until the downfall of one of them....

Prior to Cromwell's appointment, the role of Principal Secretary had not been especially important or prestigious – previous great ministers such as Wolsey, or Cardinal Morton in Henry VII's reign, had based their influence on the Lord Chancellorship, but from Cromwell's time to the current day, the position of Secretary of State has been one of the great offices in English, then UK government.

It is this period as Secretary that has furnished the enormous mass of correspondence on which much of our knowledge of the 1530s is based –

it should, however be noted, as Cromwell's biographer Everett points out, that this might lead us to exaggerate Cromwell's level of influence. If we had records of other members of the court, a different picture might emerge.

This comprehensive management of administration, never concentrated in one man before, is the basis of the interpretation by the great Tudor historian, Geoffrey Elton, of Cromwell as leading a *'Revolution in government'*. Elton portrays Cromwell as deliberately undertaking the transformation of the rather ramshackle machinery of mediaeval government into a sleek, well-ordered, bureaucracy.

Over the following years, Cromwell remained close to the King at all times. Unlike Wolsey, or his rivals, Norfolk and Gardiner, he seldom left London, other than to travel with the King on his summer progresses. It is apparent that, although he had clerks whom he trusted completely, in particular, his nephew Richard Williams (later called Cromwell) and Ralph Sadler, he was no delegator. His friend in Antwerp, Stephen Vaughan, wrote warning him that constant *'travail of common causes'* would impair his judgement for greater things, and that *'by overmuch paining his body and cumbering his wits'* he would sink into an early grave.

The voluminous documentation that charts Cromwell's activity is almost entirely business – there is very little to give a picture of Cromwell as a personality – although his friendship for Sir Thomas Wyatt peeps out of a letter. Records also show that he enjoyed hunting and hawking and kept greyhounds. He could draw a fine bow, and played bowls, cards and dice, gambling for high stakes as was common with all Henry's court. He wined and dined his friends, ordering supplies of wine from Lord Lisle, in Calais, and employed musicians to entertain them.

The breadth of Cromwell's reading matter is, of course, unknown, but certain works of politics he definitely read, including Aristotle's *'Politics'* and Marsiligio of Padua's *'Defensor Pacis'*. We can infer, too, that he read Tyndale's *'On the Obedience of a Christian Man'* that so beguiled Henry and Anne Boleyn. Many biographers have referred to Cromwell as *'Machiavellian'*, and claimed that he was a devotee of Machiavelli's work, and perhaps even knew him in Florence in his time there. Whilst any resident of Florence would have had to go round with his hands over his ears NOT to be aware of Machiavelli in the early 1510s, their different social status would preclude any meeting. There is no certainty that Cromwell read *'The Prince'* before receiving it as a gift in 1536.

By the end of 1532, the annulment was reaching crisis point. Anne Boleyn had finally surrendered her body to the King, and he was determined to marry her. More's resignation of the Chancellorship, and the death of Warham, Archbishop of Canterbury, in August 1532 finally paved the way out of the impasse. This was to be Cromwell's moment for obtaining Henry's heart's desire through legal means.

The first step was to obtain Cranmer's confirmation as Archbishop of Canterbury. Cranmer, an apparently innocuous Fellow of Cambridge, was nominated by Henry in October 1532, and approved by Clement VII in an effort to show Henry that the Papacy was trying to be accommodating. The new Archbishop was consecrated on 30th March 1533. Cromwell had helped to draft a protestation that Cranmer then immediately made, stating that his oath to the Pope could not bind him against God's Law, or the King's prerogative.

The second step was to pass the Act in Restraint of Appeals. This Act, again drafted by Cromwell, began with a long and convoluted preamble emphasising that England was an *'empire'* and thus not subject to any external authority, not even that of the *'Bishop of Rome'*. In consequence, ecclesiastical matters such as matrimony and legitimacy were to be tried and answered within the kingdom, with no appeal. Cromwell, as a master of Parliamentary business, was careful to work with lawyers and clergy through the drafting stage, taking alterations and amendments to give the Act the best possible chance of being passed. In the event, there was very little opposition, although Archbishop Lee of York, and Gardiner, Bishop of Winchester remained opposed.

As well as preparing the Act carefully, Cromwell managed the by-elections that had occurred since Parliament was summoned in 1529, to return members favourable to the King. He also urged all supporters to attend the vote, and discouraged any suspected of not being one hundred per cent on-side, such as Sir George Throckmorton of Coughton, a stout supporter of Katharine of Aragon, from coming to Parliament on the day of the vote. There was some debate in the Commons – merchants feared that the rest of Christendom might not wish to trade with a country that had left the umbrella of Papal Supremacy. Nevertheless, the Act was carried with a majority.

Convocation, headed by Cranmer, and now the supreme ecclesiastical body in England, declared Henry and Katharine's marriage to have been void *ab initio*, and his marriage to Anne legal. Cromwell had succeeded where Wolsey had failed.

Chapter 73: Dealing with Dissent (1534 – 1535)

The final annulment of Henry's first marriage brought the case of Elizabeth Barton, known as the *'Nun of Kent'*, to a head, and Cromwell was involved in the examination and punishment of an alleged group of traitors. Barton, a serving-woman in Canterbury, began to have visions of the Virgin Mary and other saints in 1525, following a serious illness. She was examined by the local priest and Archbishop Warham himself.

Found to be a woman of virtue and blameless life, she was encouraged to become a nun. Over the following years, her prophecies and visions drew a large audience. She was even consulted by Wolsey and the King himself.

Barton's prophecies were all very conservative, discouraging Lutheranism, and supporting traditional practices – pleasing to Henry in a time when he was strongly anti-Lutheran himself. However, as the annulment case became public knowledge, Barton preached against it and drew the wrath of Henry down on both herself, and any who had listened to her. The list of her patrons included a number of high-ranking courtiers who were supporters of Katharine of Aragon, including Bishop Fisher of Rochester and Gertrude, Marchioness of Exeter.

The Nun was arrested and accused not only of leading an immoral life, but also of having made up her prophecies, under the orders of her priests. In a shameless display of greed, one of the chief accusers was Friar John Laurence who gave evidence against both her, and several of his brother friars, whilst asking to be granted the office that one of the accused would no longer need after being hanged. The Nun and five others were hanged at Tyburn and her supporters in court circles were under suspicion for some time.

Henry's chief objective of marriage to Anne achieved, there was no time for Cromwell, now acknowledged as his chief minister, to rest. The 1534 Parliament bristled with bills stopping payments to Rome, ensuring the cathedrals were brought under the King's jurisdiction, and, ominously, empowering the Crown to '*visit*' (monitor) the monasteries. It was stated that this throwing off of Papal Supremacy was not to be taken to mean that England was departing from the '*articles of the Catholic faith of Christendom*' and, at this stage, no changes in religious practice were suggested.

The next important piece of legislation that Cromwell shepherded through Parliament in 1534 was the Act of Succession which, after a preamble denying papal supremacy, settled the succession on the children of Henry and his new queen, Anne's, heirs male, and thereafter on the heirs of any subsequent wife. Any subject over the age of fourteen could be called upon to swear an oath to uphold the Act.

It was decided that John Fisher, Bishop of Rochester, who had vigorously defended the marriage of Henry and Katharine, and Sir Thomas More, former Lord Chancellor, who was believed to be opposed to the Royal Supremacy, would be asked to swear the oath. Both men refused. Fisher boldly stated his grounds, and confirmed that he would sign an oath upholding the succession in accordance with the will of Parliament and the King, but would not deny Papal Supremacy. More also confirmed that he would swear to the proposed succession, but he would not sign the oath as it stood, although he gave no statement as to what he found objectionable. Both men were attainted in November 1534 and were sent to the Tower to think on their answers. Naturally, their property was confiscated.

At the end of the 1534 session of Parliament, three final Acts were drafted by Cromwell and Audley. The Act of Supremacy, which spelt out Royal Supremacy, rather than it just being part of the Act of Succession, the Treasons Act, which enlarged the concept of treason from acts to words, and a revised Act relating to annates, that began an audit of monastery land, through a Royal Commission. This session also introduced the acts which effectively amalgamated Wales into England, and created a unified state.

Early 1535 was taken up with matter of Bishop Fisher and Sir Thomas More. They were both still in the Tower, refusing to swear the oath of succession. More and Fisher were highly respected at home and abroad as pious, learned and virtuous. Our modern unease with More's treatment of *'heretics'* did not raise any such doubts at the time. Repeatedly, Cromwell put pressure on them both.

On 7th May, 1535, he led a delegation to the Tower to request More to give his opinion on the Act of Supremacy, as the King had asked for it. More refused to discuss the matter, saying he had told the King and Cromwell what he thought when the matter was first mooted, and would say no more on the topic. Cromwell appears to have used his best endeavours to persuade More to accept the oath, saying the King would be merciful, and pointing out that, just because he was in prison, he need not think he could escape from obedience to the King. Cromwell then complained that More was encouraging others to disobey by his obstinacy. More only replied that

'I do nobody harm, I say none harm, I think none harm but wish everybody good. And if this be not enough to keep a man alive, in good faith, I long not to live. And I am dying already…And therefore my poor body is at the King's pleasure: would God my death might do him good.'

Cromwell spoke *'full gently'* on hearing this, and assured More that no advantage would be taken of anything he had said.

However, Henry was not to be satisfied. On 3rd June, Cromwell returned, in a very much sterner mood. Pope Paul III, in a misguided attempt to improve the lot of Bishop Fisher, had created him a Cardinal. Henry was beside himself with rage, seeing the honouring of a disobedient subject as a deliberate provocation. He was determined that Fisher and More would conform.

The delegation, led by Cromwell, consisted this time of Lord Chancellor Audley, the Duke of Suffolk (Henry's brother-in-law) and the Earl of Wiltshire, Queen Anne's father. The men had a copy of the oath with them, and attempted to coerce More into either signing, or saying something treasonable that would call down the new Treason Act upon him. More was obdurate, and Cromwell was frustrated, telling More he liked him *'much worse'* than before. The Councillors then departed, and sent Sir Richard Rich, the Solicitor General, to remove More's books.

Cromwell drew up an indictment upon which More was tried at Westminster Hall. The first three counts of the indictment that effectively assumed guilt from refusal to give a reason for not signing the oath were dismissed by the court. The final charge was then the only matter left.

This charge, sworn to by Richard Rich, was that in a discussion about hypothetical cases, More had denied the Royal Supremacy. There were no other witnesses than the two men. More pointed out that, if he had not answered the King or his Councillors, he certainly wouldn't have shared his inmost thoughts with Rich, whom he heartily despised and accused of perjury.

The court returned a guilty verdict and More was beheaded on 6th July 1535, just after Bishop Fisher. So far as Cromwell was concerned, it was a job well done, even if he might have preferred Fisher and More to swear the oath to reduce opposition to the King.

Chapter 74: Cromwell & Anne Boleyn (1534 – 1536)

It is often stated that Cromwell was a client of the Boleyn family, and owed his rise to Anne's favour. However, this is quite clearly not the case – he came to the King's attention through his duties in relation to legal and conveyancing matters. The fact that he may have shared the Boleyns' inclination towards Church reform, might have made him more personally disposed to helping Henry with the annulment legislation, but that cannot be shown as the cause of his rise. His relationship with the new Queen was therefore one that developed over his time as the King's Councillor.

Anne was not popular, either with the public, or with the majority of the Court. Had she borne a son, all might have been forgiven, but the child who had been so eagerly awaited was a girl. Anne then had a miscarriage at some point during 1534, and her relationship with Henry continued to wax and wane. Chapuys reported as early as Christmas 1534 that Henry had consulted Cromwell as to whether he might throw off Anne, without having to return to Katharine, but since Henry and Anne had a notoriously volatile relationship, not much weight can be given to rumours at this point.

Chapuys also told Cromwell that the King and he would be held personally responsible by the Emperor should anything untoward happen to Katharine or Princess Mary, whom it was rumoured that Cromwell and /or Anne intended to have quietly dispatched.

During the late summer of 1535, Cromwell organised a summer progress for Henry, which took the court (minus Queen Anne, who was again pregnant and stayed at home to safeguard her health) to Wiltshire. Whilst there, the progress visited Wolf Hall, home of the Seymour family. The eldest Seymour daughter had, at some point, been a maid-of-honour to Katharine of Aragon, but was unnoticed by Henry at that time. Now, however, he fell in love with her. Since Anne was pregnant, he cannot have been anticipating matrimony at that point and Jane rejected his advances either from modesty, or policy. She was, nevertheless, given a place in Queen Anne's household, and Cromwell gave up his rooms at Greenwich Palace to Jane's brother, Edward Seymour, to enable Henry to meet Jane in the bosom of her family.

January 1536 brought drama at court. Katharine of Aragon died, Henry was thrown violently from his horse, causing a concussion lasting some hours, and Anne miscarried *'of her saviour'*. Katharine now dead, there was the possibility of rapprochement with her nephew, the Emperor Charles, and a return to the traditional alliance between England and Burgundy. Had Anne borne a son, she would have been unlikely to accommodate such an alliance, but, with only a daughter, and Jane waiting in the wings, Anne was looking increasing expendable. It appears she had also quarrelled with Cromwell, threatening to have his head off his shoulders.

Cromwell began to investigate Anne and to sniff out gossip, which gave him enough material for the King to grant him a commission on 24 April, 1536 to enquire as to whether there was sufficient evidence to bring Anne to trial. The vast majority of observers, then and now, believe Anne to have been quite innocent of the charges of adultery and incest with five men that were brought against her. One confession (by Mark Smeaton) was obtained, probably through torture at Cromwell's own house. Historian George Bernard believes there may be some truth in the charges. True or not, matters were not to be left to chance – the court, headed by Anne's uncle, Norfolk, knew the sentence required, and an executioner had even been employed before Anne's trial began.

Cromwell, having tidily swept away another of Henry's problems, could bask in his title of Baron Cromwell and his new position of Lord Privy Seal, the office of which Anne's father had been deprived. Keen to hitch himself to the rising Seymour star, he arranged the marriage of his son, Gregory, to Elizabeth Seymour, Queen Jane's sister. His son was now brother-in-law to the King! Quite a step up for the son of a Putney blacksmith.

Chapter 75: Cromwell & Lady Mary

On the fall of Anne Boleyn, Henry's elder daughter, who had been degraded from the rank of Princess when Anne's daughter was born, wrote to Cromwell, requesting him to intercede for her with her father. She had consistently refused to accept the annulment of her parents' marriage, and had been disgraced and banished from her father's sight, to live, bullied and humiliated by Anne's relatives, in the household of the baby Elizabeth. Now, with Anne dead, she hoped to regain her father's favour. The fact that Lady Mary wrote to Cromwell in the summer of 1536 shows that even Henry's own daughter knew that, by now, Cromwell was the man he relied on to deal with day-to-day matters.

Cromwell must have been in a quandary. Whilst a King who had had his own wife executed might not baulk at meting out the same treatment to a disobedient daughter, even though he had once dearly loved her, such a step would be controversial, to say the least. In the summer of 1536, Henry had one adult daughter (Mary), an illegitimate son who was on his deathbed (Richmond) and a three-year-old daughter (Elizabeth), child of a woman executed for adultery. By custom, the succession, if none of these children were legitimate heirs, would fall to James V, King of Scots. If Mary were dead, that would be the most likely outcome, and deeply undesirable to all of England. In addition, proceeding against Mary might bring more than angry words from her cousin, Emperor Charles.

The best route out was to persuade Mary to accept the Act of Supremacy. Cromwell arranged for the Duke of Norfolk – a man of supreme tactlessness – the Earl of Sussex and a Bishop to visit Lady Mary and demand that she take the Oath of Supremacy. She refused.

Pressure had to be stepped up. Cromwell enlisted Chapuys, the Emperor's Ambassador, to point out to Mary the danger she stood in. Simultaneously, he wrote to her himself, saying:

'If you do not leave all sinister counsels, I take leave of you for ever and desire you to write to me no more, for I will never think you other than the most ungrateful, unnatural, and obstinate person living, both to God and your most dear and benign father.'

He accompanied this tirade with an obsequious letter for Mary to copy, acknowledging her father as Supreme Head of the Church, rejecting the Pope and agreeing that her parents' marriage had been unlawful and incestuous. Mary, finally bullied into submission, signed, whilst sending a message to Rome that it had been done with mental reservations.

On 5th July that year, Cromwell wrote to Bishop Gardiner of Winchester (later Mary's own Lord Chancellor) that 'my Lady Mary is a most obedient child to the King's Highness and is as conformable as any living faithful subject can be.'

Henry probably felt no small measure of gratitude to Cromwell for fixing this problem. Queen Jane, too, was grateful, and she immediately invited Mary to court and showered affection and gifts on her.

Chapter 76: Dissolution of the Monasteries

In 1534, Chapuys had noted that the King *'is very covetous of the goods of the Church, which he already considers his patrimony'* and, as was noted above, legislation in 1534 had implemented a valuation of all monastery lands. By October of that year, Cromwell was drafting a plan for how the wealth of the Church could be better disposed of, including the suppression of monastic houses with fewer than ten inmates, and diversion of the revenues to the Crown. The valuation survey was completed and compiled as *'Valor Ecclesiasticus'*, the most wide-ranging survey of land since the Domesday Book. *Valor Ecclesiasticus* determined that the Church was worth some £800,000 per annum. As well as the valuations, the commissions to the surveyors had required them to report on the conduct of the monastic establishments.

Debate has continued for nearly five hundred years as to whether the monasteries were full of corruption, licentiousness and poverty of true religious life, or whether the odd bad example (inevitable in any organisation) was blown out of all proportion to condemn the monasteries, root and branch. Cromwell, personally, seems to have been antithetical to the concept of religious life and was thus mentally prepared to believe everything that confirmed his idea that the monasteries were anachronistic, decadent and potentially harbouring enemies of the King's supremacy, as well of course, as being awash with cash.

On 21st January 1535, the King gave Cromwell the office of Vicar-General, granting him the power to undertaken visitations (as inspections by ecclesiastical superiors were known) of all monasteries and colleges of priests. Cromwell appointed four men to carry out the tasks on his behalf. All of these men had worked with him previously and none of them were known for their scruples. A list of seventy-four questions was drawn up, to probe the innermost details of monastic life.

The initial plan was merely to close the smaller monasteries, and send those inmates who wished to continue in the religious life, to larger houses. It just so happened that plenty of evidence was found of corruption and bad practice in smaller houses, and when the bill to suppress them was introduced to Parliament, the Commons were so shocked, that cries of *down with them* were heard. Of the 300 or so monasteries below the threshold of £200 that had been set, 244 were dissolved, and 47 granted licences by the King to remain open. Crown revenues were handsomely increased.

With a huge bounty of land now free for redistribution, Cromwell was inundated with requests to persuade the King to grant some humble petition. The Court of Augmentations was instituted, which Richard Rich, Solicitor General, and Thomas Pope presided over as Chancellor and Treasurer. Cromwell and his men profited handsomely, but it is fair to say that many others of Henry's courtiers did too, and often those opposed in principle to the Royal Supremacy.

In 1536, Convocation, presided over by Cromwell as the King's Vicegerent in Spirituals, promulgated the Act of Ten Articles, a declaration of faith that challenged traditional Catholic teachings and began to give an opening to reformist, even Lutheran views. Cromwell then, on his own account, without consulting Convocation, gave orders for parish priests to preach on the Royal Supremacy, and to teach children the Creed and Paternoster in English as well as laying down rules for clerical behaviour, and stipulating how much priests should give in alms. An English Bible, too, was to be in every church from 1st August 1536.

Whatever the views of the Cromwell, the King, and his immediate circle on the legislative and religious developments of the period 1529-1536, many outside the south-east of England were very much less content. Rebellion broke out, first in Lincolnshire, and then, more seriously in Yorkshire. Suffice to say that, after a near-brush with civil war, during which Cromwell was repeatedly cast as the villain by the commons who complained, in time-honoured way, about the King's *'evil counsellors'* to avoid seeming to criticise the King, the rebels were overcome. The opinion, not just of the rebels, but of many of Henry's people was encapsulated in the words of Lord Darcy, before his execution.

'Cromwell, it is thou that art the very original and chief causer of all this rebellion and mischief and art likewise causer of the apprehension of us that be noble men and dost daily earnestly travail to bring us to

one end and to strike of our heads and I trust that, or [before] thou die, though thou wouldst procure all the noblemen's heads within the realm to be striken off, that still there one head remain that shall strike of thy head.'

Nevertheless, Cromwell was riding high. The disturbances of the Pilgrimage of Grace meant that coerced dissolutions of the larger monasteries was politically impossible, but enough pressure was brought to bear for them to surrender voluntarily. Cromwell also continued to act as the King's right hand man, particularly in the passage of the Act of Proclamations which, despite opposition from the Lords, who feared its use might be arbitrary, confirmed that the King's Proclamations, in relation to statutes passed by Parliament, had the same force as the statutes.

In 1539, too, many of Cromwell's enemies were disposed of in connection with the Exeter Conspiracy. It seemed that the Lord Privy Seal could not fail.

The tide, however, was about to turn.

Chapter 77: Cromwell's Downfall (1539 – 1540)

Henry VIII was widowed in October 1537, when Queen Jane died in childbed. Cromwell almost immediately sought a suitable replacement – preferably a wealthy, healthy princess who would counterbalance the threats to England from the France and the Empire, which were still making noises about invading England to restore Papal authority. He lit upon the sisters of Wilhelm, Duke of Cleves, as likely candidates. Cleves, like England had thrown off Papal authority, but had not gone far down the road of Lutheranism. It was also one of the duchies that made up the Empire, so an alliance would be bound to irritate Emperor Charles.

Hans Holbein, Henry's court painter, and probably a friend of Cromwell, was sent to paint the Ladies Amelia and Anna. The portrait that was delivered of Lady Anna was so delightful that Henry was prepared to ally with a more religiously radical regime. The wedding was arranged and Anna of Cleves duly arrived in England. Henry, not quite as young and handsome as he had once been, raced to meet her, disguised as a merchant. Anna, sick and weary after a dismal channel crossing, not recognising in the corpulent, aging, burgess the romantic prince of her dreams, greeted him coldly and failed to exert any charm she may have had. Henry was not impressed. Always gentlemanly in his demeanour to ladies, he treated Anna with the utmost courtesy, but he expressed his private feelings to Cromwell saying that '*She is nothing so fair as she hath been reported*' and that he would not put his head into the '*yoke*' of marriage with her, if there were any alternative.

No alternative could be found and the marriage went ahead. No doubt Cromwell was hoping that Henry would overcome his personal repugnance and settle down with Anna. But Henry could not overcome his feelings – and was soon engaged in a more pleasing relationship. The Duke of Norfolk's niece, Katheryn Howard, was one of Anna's new maids-of-honour and the King became infatuated.

Norfolk, who had resented Cromwell becoming Henry's chief minister instead of himself, and Cromwell's old sparring partner, Bishop Gardiner, who was implacably imposed to the innovation in religion, with which Cromwell was increasingly associated, saw their chance. Cromwell's patronage of Robert Barnes, an ardent reformer who was accused of heresy, was an opportunity for Gardiner to tar Cromwell with the same brush, knowing that Henry, who was becoming increasingly concerned about a drift away from Catholic doctrine, would not tolerate heresy in his chief minister.

Through a masterly handling of the opening session of the new Parliament in April 1540, Cromwell managed to diffuse the growing religious controversy. He also resigned his position of Secretary to two of his supporters, to try to increase his support on the Privy Council. Norfolk and Gardiner, however, were just biding their time.

Cromwell was promoted again, to be Earl of Essex and Lord Great Chamberlain, a largely ceremonial post and the French Ambassador believed him to be as high in Henry's favour as ever. But on 10th June 1540, the blow fell. Cromwell attended a Privy Council meeting at Westminster. The King was absent and the other Councillors had all assembled before Cromwell's arrival. On entrance, he looked for a seat, and was told that there was no seat for him amongst gentlemen. Norfolk then arrested him for high treason and personally tore off the collar of St George that Cromwell wore as a Knight of the Garter. Not surprisingly, Cromwell protested his innocence, but no notice was taken and he was dragged off to the Tower. Norfolk would not have taken such a step without Henry's approval, and yet it is difficult to believe that Henry can really have given credence to such spurious claims as that Cromwell wanted to marry Henry's daughter, Mary, and seize the throne. He must have been convinced that Cromwell's repeated conferences with the German Lutherans meant that Cromwell himself was infected with 'heresy'. If that were the case, there could be no mercy.

Cranmer wrote to Henry, almost protesting Cromwell's innocence:

'Who cannot be sorrowful and amazed that he should be a traitor against Your Majesty – he whose surety was only by Your Majesty...who studied always to put set forward whatsoever was Your Majesty's pleasure...For who shall Your Grace trust hereafter, if you might not trust him?

Cromwell wrote to Henry from the Tower, *'with the quaking hand of the most sorrowful heart of your most sorrowful subject and most humble servant and prisoner.'*

He had never knowingly committed any offence against the King, and if, in the course of his multifarious tasks he had accidentally broken any law, he begged for mercy.

Henry believed that Cromwell might still be of some use to him. He wanted his marriage to Anna annulled and Cromwell could help him to achieve that end. Not only was the delicious morsel of Katheryn Howard being laid before him daily by Norfolk and Gardiner, but the political motive for the marriage had also disappeared, as François I of France and the Emperor Charles were once again fighting for Milan.

Cromwell confirmed that Henry had entered the marriage unwillingly, and not consummated it. The marriage was annulled, and Anna, after initial hesitancy, accepted the King's terms with a good grace, remaining in England, honoured and respected, as the King's *'sister'* and friend. Cromwell, although just as keen to please, received no benefit from his help. An Act of Attainder had already been passed, condemning him to death. Nevertheless, he wrote again to Henry pleading for *'mercy, mercy, mercy'*.

His words fell on deaf ears. Unlike Wolsey, with whom Henry had had a warm, personal relationship, Cromwell was no more to him than a servant. There was no hesitation. Cromwell, now stripped of his new titles, was executed on 28th July 1540. In the speech from the scaffold purported to be his, he confirmed his faith in the Catholic Church, and all of its sacraments. After a bungled execution, requiring at least three blows, his head was displayed on London Bridge, no doubt as a mark of gratitude for a man who had served his king so faithfully. The King mourned by marrying Katheryn Howard the same day.

Aspects of Thomas Cromwell's Life

Chapter 78: Cromwell & the English Bible

Contrary to popular belief, there was no absolute prohibition on Bibles in the vernacular prior to the Reformation. There had been a translation into French as early as the late thirteenth century and into Czech in the fourteenth century. The reality was that, before the printing press, and the growth of lay education in the fifteenth century, almost the only readers were the clergy, and the more academically inclined nobles, who could all read Latin, so there was little market for Bibles in any other language.

The first printed Bible was an edition of the Vulgate (ie the standard Latin Bible, first translated in the late fourth century by St Jerome and his assistants, from the original Hebrew, Aramaic and Greek). It was printed 1454, in Mainz and was designed to be look just like a hand-written manuscript. This was followed by a printed version of a Czech translation in 1488.

Towards the end of the fifteenth century, scholars, particularly Erasmus of Rotterdam, questioned the validity of Jerome's translation, and Erasmus went back to the original Greek to produce a revised edition of the Gospels – a work that produced some controversy, as potentially challenging Catholic orthodoxy. Simultaneously, in the spirit of renewal of religion that Erasmus and the other Humanists were fostering, there was pressure for translations of the Bible into local languages to enable Christians to read the word of God for themselves. The Church authorities were somewhat suspicious, but translations were not forbidden per se, they just had to be licensed by the appropriate authority – usually the Primate or a resident Papal Legate.

In England, there were early Anglo-Saxon translations of part of the Gospels, but the first full translation had been done in the late fourteenth century, by John Wycliffe. Wycliffe had been condemned as a heretic, and his translation was forbidden from 1407 onward. His followers, known as '*Lollards*', continued as an underground movement, and preserved copies of his Bible, despite the fact that being caught in possession of it attracted a death sentence.

The concern over the Lollard heresy had led to a repressive attitude in England to all translations of the Bible. In Europe, translations were appearing in the 1520s in countries that would remain within the Catholic fold, as well as those moving towards Lutheranism. The New Testament was published in French in 1523, and the whole Bible in 1530 by Lefevre, under the protection of François I and his sister, Marguerite, later Queen of Navarre; simultaneously, Luther's translation of 1523 was an early best-seller in Germany. During the 1520s and 1530s translations appeared in Swiss, Dutch and Tuscan.

There was a growing demand for an English translation to enable the Word of God to be read by all. Supporters of the Bible in English during the 1520s were called '*evangelicals*', they were not necessarily Lutherans, and many who supported a more Biblically based faith never left the Catholic Church. However, there was one man whose desire for an English translation was only part of his wider conversion to the more personal faith espoused by the Reformers – William Tyndale.

Tyndale, a notable scholar and linguist, hoped to make a full English translation from the original Greek and Hebrew. He approached Cuthbert Tunstall, Bishop of London, in 1523 for a licence. Tunstall, although he was himself a scholar and a collaborator with Erasmus, felt that Tyndale was too radical and refused to be involved with his plans.

Tyndale left for the Low Countries, and began translating part of the New Testament in 1524. A second, full, translation followed in 1526, printed in Worms. Copies of Tyndale's work were smuggled into England, in bales of cloth, at 9d per set of octavo sheets. There had been no softening on the position that possession of unlicensed English Bibles was punishable by death. However, the growth of the printing press meant that the sheer quantity of volumes that could be brought in rendered its dissemination unstoppable.

Bishop Tunstall, in an ill-considered act, burnt Tyndale's works after condemning them as heretical at St Paul's Cathedral. The sight of Bibles being burnt made many uneasy, even those who were not inclined towards Tyndale's Lutheran views, which supported Justification by Faith alone and undermined the Catholic belief in prayers for the dead.

Cromwell is usually described as a radical in religious matters, an early Protestant (although the term was not in common currency until after his death), but there were many shades of evangelicalism between the strict conservatism of men such as Bishop Gardiner, Cromwell's nemesis, and 'heretics' such as Tyndale. Whereas Anne Boleyn and her family, and Archbishop Cranmer are referred to by Eustache Chapuys, that inveterate reporter of gossip, as *'Lutherans'* he does not use that term of Cranmer.

Cromwell's Will, made after September 1532, asks for the intercession of the Virgin and the Saints, allocates money for several houses of friars, and for prayers for his soul, a traditional Catholic practice that by 1532 was excoriated by Tyndale and Luther. His stance was certainly anticlerical - the Chronicler, Edward Hall, himself having reformist tendencies recorded that Cromwell *'could not abide the snoffyng pride of some prelates'*, but whether he supported doctrinal changes in the early 1530s is questionable.

Cromwell moved in intellectual circles, and a later correspondent wrote that he treasured the memory of *'divers dinners'* at Cromwell's home at Austin Friars where he had heard *'such communication which were the verye cause of the begynninge of my conversion'* but he also maintained friendships with conservatives such as Edmund Bonner, later Bishop of London under Mary.

Exactly why and when Cromwell himself first read an English Bible is unknown. According to John Foxe, on one of Cromwell's trips to Rome in the 1510s he had memorised Erasmus' New Testament. This would certainly suggest a lively interest in religion, beyond just form, and together with his naturally inquiring mind would probably have led him to read Tyndale's work. With his contacts in the cloth trade he would have had easy access to a contraband copy, most likely through his friend and associate in Antwerp, Stephen Vaughan, whom Cromwell later warned that he was becoming suspect for Lutheran views.

Whether or not Cromwell entertained Lutheran doctrinal views cannot be proven but what can be, is his commitment to the Bible in English. Foxe, in his *'Book of Martyrs'* wrote that Cromwell's

'whole life was nothing els, but a continuall care and travaile how to advaunce and futher the right knowledge of the Gospell'.

In 1534, the Convocation of Clergy, now the governing body of the English Church, under the King, petitioned the monarch for a full translation of the Bible for the edification of his subjects. It was suggested that Tyndale might be employed to do it, on condition that he ceased to write the offensive polemics against the King's annulment that had poured from his pen. Henry, although he was prepared to consider an English Bible, was apoplectic at the thought of encouraging Tyndale whom, according to Cromwell, he considered to be *'replete with venomous envy, rancour and malice'*.

A translator more acceptable to the King would have to be found.

Miles Coverdale was a Cambridge graduate, who was ordained priest in 1514, before becoming an Augustinian Friar. Amongst his circle of acquaintances were Robert Barnes, later burnt for heresy, Sir Thomas More, and Cromwell. Coverdale's views became more evangelical as time passed, and he spent the years 1528 – 1534 abroad. By 1535 he had completed a translation of the Bible, which was the first full translation, and much of which found its way into the King James' Authorised Version of 1611. Two more editions of the 1537 work were published, and, although it was not an official translation, it appeared in many parish churches from 1st August 1537, from which date all churches were to have an English Bible.

The title page, designed by Holbein, shows Henry VIII brandishing the Sword of Justice in one hand, and giving the Word of God to his bishops with the other. The work is dedicated to Henry saying

'He only under God is the Chief Head of all the congregation of the Church'.

Coverdale was now free to return to England, where he arranged a further printing of his New Testament, bound together with a copy of the Vulgate.

Another translation appeared in 1537, also licensed for use. This was the Matthew Bible, a combination of translations from Coverdale, Tyndale and Thomas Matthews, chaplain to the Merchant Adventurers in Antwerp. This Bible was Archbishop Cranmer's personal favourite and was to be used until the Bishops should *'set forth a better translation'* although he admitted to Cromwell that this would probably not be achieved until *'the day after Domesday.'*

In fact, Cranmer had already taken steps for a new translation and allocated sections to different bishops for translation. The fact that one of these was the conservative Gardiner, Bishop of Winchester, confirms that a desire for an English Bible was not a hallmark of Lutheranism, especially as Gardiner, unlike many of the others, completed his section – the Gospels of Luke and John.

Nevertheless, it was agreed, presumably between the King, Cranmer and Cromwell, that the first authorised translation would be a revision of the Matthew Bible, supervised by Coverdale and with additions from Sebastian Munster's rendition of the Old Testament from the original Hebrew.

On 5th September 1538 Cromwell, as the King's Vicegerent in Spirituals, ordered that the Bible be available in all churches by All Saints' Day (1st November), although, in the event, the new translation was delayed.

There was a lack of facilities for printing such a large work, and the copies needed, in London, so Bishop Gardiner was asked to obtain a licence from François I for its production in France. The licence was granted, but the French Inquisitor-General smelt heresy and tried to have the book impounded. Fortunately, Coverdale and the printer, Richard Grafton, managed to escape France with the type, the printing press and the sheets completed to date. The work was finished and issued in London in April 1539.

The resulting tome was known as *'The Great Bible'* not for its brilliance, but for its size – it was to be of a size to be read and consulted by every parishioner.

Cromwell's desire to see the Bible in English, available to everyone, cannot be denied, yet he saw no harm in turning a profit from it too. He invested £800 in the printing, and obtained a monopoly of the profits of the first five years of print runs. The book was to be of the largest volume, printed on good quality paper, and to cost 10 shillings – Cranmer had thought 13s 4d reasonable. The parish priest and his flock were to share the purchase price between them. Whilst unlearned folk were not to dispute on the content of the Bible, everyone was to be encouraged to read *'the very lively word of God that every Christian person is bound to embrace, believe and follow'*.

Chapter 79: Following the Footsteps of Thomas Cromwell

The numbers in the article below correspond to those on the map which follows.

Thomas Cromwell came from a modest background, so tracking his movements during the early part of his life is not easy. The Cromwells were originally from Norwell in Nottinghamshire (1) but by the time of his father's birth, they were settled in south-west London. Thomas was brought up in Putney, where they had a house not far from the River Thames in Brewhouse Lane (2). An exact date for Cromwell leaving home is not known, but it is likely to have been around the turn of the sixteenth century. For the next ten years or so, he travelled in Europe, first in the French army, although he apparently left after the overwhelming defeat at Garigliano in 1503, and then in Florence, the centre of the cultural renaissance that was spreading across Europe. Following that, he lived and worked in Antwerp for a period, during which time he made a range of contacts with merchants involved in the cloth industry.

On returning to London, around 1512, he seems to have set up home in Fenchurch Street (3). The street is still there, but no trace remains of any sixteenth centuries homes. It is likely he lived here with his wife,

Elizabeth Wykys, whom he married some time before 1516, as he developed a career as lawyer, cloth merchant and moneylender.

One of Cromwell's earliest recorded legal clients was the Guild of the Church of Our Lady, Boston, Lincolnshire (4) – the church itself is now known as the Boston Stump. He made a successful visit to Rome on the Guild's behalf.

When Cromwell entered Wolsey's service, sometime around 1519, he was employed on property and financial matters. His most important role, which he carried out with remarkable diligence, was the dissolution of the religious houses whose revenues were to be diverted to the building of Wolsey's colleges at Ipswich (5) and Oxford (6). He also oversaw the building works, and the entire setting up of the new foundations. This activity necessitated a good deal of riding about between the various locations involved.

In 1523, Cromwell entered Parliament. At that time Parliament usually met in Westminster Hall (7), the fabulous hall dating from the reign of Richard II, that still remains, and has witnessed so much of English and British history. The Parliament lasted seventeen weeks, and Cromwell wrote to a friend that matters ended pretty much as they had begun.

Whilst in Wolsey's household, Cromwell would have spent a good deal of time at York Place (8). This was rebuilt by Henry VIII as the royal palace of Whitehall. Cromwell was closely involved in both the legal niceties required for Henry to have a valid title to the lands, and also the refurbishment works.

Hampton Court (9) too was a place where Cromwell would have spent a good deal of time, both in service to Wolsey, and later, when it was one of Henry VIII's favourite palaces.

Cromwell was aware of how unpopular Wolsey had made himself through his extravagance and magnificent style of life, thought by the nobility to be quite incompatible with his humble beginnings. Cromwell was certainly not going to make that mistake. He had a house near the convent of the Austin Friars (10) in the City of London. Again, the street name remains, but there are no traces of sixteenth century life. Here he seems to have spent much of his personal life, wining and dining the city merchants who were his friends. He also had an official residence at Rolls House, Chancery Lane (11), in his capacity as Master of the Rolls. This has since been replaced with the Maughan Library, a neo-gothic fantasy.

Service to the King had its rewards – Cromwell built up an impressive property portfolio in and around London. Amongst his properties, he had a house at Stepney (12), where he interrogated Mark Smeaton in a quest to find evidence against Anne Boleyn, and estates out of town at Mortlake (13) and Ewhurst (14). No traces of these survive.

Although he had property outside the capital London, Cromwell was always a Londoner, and even in death, he remained within a stone's throw of the City. His final days were spent in the Tower of London (15), and his remains lie there still.

Key to Map

1. Norwell, Nottinghamshire
2. Brewhouse Lane, Putney, London
3. Fenchurch, London
4. St Botolph's Church, Boston, Lincolnshire
5. Ipswich
6. Christ Church, Oxford
7. Westminster Hall, London
8. York Place, London
9. Hampton Court Palace, Surrey
10. Austin Friars, London
11. Rolls House, London
12. Mortlake, Greater London
13. Stepney, London
14. Ewhurst, Surrey
15. Tower of London, London

Chapter 80: Book Review

Cromwell was frequently referred to in contemporary correspondence and also makes an appearance in Cavendish's *'Life of Wolsey'* and Foxe's *'Acts and Monuments'*. A comprehensive study of his life and letters was undertaken by Merriman in 1901. He came to the fore again in G R Elton's reappraisal of the Tudor period in the 1950s. Current biographies are by Hutchinson (2006), Borman (2014) and Everett (2015). We have reviewed Everett's biography here.

The Rise of Thomas Cromwell

Author: Michael Everett

Publisher: Yale University Press

In a nutshell A truly comprehensive study of Cromwell's early career, both before and after he joined the King's Privy Council. Ideal for anyone who wants to see a biography built up from the details of daily activities.

When I saw that a new biography had been published of Cromwell, I couldn't help a groan – I had already immersed myself in several other works for our Person of the Month feature, and I did not want to read the same facts again, in a different format. However, I could not have been more wrong, this book is well worth reading – no matter what you have read on Cromwell, you will find something new here.

Everett has taken a completely new approach, and concentrates on Cromwell's practical life as a solicitor, conveyancer, surveyor and receiver of rents, first for Wolsey, then for Henry VIII. The basis of Everett's thesis, is that Cromwell didn't make an instant leap from nobody to Henry's right hand man. His position was built up by proving his capabilities in financial and administrative matters related to Crown revenues and building works, before he began to be involved in political affairs. He did not, as is sometimes claimed, start out with the ambition of replacing Wolsey as the King's chief minister, rather, his efficiency and dispatch in business made his rise inevitable in a court where the King and the other senior councillors tended to delegate.

Everett is an absolute stickler for proof, nothing that is not documented is asserted, although different perspectives are discussed.

The book makes two points that are well worth considering – first, Everett draws our attention to the risk of assuming that Cromwell's role was greater than anyone else's, just because of the mass of documentation that has survived. Cromwell's papers were seized on his downfall and became part of the Crown archive, and because they are so voluminous, they are relied on extensively. Would a different picture emerge if a similar hoard of papers were discovered, relating to another minister or courtier?

The second point, which emerges from the details that Everett has so painstakingly drawn together, is that Cromwell acted in concert with others, particularly in the early days as a Privy Councillor and he also shows that Cromwell, although influential with the King, certainly did not get everything he wanted. Henry distributed patronage to reflect his own needs – he would listen to Cromwell, but he listened to others, too.

Everett's style is clear and matter-of-fact. He has obviously spent a huge amount of time and care on collating original sources and reviewing accepted datings of letters and documents. There are no flights of fancy, or attempts to understand people's inner motivations where there is no evidence – as he says, amongst all of the papers, there is almost nothing relating to Cromwell's personal life. The sheer quantity of detail means the book drags a little in the middle, but this is an academic study, not a work of popular history, so perhaps some tedium is inevitable.

Although the book is very factual, what I derived from it will influence how I read other biographies in future. Everett demonstrates, although he does not actually articulate the argument, that we have a tendency to read earlier events in the light of later happenings. Thus, because Cromwell became all-powerful earlier biographers infer that he set out with this ambition in mind. Everett avoids this trap by writing forward, rather than with hindsight, giving a much more realistic picture of how life unfolds for most of us – being in the right place at the right time is worth any number of plans.

Next time I read any biography, I will try to erase from my mind any knowledge of the future that will lead to misinterpretation of the present.

Disappointingly, Everett stops in 1534, before the exciting events of the downfall of Anne Boleyn, the Dissolution of the Monasteries, the Pilgrimage of Grace and the Exeter Conspiracy. I sincerely hope he brings out a second volume to cover Cromwell's involvement in these momentous events.

Part 7: Lady Penelope Devereux: Sir Philip Sidney's Muse

Introduction

Penelope Devereux was one of the leading lights of the late Elizabethan and early Stuart courts. Her beauty and charm, coupled with her intelligence and education, led her to be the centre of the circle of soldiers and patrons of art around her brother, the Earl of Essex. Like Essex, however, she was impetuous and single-minded and could not resist flirting with intrigue and danger.

Penelope led the life of a great lady, travelling extensively between the homes of both her family of origin and her those of her husband, as well as attending court in and around London.

In an age when even aristocratic women, once they were married, tended to be confined to hearth and home, Penelope led a life of excitement and novelty. Far from the docile, submissive wife that was the Elizabethan ideal, Penelope was a force to be reckoned with.

Part 7 contains Lady Penelope Devereux's Life Story and additional articles about her, looking at different aspects of her life.

Family Tree

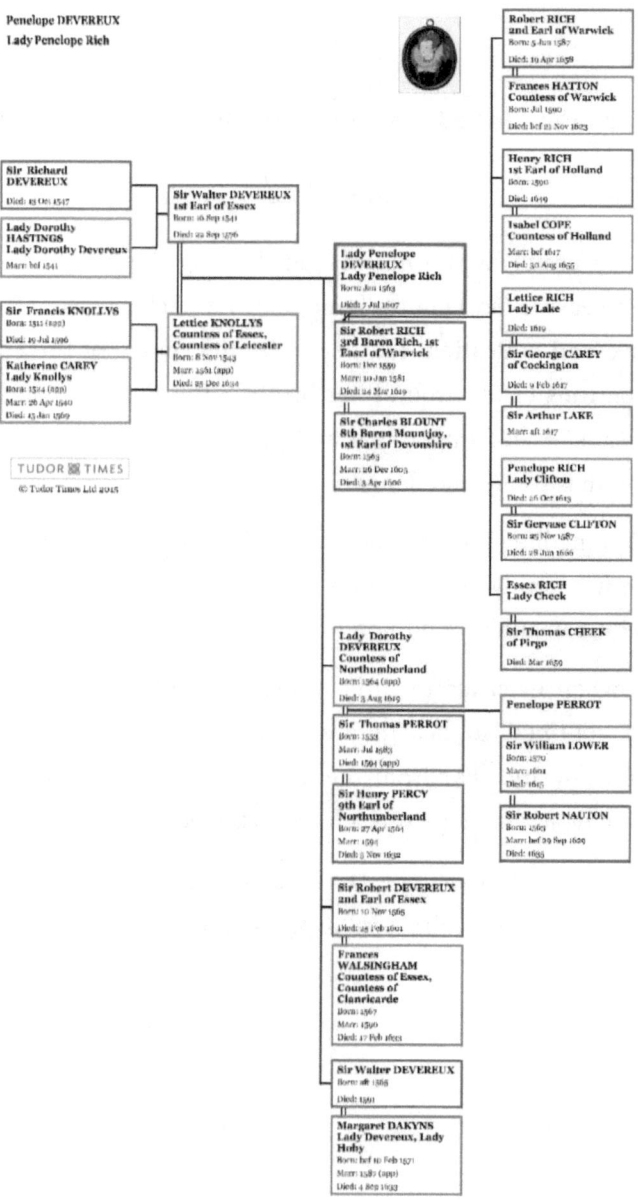

Lady Penelope Devereux' Life Story

Chapter 81: Childhood & Youth (1563 – 1581)

Lady Penelope Devereux was born into a family high in the favour of Elizabeth I. Her mother's family were blood relatives of the Queen: her grandmother, Katherine Carey, being the daughter of Mary Boleyn, Elizabeth's aunt. Katherine was a great favourite with the Queen all her life, and her husband, Sir Francis Knollys, was one of Elizabeth's chief ministers until his death in 1596. The Knollys' daughter, Lettice, had been a maid-of-honour to the Queen until marrying Penelope's father, Walter Devereux, Viscount Hereford in around 1561.

Penelope's paternal family, the Devereux, although not so closely related to the Queen as the Knollys, were, like most members of the aristocracy descended from Edward III and Penelope's grandfather and great-grandfather had received favour from Henry VIII. Both the Knollys and the Devereux families had embraced the Reformation with vigour.

Penelope spent her early childhood at Chartley Manor in Staffordshire, eldest of a family of four (a fifth child died young). Her surviving siblings were Robert, Walter and Dorothy. In the fashion of the time, Penelope and Dorothy received a thorough education, of a level that in earlier, and later, times, would have been confined to the sons of the family. Penelope's tutor was Mathias Homes, a Cambridge man of strong Protestant views. She studied French, Spanish and Italian, as well as the courtly accomplishments of dancing, singing and playing the lute.

Penelope's father was zealous in the service of the Queen, being one of Mary, Queen of Scots' custodians, and instrumental in the suppression of the Rebellion of the Northern Earls in 1569. In recognition of his merits, he was granted the Earldom of Essex in 1572. The following year, Elizabeth gave Essex a licence to colonise Ulster in Ireland, controlled by the O'Neills and the Scots. The venture was undertaken at his own cost, and was a disaster, militarily, financially and personally. He returned to England in 1575, with a view to rebuilding his fortunes at home, but in September of that year was created Earl Marshal of Ireland a post necessitating a return to Ireland. He arrived in Dublin in September 1576, but died within a few weeks, of dysentery.

Her father's will left dowries of £2,000 each for Penelope and Dorothy, but the disastrous Irish expedition had left his estates impoverished, and payment of these dowries would be a serious burden on the inheritance of his son, Robert, now the 2nd Earl. In regard to Penelope's marriage, the Earl had expressed a wish for her to marry Philip Sidney, the nephew of Robert Dudley, Earl of Leicester, Queen Elizabeth's favourite. Philip had been with Essex in Ireland and Essex had conceived a great affection for the younger man. There was no formal agreement prior to Essex' death, and Sidney's father, Sir Henry Sidney was not in favour of the match. Sir Henry, who was Lord Deputy of Ireland, had disagreed with Essex' policies there, and disliked him personally. This, coupled with the fact that Penelope was not yet of marriageable age, meant the match went into abeyance.

With their father dead, the wardship of the Devereux children was now at the Queen's disposal. Essex had expressed a wish for his heir, Robert, to be placed in the guardianship of Sir William Cecil, Lord Burghley, whilst Penelope was to be put in the care of Essex' cousin, Henry Hastings, 3rd Earl of Huntingdon and his wife, Katherine Dudley. Such arrangements were perfectly usual, and in no way expressed a distrust of his wife, Lettice.

Although Huntingdon had a respectable claim to the throne as the great-grandson of Margaret Plantagenet, Countess of Salisbury, and the grandson of Henry Pole, Baron Montague, who had been executed in the Exeter Conspiracy, Elizabeth I trusted him, and he was her Lord Lieutenant of the North. Penelope's home was now the King's Manor at York.

Lady Huntingdon was not only the sister of the powerful Robert Dudley, Earl of Leicester, but also the aunt of Penelope's intended bridegroom, Philip Sidney. Although she had no children of her own, Lady Huntingdon was renowned for her management and upbringing of young gentlewomen. Both the Earl and Countess were committed Puritans, and the household lived under a rather stringent regime of daily prayers, Bible readings and sermons, which Penelope's later career suggests she may have found rather onerous.

Not long after Penelope left for York, her mother, Lettice, married the Earl of Leicester. When Queen Elizabeth discovered the marriage, she was furious, and Lettice was banned from court for the rest of her life. Nevertheless, Elizabeth was not inclined to blame Lettice's children for her misdemeanours, and Lady Huntingdon brought Penelope to court, presenting her at Whitehall on 30th January 1581.

Chapter 82: Court & Marriage (1581 – 1590)

During 1581, Penelope was in close attendance on the Queen. It was a period of extravagant display, as Elizabeth, for the last time, entertained thoughts of marriage, on this occasion with the French Prince, the Duc d'Alencon. There were masques and jousts to attend, and even the celebrations surrounding the return of Francis Drake from his circumnavigation of the globe. The whole court attended at Deptford when Elizabeth knighted him. However, as Penelope was now eighteen, and was not formally appointed to the role of maid-of-honour to the Queen, the time had come for her marriage to be arranged.

Philip Sidney was struck off the list by her guardian. From having been the heir to both his uncles (the Earls of Warwick and Leicester), he had now been supplanted by Penelope's new half-brother, Robert Dudley, Lord Denbigh. Sidney was therefore not a particularly good prospect for the daughter of an Earl, and Penelope's dowry was somewhat in doubt.

Instead, Huntingdon proposed a marriage with Robert, 3rd Baron Rich, a major landholder in Essex, and of a similar age to Penelope. Rich, as a second son, had inherited unexpectedly. Not anticipating that he would become a Baron, he had entered the House of Commons representing Essex on 2nd February, 1581, then inherited the Barony (which debarred him from the Commons) on 27th February the same year. Lord Rich would have appealed to Huntingdon as he was a radical Puritan, supporting Calvinist preachers, and later, running into disputes with the conservative John Aylmer, Bishop of London.

Penelope and Lord Rich were married in the autumn of 1581. There was trouble over her dowry, as the Essex estates were still in dire financial straits. Her grandfather, Sir Francis Knollys, assisted to the tune of £500. It was later claimed that Penelope had protested against her marriage, and that Rich was a harsh husband, but, since the source was her second husband, it may be prejudiced. It is certainly the case that Lord Rich was less well-educated than his wife, so perhaps they did not have a great deal in common. Nevertheless, personal compatibility, although desirable, was not the primary motive for a marriage and it seems unlikely that Penelope would have expected to marry for love.

Whatever Penelope's thoughts as a young bride, she was able to continue her life at court in the immediate aftermath of her wedding.

She appears to have taken the court by storm. Her looks, charm and grace were praised both then, and for the rest of her life. She seems to have had a beauty and charisma that did not fade with age or repeated childbearing. Her most famous conquest was none other than the Philip Sidney her father had intended her to marry. She was the inspiration for his sonnet cycle *'Astrophil and Stella'*. Whether the relationship ever became more than one of courtly sighing and hand-kissing cannot be known for certain, but there is no evidence for anything more.

Penelope spent the next few years between the Rich's London home at St Bartholomew's and their estates in Essex, primarily at Leez Priory. She maintained a copious correspondence with her mother and her siblings, being particularly close to her brother, Robert, 2nd Earl of Essex, naming her second daughter after him – Essex Rich.

Chapter 83: War & Intrigue (1585 – 1595)

Penelope's brother, the young Earl of Essex was growing in favour with the Queen, promoted by his step-father, Leicester. In 1585, Elizabeth, after years of importuning by the Puritan party at court, finally agreed to aid the Protestant Netherlands against the Catholic Philip of Spain, who was the hereditary ruler. Leicester led an army onto Flanders, and Essex and Philip Sidney accompanied him. Initially, Leicester had asked for Penelope's husband, Lord Rich, to take part, *'though he be no man of war'* but in the event, Leicester changed his plans and Rich remained at home.

Sidney died at Zutphen, and became the stuff of legend. Essex, to whom he bequeathed his sword, married his widow, and attempted to emulate Sidney's glory. We cannot know whether Penelope felt anything stronger on the death of Sidney than the general outpouring of grief that accompanied his passing. The tale that, on his death bed, he confessed to adultery with her, has been shown to have no contemporary basis.

Following his return from the Netherlands, Essex rose rapidly in Elizabeth's favour, taking on Leicester's role as Master of the Horse, and spending long hours with the queen, gambling, playing cards, dancing, and, ominously, quarrelling vociferously with her.

The war in the Netherlands rumbled on, and Spain sought revenge for Elizabeth's interference. Rumours grew of a huge armada to be sent against England. Lord Rich was responsible for the militia in Essex, whilst Leicester and Essex were with the Queen at Tilbury. Penelope was probably either at Leez or with her mother at the Leicesters' home at Wanstead.

The strain of the Armada campaign was too much for Leicester, and to the great grief of his wife, and Penelope, as well as the Queen, he died shortly after. Lord Rich attended the funeral, as did Sir Christopher Blount who had been Master of the Horse to Leicester, and within the year was to comfort the grieving widow. He and Lettice were married in early 1589, giving Penelope a second step-father, who was also a close friend of her brother.

In October 1589, Penelope, Lord Rich and Essex entered into a correspondence that was at best foolish, and at worst, treason. They wrote to King James VI of Scotland, pledging their support for his succession to the English crown, which, they hinted, could not be long in coming. Penelope, who had the code name '*Rialta*', even sent him a miniature of herself. King James seems to have been rather circumspect in his responses. He knew he was Elizabeth's preferred successor, and was too wily a hand to risk annoying her (and losing the pension she paid him) by trying to step into her shoes before time.

Penelope's reasons for embroiling herself in such a risky undertaking can only be guessed at. Her biographer, Sally Varlow, suggests her actions were justified, as Elizabeth's failure to promote Essex to a prime place in government, together with Elizabeth's continued harshness towards Lettice, were symptoms of a corrupt government that did not deserve their long-term loyalty. A less partisan view might be that Penelope and Essex, for all their intellectual brilliance were politically naïve, and were demonstrating the factionalism that was to dog the last decade and a half of Elizabeth's reign. Although Elizabeth was deeply attached to Essex, she did not rate his political skills particularly highly, and, taking the long view of her reign, she seems to have been an excellent judge of character.

At some time during the early 1590s Penelope began an affair with Sir Charles Blount, a friend of Essex (and distant relative of her step-father). Blount was a military man who had seen action in the Netherlands and in the Armada engagement. On his first coming to Court, Essex had seen him as a rival for royal favour, and had insulted him, provoking a duel. Blount won a swift victory, wounding his opponent in the thigh, and the two became fast friends. In the early days of Blount's affair with Penelope, they kept the relationship quiet, but she bore him at least three children, possibly five, all of whom were accepted by Lord Rich as his own, although he cannot have been in much doubt about their paternity. Penelope even named her son Mountjoy, the title Blount inherited in 1594. Given that Rich was protecting her from public shame by accepting her children, this seems a rather tasteless choice.

Chapter 84: The Jesuit Mission (1594)

Any biography of Robert Devereux, Earl of Essex characterises him as rash, impetuous, a risk-taker and of poor judgement. It would seem that Penelope had some of the same characteristics. Not content with a potentially treasonable correspondence with the King of Scots, and an affair that was obvious to anyone who knew her, Penelope was also involved in the far more serious business of harbouring a Catholic priest.

By the 1590s, it was treason for any Englishman to be ordained as a priest in the Roman Catholic Church or for any Jesuit or priest ordained after the Queen's accession, to be in England. It was a crime to hear the Catholic mass, and it was a crime to harbour or give succour to any priest.

The Government was at pains to explain that persecution was not for the matter of being Catholic, but for the political dimensions of support for Spanish invasion and undermining of the Queen's legitimate rule. Persons caught harbouring a priest would be subject to fines, confiscations, imprisonment, and potentially, for repeated offences, death.

Despite this, Penelope hid Father John Gerard, one of the most important men in the Catholic hierarchy in England, in her own house at Leez. Gerard had been staying with the Wiseman family at Braddocks Manor, near Thaxted. The Wisemans were connections of Lord Rich, and despite their very different religious beliefs, Penelope was godmother to one of the Wiseman children. Mrs Wiseman, after one of the raids on her house, spent time with Penelope at Leez, and arranged for her to receive Gerard. He came to Leez in the early spring of 1594, in the guise of a visiting friend.

According to his later account, Penelope was close to conversion, but wanted to consult Mountjoy. Mountjoy, a man of intellect and education, prepared questions for Father Gerard, with the assurance that if they could be answered satisfactorily, he, too, would convert. Whether the answers were unconvincing, or the risk was too high, Mountjoy, and hence Penelope, remained unreconciled to Rome but she seems to have remained sympathetic to the Catholic cause, a position which, later, endeared her to Queen Anne of Denmark.

At this distance, we cannot know whether Penelope's interest was religiously motivated, whether she was a natural risk-taker and wanted to provoke her husband and family, who were largely on the Puritan end of Protestantism, or whether she was taking up a chic cause. It certainly appears that the young and fashionable court circles of the 1590s flirted with Catholicism, perhaps as a natural reaction to the control that Burghley, Walsingham, Knollys and the rest of the staunchly Protestant old guard exerted. It may be that she was naturally compassionate and sought to save Gerard from the dreadful death he would have suffered had he been caught by the authorities. (He was later caught, imprisoned, tortured, and escaped.)

Chapter 85: Penelope & Essex (1590 – 1600)

Penelope's relationship with her brother was always close. During the 1590s, as she spent less time at Leez, and pursued her relationship with Mountjoy, she took on a role as Essex' chief supporter, friend and hostess. Her sister-in-law, Frances Walsingham, who had previously been married to Sir Philip Sidney, seems to have happily taken a more retired position. Frances was regularly pregnant, but suffered several miscarriages and infant deaths, as well as having to tolerate a husband who was a notorious philanderer.

In 1593, Essex became one of Elizabeth's Privy Councillors, yet he was not satisfied. He wished to supplant the Cecils in Elizabeth's favour, and, aided by Penelope, spent much time and money building up an information network (or spy-ring, depending on your point of view) across England, France and Spain. He too, despite the strongly

Protestant background from which he and Penelope came, was flirting with the many disaffected Catholics who had been given new courage by the Jesuit mission.

During the 1590s both Essex and Mountjoy were involved in military campaigns. Finally, in 1599, Essex took command of the campaign in Ireland, which proved as disastrous for him as it had for his father. He disobeyed direct commands from the Queen, and wasted money and men. He returned to England, in contravention of orders, and was questioned by the Privy Council in a five-hour session, that concluded that he had deserted his post, and made a dishonourable truce with O'Neill leader of the Irish rebels (as the English government characterised them).

Essex was committed to house arrest at one of his London homes, York House. Whilst he was confined there, he suffered some illness, perhaps a fever caught on campaign, or perhaps stress-induced. Both Penelope and her sister, Dorothy, now Countess of Northumberland (after a secret first marriage that had brought down the wrath of the Queen), received permission to wait upon the Queen to beg permission for him to move to somewhere with *'better air'* and to be allowed to see him. Making a show of mourning by dressing in black from head to foot, they went to Richmond. The Queen received them kindly, but she would not budge. Penelope continued to plead, sending letters, presents and jewels to the Queen, which the Queen accepted, without changing her mind.

Eventually, one of Penelope's letters went too far. Her enthusiasm for her brother's cause, and her conviction that the Cecils were up to no good, was read as a hint that rebellion was in the air, and she was summoned before the Lord Treasurer, Sir Thomas Sackville, later Earl of Dorset, to explain her actions. She hastily followed up with another letter to the Queen, protesting loyalty. Not long after, she was accused of having allowed copies of the earlier, suspect, letter, to be distributed and was summoned again to the Privy Council. Taken ill, either really, or politically, she was excused attendance, and retired to the country. Her distress was probably added to by the dispatch of Mountjoy to Ireland to replace Essex. Penelope was again interrogated about her offending letter, but the Queen, at length, forgave her, whilst complaining that she *'showed a proud disposition'* and had been very negligent in allowing her correspondence to be circulated.

At last, it appeared that the Queen would forgive Essex too and he was released from house arrest in August 1600. But this was not a complete restoration - Elizabeth refused to renew his main source of income, the monopoly on sweet wines, which had been granted in 1589.

Financially ruined, and increasingly paranoid, Essex fortified Essex House, with his wife, Frances, and Penelope in support. After taking several Privy Councillors hostage, Essex, together with his chief supporters, the Earl of Southampton and Penelope's step-father, Sir Christopher Blount, rode through the streets of London, trying to gain followers to overthrow the Cecils, whom he continued to blame for his disfavour with the Queen. The Londoners were underwhelmed and Essex retreated to his house, sending Penelope and Frances away.

Essex was captured and sent to the Tower and Penelope was placed under house arrest with Sir Henry Sackford. Following his trial (in which Lord Rich was one of the judges), Essex was adjudged guilty. Afterwards, he requested that members of the Council be sent to the Tower to hear the *'truth'*. This consisted of denouncing both Mountjoy and Penelope whom, he claimed, had pushed him into treason:

'I must accuse one who is most nearest to me, my sister who did continually urge me on...'

He added that *'she must be looked to, for she hath a proud spirit.'*

This disloyalty must have been an agonising blow to Penelope who herself remained under house arrest, and was questioned by the Privy Council. During her interrogation she pointed out that, far from being the instigator of Essex' treason, she had:

> 'been more like a slave than a sister, which proceeded out of my exceeding love, rather than his authority'

Essex was executed on 25th February 1601, together with Sir Christopher Blount, Penelope's step-father. Eventually released, Penelope herself was sent home to her husband. Meanwhile, Mountjoy had been running the most successful campaign in Ireland of the whole Tudor era, whilst secretly corresponding with King James.

Chapter 86: Court Favourite (1603 – 1605)

The covert correspondence with James VI of Scotland at last paid off. When Elizabeth finally died on 24th March 1603, Penelope was chosen by the new king to travel to Berwick to accompany his wife, Anne of Denmark, south to her new kingdom. Penelope was some eleven years older than the new Queen, but they formed a very warm relationship and she was appointed as one of the Queen's most senior attendants. In a sign that the Devereux were now back in favour, James permitted the late Earl's three children to be restored in blood, and receive their father's estates.

Penelope was so high in favour with both King and Queen, that, on 17th August 1603, at a ceremony at Farnham Castle, she was given the rank of the Earldom of Essex, in the seniority it had had under the Bourchier earls. This elevation gave her rank above all the baronesses, and most of the Earls' daughters. Penelope's great-great grandmother, Cecily Bourchier, had been the grand-daughter of the 1st Earl of Essex.

Over the next three years, Penelope became one of the leading lights in the Jacobean court, taking part in the elaborate masques and entertainments that Queen Anne patronised.

Mountjoy, having brought the Irish war to a successful conclusion (from the English perspective), returned to London in 1603, and received the title of Earl of Devonshire from James I as well as being appointed as a Privy Councillor. He and Penelope now lived together openly.

In 1605, Lord Rich sought a divorce from the Church Commissioners. Whether he chose to instigate proceedings because the open co-habitation of Penelope and Mountjoy was a step too far, or whether Penelope requested the divorce, which is the contention of her biographer, Sally Varlow, is unknown.

The divorce was granted on 14th November 1605, on the grounds of Lady Rich's adultery with a man whom she refused to name in court. Archbishop Bancroft, pronouncing the sentence even went so far as to condemn Lord Rich for his hardness to his wife, and made derogatory remarks about Rich's Puritan leanings.

As the marriage had been legal, and produced off-spring, the divorce was *'from bed and board'*, rather than an annulment, which would have required an Act of Parliament. The Church of England, whilst permitting divorce, did not allow remarriage during the life-time of the other partner (a position that remained unchanged until 2002) and both Penelope and Lord Rich were ordered to live celibate lives.

Penelope and Devonshire immediately flouted the Church's rules and went through a marriage ceremony conducted by Devonshire's chaplain, William Laud, (later Archbishop of Canterbury) on 26th December 1605. This action called down a storm of anger and retribution on their heads.

King James, angered that they had defied the law, banished Penelope from court, telling Devonshire he had won '*a fair woman with a black soul.*' Devonshire now wrote to James, explaining why he believed the marriage to be legal. One of his arguments was that Penelope had not freely consented to her marriage to Rich. Free consent was a fundamental requirement for valid matrimony. James remained unconvinced and Penelope remained banished.

In the Spring of 1606, Devonshire, as a Privy Councillor, was obliged to attend the trials of the Gunpowder Plotters, many of whom were members of Penelope's extended family. In particular, her sister's husband, the Earl of Northumberland, was a prime suspect, despite all of the other plotters denying he was involved. At the end of March, Devonshire failed to make an appearance at the trial of the Jesuit, Father Garnet. His health was had been ruined by his campaigning, and he had been taken ill at Wanstead.

Penelope, pregnant again, raced to join him, and he spent his last days trying to protect the inheritance of their children. He died on 3rd April 1607, aged forty-three, with Penelope at his side. The shock and grief caused Penelope to miscarry.

Devonshire's record of service in Ireland was not forgotten, and he was given a ceremonious funeral at Westminster Abbey, followed to his grave by the Earl of Southampton (who had narrowly escaped execution with Essex), Suffolk and Nottingham. In a clear sign that his marriage to Penelope was not recognised, her arms were not shown quartered with his, as was customary for a wife.

Prior to their marriage, Devonshire had created complex legal and financial arrangements that would enable his children by Penelope to inherit his estates. The desire for a legal heir, which was so central to sixteenth century thought, may well have been a motivating factor in their speedy marriage.

As Devonshire had anticipated, his Will and property settlements were hotly contested. Various members of the Blount family, who saw an opportunity for taking control of Devonshire's vast estate, suggested that he had been unduly influenced; that he was not of sound mind; and that he regretted his relationship with Penelope.

Probate was granted in the Canterbury Court, then appealed, then confirmed again. Eventually, a charge of fraud was brought against Penelope in the Star Chamber (the Privy Council and senior judges in session). She was described as *'an harlot, adulteress, concubine and whore'*.

Before the matter was settled, Penelope died on 6th July 1607. The location is unknown, but it was probably Essex House. Conflicting stories circulated – one that she had regretted her liaison with Devonshire, and wished to be reconciled to Lord Rich, dying firmly in the Protestant religion she had been brought up in. Father Gerard, however, claimed that, at the last, she converted to the Catholic faith.

*

Penelope was later described by Archbishop Laud as *'A lady in whom lodged all attractive graces of beauty, wit and sweetness of behaviour'* and it is very apparent that she was able to charm both men and women, being beloved by her family, friends and servants. Nevertheless, it is hard to escape from the conclusion that she was also rash and spoilt, unable to perceive that there might be other priorities than the advancement of her family, or the indulgence of her desires.

Aspects of Lady Penelope Devereux' Life

Chapter 87: Poetry & Patronage

Elizabeth I's court was the centre of a great flowering of literature, music and drama with the Queen herself being an accomplished musician and a fair hand at writing verse. The courtiers with whom she surrounded herself were expected to be able to provide intellectual amusement and stimulation, not just administrative or military prowess. This emphasis on culture led to the patronage by leading courtiers of painters, poets, playwrights and actors.

This patronage was similar to that already extended by higher members of society to their lower-ranking '*clients*' and might take the form of money, advancement to posts in the patron's gift, help in legal matters, or support for advantageous marriages. In return, the artist (usually, but not always, men) would dedicate his work to the patron. The higher ranking your patron was, the better chance you had of selling your work and being recognised, so artists were always seeking recognition from the elite.

When Penelope Devereux came to court in the 1580s, other courtiers who were at the centre of the cultural life of the court included Mary Sidney, Countess of Pembroke, and her brother, Sir Philip Sidney, whom Penelope's father, the Earl of Essex had wished her to marry. Essex described Sidney as

'so wise, so virtuous, so goodly; and if he go on in the course that he hath begun, he will be as famous and worthy a gentleman as ever England bred' and expressed the hope that 'if God do move both their hearts ... he might match with my daughter [Penelope].'

The Sidney siblings (who were also niece and nephew to Penelope's step-father, the Earl of Leicester) were two of the most talented members of the court. The Countess gave patronage to the poets Michael Drayton, Ben Jonson, Edmund Spenser and many others, as well as writing and translating herself, and completing works unfinished at Philip's death.

Both Philip Sidney and the Countess were dedicatees of literary works, he receiving some forty dedications, and she a few less. In fact, the Countess of Pembroke received the second highest number of dedications to a non-royal woman of the whole Elizabethan and Jacobean era, preceded only by Lucy Russell (nee Harington), Countess of Bedford.

By 1581. when Penelope appeared at court, Philip, then aged 27, had already produced *'The Lady of May'* dedicated to the Queen, and the first version of *Arcadia* – a 180,000 word romance he referred to as a *'trifle'* – and he was now about to embark on a sonnet cycle which took Penelope Devereux as its heroine.

Whether he was actually in love with her, or whether she seemed a suitable subject – she was fair-haired, dark eyed, and beautiful – is unsure. It seems unlikely that he would compose sonnets featuring someone to whom he was completely indifferent, but, of course, admiring a court beauty who was married to another man is not the same as being in love.

The cycle of sonnets, 108 in number, was entitled *'Astrophil and Stella'*. The poet tells of his attraction to the lady, who is, of course, unattainable, and his struggles to overcome it, before dedicating himself to public service. The work was not initially printed, but circulated in manuscript form until published in 1591, after Sidney's death.

Penelope has been recognised as the heroine from the frequent use of the word *'rich'*, her married name, and juxtapositions of the word implying her husband, Lord Rich (who was, as it happened, extremely wealthy) did not deserve her:

But that rich fool who by blind Fortune's lot

The richest gem of love and life enjoys,

And can with foul abuse such beauties blot;

Let him, depriv'd of sweet but unfelt joys,

(Exil'd for aye from those high treasures, which

He knows not) grow in only folly rich.

From Sonnet 24 – Astrophil and Stella – Sir Philip Sidney

There is no record of Penelope's reaction to the sonnets – but it is hard to imagine that any woman of nineteen would be less than charmed and flattered by being the focus of a man who was much admired at court. Her feelings for Sidney are unknown – the convention of the sonnet cycle is that she should disdain his love. There is certainly no evidence that she had any illicit relationship with him.

As well as being Sidney's muse, Penelope inspired or was the dedicatee of other works. It is argued in *'Sir Philip Sidney and the Circulation of Manuscripts, 1558-1640'* by H R Woudhysen that she was the inspiration for several of the secular songs written by the famous Elizabethan composer, William Byrd. More certainly, Edward Paston dedicated his translation of *'Diana'* by the Spanish writer, Montemayor, to her and the lutenist Charles Tessier set several of the Astrophil sonnets to music.

Penelope's interest and involvement in culture continued, and she was closely associated with the extravagant patronage extended by Queen Anne of Denmark in the early 1600s.

Chapter 88: Queen Anne's Masques

Anne of Denmark became Queen of Scots in 1589; and Queen of England when her husband succeeded Elizabeth in March 1603. As Anne was pregnant at the time of James' accession to the English throne, she did not immediately accompany him south, instead, remaining in Scotland with a view to travelling when she was delivered. Sadly, the pregnancy ended in a miscarriage in May 1603. Soon after, she set out for her new kingdom.

James had arranged for a number of great ladies of the English court to meet the Queen, one of whom was Penelope Devereux, Lady Rich, who had been in secret contact with James since the 1580s.

Anne appears to have taken an immediate liking to Lady Rich, although she was some eleven years older than the 29 year old Queen. Anne also became intimate with the younger Lucy, Countess of Bedford, whom she selected as her chief Lady of the Bedchamber. Lady Bedford and Penelope were well acquainted, as Lucy and her husband had been intimates of Essex, and Lord Bedford had been involved in the rebellion of 1600.

Penelope, too was appointed to the Queen's service.

Queen Anne, like Penelope and Lady Bedford, was an avid patron of poetry and theatrical works. The Queen commissioned works, and all three ladies were dedicatees of poetry and prose. In particular, Anne was a patron of the masque – a stylised hybrid of play, ballet, musical interlude and poetry.

The playwright, Ben Jonson, wrote his first work for the Queen in June 1603, when he penned a welcome for her and Prince Henry, to be recited at the arrival at Sir Robert Spencer's home at Althorp, Northamptonshire (Sir Robert was an ancestor of the late Diana, Princess of Wales).

Thereafter, with the exception of 1604, Jonson wrote all of the Christmas masques for the court, and worked closely with the architect, Inigo Jones, as set designer.

The budget for clothes, for dancing masters, for instruments and musicians was enormous. The first two masques – *The Twelve Goddesses*' of 1604 and the *'Masque of Blackness'* of 1605 cost some £2,000 each. The scenery was complex and elaborate.

Whilst the singing and recitation were generally performed by professional actors, the dancing was undertaken by members of the Court, from the Queen downward. To be asked to take part was a great honour, as the standard of dancing and acting was high – these were not family Christmas games, with everyone laughing if a player tripped or stood on his partner's toe. The masques were intended to demonstrate the wealth and power of the two crowns of England and Scotland. Observers from foreign courts were impressed by the extravagance of the spectacles the Queen arranged

'*in everyone's opinion no other Court could have displayed such pomp and riches*' reported the Venetian Ambassador about the Christmas masque of 1604.

The evening usually opened with the '*antemasque*' which was intended to look like an amateur romp, with bawdy dancing and low humour – perhaps rather in the style of the play in '*A Midsummer Night's Dream*'. Then the masque proper would begin, with formal dancing, created from intricate choreography which had been practised for weeks, accompanied by viols or lutes. Finally, the masque participants would dance familiar court dances, such as the galliard, with members of the audience.

Penelope Devereux took part in at least two masques, the first being *'The Vision of the Twelve Goddesses'*, by Samuel Daniel produced for Christmas 1603. It was performed on Sunday, 8th January, 1604, at Hampton Court.

The masque opened with Night requesting her son Somnus to send a dream to the courtiers. They were to see a Temple of Peace with the priestess, Sybil. Iris, the god's messenger, then appeared to Sybil, telling her that twelve goddesses were about to appear. The ladies came in threes, preceded by the Three Graces. The first wave of goddesses was Queen Anne as Pallas, the Countess of Suffolk as Juno, and Penelope as Venus.

The goddesses danced *'with majestie and arte'*, forming squares, triangles and circles. They then selected gentlemen from the audience to dance with, before retiring back to the heavens.

The second masque in which Penelope took part was the *'Masque of Blackness'*, commissioned by Queen Anne for Twelfth Night 1605. Her instruction to Ben Jonson, was that she wished her ladies and herself to be disguised as 'blackamoors'. Their costumes were of blue, silver and pearl, and they were made up with black face-paint.

The scene opens with the Queen and her ladies sitting in a sea-shell, representing the water goddesses who are the daughters of the god Niger, and grand-daughters of Oceanus. Oceanus and Niger discuss the fact that the goddesses, who are supremely beautiful, have been upset to learn that the northern poets prefer fair-skinned beauties.

Niger has tried to reassure them, pointing out (with a level of cultural sensitivity that perhaps may surprise us) that they are perfect as they are, and should not seek to bind themselves to European ideas of beauty. Nevertheless, the water-goddesses resolve to ask the moon-goddess Aethiopia for help. She recommends moving to less sunny climes, suggesting places ending in –atania. The water goddesses have tried moving to Acquitania, Lusitania and Mauretania, but to no avail. *(I think we can see where this is going...Ed.)*

At this point the water-goddesses dance in pairs.

Niger begs Aethiopia to help again, as his daughters have been such faithful worshippers. She appears and tells them to visit Britannia, where the wisdom of the sun-lit King represents such a light of Reason, that it will whiten even a black-skinned Aethiopian. The water-goddesses are to travel to Britannia, and the light of his countenance will transform them. More practically, they are to bathe once a month in sea-dew, and in a year, when they return, they will be white.

The water-goddesses then dance with the audience.

Penelope's role was Ocyte, the water-goddess representing swiftness, and her partner was Katherine Knyvett, the Countess of Suffolk, whose first husband had been Lord Rich's elder brother.

Penelope's inclusion in these extravagant events is a testament to her grace, skill in dance, and beauty, as well as to her warm relationship with the Queen.

Chapter 89: Following the Footsteps of Penelope Devereux

In common with the vast majority of women of the Tudor period, Lady Penelope Devereux never travelled abroad. She did, however, travel frequently and reasonably extensively within England and Wales.

The numbers in the article below correspond to those on the map which follows.

Penelope was born at Chartley Manor (1) in Staffordshire, a modern house built after the Battle of Bosworth. It was constructed in the grounds of the twelfth century Chartley Castle, which was considered old fashioned and uncomfortable. During the 1580s, when Chartley was owned by Penelope's brother, Mary, Queen of Scots was imprisoned there, but it is very unlikely that Penelope would ever have seen her. Today, the original manor house has disappeared, and what was formally the home farm is now called Chartley Manor Farm. Ruins of the castle remain.

Penelope's father, the Earl of Essex, was an extensive landowner in South Wales and the Marches, and it is probable that Penelope visited the Bishop's Palace at Llandyfai (Lamfey) in Pembrokeshire (2) where her father spent a good deal of his time, as did her brother, Robert, 2nd Earl of Essex, in the 1580s. Today, the Bishop's Palace is an impressive ruin, in the care of Cadw, the Welsh heritage body.

During her childhood, and later, Penelope would also have spent a good deal of time at Blithfield Hall (pronounced Blifield), Staffordshire (3), the home of the Bagot family, who acted as agents, factors and personal attendants to the Devereux. The Hall of the Penelope's day has been somewhat embellished, but remains in the hands of the Bagot family. It is not open to the public.

In the aftermath of her father's death, Penelope's mother, Lettice Knollys, took Penelope and her sister, Dorothy, to the houses of various different friends and relatives. One of the main locations where Penelope spent time then, and later, was Grey's Court, near Rotherfield Greys in Oxfordshire (8). Originally owned by the Grey family, it was granted to Robert Knollys in 1514, and completely remodelled by Penelope's grandfather, Sir Francis Knollys. He and his wife, Elizabeth I's cousin Katherine Carey, lived there when they were not at court. It is now in the hands of the National Trust.

Around a year after her father's death, Penelope became the ward of the Earl of Huntingdon, and travelled north to his home at King's Manor, York (4). Formerly the Abbot's House at the Abbey of St Mary, York, the property had been turned into a private residence at the dissolution of the Monasteries, some forty years previously. Today King's Manor is a conference centre.

In 1578, Penelope's mother married again. Her husband, Robert Dudley, Earl of Leicester, was Queen Elizabeth's most favoured friend and courtier, and possessed of extensive land and property. Penelope was close to her mother and step-father and, through the course of their marriage, spent considerable amounts of time at Leicester's various properties.

The principle property that denoted Leicester's wealth and status was the magnificent Kenilworth Castle (5), a few miles north of Warwick. It is unlikely that Penelope was at the extravagant entertainment that Leicester staged for Elizabeth at Kenilworth in 1575, but she would no doubt have heard about it.

The other properties Leicester owned were Wanstead House (6), that he had bought from Lord Rich, whom Penelope was to marry, and Leicester House (7), in the Strand. Both of these properties were to figure large in Penelope's life. She frequently visited Wanstead when it was her mother's home, and later, it is where she spent most of her short married life with the man she considered to be her second husband. After Leicester's death, Leicester House became the property of Penelope's brother, Robert Devereux, Earl of Essex, and, with great originality, was renamed Essex House. Penelope was at Essex House with her brother when he mounted his foolish attempted coup against the Cecils, which ended in disaster and execution. None of these houses remain.

When Penelope married for the first time in 1581, her principle homes were Leez (or Leighs) Priory, Essex (9) – now a rather sumptuous country house hotel - and a town house near St Bartholomew's in London (12). This had been part of the Priory of that name, but had been granted to Penelope's father-in-law, the notorious Sir Richard Rich whose perjury had condemned Sir Thomas More. No trace remains of this property. Lord and Lady Rich, as Penelope was now styled, also owned Rochford Hall, Essex (11), which was the main residence of her widowed mother-in-law, and coincidentally, had probably been the married home of her own great-grandmother, Mary Boleyn. Rochford Hall still stands, partially a golf club, with some residential properties.

Penelope also frequently visited the Walsingham home in Seething Lane, London (13). Sir Francis Walsingham's daughter, Frances, married Penelope's brother, the Earl of Essex, and the two women seem to have been friends, with Penelope visiting frequently, and acting as godmother to Frances' children.

After Leicester's death, Lettice married for a third time, but was again widowed when her husband, Sir Christopher Blount, lost his head alongside her son, the Earl of Essex. Following this double tragedy, she spent a good deal of time at Drayton Bassett (11) in Staffordshire, not far from Chartley, and Penelope visited her there regularly. Penelope however, although singing small after Essex' death for the rest of Elizabeth's reign, came into her full glory in 1603 with the accession of James VI of Scotland to the English throne.

Throughout the 1580s and 1590s the Devereux siblings had been maintaining covert links with James, and the effort now paid off. Penelope was sent to Berwick-upon-Tweed (14) to greet the new Queen, Anne of Denmark, as she crossed into her new kingdom. The Queen was charmed with Penelope, who became one of her ladies of the

Bedchamber, and returned to a full court life, living at Whitehall, Richmond, Hampton Court and the other royal palaces.

In 1603, at Farnham Castle (15), Penelope was raised to the rank of the earldom of Essex, despite being only the wife of a Baron. In the status conscious 1600s this was a significant mark of royal favour. In this case, however, pride came before a resounding fall. Penelope's illegal second marriage to her long-time lover, the Earl of Devonshire, horrified the King, and she was banished from Court.

She spent most of the short period of life left to her at Wanstead House, before dying in July 1607. Her places of death and burial are unknown, although both probably occurred within the environs of London.

Key to Map

1. Chartley Manor, Staffordshire
2. Bishop's Palace, Lamphey (Llandyfai), Pembroke
3. Blithfield, Staffordshire
4. King's Manor, York
5. Kenilworth Castle, Warwickshire
6. Wanstead House, Essex
7. Leicester (later Essex) House, The Strand, London
8. Greys Court, Rotherfield Greys, Oxfordshire
9. Leighs (Leez) Priory, Essex
10. Drayton Manor, Drayton Bassett, Staffordshire
11. Rochford Hall, Essex
12. St Bartholomew house, nr St Bartholomew-the-Great Church, London
13. Walsingham House, Seething Lane, London
14. Berwick-upon-Tweed
15. Farnham Castle, Surrey

Chapter 90: Book Review

Surprisingly, there are few biographies of Penelope – seen as a disgrace to her sex, she has been overlooked by writers for four hundred years. Sally Varlow's extremely detailed biography is the first modern work.

The Lady Penelope

Author: Sally Varlow

Publisher: Deutsch

In a nutshell: A wealth of facts, and very readable, but marred by its partisan perspective and fictional style.

There was a lot to like in this book. Prior to reading it, I knew very little about Lady Penelope Devereux, other than that she was the great-grand-daughter of Mary Boleyn; the step-daughter of Robert Dudley, Earl of Leicester, Elizabeth I's long-time favourite; and the sister of Robert Devereux, Earl of Essex, Elizabeth I's last favourite.

Now, thanks to Sally Varlow's painstaking accumulation of detail, and engaging style, the charm, wit and beauty that made Lady Penelope the muse, not just of Sir Philip Sidney, but of poets, musicians and playwrights, leaps from the page, as does her warmth and generosity towards her family and friends.

Varlow also considers the relationship between Lady Penelope and her first husband, Lord Rich, more temperately than is often done. She shows that, for the early years of their marriage at least, the two got along as well as most partners in arranged marriages, and she also gives a plausible explanation of Rich's ongoing willingness to turn a blind eye to Lady Penelope's relationship with Lord Mountjoy.

One of the most interesting aspects of late sixteenth century life that the book illustrates, is the fluid nature of religious allegiance. Lady Penelope's grandfather, father, guardian, step-father and husband were all strong adherents of the Protestant, even Puritan cause, yet she herself flirted with Catholicism, apparently almost converting under the eloquence of Father John Gerard.

Unfortunately, the very charisma that Lady Penelope exerted in her own time, seems to have unduly influenced the author, too. The book crosses the line between a positive interpretation of the subject, and an almost novelistic identification with her.

Whilst I prefer biographers to at least like their protagonist, this should not render them completely blind to their flaws, nor should it cloud their judgement on the subject's interaction with the wider world. The author seems to struggle to understand that Elizabeth I had a duty beyond pandering to the sense of entitlement that seems to have permeated Penelope and Essex's whole life. Just because Essex wanted to be her chief minister, and Penelope wanted it for him, does not mean that Elizabeth should have placed him in that role. Varlow, however, gives the impression that this failure on Elizabeth's part to promote Essex to the level of his own view of himself, was a reflection of the Queen's '*corrupt*' government.

One of Varlow's recurring theories, is that Elizabeth I favoured Lady Penelope, not just as the descendant of Elizabeth's aunt, Mary Boleyn, but because her grand-mother, Katherine, rather than being the daughter of Mary's husband, William Carey, was, in fact, the illegitimate daughter of Henry VIII. Whilst the evidence adduced by the author that Katherine Carey was Henry's daughter is certainly plausible, the argument is far from bearing from the *'almost-certain'* weight that she gives it. There is no evidence relating to the length of Henry VIII and Mary Boleyn's relationship – it may have gone on for several years, as Varlow contends. Equally, it might have been a brief fling. Further, to claim that Mary Boleyn would not have slept with her husband because she was having an affair with the King, cannot be more than speculation.

Overall, the book was enjoyable and informative, giving an interesting insight into the factional politics of the late Elizabethan age but, in my view, it would probably have been better as a novel.

Part 8: James V: Scotland's Renaissance King

Introduction

James V became king aged only eighteen months, and during his minority was at the mercy of the various factions that sought to control the Government – much of the political turmoil being an off-shoot of wider European conflicts. Once he took control of Government himself, James quickly showed that he was made of stern stuff – setting out to tame his nobles and impose his authority, whilst gaining a reputation amongst the ordinary people as a giver of justice.

He was an indefatigable traveller – partly for political purposes, but also to indulge his love of hunting. James also, unusually for a king, spent several months abroad when he visited France to find a bride.

James was not just a soldier, a politician and a judge, all traditional roles of Scottish kings: he was also a musician, a poet and a lover of art and architecture – a true Renaissance Prince.

Part 8 contains James V's Life Story and additional articles about him, looking at different aspects of his life.

Family Tree

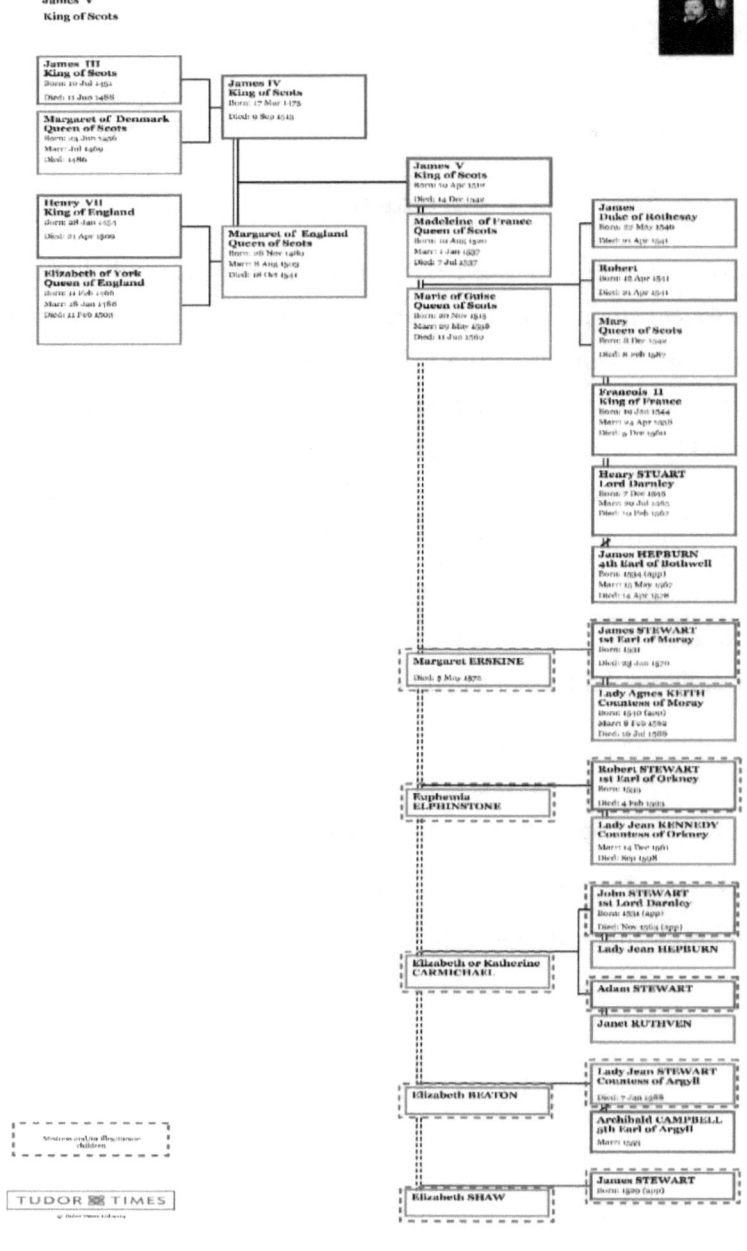

James V's Life Story

Chapter 91: The Early Years (1512 – 1515)

James was his parents' third son, but the first to survive for more than a few months. He was born to the 39-year-old James IV of Scotland, and his wife, Margaret Tudor, at Linlithgow Palace. The marriage of his parents had been intended to reconcile the age-old rivalry between their countries, but unfortunately the *'perpetual peace'* envisaged had not materialised. When James was eighteen-months old, his father marched into England at the head of a huge army, which was shattered at the Battle of Flodden on 9th September 1513 by an army led by Thomas Howard, Earl of Surrey, Lieutenant to Margaret's brother, Henry VIII. James IV and a large proportion of the senior nobles were killed, leaving baby James as king.

The immediate effect of Flodden was to leave Margaret Tudor, under the will of James IV as *'tutrix'* and Governor for James, now King James V, and his tiny heir, Alexander, Duke of Ross, born at the end of the following April. The widowed queen interpreted this role as one of a *'regent'* holding complete power. Margaret was keen to have the position of ultimate authority, as, surrounded by the remaining Scots nobles she felt herself and her young sons to be extremely vulnerable. Her own uncles, Edward V and his brother Richard, Duke of York, had not survived a regency, although they were considerably closer to adulthood than young James V.

Hovering over Margaret and the children were the supporters of John Stewart, second Duke of Albany, who claimed that, as Albany was next prince of the blood, he ought to be appointed Governor in line with the usual Scots custom.

Despite the general misgivings about a Queen who was perceived as pro-English, and strong support for the pro-French Albany, led by James Beaton, Archbishop of Glasgow, Queen Margaret's position was upheld by the Estates (parliament) at Stirling. James was crowned on Wednesday, 21st September 1513 in the Chapel Royal at Stirling Castle, by Archbishop Beaton, to the accompaniment of sacred music, including the Mass for ten voices, *Dum Sacrum Misterium* by Robert Carver, one of Renaissance Scotland's most talented musicians.

Various nobles were appointed to support Margaret, including the Earls of Angus, Huntly, Lennox, Morton and Argyll and a core Council of six was nominated including Lord Hume, Chamberlain; Patrick Paniter, Secretary; Elphinstone, Bishop of Aberdeen, Keeper of the Privy Seal and guardian of the King and Archbishop Beaton, Chancellor. The treasury was found to be empty, but it is apparent from correspondence that 18,000 gold crowns sent by Louis XII to support James IV had been paid over to Margaret by James IV, for safekeeping. In a time when the funding of Government was the King's responsibility, Margaret should have repaid the money to the treasury, but she held onto it, claiming it was to cover her jointure. She effectively stole the money from the Scottish Crown.

In October, Louis XII of France sent his condolences on the loss of James IV. Since Flodden had been a by-product of English-French hostilities, this was the least he could do. Louis told Margaret that he would neither make peace with Henry, nor permit Albany to travel to Scotland without knowing her wishes. In November, the full Scots Council, whilst accepting that Margaret was the legitimate tutrix, sent Islay Herald to France to ask King Louis to send Albany to them for the defence of the realm. Henry warned Margaret that she should try to prevent Albany returning, and encouraged her in her fears that the Council aimed to take the Governorship from her.

Queen Margaret, having begun well with the rapid organisation of her son's coronation, then placed her position at risk by marrying 24 year old Archibald Douglas, 6th Earl of Angus. Angus was described as a *'young, witless fool'* by his own uncle, Gavin Dunbar, Dean of Moray.

Queen Margaret's match horrified the other nobles and the Scots Estates. It was inconceivable to the sixteenth century mind that a woman could act independently of her husband. For her nobles, it was a truth universally acknowledged that she would be led by Angus, to the detriment of all of the rest of them and they seized on the clause in the will of James IV, stating that remarriage would render his widow ineligible to act as regent. Margaret was determined to hold on to her position and from this time forward, Scotland was plunged into feuding.

Despite having lost her husband to her brother's army, Margaret had all of the English princess's animosity towards France and all of a queen's dynastic eagerness to ensure that her own son should come safely into his kingdom. She turned to Henry to protect her and her sons. In particular, she wanted him to either send an army to protect her and young James, or at the very least, prevent the dispatch of Albany from France. In the aftermath of Flodden, it is hardly surprising that such a course of action led many of the Scots lords to distrust her.

Henry declined to send the army and gave little practical assistance, not even accepting Margaret's proposals for a permanent peace in the troublesome Border region. He did, however, try to persuade Margaret and Angus to take themselves and her sons to England, no doubt with a view to instituting a regency council composed of English sympathisers, and the young king held in England as, effectively, hostage for their good behaviour.

In due course discord amongst the Scottish Lords and between them and Margaret, erupted in a heated dispute over the Archbishopric of St Andrew's. Margaret put forward Angus' uncle, Gavin Douglas. This was opposed by Hepburn, already Prior of St Andrew's. A third candidate for the Archbishopric was Alexander Forman who was the preferred choice of Lord Home.

Gavin Douglas took possession of the Castle of St Andrew's and was besieged by Angus, leaving Queen Margaret and her sons at Stirling. As soon as Angus was out of sight, Lord Home (Lord Chamberlain) and the Earl of Arran raced to Stirling to compel Margaret to attend the Council at Edinburgh where she was forced to give up the Governorship in favour of Albany, having refused a compromise that would have given her guardianship of James, and Albany the political power. Meanwhile, the Earls of Lennox and Glencairn, supporters of Albany, took control of Dumbarton Castle, further lessening respect for the crown.

Albany had been born and brought up in France and Queen Margaret and King Henry continued to put pressure on the new King of France, François I, to hold him back from sailing, but to no avail. François prevaricated for a bit then claimed that as he had already promised the Scots to send Albany over, he could not '*in honour*' refuse. Albany therefore arrived at Dumbarton accompanied by eight ships on 18th May 1515 and was installed as Governor of Scotland. His position was formalised by the Estates on 12th July, and Margaret was deprived of her position.

The Council decided that Queen Margaret was no longer to be permitted to keep control of James and his brother as it was material to the effective carrying out of the regency that the King be supervised by the Governor. Nevertheless, she defied the decree and determined to hold onto the boys. She suggested a compromise, whereby the boys would be surrendered to lords chosen by herself, to include her husband,

Angus and supporter Lord Home, but Albany refused and besieged Margaret and her sons in Stirling Castle. The Queen eventually surrendered in August, and in one of his first public appearances after his coronation, three year old James symbolically handed over the keys of the castle. On 20th August 1515 James was formally put in the charge of Albany. At the same time, Henry VIII, largely through the efforts of Thomas, Lord Dacre, Warden of the East and Middle Marches, continued to sow dissension by recruiting Scottish supporters through a mixture of bribes, threats, and fomentation of internal disputes – in particular encouraging Lord Home to defect. Home had been offended by some act or remark of Albany's and thereafter could be relied upon to do almost anything to provoke Albany, regardless of the greater good of Scotland. One of his actions was to help Margaret escape for England in September 1515. They were accompanied by Angus and the Earl of Arran. Both Angus and Arran returned and made peace with Albany, but Margaret did not return until 1517.

Chapter 92: Factions and Rebels (1515 – 1528)

James was now, at the age of three, effectively an orphan. For the next thirteen years the various factions ranged at the Scottish court attempted to control his person, and the government. In order to prevent any one group gaining control, it was agreed that various nobles would rotate the guardianship of the king, who was housed in the main defensible castles in Scotland's central belt – usually Edinburgh or Stirling. His most immediate care-giver was Sir David Lindsay of the Mount who was a surrogate father, carrying James in his arms, teaching the little boy to dance and play the lute, and telling him stories. James also had official tutors, the poet, Gavin Dunbar, who remained in post until 1525, John Bellenden, Archdeacon of Moray and William Stewart, a scholar.

James, though he proved to be a shrewd and intelligent man, was not academically inclined. Unlike his Tudor cousins, Mary I, Elizabeth I and Edward VI, he had little skill in languages. He was, however extremely musical (although with a poor singing voice) and able to write poetry in Scots. His chief prowess was in the knightly and athletic accomplishments of the mediaeval king – hunting, jousting, and running at the ring. Once adult, he also showed an appreciation of material beauty and architecture.

By early 1517, Albany was itching to get back to France. He had left his extremely rich wife, Anne, Countess of Auvergne, and his children behind, and he was also eager to take part in what François I hoped would be a continuing series of victories in Italy over Imperial and Spanish forces. Albany nominated a Council to govern in his absence, with Sir Antoine d'Arcy, the *'White Knight'* as his deputy. D'Arcy was well-known in Scotland, having taken part in James IV's tournaments. On arrival in France, Albany was able to negotiate a new treaty in favour of the Franco-Scots Auld Alliance. The Treaty of Rouen of 20th August 1517 committed both countries to mutual aid against any attack by England and also agreed a match for James with a French princess.

Just before Albany's departure, Queen Margaret returned from England, with her daughter by Angus, Lady Margaret Douglas. She was allowed to see James, but he was not permitted to live with her.

Albany's Council of seven soon fell out amongst themselves. D'Arcy was assassinated on 17th September 1517 by the adherents of the Lord Chamberlain, Lord Hume, and replaced as deputy-Governor by the Earl of Arran, next in line to the throne after James and Albany (the little Duke of Ross having died in early 1517). This went down very badly with the Earl of Angus, who, whilst living with another woman, and flagrantly spending Margaret's money, still thought he should be in charge of his step-son's government.

Eventually Angus and Arran came to open blows at the Battle of the Causeway, which was a running battle along the High Street of Edinburgh on 30th April 1520. During the fracas, various members of the Arran party were killed. This fanned the flames of the feud between the Douglases and Hamiltons, Angus' and Arran's kin respectively. Angus' relationship with Margaret had also broken down completely, and she sought a divorce.

In November 1521, Albany returned, and Margaret now gave him her complete support – he had proved a far more respectful and considerate friend than her brother or her husband. Henry VIII moved between alliances with France, which was generally positive for Anglo-Scots relationships, and with the Empire, which was not. Additionally, as the 1520s unrolled, Henry was becoming more concerned about the lack of a male heir. If female inheritance were disallowed (English law did not prohibit it, but it was not a welcome notion), then James V was his uncle's nearest male successor. Henry would always see James in the light of this unwelcome slur on his masculinity.

Angus was banished to France, and rumours spread that Margaret and Albany would marry. Henry VIII add fuel to the flames with an offensive letter to the Estates, claiming that James had been put in the care of a stranger of *'inferior repute'* and that Albany's supposed intention to marry Margaret would put James in danger. Margaret was incensed and wrote a stiff reply, pointing out that if Henry continued to be hostile, *'the world will think he aims at his nephew's destruction'* – a pointed dig at a man who was Richard III's great-nephew.

The Scots Council, led by Archbishop Beaton, also responded, questioning the possibility of amity between the countries if Henry continued to undermine Albany. Nevertheless, the Scots nobility was not interested in involvement in large-scale military action against England and many of them were very interested in the bribes and promises liberally scattered around by Henry's warden, Dacre. There were large scale border raids led by the Earl of Surrey and Dacre in 1523 in which Jedburgh was attacked and Ferniehurst Castle burnt. Albany was losing his grip on events, and perhaps any will to continue in his role, without more support from the Scots nobles. It was a thankless task, and he left once more for France in 1524, claiming that he had left the country in '*excellent order*' and might return at any time. In fact, he never returned to Scotland although he still took some part in Scottish affairs abroad, particularly in the early 1530s in relation to James' marriage.

Angus now returned to Scotland. From France, he had gone to England where he and his brother, George Douglas, struck up an even closer alliance with Angus' brother-in-law, Henry VIII. For the remainder of James V's reign, Angus and his brother remained in the pay of the English, and promoted English interests, certainly over French interests, and frequently, it would seem, over Scottish interests. It is, of course, possible that they genuinely have believed that a Scotland subjected to English overlordship was a desirable outcome for the country. Henry VIII consistently favoured Angus and his plans over those of Queen Margaret.

Despite their failed marriage, both Margaret and Angus wanted to promote James as old enough to rule without Albany as Governor. The English, too, were in favour, seeing it as an opportunity to keep Albany and the French out. The obstacle to the plan was James Beaton, Archbishop of St Andrew's who remained wedded to the French alliance. Henry, and his chief minister, Cardinal Wolsey, hatched a plot with Lord Dacre to kidnap Beaton, on the pretext of Beaton attending a conference to settle matters on the border. Beaton was too shrewd to fall for it and proposed sending others in his place. As the English had never really intended a peace conference, the idea was abandoned now that the object of capturing Beaton could not be fulfilled. Henry continued with his plans to bribe Scotland into submission, sending money to Arran, and to Margaret and paying for a bodyguard for James.

On 26th July, 1524, James and his mother rode from Stirling to Edinburgh where the nobles swore allegiance to the King, and on 20th August the Estates declared the Governorship of Albany to be ended. James had turned twelve that spring.

Chapter 93: Subjection to Angus (1524 – 1528)

Whilst the nobles, sweetened with English bribes, were prepared to throw off Albany, there was no realistic prospect of James being able to rule unaided. It was ordered by the Estates that Queen Margaret should *'have the rule of her son'* and that he would have four guardians amongst the lords who would take turns to supervise the King, changing quarterly.

Angus was not happy with this, and attempted in November 1524 to seize control of him, but was repelled from an assault on Edinburgh Castle. James and Margaret then established themselves at Stirling, and Angus and Beaton made some sort of private deal. Nevertheless, the rotation of the King's guardianship continued, and included a turn for Angus.

Slightly more cordial relations were established with England during 1524, and in December, Henry VIII wrote to Pope Clement VII, asking him to confirm James' (or rather, Margaret's) nomination for a bishopric. Henry also wrote to James, thanking him for his *'good understanding'* of Henry's letters, *'as proceeding from the fresh wit and great towardness of wisdom which is reported to be in him (James)'*.

He went on to assure James that one of his own principal concerns was James' safety and honour. All the blame for the troubles of the past eleven years were obviously the result of Albany's machinations and henceforward Henry and James could live in perfect peace (provided James followed his uncle's advice, of course).

During 1525, France suffered a major defeat at the hands of the Emperor Charles at the Battle of Pavia, so had little time or inclination to get further involved in Scots affairs. With a weakened ally, and many of the Scots Lords in English pay, the Estates agreed a three-year truce with England in July of 1525, which was eventually ratified in June 1526. The Estates of 1525 consisted of some ten earls, nine senior lords, five lesser lords, eight commissioners for burghs and twenty clergy.

In June 1526, the lord in charge of James, according to the scheme of rotation, was Angus. On 14th June, James was declared to be of full age. According to Scots law, James could now cancel any grants made during his minority, however, Angus had no intention of letting him wield authority. His plan was to control James, whilst negating any arguments that the King should move to another guardian once Angus' term ran out. James was furious, but unable to escape from Angus' clutches.

His anger towards the whole Douglas clan grew during this period, and, as Angus was strongly representing Henry VIII's interests, the seeds of suspicion between uncle and nephew were sown. A new Privy Council, largely made up of Angus' supporters was appointed, with himself as Chancellor.

In 1526, Queen Margaret wrote to Henry VIII, saying that James, despite being recognised as of age by the Estates was in *'thraldom'* to Angus, and had been forced by Angus to write various letters to Henry and the Pope criticising Archbishop Beaton.

James, desperate to escape from Angus, made an agreement with the Earl of Lennox, and a scheme was hatched to rescue the King when he rode with Angus to the Borders, to attempt to punish the notorious reivers, the Armstrongs. Lennox' ally, Scott of Branxholme, mounted an ambush (known as the Battle of Melrose) to rescue James, but Angus had the support of Lord Home's men, and retained control.

James did not give up, and a further armed confrontation took place at Linlithgow, when Lennox again brought soldiers, but was defeated by Angus, now allied with Arran. During this confrontation, George Douglas told James that they would hang onto his person, even it if meant him being torn in pieces. Lennox was killed, Arran cried crocodile tears, and then withdrew from Angus' party. Angus was reconciled to Beaton (at the price of a large bribe) but his brother suspected Beaton's motives. Angus, according to Henry VIII's envoy was *'gentle and hardy, but wants wit.'*

In January 1528, James, presumably forced by Angus, wrote to Cardinal Wolsey in England, asking him to request Henry VIII to prevent the return of the Duke of Albany, although the likelihood of Albany wanting to return was small.

Chapter 94: James Takes Power (1528 – 1534)

At Easter 1528, now aged sixteen, James called his Privy Councillors together and confronted Angus, claiming that he was promoting his own relatives at the King's expense; failing to keep peace in the Borders (thus undermining the three year truce with England) and offending foreign ambassadors. Angus promised to mend his ways, sending a force to the Border to hang a few outlaws, and summoning troops.

In May James wrote to Henry VIII that these troops, far from being levied to protect the Borders, were part of a plot by Angus to kill him (James). Somehow, between 27th May and 30th, James gave Angus the slip, and appeared at Stirling, where his mother was in residence. James was now supported by Arran, Beaton (who, as anticipated by George Douglas, had double-crossed Angus), Lord Maxwell and the Earl of Argyll. In his triumph, he wrote to his uncle, Henry VIII, proclaiming that Angus and his brother had been commanded to give themselves up, but had disobeyed and were wreaking havoc in the country.

The Estates were summoned for 2nd September, and Angus should have attended, but failed to do so. He claimed that his disobedience in not giving himself up was justified as he and his supporters would have been in danger of their lives. As for the troops that had been gathered in May, it was done by the King's own command to take reprisals against the Border warlords.

Angus retired to his castles, first Coldingham, then Tantallon, which he fortified (but *'not to the prejudice of the King'*). He still hoped to negotiate from a position of strength. James besieged Tantallon, but his artillery was captured by Angus (who returned it so as not to offend too deeply).

The three-year truce with England had expired, and Henry and James' commissioners met to agree new terms. The English initially sought the reinstatement of Angus, but the Scottish commissioners refused, and queried why Henry would want to support a rebel. It also became apparent to Henry and Wolsey that Angus had nothing like the support in Scotland that he had previously claimed.

The English, now aiming to ally with France against the Emperor (partly in the hope of French support for Henry's annulment, which was largely occupying his mind) chose not to press the point of Angus' reinstatement and peace was renewed. This did not stop the English from continuing to subsidise Angus' in *'doing all the mischief he could'* in subsequent years.

A five year peace was concluded in December 1528, and Angus and his daughter, Lady Margaret Douglas, who had been held by her father as a bargaining chip against her mother, Queen Margaret, were exiled to England. This did not prevent him working to undermine James from the safety of England.

James took up his authority with panache, rewarding and promoting men who had supported him, or been close to him such as Gavin Dunbar, who was now appointed as Chancellor. One of James' early actions was to set about improving matters on the Border, where he led an expedition in 1529 with the aim of punishing criminals. Unfortunately, it met with little success.

He also wrote to Henry VIII, thanking for his support during his minority (presumably his tongue was firmly in his cheek) and then explaining his own activities in trying to keep the peace. He mentions that the Earl of Northumberland has been rather slack about attending the regular meeting days, and was not redressing the crimes of English subjects in Scotland.

The following year (1530), suspecting some of the nobles with interests in the Border of undermining his authority, he arrested a number of them, including the Earl of Bothwell, and Lords Home and Maxwell. He then gathered a larger force and captured a large number of miscreants, some of whom gave surety for good behaviour, but some were executed. Although James has subsequently been criticised for severity, the men executed were blackmailers (in the sixteenth century sense of extorting protection money), thieves and burners of women and children in their homes.

James also faced trouble in the Highlands and the Isles. The Isles had only been integrated with the Scottish Crown in the reign of his father,

James IV, and there was continued strife between the different clans, and between them and the central authority.

Under Albany, Argyll had effectively been given lieutenancy over the southern Isle, and the Earl of Huntly over the northern lands. Both protested their loyalty and eagerness to pacify the clans for the benefit of the King, but clan feuds and revenge seem to have been part of the plan. In 1530, Argyll, who had been a supporter of James against Angus, sought permission to proceed against Alexander of Islay. After some hesitation, this was granted, but Argyll died shortly after.

With the help of James' illegitimate half-brother, the Earl of Moray, and the new Earl of Argyll, the clan chiefs submitted, but complained about Argyll's actions. James investigated, and stripped Argyll of his offices, granting them to Alexander of Islay. One of the underlying causes of this renewed trouble in the Highlands and Islands, was MacLean of Dowart's ill-treatment of his wife, Argyll's sister. He is said to have chained her to a rock, and left her to drown. She was rescued by a passing boat, and her brother, in revenge, broke into MacLean's bedchamber when he was in Edinburgh in 1523, and stabbed him to death.

Flexing his muscles, James wrote a very short letter to Henry VIII, saying that he could not grant Henry's continuing requests for the restoration of Angus to office, without '*great inconvenience*' and asking him to desist from intervening in the matter.

The exertion of control by James was not popular with his lords either in the Borders or the Highlands, and there was an attempt led by Bothwell, Argyll, Maxwell, Moray and others to overthrow him. James managed to suppress this, by dint of reconciliation with Moray. He then set about giving Henry VIII a taste of his own medicine by paying for Highlanders to assist Irish rebels against England.

Border raids continued, with James and Henry writing to each other, blaming the other's officers for not keeping the peace and giving redress as required. In 1532, eager to improve relations with France, in support of his annulment, Henry was more conciliating to James, suggesting that he attend the planned meeting at Calais, between Henry and François, and inviting James to travel there via England. He also sent expensive gifts. James declined to visit on this occasion.

Eventually, a further truce was agreed in May 1534, to last a year longer than the death of either monarch. Again this was part of a wider peace between France, England and Scotland. James received the Order of the Garter from England, and the Order of St Michel from France in token of everyone playing happy families.

Following James' election to the Order of the Garter, Henry sent Lord William Howard (brother of the Duke of Norfolk) and Garter King of Arms to take James the accoutrements of the Order, including the Garter Book. The book itself was an elaborate and expensive confection. Written on vellum, with illuminated letters and arms, it was bound and gilded, covered in purple velvet, and laced with purple silk laces. Attached by green and white silk laces were the seals, and the bag was enclosed in a bag of red satin, lined with red sarcenet and drawn with red silk laces. The bag was ornamented with Venetian gold, and encased in a box.

Chapter 95: Love and Matrimony

James IV had been a notorious womaniser, but James V looked fair to outdo his father in this respect. He had children by at least five different women during the decade from 1528. These relationships are remembered because they were with women of the nobility – he probably had numerous other mistresses as well. James took responsibility for his children and, unlike in England, there seems to have been little stigma attached to illegitimacy, although it debarred them from the Crown.

The most important of the ladies in James' life was Margaret, daughter of the 5th Lord Erskine. Margaret bore him a son in 1531, James Stewart, later Earl of Moray, Regent of Scotland. Another mistress was Elizabeth Beaton (or Bethune), great-niece of the Archbishop. Elizabeth's daughter, Jean Stewart, became Countess of Argyll and a close friend of her half-sister, Mary, Queen of Scots.

A marriage had been mooted between James and his cousin Mary, daughter of Henry VIII and Katharine of Aragon, as early as 1524. This would, to an extent, have solved Henry's succession problem, if they had married young and produced a son. But there were obstacles – first, Henry wanted a son of his own; second, the English were adamant that they did not want a Scottish King; and third, after the annulment proceedings began, which would render Mary illegitimate, James declined to take an interest in tarnished goods.

James also considered marrying Margaret Erskine, but to do that she would need to have her marriage to Sir Robert Douglas of Lochleven, which had taken place in 1527, annulled. James made the request of Pope Clement VII, but it was refused, and James was either less enamoured of Margaret than Henry was of Anne Boleyn, or more genuinely religious. He accepted the Pope's ruling.

Other candidates for the post of Queen of Scots were Catherine de Medici (niece by marriage of the Duke of Albany). Catherine was also a niece of the Pope, and as Duchess of Urbino in her own right, was a promising bride. She was soon snapped up by François I for his own son (the thought of Catherine de Medici as Queen of Scots is fascinating....). There was also Mary of Austria, the widow of the King of Hungary, and Regent of the Netherlands for her brother, Emperor Charles. Other possible brides were Christina of Denmark, the Emperor's niece, and Isabelle, sister of the King of Navarre.

The Treaty of Rouen of 1517 had envisaged a French princess as a bride, and James now decided that this was still the right answer. King François' eldest living daughter, Madeleine, suffered (probably) from tuberculosis, and François was reluctant for her to marry. Instead, in 1534, he offered Marie of Bourbon, daughter of Charles, Duke of Vendome. Marie was a '*princesse du sa*ng', that is, a lineal descendant of Louis IX and thus worthy to be a queen. Albany was in favour of the match, and set his secretary, Nicholas Calvinet, to work with James' Secretary, Thomas Erskine of Brechin, to agree terms.

James demurred – he wanted a daughter of François. He informed François that anything else would be a departure from the Treaty of Rouen, and require the consent of the Estates. François offered the same dowry as he would give with his own daughter which partially satisfied James, who then sent an envoy to meet Marie and report on her looks and deportment. If the envoy considered her suitable he could confirm her dowry with François, and arrange for her dispatch to Scotland, before winter.

Eventually, agreement was reached on 29th March 1536. James however, rather than waiting for Marie to be delivered to him, resolved to visit France in person. He instituted a Regency Council consisting of Archbishops Beaton and Dunbar, the Earls of Eglinton, Montrose and Huntly and Lord Maxwell. He set sail from Leith but was driven back to shore and took refuge in Whithorn, Galloway, before embarking again from Kirkcaldy on 1st September, 1536, with numerous earls in attendance and a huge retinue. The King's flagship was the *Mary Willoughby*.

On arrival in France, he went first to Marie of Bourbon's home, at St Quentin, but, for unknown reasons, broke off the match. Later chroniclers say that Marie was disabled in some way, based on a comment of Marguerite d'Angouleme, sister of François, that Marie was '*sore made awry*', but, presumably, if that were the case, James would already have known. Marie's death in 1538 was attributed by the chronicler Leslie to her distress at being jilted by James.

When he left St Quentin, James headed south to meet François, and insisted that he would only marry Madeleine. Perhaps he fell in love with the sixteen year old girl, or perhaps he wanted the prestige of being the King of France's son-in-law. It appears, however, that Madeleine was just as keen as James, saying she wanted to be a Queen before she died. François, although certain that the Scottish climate would be his daughter's death-knell, eventually agreed. The marriage treaty, signed at Blois, renounced any claim by Madeleine or her children to the Crown of France. Her jointure was to include the earldoms of Ross, Strathearn, Orkney and Fife as well as several palaces and lordships. The dowry and wedding gifts her father gave were munificent.

James and François appear to have got on well, and James certainly enjoyed his stay in France to the utmost.

On 1st January 1537, he and Madeleine were married at Notre Dame. They left France in May 1537, travelling up the channel, with an escort of ten French vessels. Sailing up the English coast, they purchased fresh fish and meat from Bamburgh and other towns along the Northumbrian coast.

Madeleine was richly provided with jewels, furs, silver plate, furniture and hangings, to make her new home comfortable. She also had a long train of attendants, including her former governess and doctors as well as her furrier, butcher and secretary.

Sadly, despite all the cosseting that James and her father could give her, Madeleine died on 7th July, 1537, having been Queen of Scots for just six months. She was buried at Holyrood Abbey.

James mourned her sincerely, but personal grief could not interfere with government diplomacy, and in June 1538 he married a second time, to Marie of Guise, niece of the Duke of Lorraine, and widow of Louis d'Orleans, Duke of Longueville.

Chapter 96: James as King

Throughout his reign, James made sustained and widespread efforts to improve justice and the rule of law throughout his kingdom. One of his acts was the founding of what is now the Court of Session of the highest civil court in Scotland. He also commissioned the Register House within Edinburgh Castle, for the housing of national archives at a cost of £120 Scots.

James was keen to portray Scotland as an important kingdom in its own right. He spent lavishly on renovating and improving the palaces of Stirling and Falkland in particular, creating Renaissance fantasies similar to those to be found in the Loire valley. One of his greatest expenditures was on his series of tapestries, now recreated at Stirling Castle.

He also played a complex diplomatic game. With England in the grip of religious turmoil, James took the opportunity to increase his standing with European powers and isolate England. In particular, he took care to increase his position with the Emperor Charles, at one time hoping for a marriage with a relative of his. James also kept a cordial relationship with his own cousin, Christian of Denmark.

In one of the least attractive actions of his reign, James took revenge on the sister of Angus. Lady Janet Douglas, Lady Glamis, was accused in September 1528 of having poisoned her husband, John Lyon, 6th Lord Glamis. The charge was dropped, and Janet was given a licence to go on pilgrimage. But in December of the same year, she was accused of having abetted Angus in holding the King against his will. This charge, too was dropped, and she married again.

James, however, had a long memory, and in July of 1537, Janet was again arrested, charged this time with conspiring to poison the King, of witchcraft and also with corresponding with her exiled brothers, the Earl of Angus and George Douglas. English commentators (who may well have been biased) said there was little evidence against her, but nevertheless, she was burnt to death – the standard punishment for a woman accused of treason or witchcraft.

In May 1540, James and Marie had a son, another James. With the succession hopefully now assured, King James set out on a journey round his kingdom. In a fleet of twelve ships, he set sail in June, accompanied by the Earls of Huntly and Argyll, as well as Cardinal David Beaton, who had followed his uncle, James Beaton, as Archbishop of St Andrew's on the elder Beaton's death in 1539.

The progress stopped at numerous places along the Scottish coast, the court would then disembark and camp near the sea-front, before embarking on hunting and hob-nobbing with the local gentry as well as holding Justices in Ayre. The purpose of the progress was three-fold – for James to show himself to his people at all levels of society; to show his power to any nobles who thought they were far enough away from the King to disobey him; and to see justice done, one of James' priorities.

He was back in the south in time for Marie to conceive and bear another son in April 1541. In a tragedy for the couple that is hard to imagine, both little boys died on the same day – 28th April, 1541 (some accounts say within a couple of days of each other). The Dowager Queen, Margaret, wrote to Henry VIII at the end of May about the distress of both parents. Queen Margaret herself was ailing, and died in October of that year, at her castle of Methven. James ignored her request (she had not made a will) that her jewellery be given to his half-sister, Lady Margaret Douglas, now a leading light of Henry's court, and kept it himself.

During 1541, the idea of a meeting between James and Henry VIII was mooted. Such a meeting had frequently been talked of, and both sides had made soothing noises about its desirability, but no concrete arrangements had ever been made, although there had been detailed discussions in 1536.

Henry decided to make a progress to the north of England, to exert his authority and overawe with his presence following the Pilgrimage of Grace. It was suggested that James should travel to meet Henry at York, where Henry arrived, accompanied by his fifth wife, Katheryn Howard, on 16th September 1541. The English royal party waited for some ten days, but James did not appear. With no legitimate children, and a not-unfounded fear of kidnap, James, who had carefully never actually committed himself, declined to make the journey.

Henry was outraged at the insult, which was yet another nail in the coffin of Anglo-Scots relationships. With the death of Queen Margaret the following month, there was no-one who could even try to make peace between uncle and nephew.

During 1540, James had promulgated new ordinances for the army. Every man between sixteen and sixty was liable to be called out for defence, and had to be ready to muster at the named point within 24 hours of the call, armed and arrayed in a jack or brigandine (a protective corselet that covers the upper body, padded and with small metal plates sewn in to deflect arrows), together with gloves and a gorget (neck protector).

Scots armies were traditionally made up of *'schiltrons'*, that is, phalanxes of foot-soldiers in tight formation bearing extremely long spears or pikes. The weapons the ordinary men were to bring could include any of: spear, pike of six ells in length, culverins, hand bows and arrows, cross bows, halberds, axes or two-handed swords. Only earls or lords could be mounted, and any horses brought by lesser men were to be used for carriage.

With the final breakdown of amity between James and Henry, it seemed that military action might be necessary.

In June 1542, Thomas Howard, 3rd Duke of Norfolk, accompanied by Sir Robert Bowes, invaded Scotland at the head of an army of 8,000 men, including Douglas supporters. The Earl of Huntly, and Lord Home met the invaders near Kelrose, and scored a decisive victory at the Battle of Haddon Rig. Bowes, who had had charge of a party sent to harass Jedburgh, was taken prisoner, but soon released.

Following this, James sent further dispatches to England, in July and August to make peace. His overtures were not accepted, and the Duke of Norfolk mustered an army of some 20,000 that crossed the border at Berwick and set about the usual burning and pillaging around Kelso and Roxburgh.

James called his levies to meet at the Borough Muir, just as his father had done in 1513. His army numbered somewhere up to 30,000 – it is difficult to be more accurate as contemporary sources tend to exaggerate numbers. He set out towards Fala Muir (where the Battle of Pinkie would be fought some five years later), but was greeted by the news that Norfolk and his men had retreated homeward. At this point, James wanted to carry the war into the enemy camp, but his nobles refused to support him. They did not want war with England.

James was obliged to disband the majority of the troops, but retained about 18,000, who were sent to attack in the west. James himself rode with the army, but mindful of the dire consequences of his father's death in battle, did not plan to take part himself, instead remaining at Lochmaben, about twenty miles inside the Scottish Border. He had also complained of illness in a letter to Queen Marie, which may have been another factor in him not joining the army.

The Scots crossed the border and advanced southward to cross the River Esk near Longtown. The English were surprised, having expected Haddon Rig to be followed up by a crossing on the east, but the Warden, Sir Thomas Wharton, an extremely experienced commander, rustled up a defensive body of about 3,000 and proceeded north from Carlisle.

With the numbers the Scots had, it seemed that victory was a foregone conclusion, but matters went awry. There was quarrelling and dissension amongst the Scots leaders. Lord Maxwell and Sir Oliver Sinclair both claimed to be in command. The Scots plan had been less one of a battle, and more a retaliatory raid, and, when Wharton approached on 24th November, 1542, the Scots were not in battle array but were busy about cattle-rustling and burning of farmsteads. The Scots were trapped between the rivers Esk and Lyne.

After intense fighting, the Scots broke and attempted to flee across the Solway Moss. The English captured the Scots artillery and the royal standard – a terrible humiliation. Whilst casualties in the fighting were small, many Scots were drowned in the Moss, and some 1,200 were taken prisoner, including the Earls of Cassilis and Glencairn and Lords Maxwell and Fleming.

Nevertheless, this defeat need not have been a worse outcome from Scotland than many of the other Border skirmishes. James, although humiliated by the loss of his royal standard, and many of his nobles, could have rallied and continued with his reign – England did not have the resources to occupy and subdue Scotland for the long term. James, however, was not just sick, he was dying.

He rode from Lochmaben to Linlithgow, where Queen Marie was awaiting the birth of their third child, then on to his favourite palace at Falkland. He heard the news of his daughter's birth on 8th December, but died on the night of the 14th – 15th or possibly 15th – 16th of December. Chroniclers liked to say he died of a broken heart, following the misery of defeat at Solway Moss, but the truth is more prosaic – he died of that perennial curse of soldiers, dysentery, or possibly cholera.

The last words ascribed to him (although they are probably apocryphal) are *'It cam' wi a lass, and it'll gang wi' a lass'*, reference to the Stewarts' inheritance of the throne through Marjorie, daughter of Robert the Bruce. He was aged thirty. James was buried at the Abbey of Holyrood, together with Queen Madeleine and his sons by Marie of Guise.

*

James had been an effective king for the fourteen years of his personal rule. He was not as personally popular with his nobles as James IV had been, seeming to have more of the suspicious temperament (not without reason!) of his grandfather, James III. Had he not died so prematurely, it is likely that he and Queen Marie would have had more sons, and the fate of the British Isles might have been quite different.

Aspects of James V's Life

Chapter 98: Religion and Reform

James V was castigated by English Protestant writers of the nineteenth century as *'priest-ridden'* and superstitious. Even later writers cite the prominence of ecclesiastics such as Cardinal Beaton as proving that James was a benighted bigot. However, this interpretation is so heavily influenced by the partisans of the Knox and the Scottish Reformation that it hardly reflects the truth of politics and religion in Europe in the first half of the sixteenth century.

Whilst James IV had been a promoter of learning, a supporter of Erasmus and a well-informed and educated man himself, the vast majority of the upper classes in Scotland were still of the mediaeval mind-set that left learning to clerics, and lawyers. There was neither the wealth, nor the stability in society that could support the level of patronage of education that was beginning to be seen in England, through patrons such as Lady Margaret Beaufort and Bishop Fox. James V's education had been truncated, and, although he was an intelligent man, there is no sign of him having an academic bent.

With no highly educated men outside the Church, and, to a lesser degree, the law, it was natural that James, in common with every mediaeval and early modern king, should have clerics as his chief advisors. The appearance of the layman Thomas Cromwell as Henry VIII's most prominent minister was almost unprecedented.

As the Church was almost the only career open to an intelligent man of good family, who was not the oldest son, the higher ranks of the clergy were filled with men who may have had little or no real religious conviction, beyond unthinking conformity to traditional beliefs and practices. It was also a convenient way of securing lands and income for illegitimate sons, particularly for kings, who arranged benefices for them when they were well below the canonical age.

James IV's illegitimate son, Alexander, who was tutored by Erasmus, was an archdeacon at nine years old, and Archbishop of St Andrew's (the primacy) at a mere eleven. James V's own brood of sons benefited similarly with at least six of them being preferred to office whilst children, including the priories of St Andrew's, Whithorn and Charterhouse.

In Scotland, as elsewhere, the senior ecclesiastical offices gave access to lands and relatively high incomes. Although the Pope was the ultimate decision maker, since he did not usually have any day to day knowledge of the offices in question (apart from the Bishoprics) he tended to accommodate requests from the King, or other ecclesiastics or nobles whom he wished to favour (or, sadly, but truly) those who paid the largest bribe. Whilst an office was vacant, or if the holder were a minor, the income would slip into the King's pocket.

Earlier Scottish Kings had negotiated an eight month period for them to nominate a new Bishop; James pursued his rights in the matter of benefices vigorously, and frequently wrote to Rome complaining if his wishes were not respected.

After the Battle of Flodden, when the Pope had been strongly in favour of the English position, Henry VIII petitioned Pope Leo X to rescind the Scots King's right to recommend bishops and to insist that Henry be consulted over the filling of the many bishoprics left vacant after the battle. Unsurprisingly, the Scots were infuriated by this interference. The quarrel came to a head over the filling of the

Archbishopric of St Andrew's (vacant as Alexander Stewart had fallen at Flodden).

The story is complex, but worth telling, as it is a microcosm of how the whole ecclesiastical system was run.

There were five contenders in the race.

Queen Margaret, supported by Henry VIII, nominated Gavin Douglas, uncle of her new husband, the Earl of Angus. Douglas immediately occupied the Archbishop's castle. The Pope had his own candidate, his nephew, Cardinal Innocenzo Cibo. Albany (who had not yet been appointed Governor, and was still in France) was in favour of Andrew Forman, Bishop of Moray, Bishop of Bourges and Commendator of several abbeys. The fourth nomination, by the Council, was Bishop Elphinstone of Aberdeen. Fifthly, there was John Hepburn, who was already Prior and Dean of St Andrews and had begun collecting the income.

The Pope, Leo X, sent an envoy to take possession for Cibo but he was refused entry to the country by the Council, who then wrote, in King James' name, protesting against this encroachment on the Crown's privilege of nomination. The Pope reconfirmed James' rights, and dropped Cibo, doing a deal with Forman who agreed to resign his bishopric of Bourges in Cibo's favour. Forman was then appointed by Leo.

Hepburn besieged Douglas and drove him out of the castle. The Council wrote to the Pope, claiming that Forman was a rebel and should not be granted the Archbishopric. When Forman arrived in Scotland, he was prevented by the Council from leaving his Priory at Whithorn, but, after Albany's installation as Governor, the Council was persuaded to accept him as Archbishop (Elphinstone considerately having died in the interim) and in the following year, he also became Papal Legate.

Hepburn and Douglas compromised their differences by an exchange of cash, and the grant of one of the minor offices of Douglas to a Hepburn relative, whilst Douglas received the Bishopric of Dunkeld.

This unedifying spectacle was typical of Church governance and undermined respect for the Church. As elsewhere in Europe, the senior clergy also flagrantly broke their vows of celibacy, many having long term relationships and children, disgusting on-lookers with their blatant hypocrisy.

Queen Margaret's secretary described the situation:

'Every man taks up abbacyis that mayest: thay tary not quhilk (until) benefices be vacant: thai tak tham or (before) thai fall…'

In 1517, when Luther took up his pen to complain of the conduct of the Church hierarchy, his arguments fell on fertile ground all over Europe, and Scotland was no exception.

The first mention of Luther is in the Parliament of 1525, which James presided over, although he was still under the control of Angus. Parliament passed *'An Act Anent (concerning) Heresy'* which proclaimed that importing and/or reading his works, on pain of forfeiture. The majority of the works – Luther's writings, and perhaps early translations of the Bible – were likely to have come into Scotland through its eastern ports, where trade with Germany and the Low Countries was frequent. This prohibition was repeated and amplified in the Parliament of 1535. Merchants bringing such books in were to have their ships confiscated.

James' own education had been in the hands of Gavin Dunbar, who became Archbishop of Glasgow in 1524, and, exceptionally, was permitted by the Pope to operate outside obedience to the Primate, the Archbishop of St Andrew's (by this time James Beaton, Forman having died in 1521). James obviously trusted Dunbar, who was granted the office of Chancellor as soon as James could act for himself. Relations between Dunbar and Beaton were poor and even worse with James Beaton's successor as Archbishop, Cardinal David Beaton, who was translated there in 1539.

Dunbar was a cleric of the old school – pluralist, militant and a politician rather than a man of religion. However, he was happy to use his spiritual power to political effect. In 1525, in pursuit of the truce with England, he issued a curse on the Border Reivers, which is wonderful to hear. This *'monition'* which was to be read by every parish priest to his congregation is pages long, but a couple of choice sentences illustrate:

'I curse thair heid and all the haris of thair heid; I curse thair face, thair ene [eyes], thair mouth, thair neise, thair toung, thair teith, thair crag [neck], thair schulderis, thair breist, thair hert, thair stomok, thair bak, thair wame [womb], thair armes, thair leggis, thair handis, thair feit, and everilk part of thair body, frae the top of thair heid to the soill of thair feit, befoir and behind, within and without..... I curse them within the house, I curse thaim without the house, I curse thair wiffis, thair barnis [children], and thair servandis participand with thaim in thair deides. .. thair cornys, thair catales, thair woll, thair scheip, thair horse, thair swyne, thair geise [geese], thair hennys, and all thair quyk gude [livestock].'

There was the issue of money, as well. One of the defining grievances against the Catholic Church all over Europe was the wealth of its upper ranks and, often, the monasteries, whilst parish priests were frequently poor and ill-educated. The doctrine of purgatory and payment for Masses for the dead, weighed heavily, and the payment of the best cloth and a cow for funeral masses impoverished many.

With traditional churchmen such as Beaton and Dunbar in charge, there was little chance of any interest in Church reform, particularly where it questioned Church authority, and in 1528, the first Protestant martyr in Scotland, Patrick Hamilton, Abbot of Ferne was burnt. Hamilton had had plenty of warning that he was to be arrested, and Beaton had intimated that his escape was desirable but he had not left Scotland by the time men arrived to arrest him. Hamilton was well connected – nephew to Arran, Albany and Lennox, and second cousin to the King, but this did not save him from a mismanaged burning that lasted six hours because wet fuel was used. His example of fortitude did, however, sway many to listen to the message of reform.

In 1539, a further five men were burned in James' presence. Burning was the punishment prescribed by law for heresy in Scotland and across Europe – if a heretic refused to recant, the secular authorities had no choice but to carry out the sentence. In other instances, such as that of David Stratilon in 1534, it appears that James exhorted the accused to recant.

For James, there was a political element to his faith, as well as a religious one.

In the early 1530s when his uncle, Henry VIII, was renouncing Papal authority, he made overtures to James to join him. Henry and his ministers became increasingly concerned about the risk of invasion by France or the Empire to uphold traditional religion, and it would have been a great comfort to him to know that Scotland, the back door to England, would join him. He suggested James join with him in rejecting the '*pretended*' authority of the Bishop of Rome, who sought to keep princes in ignorance. James responded that he would:

'*hold by God and Holy Kirk as our ancestors have done these thirteen hundred years.*'

A later suggestion to James that the monasteries ought to be put down to enable him to take their property was met with the answer that he could not see any benefit in so doing:

'[they have stood] these many years, and God's service maintained and kept in the same, and I might have anything I require of them...'

For James, the advantage lay all on the side of conformity. The more unpopular Henry was with the Pope, and the European monarchs, the more they would caress him. In 1532, James instituted the College of Justice, the forerunner of the Court of Session. To do this, he needed money, and Clement VII agreed to the taxation of clergy – which seems only fair as Church lands in Scotland were worth about ten times the value of Crown land. James was thus able to access Church wealth without going to the extremes of Henry VIII's dissolution programme.

James was further honoured by the Pope (Paul III) in 1537, who dispatched a cap of maintenance and sword to the King, as he travelled through France. James tipped the Papal messenger 400 crowns and gave him a horse trapped in velvet.

James could not, of course, be unaware of the need for change, and happily listened to satire upon the ignorance, superstition and venality of the average priest, composed by his childhood mentor, Sir David Lindsay of the Mount.

But there was a difference between condemning poor practice and rejecting the authority of the Church or its doctrines. The Parliament of 1541 clearly set out the official position of James and the three Estates, with legislation that comprised the following for management of the Church (paraphrased – see Acts of Parliament of Scotland):

1. The Holy Sacraments were to be honoured, as in time past
2. The Virgin Mary was to be worshipped and reverenced and prayed to intercede with the Holy Trinity for the welfare of the King and Queen and for peace and concord amongst Christian people. The saints were also to be honoured and invoked.

3. There was to be no questioning of the Pope's authority, on pain of death and confiscation
4. Reforming kirks and kirkmen – a long list of exhortations for clerics to set a good example and look after their parishes and parishioners in accordance with church teaching
5. There were to be no private conventions to dispute scripture
6. Abjured heretics may not discuss religion, abjured or suspected heretics may not hold office
7. There is to be a reward for those that reveal conventions for disputing scripture or heretics
8. No-one is to damage or dishonour statues of the saints
9. It will be treason for anyone to try to install a bishop or abbot, other than as nominated by the King of the Pope.

In other orders, James forbad the Church to exact death duties.

With a King and clergy committed to holding to the old faith, it seems unlikely that the Reformation would have gained much ground in Scotland, had James lived, especially if he had kept up pressure for internal reform. His early death, however, opened the door to a much more radical change in religion, with the appearance of George Wishart and John Knox.

Chapter 99: The Gudeman of Ballengeich

A story is often told that James V would dress up (or rather, dress down) as a yeoman farmer, and would walk amongst his subjects incognito, calling himself the Gudeman of Ballengeich (ie the tenant farmer of Ballengeich, a place near Stirling). Thus disguised, James would find out about life from the perspective of his subjects, rather than just hearing what his nobles or clergy told him. Whether the facts are true or not, the story points to a belief that James was interested in the life and fate of the common man, and this certainly seems borne out in his attitude to one of his chief roles, that of giver of justice.

In England, the role of judge had long been delegated from the King to professional judges, but in Scotland, it remained an important part of his kingship.

He would travel to the '*caput*' or main town in the various sheriffdoms (from which the word shire derives) and hear the most serious case at sessions called Justices in Ayr. These would last from four to seven days, with Sundays always excluded. The day to day matters of justice were dealt with in the Barons' courts, with the baron, or laird, having '*right of pit and gallows*' and jurisdiction over '*life and limb*'.

The justice system in Scotland was complex, but important features include the fact that prison as a punishment did not, for the main part, exist. The pannel (accused) would be held in the sheriff's gaol, but only until the trial. If he were filed (convicted) his punishment would be either a physical one – hanging, the stocks etc, or being outlawed for a sum of money – what we would term a fine.

In addition, criminal justice was not just a matter between the Crown and the wrong-doer, but was also a matter for the victim. The criminal would need to compensate the victim (or his family) through assythment, for which he would have to find sureties until it were paid. Once assythment had been agreed, the malefactor would be outlawed for a sum and the King would grant a pardon, conditional on that being paid. There were variations around this, if the victim could not be satisfied, or there were no sureties. In some cases, the King could grant a pardon without the victim being satisfied, but this was rare.

The Justices in Ayre were not generally courts for the finding of guilt, instead, pannels who had agreed assythment were brought forward for pardon, and to be brought back into the king's mercy. An important part of the system was the use of sureties. These were the kinsmen and the laird of the pannel, who would also come into the court and, collectively, assume responsibility.

There seem to have been few crimes for which assythment, and subsequent pardon was not possible, even murder. One such was '*common*' theft, which was a general accusation of theft but without a specific victim identified, so no assythment could be made. Common thieves were frequently hanged. This was the charge usually brought against the border reivers.

One of the most well-known cases of James dispensing justice, rather than granting pardon following assythment, was that of Johnny Armstrong. Armstrong and his clan were notorious reivers – raiding across the border, stealing cattle, raping, murdering and burning. In 1530, when James set about trying to reduce the levels of crime in the area, he promised Armstrong safe-conduct, but then broke his word and hanged Armstrong and thirty-six of his clan.

He also personally heard the case of William Cockburn of Henderland, panneled and fined for inbringing (abducting) an Englishman and his son. Cockburn was beheaded and his goods forfeit to the Crown.

At the same Justice in Ayre, on 18th May 1530, Adam Scot of Tuchelaw was found guilty of taking black-mail (protection money) from poor tenants, and was similarly beheaded.

A major problem with the justice system was identified as the frequent '*non-compearance*' (non-appearance) of the pannels, meaning that justice was protracted and that the injured could gain no relief. A statute of 17th June 1535 was enacted to deal with that, by proclaiming that a second non-attendance would result in confiscation of goods and the accused being '*put to* (the) *horn*' – that is, the town crier would wind his horn three times, then publicly declare him a rebel. Additional provisions were made for restitution of costs where one party falsely accused another, and unusually, gave a punishment of imprisonment of a year and a day, for failure to pay the costs.

Later acts required the bailiffs and stewards of the court to attend in person to ensure justice was properly done and that cases were to be heard within fifteen days.

When James first became king, there was no separate court for civil cases – everything was disposed in the Baron's court, or at the Justice in Ayre.

In 1531, Clement VII issued a Papal Bull, granting James the right to tax Church property to fund a new civil court.

On 17th May 1532, legislation was brought into Parliament for the setting up of a

'college of cunning and wise men, both of the spiritual and temporal estate, for the doing and administration of justice in all civil actions'

The court was set up with 14 judges, half laymen, half clerics, and was to sit for three terms in each year. Justice was to be administered equally to anyone before the court. There was provision for the Lord Chancellor to preside, were he available.

Additional rules were set out for how defendants were to be summonsed, for removing notaries who were not competent, and for ensuring that notaries were properly introduced to the courts. Losers of lawsuits were to pay the other party's expenses, as modified by the sheriff. Documents brought in evidence had to be signed as well as sealed, or witnessed if the person could not write.

The college was the forerunner of the present Scottish Court of Session, the highest civil court, and preserved in the Act of Union of 1707 *'for all time coming.'* James could be justly proud of his creation.

Chapter 100: French Fashions

In February of 1536 a marriage was agreed between James and Marie of Bourbon, daughter of the Duke of Vendome, a relative of King François I of France. The original intention of the Treaty of Rouen of 1517, had been for James to marry a daughter of the King, but his two elder daughters had died young, and the next in age, Princess Madeleine, who was not quite sixteen, was in frail health, probably suffering from tuberculosis. François therefore proposed Marie of Bourbon, offering her with a dowry as great as that of a Princess of France.

James, after initially protesting, and seeking a bride amongst the flock of female relatives of the Emperor, whether genuinely, or to concentrate François' mind, agreed to the match. He gave authority to the Duke of Albany to conclude negotiations and send the bride to Scotland. For some reason, however, he changed his mind about waiting at home for his bride, and decided to go to France to fetch her himself.

He requested a safe-conduct to travel through England, but this was refused. The Duke of Norfolk wrote to Henry VIII and the Council, saying that, although he was surprised that James had not asked Henry directly, he did not think there could be a problem with James' request, other than in the matter of expense.

Henry replied, that no King of Scotland could be entertained in England except as a vassal, for 'there never King of Scots into England in peaceful manner otherwise'. In addition, since James had failed to meet Henry as previously mooted, citing that he feared betrayal, Henry could not allow him or his wife to travel through England, because if there were any mishaps, Henry would be suspected.

Following this ungracious response, James was obliged to sail all the way. In July, he set out, but was driven back by storms. After regrouping, on 1st September 1536 he sailed again from Kirkcaldy, in Fife (or possibly Leith), with seven ships, landing at Dieppe on 11th of the month. He took no chances with leaving potential troublemakers at home, and was accompanied, amongst others, by the Earls of Argyll, Rothes and Arran and the Lords Fleming (his brother-in-law) and Maxwell.

There is some inconsistency as to whether James went first to Paris, or to the Duke of Vendome's chateau (variously reported as at St Quentin in Picardy, but more likely the Vendome chateau near Tours), but little doubt as to what happened in either place.

Lindsay of Pittscottie claims that he went to the chateau in disguise, but that Marie recognised him from a painting she had been given, and picked him out. Her perspicacity may have owed something to the fact that he would be obviously foreign, spoke poor French and was red-headed.

For some undisclosed reason, having met Marie and spent eight days at her father's home, near Chartres, being feasted and honoured, and practically smothered in cloth-of-gold, James no longer wished to go through with the match (it is unlikely she would have been allowed to refuse). Marie of Bourbon died the following year – according to Pitscottie, she pined away following the heartbreak and dishonour of being jilted.

When James arrived in Paris the French court was not in residence so James amused himself, apparently '*incognito*', much to the disgust of Sir George Douglas, brother of James' enemy, the Earl of Angus, and currently in Paris in English pay. According to Douglas, James, who had '*beggared Scotland*' to take £19,000 Scots to cut a magnificent figure in France, ran up and down the streets of Paris, with no more than a couple of servants, buying everything in sight, fondly believing himself unrecognised, whilst the shopkeepers pointed and whispered *'Voila le roy d'Ecosse'*. Perhaps it was a matter of etiquette, that, until he had waited upon the King himself, he should not admit to being in the country.

In his running up and down the streets, James did some serious shopping. He purchased a great diamond, fifty-five spears, some for tournaments, others for battle, tipping the spear-makers lavishly, and four white feathers at a cost of 12 francs for his bonnet (as a comparison, the diamond cost him 8,787 francs).

In due course James travelled to La Chapelle, near Lyons, where the King and court were in residence, in deep mourning following the death of François' eldest son. Some reports have Madeleine as present, although too ill to ride, others state that she and James did not meet until the court was at Amboise. With the appearance of his royal guest, François was roused to activity. James made a good impression, and there are reports of the two Kings hunting together at the Chateau of Loches, in the Loire.

Perhaps the loss of his son (his third child to die) made François reluctant to disappoint his daughter, who, despite her illness, apparently wanted to be a Queen. More romantically, she and James may have become genuinely attached – although there was an eight year age gap. It is certainly likely that James was attached to the French alliance in principle, and the 100,000 livres tournois dowry plus an annual pension that was on offer. Despite his misgivings about sending her to the damp climate of Scotland, François agreed to the marriage, and they were betrothed on 26th November 1536.

The court returned to Paris, and on 31st December made a state entry. James made a splendid figure, dressed in crammasy (red or crimson) velvet, lined with red satin with raised gold work and 116 22-carat gold buttons, with lapis-lazuli. According to his wardrobe inventory, he had another fifty similarly elegant and extravagant outfits. Complaint was made by the burgesses of the French Parliament that they had been obliged to dress in their red coats and process in front of anyone other than a King of France, but François replied that he wished James to be treated with as much honour as himself.

On 1st January 1537, James was led in procession by François to the cathedral of Notre Dame, where he married Princess Madeleine. Once married James continued shopping, buying quantities of textiles and tapestries. He also received twenty fine horses from François, all trapped with enamelled harness. François gave Madeleine the run of his cloth stores, allowing her to take as much cloth-of-gold, velvet and satin for her clothes and those of her ladies-in-waiting as she liked. The young Queen also received quantities of jewels from her father.

Whilst in Paris, James bought two huge beds, furnished with green velvet and damask curtains and counterpanes. The fabrics had come from Genoa and Florence, and, in total there were some seventy yards of fabric used. The craftsman who made the bed hangings, one Guillaume Petit, was paid twenty crowns to up sticks with his wife and children and move to Scotland.

The young couple left for Scotland in mid-May (after a delay owing to Madeleine's illness) and arrived on 19th May 1537.

Once home, James was determined to recreate what he had seen in France, on both the inside and outside of his palaces. He had been accompanied to France by a French mason, Moses Martin, who was already in his employ. Martin was named as master-mason not long after arrival in France. This suggests that James was planning before he left home to find out more about the latest styles in architecture. François' spending on the chateaux of the Loire was no doubt famous in every court in Europe.

Queen Madeleine, and later, James' second wife, Marie of Guise, both received Falkland Palace and Stirling Castle as parts of their jointure and both properties received extensive make-overs, partially funded by the lavish dowries that both ladies received. (Marie's was only two-thirds of Madeleine's, but still a princely sum.) More beautiful beds were furnished, and the King expanded his collection of tapestries.

Stirling Castle today has been renovated to show how the royal apartments looked in the 1540s, after James' death, but still occupied by his widow, and heavily influenced by French Renaissance taste.

Chapter 101: Following the Footsteps of James V

The numbers in the article below correspond to those on the map which follows.

On Saturday, 10th April, 1512, James V was born in Linlithgow Palace (1), which had been his father, James IV's, *'morning gift'* to his bride, Margaret Tudor. The palace, which is now an evocative ruin, was one of the most modern and comfortable in Scotland. He was baptised the following day, which was Easter. Despite his parents' marriage having been intended to promote peace between England and Scotland, within eighteen months the countries were at war, and James IV was killed at the Battle of Flodden. Young James was now King, aged seventeen months.

Margaret took him to Stirling (2), one of the most defensible castles in all of Scotland, situated at the crossing point on the Forth that had seen numerous battles, including Bannockburn, two hundred years before, and Sauchieburn in 1488. James was crowned in the Chapel Royal at Stirling on 21st September.

During James' minority, there were constant quarrels over guardianship of his person, and he was usually moved between Stirling, Edinburgh Castle (3), and Holyrood Palace (6). In September 1517, an outbreak of plague in Edinburgh led to him being moved to Craigmillar Castle (4), about three miles south-east of the city centre. He also spent time at Dalkeith Castle.

In 1524, James was declared of an age no longer to need a Regent or Governor. Instead, he was to be under the guardianship of his mother, and various lords who would take turns to supervise him. Matters did not go as expected, and Archbibald Douglas, 6th Earl of Angus, and estranged husband of Queen Margaret, took control of James.

For the next four years, Angus ruled James and the Government, setting himself up as Chancellor, and giving key offices to his friends and family. James chafed under his government, but despite a couple of attempts was unable to break away until May 1528. Accounts vary as to whether James was at Edinburgh or Falkland Palace (5) when he managed to escape to Stirling in May.

Now sixteen, James began his personal rule. One of his early actions was to march on Tantallon Castle (7), Angus' stronghold on the northern coast of Lothian and besiege it. The King arrived with impressive artillery but despite battering away for nearly three weeks could not mount an effective attack. He was unable to capture the castle or Angus (who was elsewhere) and lifted the siege. In May 1529, Angus, still being hunted by James, managed to slip away to England. Tantallon was taken into royal hands.

Over the next few years, James travelled extensively around the south of Scotland, largely in the cause of putting an end to the constant lawlessness in the Borders. During two expeditions of 1529 and 1530, he visited Haddington, Jedburgh, Peebles, Lindores, Crammald (now

Cramalt Tower) and Magetland (the area around today's reservoir of Megget Water).

He also ventured further north, to Allan Water, Perth, Dundee and Dunkeld. He did not generally stay anywhere for more than a few days, and most trips were from his main residences at Stirling, Edinburgh (both the Castle and the Palace at Holyrood) or Linlithgow and then back.

One of James' chief interests, as for so many noblemen of the time, was hunting. There are frequent references in the Lord Treasurer's accounts for the expenditure on dogs, horses and hunting equipment, as well as for hunting trips, particularly near the delightful Falkland Palace, the hunting lodge that he spent significant sums of money upgrading.

In the summer of 1533, he went further afield on a hunting trip, to Blair Atholl Castle (10), seat of the Earl of Atholl. The whole court went on the jaunt, James, Dowager Queen Margaret, the Papal envoy who was visiting and the King's councillors. During the visit, some 600 animals were slain – deer of various kinds, wolf, foxes and even wild cats. The Earl had built a splendid wooden palace for the King, which, on departure, was burnt. James told the astonished Papal Envoy that it was the custom for countrymen to burn the place they had slept in the night before!

After leaving Blair Atholl, James went on to Dunkeld and Perth, before travelling west to Glenorchy and Inverary (9).

On 1st September 1536, James set sail from Kirkcaldy to visit France, where he spent some nine months, returning in May of the following year with his bride, Madeleine of France. Madeleine took up residence at Holyrood Palace, but died within two months of her arrival, and was buried in the Abbey. The mourning for the young Queen was intense, and orders had to be given for black cloth to be brought in from Dundee to Edinburgh for mourning clothes, the city having run out of black. A further order was given, preventing any increase in the price of black cloth.

The following June, a new wife and queen arrived, Marie of Guise, at Balcomie Castle (8) in Fife. James and Marie were married at St Andrew's, where they then spent six weeks before moving to Cupar, to Falkland for hunting and then on to Stirling and Linlithgow.

On 1st March 1539, James was at Edinburgh, where he witnessed the burning of five '*heretics*', before returning next day to his Queen at Linlithgow. Whilst James and Marie do not seem to have been particularly attached to each other, they spent plenty of time together, hunting, visiting the shrine of St Andrew's and enjoying their building projects. According to one source, they went on a pilgrimage in their ship, the Unicorn, to a shrine on the Isle of Man (12), but it seems unlikely. At some point (the dates are unclear) they also travelled to Aberdeen (13), and spent some two weeks there.

Whilst at Falkland Palace, it is likely that James would have visited his menagerie. These were popular symbols of Renaissance power, and James was the happy possessor of various wild animals, including a lion. The creature had been bought in Flanders, where James' man was outbid by his uncle's, but Henry VIII then sent it as a gift.

During the summer of 1540, James went on an extended tour, by sea, around Scotland. He was not accompanied by his Queen, possibly because she had only just had a baby, or perhaps he saw the mission as essentially a demonstration of power in areas of Scotland that were not fully controlled by the Crown, and hence potentially dangerous.

He sailed with some twelve ships as far as the Orkneys (which had come to Scotland as surety for the dowry of his grandmother, Margaret of Denmark, and never been redeemed), and then through the Hebrides and the Western Isles.

In the Spring of 1541, James' second legitimate son, Robert, was born, but both he and his older brother died on 21st April of that year. Both King and Queen were distraught. The children were buried at Holyrood, next to Queen Madeleine.

During 1541, James seriously considered visiting England, to hold a conference with his uncle, Henry VIII at York. It appears that the English thought this was a definite arrangement, whilst James did not believe he had actually committed himself to it. James' failure to appear at York was held against him by Henry, who believed he had been humiliated by his nephew. Later that year, James attended the funeral of his mother at Perth.

The uneasy peace that had obtained between Scotland and England since the late 1520s (border raids by local reivers excepted) began to break down. By and large, border raids were ignored as casus belli unless they took place under the direct orders of either King or were led by his lieutenants. In early 1541, the English Duke of Norfolk led a massive raid into the south-east of Scotland, but was defeated by Scots, under the leadership of George Gordon, 4th Earl of Huntly, at Haddon Rig (14).

What was intended as a retaliatory raid, in the west went horribly wrong when James' troops were scattered or imprisoned at Solway Moss (15) on 24th November 1542. Within three weeks of the battle, James had died at Falkland Palace. He was interred next to Queen Madeleine and his sons at Holyrood.

Key to Map

1. Linlithgow Castle
2. Stirling Castle
3. Edinburgh Castle
4. Craigmillar Castle
5. Falkland Palace
6. Holyrood Palace

7. Tantallon Castle
8. Balcomie Castle, Fife
9. Inverary
10. Blair Atholl Castle
11. Crawford Castle
12. Jedburgh
13. Aberdeen
14. Haddon Rigg
15. Solway Moss

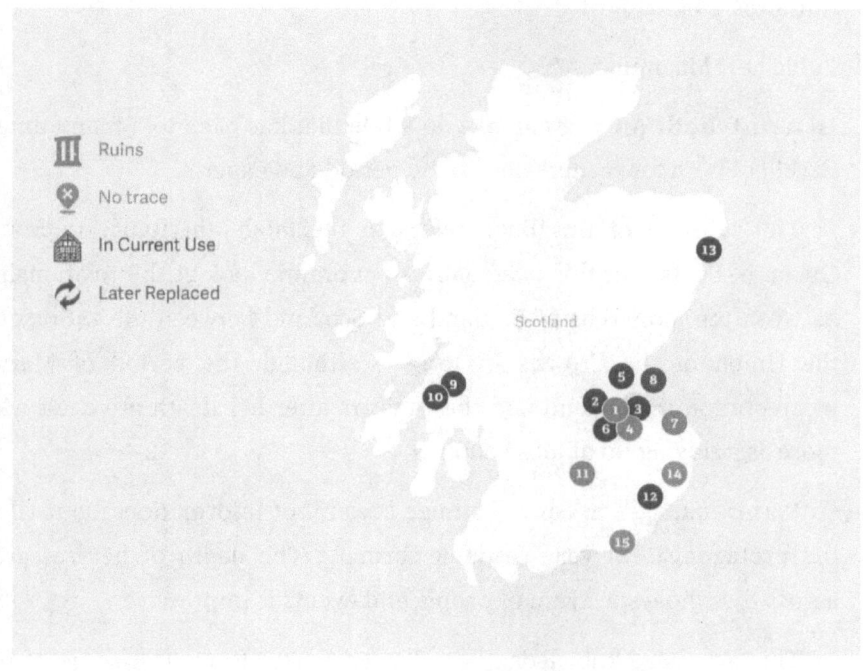

Chapter 102: Book Review

There is a dearth of modern, easily available books on James V. Most works touching on him are broader histories, or dense academic works concentrating on a particular theme. The most accessible information is in Linda Porter's *'Crown of Thistles'*

Crown of Thistles: The fatal inheritance of Mary, Queen of Scots

Author: Dr Linda Porter

Publisher: Macmillan

In a nutshell: An original take on a tale that has been told many times. Excellent both for readers new to the period and experts.

The sub-title of this book refers to the fatal inheritance of Mary, Queen of Scots, but this is actually a panoramic look at the relationship between the monarchs of England and Scotland between the 1480s and the Union of the Crowns in 1603 – although the period of Mary's incarceration in England and the 15 years after her death are dealt with more as a tidying up of loose ends.

Porter manages to convey a huge amount of information about all of the protagonists in very readable format. The depth of her research across the whole spectrum of people and events is impressive.

This extensive knowledge has allowed Porter to contest some of the frequently repeated judgements on many of the people and events involved. For example she is kinder to Margaret Tudor, the widow of James IV than most historians have been – seeing Margaret as well-intentioned and determined to do the best for her son's realm. She also challenges the frequently repeated assertion that, post-Flodden, with a generation of leaders dead on the field, Scotland descended into chaos.

This is not, however, a dreary recitation of political facts. Porter covers a wide range of topics, from the architectural interests of Henry VIII, and the literary pursuits of James V, to the religious views of John Knox and the Machiavellian plotting of Mary's mother-in-law, Catherine de Medici.

Porter's Mary, too, is more nuanced than is often the case. She is shown as physically extremely courageous, charismatic, resourceful and politically shrewd in many ways, but Porter hints, although does not conclude, that Mary was probably aware of the plot to murder Darnley, even if she were not directly responsible.

Mary's actions after the death of Darnley seem to fly in the face of common sense, but hindsight is a marvellous thing, and it is difficult to unknow the results. At the time, Mary was surrounded by factions and traitors and each individual choice she made can be justified, although the outcome was disastrous. Her worst mistake of all was stepping into the fishing boat that took her across the Solway Firth and into twenty years of incarceration at the hands of her cousin, Elizabeth I.

The book is a weighty tome, but I wish it had been longer. An exposition by Porter of the years of plot and counterplot as Mary was pitted against Elizabeth's spymaster, Sir Francis Walsingham would make gripping reading.

Part 9: Lady Katherine Grey: Tudor Prisoner

Introduction

Lady Katherine Grey is very little known compared with her older sister, Lady Jane, yet her life in many ways encapsulated the problems of the Tudor succession, and the difficulties that almost everyone of royal blood encountered. First, a pawn in the plans of the Duke of Northumberland, and then disliked and distrusted by Elizabeth I, she sought to find happiness in marriage, but suffered imprisonment and separation from her husband.

Katherine's life was lived in the east and south of England, in the houses of the nobility and gentry in the country and the grand town houses and palaces of London, including that most dreaded of fortresses, the Tower of London.

Part 9 contains Lady Katherine Grey's Life Story and articles 'following in [her] footsteps'. Katherine's life was defined by her royal blood. As a potential heir to the crown in a country riven with dynastic and religious uncertainty, her life was not her own.

LADY KATHERINE GREY

Family Tree

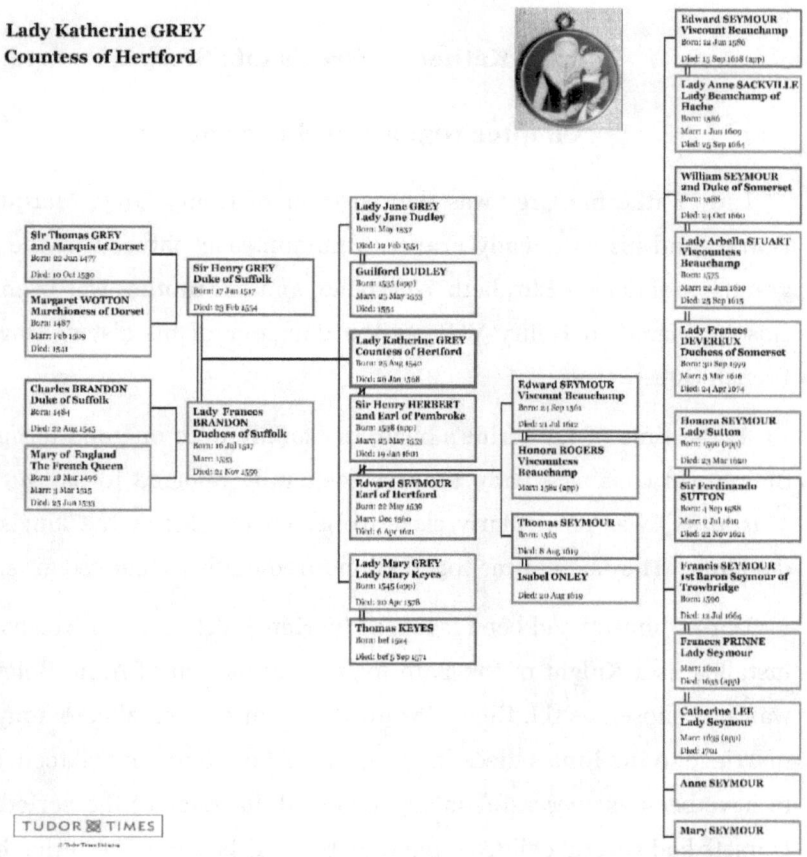

Lady Katherine Grey's Life Story

Chapter 103: Katherine's Family

Lady Katherine Grey was the daughter of Henry Grey, Marquess of Dorset, and his wife, Lady Frances Brandon. Her father was the great-grandson of Queen Elizabeth Woodville, and her mother was even more closely related to Henry VIII, as the daughter of his sister, Mary, the French Queen.

At the time of Katherine's birth, her family were on good terms with their royal cousins. Lady Frances (generally referred to as '*My Lady Marquess*') was particularly close to her cousin, Mary, the king's elder daughter. They spent time together and frequently exchanged gifts.

Dorset himself had been favoured by Henry VIII, and, as well as being installed as a Knight of the Bath for the coronation of Anne Boleyn, he was also chosen as the King's Sword Bearer at the actual ceremony. His marriage to the King's niece in 1533, when they were both sixteen, seems to have been as successful as any arranged marriage of the period. The Dorsets had several children, but only three girls, Jane, Katherine herself and Mary, survived infancy.

The young family were brought up largely at Bradgate Park, Leicestershire, and received the best education available. Dorset was strongly inclined to the Reformed faith, and, whether or not his wife totally agreed with him, his daughters were brought up in it. The Grey sisters benefited from the great leap forward in female education that occurred during the last quarter of the fifteenth century, and the first half of the sixteenth. As well as the traditional education of upper class women in household and domestic management, courtly skills such as music, dancing and hunting of various sorts, the girls received an academic education that included Latin and Greek.

The tutor in the Grey household was John Aylmer who had been patronised by Dorset for some years. He later (1577) became Bishop of London, and was a supporter of the legitimacy of female rule (although in a rather half-hearted manner that didn't endear him to Queen Elizabeth). The other men involved in the education of the Grey sisters were their parents' three chaplains – John Haddon, a Fellow of Trinity College, Cambridge; Thomas Harding, holder of the Regius Chair in Hebrew at Oxford, and John Willock, a former Dominican friar. All four of these men who influenced Katherine's education were, at that time, convinced reformers. (Harding later returned to the Catholic fold, and was treated to an excoriating written attack from Jane Grey). All his life Dorset was a keen supporter of scholarship and learning, particularly in the more radical elements of the Reformed faith.

Chapter 104: Royal Succession

When Katherine was seven years old, she came to hold a place in the English succession. The Act of Succession of 1544 named Henry's three children, Edward, Mary and Elizabeth, in that order (ignoring the fact that both daughters had been declared illegitimate). With no further stipulations, the Crown would then have passed from Elizabeth to her heirs under common law – the descendants of her oldest aunt, Margaret, Queen of Scots. However, the 1544 Act had a further provision, permitting Henry VIII to change the succession, should he so wish. Henry took advantage of this latter clause, making a new will not long before his death in January 1547, which had a different effect, putting the line of his younger sister, Mary, the French Queen, directly after

Elizabeth and naming *'the heirs of the body of Lady Frances'* to follow Elizabeth.

Thus, in January 1547, on the accession of Edward VI, Lady Katherine Grey became fourth in line to the throne – a great step up from the position of eighth which she would have held under common law. Nevertheless, it seems highly unlikely that Katherine would have known anything about it, or understood it if she had.

As King Edward's reign began, Katherine continued her education, dividing her time between Bradgate and Dorset House in London. But intrigue was beginning to surround the family. The Lord Protector, Edward Seymour, Duke of Somerset, had not chosen to avail himself of the advice of his younger brother, Sir Thomas Seymour, nor that of Dorset and this caused resentment. In the later years of Henry's reign, Dorset had taken rather a back seat. He was not generally popular in Government circles: he was considered to be *'without sense'* – a reputation he soon lived up to.

Dorset was also disgruntled at the rash of new titles being handed out. Ahead of him in rank had been only the Duke of Norfolk, and his wife's half-brother, the Duke of Suffolk. Now, Edward Seymour had appropriated a Dukedom, and raised his friend, William Parr, brother of Queen Katherine, to a Marquessate as well. Thomas Seymour and Dorset, resentful at being left out of the Privy Council under Henry's will, began to look for other means of increasing their influence.

Seymour smoothly married his former sweetheart, Katherine Parr, the Queen Dowager. He also began a flirtation (to put it mildly) with his new wife's stepdaughter, the Lady Elizabeth. He persuaded Dorset that, if Dorset's elder daughter, Lady Jane, were committed to his care, he would be able to arrange a marriage between her and the King. Dorset agreed to sell Jane's wardship for £2,000. This was by no means an unusual step – most aristocratic adolescents were sent to live in other households, although it was less common to transfer the wardship and marriage if the parents were still alive. With Jane's departure, Katherine was now the eldest daughter at home. She began studying Greek under the tutelage of Thomas Harding.

Chapter 105: Unrest

In September 1548, following the death of Katherine Parr in childbed, Jane returned home. Seymour's initial attempts to have her returned to his care, to a household to be presided over by his mother, were rejected by both Dorset and Lady Frances. He persisted, however, and Jane went back to Sudeley. Seymour was becoming more and more reckless in his plotting to obtain power by undermining his brother, Somerset, and Dorset supported him. By March 1549, Seymour had over-reached himself and was executed. Katherine was reunited with her sister again when Seymour's household was broken up.

During the summer of 1548, the rituals of the old religion had been swept away. Use of the rosary was forbidden and a wave of iconoclasm smashed images and stained glass. Prayers for the dead were abandoned, and the chantries, where priests had been paid to pray for souls for all eternity, were closed. For Katherine, brought up in a household that had already eschewed these rituals, little would have changed, but for the vast majority of the population, these changes were not welcome. Katherine, now nine, would probably have been old enough to be aware of the state of the country.

In the west, in the summer of 1549, the Prayer Book rebellion attempted to overturn the new Protestant Communion service. In the east, where Protestantism was more popular, there were uprisings against the enclosure of land – near Bradgate various enclosures had the fences torn down. Matters were compounded by the declaration of war by the French on 17th August, in support of their Scottish allies. The country was in uproar.

Both rebellions were harshly crushed, and, in the fighting, Katherine's uncle, Sir Henry Willoughby, was killed, leaving her cousins as orphans. The oldest, Thomas, came to Bradgate as Dorset's ward and he and his younger siblings, Margaret and Francis, spent a good deal of time with the Grey sisters.

As well as gentry cousins, the Greys had far more impressive relatives, and in November 1549 the Greys travelled to Beaulieu in Essex for a visit to their cousin, the Lady Mary, sister of the King. Lady Mary and Lady Frances had been close friends, although religious differences were beginning to drive a wedge between them. Lady Mary was a staunch conservative, and objected strongly to the religious changes of 1549, whilst the Greys had embraced them – according to Spanish reports, Dorset was *'entirely won over to the new sect.'* Nevertheless, Lady Mary showered gifts upon the three girls.

Chapter 106: Ambition

In the aftermath of the summer rebellions, a coup, led by John Dudley, Earl of Warwick overthrew Somerset as Protector. Warwick became Lord President of the Council, and appointed Dorset to a place on it. All of the chief men on the Privy Council were now Protestants (although the term was still not generally used).

Dorset's new position on the Council led to a clutch of honours and offices being granted to him, and the family resided mainly at Dorset House, in London, to give access to the Court.

Based on a passage in one of the Grey tutors, Roger Ascham's, book, *The Schoolmaster*, Dorset and Lady Frances have been characterised as abusive parents, certainly in relation to Katherine's older sister, Jane. Ascham reports that Jane complained, in effect, that nothing she could do pleased her parents, who punished her with nips and pinches.

The biographer of the sisters, Leanda de Lisle, puts this plaint into context, citing more contemporary accounts that suggest that Jane was no more harshly treated than any of her contemporaries, and also pointing out that Jane was a young teenager – an age recognised even in the Tudor period as being one when rebellion against parental authority was normal, although they believed it had to be firmly nipped in the bud.

There are no records of how Katherine felt about the strict regime of study, but she was not destined for greatness like Jane (whom Dorset still fondly believed might one day marry Edward VI) and was not encouraged to be the paragon of learning that her older sister was. Whether this is a reflection of the differing intellectual capacities or tastes between the girls, or the amount of effort expended on Jane, cannot be known. Certainly, Jane was exceptionally intellectually gifted, whilst Katherine seems to have been less interested in academic pursuits.

In 1550, grief struck the family when Lady Frances' two half-brothers, Henry, 2nd Duke of Suffolk, and Charles, died on the same day of the sweating-sickness.

The Duke of Somerset had never been content with having been ousted from the Protectorship and was hoping to be reinstated. Warwick could not stomach the idea, and found means to undermine him, claiming there was a plot by Somerset to capture and murder Warwick and Northampton.

In another round of new honours, orchestrated to strengthen Warwick and his supporters on the Council, the Dukedom of Suffolk was recreated for Dorset and Lady Frances. Warwick was promoted to the Dukedom of Northumberland, and William Herbert, brother-in-law of the late Queen Katherine Parr, and another evangelical, became Earl of Pembroke. Somerset was arrested, and the new Duke of Suffolk signed the warrant for his removal to the Tower of London, from which he never emerged – Northumberland and Suffolk both sat as judges at his trial.

The Suffolks were riding high and were often at court. On the visit of Marie of Guise, Dowager Queen of Scotland, Frances sat at her left hand at the feast (Lady Mary having declined to attend).

In religious matters, what had begun as evangelicalism and the desire to hear the Word of God, was now moving towards the joylessness that was later associated with Puritanism. In the Suffolk household, the sisters were discouraged from music, and the servants forbidden to play cards. Plainness of dress was also becoming all the rage amongst the '*Godly*' in contradistinction to conservatives such as Lady Mary who continued to dress resplendently. Ascham reported that the precocious Lady Jane, on receiving a magnificent dress from Lady Mary, refused it with an insolent message – a step much admired by the evangelicals.

In 1551, a new Prayer Book was prepared. It was far more evangelical in tone than that of 1549, and the Archbishop of Canterbury, Thomas Cranmer, was not entirely happy with some of the more radical proposals – for example, he insisted on the retention of kneeling to receive Communion. For the Greys however, it was very welcome.

Chapter 107: The King's 'Devise for the Succession'

Northumberland's influence over the young king grew. He even persuaded the King to over-rule the Earl of Cumberland's refusal to permit the marriage of his daughter, Margaret Clifford (Frances' niece) to his own fourth son, Lord Guilford Dudley. This marriage, was not, however, to take place. Instead, Northumberland looked to move his family a step closer to the throne with the marriage of Guilford to Katherine's sister Jane (third in line). Edward VI was ill, and the Lady Mary was reminding the Privy Council of her position as heir. She rode to London in February with a huge retinue, and the Duchesses of Northumberland and Suffolk joined her train as she visited her brother.

Although Edward opened Parliament on 1st March 1553, no substantive business was done, and he was not formerly announced as of age. Soon after, he made a will, called his *'Devise for the Succession'*. Edward was fourteen, exceptionally well-educated and intelligent. The influence of Northumberland and his radical tutors had given him a deep commitment to the Reformed Faith, and his great fear was that the Lady Mary would undo all his good work. Besides, the idea of female rulers was even more unpopular with the Reformers than it had been with Catholics. Bible study had dwelt a good deal on the wickedness of women and their duty of obedience. A particular scourge of womankind was John Knox, later to write his *'First Blast of the Trumpet against the Monstrous Regiment of Women'* and Knox was a chaplain at Edward's court.

The King's Devise named as his heir, the heirs male (not yet born), first of Frances, then of her three daughters, then of her niece, Margaret Clifford, daughter of Eleanor Brandon. In the event of a minority, the boy's mother was permitted to be Regent, provided she did everything her male Councillors advised. If no males had been born by the time of the King's death, Frances was to be Regent – Suffolk must have danced with glee.

For the Privy Councillors, this meant that there were four young women available to be snatched up as matrimonial prizes, by whom they could, potentially, make their sons King. Lady Mary Grey and Lady

Margaret Clifford were too young (both only 8 years old), so this left the two older Grey girls.

In early 1553, Katherine and Jane were married in a triple arrangement. Katherine was married to Henry Herbert, the son of William Herbert, Earl of Pembroke, nephew of the late Katherine Parr; Jane was married to Northumberland's fourth, but oldest unmarried son, Guilford, and Katherine Dudley, Northumberland's daughter, was married to Henry Hastings, who was a great-grandson of Margaret Plantagenet, Countess of Salisbury, and thus carried royal York blood. Ominously, the King was too ill to attend any of the ceremonies, contenting himself with sending presents of *'rich ornaments and jewels'*

The ceremony between Katherine and Herbert took place on 25th May 1553 at the Northumberland residence, Durham House. It was a day of traditional celebrations – feasting, jousting and masquing. Whether Northumberland engineered the marriage of Katherine as part of a wider plot to secure the succession to Jane and his son, is a matter of debate amongst historians.

As more emphasis is placed on Edward's own responsibility for the *'Devise'* so less is placed on Northumberland. Professor Ives, in particular, believes the marriage of Katherine and Herbert was a routine aristocratic arrangement, and that, far from Pembroke being his crony, the two men did not get on well. The counter-argument might be that Pembroke was given the second prize of Katherine, in order to gain his support for the marriage of Jane to Northumberland's son. Support for this may be found in the correspondence of the Imperial Ambassador, who claimed that the marriage was made for Katherine at Northumberland's *'intercession.'*

Katherine was twelve, which was the age of consent for marriage, but generally considered to be too young for consummation. Nevertheless, she went to live at the Pembroke home at their London property,

Baynard's Castle, together with her fifteen year old husband. He had been in poor health at the time of their wedding, but soon made a recovery and the young couple grew fond of each other.

Meanwhile, Edward, close to death, had made another change to his *Devise*. It was apparent that no boys would be born before he died, so he bequeathed the throne, not to Frances, but to Lady Jane and her heirs male. As Jane was now firmly under the thumb of Northumberland (or so the Duke thought) Northumberland could picture a world in which his pre-eminence continued for some time.

Chapter 108: The Queen's Sister

On 6th July 1553, Edward died, and the following day the Mayor and City dignitaries swore oaths of allegiance to Queen Jane. Katherine was still living at Baynard's Castle with her husband and father-in-law, Pembroke. She could look forward to a glorious future as sister to the Queen and Countess of Pembroke with a husband she was growing to love – for a Tudor noblewomen, life could hardly promise to be more enjoyable.

By 19th July, however, the Lady Mary had triumphantly overturned the coup. On that day, Pembroke, convened a meeting of Councillors and the Lord Mayor at Baynard's Castle and they agreed that they would process to Cheapside to proclaim Mary as queen.

When the news arrived at the Tower, Suffolk was persuaded to proclaim Mary Queen from Tower Hill, and then inform Jane that her reign was over. Suffolk and Frances then left Jane to her fate with the Dudleys and went to Baynard's Castle.

Before long, Suffolk was under arrest in the Tower, but Frances had raced to intercept Mary at Beaulieu, and beg her forgiveness, placing as much blame as she could on Northumberland, and pleading that Suffolk had been coerced and poisoned by the Duke.

Mary, who was of a forgiving nature (leaving religion aside) promptly issued pardons for Frances and Suffolk, and was only dissuaded from doing the same for Jane by the urgings of the Imperial Ambassador.

Katherine was now placed in a very unhappy position as Pembroke, who had also been pardoned, sought to distance himself from the debacle of the coup. He wanted the marriage between Katherine and his son annulled. The young couple, who had become attached to each other, swore that despite her youth (she was still not quite thirteen years old) they had consummated the marriage. Even if that were true, which is unlikely, no-one was prepared to listen to them and she was packed off back to her mother.

Had Suffolk been prepared to pay even lip-service to Mary's re-introduction of the old faith, and accept her decision to marry Prince Philip of Spain, it is likely that both he and Jane would have had their lives spared. Instead, he first stirred up trouble in religious matters, and, according to the Imperial Ambassador, this annoyed the Queen

'The Duke of Suffolk is doing bad work in connection with religion, and the Queen is angry with him for his manner of abusing her clemency and good nature'

He then became involved in outright rebellion, taking part in what is known as Wyatt's Rebellion, an uprising that sought to overthrow Mary and replace her with Elizabeth, who was of a more Protestant bent, although nowhere near so radical or idealistic as Jane Grey. The revolt was a complete failure, and, whether the intention was to replace Mary with Elizabeth, or with Jane, the result was the same. Death warrants for Jane, her husband Guilford, and Suffolk were signed.

Mary still hoped to save her young cousin, both body and soul, and delayed the execution in the hope that Jane could be converted to the Catholic faith, sending a priest of her own, Dr Feckenham, to try to persuade her. Jane was steadfast in her religion, and glorying in martyrdom as only a sixteen year old idealist can, accepted her fate. One of her last actions was a gift to Katherine, of her Greek New Testament, with a message written on the blank leaves. The letter is strongly evangelical in tone, exhorting Katherine to put away the things of the world and be prepared for death at any time:

'I have here sent you, my dear sister Katherine, a book, which although it be not outwardly trimmed with gold...yet inwardly it is of more worth than all the precious mines that the vast earth can boast of. It is the book, my only best and best-loved sister, of the Law of the Lord. It is the Testament and last will...which shall lead you to the path of eternal joy and if you with a good mind read it, and with an earnest mind do purpose to follow it, it shall bring you to an immortal and everlasting life..... It shall teach you to live, and shall learn you to die...My good sister, once more again let me entreat you to learn to die; deny the world, defy the devil, and despise the flesh, and delight yourself only in the Lord. Be penitent for your sins, and yet despair not; be strong in faith, yet presume not; and desire with St Paul to be dissolved and to be with Christ, with whom, even in death, there is life...Now as touching my death, rejoice as I do, my dearest sister, that I shall be delivered of this corruption, and put on incorruption: for I am assured that I shall, for losing of a mortal life, win one that is immortal, joyful and everlasting....I pray...(that you may) die in the true Christian faith, from the which (in God's name) I exhort that you never swerve, neither for hope of life nor for fear of death...Fare you well, good sister, and put your only trust in God, who only must help you.'

Jane and Guilford died on 12th February 1554 and within two weeks Katherine also lost her father to the axe. He, too, was steadfast in his evangelical faith.

Frances was now left to salvage what she could from the ruin of her husband's mixture of ambition, religious zealotry, and lack of political skill. The Suffolk estates were forfeit to the Crown, but within a couple of months Queen Mary had re-granted various of the family's possessions.

Chapter 109: The Queen's Cousin

By July 1554, France, Katherine and her younger sister, Mary, were at court, granted positions of honour in the Queen's Privy Chamber. That month was a busy one for Queen Mary and her ladies. On 25th she was married at Winchester Cathedral to Philip of Spain. Katherine and her former husband were both present at the celebrations, Katherine in a new red velvet gown provided by the Queen. On their return to London, Mary and Philip, with the rest of their train, spent the night at Suffolk House before entering the capital. One wonders how Katherine viewed her old home, now housing Mary and Philip as sovereigns, rather than Jane and Guilford.

Katherine was making friends amongst her fellow courtiers, including Elizabeth (Bess) Hardwick, wife of Sir William Cavendish. Katherine was godmother to their first child, and using her privilege of choosing the name, selected Elizabeth. This has been read as a signal that Katherine was showing support for her cousin Elizabeth, and the Protestant faction, but, since Katherine was only fourteen, and at no time displayed either religious zealotry or any political cunning whatsoever, it is probably safer to assume that she just named the baby after the mother.

Katherine's best friend, however, was Lady Jane Seymour, daughter of the Duke of Somerset, and his second wife, Anne Stanhope. Named for her aunt, Queen Jane, the young Jane Seymour had been brought up to be nearly as intellectually precocious as Katherine's sister and a strong adherent of the Reformed faith. She too, had once been considered as a possible bride for her cousin, Edward VI. Now, the girls idled away their hours in the time-honoured pursuits of young women – chatting, and sharing confidences about the young men they fancied. Katherine, unhappy at the dissolution of her marriage to Herbert, still hoped that they would be reunited.

Herbert was also making his way at court, and in 1557 would be amongst the young men who went to France in the army led by King Philip against Henri II. At first victorious in the Battle of St Quentin, Philip's accustomed hesitancy meant that he failed to follow up the victory in a march to Paris. Henri II, desperate for revenge, retaliated by an onslaught on the poorly provisioned and defended town of Calais, which fell in January 1558 – the last remnant of Henry II's empire that had stretched from Hadrian's Wall to the Pyrenees.

The loss of Calais infected the Queen and the court with depression, at the beginning of a terrible year for the whole country – poor harvests, worse weather, and a virulent strain of influenza scourged the country. Lady Jane Seymour fell ill, and returned to her mother at Hanworth House for nursing. Katherine went with her and spent the summer of 1558 in a combination of care for her friend, and young love.

For Lady Jane's brother, another Edward Seymour, was also at Hanworth. Seymour was a year or so older than Katherine. The young couple fell in love, and aided by Lady Jane, passed messages and notes between each other. He even asked his sister to find out whether Katherine would marry him.

At this point, scenting danger, Seymour's mother intervened, no doubt pointing out to the young man that to marry a woman of royal blood, without the Queen's express permission, was an act likely to end in the shedding of tears, if not the shedding of blood.

Seymour, in the time-honoured fashion of adolescents, shook off his mother's advice, and maintained that there was nothing wrong with Katherine and he being together, either at home or at Court, unless the Queen forbade it.

At the end of the summer, Katherine and Jane Seymour returned to Court. Jane was better, but this illness may have weakened her lungs. The Queen however, was now seriously ill. She too, had caught the influenza, and was still suffering from whatever disease (possibly ovarian cancer) had falsely led her to believe herself pregnant. By mid-November, forty-two year old Mary was dead. Katherine, as one of her ladies, would have been involved in the preparations for the funeral. Her feelings for the queen as she watched over the body during the month-long lying in state are likely to have been mixed. Mary was responsible for the death of Katherine's father and sister (no matter how much they may have deserved it by the standards of the time) yet she had been forgiving and generous to Frances and Katherine herself.

But there were not just her personal feelings of either grief or rejoicing. Katherine was now heir to the throne under the terms of Henry VIII's will.

Chapter 110: The Queen's Heir

In later years, when quizzed on Mary, Queen of Scots, another possible successor, Elizabeth asked drily '*..think you.. that I could love my own winding sheet?*' and that dislike of her possible heirs manifested itself within days of her accession. Katherine was demoted from Queen Mary's Privy Chamber, the inner sanctum of the court, to the Presence Chamber, a place to which any member of the nobility or higher ranks of the gentry had access. She had a part, with other ladies of the court, in the coronation procession through London, but no special treatment.

On the bright side, her lover had had his father's earlier title of Earl of Hertford resurrected and bestowed on him in a new creation. The Duchy of Somerset, however, was not re-granted. It can probably be inferred from this, that no rumour of an attachment between Katherine and Hertford the preceding summer had reached Elizabeth. She certainly wouldn't have wished to promote a young man who had been sniffing around an heir to the throne.

There was immediate pressure on the new Queen to marry, but Elizabeth prevaricated. With hindsight, her choice not to marry looks like a brilliant decision, but we cannot infer that Elizabeth ever made that deliberate choice – at least, not in the early years of her reign. Mediaeval and Tudor minds just did not consider a state of non-marriage as a possible choice (with the exception in earlier times of entering a religious order). At the lowest levels of society, marriage was more or less an economic necessity, as neither men nor women could function alone as an effective economic unit. Higher up the social scale, it was a duty to marry to beget heirs, and at the top of the hierarchy, it was a self-evident truth that a monarch should beget a legitimate heir as soon as possible.

Elizabeth's hesitations were around when she ought to marry and to whom, given that both a home-grown consort, and a foreign prince had draw-backs. So long as she did remain unmarried, however, her heir was likely to be courted, as she had been during Mary's reign. It was thus prudent to treat any pretensions to being her successor that Katherine might have, coldly.

Katherine was well aware of the meaning of her demotion, complaining to Count Feria, the Spanish Ambassador that:

'the Queen [did] not wish her to succeed in case of her (Elizabeth's) death without heirs.'

Feria, who knew Katherine well, as he was to marry Jane Dormer, one of Katherine's former colleagues as maid-of-honour to Queen Mary, described her as *'dissatisfied'* and *'offended'* at Elizabeth's treatment of her. It was also reported that she had spoken disrespectfully to the Queen.

Chapter 111: Politics

Wider European politics now came into play. With Mary's death, England's alignment with Hapsburg Spain and Empire was weakened, but the French (who previously had intrigued to overthrow Mary in the Wyatt Rebellion with the ostensible goal of putting Elizabeth on the throne) were now promoting the claims of Mary, Queen of Scots. The Hapsburg interest would be best served by a marriage between Elizabeth, and her former brother-in-law, Philip II, or with one of his Imperial cousins. If that could not be achieved, then the Hapsburgs needed a viable alternative to Mary, Queen of Scots to support. Katherine Grey might be the very one!

Feria courted Katherine's support. He suggested that a Spanish or Imperial husband might suit her, and she agreed that she would not marry without his agreement, nor change her religion – Katherine had conformed to the reintroduced Catholic practices of Mary's reign. There were rumours that Feria even went so far as to arrange an abduction of Katherine with a view to smuggling her to Spain. From the extant records, it is impossible to tell whether Katherine was privy to this plan. It was abandoned when Henri II of France died, the Spanish believing that his heir, the young François II, was much less likely to consider invasions of England – he was too young and untried to begin his reign with extravagant military ventures, even in favour of his young wife, the Queen of Scots.

Katherine's statement that she would not change her religion without consulting Feria (if his remarks are to be believed) is unlikely to have been a genuine declaration of Katherine's religious views. So far as is recorded, she complied with the Act of Uniformity, and all of the support for her position as heir was grounded on the belief that she was a Protestant. Katherine may have made this comment to leave open the idea of a Spanish match. She probably warmed to the idea, as during the summer of 1559, Hertford seemed to have lost interest in her.

He initially excused himself from attending the Queen's progress that set out from London on 17th July 1559. They met again, however, at Eltham, and were soon deeply in love. It was an enchanted summer for the young couple – masques, banquets, hunting parties and dancing filled the days and the fragrant summer evenings at Eltham and Nonsuch. Hertford's intentions were strictly honourable, and later in the year, probably in September or October, he formally requested Lady Frances to sanction his marriage to her daughter.

Lady Frances and her second husband, Adrian Stokes, were pleased with the plans, but they were well aware that the Queen might not approve. Their advice to Hertford was to persuade as many of Elizabeth's advisors and Privy Councillors as possible of the benefits of the match. A letter was drafted for Frances to send to the Queen, once there was sufficient support for the match, asking the Queen's consent. Frances also confirmed with Katherine that she wished the marriage to take place – the fashion for arranging marriages for young people without consulting them was beginning to fade.

Hertford's initial feelers to Privy Councillors met with the advice that he should not attempt to rush matters. Whilst Katherine was waiting to formalise the betrothal, her mother, who had been ailing for several years, died. The funeral, paid for by Elizabeth, in an unusual access of generosity, took place in Westminster Abbey. Katherine, her eldest surviving child, was chief mourner, following the coffin. The funeral was conducted according to the rites and ceremonies laid down in Elizabeth's Act of Uniformity, which, although Protestant, was not as radical as the faith that had been espoused by Frances' husband and Jane.

Chapter 112: The Queen's Rival

Katherine was now in a sort of limbo – in mourning for her mother, not yet betrothed although she was nearly twenty, by which time most girls of her class were married, and with no formal role at Court. She was still, however, being courted by the Spanish, who were gleeful at the prospect that Elizabeth's open infatuation with Lord Robert Dudley was causing murmurs of disquiet. If she were overthrown in favour of an heir over whom they had more influence than on the steely Elizabeth, England might be brought back into the Hapsburg sphere.

In early 1560, rumours had reached the France and the Low Countries about Spanish plans. One of Cecil's informants, John Middleton wrote:

'I am told that there is practising for a marriage to be made betwixt the Prince of Spain and the Lady Katherine Grey, which is not of the best liked for divers respects, and by some hindered.'

Elizabeth, who was having probably the most enjoyable six months of her life pursuing a passionate, if platonic, relationship with Dudley, was not blind to the overtures being made to Katherine by Spain. She decided to out-charm the Spanish Ambassador by suddenly taking Katherine by the hand, restoring her to the Privy Chamber and keeping her at her side – even saying she might adopt her cousin – a scheme as far-fetched as may be imagined!

Meanwhile, Hertford's sister, Lady Jane, and their brother, Henry, were promoting the marriage – passing billets-doux between the young lovers and facilitating secret meetings. It is clear that at these meetings, nothing more intimate than hand-holding took place.

As another attempt to downplay Katherine's importance, Sir William Cecil, Elizabeth's chief minister, told the Spanish Ambassador that, in the event of Elizabeth's untimely demise, a third queen-regnant in a row would be quite unacceptable, and that Henry Hastings, Earl of Huntingdon and great-grandson of Margaret Plantagenet, Countess of Salisbury, would be preferred.

Huntingdon was a committed Protestant. Known as 'the Puritan Earl', he was a brother-in-law of Lord Robert Dudley. It is evident, nevertheless, that Cecil, although he would prefer Elizabeth to marry suitably and beget children, favoured Katherine as her heir. There was talk of marrying her to the son of the Earl of Arran, who was Mary, Queen of Scots' nearest male heir, although he was also a suitor for the Queen.

Scandal regarding Elizabeth and Dudley reached epic proportions when his wife, Amy Robsart, was found dead in mysterious circumstances. Had the Queen then married him, she would surely have lost her throne, if not her life. Elizabeth might have loved Dudley, but she loved her crown, her honour and her country more. She soon made it clear that there would be no marriage.

In the light of this cooling of the Queen's relationship with her favourite, her marriage to a suitable European prince once again moved to the top of the her Council's agenda. Cecil took the opportunity to warn Hertford that he should back off from plans to marry Katherine.

Chapter 113: Secret Marriage

It is difficult to imagine that Katherine, who had borne the loss of her sister for attempting to interfere with the succession, can really have been so naïve as to believe that Elizabeth would easily forgive a marriage that was not sanctioned by her, especially as Katherine had shown herself disgruntled when the Queen had not acknowledged her openly as her heir.

Perhaps she believed that marriage to a known Protestant of good standing would actually enhance her position – certainly those nobles in favour of a Protestant succession would welcome a married woman with a son rather than another childless queen. Perhaps Katherine thought that Cecil's tacit support would be enough to extricate her from any problems. Perhaps, though, it was just love.

Hertford took Cecil's warning seriously and backed off – even flirting with another lady. Katherine was distraught and wrote to him. Unable to distance himself from her, Hertford wrote a reassuring letter, suggesting a secret betrothal, to which Katherine agreed. Betrothal was as binding as marriage and could only be set aside with the Church's permission. Hertford and Katherine exchanged promises with his sister, Jane, as witness. Katherine received a diamond betrothal ring, and Hertford commissioned a gold wedding ring, inscribed with verses of his own invention.

Whilst betrothal was binding, it could be dissolved with Church sanction. For marriage, consummation must take place, and Katherine and Hertford were no doubt eager to fulfil the requirements.

The next time the Queen left Court, for a hunting trip, Katherine cried off, claiming she had the tooth-ache. She and Jane were allowed to stay behind. The next day, they left Whitehall and went to Hertford's house at Cannon Row. Hertford later testified that the date had not been prearranged, that they had just agreed that Katherine would come as soon as she could. Hertford sent most of his servants away, although some of the kitchen staff remained, and they later testified to Katherine having come to the house on that day.

Whilst Hertford and Katherine greeted each other, Jane slipped out to find a priest, although whether she just picked the first one she saw, or whether the groom had previously engaged him is unclear. The wedding service, according to the authorised Book of Common Prayer, was completed, and Jane left the couple together.

The marriage thoroughly consummated, Katherine and Jane returned to Whitehall. Over the next few months, Katherine and her new husband took every opportunity they could to be together. It was pretty much an open secret, at least amongst their servants and immediate friends, that they were sleeping together, even if no-one knew about their marital status. Katherine was taxed on the matter by Elizabeth's friend, Geraldine, Lady Clinton, but denied that she was *'familiar'* with the earl.

In early 1561, Cecil, still concerned that Hertford was paying too much attention to Katherine, suggested that he might like to travel abroad. A suggestion from Cecil was as good as a command, but Hertford, although he was probably thrilled at the idea of seeing France and Italy at Crown expense, hesitated. His mother wrote to Cecil that she was happy for Edward to go abroad, and that Cecil was to overrule his wilfulness. The Duchess mentioned that she would like him to be *'matched to some noble house to the Queen's liking'*. With pressure from the Duchess and Cecil, Hertford agreed. He told Jane that he would go, and she broke the news to Katherine.

Katherine thought that she might be pregnant. If she were, according to Hertford, there could be no solution but to tell the Queen of their marriage and hope she would be forgiving. Katherine hesitated. Perhaps she wasn't pregnant after all. Soon, her own health was the least of her preoccupations. Her friend, and now sister-in-law, Jane, was mortally ill, and died on 29th March 1561. She was buried in Westminster Abbey, next to Katherine's mother.

Both Katherine and Hertford grieved for Jane, and this may have affected Katherine's health. She could not tell Hertford for certain whether she was pregnant. He told her that he would not leave for Europe if she were, but if not, he would go. Nevertheless, he would '*not tarry long*' if it transpired she was going to have a baby.

Before his departure, Hertford drew up a will, granting Katherine lands to the value of £1,000 per annum, which he gave to her, together with some ready cash, and then departed for Europe. Cecil took the opportunity to warn Katherine again about the risks of consorting with the Earl without royal approval.

It was far too late for Katherine to draw back now. She was certainly about to bear a child, and the Queen, after the short period of favour, had once again turned hostile. Only twenty, with her husband abroad and not answering the letters she sent, her parents and older sister dead, and her best friend and sister-in-law also gone, Katherine panicked. She cast about for another solution, and remembered her first husband, Henry Herbert. If she had actually been validly married to him back in 1553, Elizabeth could not reasonably be angry with her for that, and any affair she might have had with Hertford would not have the taint of treason.

She wrote to Herbert, saying she believed they were still married. At the time of the annulment, they had pleaded to stay together, so perhaps she believed he would be fond enough of her to accept paternity of her child. Herbert began to court her, sending pictures and gifts, whilst Katherine still sought to contact Hertford. On discovering this, Herbert withdrew his attentions and sent her a stinging letter, accusing her of '*whoredom*' and attempting to '*entrap*' him with sugared bait. He demanded the return of the letters he had sent her. Katherine did not immediately comply, leading him to write a further letter, threatening her with exposure if she did not send his notes back.

Chapter 114: The Queen's Prisoner

That summer, the Court progressed through the eastern counties, arriving in Ipswich on 5th August 1561. The same night, Katherine confessed her pregnancy to a lady by the name of St Loe. The identity of this lady is disputed. Biographers of Bess of Hardwick usually assume it to be her. This would seem a perfectly reasonable proposition – as noted earlier, Katherine was the godmother of Bess' daughter by her second marriage to William Cavendish. Katherine's biographer, Leanda de Lisle, however identifies St Loe (or Sentlow) as Bess' sister-in-law. Whoever the recipient of Katherine's confidences was, she was refused to get involved.

The next day, Katherine sought out Lord Robert Dudley, and confessed all. Lord Robert agreed to be *'a means to the Queen's Highness'* and told Elizabeth the whole tale. Elizabeth was incandescent – as she would always be when secret marriages were revealed. Whilst the main thrust of her anger was in Katherine's threat to the succession, any hint of immoral behaviour at her court reflected badly on her, and gave fodder to the gossips who speculated about her behaviour with Dudley.

Katherine was immediately arrested and sent to the Tower, and Hertford recalled from Europe.

Orders were given to Sir Edward Warner, the Lieutenant of the Tower, to question Katherine strictly. Warner had been Lieutenant during the brief reign of Lady Jane Grey, and he must have regretted seeing her sister brought to the Tower. He was also detailed to find out who had known about the secret match and to tell Katherine that her only hope for mercy was to tell the complete truth.

Hertford, who had returned as commanded, was arrested when he docked at Dover, and despatched to the Tower as well.

Over the succeeding weeks, the couple were interrogated numerous times by the Privy Council, as was Katherine's step-father, Adrian Stokes, who had been involved in the early discussions between Hertford and Frances about a possible marriage. Their accounts of their courtship, betrothal and marriage did not tally entirely, particularly in that Hertford did not recollect Frances ever having drafted a letter to the Queen – although, of course, he may not have known of it. Hertford's mother, Anne, Duchess of Somerset distanced herself from her *'unruly child'* with a letter to the Queen protesting her own loyalty.

The couple remained in the Tower, forbidden to have contact. Katherine delivered a son on 21st September 1561. He was christened Edward, for his father and grandfather, and a couple of the Tower officials served as his god-parents. Elizabeth, further enraged by the birth of a son to her potential heir, kept the couple in prison.

Whilst this seems harsh, they had, in fact broken the law – a Statute of 1536 had forbidden the marriage of a member of the royal family without the sovereign's permission. Elizabeth was making quite clear that her personal preference for the succession was the traditional route of primogeniture, which would put Mary, Queen of Scots' claim first, but she would not make any official declarations on the topic. Elizabeth also believed that there was more to the matter between Katherine and Hertford than love-sick youth, hinting that some of her Councillors were behind the match.

In the outside world, Cecil and Elizabeth's other councillors were pushing for settlement of the succession by a Parliamentary act. For Elizabeth this was anathema – to suggest that the succession be laid down by Parliament was to suggest that the sovereign answered to Parliament, rather than the reverse. For this reason, if no other, she would always prefer the claim of the Queen of Scots – above all, monarchs should stand together to enforce their rights.

With this level of pressure on her, Elizabeth was determined to undermine Katherine's claim – showing her as the mother of a bastard child would certainly not do her credibility any good. On 31st January, 1562, an ecclesiastical commission was set up, under Matthew Parker, Archbishop of Canterbury, and the details of the couple's union examined.

What constituted marriage was not absolutely clear-cut. Prior to the Reformation, the general view was that consent, a statement that the couple were marrying or planning to marry, plus consummation was sufficient, provided both parties either agreed they had consented, or there were witnesses to the promise. The Book of Common Prayer adopted in 1559 required banns to have been read on at least three Sundays, or a licence to have been given by the Archbishop to obviate the need for banns, but this irregularity did not necessarily invalidate the match.

In this case, much was made of the fact that no witnesses could be produced – Jane Seymour was dead, and the couple had not bothered to find out the name or address of the priest who had officiated. If any official efforts were made to track him down, they failed, either for lack of rigour or because he preferred to avoid the role of scapegoat. The Commission, therefore, in a decision that can hardly have come as a surprise to anyone, in view of the Queen's attitude, declared the marriage invalid on 12th May 1562, and the baby Edward as illegitimate.

Chapter 115: Punishment

Despite the judgement, Katherine and Hertford themselves stuck to their belief in the validity of their marriage. Still languishing in the Tower (although in all the comfort appropriate to her status, with her pets) Katherine clearly inspired sympathy for her plight. On at least two occasions, the gaolers turned a blind eye to a couple of unlocked doors that led to meetings. These meetings led to Katherine falling pregnant again. It would be difficult for the illegitimacy of this child to be impugned, as both parents had stated their belief in their marriage in front of no less a witness than the Archbishop of Canterbury himself!

In the summer of 1562, the succession question became urgent as Elizabeth fell ill with small-pox. Katherine's claims were pressed by some of the Council, but others preferred Mary, Queen of Scots, the Earl of Huntingdon, or the Countess of Lennox (who in strict primogeniture would follow Mary of Scotland and had the advantage of being born in England). Elizabeth recovered, but the new Parliament (carefully managed to ensure a Protestant majority) pushed her to name a successor.

Elizabeth refused. She assured the Commons that she had every intention of marrying and begetting an heir – she just wasn't able to say exactly when. Into this tense situation, Katherine's pregnancy was announced. The scale of Elizabeth's fury was beyond measure. The Lieutenant of the Tower was to be imprisoned for enabling the meetings to take place, and on the day the child (another boy, named Thomas) was christened in February 1563, Hertford was brought before the Star Chamber for further interrogation. The story of how he had bribed the warders was revealed, together with details of his visits to Katherine.

Hertford was found guilty on three counts – deflowering a royal virgin, breaking out of his prison, and repeating his criminal behaviour.

He was fined £15,000 in total and ordered back to the Tower to remain there at the Queen's pleasure.

Katherine and Hertford both remained in the Tower, and now there was no hope of meeting. Hertford wrote importunate letters to Dudley, asking him to intercede with the Queen, even sending her a pair of gloves as a sweetener, but to no avail.

Katherine's relatives also pleaded on her behalf. In March 1563, Lord John Grey, her uncle, wrote a strongly worded letter to Cecil, expatiating on Katherine's misery and condemning the Queen's hard-heartedness:

'In faithe, I wolde I were the Queene's Confessor this Lent, that I might joine her in penaunce to forgeve and forget; or otherwise able to steppe into the pulpett, to tell her Highnes, that God will not forgeve her, unleast she felye forgeve all the worlde...'

It is unlikely that Cecil shared these sentiments with the Queen!

Chapter 116: House Arrest

The summer of 1563 saw an outbreak of plague. By August, the number of deaths had increased to such a level that Elizabeth was begged to send Katherine, her children and Hertford out of London for their own safety. She agreed, and Katherine, together with her younger son, was released to the custody of her uncle, Lord John Grey, at Pirgo in Essex. Lord John was warned Katherine was only being released from the Tower for fear of illness, not to be free.

Hertford was permitted to live with his mother at Hanworth House. Katherine's oldest son went with his father, to be brought up by Anne, Duchess of Somerset.

Once Katherine had arrived at his home, Grey wrote again to Cecil, assuring him of Katherine's penitence. In a rather ironic testament, both to Elizabeth's fears in regard to naming a successor, and her parsimony, Hertford was obliged to defray the costs of Katherine's household, despite the validity of their marriage being denied. Her household consisted of three ladies, three man-servants, a 'lackey', a nurse for the baby, and a two women to wash both her's and the baby's linen.

In addition she had a quantity of furniture, including five pieces of tapestry, a 'changeable' (presumably what we would call 'shot') silk damask bedspread, a red and gold-striped silk quilt, numerous pillows of different levels of softness, footstools and cupboards. Whilst this sounds rather grand, apparently the furniture was largely worn out and shabby. It had also been damaged by Katherine's own monkeys and dogs during her time in the Tower.

In November, Katherine wrote a humble letter to the Queen, begging her pardon and mercy. It was forwarded by Grey to Cecil, with a view to having it first approved and then forwarded by Robert Dudley – this would be Katherine's best hope of forgiveness.

Elizabeth remained adamantine in the face of Katherine's pleading. Katherine then seems to have fallen into depression. Lord John informed Cecil in December 1563, that she was constantly weeping, would not leave her room, and was not eating properly.

Katherine wrote yet another humble letter to Cecil, but, perhaps rather tactlessly, signed it *'Katheryne Hartford'*. She also wrote to her husband, in a letter recently brought back into the light by her biographer, Leanda de Lisle, it having lain hidden after its original Victorian compiler declined to publish its unusually explicit content. Katherine wrote that she

> *'long[s] to be merry with [him] as when [their] little sweet boy in the Tower was gotten...'*

Chapter 117: The Succession Question

Katherine was a figure of sympathy for many – why should she not marry at her pleasure? But others considered the behaviour of the young couple as foolish at best, and treasonable at worst. Whilst the country outside London was still, in the early 1560s, traditional in religious practice, London was at the forefront of Protestant thought. Katherine's sister, Lady Jane Grey, was considered a Protestant martyr, and there were several publications, including John Foxe's *'Book of Acts and Monuments'* (Foxe's Book of Martyrs) that capitalised on the Grey adherence to the new faith. Katherine, now with two sons, was their prime candidate for the succession.

Her claims were tabulated in a book by the MP John Hales, possibly aided by Cecil (certainly Lord Robert thought so, and Nicholas Bacon, Keeper of the Great Seal, agreed). Hales, who was the Member of Parliament for Lancaster, had been a member of Edward VI's Government, and was an associate of the more Protestant leaning of Elizabeth's ministers. He not only espoused Katherine as heir, but also declared that her marriage was legal, despite the findings of the Archbishop's Court. Not content with writing his book, he brought the matter up in the House of Commons – this led to a speedy dispatch to the Fleet prison, followed by a sojourn in the Tower, and then house arrest for almost the rest of his life. Such was the danger of meddling with the succession, and Katherine and Hertford too, continued to face the consequences.

Whatever Elizabeth might have wanted to do (and there is no evidence that she had anything but dislike for her Grey cousins), to free Katherine would have undermined her strategy to keep the succession in abeyance, or if she couldn't avoid specifying an heir, settle it on Mary, Queen of Scots, whom she hoped to neutralise by arranging a marriage for her with her own favourite, Robert Dudley. Hertford was returned to the Tower on 26th May 1564, and Katherine moved to even stricter supervision under Sir William Petre at Ingatestone Hall. Her uncle was too partisan, and was sent to the Tower himself to contemplate the Queen's displeasure.

More pleas were made – from the Duchess of Somerset to Cecil, and Hertford to Dudley, who counselled patience. Sometime during the summer, Hertford was released to the custody of Sir John Mason, who heartily disliked him, while Katherine remained at Ingatestone.

Despite her imprisonment, she was still seen as a potential heir to the throne. In 1565, Philip of Spain thought it possible that she would be named as successor as an act of revenge by Elizabeth and the English Parliament following the marriage of Mary, Queen of Scots to Lord Darnley, who was the nearest male heir to Elizabeth. However, it did not happen.

Chapter 118: The End

Katherine was to stay at Ingatestone for two years, before being moved in May 1566 to the home of Sir John Wentworth at Gosfield Hall, a distant cousin of Hertford's. Sir John was not happy at the arrival of such a troublesome prisoner. Well into his seventies, he declared that he would rather be imprisoned himself than be custodian of Katherine. He pointed out how easy it would be for her to escape. Katherine did not attempt to escape, but she and Hertford still corresponded.

During 1566, calls for the succession to be assured were again brought forward by Parliament, with Katherine still favoured by the majority of the Protestant faction - although not all. Dudley was inclined to support the claims of Mary, Queen of Scots, who now had a son. Elizabeth, with her usual skill, managed to evade the issue yet again.

Then came the bombshell that overshadowed politics in England and Scotland for the next twenty-five years. The Queen of Scots' husband, Lord Darnley, had been murdered, and Mary deposed, accused of complicity in his death. Yet another wave of uncertainty over the succession washed over Elizabeth and her ministers, with the rival factions supporting Katherine and Mary each pushing their own candidate forward. Meanwhile, Katherine herself was still isolated in Essex, although she was now permitted to enjoy the rents of some of the lands previously owned by her parents.

By the end of 1567, poor Sir John Wentworth had died, and his widow and executor were at their wits' end with no orders as to what to do with their young prisoner. She was moved to even stricter confinement at Cockfield Hall in Suffolk, under the wardenship of a protesting Sir Owen Hopton.

As soon as he saw her, Hopton realised that Katherine was ill. He requested that the Queen's own doctor, Dr Symonds, be sent to treat her. Katherine however, did not want to get better. She lay in bed, depressed, not eating and with no hopes for the future. She listened to the psalms being read to her and although the Hoptons exhorted her to brace up and take comfort, she would not.

At the end, she confirmed the Protestant faith in which she had been brought up, saying that *'[she] believe[d] to be saved by the death of Christ.'* She then sent a last request to the Queen, to hold her children blameless for her own offences, and to ask Elizabeth to set Hertford free. To her husband, for so she was certain that he was, she left the diamond betrothal ring, her wedding ring, and a ring with a picture of herself set in it. Katherine died on 27th January, 1568, at the age of twenty-eight.

Elizabeth made a polite show of sorrow, and ordered a suitably grand funeral, complete with Katherine's arms of England, quartered with France, differenced for her descent. A sum of £140 was sent to Hopton for Katherine's final expenses and the costs of the funeral. Katherine was buried in the parish church of Yoxford, rather than in Westminster Abbey with her mother.

Hertford, surprisingly, seems to have learnt little from his experiences. Although after Katherine's death he was released and restored to the normal activities of a peer of the realm, he made two further secret marriages and had another couple of sojourns in the Tower.

After the accession of James I, Hertford managed, in 1608, to track down the clergyman who had married him to Katherine. It seems extraordinarily unlikely that the man, who had not come forward previously, should both still be alive, and identifiable. A suspicious mind might think that either Hertford knew where he was all along, or that he found someone willing to play the part. Nevertheless, there he was, prepared to swear that Hertford and Katherine had been legally married.

The incentive may have been his grand-son's secret plan to marry the Lady Arbella Stuart, who had a strong claim to the throne. Hertford died in 1621, having outlived Katherine by over 50 years. Their grandson had Katherine's body exhumed, and she now rests, finally at Hertford's side, in a grand tomb in Salisbury Cathedral.

Aspects of Lady Katherine Grey's Life

Chapter 119: Following the Footsteps of Katherine Grey

Katherine's childhood was typical of the nobility of the time – regular visits to London and the court, long summer months in the country, and a round of visits to family and friends. Unfortunately, she also spent a third of her life as a prisoner – first in the Tower of London, and then under house arrest in Essex and Suffolk.

The numbers in the text below correspond to those on the map which follows.

*

Katherine Grey was probably born at her parents' town house in London. Dorset House (1), in the City of London. Originally Salisbury Court, and the possession of the Bishops of Salisbury, Dorset House was located near the current City Thameslink station, clues to its location being in the names of Salisbury Court and Dorset Rise.

As well as their town house, the Dorsets owned Bradgate House (2) in Leicestershire. Building at Bradgate began around 1499 under the aegis of Thomas Grey, 1st Marquess of Dorset, Katherine's great-grandfather, who was the son of Queen Elizabeth Woodville, by her first marriage. The house, built in the fashionable, and expensive, red-brick favoured by the Tudor elite, was completed around 1520. Although it was not a small property, it was more in the nature of a country house, than a great mansion or castle. The remains of the house are still visible today.

During Katherine's girlhood, she would have spent a good deal of time here, particularly in the summer when nobles left London to avoid the diseases that tended to spread in the warmer months. During the hunting season, too, the Dorsets would spend time here – Leicestershire was (and is) considered one of the prime areas for hunting in England, and the vast parks surrounding the house would have been stocked with deer.

Part of aristocratic life was visiting relatives and friends. Katherine frequently visited the Willoughbys of Wollaton who were her paternal relatives. Lady Anne Grey, Lady Willoughby (d. 1548), being her father's sister. The two families remained close. When Sir Henry Willoughby died fighting for the Crown during Kett's Rebellion in 1549, the young Willoughbys, Francis, Margaret and Thomas, were placed in the care of their mother's relatives.

Thomas Willoughby was placed with the Dorsets and the other two with Dorset's half-brother, George Medley, at Tilty (3) in Essex. This was another house frequented by Katherine. Formerly a Cistercian Abbey, just before its dissolution, the Abbot had granted Dorset's mother, Margaret Wotton, Marchioness of Dorset, a sixty-year lease of buildings and land. Although the matter was looked into – fraud being suspected in a lease granted when the monasteries were being dissolved - it was found to be a legitimate transaction. No traces are left of Tilty today, although the parish church where the family probably worshipped, remains.

Another house in Essex where Katherine visited at least once, was Beaulieu (4), or Newhall. This was the home of her mother's cousin, the Lady Mary, daughter of Henry VIII. Near Chelmsford, the palace was built by Henry VIII in the 1520s – a recent excavation by Channel 4's Time Team found significant remains of the construction, again in the fashionable red-brick. The property was then granted to George Boleyn,

Lord Rochford, brother of Queen Anne Boleyn, before reverting to the Crown and being given to the Lady Mary in 1537. A private school now occupies the site.

When Katherine's father was granted the Dukedom of Suffolk, on the death of both her half-uncles in 1551, the family inherited a grand new town house, Suffolk House. The property was formerly Norwich House, the town house of the eponymous bishop, but was frequently used by courtiers. In 1528, it was suggested as an appropriate lodging for Cardinal Campeggio who had come to hear Henry VIII's annulment case. However, the idea was rejected because

> *'that lewd knave Jamys that nevyr did good hath so paynted Norwyche place to the Cardynall that it seemyth that logyng hym ther ye wold have logyd him in a pygge stye.'*

In 1536, this *'pig-sty'* was granted to Katherine's grand-father, Charles Brandon, Duke of Suffolk, in exchange for a house he had at Southwark. It reverted to the Crown following the execution of Katherine's father, and was variously used by Archbishops of York, the Lords Keeper, and even the Earl of Essex. No trace of the house remains today.

Another house, similarly located on the Strand, leading down to the Thames that Katherine would have known, was Durham House (6). Again, the palace of a Bishop, it was frequently used in the sixteenth century by royalty. Katharine of Aragon was lodged there during her widowhood, and Edward VI lived there before acceding to the throne. Under Henry VIII's will, it was granted to his daughter, the Lady Elizabeth, but the Duke of Northumberland contrived to wrest it from her, but not without her *'conceyvinge some displeser'* against him.

For Katherine, it was a significant location as the place where she was married to Henry Herbert, son of the Earl of Pembroke, on 25th May 1553.

Following her marriage, Katherine went to live at Baynard's Castle with her in-laws. Baynard's Castle had been the London home of Cicely Neville, Katherine's great-great-grandmother during the reign of Edward IV. In 1509, it was granted to Katharine of Aragon, and also formed part of the jointure of Anne of Cleves, on her marriage to Henry VIII. On Henry VIII's death it was granted to William Herbert, 1st Earl of Pembroke, and his wife, Anne Parr, sister of Queen Katherine. Katherine Grey was only resident here for a few weeks, as, following the failure of the coup intended to put her sister on the throne, Pembroke disowned the marriage, and sent her back to her mother.

Katherine spent the next few years as maid-of-honour to the new queen, Mary I. She would have lived at Whitehall, Greenwich, Hampton Court, Richmond and St James' Palaces, amongst other royal properties. She was present at the marriage on 25th July 1554 of Mary and Philip of Spain at Winchester Cathedral (8).

During the summer of 1558, Katherine spent several weeks at the manor of Hanworth. This was another royal property – it had been one of the dower houses of Katherine Parr. In the 1550s, it was occupied by Anne Stanhope, Duchess of Somerset. The Duchess, despite being a strong adherent of reform, and the widow of Protector Somerset, had always had a good personal relationship with the Queen Mary, and her daughter, Lady Jane Seymour, was another of the Queen's maids-of-honour, and Katherine's best friend.

The two girls were at Hanworth for Jane to convalesce after a bout of influenza that had almost carried her off. Katherine was courted by Jane's brother, Edward Seymour. On returning to court, the girls found that, whilst Jane had recovered from the influenza which, the Queen had now caught it, and had no hope of recovery. Katherine would have been at the Palace of St James where Mary died, and attended her funeral at Westminster Abbey in December 1558. In the following year, she attended her mother's funeral, also in the Abbey. Duchess Frances had spent her last years in her home at Sheen (9), near modern day Richmond-on-Thames.

Katherine remained at court under the new queen, Elizabeth I, although Elizabeth had far less time for her than Mary had had, and demoted her from the Privy Chamber. In due course, Katherine's romance with Edward Seymour (now Earl of Hertford) was rekindled, and in late 1560, aided and abetted by her friend Jane Seymour, the couple were secretly married at his house at Cannon Row, Westminster (10).

On discovery of the match, the wrathful Elizabeth clapped both Katherine and Hertford into the Tower of London (11), where they remained until the summer of 1563. When plague broke out, Elizabeth was persuaded to send Katherine, still as a prisoner, to her uncle, Lord John Grey's, home at Pirgo (12) in Essex.

Because Lord John was considered too lenient, and was also suspected of involvement in John Hales' book promoting Katherine's rights of succession, she was moved to Ingatestone Hall (13) under the care of Sir William Petre. Ingatestone Hall remains, a wonderful Tudor house that is frequently host to Tudor re-enactments.

Before too long, Katherine was on the move again, this time to Gosfield Hall, Essex, home of Sir John and Lady Wentworth, distant relatives of Hertford's. The property, built in the late 1540s, still remains standing and is used as a wedding venue. On the death of the elderly Sir John, Katherine was moved to what would be her final home-cum-prison, Cockfield Hall (14) in Suffolk.

Cockfield Hall still exists, although the building has been refurbished and is in largely eighteenth century style. Here, although her custodian, Sir Owen Hopton, did his best to restore her to health, Katherine succumbed to illness, exacerbated by depression and died in 1568. Originally buried in the parish church at Yoxford, she was moved fifty years after her death to lie beside Hertford in and elaborate tomb in Salisbury Cathedral (15).

Key to Map

1. Dorset House, London
2. Bradgate, Leicestershire
3. Tilty, Essex
4. Beaulieu, Essex
5. Suffolk House, London
5. Durham House, London
6. Baynard's Castle, London
7. Hanworth Manor, London
8. Winchester Cathedral, Hampshire
9. Sheen, London
10. Cannon Row, London
11. Tower of London
12. Pirgo, Essex
13. Ingatestone Hall, Essex
14. Cockfield Hall, Essex
15. Salisbury Cathedral

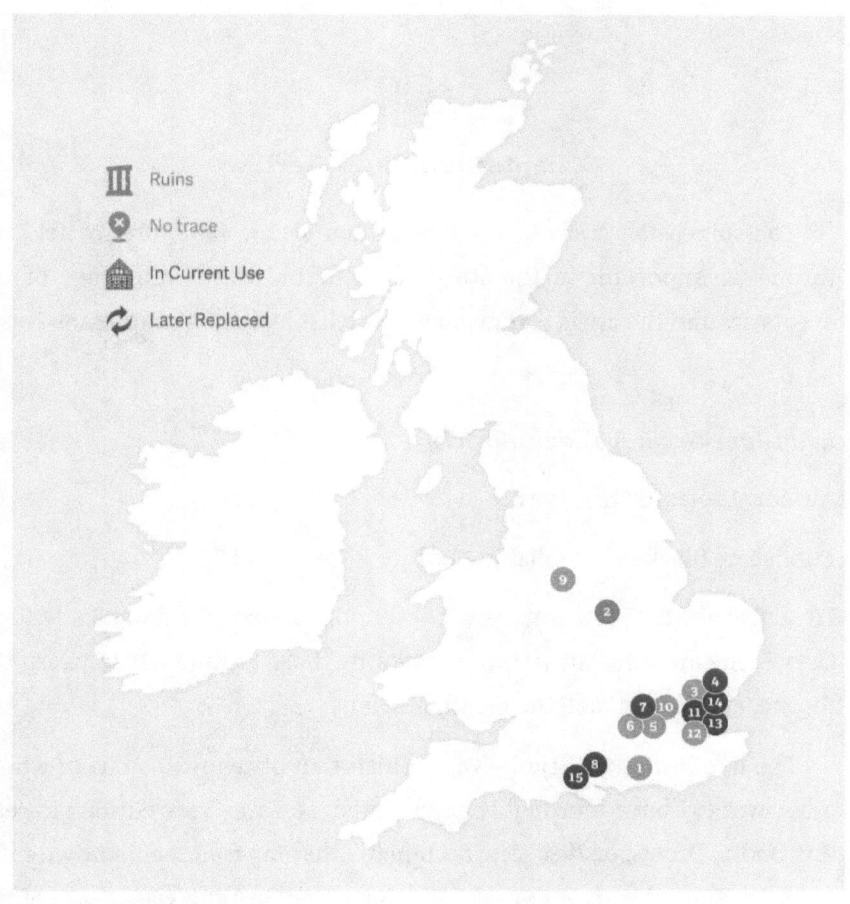

Chapter 120: Book Review

The succession crisis of 1553, when her sister, Jane, briefly held the throne, is important in the story of Katherine Grey. Coverage of the events around the crisis was given a new twist by the late Professor Ives.

Lady Jane Grey: A Tudor Mystery

Author: Professor Eric Ives

Publisher: Blackwell Publishing Ltd

In a nutshell Professor Ives' contention is that, far from Lady Jane Grey being an innocent victim of a plot by those around her to usurp the throne, she was, in fact, the legitimate heir.

The late Professor Eric Ives is an historian of renown, some of whose other works I have thoroughly appreciated, so I was very curious to read this book. Professor Ives' central tenet is that far from being an attempt at usurpation, the accession of Lady Jane Grey in 1553 was a case of the Crown passing to the legitimate heir, and that her overthrow by Mary was the result of rebellion. This is not, of course, the received opinion, and I was eager to be convinced by new information or arguments. The '*mystery*' of the book is how such an overthrow was achieved.

The format of the book, too, is slightly unconventional, in that rather than a narrative of events, he begins by describing each of the main protagonists in detail. This is very helpful, as it prevents lots of asides when the main action of the book is presented. Unfortunately, Ives' predilection for Jane Grey results in a number of repetitions of incorrect facts and misogynist comments about Mary. For example he claims that

Mary's mother, Katharine of Aragon, encouraged her to see herself as *'half a Hapsburg'*. Neither Katharine nor Mary had any Hapsburg blood whatsoever. Nor is a description of Mary, aged 37, as *'ageing'* likely to have been used of any male in the story. In fact, he refers to Northumberland's achievements at *'barely forty'* as *'unique in Tudor England.'*

Passing on to Edward VI, the information about the development of Edward's authority, and how he moved from being a spectator in government, to beginning to formulate policy, is very persuasive. In particular, the detail about the development of the Devise for the Succession is comprehensive, although I found the statement that Edward *'never even thought of his half-sisters'* as possible heirs bizarre. Of course he must have thought of them, as they were named in his father's Will, and, in any event, within a few paragraphs Ives writes that Edward was deliberately creating a Will that *'mimics Henry VIII's own.'*

Ives then goes on to consider the legality of Edward's Devise. He first states that Parliament hadn't *granted* Henry VIII the right to change the succession, because that would suggest that Parliament was of higher authority than the King, not the position in the sixteenth century constitution, but merely recognised Henry's right. Thus, if Henry VIII had the right to change the succession by Will, so had Edward VI. I am not entirely convinced by that argument, as, although Parliament was not above the King, it was not necessarily the case that the King was above the law, although this was undoubtedly a murky area, not tested until the Civil War. It also does not accord with the wording of the act, which says:

'by the authority of the same (the Lords Spiritual and Temporal and the Commons) your highness shall have full and plenary power... to give, dispose etc.'

However, Ives establishes, to his own satisfaction, that Edward's Devise for the Succession document was legal and thus, the proclamation of Jane as Queen on Edward's death was fully justified, and totally in accordance with Edward's wishes. This raises the other plank of Ives' argument, which appears to be a complete exoneration of the Duke of Northumberland from any responsibility for the matter at all.

Ives contends, first, that the three marriages of May 1553 between Northumberland's son and Lady Jane, Pembroke's son and Lady Katherine Grey, and Northumberland's daughter to the son of the Earl of Hastings, were no more than the usual aristocratic arrangements. He even goes so far as to say that *'the evidence is that the initiative for Jane's marriage did not come from Northumberland at all,'* and that suspicion about Northumberland's motives was a post-event justification. He also adduces evidence that the other Privy Councillors were equally involved, although whether they were genuinely inclined to accept Edward's Devise, or brow-beaten by Northumberland as they claimed, is debated. Ives' view being that of Mandy Rice Davies in the Profumo Affair – *'Well, they would say that, wouldn't they?'*

Having identified that there was widespread support for Edward's Devise, Ives claims that this support was forthcoming because Henry's attempt to settle the Crown on illegitimate off-spring was a subversion of common law that had made all property owners uneasy, and thus the choice of Lady Jane as successor was entirely consistent with a return to the rule of law. Unfortunately, he does not then address the question of why, if common law should be followed, Edward's heir was not Mary, Queen of Scots? Or Henry Stuart, Lord Darnley? Even Lady Frances, rather than her daughter? All three of them would precede Jane Grey under common law.

Moving on from the legal issues, Ives addresses the events themselves, from the perspective that Mary's refusal to accept Jane as

Queen was an act of rebellion. The clear inference he draws is that the Privy Council just could not encompass the thought that Mary might rebel and therefore did not prepare thoroughly to circumvent it, rather than that they themselves were half-hearted. He also postulates that there was little objection to Jane's accession amongst the nobility or gentry, or even the population of London. He also disputes accounts that Northumberland had difficulty raising men.

This interpretation paints Ives into a corner. If everyone who counted supported Jane, and the commoners were happy to serve in her army, where did it go wrong? It wasn't even the defection of the six ships sent to patrol the Suffolk coast, and the dispatch of their guns to Mary, which is often postulated as the root of her success.

Instead, Ives sees the collapse of Jane's support as the fault of the Earls of Arundel and Pembroke who would not take military action themselves. The final section of the book deals with the aftermath of the crisis.

Whilst I hesitate to criticise such an eminent historian as Professor Ives, I cannot help but feel that the arguments in the book lack a certain level of logical integrity and don't necessarily follow from the information presented. The mystery is not really solved. Nevertheless, in spite of my reservations, I would recommend the book as a detailed account of the events of the summer of 1553.

Part 10: Sir William Cecil: Elizabeth I's Chief Minister

Introduction

Sir William Cecil, Lord Burghley was the longest-serving and most successful politician of the Tudor age. First as Privy Councillor to Edward VI, and then as Elizabeth I's Secretary and Treasurer, he profoundly influenced the religion and politics of the second half of the sixteenth century. Scourge of the Catholics, and implacable enemy of Mary, Queen of Scots, Cecil's life was devoted to fulfilling his vision of a Protestant nation.

Cecil was a Lincolnshire man, born and bred, and he always saw that county as his own. But as a politician, he needed to keep close to the centre of power and he spent the majority of his life in and around the capital, building several houses to reflect his status.

This book contains Sir William Cecil's Life Story and additional articles about him, looking at different aspects of his life. Whilst politics were central to Cecil's life, he was also a scholar and a bibliophile. Widely read, hungry for knowledge and fascinated by architecture and maps, he took an interest in topics as diverse as gardening, navigation, astronomy and alchemy. Cecil was a family man, close to his parents, siblings and second wife, but not all his personal relationships were successful.

SIR WILLIAM CECIL

Family Tree

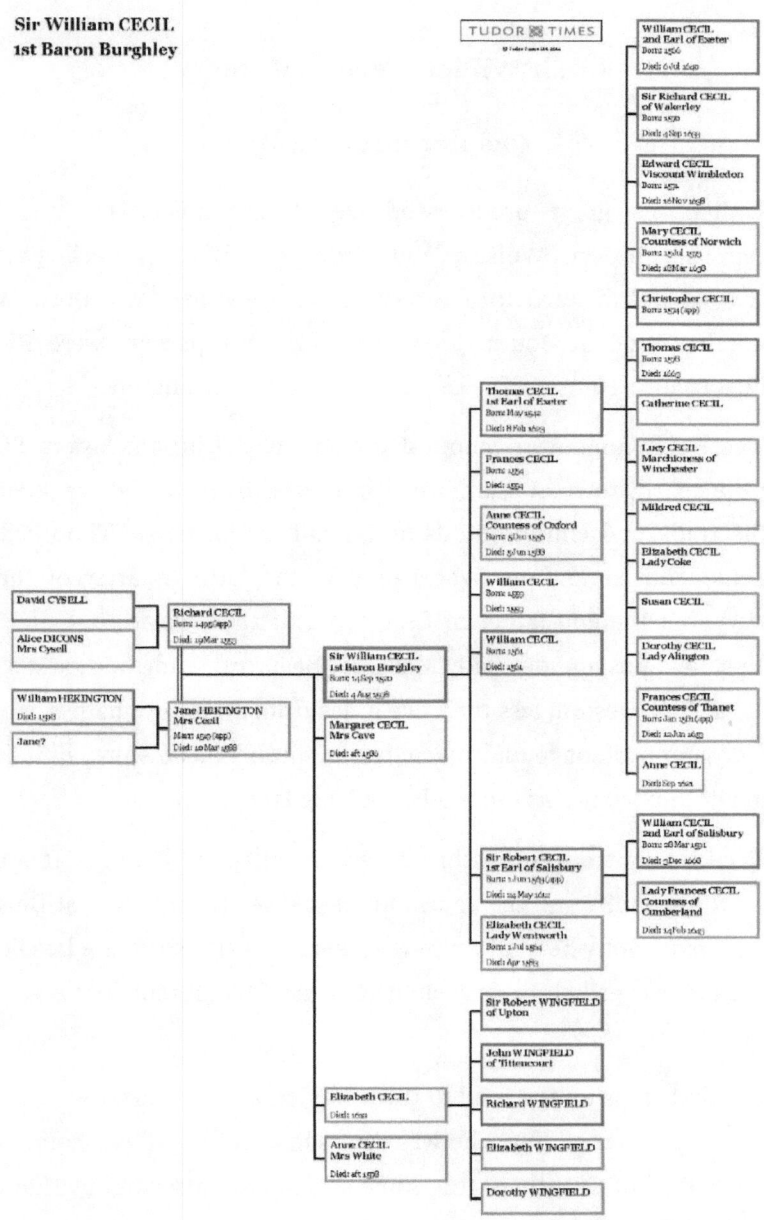

Sir William Cecil's Life Story

Chapter 121: Education

Unlike his great predecessors as chief minister to the Tudor monarchs, Morton, Wolsey, and Cromwell, William Cecil probably always looked forward to a career in the royal service. Born in late September 1520 at Bourne in Lincolnshire, his parents were Richard Cecil, a Page in Henry VIII's chamber, and Jane Hekington.

The Hekingtons were amongst the elite of the urban class in Bourne and the nearby town of Stamford. They were town councillors, members of the trade and church guilds and small landowners. The Cecils (or Syssells) had come from Wales only in the latter quarter of the 15th century, but the god-father of Cecil's grandfather, David, one Sir David Philips, held posts under Lady Margaret Beaufort. Lady Margaret's great estate at Collyweston, less than five miles from Stamford made her one of the most important feudal magnates in south Lincolnshire, quite apart from her importance as the mother of King Henry VII.

Cecil thought of Lincolnshire as his '*country*' all his life. It was the heart of his family and the enormous estate he created there at Burghley was the patrimony he left to his eldest son. It was also where he chose to be buried. Nevertheless, from an early age, his path took him away from home.

His first steps on the road to royal service were educational. The only boy amongst four siblings, he was sent some 15 miles from home to the King's School at Grantham (the same school later attended by that other illustrious son of Lincolnshire, Sir Isaac Newton). King's School was founded by Henry VII's Lord Privy Seal, Bishop Richard Foxe, also a Lincolnshire man.

The school, which still survives, is in the shadow of the enormous church dedicated to St Wulfram which must have been a focal point for the pupils, whose education was largely aimed at entry to the church or the law. There, Cecil would have practised the religion of his forefathers, surrounded by candles, relics, images of the saints and prayers for the dead.

After a short period at Grantham, Cecil was moved to a school closer to home, the new chantry school at Stamford, where he remained under the supervision of the priest-cum-school master, Libeus Byard, until he was about 14. Then, in 1535, he went to Cambridge. The college he attended, that of St John the Evangelist, again had local connections. It had been founded under the will of Lady Margaret Beaufort by her friend and confessor, John Fisher, Bishop of Rochester. Both Lady Margaret and Fisher were renowned for their piety and their learning, encouraging the Humanist expansion of learning of the late 15th century which became a feature of St John's. Greek, Hebrew and medicine were on the curriculum, in addition to the subjects taught at the other Cambridge Colleges.

When Cecil arrived, he was flung into a maelstrom of political, educational and religious upheaval. The King, Henry VIII, in his quest for an annulment of his marriage to Katharine of Aragon, had rejected the authority of the Pope, an act which Bishop Fisher refused to accept, with fatal consequences. After his execution, which took place in June 1535, about a month after Cecil's arrival, Cromwell sent an order to St John's to have every monument or reference to Fisher defaced.

Whilst Henry had largely intended that the change in overall authority in the church should be the only alteration, the spirit of reform was abroad, and the principles of Luther and other reformers were spreading like wild-fire amongst the intellectuals of the day. St John's College contained a circle of men who would go on to be the first generation of scholars and academics in England who could be termed Protestant.

The group included John Cheke, whose novel approach to the pronunciation of Greek had created waves in traditional academic circles; Roger Ascham, later tutor to the Lady Elizabeth and Lady Jane Grey; and Sir Anthony Denny who had a role in the education of Edward VI. When Cecil arrived, he was drawn to this set and embraced their religious stance, first evangelicalism, concentrating on the importance of the scriptures; then the doctrine of Justification by Faith alone, and finally the rejection of the Mass as predicated on the doctrine of transubstantiation (ie that Christ was really physically present in the bread and wine).

Cecil remained in Cambridge for some five years, leaving in 1540 to complete his education at Gray's Inn in London, where he was admitted to the Bar on 6th May 1541. With strong reformist views, a church career was not on the cards, and a training in civil law was the most obvious home for his talents.

Chapter 122: Councillor in Training

According to Cecil's later reminiscences, he was a member of the Parliament that sat between 16 January 1542 and 28th March 1544, although there is no record of which constituency he represented, nor whether he sat for the whole period or came in on a by-election. This was the Parliament that passed the Third Act of Succession. This Act laid down the order of succession after Henry VIII's son Edward and any child he might have by Katherine Parr, if neither Edward nor such additional children had legitimate heirs. In that case, the crown was to be inherited by Henry's elder daughter, Mary, and her heirs, then, if she had none, his younger daughter, Elizabeth, and her heirs. It also permitted Henry to name, by his will, heirs to follow on from Elizabeth if she had no children. The Act designated as treason any attempt to subvert this arrangement.

During his time in Cambridge, Cecil had become acquainted with John Cheke's sister, Mary, whom he married in August 1541. Her mother, Agnes, was a widow and an established vintner and property owner in Cambridge. She was not, however, of the gentry class, and for this reason (or perhaps the very prompt arrival of their son, Thomas), Cecil's father did not approve of the match. It was unusual for a man of Cecil's class to marry without parental consent, so we might infer that it was a love match, perhaps precipitated by pregnancy. By the end of May 1543, Mary, back in Cambridge, had died, and been buried at her mother's, rather than her husband's expense. For the time being, little Thomas Cecil stayed with Agnes Cheke.

Freed from his hasty marriage (there is no evidence about how he reacted to Mary's death), Cecil was able to make a far more advantageous match. His second wife, whom he married on 21st December 1545 was Mildred Cooke, daughter of the courtier, Anthony Cooke.

The marriage was probably arranged by Cecil's father who would have known Cooke, since the latter was one of the King's '*spears*' or bodyguards. Cooke was an exceptionally learned man, and was at the forefront of promoting intellectual education for women. His five daughters, Anne, Mildred, Elizabeth, Margaret and Katherine, learnt Greek and Latin, and both Anne and Mildred became known for their scholarship. Given Cecil's intellectual interests, it seems likely to have been a match to suit both parties. This marriage drew Cecil further into the circle of Reformers and scholars whose influence in the last years of Henry VIII was growing.

This circle included illustrious figures – Queen Katherine Parr, Katherine Willoughby, Dowager Duchess of Suffolk, and Edward Seymour, Earl of Hertford, the King's brother-in-law who all became known to Cecil, and the Duchess of Suffolk remained a lifelong friend. The relationship with Hertford was particularly important as he was likely to be of some importance during the reign of Henry's successor: a time that could not be long in coming. Henry's health was declining as his weight ballooned.

Chapter 123: Somerset's Man

When Henry VIII died in 1547, Hertford became Lord Protector, and Duke of Somerset. By the middle of that year, if not before, Cecil was in his direct employ. Within a year, Cecil had the post of Master of Requests – that is, he had the responsibility of reviewing petitions made to Somerset and sending them on to the appropriate divisions of the Courts at Westminster (not to be confused with the role of Master of the Court of Requests, a legal office).

Despite the fact that Somerset had fallen out with the Queen Dowager, Katherine Parr, Cecil remained on good terms with her. He wrote an effusive introduction to her devotional work, the *Lamentations of a Sinner*, which he registered for her at Stationer's Hall in late 1547. This friendship with her step-mother may have been the root of Elizabeth and Cecil's acquaintanceship.

In the political world of the sixteenth century, a system of favours and place-seeking for friends and family that we would consider corrupt, was the norm. The mediaeval concept of *'good-lordship'* whereby the lower ranking person (both men and women) gave service, or gifts in return for the higher-ranking individual putting them forward for plum jobs continued, although, as the century progressed, it began to be questioned. Cecil was now in a position to do favours for people, and he began to be seen as a man of influence.

One of Somerset's pet projects was the forcible absorption of Scotland into English domination. The project had been begun by Henry VIII, when his nephew, James V, died, leaving a week old baby as queen. Henry had leapt at the idea of marrying her to his son, Edward. The Scottish Regent, Arran, initially in favour, could not force the scheme through his Parliament, and the little Queen Mary was hidden away from the risk of abduction by her terrifying great-uncle. Henry, with Somerset as his lieutenant, had made war on the recalcitrant Scots. Somerset, a notable soldier, continued the policy, and led an army north in person.

Cecil was part of this force, not, officially as a soldier, but as a judge of the Court of the Verge. This court was responsible for jurisdiction in disputes involving members of the sovereign's court that took place within a 12-mile radius of wherever the sovereign happened to be. Presumably it was considered likely that there would be disputes between men on campaign. Whilst away, Cecil and his colleague, William Patten, kept journals. Patten used their memoranda to write his book '*The Expedition into Scotland*' published in 1548. The expedition was, from the English perspective, extremely successful, culminating on 10th September 1547 with the Battle of Pinkie Cleugh, which effectively annihilated Scotland's army, and allowed the English, including Cecil, to burn Leith and besiege Edinburgh.

This vision of incorporating the neighbouring kingdom into a single, Protestant, country of Britain, followed Cecil throughout his life, and much of his later policy as Elizabeth's chief minister, was undertaken with the goal of achieving it.

Somerset's rule also introduced extensive religious reforms, which Cecil wholeheartedly supported. Change began to be visible in churches in the summer of 1547, when, as well as reinforcing the requirement for an English Bible and a copy of Erasmus' *Paraphrases* to be in every parish church, the incumbents were exhorted to remove anything that could tend to idolatry or image worship. The statues of the saints and the holy relics which had been objects of veneration for hundreds of years began to be removed, although wholesale destruction did not happen until after the passing of the Chantries Act of 1548.

This Act disbanded the religious guilds that had been such an important feature of mediaeval life: that mixture of civic duty and religious devotion that had built the churches and cathedrals, and instituted a whole system based on belief in the doctrine of purgatory. Now, prayers for the dead were outlawed, the chantries which had been endowed for priests to say Masses for souls for the dead were torn down, and a wave of window-smashing, and destruction of images rolled over the country.

The chantries had been staffed by priests who, when they were not saying the obligatory Masses (a priest could only offer two per day), frequently taught the local children. In just such a chantry school at Stamford had Cecil received his own education. Now, although Cecil was committed to reform, he used his influence to have a private act passed re-founding his old school as a Grammar School, affiliated to St John's College, Cambridge and under the mastership of his old teacher, Libeus Byard.

Not everyone was happy with these religious changes. In particular, Stephen Gardiner, Bishop of Winchester, who had led the conservative faction in Henry VIII's last years, objected strongly to religious changes being made before Edward VI reached his majority. Cecil was sent by Somerset to try to persuade Gardiner to conform to government policy, but met with no success. Gardiner preached a very public sermon, condemning the changes.

Then came the 1549 Book of Common Prayer. Probably the work of Thomas Cranmer, Archbishop of Canterbury, it changed church services from Latin to English, and reduced and changed some of the ceremony and ritual. It was based on the traditional Sarum rite of the English Church, and its central ceremony of the Eucharist was ambiguously worded, allowing for both Catholic and Protestant interpretation. Nevertheless, for the more conservatively minded (which was the vast majority of people outside London and East Anglia, where Protestantism flourished), it was unacceptable. Cornwall rose in revolt - in the Prayer Book Rebellion.

Almost simultaneously, in the east of the country, there was a rebellion motivated by economic factors, led by Robert Kett, eventually put down by John Dudley, Earl of Warwick.

Somerset's inability to control events and his high-handed attitude to his colleagues on the Council had lost him popularity, and in the autumn of 1549 he was relieved of office. His friends and colleagues also suffered, and on 24th November 1549, William Cecil was dispatched to the Tower of London.

Chapter 124: Working with Northumberland

Cecil spent eight weeks in the Tower, although comfortably housed, and not subject to any mistreatment. He was released on 25th January 1550, to find that the new man in charge was Dudley, Earl of Warwick. Over the following year the power struggle between Somerset and Warwick continued. Cecil, reading the writing on the wall, abandoned his old master and began to work with Warwick.

On 5th September 1550, in a ceremony at Oatlands Palace, Cecil was given a place on the Privy Council as Secretary to the King. This was an important position, giving access to the monarch, and involving Cecil in all state business. He shared the office with Sir William Petre. Cecil also continued to work with in a more direct capacity for Warwick as his secretary.

As the impetus for Protestant reformation grew, the Privy Council became increasingly concerned about the non-compliance of the Lady Mary, the King's half-sister and heir, to the 1549 Act of Uniformity. Mary refused to countenance any changes to the services laid down in the time of her father, on the stated grounds that, during the King's minority, the Council had no power to change religion. It was widely known, however, that her objections were religious, rather than political. A number of attempts to force her to conform, by imprisoning her household officers, had failed. Mary remained intransigent.

In August 1551, Mary received a letter in the King's name. She received it very properly, kneeling and kissing the seal. But Mary had a sarcastic turn of phrase, and as she read it, she commented aloud:

'Ah, good Master Cecil took much pain here.'

Mary's powerful cousin, the Emperor Charles V, intervened and secured permission for her to hear the traditional Mass, privately. Mary flagrantly abused this privilege, inviting all and sundry to her chapel, but the English government was not in a position to take action. Nevertheless, the drive for reform continued, and Cecil hosted a debate at his house in Canon's Row, Westminster, during which five scholars, including Cecil himself, debated against the doctrine of transubstantiation (that Christ was really, physically, present in the bread and wine). Two men argued in favour of this Catholic interpretation.

Soon after this, on 11th October, 1551, Cecil was knighted in a ceremony at Hampton Court. This was also the occasion for Warwick to be promoted to Duke of Northumberland, making him of equal rank with Somerset, and Henry Grey, Marquess of Dorset and the new Duke's crony, to the Duchy of Suffolk. Tensions between Northumberland and Somerset continued. Cecil seems to have had little hesitation in supporting his new master, and, when Somerset was executed in January 1552, there were no repercussions for his erstwhile friend.

In August 1552, the powerful Scottish preacher, John Knox, arrived at the English Court, taken by Northumberland, who had heard him preach in Newcastle and appointed him as his chaplain. Cecil and Knox seem to have developed, if not a friendship, then at least a position of mutual respect. Knox was at the radical end of Protestantism. He preached in front of Edward VI and Cranmer, Archbishop of Canterbury. What he had to say shook the court. Cranmer, persuaded by the types of argument and debate that Cecil had hosted, had revised the 1549 Prayer Book into a more Protestant version, clearly denying transubstantiation, but commanding Communicants to kneel as a sign of respect. Knox claimed this was idolatry, infuriating the Archbishop. Cranmer became even more enraged when a body of evangelical preachers was engaged by the Privy Council to review his Prayer Book – this included Knox.

Knox was invited to become Bishop of Rochester, but refused. Northumberland wrote to Cecil, explaining that, if Knox could be persuaded to accept, he would firstly, keep Cranmer on his toes, and secondly, stop preaching excessively radical doctrines in the North, and attracting crowds of Scots from over the border. Knox discussed the matter with Cecil, telling him that he would decline the bishopric.

Cecil refused to be Knox's messenger, telling him would have to break the bad news personally. Northumberland was disgruntled, and told Cecil that

'[he loved] not to have to do with men which be neither grateful nor pleasable...'

Cecil continued to correspond with Knox, and it is likely that Knox's views on the necessity for reform in Scotland (still officially Catholic, and ruled by the Queen Dowager, Marie of Guise, as Regent for Mary, Queen of Scots, who was in France) influenced his views on Anglo-Scottish policy.

Cecil was also, perhaps, influenced by Knox's announcement in January 1553, that there were secret traitors, just waiting for Edward VI to die, so that they could bring back Catholicism. Certainly, there were others who believed that for Mary to succeed would spell disaster, and so was born the scheme to change the succession from that laid down in the Act of Succession 1544.

Chapter 125: The 1553 Succession Crisis

In early 1553, Edward VI drew up a *'Devise for the Succession'* which attempted to overturn the Act of Succession 1544. The King's initial plan had been to find a male, Protestant, successor (overlooking the male, Catholic, Lord Darnley, and his own half-sisters). But by June, Edward's time was running out and there was no time for more boys to be born. He settled the succession on his evangelically Protestant cousin, Lady Jane Grey.

The level to which Edward was influenced by Northumberland has been a matter of some debate. There can be little doubt that Edward wanted to preserve his Protestant reformation, and that he would prefer to be succeeded by Lady Jane than by his sister Mary. Equally, Northumberland would benefit as he was Lady Jane's father-in-law. Cecil's level of involvement is also difficult to pin down precisely. We might infer that he would have preferred the crown to pass to Jane – they were of similar mind in religious matters. There was also a family connection – Jane's cousin, Frances Grey of Pirgo, was married to Cecil's brother-in-law, William Cooke. That may seem a rather distant connection today, but, in the sixteenth century, the extended family was an important network of influence.

There is no evidence of Cecil's state of mind, and the detailed record of his actions is contained in the exculpatory letters he sent to Queen Mary after the event, so we might suppose he gave himself the benefit of the doubt when telling her his story.

In spring of 1553, Cecil was absent from court – his father had died, and he himself had taken to his bed with an illness that lasted for nearly two months. On his return in May, he discovered that the King had no hope of surviving the summer and that there was a plan to subvert the succession. He avoided Privy Council meetings, so as not to be involved. Fearing trouble, he arranged for his money and valuables to be hidden.

On 11th June, he was obliged to attend a Council meeting, at which Lord Chief Justice Montague had been invited by the Privy Councillors (including Cecil himself) to attend to give evidence as to the legality of changing the succession without an Act of Parliament. King Edward told Montague he wanted his '*Devise*' implemented, but Montague informed King and Council that to implement it would be treason, as defined by the Act of 1544. The King's personal Devise could not trump an Act of Parliament. This was never going to be music to a Tudor king's ears – even one so young as Edward. Montague was ordered to do as he was told and draw the Devise into legal form. He resisted as long as he could, trying to persuade Edward to call Parliament to make the changes required.

The King was not willing to wait, so, bullied and threatened with dire consequences by King and Council, Montague drew up the document, first requesting a pardon under the Great Seal. In the background, Cecil shared his misgivings with some of his friends and family – including his wife's brother-in-law, Nicholas Bacon. Bacon's wife, Anne Cooke, was a close friend of the Lady Mary's, so it was politic to get his doubts into the right ears.

Once the legal document was drawn up, Cecil, like all the others, added his signature. He claimed however, that he signed only as a witness of the King's intention. No doubt he, like all of his colleagues, was praying for the King to live long enough for the Parliament that had been summoned to relieve him of the taint of treason which clung about them all.

Edward, however, did not live long enough. He died on 6th July 1553, and Cecil was now faced with the choice of committing active treason by supporting Lady Jane, or not. Jane's new Privy Council wrote an offensive letter to Mary, pointing out that as she was illegitimate she could not inherit. Cecil, although he declined to write the offending missive, signed it. He also avoided writing any other letters that were blatantly treasonable, such as orders to the Lords Lieutenant of the counties, or Jane's Accession Proclamation. He did, however, take the oath of fealty to Jane.

Cecil then began (or so he later claimed) to actively undermine Jane's authority. He sounded out his fellow Secretary, Sir William Petre, the Earls of Winchester, Bedford and Arundel and Lord Darcy, with a view to handing over Windsor Castle to Mary. Whether this counter-coup was real, or would have been successful, became, in the end, a moot point. Mary was victorious, and by early August was on her way to London to claim her crown, and to meet a Privy Council, including Cecil, that had suddenly discovered that it had supported her all along.

Cecil raced to meet her, sending his servant, Robert Alford, in advance, and travelling with Nicholas Bacon. He also composed a detailed defence of his actions. He finally came into Mary's presence on 31st July at Ingatestone Hall.

Whether Mary believed his protestations is debatable. However, her policy from the beginning was to accept the grovelling from the councillors, and let them pin all of the blame on Northumberland and his two closest allies.

Cecil's last act as Secretary to Edward VI was to march in his funeral procession on 8th August, 1553.

Chapter 126: Mary's Reign

Cecil was not immediately reappointed to public office as some of his former colleagues, such as Paget and the Earl of Winchester were. He retired to his house at Wimbledon with his family, and, to public view, lived quietly. It seems, however, from evidence presented by his biographer, Stephen Alford, that he was giving support to men undermining the new government. In particular, he hoped to mke life difficult for his old adversary, Gardiner, Bishop of Winchester, now, having been released from the Tower, Lord Chancellor.

A man named Day, working at least in part with Cecil's brother-in-law, William Cooke, was running a secret printing press from land owned by Cecil in Lincolnshire. The works he printed attacked the new government's stance on religion and produced hagiographical works about Lady Jane.

On religious matters, Cecil conformed. Other Protestants were not willing to bow to the restoration of the old faith and went into exile. These exiles included Cecil's friend, Katherine Willoughby, Dowager Duchess of Suffolk and her new husband, Richard Bertie, as well as Cecil's father-in-law, Sir Anthony Cooke. Others stayed home. Sir Nicholas Bacon remained in his post at the Court of Wards and Liveries, with his wife now a Gentlewoman of the Privy Chamber. Roger Ascham, Cecil's old friend from Cambridge, was the new Queen's Latin Secretary. Sooner or later, it seemed likely that Cecil would return to office.

In the meanwhile, Cecil retained a connection with the Queen's sister, and, for the time being, heir, Elizabeth. He had become steward of some of her lands in Lincolnshire, early in the reign of Edward, and continued in that post.

Cecil's chance at rehabilitation came in 1554 when he was commanded to act as host to one of the Secretaries of Philip of Spain, who had arrived in England and married the Queen in July 1554. He then gained a further step when, with what might have been an exquisite sense of irony on the part of Queen Mary, Cecil was sent to Brussels to greet Reginald, Cardinal Pole and escort him back to England after an exile of nearly thirty years.

Pole was returning to England to take up the position of Archbishop of Canterbury, and to return the country to the Roman fold. Surprisingly, Pole and Cecil got on well. Pole (who was later traduced as a heretic by the Pope himself, for his reforming stance) wanted to reform Catholicism in many of the ways that had been first mooted, back in the 1520s, and the scholar in both men appreciated the other.

In early 1555, it looked as though Mary would have a child, reinforcing the return to Rome, and, from Cecil's perspective, the best thing to do was to accept reality and make the most of the new situation. He continued to build links with Mary's Privy Council, and even sent her a gift. Slow integration continued, and in 1555 he was part of a delegation that travelled to Brussels to treat of peace between France and Spain. He then spent a couple of months travelling.

Cecil was returned to Parliament in 1555, where he was one of the opponents of a government bill to confiscate the lands of the Protestant exiles. It was a subject to touch him closely, with many of his friends abroad. The bill was defeated when the opponents locked the supporters out of the House and forced a count. The government was not happy with this misconduct by the Commons, but took no action, beyond sending stern reprimands.

Cecil had purchased the lease of the Rectory of Wimbledon back in 1549. The Manor of Wimbledon (Crown land) was now granted to Pole, and Cecil lobbied hard to become his steward for the land, a position granted in 1556. The Cecils continued to show public conformity to Catholicism. Mildred attended one of Pole's great public sermons, and the couple attended Mass in St Mary's Church, Wimbledon at Easter 1556. As he was '*rector*' of the parish, the offerings from the Easter Mass, less the costs of bread, wine, candles etc went into his pocket.

Meanwhile, those who would make no outward show of conformity were punished with increasing severity – nearly three hundred people, some of whom were Cecil's former colleagues, such as Cranmer, and the Bishops Latimer and Ridley, were burnt. Sir John Cheke, his brother-in-law, although he had initially deplored those who hid their Protestant beliefs, was offered the choice of recantation, or burning. He chose the former.

During these years, the Cecils visited their friends and family, waited on their patrons at court, and began a family. Their first child, Frances, born in 1554, lived only a few hours, but their second, Anne, born in 1556, survived. They attended christenings and weddings, frequently amongst Mildred's Cooke, Bacon, Grey and Hoby connections. Cecil was also continuing to make himself useful to Mary's Councillors and visiting Cardinal Pole.

Things began to change in 1558. The loss of Calais weighed heavily on the Queen and her government, and Mary's renewed hope of pregnancy was not widely believed to have firm foundations. Her health was failing, and the prospect of Elizabeth becoming Queen became closer. During February 1558, Cecil paid a visit to Elizabeth, ostensibly, no doubt to discuss his stewardship of her lands, but perhaps with other intentions, too. By October, it was only a matter of time before Elizabeth became Queen. King Philip's Ambassador, Count Feria, wrote to the King, noting that it was likely that Cecil would be appointed to her government. He described Cecil as:

'...*said to be an able and virtuous man but a heretic.*'

On 17th November, 1558, both Queen Mary and Cardinal Pole died of influenza. Cecil was at Hatfield on that day, with Elizabeth, and they were already planning for the future.

Chapter 127: Urgent Problems

On 20th November, 1558, Cecil was sworn to Elizabeth's Privy Council, and took the office of Master Secretary. In addition to the usual oath of office, it is recorded that Elizabeth gave the great charge of his office to Cecil with the following words:

'This judgement I have of you, that you will not be corrupted with any manner of gift and that you will be faithful to the state, and that without respect of my private will you will give me that counsel that you think best. And if you know anything necessary to be declared to me of secrecy, you shall show it to myself only, and assure yourself I shall keep taciturnity therein, and therefore herewith I charge you.'

Their political partnership was to last for forty years – not without differences in many areas of policy, but ultimately in the forging of a nation state that truly brought England from the middle ages, to the discernible parent of the United Kingdom of the twenty-first century.

On Elizabeth's succession there were four major problems facing her government: the war with France, the rebellion in neighbouring Scotland, religion and the succession. Cecil had decided views on all of these, generally more radical than Elizabeth's.

First, there was the ongoing war. England was Spain's ally in the ongoing round of the interminable Franco-Spanish war that had begun in the 1490s. Although the current outbreak had brought initial success for them, at the Battle of St Quentin in 1557, this had been followed up by the loss of Calais and the decided coolness of Spanish efforts to help recapture it. France and Spain finally made a lasting peace at the Treaty of Cateau-Cambresis, and, although whilst Mary lived, her husband, Philip II tried to include the return of Calais as part of the deal, once he was no longer King of England, he had less interest in pursuing it. England was in no financial position to prosecute the war alone, and had little option but to join in the treaty as agreed. Cecil saw this as evidence of the Catholic powers putting their differences aside to isolate Protestant England.

The nightmare scenario he envisaged was the use of Scotland by France as a back-door into England. The King of France's daughter-in-law was Queen of Scots, and, in the opinion of Catholic Europe was the rightful Queen of England, following Mary I's death. Now it was no longer preoccupied with Spain, France would invade on two fronts.

The solution to this, in Cecil's view, would be for England to support the Lords of the Congregation. This was a group of Scots nobles who, largely under the influence of John Knox, had converted to Protestantism, and who were no longer as convinced as they had been in the 1540s that France was a friend, and England an enemy. The Lords rejected the authority of the Queen Regent, Marie of Guise, who had called for French troops to regain control. Cecil was in constant communication with the Lords and was certain that England should send money and men to help them.

Unfortunately, he was having trouble persuading Elizabeth of the merits of supporting rebellious subjects. Throughout her reign Elizabeth hesitated to support rebels against their lawful prince. For her, solidarity amongst monarchs was more important than solidarity with her co-religionists, especially as the more vocal Protestants like Knox had far more extreme religious beliefs than hers. For Cecil however, the opposite was true. He believed, and would continue to try to persuade the Queen, that England should support Protestant rebels against their Catholic masters.

In 1559, John Knox sought a safe conduct to travel through England. Elizabeth trenchantly refused. Not only was he encouraging rebellion, he was also undermining her own position as Queen with his diatribes against women rulers. Knox had loudly criticised Marie, and also the late Mary I, in his '*First Blast of the Trumpet against the Monstrous Regiment of Women*' excoriating female rule.

The offensive language of the '*First Blast...*' was an affront to Elizabeth. Every attempt of Knox to dig himself out of the hole he had created by claiming that he had not meant to offend her failed. He did suggest that, provided she admitted that she was an exception, with a special dispensation from God from His usual laws against women rulers, then no-one would be happier to maintain her authority than himself.

On the other hand, if she believed that she was Queen because of custom and law, *'her ingratitude [would] not long lack punishment.'*

He asked Cecil to share his views with Elizabeth. One can only imagine Cecil's reaction to such inflammatory language. He declined to answer Knox and certainly didn't communicate his views to Elizabeth. Nevertheless, Cecil was determined to help the Scots Lords and under his control, the Privy Council wrote encouraging words, but there was still Elizabeth to persuade.

Then the Queen of Scots committed what, with hindsight, was probably the greatest mistake of her life. Only sixteen, newly married and crowned as Queen of France (Henri II having died in July 1559), she accepted the Catholic, French view that, in law, if not in fact, she, Mary, was the rightful Queen of England. She quartered her arms with those of England and she and her husband called themselves Kings of France, Scotland and England. For Cecil, this was proof positive that Mary was Elizabeth's bitter enemy, and, for the rest of Mary's life, he sought every possible means to undermine her, and eventually, dispatch her.

Elizabeth, not yet secure on her throne, although furious at Mary's action, still had to be persuaded to act. Initially, Cecil failed to induce his colleagues on the Council to do more than make encouraging noises: not even his brother-in-law, Nicholas Bacon was convinced. It was not until they heard that a French fleet had put to sea in support of the Scottish Regent that the whole Council recommended to Elizabeth that she support the Lords. The Queen, however, rejected their advice out-of-hand. It was only in February 1560, after months of argument, that Elizabeth agreed to give the Lords military assistance.

Cecil travelled north to Edinburgh, where he agreed the Treaty of Edinburgh with the Lords. From the point of view of Cecil and the English, the Treaty was a triumph. From the perspective of the legitimate government of Scotland, Queen Mary and her husband, it was quite unacceptable. The Treaty provided that, if Mary failed to ratify its terms, the English would be free militarily to protect the Protestant religion in Scotland, and prevent French intervention. It also acknowledged Elizabeth as the legitimate Queen of England. Mary never ratified the treaty, but the clauses relating to the withdrawal of French troops were fulfilled.

Chapter 128: The Religious Settlement

Whilst the vast majority of the populace outside London and the South East were largely Catholic in their habits and customs, Elizabeth's immediate advisors were generally Protestant, and many had either been exiles from Mary's rule or had been hiding their religion under a cloak of conformity and were now eager to continue the Protestant reformation begun in Edward's reign. This prevalence of Protestants in her government, led by Cecil, together with a growing dislike of religious persecution (although we need to be careful not to read contemporary reaction solely through the eyes of the martyrologist and vehement Protestant John Foxe) meant a break with Rome was inevitable.

The Pope, Paul IV, not certain of Elizabeth's views, and an inveterate enemy of Spain, was hopeful that she might prove a more biddable member of his flock than Mary had, but he was doomed to disappointment. Whilst Elizabeth never discussed her legitimacy or otherwise, it would be hard for her to accept the Roman Catholic position on her parents' marriage - that it was bigamous and unlawful.

Prior to the meeting of her first Parliament, the law was observed at Elizabeth's court and elsewhere, and the Catholic Mass continued, although Elizabeth showed her rejection of transubstantiation by walking out of Chapel when the priest elevated the Host. Nevertheless, her religious preferences were conservative, and her preferred resolution would have been the reinstitution of the ambiguous 1549 Book of Common Prayer, with acceptance of the monarch, rather than the Pope, as Supreme Head of the Church in England.

A bill to restore Church supremacy to the monarch was introduced in Elizabeth's first Parliament. Guided by Cecil's father-in-law, Anthony Cooke, newly returned from exile, and his brother-in-law, Nicholas Bacon, it eventually passed through the Commons, although not easily. It went to the Lords, where there was strong opposition from both peers and bishops. The Archbishop of York (the senior ecclesiastic, as the see of Canterbury was vacant) pointed out that as a woman could not be a priest, she could not possibly be the head of the Church. The arguments continued, and, instead of the quick return to the Protestant regime of Edward, Cecil found himself stymied.

As the Lords and Bishops could not be punished for their speeches in Parliament, he came up with a scheme to trap the Bishops into appearing to disobey an order from Elizabeth's Council during a debate elsewhere on religion. A couple of the most recalcitrant were sent to the Tower and the others given the opportunity to rethink their objections when a new Supremacy Bill came forward. Again, the Lords were divided, but although all of the Bishops rejected it, the absence of two of them in the Tower, and the strange non-appearance of Dr Feckenham, the Abbot of Westminster, who had led the calls for refusal, meant that the bill was carried by three votes.

The law of the land, enshrined in the Act of Uniformity 1559 now stated that all ministers (not priests) of the Church of England must use the 1559 Prayer Book, which mirrored the 1552 book, amended by deletion of some statements highly offensive to Catholics about the

Bishop of Rome, and removal also of the clear statement that the bread and wine do not change.

To encourage consistency and acceptance of the new rules, every person was to attend the parish church and hear the prescribed service each Sunday, on pain of a fine of 1s. Gentlemen who had their own chapels were exempted, a proviso that saved the position of many of the Catholic nobles, who continued to hear Mass privately. The programme of education of the laity and reform of the clergy which had been part of Mary and Cardinal Pole's plan continued, but with a Protestant bent. In particular, clergy were permitted to marry, something Elizabeth heartily disliked. It was all Cecil could do to persuade her to accept it and, throughout her life she would either ignore, or be rude to, clerical wives. Where he had no success was in the matter of candles and flowers in the Queen's own chapel.

Chapter 129: The Succession

The issue that consumed a vast proportion of Cecil's time in the 1560s was that perennial Tudor favourite, the succession. In accordance with the powers granted in the 1544 Act of Succession, in his Will, Henry VIII had nominated the heirs of the Lady Frances to succeed. With her eldest daughter, Lady Jane Grey now dead, this right devolved on her second daughter, Lady Katherine Grey.

Although there can be no doubt whatsoever that Cecil wanted Elizabeth as queen, and for her to marry and bear an heir, he was quite content with the notion of Lady Katherine as a successor. She was a family connection, and presumably a Protestant, although she had never been as ardent as her sister and had cheerfully conformed under Mary. Mary had treated the Greys kindly, but had made it pretty clear that her personal choice, lacking an heir of her body, would be another cousin, Lady Margaret Douglas, Countess of Lennox, a good Catholic, with a son.

Elizabeth cordially disliked the Grey sisters, and demoted Lady Katherine from her position in the Privy Chamber. She disliked Lady Lennox even more, but was content to play her various cousins off against each other. Elizabeth abhorred any mention of the topic of the succession and never, in all her long life, made an unambiguous statement about it. However, we can infer from some of her comments that she believed her legitimate heir was Mary of Scotland, a view probably shared at the beginning of her reign with her largely Catholic nobles, none of whom wanted interference with the usual laws of inheritance.

For Cecil and the Protestants, however, the idea of Mary of Scotland as queen was their worst nightmare. All of their energies therefore went into persuading Elizabeth herself to marry as soon as possible. Writing to Sir Nicholas Throckmorton, England's Ambassador to France, Cecil said:

'God send our mistress a husband and by him a son, that we may have a masculine succession.'

Elizabeth never rejected the concept totally. Whilst we can look back and consider that her eventual non-marriage worked well, it is not clear that that was a conscious decision by the Queen herself. It was more that the right candidate never appeared. The princes of Europe were generally Catholic, and the example of the trouble caused by her predecessor's choice of a foreign king didn't seem to make that a good idea.

But marriage to one of her own subjects was also fraught with difficulty. The Scottish Earl of Arran, heir in 1560 to Mary, Queen of Scots until she remarried and had a child, suggested his own son, but

Elizabeth didn't care much for that idea – fortunately, as the gentleman in question went mad in 1562 and spent the rest of his life in confinement.

Elizabeth's own closest male heir was the young Lord Darnley, son of Lady Lennox, but in 1560 he was only fourteen. The next male heir was Henry Hastings, Earl of Huntingdon, descendant of both the Duke of Buckingham, executed in 1521, and Margaret, Countess of Salisbury, executed in 1541. He was Protestant, even Puritan, but he was already married to Katherine Dudley, daughter of the late Duke of Northumberland.

Cecil and the Privy Council sought out candidates everywhere, but they were hampered not just by the lack of choice but by Elizabeth's own feelings. During the early 1560s it was apparent to every on-looker that Elizabeth was deeply in love with her Master of Horse, Lord Robert Dudley. He was constantly at her side. They danced, hunted, gambled and laughed together.

Fortunately, from the perspective of Cecil, Dudley was not free to marry. His long-suffering wife was stuck in the country whilst Lord Robert sat up till all hours flirting with the Queen. Nevertheless, Cecil was horrified by the Queen's imprudent behaviour and pleaded with her to moderate her public conduct, especially when foreign rulers, who were still considering marriage treaties, began to suspect that the Queen was sleeping with Dudley – a charge she always denied.

Matters came to a head in September 1560 when Cecil told the Spanish Ambassador that he was so appalled by Elizabeth's behaviour that he was planning to resign, especially, said Cecil, as Elizabeth and Dudley were planning to kill Lady Dudley. It seems quite astonishing that the cautious Cecil would have said such a thing to a foreign ambassador, had he not had an ulterior motive, particularly as, within days, Lady Dudley was indeed dead in suspicious circumstances.

Whatever Cecil's motivation for his bizarre comments, the result of events was that Elizabeth could never marry a man whose wife was rumoured to have been murdered – that threat, at least, was over, although Dudley did not cease to hope for another fifteen years.

But, as if Elizabeth's headstrong behaviour were not enough, Cecil's own preferred candidate for her successor, Lady Katherine Grey, had called forth the Queen's wrath by a secret marriage and pregnancy. Cecil was quite unable to deflect Elizabeth's wrath from the offending girl, who was sent to the Tower.

In 1563, the House of Commons, at the suggestion of the Privy Council, brought forth a petition to the Queen, requesting her to name her successor. Elizabeth listened politely, then, saying it was an important matter, which required much thought, agreed to consider the request. The Lords then followed suit, receiving the same answer. This was not good enough for Cecil, who drafted articles for a bill to deal with the disaster of Elizabeth's death. Instead of the Crown passing automatically to her heir (whether that were considered to be Mary of Scotland or Lady Katherine Grey), regal authority would pass to a Privy Council of twenty-four until such time as Parliament selected an appropriate, Protestant, monarch.

Not surprisingly, this draft bill failed to receive any support from Elizabeth. She would not be forced by Parliament, the Privy Council, Cecil or anyone else to derogate from the principle that monarchs rule by God-given right, not through appointment by Parliament.

Cecil's efforts to persuade Elizabeth to name a successor rumbled on, without success, at least until after the death of Mary, Queen of Scots in 1587. By then, her obvious heir was Mary's son, James, who, as a Protestant, would be able to fulfil Cecil's dream of a single, British, Protestant state, although Cecil did not live to see it.

Chapter 130: Marriage Negotiations

The only cure for the succession problem, in Cecil's eyes, was marriage for Elizabeth. Throughout the 1560s and 1570s, he continued to press her to choose a husband. Her first suitor had been Philip of Spain, widower of Queen Mary, but he soon gave up pursuit, marrying Elisabeth de Valois as part of the Treaty of Cateau-Cambresis. Although Cecil would have disliked his Catholicism, he was, at least a known quantity.

Then there was Philip's cousin (and nephew), the Archduke Charles, son of Emperor Ferdinand I. Archduke Charles, also being touted for Mary, Queen of Scots, was the front-runner in the period 1564 – 1568 (early negotiations in 1560 having collapsed). Whilst he was Catholic, the Imperial Hapsburgs were more emollient on religious matters than the Spanish branch of the family and Cecil re-opened negotiations in 1565. The Austrians, however, were wary, after the previous failure.

There was another Charles in the frame, too. Charles IX of France was promoted by his mother, the Queen Regent, Catherine de Medici. His age (he was only fourteen) was rather a drawback, as Elizabeth was now thirty. He was also described as *'pale and not greatly timbered (skinny)'*. She firmly rejected the unappealing prospect of marriage to a teenager, and decided that the Archduke was her favourite choice. She had heard how happy the Archduke Charles' parents had been, and was confident he would be a loving husband. She could not, however, marry him sight unseen – would he visit her?

At this point, the Imperial Ambassador began to smell a rat, and wrote home that:

'She was determined not to marry and therefore found none who pleased her...'

Meanwhile, Mary of Scotland had married Lord Darnley, to the consternation of all of Elizabeth's advisors – the merging of their two claims to the English Crown, and the likelihood that Mary would have a child seemed to increase the threat to their unmarried queen. Elizabeth, overcome by stress, gave way to an emotional outburst, screaming at Cecil, Dudley and others that their pressure on her to marry would ruin her.

Cecil reassured her that they were her loyal subjects, and would never try to force her against her will, but, regardless of his gentle words, the pressure continued, with further petitions from Parliament.

In 1567, the match with Archduke Charles was finally abandoned when a religious compromise in which he would be permitted to hear Mass in private, provided he also attended the Protestant service with the Queen, did not garner sufficient support in the Privy Council.

By 1570, it appeared that Elizabeth was regretting her failure to marry and secure an heir. In that year, following the Rising of the Northern Earls, in support of Mary, Queen of Scots' succession to the throne, the Pope had finally excommunicated Elizabeth and released Catholics from their duty of obedience to their monarch. In the face of this massively increased threat to her security, Elizabeth needed allies and told the French Ambassador that she intended to marry, not because she wanted to, but to satisfy her subjects. Even Cecil was convinced by her change of heart, writing:

> 'If I be not much deceived, her Majesty is earnest in this.'

She turned to France for a possible mate. Having rejected Charles IX on the score of the disparity in their ages, she now looked to his younger brother, Henri, even younger, and rumoured throughout Europe to be bisexual (although that term was not used). Initially, Henri was unenthusiastic, and made extremely ungallant remarks about his intended bride, but was talked round by his mother, Catherine de Medici. His religion, however, was the bugbear. Again, an arrangement whereby he could hear Mass privately, if he accompanied Elizabeth to chapel, was mooted. Cecil, although he hated Catholics, and the French in equal measure, wrote to Sir Francis Walsingham, English Ambassador in Paris that:

> *'I see the imminent perils to this state… that I cannot but persist in seeking marriage for her Majesty.'*

But it was not to be. Elizabeth still dithered, and Henri soon reverted to his original refusal.

The final contender for Elizabeth's hand, and the man whom she perhaps might have married, was the younger brother of Charles IX and Henri. This was François, Duke of Anjou. Although Catholic, he had been instrumental in achieving tolerance for the Huguenots in France, so might be persuadable on religious matters. He had also been active in the Low Countries on the side of the rebels against Spain, which would play well with those of Elizabeth's advisors, including Cecil, who wanted her to intervene there. If Anjou could lead troops there on behalf of England, rather than France, that would be a great strategic advantage. Cecil, together with the Earl of Sussex, supported the match, whilst Dudley (now Earl of Leicester) and Walsingham opposed it.

Negotiations continued, and Anjou sent his envoy, Jean de Simier, to England to woo Elizabeth on his behalf, with a level of success that horrified the opponents of the match, particularly Leicester. Eventually, Anjou even came himself, and he and Elizabeth became surprisingly close.

After all the urging to Elizabeth to marry that had been going on for twenty years, when it looked as though she was finally about to take the plunge, her advisers and the public began to back-track.

Cecil wrote one of his lists of pros and cons – in favour was the fact that, despite being forty-five, Elizabeth was in good health, and would still be able to bear a child. Against the proposition, he noted that she '*misliked*' the idea of marriage.

A tract criticising the marriage, snappily called '*The Discovery of a Gaping Gulf wherein England is like to be swallowed by another French marriage if the Lord forbid not the banns by letting Her Majesty see the sin and punishment thereof*' was circulated in the streets of London. The Privy Council rounded up as many copies as they could but Elizabeth was incandescent at this public criticism of a foreign prince, a guest in her realm and her potential husband. The author, a Puritan by the name of John Stubbs, was sentenced to lose his hand. The expected reprieve was not forthcoming, and the brutal punishment was carried out.

Elizabeth however, was not blind or deaf to the dissension within her Council, and, although negotiations carried on until 1581, this domestic uncertainty, together with her innate reluctance to marry, led her to call the negotiations to a halt on. In order to keep some of the advantages of the match, she lent Anjou money for campaigning in the Low Countries.

Once the match with Anjou had been broken off, it was clear to everyone that Elizabeth would never marry.

Chapter 131: Religious Dissent

Following the Act of Uniformity in 1559, Elizabeth was content that religious reform had gone far enough, but not everyone, including probably Cecil, agreed. Increasing in volume, were the radical Protestants, who became known as Puritans because of their objections to wearing the vestments laid down by the Act, and who strove throughout Elizabeth's reign to take reform further.

It can be inferred that Cecil was a supporter of a more radical settlement than Elizabeth eventually allowed. He favoured clerical marriage, which she did not; he pointedly refused to support Archbishop Parker's attempts to enforce conformity in the wearing of vestments, and he also supported the later Archbishop, Edmund Grindal in the dispute over *'prophesyings'* with Elizabeth that ended in Grindal being relieved of his duties. But for Cecil, the enemies were the Catholics.

In 1558 Catholics were far and away the most populous group in the country, but, like most people in most times, the majority were not interested in religious martyrdom, and whatever their private thoughts, and sometimes practices, they attended church. Over the course of Elizabeth's reign, as new generations were brought up under the Act, the bulk of the population became Anglicans – essentially Protestant in doctrine, but dressed in the pared down Catholic clothes of ceremony.

A hard core of Catholics remained, and, as time went on, became more troublesome as religion and politics began to mix. In 1568, when Mary, Queen of Scots was deposed and fled to England, the Catholic party wished her to be openly recognised as Elizabeth's successor, and some even believed that she should already be Queen. For Cecil, this was an intolerable situation – he genuinely believed that the succession of Mary would lead to the re-imposition of Catholicism, and he feared that Elizabeth would be assassinated in order to bring the day forward.

Cecil heartily concurred with the advice of his close colleague, Sir Francis Walsingham that *'it is better to fear too much, than too little'*. He saw plots everywhere, and his whole energies were directed to circumventing them, by fair means, and sometimes by foul.

Cecil's obsession with Catholic rebels at home, and his desire to support Protestant rebels abroad, had contributed to deteriorating relationships with Spain. The impounding, on Cecil's advice, of three Spanish ships carrying gold to the Low Countries for their armies that had taken refuge in Plymouth Sound, caused a serious rupture in diplomatic relationships. Many of Elizabeth's other Councillors, who were becoming restive under Cecil's dominance, felt he was provoking Spain too far.

A plan was hatched for Mary, Queen of Scots to marry Thomas Howard, 4th Duke of Norfolk, and a Protestant. Norfolk and Cecil were on bad terms. The proposal was supported not only by Norfolk's brother-in-law, the Earl of Westmorland, but also by the Protestant Earls of Leicester and Pembroke, and the Catholic Earl of Arundel. The Catholic Earl of Northumberland was not convinced of the merits of the plan, as he did not want Mary to marry a Protestant.

Elizabeth rejected the idea out of hand, and rebuked those Councillors who were criticising Cecil's handling of foreign policy. But negotiations continued in secret. In July, on a day when Cecil was absent from the Privy Council, the majority agreed that if Mary married a Protestant, she could be freed. Still no-one dared to tell the Queen, until, on 6th September 1569, Leicester confessed all.

Norfolk withdrew from court, then, when he refused to answer Elizabeth's summons to Windsor, it was assumed that he had gone to his East Anglian estates to raise an army. In fact, he hadn't, and on 1st October wrote to Westmorland to desist from insurrection, whilst he returned to London to throw himself on Elizabeth's mercy.

The northern Earls, Northumberland and Westmorland decided to act anyway, although their activities were disorganised and somewhat half-hearted. Cecil's worst fears were recognised when they raised an army and marched to Durham Cathedral, where a full Roman Catholic Mass was offered. But, as with the Pilgrimage of Grace, thirty years earlier, the south was controlled by the government, and there was little support for the rising beyond the northern counties. By November, Cecil was reporting that:

> 'Our northern rebellion is fallen flat to the ground and scattered away.'

Cecil emerged from the affair stronger than ever, and his anti-Catholic stance seemed vindicated. Unpleasant rumours that he and Bacon were conspiring to have Norfolk (imprisoned in the Tower) murdered, were brushed off.

In 1570, the stakes were raised when the Pope finally excommunicated Elizabeth. In his Bull, *Regnans in Excelsis*, he not only pronounced the Queen a heretic, but also absolved all of her subjects of any oaths of allegiance they might have sworn to her. Even more provocatively, the Bull stated that any who obeyed the Queen would be cursed. The words '*I told you so,*' must have been trembling on Cecil's lips when Elizabeth heard that this was the result of her toleration of private Catholic practices, and her reluctance to deal too harshly with the Queen of Scots.

The Bull backfired spectacularly. The majority of law-abiding Catholic subjects had absolutely no intention of defying the Queen, or attempting to overthrow her. Even Philip of Spain thought the Bull was the wrong approach. For Cecil, it was grist to his mill. Parliament was called and new laws introduced to not only make it high treason for anyone to '*reconcile*' to Rome, but also, it became treason to have any '*vain and superstitious things*' such as crosses, relics, Agnus Dei etc, that had been blessed by the Pope or a priest.

The Commons removed the exemption from the Act of Uniformity, which had allowed gentlemen with private chapels to attend service there, rather than in the Parish Church, according to the authorised rite. They also tried to impose a requirement to take Communion, which would immediately identify every Catholic who refused. This latter clause was hotly debated. It was one thing to impose attendance, it was quite another to force someone to receive Communion.

The Lords (where Cecil was now seated as Lord Burghley) were not unanimous. At least four of them (Lords Vaux and Windsor and the Earls of Worcester and Southampton) voted against it. The Queen then vetoed the bill. She still would not force consciences (at least, not those of noblemen), provided outward conformity was observed. The cost of failure to attend church however, was increased, from 1s to £20, enough to ruin most families if they persisted in recusancy.

During the late 1570s, a new Catholic threat became apparent as the English seminary, established in Rome by the Englishman William Allen, and later taken over by the Jesuits, began to send priests into England on a mission both to reinvigorate the recusants, and convert people to the Roman Catholic faith. Within the movement there were many who wanted to concentrate only on religion, and not to embroil themselves in politics. In support of this, the Bull, *Regnans in Excelsis* was modified by Pope Gregory XIII who permitted English Catholics to obey the Queen in civil matters.

One of the most famous of these missionaries was Edmund Campion, who entered England in 1580, and was captured in 1581, tortured, condemned for treason, and hanged, drawn and quartered. There was much unease at the idea of persecution for religion. In 1583, Cecil wrote a tract, the *Execution of Justice*, defending the deaths of Campion and others and the allegations of torture. In it, he wrote that the torture of Campion had not, contrary to rumour, been so great that he could not walk. He also added that the rack had been managed

'ever by those that attended upon the Examinations charged to use it (the rack) in as charitable Maner as such thing might be.'

None of the men questioned had been asked about their religion, only about political matters, and whether, if the Pope commanded them to rebel, they would do so.

As for Alexander Bryant, from whom food and water had been withheld until he was obliged to lick the stones of his prison, well, it was his own fault. In an effort to gain a sample of his handwriting, he had been told to write something, anything, and had refused. He was then told he could have food and water if he would write his request down. His refusal to request food could hardly make the authorities guilty of starving him.

In Cecil's eyes, the hounding of Catholic priests was completely justified – they sought to overthrow the Protestant state, and kill the Queen. It was apparent that Spain was planning invasion, and the Queen of Scots was still attracting plots. Every weapon had to be used to protect England.

He wrote further advice to the Queen on how to manage Catholics who were suspected of supporting invasion. They should not, he advised, be asked to swear an oath that they would fight against any Popish invasion plans. To ask that would be to render them '*desperate*', and his view was that desperate men would do desperate deeds. Besides the only way to get rid of desperate men is to kill them, and '*there are so many it would be as hard and difficult as it would be impious and ungodly*'.

Instead, the suspects should be asked to swear that anyone who refused to fight invasion plans ought to be condemned as a traitor. He believed that most would take the oath, as they were not being asked to comment on what they would do in the circumstances. Refusal to take it would immediately show the person as a traitor, but would not be a religious question.

In 1586, yet another plot against the Queen was discovered. It is certainly possible that the Babington Plot was a sting, manufactured by Cecil and Walsingham, but the Queen of Scots fell into the trap. Cecil was determined that this would be her end, and, when she was condemned in a trial at Fotheringhay Castle, over which Cecil presided, he pleaded with Elizabeth to sign the death warrant.

Elizabeth hesitated for weeks, but eventually signed it. Immediately the signed document was given to the Privy Council, which, before the Queen could change her mind, was sent to Fotheringhay and carried out. When she discovered what had happened, the Queen's rage, real or feigned, knew no bounds. She banished Cecil from court and refused to see him for months.

Still the Catholics refused to go away, and for the remainder of Elizabeth's reign the spectre of a Catholic invasion, supported by internal traitors, remained. Nevertheless, after the defeat of the Armada in 1588, it became obvious that there was no widespread support for foreign invasion or a forcible return to Rome. Although the penalties for recusancy were ruinous, and the government continued to vigorously seek out priests, dragging them from their priest holes, and fining and imprisoning those who harboured them, the level of fear somewhat subsided.

Chapter 132: Foreign Policy

Negotiations for Elizabeth's marriage were, of course, just one strand in England's foreign policy. Cecil's long-term goal of creating a single, Protestant, British state, and helping co-religionists across Europe was manifested in other ways, not always successfully, as Queen and minister did not necessarily agree on either aims or the right method to achieve them. Cecil was always a proponent of supporting of supporting Protestants abroad, although, conceptually, this had little appeal for Elizabeth who did not wish to give succour to people in rebellion against lawful authority.

England also needed to steer a course between the two European giants, France and Spain. Spain, and its associated territories, the Netherlands, had, historically, been England's ally. In particular, the Netherlands was the greatest market for English exports. Difficulties arose when the Netherlands wanted to throw off the dominion of its Spanish king, Philip II. Philip, from having been friendly disposed towards England, whose king he had once been, decided that it was his role in life to re-impose the Roman Catholic religion both in the Netherlands and England.

Queen and minister were at odds on what should be done. Cecil was eager to support the Netherlands, because a proportion (although not all) were Protestant. Elizabeth baulked at undermining royal authority. The other stumbling block was the activities of the French – they, too, were involving themselves, with a view to taking over the Netherlands. From Elizabeth's perspective, the possibility of French control was worse than Spanish.

In March 1572, England closed its borders to Dutch *'Sea-Beggars'* who had been capturing Spanish shipping in the Channel. This brought about a rapprochement with Spain – relations having been frosty since the unravelling of the Ridolfi Plot, although by June, Philip was complaining that English interference was undermining his authority and Burghley (Cecil had been promoted to Baron Burghley that year) was informed that

'[King Philip] has sworn that he will be revenged in such sort, as both the Queen and England shall repent that ever they did meddle in any of his countries.'

On 24th August 1572, something occurred that reinforced Burghley's view of the urgent need for England to support co-religionists abroad. On that day, one of the worst massacres in Western European history since the fall of Rome began, carried out by the Catholics of France, against their Huguenot (French Protestant) countrymen. As many as 30,000 were killed in the days and weeks that followed.

At some point in 1572 (the memorandum is not accurately dated) Burghley set out the pros and cons of aiding the Dutch. We may infer, from the first article, that he did not share the note with the Queen.

'Objections – First, for that her Majesty being by sex fearful, cannot but be irresolute.

Secondly, in respect her Majesty is not furnished with such store of treasure as were requisite for a prince that is to enter into wars (money being the sinews of the same).

Thirdly, she is unfurnished of expert soldiers fit for the wars.

And again, (1) the wars may seem unjust and to maintain rebels

(2) In respect of the ancient league between [England] and [Spain];

(3) The greatness of the Prince with whom she is to contend [Philip]

(4) For that another [France] may grow over great.[1]

In favour of involvement, Burghley listed the fact that Spain had supported the Rising of the Northern Earls, that Philip's previous Governor in the Netherland, the Duke of Alba had slandered Elizabeth, that Spain was behind the Papal Bull excommunicating Elizabeth, and, most of all, that Philip was supporting Mary, Queen of Scots, and had sent a ship full of bullion to her party in Scotland (at that time torn

---

[1] http://www.british-history.ac.uk/cal-cecil-papers/vol2/pp29-42 Words in [] added.

between the Queen's Party and the King's Party). Positives to be gained were that:

By joining the enterprise her Majesty shall advance the cause of the religion; (2) her Majesty with her confederates shall give liberty to all Europe[2]

And further, that her intervention would take the glory away from the French Guise party that was supporting the Dutch – even though at home the Guises were militantly Catholic and violently supressing the Huguenots.

Although accused of interference, Elizabeth forbore to send troops to the Dutch leader, William of Orange in December of that year.

Elizabeth then made strenuous efforts to broker a peace when Philip's new deputy in the Netherlands, Don Luis de Requesens y Zúñiga, took a more conciliatory line with the rebels. The Spanish agreed to remove their troops, provided Catholicism was imposed and maintained. Elizabeth thought the Dutch should accept this compromise, and was displeased that William of Orange refused to do so. His desire for religious tolerance, was, she thought, quite indefensible and in 1575, Burghley was commanded to write to all the ports forbidding the landing of William of Orange or any of his supporters.

After Requesens' death in March 1576, and before the arrival of the new Governor, Philip's half-brother, Don Juan of Austria, the unpaid Spanish army sacked Antwerp, uniting the disparate rebel forces against Spain. Don John, whose ultimate mission appears to have been an invasion of England, followed by marriage to Mary, Queen of Scots and the taking of the English throne, was forced to comprise with the Dutch.

---

[2] ibid.

The Pacification of Ghent was agreed amongst Netherlandish states, agreeing to raise an army to resist Don Juan and Spain. Don Juan accepted terms, in the Perpetual Edict, agreeing that Spanish troops would return home. He planned to send them via England. Elizabeth immediately refused to allow them safe passage, believing it was but the cover for an invasion. Don Juan then broke the terms of the Perpetual Edict by capturing the town of Naumur.

Finally driven to involvement, Elizabeth authorised the sending of a large amount of cash to the Dutch. She was obliged to pawn her own jewels to raise it. She would not, however, openly intervene, instead, she carried on the discussions about a marriage to François, Duke of Alençon (later Duke of Anjou) with a view to controlling French activities in the Netherlands.

Over the following ten years, tensions escalated. More plots were uncovered to put Mary Queen of Scots on the throne; France was scarred by ugly and repeated religious civil wars, and the Dutch and Spanish continued to fight. In the early 1580s, Elizabeth was persuaded to direct intervention, although she and Burghley had qualms about the cost, and the risk of provoking Spain to the point of no return. The Earl of Leicester was sent to represent England, and to lead her forces. Nothing was fully resolved, and, in the end, Leicester was withdrawn in 1587.

With the execution of Mary, Queen of Scots in 1587 which, for Burghley, was the triumphant vindication of his long campaign against her, there was no possibility of averting war with Spain. In another of his detailed memoranda, Burghley set out the best way to organise the Queen's troops and navy to forestall invasion.

He calculated the number of ships available to be 37, with 6,000 men, plus some further merchant shipping. He also hoped that some additional ships might be obtained from the King of Scots, since he might reasonably expect to succeed Elizabeth. The ships were to be divided into two fleets, one part to protect the entry to the channel from the west, and the other part at the eastern end. In all, he calculated that the costs of the ships, together with paying the men, victualling the ships, and providing arms would amount to some £60-70,000. In addition, an army would need to be raised and paid – at least £24,000 for two months. Then there was the necessity for men for the Scots border, for Ireland and for Kent, costing at least a further £20,000. He calculated that the costs the Queen had already incurred in the Netherlands were at least £130,000 per annum.

With these costs, and a treasury that was not overfull (inflation was a scourge in the sixteenth century), it was not surprising he also weighed up the advantages of making a treaty with Spain, even at that late point. For Burghley, though, no peace could be entered into unless Spain were willing to cede religious toleration to the Protestants in the Netherlands – he does not seem to have reflected that a similar religious toleration might be granted at home to Catholics.

With the defeat of the Armada of 1588, the worst threat to English security was past, although Spain made several further attempts to invade. With the accession in France of Henri of Navarre, a Huguenot who converted to Catholicism saying *'Paris is worth a Mass'*, there seemed less to fear from France as well.

Chapter 133: The Last Years

The last years of Burghley's life were by no means quiet, but after 1588, both he and Elizabeth seemed to enter a new phase. On the personal front, he suffered the loss of his mother, his wife and his daughter within the space of a year. His old colleagues and friends, the Earl of Leicester, Sir Francis Walsingham and Sir Christopher Hatton, died in the period 1588 – 1591 and their places at the Council table were being taken by a new generation.

Chief amongst these was Robert Devereux, Earl of Essex, who had been Burghley's ward. It was soon apparent that Essex was going to follow a very different path in the advice he gave the Queen than Burghley had. Essex loved the glory of war – he saw Burghley's cautious approach as pusillanimous at best, and perhaps even cowardly. He believed that England should carry the war against Spain into the enemy camp.

Whilst Essex retained his personal respect for Burghley, he did not extend such courtesy to Burghley's son, Robert Cecil, who was now also a member of the Privy Council. Robert and Essex were so temperamentally different that it was hard for them to work together, and their constant jarring created factions at court that Elizabeth was no longer able to control. The Essex faction criticised Robert Cecil, and by extension, Burghley's rule – accusing them of financial irregularity and corruption.

Burghley himself was in declining health. He had complained regularly over the years of gout, of being over burdened with work, and of needing rest. Indeed, one might believe him to be of a somewhat hypochondriacal turn of mind to read all of his complaints about headaches, stomach-aches, sore eyes and trembling hands. A constant refrain was '*I have been and yet am, not in sure health.*'

But by the 1590s, with Burghley well into his seventies, we might perhaps believe that he was indeed ill. He began to spend months away from the court. In April 1591, he attempted to retire, but Elizabeth, not seeing any diminution in his abilities refused. In a letter to him she called him by the pet name of Sir Spirit – it was her custom to give her favourites nicknames – and teased him about becoming the *'hermit of Theobalds.'*

His work carried on. Trouble in Ireland was mounting, and there was no easy solution as Spain funded the rebellion of the Irish Earls. The English had never had a complete domination of Ireland, and the Reformation had not penetrated much beyond the handful of Anglo-Irish in Dublin. Much of Burghley's advice was now given to Elizabeth via the mouth of Robert, as he spent increasing time confined to home with illness.

Vast amounts of correspondence on subjects as disparate as the funeral arrangements to be made for Henry Hastings, Earl of Huntingdon, Lord President of the Council of the North, and the state affairs at the court of the Duke of Brunswick were still delivered to him personally.

In 1597, he began to settle his affairs. He drew up regulations for an almshouse for thirteen poor men of Stamford, to be located near to the site of the school he had attended seventy years before. Although he had eschewed the mediaeval idea of prayers for the dead, yet, in his rules about the requirements for the inmates to wear his livery and attend church each Sunday, on pain of a fine, perhaps there was a trace of the old belief that the prayers of the living could help him, once dead.

He wrote his Will, carefully dividing his lands between his elder son, Thomas, who was to have Burghley and the family estates around Stamford, and Robert, who was to have Theobalds.

In April 1598, he was given leave to absent himself from the annual Garter ceremony. He then travelled to Theobalds for a few weeks in June before returning to London and attending council meetings.

Finally, he took to his bed at Cecil House, where Elizabeth came in person to see him and fed him with her own hands. By 21st July he had an infected throat, perhaps a quinsy, and he died on the morning of 4th August, 1598. One of his last known letters was to his son, Robert, in which he summed up his life of service:

'Serve God by serving the Queen, for all other service is indeed bondage to the Devil.'

Aspects of the life of Sir William Cecil, Lord Burghley

Chapter 134: Key Dates in his life

1520	Born, 14th September, Bourne, Lincolnshire
c. 1528	To school at Grantham
c. 1530	To school at Stamford
May 1535	To St John's College, Cambridge
1540	Began studying at Gray's Inn, London
6 May 1541	Admitted, Gray's Inn
August 1541	Married Mary Cheke of Cambridge, sister of John Cheke
May 1542	Birth of son, Thomas, later Earl of Exeter
22 February 1544	Death of Mary
24 December 1545	Married Mildred Cooke, daughter of Sir Anthony Cooke
1543 – 44	May have sat in the House of Commons. This Parliament passed the 3rd Succession Act
c. 1545	Enters the service of Edward Seymour, Earl of Hertford
1545	Recorder of Boston

28 January 1547	Death of Henry VIII
February 1547	Earl of Hertford becomes Lord Protector and Duke of Somerset
1547	Justice of the Peace, Lincolnshire
1548	Master of Requests for Duke of Somerset
1549	Buys lease of the Rectory, Wimbledon
1549	First Book of Common Prayer
6 July 1549	Custos Rotulorum for Lincolnshire
10 September 1549	Present at Battle of Pinkie
24 November 1549	Arrested and imprisoned in the Tower of London
25 January 1550	Released from the Tower
5 September 1550	Secretary to Edward VI and appointed to Privy Council
c. 1550	Steward to the Lady Elizabeth of her lands in Lincolnshire
11th October 1551	Knighted
Before 1552	Court of Augmentations for Lincolnshire
22nd January 1552	Execution of Edward Seymour, Duke of Somerset
1552	Second Book of Common Prayer

19 March 1553	Death of his father, Richard Cecil
12 April 1553	Chancellor of the Order of the Garter
6 July 1553	Death of Edward VI
8 August 1553	Took part in funeral of Edward VI at Westminster Abbey
22 August 1553	Execution of John Dudley, Duke of Northumberland
1554	Birth and death of Frances Cecil
1554	Travelled to Brussels to meet Cardinal Pole and escort him home
1555	Member of the House of Commons
1556	Steward of the Manor of Wimbledon for Cardinal Pole
5 Dec 1556	Birth of Anne 'Nan' Cecil, later Countess of Oxford
17 November 1558	Death of Mary I and accession of Elizabeth I
20 November 1558	Sworn in as Privy Councillor and Secretary
1559	Birth and death of William Cecil (I)
1559	Act of Uniformity
c. 1560	Steward of Stamford, Lincolnshire
1560	Acquired Theobalds
1560	Visited Scotland to negotiate Treaty of Edinburgh

1561	Birth and death of William Cecil (II)
1563	Birth of Robert Cecil, later Earl of Salisbury
1563	Elected senior Knight of the Shire for Northamptonshire and Lincolnshire
1563	High Steward of Westminster
1564	Birth of Elizabeth Cecil, later Lady Wentworth
10 January 1568	Master of the Court of Wards and Liveries
1568	Lord Lieutenant of Middlesex
1569	Rising of the Northern Earls
April – June 1571	Lord Keeper of the Privy Seal
7 September 1571	Execution of Thomas Howard, 4th Duke of Norfolk
25 February 1572	Created 1st Baron of Burghley
July 1572	Lord Treasurer
4 August 1572	The Massacre of St Bartholomew
1572	Overseer of the Queen's Majesty's Works
April 1583	Death of Elizabeth Cecil, Lady Wentworth
1585	Steward of the Honour of Bolingbroke, Lincolnshire

1587	Lord Lieutenant of Lincolnshire
8 February 1587	Execution of Mary, Queen of Scots
1588	Lord Lieutenant of Essex and Hertfordshire
10 March 1588	Death of Jane Heckingon, Mrs Cecil, his mother
5 June 1588	Death of Anne Cecil, Countess of Oxford
7 August 1588	Defeat of Spanish Armada
4 April 1589	Death of Mildred Cooke, Lady Burghley, his wife
15 July 1598	Last attendance at a Council meeting
4 August 1598	Death of Sir William Cecil, Lord Burghley

Chapter 135: Family Life

Marriage

William Cecil first married in around August 1541. His bride was Mary Cheke, sister of his friend and tutor at Cambridge, John Cheke. Almost nothing is known of Mary, other than that her father had died before 1541, and that she lived in the house of her mother, Agnes, who was a vintner and small business-woman, established near St John's College. As well as John, Mary had four other siblings, Elizabeth, Alice, Magdalen and Anne, who lived to adulthood. We can infer that Cecil was on good terms with the whole family, as Anne Cheke's son, Hugh Alington, later became one of his secretaries.

At the time of Cecil's marriage to Mary, her brother had not yet achieved the prestige he attained later as Regius Professor of Greek, and tutor to Prince Edward, and so, from the point of view of Cecil's father, the match was a disappointment. The purpose of matrimony was to extend a family's influence, not the indulgence of private affection. Soon after his marriage, Cecil was sent to Gray's Inn to continue his studies, but was obliged to leave Mary behind. Presumably, still financially dependent on his father, he could not afford to maintain her in London.

In May, 1542, Mary gave birth to a son, Thomas. In February of the following year, she died, although the cause is unknown, as is the frequency with which she and Cecil met during the years of their marriage. Based in London, he would have had little spare cash for visiting her. After her death, Thomas remained in Cambridge with his grandmother, Agnes Cheke. Agnes paid Mary's funeral expenses of 6s 8d.

There is no record of Cecil's reaction to Mary's death, but, since he continued to be close friends with John Cheke, we can suppose that they shared their grief.

Cecil's second marriage was far more to the taste of his family. The lady was Mildred Cooke, one of the seven (or possibly eight) children of Anthony Cooke, who, like Cecil's father, was a member of Henry VIII's household. Mildred is usually listed on genealogical sites as the eldest daughter, but, given the naming practices of the time, it is more likely that Anne was the eldest, named for her mother and grandmother. Mildred was named for her step-grandmother.

Cooke was a member of the royal bodyguard, but there was certainly more to him than brawn. Like his new son-in-law, he was trained for the law, although, in Cooke's case, his Inn was Inner Temple. Cooke was a dedicated promoter of education, and his five daughters received the same education as his sons, in Latin and Greek. Two of them, Anne and Mildred, became noted scholars, whilst a third, Elizabeth was known as a poet and accomplished musician. Anthony Cooke was later involved in the tuition of Edward VI, although he was not formally the Prince's tutor.

Mildred was described (in bad verse!) as:

'Cooke is comely and thereto

In books sets all her care

In learning with the Roman dames

Of right she may compare.'

On this second marriage, which took place on 24th December 1545, Richard Cecil granted William and his bride land in Rutland and Leicestershire. Presumably Mildred also brought a dowry in either cash or land. This enabled them to set up a household, although there was no thought of leaving London.

Cooke was a member of the Reforming faction at Henry VIII's court, and all of his children followed him in this regard – two of his daughters later being known for their Puritan views. Cecil would have felt quite at home in these circles.

There is no information as to exactly where Cecil and Mildred lived immediately after their marriage – most likely, they had lodgings near Gray's Inn. In 1549, once Cecil was a member of the household of the Duke of Somerset, they took up residence at the Rectory, Wimbledon, although they also had a town house in Cannon Row, Westminster. Sharing their home at Wimbledon were Cecil's sister Mary, and Mildred's sister Elizabeth, as well as two wards – Arthur Hall and John Stanhope.

Whilst Cecil was serving Somerset, Mildred was developing her relationship with his wife, Anne Stanhope. She translated a sermon by St Basil the Great on the biblical book, *Deuteronomy*, that she dedicated to the Duchess, and signed, herself, in the usual deferential sixteenth century fashion as the Duchess' *'humble servant and debtor'*.

During these first years of married life, there were family visits to pay: to Burghley to see the senior Cecils, with side visits to Katherine, Dowager Duchess of Suffolk at Grimesthorpe, and Lord Clinton (once married to Bessie Blount): to Ingatestone Hall to visit Cecil's colleague, Sir William Petre; and, later, to Bisham to visit Mildred's sister, Elizabeth, who married Sir Thomas Hoby.

A Growing Family

One of Mildred's attractions as a match for Cecil had been her connections, and the promise of this seemed to be fulfilled when her brother married the cousin of Lady Jane Grey, a young woman who, in the early 1550s was talked of as a possible wife for Edward VI. In the event, Lady Jane was proclaimed Queen herself, with disastrous results. Whilst the plan for Jane to take the throne was being hatched, Cecil was covering his back with carefully placed statements to his friends and family, suggesting reluctance to be involved. He even wrote to Mildred, asking her, in the event of his death in the commotion likely to follow an attempt to subvert the succession, to continue to look after his son, Thomas. Should she decide to marry again, she should chose a man of good (ie Protestant) religion.

No children other than Thomas were mentioned, because, although Mildred's mother had had at least seven children in fairly quick succession, she and Cecil seem to have had some difficulty in beginning a family, and during Edward VI's reign, so far as is known, they had no children.

Thomas seems to have moved to live with William and Mildred when they took the house in Wimbledon. However, it appears that family life was difficult. Cecil did not get on well with his son, either when he was a child, or later. He admitted in May 1561 that

'To this hour I never showed any fatherly favour to him but in teaching and correcting.'

The result was, that, although there was never any open breach, there was little warmth between them. There is a record of them practising archery together in 1556, when Thomas was about eighteen. Hopefully, it was an enjoyable event, although one can image Cecil may have spent much of the afternoon carping at Thomas' style.

On Mary's accession, Mildred's sister, Anne, who was married to the Master of the Court of Wards, Sir Nicholas Bacon, became a part of the new Queen's household. Later, a third sister, Margaret Cooke, also served Queen Mary. This link to the Queen's household helped to maintain the Cecils' profile during Mary's reign, and both Cecil and Mildred visited Cardinal Pole and attended some of his sermons.

In 1554, Mildred gave birth to her first known child, a daughter, named Frances, presumably for Frances, Duchess of Suffolk, who, despite the execution of her husband and daughter, Lady Jane Grey, remained in favour with Queen Mary. Cecil later wrote of the arrival in his commonplace book:

'Between 11 and 12 this night my wife gave birth to a daughter called Frances but after a few hours the tiny girl departed this mortal life and was buried at Wimbledon.'

In 1555, Cecil paid the dowry of his sister, Elizabeth, on her marriage to Robert Wingfield. He did not forget his father-in-law, who had chosen to leave England on Mary's succession, for the more attractive, Protestant air of Strasbourg. Cecil sent him money regularly, and, no doubt thinking of him as well as his other Protestant friends, voted against a government bill that year to deprive exiles of their lands.

The Cecils were invited in July of 1556 to visit their friend, Sir Philip Hoby, at his home at Bisham. Sir Philip even offered to send a carriage for Mildred, as she was expecting. Probably fearing the jolting of the unsprung carriages of the time, the Cecils declined. Their carefulness paid off, as, on 5th December, a healthy daughter was born, named Anne, presumably for Mildred's mother and sister, or perhaps for her godmother Anne, Lady Petre. The Petres also gave a sumptuous gift of a gilt salt cellar.

Sir Philip Hoby also sent his congratulations, lamenting slightly that Anne was not that far more worthy creature, a son:

'Of my lady's daughter (in hope of a son hereafter), I trust ye be now no sorrowful man.'

Congratulations were also received from Cecil's father-in-law, no doubt now relieved that his daughter was finally showing signs of knowing her duty. He hoped that Mildred would *'increase [Cecil] with many sons and daughters, though she were not hasty at the beginning.'* These words tend to dispel any thoughts that Mildred had suffered many miscarriages or infant deaths previously.

Cecil adored his little girl, referred to as Nan, or even Tannikin, in family correspondence. When she was nine, he even wrote a poem for her – rather different from his usual dry outpourings. It went with her New Year gift of a toy spinning wheel. Ever the improving father, the gift was to encourage her *'some thrift to feel'* in learning a housewife's tasks.

William and Mildred had two more children who lived to adulthood. Robert, born 1 June 1563, and Elizabeth, born 1 July 1564. There were two short-lived boys, both named William, who were born in 1559 and 1561. Robert too, although he survived, was not especially robust – he had some physical deformity which gave him a curvature of the spine.

Thomas

In 1561, Cecil's oldest child, Thomas, was ready to embark on adult life. He had been well educated by Cambridge tutors (although there is no record of him attending the university – his masters came to him). He had also been taught the appropriate courtly arts of dancing and music. Thus armed, Cecil sent him to Paris to practice his French and learn to be a courtier.

Thomas was to be accompanied by one of his father's clerks, Thomas Windebank, who was furnished with £90 in gold for the trip. Obviously, Cecil didn't believe his son was sufficiently mature to hold the cash himself. The original plan was for Thomas to spend time both at the French court, where Cecil's friend, Sir Nicholas Throckmorton, was Ambassador, and also to meet other Englishmen – chief of whom was the Earl of Hertford who had been sent abroad earlier that year. When the scandal of Hertford's secret marriage to the Queen's cousin, Lady

Katherine Grey, came to light, Cecil was quick to send a message to Thomas to avoid Hertford's company.

Unsurprisingly, given his first taste of freedom, Thomas did not always behave in ways his father approved of. There was the usual problem of the expenses of a young man outstripping his allowance. In particular, Thomas' purchase of a horse drew disapproving letters from his father. A man of Thomas' age and station in life should be content to walk. Cecil summed up his fears by writing to Windebank that he feared Thomas would return *'like a spending sot [drunkard], meet to keep a tennis court.'* Why tennis-court-keeping or using should be disgraceful is a mystery, but clearly it upset Cecil. He continued to send reprimands and harsh messages about his disappointment in his son's behaviour to Thomas until the young man returned.

Whether Thomas were the ideal son in terms of his behaviour or not, he quickly proved that he could fulfil the obligation on every gentleman to marry well. In 1564, he married Dorothy Neville, the daughter of John Neville, 4th Baron Latimer, who had once been step-son to Queen Katherine Parr. Whilst his father had a small family by the standards of the day, Thomas and Dorothy produced thirteen children. His descendants continue to hold the Marquessate of Exeter.

Thomas played little part in public life. He was an officer in the army sent by the government to repress the Rising of the Northern Earls in 1569, and, bizarrely, together with his half-brother, Robert, was intended to be the target of a kidnapping plot a couple of years later. The conspirators, whose primary plan had been to assassinate William Cecil (by then Lord Burghley) as part of their overall scheme to enthrone Mary, Queen of Scots, had planned to capture the Cecil brothers to ransom them should the murder of Cecil go awry. Nothing came of this, or any other of the various assassination plots of Elizabeth's reign.

A request by Thomas in 1575 for a passport to travel abroad was refused by the Queen, and we can infer that Cecil had asked her to reject it, as he did not want Thomas to travel whilst the latter's eldest son, another William, was underage.

As time passed, Thomas and his father seem to have been on better terms. In 1575, Thomas wrote, requesting Cecil to ensure that Mildred and Anne should visit Wimbledon. It would, he said, presumably without sarcasm, be *'a comfort unto my wife and me, and an honour to my poor parsonage.'*

Anne and Elizabeth

Anne was the second of Cecil's children to marry. A betrothal had been arranged for her when she was twelve, in 1568. This was to Philip Sidney, son of Sir Henry Sidney, President of the Council of Wales, and his wife, Mary Dudley, daughter of Cecil's old master, the Duke of Northumberland. Although contracts were signed, the wedding was never carried out. Instead, Anne made what was, on paper, a far grander match – to a man well known to her before-hand – Edward de Vere, Earl of Oxford. Oxford was one of Cecil's wards, and had joined the household in 1564 when he was thirteen. Cecil, responsible for his upbringing and his estates, made careful arrangements for both.

The couple were married on 19 December 1571, in the presence of the Queen. The marriage turned out to be one of the most miserable of the era. In 1573, Oxford had licence to travel abroad. Whilst he was away, Anne gave birth to a daughter, whom she named Elizabeth. Oxford thanked Cecil for sending him the news and dispatched presents for Anne, but, when he returned home, he refused to acknowledge the child and sent Anne back to her parents, with bitter words. He had, apparently, some *'mislikings'* of Anne or her behaviour, but he refused to specify what. In an age when female chastity was considered her most important virtue, the disgrace that Anne suffered when rejected by her husband, and the hints that her daughter was not his, must have been hard for her to bear. Cecil and Mildred stood by her throughout, and for the next few years, she lived with them.

At some point in the early 1580s there was a partial reconciliation between the Oxfords. Anne produced a son, who died within a few hours, and then two more daughters, Bridget and Frances. Nevertheless, there were long periods when the Earl would refuse to have anything to do with his wife, and would leave her to live at her parents' expense. Anne died young, only 31, on 5 June 1587. She was buried in Westminster Abbey.

Cecil's other daughter, Elizabeth, did not make so grand a match as her sister. Aged 18 in 1582, she married the 26 year old William Wentworth, son of Lord Wentworth, an old friend of Cecil's. It appears from the correspondence, that the couple fell in love, and Wentworth requested his father to make overtures to Cecil. Perhaps chastened by the unhappiness of Anne, Cecil did not seek to make a second grand match, and Elizabeth and Wentworth were married in February 1582. But this marriage too, ended badly. The groom was dead by November, and Elizabeth followed him to the grave in April 1583.

Robert

Cecil's second son, Robert, was initially more successful in his marital career than his sisters. He married Elizabeth Brooke, the daughter of 10th Lord Cobham in 1586, when he was 22. The couple had three children before Elizabeth's untimely death in 1597. Robert mourned her deeply and, unusually, never remarried. His descendants are the Marquesses of Salisbury.

Robert was certainly more successful in his political career than his brother. It seems that Cecil groomed him from an early age to be his political heir. Perhaps Robert's physical infirmity made him more interested in studying and politics, or perhaps Cecil had learnt from the mistakes he made with Thomas and spent more time with his younger son. Robert received expert tuition in Latin, Greek, Mathematics and all of the other subjects considered essential to the Humanist education. He then went on to study law at Gray's Inn, where he was admitted in 1580. Following that, he travelled abroad for a short period.

Whatever the reason, Cecil made every attempt to promote Robert's career at court.

Like his brother, twenty years before, Robert travelled abroad for a short period, studying at the Sorbonne. When he came home, he sat in the House of Commons for Westminster. By 1587, Cecil was promoting him to the Queen as a suitable man to take over some over some of his duties, a message he repeated over the next few years. Eventually, in 1596, Elizabeth appointed Robert to the role of Secretary – the position Cecil had held when she first came to the throne. But such a promotion caused a good deal of envy at court – particularly in the faction surrounding the Earl of Essex, and his sister, Lady Penelope Rich.

The late 1580s were a time of loss for Cecil. In the period 1588, he lost his daughter Anne, his mother (who must have been getting on for ninety), and then, in 1589, his wife of over forty years. His grief was heavy. He wrote that they had

'lived in continual love without any separation or any offence.'

Mildred was buried with her daughter, Anne, Countess of Oxford in Westminster Abbey. Cecil paid for a sumptuous monument, in which the two of them are surrounded by the kneeling figures of Anne's daughters, Lady Elizabeth, Lady Bridget and Lady Susan de Vere, and Mildred's son, Robert.

Despite this, when his own time came, Cecil chose to be buried in Stamford, by the side of his parents, in the country he always thought of as his.

Chapter 136: Architect & Builder

In modern parlance, Cecil was a workaholic. He worked by day and night, writing the vast majority of his letters in his own hand, and working out arguments by creating long lists of pros and cons. But even the busiest man needs some outlet for his creative energies, and Cecil's artistic bent found its expression in architecture. Architecture was one of the most fashionable pursuits of gentlemen in the Renaissance period – it was used to express power and wealth as well as taste and education, and there is no doubt Cecil wanted to indicate that he possessed all of those attributes.

During his long life and political career, Cecil built three vast properties that typified the Elizabethan style. Sadly, only one remains - Burghley House. The other two, Cecil House on the Strand, London, and Theobalds (bizarrely, pronounced Tibbalds), near Cheshunt, in Hertfordshire, just north of London, have left no traces. Nevertheless, from the copious records kept, we can learn a bit about them. He also built or renovated two other houses – one named Pymmes at Edmonton (not far from Theobalds) and one at Chelsea, in London, although we cannot find any direct evidence of ownership or any reason for him to have a property there.

Architecture was a taste that Cecil first seems to have developed during Edward VI's reign. His patron, the Duke of Somerset, built the vast Somerset House in the Strand – the first great construction by a subject since Wolsey had created Hampton Court, some thirty years before. Whilst he was Somerset's Master of Requests, it is likely that Cecil visited frequently, and, it appears he was impressed by it, as the West Gate he built at Burghley resembled the earlier construction.

Other members of Somerset's household who were friends of Cecil's were Sir Thomas Smith and Sir John Thynne, builders of Hill Hall, Essex (now owned by English Heritage) and Longleat, in Wiltshire, respectively. Longleat, currently lived in by a descendant of Thynne, is similar in style to Burghley House, and we can speculate that Cecil and Thynne conferred.

The fall of Somerset did not put an end to architectural discussion at court – the Duke of Northumberland was also interested in the practice, and sent John Shute, author of the first English treatise on architecture, to Italy. Doubtless Cecil was fascinated by what Shute discovered there and would have read Shute's work - *The First and Chief Grounds of Architecture.*

As well as Somerset House and Longleat, another model for Burghley was Sir Thomas Gresham's new Exchange, in the City of London, the stone loggia (an open arcade) of which was originally copied at Burghley, although it was later covered in.

According to his early biographer, the Rev. W.B Charlton, who was chaplain to the Marquess of Exeter in the 1840s, Cecil's father, Richard, was granted the former priory of St Michael's, Stamford together with 299 acres of arable land in 1539. This became the nucleus of the modern Burghley estate, and Cecil began working on it after his father's death in 1553. It remained the principal house of his mother, Jane, until her death in 1588. The original works, carried out in the 1550s and 1560s, were later replaced with even grander edifices.

Cecil's great masterpiece was Theobalds. He acquired the land, just west off what is now the A10 some time around 1560. He probably chose the location as handy for travelling between Cecil House in the Strand, and Burghley. Information about one of his journeys between his previous house in Wimbledon and Burghley show that this is the route he customarily took.

Major works seem to have begun in the late 1560s – in 1572 alone, he spent £2,700. The property was finally finished in 1585. There are some 18 drawings still extant in the archives at Hatfield House (which Cecil's son, Sir Robert, acquired in exchange for Theobalds when James VI & I made clear his desire to own the great pleasure palace himself). From the annotations on the drawings, it can be inferred that Cecil himself was, at least in part, his own architect and designer. He appears to have been able to draw well – there is a note from a mason at building asking him to send a detailed drawing, so that he can understand what is required.

Once completed, the house was vast – the domestic parts of the building set around two large courtyards or quadrangles, and smaller ones for the buttery, the dial (clock) and the dovecotes. There was also a long gallery and a hall.

The main quadrangle, Fountain Court, was 86 ft square and housed a water feature of black and white marble. On the east of the court was an open loggia, floored with Purbeck marble, presumably for walking in to catch the evening sun.

The location made Theobalds a convenient place for Elizabeth I to travel to when she wished to leave London for a spot of hunting. She paid Burghley repeated visits over the years, the first being in 1564, when she apparently complained that her bedroom was too small, leading him, or so he claimed, to enlarge the house. It was still not complete by the time she arrived again on 22nd September 1571. Rather than the Queen bringing a gift with her for her hostess, she was the recipient of some verses (one's ears cringe at the thought) and a picture of the house.

Whether it was the house or the company she most enjoyed, she visited again in 1572, 1575, 1577, 1583, 1587, 1591, 1593, 1594 and 1596.

Sometimes her stay was of brief duration, but on other occasions she brought a large retinue with her. Elizabeth, perennially short of money, and of a thrifty turn of mind, was always happy for her courtiers to support some of the financial burden of the court. In 1583, she was accompanied by her friend, Robert, Earl of Leicester; his brother, the Earl of Warwick; her other favourite, Sir Christopher Hatton; Cecil's companion and colleague, Sir Francis Walsingham; the Queen's cousin, Lord Hunsdon, and several others.

Ten years later, she visited for nine days at a cost to Cecil (who was also of a frugal nature, and must have wilted under the bills) of nearly £3,000. With such sumptuous hospitality available, it was not unknown for Elizabeth to invite foreign ambassadors and dignitaries to wait upon her at Theobalds – the house and gardens were beautiful, and Cecil was picking up the tab!

To give this sum some context, his usual weekly bills at Theobalds were around £80 and his annual stabling bill was about £667. He paid £10 per week for the local unemployed to work in the gardens, and distributed £1 per week in charity. According to custom, even when Cecil was not in residence himself, there was provision for a table of gentleman and two tables of *'inferior'* persons for dinner each day. His silver plate weighed some 14,000 pounds (c. 6,350kg).

One of Cecil's favourite recreations was to ride around his gardens at Theobalds, on a mule.

Elizabeth would also visit Cecil at his town house, dining there on at least one occasion and attending the christening of his daughter, Elizabeth, to whom she stood as godmother. Cecil House, of which no trace now remains, was located on the Strand, north of where the Savoy Theatre now stands. It was built of brick, with four turrets and two courtyards. On the east range were the family's private apartments. To the north, the gardens stretched as far as what is now Covent Garden.

Cecil's interest in building presumably led to his appointment as Overseer of the Queen's Majesty's Works in 1572, although his job was probably to oversee the finances. The Comptroller of the Works, from 1556 – 1596, was one Thomas Fowler, with whom Cecil was on good terms, as may be inferred from the fact that Fowler bequeathed his house to Cecil, should he wish to accept it. Other men within the office were Thomas Graves, Surveyor of the Queen's Works from 1578, Henry Hawthorn and John Symonds; drawings from the men remain in the archive at Hatfield. Graves seems to have worked for Cecil on the manor house at Pymmes, which Cecil purchased in 1582, paying £250 for six acres of pasture and a manor house. Once completed, it was lived in, after his marriage, by Cecil's younger son, Robert.

Chapter 137: Bibliophile & Map Collector

Sir William Cecil was educated at St John's College, Cambridge, one of the most advanced of the colleges at the time. His friends and colleagues there were all followers of the new humanist ideas that promoted the examination of original texts rather than the endless interpretations and reinterpretations of the works of the mediaeval scholars.

With the fall of Constantinople in 1453, the last remnants of the Roman Empire, a torrent of ancient manuscripts found its way into Europe, in Greek as well as Latin, which inspired the generations that followed to study Greek and classical Latin, rather than the mediaeval Latin into which it had metamorphosed. During his time in Cambridge, and after, Cecil was friends with some of the foremost scholars of the century – Roger Ascham, John Cheke, Thomas Smith. He himself, although never inclining to a career as an academic, never lost his interest in intellectual matters, even though his own writing style was somewhat turgid.

Throughout out his life, Cecil sought to learn, to gather facts and to know as much as he could about myriad topics, and this was reflected in a passion for collecting books and maps. Between January 1554 and December of the following year, a period during which his political career had taken a pause, there are seventy entries in his accounts for book purchases from the London book-seller William Seres. They include titles on cosmology, geography and navigation, reflecting his interests in maps and the physical world.

On his death in 1598, his will directed that his elder son, Thomas, should inherit *'all my books in my upper library over my Great chamber in my.... house in Westminster'* together with *'all my evidence and rolls belonging to my pedigrees'*. In common with most gentlemen of the era, Cecil liked to study genealogy and family trees, mainly in the hope of finding illustrious ancestors.

On a sale of some of the Cecil family's possessions in 1687, the inventory for books listed some 3,645 books and 249 volumes of manuscripts said to be his. The collection is now in four main parts – a great many are in the Cotton Collection at the British Museum, some are in the National Archive, a substantial portion is at Trinity College, Dublin, of which Cecil was Chancellor, and many remain at Hatfield House.

The collection includes mathematical, surveying, mapmaking, artillery building, town planning, and hydrography works.

One of the books in the collection is his Commonplace book (a kind of journal in which information was gathered, notes made and expenses recorded). Cecil's has a cover of vellum, folded to make a pocket, in which is stored a map of Sicily and one of the British Isles. It also has the distances and travel information for journeys between Antwerp and Dunkirk and Augsburg; and London to Edinburgh. Presumably the information dates from his trip to the continent during Mary's reign, and his expedition to Edinburgh to negotiate the eponymous treaty in 1560.

It appears that whilst Cecil liked maps, it was a cerebral matter, rather than a desire for travel, as, according to Henry Peacham's book, *The Compleat Gentleman*, published in 1622:

> *'If anyone came to the lords of the council for a licence to travel, he would first examine him of England; if he found him ignorant, would bid him stay at home and know his own country first.'*

In 1563, Laurence Nowell, an early antiquarian and manuscript collector who worked for Cecil, wrote to him in for support for a map making project. Nowell, using the best butter, referred to Cecil's *'marvellous pleasure in geographical maps, above all other monuments of the noble arts.'* Cecil commissioned him to undertake a map of a part of the coast of Ireland, and it is likely that Nowell created Cecil's pocket map of the British Isles referred to above.

Cecil also collected maps from abroad. On 20 February 1567 he wrote to Sir Henry Norris, the English Ambassador to France, saying *'if there be any charts newly printed, I pray you send me a calendar thereof.'* Norris must have found some, as there is a letter from the following July, thanking him for the chart of Paris.

In around 1566, Cecil acquired a collection of engraved maps, compiled in Rome. It is likely that Nowell acted for him.

On 20 May 1570, Cecil acquired one of the earliest copies of *Theatrum Orbis Terrarum* the first modern atlas, published that year by the Flemish cartographer, Abraham Ortelius. Cecil hand-wrote his own notes on it.

He also kept detailed notes on the county atlases he collected. These were created during the period 1574 – 1578 by Christopher Saxon. They were engraved plates, and were delivered to Cecil as they were completed. On them, he annotated all the justices in England and Wales, added and corrected place names as well as supplementing the maps with historical, topographical and geographic notes and tables of roads and posts.

In addition to Saxon's maps, he collected a further 18 manuscript and two other printed maps of the British Isles, before 1595. These were remarked on by a foreign visitor to Theobalds, who noted hanging on the walls:

> 'correct landscapes of all the most important and remarkable towns in Christendom' and in another room, 'the Kingdom of England, with all its cities, towns and villages, mountains and rivers.'

His interest in maps was obviously widely known. He received presentation copies of the Dutch hydro-cartographer Lucas Waghenaer's work *De Spieghel Der Zeevaerdt*. This was translated into English on the orders of the Privy Council, by Anthony Ashley. Cecil took two copies, one to admire, and the other to use as a working copy.

He also had a plan of the Spanish palace, the Escorial, and maps of Guiana sent to him by Sir Walter Raleigh and Thomas Hariot.

Finally, Cecil's treasures included a *'lytle terrestriall Globe with a Lattin Booke that Teacheth the use of my great Globes'*. These great globes were made by Emery Molyneux and were 25 inches (c 60cm) in diameter.

Chapter 138: Following the Footsteps of William Cecil

Cecil was a Lincolnshire man, born and bred, and he always saw that county as his own. But as a politician, he needed to keep close to the centre of power and he spent the majority of his life in and around the capital, building several houses to reflect his status. He visited Scotland twice, once in peace, and once in war, and had two short trips abroad.

The numbers in the article below correspond to those on the map which follows.

*

When William Cecil was born in 1520 in the small town of Bourne (1) in Lincolnshire, it was to a family that, on his mother's side, was well-established in the district, with a history of service in the various civic offices of Bourne and membership of the religious guilds of the town. His father's family had settled in the neighbouring town of Stamford only in the last quarter of the fifteenth century, having come from South Wales, probably because of their connection, through the god-father of William's father Richard, with Lady Margaret Beaufort. Lady Margaret had an impressive estate nearby at Collyweston, and the Cecils had roles in its management. Thirty years later, William was to be steward of some of those lands on behalf of Lady Margaret's grand-daughter, Elizabeth.

William was christened in the Abbey Church of St Peter and St Paul, which, generally referred to as Bourne Abbey, still stands in the town, although the monastic buildings are long gone. At the time, the Abbey was an Augustinian foundation, at the heart of town life and Cecil's maternal grandparents are buried there.

Around 15 miles from Bourne is the large town of Grantham. Situated just off the A1, or in more romantic parlance, the Great North Road, it has been a settlement probably since Neolithic times. It was certainly in existence at the time of the Domesday Book in 1086. In the older part of the town is the enormous church of St Wulfram, noted in Simon Jenkins' *'1000 Best Churches in England'*, as having the best steeple (282 ft in height) in the country. In the shadow of this enormous edifice is the old schoolhouse (2) that Cecil would have known when he came to be educated there. Cecil probably arrived not long after the school had been re-founded by Dr Richard Foxe, Bishop of Winchester, and once Lord Privy Seal.

Perhaps because of his youth, Cecil did not remain so far from home for long. Instead, he was moved to a school rather closer at Stamford (3). Stamford, like Grantham, is a settlement on the Great North Road. It is one of the loveliest towns in the whole of England, built of the local oolitic limestone, a hard-wearing, creamy stone. The town is home to an extraordinary number of mediaeval churches, as well as one of the oldest inns in the country. The Tabard at Stamford was a thriving business, and the family of Cecil's grandmother, Alice Dicons, had some interest in it, although, contrary to rumours intended to denigrate Cecil in later life, they were not the innkeepers.

The Tabard has been renamed the George, and is well worth a visit. Stamford school still exists too, although the buildings, which are dotted around the town, almost all post-date Cecil.

At the age of 14, the usual age, Cecil went to the College of St John the Evangelist, Cambridge (4). This College had been founded in the Will of Lady Margaret Beaufort, and so had associations for Cecil's family. During this period, he met and built relationships with some of the men who would influence him in religious matters and be politically associated with him throughout his career – John Cheke, Roger Ascham, Thomas Smith and Edmund Grindal were all either studying or teaching there. His friendship with John Cheke led on to affairs of the heart. To the intense disapproval of his father, he married Cheke's sister, Mary, although she died young, leaving Cecil with a baby son.

St John's College is still a functioning college of the university, and, in fact, is one of the largest. It can be visited between March and October between 10am and 5pm and during the winter between 10am and 3.30pm. A good proportion of the buildings are those that Cecil would have known – particularly the Great Gatehouse, completed in 1519 and sporting the arms of Lady Margaret – the Beaufort Portcullis supported by her heraldic beast, the Yale. The chapel is a gothic confection by Gilbert Scott, dating from the nineteenth century.

After his five years at St John's, Cecil went to study law at Gray's Inn (5). Again, the place itself is still an Inn of Court, but the buildings have been much altered. There are remnants that Cecil would have known as a student, in the Chapel and the Hall, although both have been extensively rebuilt since his time, the Hall as early as the 1550s, so it would look familiar to him.

In the early 1540s, with his marriage to Mildred, one of the daughters of the courtier, Sir Anthony Cooke, Cecil began to spend time in and around the King's court. It was not, however, until he was working for the Duke of Somerset, early in the reign of Edward VI that we have exact information on where he lived. At that time, he bought two houses in Canon Row, Westminster (6) from Lord Paget, for around £400 cash. This was not an insignificant amount of money, but there is no information as to how he raised it.

Cecil took his first trip out of the country in September 1549, when he travelled with the English army to Scotland. He was present at the Battle of Pinkie Cleugh, and afterwards, when the English marched on Edinburgh (7).

Returning from Scotland, Cecil continued to live at Canon Row, when in London, for at least ten years, but an aspiring courtier also needed a country home. In 1549, he became interested in property in Wimbledon, and discussed with Sir Robert Tyrwhitt, the possibility of acquiring the remainder of a sixty year lease of the Rectory of Wimbledon (8).

The lands in and around Wimbledon had been owned by the Abbey of Worcester, and, at the Dissolution of the Monasteries had transferred to the Crown. There were two parts to the estate – the Manor of Wimbledon, which included a manor house and was near modern Mortlake, and the Rectory, which included a Parsonage near the Church of St Mary's, Wimbledon.

The Rector had the right of presentation of rectors to the Church of St Mary's and curates to Mortlake and Putney. He also had the right to collect the tithes and either farm the glebe (church lands) himself, or lease it out. In return, the Rector had to maintain the three churches mentioned.

The Manor of Wimbledon had been granted to Thomas Cromwell, and then to Queen Katherine Parr. The Rectory had been returned to the Dean and Chapter of the new Cathedral at Worcester, who had leased it out, and it was the remainder of this lease that Cecil now acquired. He also acquired more land, north of what is now Worple Road in Wimbledon, stretching up towards the Common. He was fined 6d in 1555 for not maintaining his gate there properly.

During Edward's reign, Cecil spent the majority of his time at Canon Row, during Mary's sovereignty he spent more time at Wimbledon. It was in either of these places that the first four children of his marriage to Mildred were born – Frances, Anne, and two babies, both named William. Only Anne, born in Westminster, survived and the others are buried in St Mary's Church.

Living at Wimbledon with him were his wife, Mildred; his sister, Margaret, later Mrs Cave; Mildred's sister, Elizabeth, later Lady Hoby; his son, Thomas, and his two wards at the time, Arthur Hill and John Stanhope. When the Manor of Wimbledon was granted by Mary to Cardinal Pole, William became his steward for the land.

In late 1549, Cecil exchanged his comfortable quarters at Canon Row, for a stint in the Tower of London. As a gentleman prisoner of means, he would not have been kept in a dank cell, but in one of the better rooms.

He would have had to pay for his own keep. His sojourn there was short, only about 5 weeks, but we can suppose he was glad to leave.

A far more enjoyable moment in a royal palace would have been on 5th September 1550, at Oatlands Palace (10) when he was given a place on the Privy Council as Secretary. Oatlands Palace, which was near the village of the same name in Surrey, has completely disappeared now – it was demolished under the Commonwealth in the 1650s. A single building on the estate, some distance from the palace, was developed into Oatlands House and parts of it are in the hotel currently on the site.

Another high point would have been at Hampton Court on 11th October 1551, when he was knighted.

It was at Ingatestone Hall, in Essex, the home of his fellow Secretary, Sir William Petre, that Cecil came to swear allegiance to Mary, after the failure of the attempt to replace her with Lady Jane Grey. Although the Queen pardoned him she did not immediately take him back into government service.

In the years when Cecil was not directly in government employ, he travelled around London and the nearby counties, visiting friends, such as the Hobys at Bisham, and his parents still in Stamford, on their property at Burghley, just south of the town. Cecil was a compulsive recorder of detail, and information exists about one of his trips to Burghley during this period, which he undertook in company with his servant, Thomas Cayworth.

The two left Wimbledon on the morning of Sunday, 2nd May, with four horses. Cecil crossed the river by the Wandsworth ferry, which delivered him close to Canon Row, whilst Cayforth had to detour up to Lambeth to take the animals across the Thames on the horse-ferry (hence the name Horseferry Road in South London today.) They slept at Canon Row that night, then, on the following day had dinner at Ware in Hertfordshire –

probably about 11am, having covered 25 miles, followed by supper at Royston, a further 20 miles. We can infer from this that they followed the route of the modern A10. The next day they completed the full 50 miles on to Stamford, probably crossing westward to the Great North Road at Huntingdon.

Cecil remained in Stamford until 13th May, on which date he and Cayworth arrived in Huntingdon in time for dinner, and supped and slept at Royston. Dinner at Ware on 14th was followed by a long ride back into London, and a ferry crossing at Westminster, arriving at Stangate on the south side. From there, they probably followed what is now the A3 to arrive back in Wimbledon for bed. The whole journey cost 14s 5d on the outward trip, and 12s 5d to return.

There were two trips abroad during Mary's reign, the first, to Brussels to escort Cardinal Pole home, and the second, also to Brussels on government business, but followed up by independent travel to Antwerp and other places. During Mary's reign, Cecil also began his refurbishment of Burghley House at Stamford (3), which he inherited in 1553

We know that Cecil was at Hatfield in November 1558, when Elizabeth received the news of her half-sister's death. From that time he was in constant attendance on the Queen at the various royal palaces, Whitehall, Nonsuch, Richmond, Oatlands and others. In 1572 he was installed as the 356th Knight of the Order of the Garter, at St George's Chapel, Windsor Castle.

For domestic purposes, Cecil and his family had outgrown Wimbledon, which was passed to his son, Thomas. Instead, Cecil developed a grand new property in the Strand. Cecil House (14) was situated more or less opposite where the Savoy Theatre is today. He lavished time and money on it, and it was here that he died in 1598.

But even Cecil House and Burghley House did not satisfy Cecil's architectural passions. He created the most beautiful of all of the Elizabeth Prodigy houses at Theobalds, near Cheshunt, on the northern fringes of London. Nothing remains of it today – another palace pulled down during the Commonwealth.

For all Cecil's ties to London, when he died, he chose to go home to Stamford. Following his death on 4th August, 1598, at Cecil House, he began his last journey. He was transported to Westminster Abbey where over five hundred people attended his funeral. Then, following his orders, his cortege which consisted of only twelve men, accompanied the black draped coach containing the coffin the 100 miles to Stamford. At each resting place the poor of the parish were to be given 40s. He was entombed next to the memorial he had built for his parents in the church of St Martin Without, a thirteenth century church on the west of Stamford, about a mile from Burghley. There he rests, alone in his sumptuous monument, awaiting the resurrection and that final passage he so firmly believed in.

Key to Map

1. Bourne, Lincolnshire
2. Grantham – School
3. Stamford – School & Church, Burghley House
4. St John's College, Cambridge
5. Gray's Inn, London
6. Canon's Row, London
7. Edinburgh
8. Wimbledon Rectory & Church, London
9. Tower of London
10. Oatlands Palace, Surrey
11. Hampton Court Palace, Greater London

12. Ingatestone Hall, Essex
13. Windsor Castle
14. Cecil House, London
15. Theobalds, near Cheshunt (Greater London)

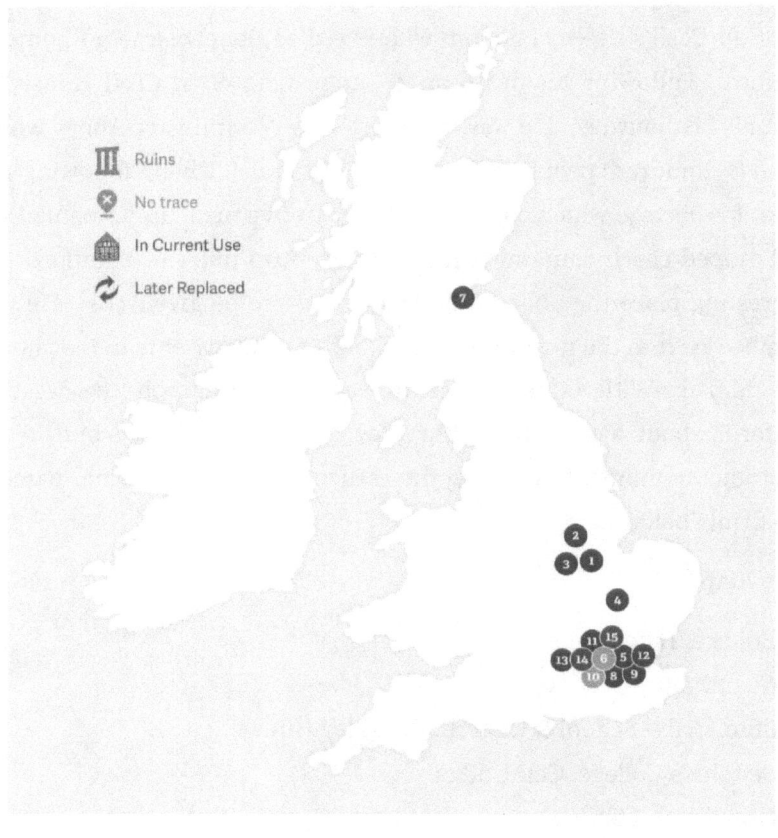

Chapter 139: Book Review

William Cecil has been the subject of many biographies over time, from the early ones written by members of his staff, to the Victorian hagiographies praising a great Protestant Statesman. Amongst modern works, the most comprehensive is that of Stephen Alford which, although not exhaustive on every topic, is a work of considerable scope.

Burghley: William Cecil at the Court of Elizabeth I

Author: Stephen Alford

Publisher: Yale University Press

In a nutshell A vast, detailed study of Elizabeth I's chief minister. William Cecil, Lord Burghley, emerges as a dedicated public servant, who believed totally in his destiny to protect Elizabeth and the Protestant state – with or without her agreement.

Stephen Alford is a Fellow of King's College, Cambridge, and has made a life-long study of the politicians of Elizabeth's court. His profound knowledge of the minute detail of every aspect of Burghley's long life and service pervade every page.

Many books portray Elizabeth and Cecil as two sides of the same coin – his role being to carry out her policy, but Alford suggests a rather different picture, perhaps supporting some of the anti-Cecil rhetoric of the day that saw him as too powerful, and tending to usurp the Queen's authority. There is no doubt that Alford's Cecil would have rejected such a view. He was devoted to the Queen's cause, it was just that he sometimes knew her interests, and those of her country, better than she did.

Alford identifies a number of occasions when Burghley, whilst ostensibly carrying out the Queen's policy, in fact, was attempting to subvert it through manipulating Parliament. In particular he cites the drafting of the petition put forward in 1566 for the Queen's marriage, which, he identifies was Cecil's brain-child, unbeknownst to the Queen, even whilst he was replying on her behalf with one of her famous '*answers answerless*'.

One of the underlying themes of the book is Cecil's obsession with the threat posed by Mary, Queen of Scots. How much of this threat he created through his own policy is left as the unanswered question – for who can know? But a case could certainly be made that his relentless undermining of her position in Scotland, and his later covering up of the forgeries in the Casket Letters, were all steps on his ultimate goal – her death.

Burghley's personality comes out well in Alford's writing – his tirelessness, his frequent ill health, his obsessive-compulsive need to control everything, from insisting on writing almost all his letters himself, to his minute directions to his son's guardian in Paris, to prevent young Thomas sitting up late over supper.

Cecil's family was important to him. His first marriage, to Mary Cheke, is over in a couple of paragraphs, but his forty-two year marriage to Mildred Cooke and their close relationship is interwoven into the story, together with his love and concern for his daughter, Anne, Countess of Oxford. Nevertheless, he was an exacting parent, and his relationship with his elder son was poor.

A man of omnivorous knowledge and interests, Alford brings out Cecil's other interests, which he pursued whenever he had leisure – architecture, gardening, map and book collecting.

Areas that could have been covered in more depth might have been Burghley's relationships with the Puritans, his views on the '*prophesying*' debate and the imprisonment of Grindal.

Another area that Alford does not explore at all (perhaps because he perceives it to be baseless sensation-mongering, which is probably true) is the hint in other studies of the period that Cecil might have had a hand in the death of Lord Robert Dudley's wife, Amy Robsart.

All in all, however, a book that is difficult to fault for its combination of depth and breadth.

Part 11: Lady Margaret Douglas: Countess of Lennox

Introduction

Lady Margaret Douglas, Countess of Lennox was the niece of Henry VIII, and both aunt and mother-in-law of Mary, Queen of Scots. Exiled at a young age from her native Scotland, Margaret was a great favourite at the English court, with a wide range of friends, both Catholic and Protestant. Imprisoned in the Tower three times, for *'matters of love'*, as she put it, but really at least twice for furthering her ambitions, her life is a microcosm of Tudor intrigue.

Lady Margaret spent her childhood in Scotland and the borders before being housed in the palaces of the English court. During her married life, she spent the majority of her time in the great houses that Henry VIII had granted her – that is, when she was not in the Tower of London!

This book contains Lady Margaret Douglas' Life Story and additional articles about her, looking at different aspects of her life. Lady Margaret's life encompassed almost every experience a sixteenth century princess could have, with the exception of execution or coronation. She was a lady-in-waiting to Queens, mistress of great estates, mother of eight children, a prisoner, a wife, and even a poet.

LADY MARGARET DOUGLAS

Family Tree

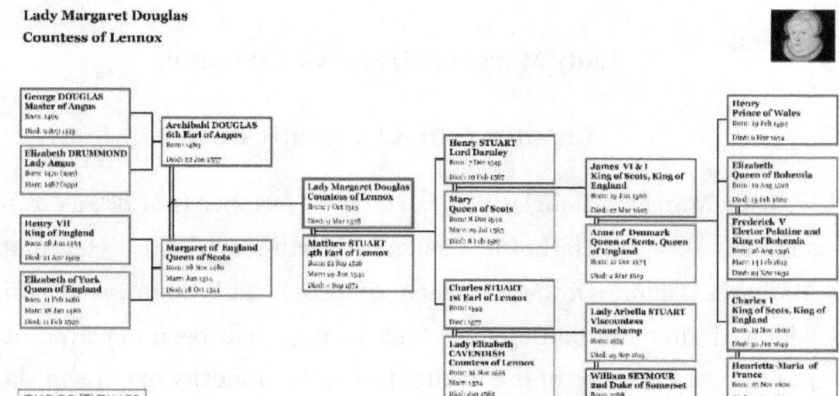

Lady Margaret Douglas' Life Story

Chapter 140: A Dramatic Birth

Lady Margaret Douglas was born on 7th October (not 8th, as in some sources) 1515, at Harbottle Castle in Northumberland. Her mother, Margaret Tudor, Dowager Queen of Scots, and Countess of Angus, widowed after the Battle of Flodden in 1513, had been deprived of her position as Governor of the Realm during the minority of her son, James V, when she married Margaret's father, Archibald Douglas, 6th Earl of Angus.

Angus, described by his uncle, Gavin Douglas, as a *'young, witless fool'*, was head of the powerful 'Red' Douglas clan, based at Tantallon Castle, and generally inclined to the pro-English party in Scotland, rather than the majority pro-French grouping. He failed to mention to Queen Margaret before their marriage, that he was already pre-contracted to marry Lady Janet Stewart of Trequair, an issue that came back to haunt both him, and his daughter.

The other Scottish nobles resented the match, believing it would lead to Angus dominating the government and invited the Duke of Albany, the young King's closest male heir, to return to Scotland from his home in France to take up the role of Governor. Queen Margaret felt hounded when she was forced to relinquish her sons and her fears were stoked by Thomas, Lord Dacre, the English Warden of the East March. Dacre requested instructions from Queen Margaret's brother, Henry VIII of England, in a letter of 7th September 1515 on what to do with Queen Margaret if their negotiation with her to leave Scotland should succeed *'as we trust verily it shall, to the great disturbance of all Scotland'*.

Eventually, Queen Margaret was persuaded to take refuge over the border and, leaving Linlithgow in secret, arrived at Harbottle a few days before her first child by Angus was due. Lady Margaret's birth was difficult, unsurprising in the circumstances. Nevertheless, she thrived, and was christened on 8th October, with Cardinal Thomas Wolsey (represented by a proxy) named as her godfather.

The fact that Lady Margaret Douglas was born in England had an important long term effect on her position. Born in England of an English mother, she was treated as an English subject, and thus eligible to inherit the Crown. A Statute of Edward III prohibited inheritance to individuals born out of the realm, although there were doubts as to whether this applied to the Crown.

Queen Margaret was very ill with sciatica following Margaret's birth. She lay immovable, barely able to sit up in bed. In the meantime, it was rumoured in Europe that Henry intended to invade Scotland. His minister, Cardinal Wolsey, maintained that there was absolutely no English intention whatever to invade Scotland, or France. Nevertheless, he added menacingly, if Albany did not mend his ways with reference to Queen Margaret, Henry would be forced to make him. Albany continued, with little success, to reach an accommodation with the Queen.

After some to-ing and fro-ing of letters, it was decided by Henry and his Council to invite Queen Margaret and her husband, Angus, south for Christmas. In the event, the party did not travel to London in November, perhaps because of Queen Margaret's continued frailty or because Henry had not yet decided on the best policy with reference to Scotland. Instead, Queen Margaret and the baby Margaret were moved in very slow stages of four or five miles each day to Morpeth, which had a few more of the creature comforts to which the Queen was accustomed, arriving on

23rd November 1515. They were met there by Angus, who appears to have returned to Scotland in the period after the original arrival at Harbottle.

Henry finally made arrangements for Queen Margaret and the baby Margaret to travel south, planning that they should set out from Morpeth on 7th April, and furnishing them with a litter and attendants. Mother and daughter set out on 8th April 1516, accompanied by Dacre and others, travelling first to Newcastle, where they were met by Sir Thomas Parr and then on to Durham.

Queen Margaret was no doubt thrilled to be travelling south at last, but, at the same time, she was in '*much heaviness*' as, a couple of weeks earlier, Angus had resolved to return to Scotland and make his peace with Albany. Whether the Queen's unhappiness stemmed from a sense of betrayal, or because she missed him, we cannot know. She would have understood Angus' need to keep his estates that were threatened with forfeiture, and, when she knew that Angus' return was inevitable, she wrote to Albany asking him to restore to Angus the castles of Tantallon and Bothwell. Henry was more condemnatory and characterised Angus' actions as '*done like a Scot*'.

Whether Angus was sorry to leave Queen Margaret is another question. On his return home, he quickly renewed his relationship with Janet Stewart of Traquair, who, in due course delivered a daughter, known as Lady Janet Douglas. He chose to set up home with Lady Janet in Queen Margaret's own dower castle in Newark, a fact which, when it came to her notice, enraged her far more than the simple matter of adultery.

Queen Margaret and the young Margaret continued to travel slowly towards London. On 3rd May, they entered London at Tottenham, as was traditional for Scots Ambassadors, before travelling to Greenwich, where the court was rejoicing in the birth of Mary, a live child at last, to Henry and Katharine, following at least four previous unsuccessful pregnancies.

Chapter 141: Scottish Years

Henry VIII saw his sisters first and foremost as a means to take and retain power for his dynasty. His view was that a Scottish regency favourable to England was an outcome to be promoted by whatever means possible. At this time, even after the live birth of Mary, it was looking increasingly likely that Henry's nearest male heir would remain the young king of Scots: a most unwelcome prospect to Henry.

At the very least if he could influence the boy through his mother, and, ideally, have him brought to England, the prospect might not be so bad. To achieve this, he needed Margaret in Scotland, not idling her time away at his expense in Westminster. Finally in December 1516, the terms of a treaty were agreed that would permit Queen Margaret to return to Scotland.

Queen Margaret and Lady Margaret, now eighteen months old, set out from London on 18th May 1517 in some state. On 15th June they were met at Berwick by Albany's deputy. Angus was also waiting for them at nearby Lamberton Kirk, and, ignorant as yet of the existence of Lady Janet of Traquair and her daughter, Queen Margaret was delighted to see him. Queen Margaret took up residence at Holyrood Palace, and, presumably, Lady Margaret was with her. The rapprochement between Queen Margaret and Angus did not last long, and Queen Margaret was soon writing to her brother.

'Also, please you to wit that I am sore troubled with my lord of Angus, since my last coming into Scotland, and every day more and more, so that we have not been together this half year.'

So far as is known, Margaret remained with her mother, but there are no records of her upbringing or education during this period. Late in 1517, Queen Margaret began to wonder if she could have her marriage to Angus annulled, but was persuaded against the idea at that time. By 1520, Margaret's parents were again on good terms, but by 1521, the relationship had broken down completely. In that year Angus, who had tried to undermine Albany's regency, was exiled to France.

Eventually, Angus travelled to England, where he was well-received by Henry, and began an alliance with his brother-in-law which required him to promote English interests in Scotland. Henry seems to have got on well with Angus, apparently preferring him to Queen Margaret, and certainly ignoring all her complaints about him.

Many writers have accepted the theory that Angus took Margaret with him to France, and then to England. However, this seems unlikely, as no mention of it is made in the records (we could fairly infer that Queen Margaret would have made huge protests to her brother). A letter that purports to date from 1524 from the Queen, complaining that Angus had kept her child from her for the preceding three years, should probably, according to the records in the *Douglas Book*, be dated to 1528. Margaret's most recent biographer, Alison Weir, concurs with this and believes that Margaret remained with her mother until at least 1525, although it is possible she was at one of Angus' castles, perhaps Tantallon, or with his other family.

Wherever Margaret was, there is no record of her education, but some information can be gleaned from later records, and the customs of the time. She would have learnt to read, and probably, but not necessarily at this time, to write. Her later writings are all in English, whereas one must suppose that during this period of her life she would have spoken Scots (Scots is a Germanic language, which developed in parallel with English from Anglo-Saxon languages, not be confused with Gaelic, the

Celtic language of the West and the Highlands). It seems likely that Lady Margaret would also have had at least some understanding of French, which was widely spoken at both the Scots and English courts.

If Margaret were brought up away from her mother, it is likely she would have been educated as was usual for young noblewomen, with an emphasis on the practical skills of running a great household - a woman of Margaret's rank would have been expected to be able to care for the estates of her future husband. It is unlikely that at this point Angus would have had any ambition for her beyond marriage to one of his fellow peers.

If Margaret remained with her mother during these years, she might have profited from a more sophisticated education such as her own mother had received, with perhaps a smattering of Latin and history. Wherever she was educated, she would certainly have been taught to sing, and probably play the lute and the virginals. Plenty of physical exercise would have been part of daily life - riding, hunting and possibly falconry.

She would also have been brought up to practise traditional forms of religion. In this regard Margaret remained loyal to the teaching of her childhood and did not move with the times. She remained an adherent of the Catholic Church throughout her life. The veneration of images and relics and undertaking of pilgrimages was as widely-practised in Scotland as elsewhere, although amongst the intellectuals of Europe these practices were being laughed at and questioned as hinting at idolatry. This scepticism did not rub off on Margaret, who was later noted as a great lover and collector of relics.

Chapter 142: Exile

After Angus was exiled in 1524, Queen Margaret requested the Pope for an annulment (although the term 'divorce' is used) on the grounds of Angus' prior betrothal to Lady Janet of Traquair. Back in England, Henry, Katharine and Wolsey were scandalised by her action, and exerted themselves to prevent it in every way. Wolsey wrote to Henry explaining his efforts at hindering the matter, as it was feared that the Queen intended to marry Albany, with whom she was rumoured to be having an affair.

In 1524, Queen Margaret persuaded the Scots Estates to declare that the regency of Albany was at an end, and that King James should now rule himself. On this, Angus returned to Scotland where he continued to make trouble for his wife and step-son. He seized James and for the next three years dominated Scottish government. His daughter's whereabouts are not known for certain, but she was probably kept close to her father's side, and thus in near proximity to her half-brother in the various royal palaces at Stirling, Linlithgow or Edinburgh Castle. In early 1525 a betrothal between Lady Margaret and the Earl of Moray, the illegitimate half-brother of Margaret's own half-brother, King James, was suggested, but it came to nothing.

Queen Margaret's divorce was finally granted by the Pope in 1526 and pronounced in Scotland by Cardinal James Beaton, Archbishop of St Andrew's with the proviso that, as Queen Margaret had undertaken the marriage in good faith, the daughter of the union was legitimate. The Queen then married Henry Stewart, Lord Methven, described by the French Ambassador, du Bellay as *'a still finer fellow than himself (Angus)'*. There is no record as to what Margaret thought, if anything, about her step-father. James V treated him with contempt.

In 1528, James escaped from Angus and his brother George, and declared the whole Douglas family as *'proscribed'* and subject to forfeit of their lands. He apparently excluded his half-sister from this, but Angus chose to interpret it as including her, and took her with him to Tantallon. James, fearful that she would be taken to England, and anxious for her return, sent scouts the length of the border to hunt for her and bring her back to her mother, where an appropriate establishment was being provided for her.

Rumours of further marriage plans arose – this time to an even more inappropriate husband – James Stewart, Captain of Doune, the brother of Queen Margaret's third husband. The idea that James Stewart had been Queen Margaret's lover before her marriage to his brother hardly seems credible, but the teller of the tale, Alexander Pringle, was a retainer of the Douglas family and no doubt could hardly find a good word to say of Queen Margaret. At any rate, he gives this mooted marriage as the reason for Angus being eager to take Lady Margaret out of the country.

James marched south with some 8,000 men to besiege Tantallon, but Angus had already left and proceeded to undertake a series of skirmishes and sieges against his King during the period of October 1528 to May 1529. On 9th October, having avoided being captured by James at Coldingham Priory, Angus sent Margaret for shelter to King Henry VIII of England's border castle of Norham. It is not clear whether she actually went to Norham, and stayed there, or returned to her father. She is next heard of in 1529, at Berwick Castle, in the care of Thomas Strangeways, Captain of Berwick.

Unsure what to do with her, Strangeways sent Carlisle Herald to Wolsey for instructions, keeping her in the meantime in some level of confinement, probably to prevent her being captured by James and Queen Margaret (or rescued, depending on Margaret's point of view, which we do not have). Wolsey, no doubt harassed by his own problems of Henry's annulment, found time to send instructions to Strangeways to keep Lady Margaret and look after her as well as possible, whilst not permitting her to leave. Strangeways replied in July 1529, pointing out that he had already had the lady in his care for three months, without any money to provide for her.

> 'Mr. Carlisle the herald hath declared to me that I shall keep still with me, in my house, the Lady Margaret, the daughter of the Earl of Angus ; and further, that I should take good heed to be sure of her ; but that she might hove as much liberty and recreation, and rather more, than she hath had. Please your Grace, even so according to your commandment sent me by the said herald, rightso I have used her before that commandment came to me. I was warned that if I took not good heed, and looked surely to her, she would be stolen and withdrawn into Scotland, which caused me to take more labor for her sure keeping; and yet I know well she was never merrier or more pleased and content than she is now, as she ofttimes repeats. My Lord of Angus, at the first bringing of her to me, desired that I would take her to my house, and he would content me both for her and for her gentlewomen, with such folk as wait upon her daily or resort to her. And I showed again to my said lord, that forasmuch as I understood that your Grace [Wolsey] was godfather to her, and seeing that my Lord of Angus was not provided with a convenient place for her to be in, I was content to take her, and do her the best service that might lay in my power, till such time as I knew your Grace's pleasure. Since the coming to Berwick of the said herald, I have showed my Lord of Angus that your express commandment to me by the said herald was, that I should keep and retain my lady still; wherewith he was very glad, and joyous that your Grace had his in such remembrance. An' it like your Grace, I have had the said lady and her gentlewomen, and a man-servant, with other of her friends and servants, at certain times, and for the most part the Earl

of Angus her father, now by the space of three months, without any manner of costs to my said lord or any of them ; and what your Grace shall further command me in this matter, or any other, I shall be ready to accomplish the same by the grace of God.'

The gentlewoman referred to is named as Isobel Hoppar who was married to Angus' uncle, another Archibald Douglas, so was probably more of a governess than a servant.

Chapter 143: Life in England

On 6th April 1530, Henry VIII paid for clothes for Margaret, but her actual whereabouts are not clear. There is a theory, supported by her latest biographer, Alison Weir, that she was sent from Northumberland to the household of her aunt, Mary, the French Queen at Westhorpe Castle in Suffolk. This is based on the content of a commemorative poem written about Margaret after her death, probably by a man who knew her. There are no contemporary records and other historians (Rosalind K Marshall, and William Fraser who collated the Douglas papers) place her immediately at Beaulieu with her cousin, Mary. In August of 1530, Strangeways requested 200 marks for the *'bringing-up'* of Lady Margaret, but the implication is that she had left his care.

By Christmas 1530 Margaret was at court and received £6 13s 4d to *'disport'* herself from Henry VIII. This gift was repeated the following year. Margaret was now in the retinue of her cousin, Mary, who was still treated as a Princess, her parents' marriage, although in dispute, not yet annulled. She would not, of course have remembered her cousin whom she had last seen in 1517, but the two girls struck up a friendship that lasted for the rest of Mary's life.

The cousins, some six months apart in age, were in the care of Mary's Lady Mistress, Margaret Plantagenet, Countess of Salisbury, cousin of their maternal grandmother, Elizabeth of York. Life in the Princess's household would have been closely regulated. At this time, Lady Salisbury was in her late fifties and likely to have been traditional in her approach to the upbringing of young ladies of the royal family. This would have been counterbalanced by the very modern education that Mary was receiving, although there is no evidence that Margaret shared her lessons. In total, there were 162 members of the household. Following Lady Salisbury in importance was Margaret herself, then ten other ladies and gentlewomen. Margaret received an annual salary of £10.

The girls spent most of their time at Mary's houses of Beaulieu and Hundson in Essex, with visits to the King and Queen at court at Easter and Christmas. They would also have seen Henry and Katharine as they moved around the various palaces on the north of London.

In their spare time the girls would have ridden, hunted, hawked and danced; played cards – in particular a game known as cent, similar to modern picquet, tables, chess and bowls and gambled on the outcome. Gambling was a permanent feature in Tudor entertainment. Mary remained a frequent gambler all her life, and Margaret presumably followed suit. There is no description of Margaret known at this age.

Henry gave both Angus and his brother George large sums of money to pay spies and undermine the Scots government, as well as for living expenses. The maintenance of Angus, his brother and daughter was set on a surer footing than random gifts of money when Henry granted the Earl a pension of £1,000 per annum in 1532. This was a munificent sum.

There is a record of a magnificent present of clothing for Margaret, her two gentlewomen and her servants in October 1531. The gift included three gowns of 11 and a half yards each – one of '*tynsen*' (tinsel or some sort of gold cloth), one of black velvet, furred with powdered ermine and one of black damask, together with kirtles and sleeves (which were separate garments) of crimson satin, black satin and black velvet, each being seven and a half yards. More yards of white satin, black velvet and crimson satin for other items, 30 ells of Holland cloth (a type of high quality linen) for underclothes, two French hoods (the curved hoods set back on the wearer's hair familiar from paintings of Anne Boleyn), 12 pairs of hose, 6 pairs of black velvet shoes for indoor use, and six of leather, lacing ribbons and garters, 12 pairs of gloves, a lb of thread, 100 needles, 2 brushes and a '*standard*' 1 and three quarter yards, by ¾ of a yard. Presumably this last had her coat of arms on it and would have been carried in front of her when she travelled. In addition, there was a generous allowance of clothing for her servants.

Margaret's reaction to this sumptuous gift is not recorded, but what adolescent girl would not have been delighted at such a present, particularly if she had inherited her mother's love of '*rich apparel*'?

Clothes were not just pretty or useful items in themselves, they were also one of the most significant indicators of rank or status. With little in the way of consumer goods and in a pre-industrial age with nothing to invest in, other than land, wealth was displayed by your clothes and jewels. The mediaeval sumptuary laws which had striven to prevent men '*aping their betters*' and hence threatening the all-important hierarchy, were re-affirmed, and even strengthened, during the Tudor period. Certain colours, such as purple, and fabrics, such as cloth of gold, could not be worn other than by royalty or the highest ranks of nobility. Interestingly, the sumptuary laws did not generally apply to women. This gift of expensive fabrics, such as tynsen and velvet, showed Margaret's high rank and the generosity with which Henry treated her.

Chapter 144: At Anne Boleyn's Court

In 1533, when Princess Mary was demoted in rank, and had her household disbanded, Margaret was summoned to court to serve the new Queen, Anne Boleyn, in the capacity of Chief Lady of the Bedchamber to Anne's recently born daughter, Elizabeth. It is not recorded whether Margaret was required to swear to the Acts of Succession and Supremacy in 1534, the former of which stated Henry and Katharine's marriage to be null and establishing Anne as his wife and Elizabeth his only legitimate child; the latter, repudiating the authority of the Pope, or Bishop of Rome as he was henceforth referred to. It seems highly likely that as the King's niece and in her position as First Lady of the Bedchamber to Elizabeth she would have been required to do so.

Nor is it apparent whether she joined Elizabeth's household in fact, as well as name. In March 1534, she is recorded as being at court, when the French Ambassador reported that Henry was offering Margaret as bride for François I of France's son, in place of the previously requested Mary.

'He [Henry] added that there were many other girls in his kingdom, and that he had a niece, daughter of the queen of Scotland, whom he keeps with the Queen his wife, and treats like a queen's daughter, and if any proposition were made for her, he would make her marriage worth as much as his daughter Mary's. I assure you the *lady* is beautiful, and highly esteemed here'

Henry and Katharine's court had always been magnificent. With Anne at his side, Henry continued to enjoy a wide variety of activities – gambling as always, but even astronomy. Anne, though not so well educated in a formal sense as Katharine, was undoubtedly a clever woman and seems to have had a biting wit which, whilst it made her many enemies who came back to haunt her, yet must have made her company exhilarating. However, wit was not enough for a Queen – she needed allies and friends – an *'affinity'* as it was called, and Anne was doing her best to create one.

The appointment of Lady Margaret Douglas, the King's own niece, daughter of a Queen, and half-sister of a King, to be her lady-in-waiting must have seems quite a coup, especially as it would separate Margaret from Mary, as Anne, perhaps jealous, but certainly frightened of Henry's lingering affection for his daughter, took every opportunity to undermine her and detach any of Mary's friends or supporters from her side. In addition, to have such a highly-born attendant would raise the tone of her household, and be some counter to the barely concealed contempt of the older court ladies – even her aunt, the Duke of Norfolk's wife, had refused to serve her, protesting her support of Katharine.

Amongst the circle of gentleman surrounding Anne, were the sons of the new gentry class that was rising under the Tudors, to the disgust of the older families, who complained of these *'new men'*. Their charm for the King was that they had no power base or affinity of their own, and were completely dependent on him for favour. The new circle of friends included men such as Anne's father, Sir Thomas Boleyn and Henry Norris, the King's closest companion since his old friend and brother-in-law, Suffolk, was less supportive of the divorce than Henry would have liked.

The ladies of Queen Anne's household were a mixture of her personal friends, largely drawn from the daughters of her mother's twenty siblings and half-siblings, and, for state occasions, the great ladies who were the wives of the highest ranking nobles. Amongst these women, Margaret was to find her friends. Many of Anne's ladies were, like Anne, on the more evangelical wing of religious thought. This is hardly surprising, as conservatives rejected (in their hearts, even if not openly) the divorce and would not be clamouring to serve her, so taking an evangelical view was likely to gain favour with Anne. For Margaret, however, this does not seem to have been a problem. Her two closest friends at this time appear to have been Anne's paternal cousin Mary Shelton, and Mary Howard, the Duke of Norfolk's daughter, who was shortly to marry the King's illegitimate son, Henry Fitzroy, Duke of Richmond. Both of these ladies, and particularly Mary Howard, were later considered as evangelicals. However, during the early 1530s religious difference had not yet hardened into the irreconcilable divide of Catholic and Protestant. In any event, although religion played a central role in the day to day life of everyone, young women in the sixteenth century enjoyed music, singing, dancing, poetry and thoughts of love just as much then, as they do now and they had ample opportunity to indulge these tastes at Anne's court.

Writing love poetry was a popular pastime amongst the erudite youth of the court and it was fashionable for lovers to write verse conversations and for poems to be written down and shared amongst friends, with each adding an answer to the previous poem. A large group of verses is contained in a manuscript, now known as the Devonshire manuscript, a collection of 183 poems, transcribed mainly in the hands of Margaret Douglas and Mary Shelton with various marginalia and comments - not always flattering to the versifiers - and in this document is a series of poems attributed to Margaret herself and her lover, Lord Thomas Howard.

Chapter 145: Courtship

By 1535, Margaret was 20 years old. This was an unusually advanced age for a noblewoman not to be married. The tentative arrangements that Queen Margaret had made for her ten years before had come to nothing, and there did not seem to be any definite prospects for her, despite the conversation with the French Ambassador.

Margaret, perhaps inheriting the romantic streak of her mother and uncle, was not content to wait, and sometime during late 1535 began a relationship with Lord Thomas Howard. Lord Thomas was the much younger half-brother of the Duke of Norfolk, with whom he confusingly shared his Christian name. Perhaps with twenty previous children, his father had run short of inspiration! Lord Thomas was some four years older than Margaret and had been honoured by Henry in being permitted to hold the canopy of estate over the baby Elizabeth at her christening. At Christmas, Howard and Margaret exchanged gifts - he gave her a cramp ring which was a fairly common gift amongst friends, and she gave him a miniature of herself.

It has been said that to begin with, Henry and Anne encouraged the match. This is based on the evidence of Queen Margaret's later letter in which she says that Henry had '*advised*' the match, however, the word advised at that time could also mean 'been informed of'. Nevertheless, there is no definite evidence that Henry was aware of the young couple's relationship at the time.

For Queen Anne, it would definitely be a welcome prospect. Any closer ties that Anne could make between her family and the King's would be to her advantage, and Henry, still eager to promote his second marriage as valid, and to raise Anne up in public estimation, would also have seen the benefits. Lord Thomas' elder brother, Lord William Howard had been dispatched in 1534 as Ambassador to Scotland where he proceeded to develop good relations with Queen Margaret who was now influential in her son's government. Margaret, as well as being in love, would have been well aware that marrying the Queen's uncle would be a good match for her.

In a complete volte face from Henry, Anne was disgraced, degraded from her rank and executed all within a period of weeks in Spring 1536.

In the aftermath of Anne's execution, and the annulment of a marriage that apparently was not valid for an unspecified reason, Henry was left with two illegitimate daughters, an illegitimate son, and the offspring of his sisters. The numbers of possible claimants to the throne was reduced by the death on 31st May of Henry Fitzroy.

The Act of Succession of 4th July 1536, passed after Anne's death had the effect, surely not Henry's ideal scenario, of making Margaret his lawful heir, James being excluded as born out of the realm. The actual wording of the Act conferred the succession on the children of Henry's new queen, Jane Seymour (whose train Margaret had held at her wedding), but since she was not even pregnant at this time, logically, in default of Mary or Elizabeth, had Henry died before Jane became pregnant, the Crown would have devolved on either James V or Margaret Douglas. At this point, Henry woke up to the fact that his niece was embroiled in some sort of love affair that had previously had his tacit acceptance, and for Margaret, her betrothal to Lord Thomas was now a source of danger. Fortunately, the match had not been consummated, which would have created a binding marriage.

On the 9th July, the members of the former queen's household were questioned. Howard admitted to the relationship between himself and Margaret, saying they had been married *de verbi di praesenti*, but consummation had not taken place. Both Howard and Margaret were clapped in the Tower and an Act of Attainder was raced through Parliament against Howard, being both introduced and passed on the same day – 18th July 1536. An Act of Attainder permitted the execution without trial of an individual accused of treason. Instituted in the early 1530s they became Henry's weapon of choice for disposing of recalcitrant relatives who had undertaken activities that, not criminal at the time, but that Henry, in the aftermath, disapproved. Howard was convicted of an attempt to *'interrupt ympedyte and lett the seid Succession of the Crowne'*.

The act imposed the death sentence on Howard and also forbade the marriage of any member of the King's family without his permission. Margaret was not included in the Act, and it was believed that the non-consummation of the marriage saved her.

Bizarrely, Sir Francis Bigod, who led the final phase of the uprisings around the Pilgrimage of Grace in early 1537, claimed in his statement that it was commonly supposed that the Act of Attainder against Thomas Howard had been instigated by Cromwell, as he wished to marry Margaret himself. It is hard to believe any credence could be given to such a rumour.

Chapter 146: Imprisonment

The sentence was not carried out immediately and Thomas and Margaret remained in the Tower throughout the summer of 1536. The example of Anne's death must have thoroughly frightened Margaret. She could not suppose that nearness of blood to the King would save her, but she perhaps put her hope in her parents or half-brother to plead for her with Henry. There is no record of Angus taking any action, although of course he may have done, but on 12th August 1536, Queen Margaret wrote an importunate letter to her brother, first marvelling that since he had known about the betrothal earlier, he could then punish her daughter for carrying it out.

She followed this by begging him, both for affection for herself, and respect for King James to allow Margaret to be sent back to a Scotland, so that *'in time coming she shall never come into your Grace's presence.'* Henry, however, had no intention of letting such a useful bargaining chip slip from his grasp and the young couple remained in prison.

It need not be thought that Margaret was confined to a gloomy dungeon, lying on straw watching the damp creep down the slimy walls and listening to the scurrying of rats in the straw. That indeed, was the fate of many prisoners, but nobles confined to the Tower were held in the upper rooms, usually in the Bell Tower or the Lord Lieutenant's own quarters. Margaret probably had her gentlewomen and servant to wait upon her, and might even have received guests. That her captivity, although frightening, was not rigid, is supported by the likelihood that she and Thomas were exchanging verses whilst in confinement. Lord Thomas appears to have been more faithful than Margaret, who eventually renounced his love. One can hardly blame her, aged 21, urged to obey her uncle the King. She would also have had in mind the shocking death of her former mistress, Anne, and many of Margaret's circle and perhaps the scene of it before her eyes, out of her prison window.

By 20th October, 1536, Margaret's mother wrote to Henry, thanking him for his '*nobleness*' towards her daughter, and confirming that she would never give her blessing to her wayward child if she did not conform to the King's will. From this we may infer that Henry had pardoned Margaret.

There is a difference in historians' accounts as to what happened next. Wriothesley's Chronicle, a contemporary document, suggests that Margaret remained in the Tower until the end of October 1537. This is the view taken by Alison Weir in her recent biography, who also cites a letter from Queen Margaret of 30th October 1537, saying how pleased she is that Margaret is no longer in the Tower. Ms Weir then notes that Margaret was conveyed to Syon Abbey by barge on 24th November 1537 and that she was at the Abbey for convalescence, rather than under house arrest.

A contrary view, is that Margaret left the Tower in November 1536, for conveyance to Syon. This rests on a letter from the Abbess of Syon that confirms she is willing to take Margaret into the precinct of the convent. The letter is catalogued in the '*Letters and Papers of the Reign of Henry VIII*' and also in the collection of letters transcribed in 1822 as '*Letters of Illustrious Ladies of Great Britain*' as pertaining to November 1536. However, Ms Weir contends that this is a misplacement, and that it should be placed in November 1537. The earlier date would seem to accord with Queen Margaret's letter of 20th October 1536 and Henry's response to it in December 1536 that although Margaret had '*used herself to her dishonour*', yet, in future, if she behaved, Henry would be good to her. This seems to imply that she had been forgiven and it was in that month that she received from him the gift of a magnificent crimson velvet chair, with 2,000 nails and silver fringe at 5s the ounce. Chairs were the preserve of the highest ranks, and this specimen must have been a splendid example. Would Henry have sent such a present if she were still in the Tower and would she have been kept there for a further ten months after being forgiven?

Furthermore, there is a letter from Margaret, again transcribed in *Letters of Royal and Illustrious Ladies of Great Britain*. Letters and Papers catalogues it in August 1536, with which Ms Weir concurs, giving it as written from the Tower. The transcription in *Royal and Illustrious Ladies* also dates it to 1536, but with no month given. It could be argued that the text, although the tone of it suggests that Lord Thomas is still alive, is more consistent with Margaret being at Syon for a couple of reasons: first, it refers to a complaint by Cromwell about her keeping excessive numbers of servants and having too many visitors. It is hard to believe that, imprisoned in the Tower, she could have had excess servants or visitors. Second, Margaret denies that her servants are an additional charge to the '*house*' and uses the expression '*house*' twice, which might seem an odd way of referring to the Tower.

Wherever Margaret was, Lord Thomas continued to languish in the Tower. Eventually, he fell ill, and before Henry could either confirm his execution, or release him, he died on 31st October, 1537. Margaret apparently took Lord Thomas' death hard, despite her protestations to Cromwell, and one of the last entries in the Devonshire Manuscript from her is a long poem with a definitely suicidal tone. Suicide was the most terrible sin of all, and it is unlikely a woman of Margaret's apparent energy and spirits would have contemplated such a terrible step for long, but the verses make sombre reading. Margaret was unable to mourn publicly for Lord Thomas. His mother, Agnes, Dowager Duchess of Norfolk was granted permission by the King to take his body and bury it

'so [on the condition] that she bury him without pomp.'

Lord Thomas was interred, with many others of the family, at Thetford Priory.

That Margaret was ill both during, and after, her time in the Tower is attested by medical expenses paid by the King, to the tune of £14 4s. Henry also paid £20 to Dr Cromer, possibly for medical services, but more likely for spiritual advice, as the payment is for *'preparations against Easter.'* There seem to be two Drs Cromer – one a physician, and the second a priest who had preached on Palm Sunday, and who was later accused of heresy. It is possible, of course, that they were one and the same.

There is no record of Margaret leaving Syon or where she went, although there is a note from Cromwell to pay her expenses there in April 1538. As the court was in mourning for Jane Seymour, it seems likely she returned to the household of her cousin, Mary, and she was certainly there by June 1538.

Chapter 147: Queen's Lady

In October 1538, Margaret was again mentioned as a possible spouse for a foreign prince. Henry suggested that, if the Emperor Charles accepted Mary for his protégé, the Infante of Portugal (Charles' nominee for the Duchy of Milan) Henry would allow Charles to choose suitable Italian princes for Margaret, the Lady Elizabeth, and the widowed Duchess of Richmond – a case of buy one get three free! Again, the negotiations went nowhere.

Henry began to look for a new wife for himself and, his choice falling on Anne of Cleves, a new household was formed for her. Margaret was to be the chief of the *'Great Ladies'*, and she was also to be part of the welcoming committee for the new Queen at Blackheath in late 1539. In recognition of her status, she was given one of the best apartments at Hampton Court.

Another of the ladies in the new Queen's service was Mistress Katheryn Howard, who was the half-niece of Margaret's former lover. She was probably about five years younger than Margaret, and far below her in rank, so it must have come as a shock to Margaret when Katheryn replaced Anne of Cleves as Queen in August 1540. Whatever her thoughts, Margaret kept them to herself, retaining a position in the Royal Household, and being given a gift of *'beads'* (a rosary) by the new Queen.

Just as Queen Katheryn's cousin, Anne Boleyn, had surrounded herself with cheerful young cousins and friends, so did Katheryn. Among her household were her various siblings, including Charles Howard, with whom Margaret struck up a flirtation. It was now three years since Thomas Howard's death, and probably four since she had actually seen him. Aged 25, it was more than time for Margaret to marry, but no plans were forthcoming.

In October of 1541, Margaret's mother, Queen Margaret, died. She requested that her goods be given to Margaret, since she had never previously given her anything but James V kept them for himself. It was some fifteen years since Margaret had last seen her mother, and there is no record of correspondence between them, but that does not, of course, mean that she did not grieve. But a more immediate worry was soon upon Margaret – the King had been informed that his pretty young wife was not chaste, and immediate enquiries began.

Katheryn Howard was arrested and sent first to Syon, then to the Tower, on charges of adultery. Margaret would have been questioned with the rest of her ladies, but was not implicated in the Queen's bad behaviour. Queen Katheryn's household was broken up on 11th November 1541, with an instruction that Margaret was to go to Kenninghall, in Norfolk, the property of the Duke of Norfolk. She was to go with her friend, Mary, Duchess of Richmond, Norfolk's daughter and widow of Henry's late illegitimate son. The Privy Council note says that she is to be sent there if '*my lord her father and she are content.*' This requirement has generally been read to refer to Norfolk and Mary because Margaret was in disgrace, but could be read to mean Angus and Margaret - suggesting that Margaret had some choice in the matter. This view may be supported by the fact that Norfolk was one of the signatories. He must have known whether he was '*content*' or not. It also seems unlikely that Mary Richmond would have been asked for her opinion.

It is only the following day, after further examinations of the Queen had taken place, that Cranmer was told to take a stern message to Lady Margaret, rebuking her for acting indiscreetly, first with Lord Thomas, and now with Charles Howard. Cranmer was to tell her to '*beware the third time.*'

Margaret appears to have stayed with the Howards at Kenninghall for some time, writing to her father from there in October 1542. She may have visited Lady Mary at Christmas 1542, when she gave the Princess a carnation velvet gown for New Year, although in Lady Mary's accounts there is a tip for Margaret's servant for delivering it. She herself would have been in mourning that Christmas – her half-brother, King James V of Scotland died in early December 1542, after a defeat at the Battle of Solway Moss. There is no reason to suppose that Margaret was personally grieved by James' death. He was the cause of her original exile to England and his personal hatred for her father, Angus had never wavered, but, of course, we do not know the state of her emotions. Angus had fought for the English at the Scots victory at Haddon Rig, immediately before Solway Moss, but the Anglo-Scots landscape now changed dramatically with James' death.

The new Scots Regent, the Earl of Arran, although head of the Hamiltons, who were enemies of the Douglas clan, was pro-English, and in favour of a policy of Church reform. He made overtures towards England, and Henry, seeing the possibility of English domination of Scotland through the marriage of his son, Edward, to the baby Queen of Scots, encouraged Angus to return to Scotland to further the match. This seemed a good plan to Henry, who let Angus travel north. Angus was restored to his lands, sworn to Arran's Privy Council, and married to Margaret Maxwell, all within a few months.

On 12th July, 1543, Lady Margaret was one of the witnesses of Henry VIII's sixth marriage, to Katherine Parr, the widowed Lady Latimer. The new Queen was a good friend of the Lady Mary, and was soon surrounded by many faces familiar to Margaret – Mary of Richmond; Anne Stanhope, Countess of Hertford; Katherine Willoughby, Duchess of Suffolk. All four of these women, and the Queen herself, were evangelists in religion, unlike Margaret or Lady Mary, but that does not seem to have caused problems.

In February 1544, Margaret, described as the *'Princess of Scotland'* was noted as one of the ladies of the Queen's suite who welcomed and entertained the Duke of Najera. She danced with various gentlemen, and, at the end, all of the English ladies were kissed by the Duke.

Having been bridesmaid to at least two, probably three, of Henry's queens, it was now Margaret's turn to be married at last.

Chapter 148: Marriage Negotiations

It is impossible to know when Margaret first heard a marriage mooted between herself and Matthew Stuart, 4th Earl of Lennox, but Henry's Council and her father were negotiating for it from July of 1543. Lennox had spent most of his youth in France, where he was an important figure in the Scots Guard around François I. He had left Scotland in the wake of his father's murder by one of the Hamiltons. This shared enmity for the Hamiltons and their leader, the Earl of Arran, was a link with Angus, but in 1543, with Angus reconciled to Arran as Governor of the Realm, it looked as though the two would be on opposing sides. Lennox returned to Scotland with the view of ousting Arran from the Governorship – a role he felt belonged to him, as, in his view, his claim to be the young Queen Mary's heir was superior to Arran's.

Lennox represented the French alliance, and hoped to marry Marie of Guise, the Dowager Queen. She held him off, but gave him enough encouragement for him to help her in her plan to move to Stirling to enable her daughter to be crowned.

At some point, Arran turned away from Henry, and dismissed the idea of the marriage between Mary and Edward, reconciling more fully with the Queen Dowager and Cardinal Beaton, the other leader of the pro-French party. The bitterness between Arran and Lennox was so strong that this influenced the latter to turn towards the English party. Arran had stated quite clearly that he would not be of the same party as Lennox, unless the latter recognised his right as *'second person of the realm'*. Lennox, claiming that place for himself, refused to do so and presumably was determined to be on any side against Arran. Marie de Guise began to suspect that Lennox, would betray the Governor and herself and warned Arran (who needed no prompting) against trusting him.

By the end of October 1543, Lennox was at Dumbarton Castle, whence a French loan of 10,000 crowns together with munitions, a Legate from the Pope, and the French Ambassador had been sent. Queen Marie told the Venetian envoy that she would have preferred the gold to be at *'the bottom of the sea'* rather than that it should fall into Lennox' hands.

Marie was right in her surmise that Lennox would betray her, as he was now in secret negotiation with the English, and was demanding, as part of his price for betraying Dumbarton to Henry's men, that not only should he marry Margaret, but that they should succeed her father, Angus, in the Earldom of Angus, even though Angus had sons by his third marriage. Angus refused to agree to this. The Dowager, Cardinal and Governor all commanded Lennox to send the money, munitions, Legate and Ambassador to Edinburgh. Sir Ralph Sadler (Henry's Ambassador) believed Lennox might send the latter two, but would hang on to the useful items. The Venetian envoy could not believe that Lennox, being a *'Lord and a Gentleman'*, would so dishonour himself, and risk the loss of the King of France's favour as well as his lands in France and expectation of more there: however it seems that Lennox's hatred and jealousy of Arran and his resentment at his rejection by Marie were stronger than his loyalty to the King of France. Whilst Henry considered his proposals, Lennox temporised with Marie, promising, but failing, to deliver the money and munitions to her.

By March of 1544, it appeared that Henry had agreed in principle to the marriage, although he made the caveat that the young couple must agree to it, once they had seen each other, as he had promised his niece *'never to cause her to marry any but whom she shall find in her own heart to love'*. This is less likely to be a reflection of Henry's romantic streak, than a loophole for breaking the match off if he changed his mind.

Chapter 149: Countess of Lennox

On 26th June, 1544, Henry and Lennox entered a treaty for the marriage. In return for Lennox abandoning his claims to the Scots throne in favour of Henry, giving up his French estates, and betraying Dumbarton and Bute to the English, he was to receive Lady Margaret Douglas in marriage, and a handsome estate. Also listed in the treaty were the lands that Margaret was to have from Lennox as her jointure, which were part of the Lennox earldom and amounted to 500 marks Scots per annum. When Henry achieved his fantasy of overlordship of Scotland, Lennox would be Governor under him, and could take any revenue over the cost of running the country and maintaining Margaret. He was also to cause the *'Word of God'* to be preached in Scotland. As Henry was still firmly Catholic in doctrine, we may suppose that this was merely to reiterate Catholic teaching, with the rejection of Papal authority.

The signing of the treaty was celebrated with a feast at which Henry, Lennox, Prince Edward and the Ladies Mary and Elizabeth were present. Margaret herself is not named, although she may have been there.

Three days later, on 29th June 1544, at St James' Palace, Margaret married Lennox after Mass, with the King and Queen in attendance.

There is no record of Margaret's initial reaction to the marriage, but we can assume that she would have been pleased, for a number of reasons, not least the fact that she was close to thirty in an age which considered the appropriate age for women of her class to be married was about twenty. The fact that Lennox himself was the same age as her, and by all accounts a personable man, was unlikely to have escaped her.

Margaret is likely to have been warmly disposed to the match for political reasons too. She was a strong supporter of Henry's policy, still being pursued by her father, Angus, of the marriage of Edward and Mary Queen of Scots. Such a match would have made her aunt-by-marriage to the next King of England, as well as cousin – never a bad idea to be closely allied to the Crown, provided that one's loyalty was not suspect.

Henry's motives for keeping Margaret single so long are likely to have been similar to his reasons for keeping his daughter, Mary, single. Apart from wanting to hang on to his bargaining chips as long as possible, he was reluctant to provide either woman with a husband who might challenge either Henry himself, or more likely, the young Edward, should Henry die before Edward was able to hold his throne firmly. He must have been strongly convinced either that Lennox would be loyal, although a talent for loyalty had not been conspicuously demonstrated by Lennox' behaviour to date, or that the English would be so solidly against a Scottish King that he would not pose a threat. Lennox became a '*denizen*' of England – that is, he swore allegiance to the English King.

On her wedding, Margaret received a generous gift of jewellery from the Lady Mary consisting of several gold brooches with diamonds, sapphires and emeralds.

Henry granted Margaret and Lennox vast swathes of land in Yorkshire. To fulfil the marriage treaty, their value had to be at least 6,800 marks Scots, or 1,700 marks English – about £1,100 English. The lands were made up of property from the Percy Earldom of Northumberland, the lands of dissolved monasteries, including that of Jervaulx, and land confiscated from rebels after the Pilgrimage of Grace. The lands were granted to the couple jointly, and entailed on their joint heirs – ensuring that, in the event of Margaret's death without heirs, they would not pass to the children of any subsequent wife of Lennox. The extent of their lands made them the second largest landowners (excluding the Crown) in the whole of the north, next only to Henry Clifford, Earl of Cumberland, married to Margaret's cousin Eleanor Brandon.

Margaret was now a Countess with vast estates. The lands they received were:

- Temple Newsam
- Temple Hurst
- Settrington
- Whorlton
- Kirk Leavington,
- Breighton
- Grange of Rookwith
- Abbey of Jervaulx together with land in Feldum and Didderston, and 6 carucates in Hutton Hang and the manor and land at Elington
- Scrafton, Caldbergh, Carlton, Arundel House and Slape Gill, with their five respective granges, which had belonged to Coverham Abbey

Chapter 150: Early Married Life

The complexities of the political relations between England and Scotland in the last years of Henry's reign are too great to cover here in detail – more can be found in the Profile of Marie of Guise. Suffice to say, that Lennox continued to support Henry's policy. Henry VIII was determined to get his money's worth from Lennox, and during much of the next few years Lennox was raising armies and spending time in Ireland and Scotland to promote the English cause in the War of the Rough Wooings. On 1st October 1545 at Linlithgow, the Scots Parliament convicted Lennox of treason and confiscated his lands.

During her husband's absences, Margaret seems to have remained at court. She was with Queen Katherine during September 1544, when Henry sent greetings from Boulogne to her, and is recorded as present at the visit of the French Ambassador to Hampton Court in August 1546. Although she is named in precedence after the Ladies Mary, Elizabeth and Anne of Cleves, it does not seem that she was '*pricked*' (chosen) to sit at the feast.

Nevertheless, Lennox and she met sufficiently frequently for her to have borne and lost a son, Henry, Lord Darnley, by November 1545, and to have a second in the following month, also named Henry. In all, Margaret was to have eight children, four daughters and four sons. There are no records of the daughters' names, or dates of birth or death, so they presumably died in infancy. Her last two sons, Philip and Charles were born in the mid-1550s, but only Henry and Charles reached manhood.

Not long before Margaret's marriage, the Third Act of Succession had been passed, which laid down the succession to the English Crown – first Edward, then Mary, then Elizabeth, with a proviso for Henry to name Elizabeth's successors (should she have no children) in his will, or by Letters Patent. This act overturned the common law, both by permitting the inheritance by two women who were, under English law, illegitimate, and by allowing the King to specify an heir who might not be the heir under common law.

Under the usual rules of inheritance, on the assumption that Mary and Elizabeth were both illegitimate, then Henry's heir was Edward, followed by Margaret's niece, the baby Queen of Scots, or, if, as was sometimes claimed Queen Mary was debarred from the Crown by foreign birth, Margaret herself. As in 1544 it was probably assumed that at least one of the King's children would have an heir, it seems unlikely that Margaret considered herself to have been wronged, especially as she probably considered that at least Mary was legitimate. She may even have thought that Henry might name her in his will to follow Elizabeth. It was not until the King, in his final will, named as Elizabeth's successors the children of Margaret's other cousin, Frances, Duchess of Suffolk, that Margaret knew herself to have been definitely passed over.

It has been speculated that Margaret had quarrelled with Henry, and that was the reason he cut her out of the succession, but there is no evidence to support this. It is far more likely that, despite his personal fondness for her, Henry could not countenance Lennox as King of England – it being assumed that any woman inheriting would naturally be subordinate to her husband. It may also have been the result of Angus finally abandoning Henry and the English alliance (see next chapter).

On Henry's death, Margaret and Lennox moved north, basing themselves at Temple Newsam, near Leeds where they concentrated on managing their estates.

As Edward's government introduced more reformist legislation it appears that Margaret became known for retaining Catholic practices, although she must have conformed sufficiently to keep within the law. Lennox' religion seems to have been a more fluid affair. He was probably Catholic in such convictions as he may have had, but had no trouble with working with Protestants in Scotland. Their sons, Henry, Lord Darnley, and Charles Stuart were brought up as Catholic, but Darnley also appears to have been willing to be flexible on religion.

During Edward's reign, the Lennoxes did not often travel to court, although Margaret was one of the great ladies who entertained the Regent of Scotland, Marie of Guise on her journey from France to Scotland, via England in November 1551.

Chapter 151: Quarrel with Angus

As noted earlier, on Angus' return to Scotland he had married Margaret Maxwell, and had at least three children by her, although only one, James Douglas, survived childhood. In August, 1547, Angus arranged for transfer of his lands to James, retaining only a life-interest, but young James died early the following year.

Angus continued in Henry's pay until June 1546, when the Scots Parliament rejected the Treaty of Edinburgh which had been agreed by Arran for the marriage of Queen Mary and Prince Edward. On 22nd August 1546, Angus, and his brother, Sir George Douglas, swore allegiance to Arran as Governor. Margaret's father and son were now on opposing sides. There can be no doubt that Margaret's loyalties lay with Lennox and the pro-English party. Henry, as may be imagined, was beside himself with the loss of the Scots marriage, and continued to try to bring it about by force. After his death, Edward's Lord Protector, the Duke of Somerset, maintained the war, during which Lennox burned Annan on 8th September 1547, a raid that was swiftly followed by the Battle of Pinkie Cleugh. Pinkie, at which Angus fought for Scotland, was a disastrous defeat for Scotland, but Somerset was unable to follow it up with any long term control.

Later that year, Angus wrote to Margaret, asking her to plead with the English government for kind treatment for his illegitimate son, (another George) and other hostages who had been taken by the English. The

Lennoxes were not inclined to help, and did not intervene to any effect. Despite his efforts, Lennox was not a successful commander, and the English never managed to gain mastery of Scotland. Eventually, the young Mary, Queen of Scots was sent in secret to France, and the pro-French party continued to rule the country until the crisis of 1559-1560.

Angus was hoping to improve his relationship with Margaret and Lennox, promising the latter some hawks, and sending letters that were loving and affectionate – dwelling on his love for Margaret and his desire to see her, and, by implication, her son, young Lord Darnley.

Margaret was not impressed. She was furious with her father, both for his perceived disloyalty to the pro-English party, and, more importantly, his actions with regard to her inheritance. In the land arrangement mentioned above, Angus had entailed the earldom of Angus to '*tail male*' – that is, in default of sons of his own line, the earldom would pass to his next male heir – at that time his brother, Sir George Douglas. This disinherited Margaret, as the Earldom of Angus had previously been heritable by women. On 15th March 1549, Margaret wrote one of the sternest letters of the period from a child to a parent. In it, she points out that George Douglas couldn't wait for Angus to die, so that he could inherit, but that if Angus had no more sons and she were passed over, '*many a man shall smart for it*'.

The full text of the letter is set out at page 567, as it is very illustrative of Margaret's character.

She also mentions that she plans to visit Carlisle, but there is no record of whether she did or not. In April 1552, there is a mention in the Privy Council of her as wishing to return home, as she is pregnant, although whether home means Scotland or Temple Newsam is not specified. Margaret does seem to have visited Scotland in 1552, perhaps for the first time since leaving back in 1528 and she probably visited Angus at Tantallon. Even if they were reconciled during this visit, Angus did not change the entail on his lands, and a dispute over inheritance flared up after his death.

Whilst the exact dates of Margaret's visit are unknown, what is clear is that Lennox and her children were retained in England. Ms Weir postulates that the visit was advantageous to the English government as it kept Margaret out of the way during the summer of 1553, when an attempt was made to put Lady Jane Grey on the throne in place of the Lady Mary.

Chapter 152: Second Lady in the Kingdom

Whether or not Margaret was out of the country when her cousin and friend, Mary, acceded to the throne, she certainly made haste to travel to London, secure in the knowledge that she would be welcomed. She was present at court on 17th October 1553 when the new Imperial Ambassador, Simon Renard arrived. Later in the year, the French Ambassador, de Noailles, reported that the Countess of Lennox, spoken of as *'My Lady Margaret'* and also Frances, Duchess of Suffolk, were sometimes given precedence over the Queen's half-sister, the Lady Elizabeth.

Margaret, whose son, Henry, Lord Darnley was now about 8 years old, seems to have seen Mary's reign as the opportunity both to promote Darnley as a possible male heir, and also to enlist the new Queen's support for Lennox' campaign to have his Scottish estates restored.

Mary certainly favoured the Lennoxes – the Earl was granted the position of Master of the Queen's Hawks, and Margaret received valuable clothes and jewellery. Darnley was the lucky recipient of some of the late King Edward's clothes, and also his lutes. Mary herself was a notable lute-player, so Margaret was probably pleased to see that Darnley's skill impressed the Queen.

It should be noted, however, that Mary also showed high favour to Edward Courtenay – the son of the Marquess of Exeter, who had been executed in 1538. Courtenay had been in the Tower since that time, sent in as a child, and now emerging as a possible suitor for the Queen. She dismissed that prospect, but, as a great-grandson of Edward IV, Courtenay had a very respectable claim to the throne himself.

Mary was determined to provide her own heir, and quickly decided to marry Philip of Spain. This caused some disquiet amongst the Protestant faction and rebellion flared up in Kent and the Midlands. The Duke of Suffolk and Courtenay were both implicated, but, as Courtenay's confession before the event had allowed the government to prepare and defeat the rebels, he was pardoned and exiled. Suffolk and his daughter, Lady Jane Grey, were executed and the Lady Elizabeth, who was suspected of complicity, was sent to the Tower. It was later claimed that Margaret had encouraged Mary to imprison Elizabeth, and perhaps to have her executed as well. Whether true or no, there does not seem to have been much love lost between Margaret and Elizabeth.

When the marriage of Mary and Philip finally took place in July 1554, at Winchester, Margaret acted as the Queen's train-bearer. Following the wedding, Margaret, although pregnant again, remained at court, acting as Mary's chief Lady-in-waiting. During Mary's reign, Margaret bore two sons, Philip and Charles, but only the latter survived.

In early 1557, Margaret's father, the Earl of Angus, died. She immediately claimed the earldom, and signed her letters as Margaret, Countess of Lennox and Angus. The difficulty was, that she was in England, and the Angus lands were in Scotland, being taken possession of by Archibald Douglas, grandson of her uncle, Sir George.

Queen Mary wrote to the Scottish Regent (now Marie of Guise, in place of Arran, or Chatelherault, to give him his new title) requesting her to support Margaret's claims. Marie sent a gracious response with reference to the Angus lands but refused to have anything to do with trying to overturn the forfeiture of Lennox' lands, saying it was a matter to be decided by her daughter, Mary Queen of Scots herself. As the said Queen was in France, and still only fourteen, this was obviously intended as a rejection. More discussions were held over the Angus lands later that year, but to little avail, from Margaret's point of view.

Queen Marie was more helpful towards the end of 1557, agreeing to further discussions on the matter, but it remained unresolved.

A slight embarrassment occurred for the Lennoxes when the Earl's brother, John Stuart, who held the French estates and titles of Aubigny, was captured, fighting for France at the Battle of St Quentin – a major victory for the allied Anglo-Spanish army. Having been ransomed, he then proceeded to fight for France at the siege of Calais, the loss of which broke Queen Mary's heart, and then to take part in border raids from Scotland. Lennox and his brother were in continued communication. Such consorting with her enemies must have raised Mary's suspicions about the trustworthiness of Lennox, and perhaps of Margaret, but no action was taken against them before Mary's death in November 1558.

Chapter 153: Suspicion

On Queen Mary's death, Margaret performed her last duty as the Queen's friend and lady-in-waiting, acting as Chief Mourner at the funeral in Westminster Abbey. She also played a part in the coronation of the new Queen, Elizabeth, although she did not have the coveted office of train-bearer. But once these duties were done, Elizabeth made it quite clear that Margaret was not welcome at her court. Elizabeth disliked all her royal female relatives and certainly did not wish to give any hint that Margaret or her son could be considered as possible successors.

The Lennoxes moved further north from Temple Newsam, spending time at their properties in Settrington, and Jervaulx, in areas of the country that the Reformation had barely touched. The Act of Uniformity of 1559 required all subjects of England to attend the Anglican service in their parish church, however, it exempted gentlemen with private chapels. It was thus possible for the Lennoxes and many others of the nobility to continue to hear the Catholic Mass. There seems little doubt that Margaret did so, and also brought her sons up in the old faith.

The Elizabethan world was awash with spies and informers – Elizabeth and Cecil had paid informers in the Lennox household, and Margaret had spies in the Queen's court. Everyone was spying on everyone else, till it becomes impossible to know where anyone's loyalties actually lay. In the Lennox household was one Thomas Bishop. He had been secretary to Lennox before his marriage, but had fallen out with Margaret to the extent that he was dismissed. He held a permanent grudge against her for this, and, although Lennox had taken pity on Bishop when he was destitute and reinstated him, he repaid his employer by spying on the family and reporting, with the blackest possible spin, everything they said and did to Elizabeth's government. Much of the information on the Lennoxes comes from this source, so should perhaps be taken with a pinch of salt.

There was continuing turmoil in Scotland. Marie of Guise was being challenged by the Lords of the Covenant who wished to institute Protestantism as the state religion. To counter them, she made overtures to Lennox, promising restoration of his estates, and also that Margaret would be confirmed in the Earldom of Angus. The Lords of the Covenant requested the English government to refuse Lennox licence to leave the country.

Margaret, with two sons, was looking to the future – in the eyes of many Catholics, including herself, Elizabeth was illegitimate. Nothing in Margaret's behaviour suggests that she sought directly to overthrow Elizabeth, but she clearly wanted her son to be recognised as heir. However, England was not the only possibility for Darnley. There was also the prospect of re-establishing him in Scotland, as Earl of Lennox and Angus, and, should the Queen of Scots not bear an heir (she was married to the young King of France, François II) then he had a claim to that throne too, through his father. Twelve year old Darnley was sent to France, at the urging of Lennox' brother, Aubigny, to congratulate François and Mary on their accession and request the return of the Lennox estates. Queen Mary was gracious, but refused the request.

Lennox, whilst ostensibly conforming to Elizabeth's policy of supporting the Lords of the Covenant, showing the government letters he had received from Aubigny, was also communicating secretly via the French Ambassador with Marie of Guise, furnishing him with a family tree, showing that the Lennox claim to be Mary, Queen of Scots' heir was superior to that of the English backed Chatelherault's.

This soon got the Lennoxes into trouble – the Council summoned them to London, and Margaret was questioned. Elizabeth's council also began to look into the matter of Margaret's legitimacy – claiming that the divorce that Queen Margaret Tudor had obtained, back in 1527, on the basis of Angus' pre-contract to Lady Janet of Trequair, rendered Margaret illegitimate. On the surface however, Elizabeth continued to support Lennox' claim to his lands.

Despite this, Darnley was being openly talked of as a possible to successor to Elizabeth, who was beset on all sides to confirm the succession. She would not name Lady Katherine Grey, the preferred Protestant choice, and she certainly would not name Mary, Queen of Scots or Darnley, both of whom were Catholic, and likely to be controlled (in the English view) by France.

Before long, the Scottish throne looked as though it might come a little closer. Francois II died in December 1560, leaving Queen Mary childless – perhaps young Darnley, now 14 to the Queen's 18, might make a suitable second husband, uniting their claims to the English throne, and strengthening the throne of Scotland?

Chapter 154: Plotting the Darnley Marriage

As soon as Queen Mary was known to be widowed, it was immediately assumed in both Scotland and England, that the Lennoxes would try to arrange her marriage to Darnley. Simultaneously, Chatelherault was hoping she would marry his son, James Hamilton, Earl of Arran, who was also a possible suitor to Elizabeth. Margaret wrote letters to Queen Mary, which were delivered in person by Darnley, who had been allowed by Elizabeth to go with her own Ambassador to offer condolences. Mary, however, was far more interested in a match with Spain, and paid little attention to the young man.

In August of 1561, Mary, Queen of Scots returned to take up personal rule of her kingdom. This completely negated any requirement for a regent (Marie of Guise having died) and so that immediate bone of contention between Chatelherault and Lennox was removed, although they still vied to be nominated as her heir. On the Queen's return, Lennox again petitioned for reinstatement of his lands, but Mary prevaricated. Thomas Bishop, the man noted above as Margaret's enemy, told the English government that Margaret was regularly communicating with her niece, and perhaps giving her more information about happenings in England than should have been shared with a foreign ruler.

Margaret was certainly promoting the idea of a marriage between Queen Mary and Darnley at this time, and Queen Mary later said that she had been pestered with endless letters, messages and presents.

In November 1561, Margaret and her children were summoned to London. The Catholic Earls of Northumberland and Westmoreland were similarly called for. The Spanish Ambassador, de Quadra, reported that Margaret feared arrest, and was determined to defend her actions by saying that the marriage of Mary and Darnley would avert civil war, in the event of Elizabeth's death without heirs. It does not appear that Margaret obeyed the summons, although what excuse she sent is unrecorded.

Margaret was also accused to the Council of seeking to prevent a meeting between Mary and Elizabeth, on the grounds that she was afraid Mary would let slip information about their correspondence. However, it is absolutely clear that Elizabeth's government, Cecil in particular, did not want Elizabeth and Mary to meet, and, if Margaret did warn Mary that to leave Scotland would risk the English capturing her capital, she probably had truth on her side – the English government was continuing to support the Lords of the Congregation against their lawful Queen, although more subtly than previously.

Queen Mary, of course, was far more interested in being named Elizabeth's successor directly, than embroiling herself with the Lennoxes, and was quite willing to inform Elizabeth's council about her dealings with them.

In January 1562, Margaret was horrified to hear that Lennox had been arrested in London and was being held at the home of the Master of the Rolls. He had travelled to London to explain some rather unfortunate missives to Scotland that had fallen into the hands of the government. Thomas Bishop, who had once again been sacked by the Lennoxes, who accused him of spreading malicious lies about them, outdid himself in his accusations against them – everything from consulting astrologers to cowardice on the part of Lennox, and illegitimacy on the part of Margaret.

There was no help forthcoming from Scotland – Queen Mary had no interest at this stage in Darnley or his parents. Another of the Lennox servants was questioned – Francis Yaxley, who seems to have been at one time a confederate of William Cecil and sat for Stamford in the 1555 Parliament (Cecil's own borough). However, whether he was a spy for the English government throughout his service to the Lennoxes, or whether he just confessed everything he could think of to save himself, will never be known. In any event, he confirmed that he had, on Margaret's behalf, been seeking to arrange the marriage of Darnley to Queen Mary.

Following this, Lennox was removed to the Tower and Margaret was arrested at Settrington and brought to London, where she was placed under house arrest with Sir Richard Sackville, in the old Charterhouse at Sheen.

Chapter 155: Serious Charges

The government now discovered that the Spanish Ambassador, de Quadra, had been fomenting a plot to put Margaret on the throne in place of Elizabeth, claiming there would be widespread support for her, if King Philip would but send help. There is no evidence that Margaret knew anything about this, but she had been in correspondence with de Quadra. Thomas Bishop, and his colleague, William Forbes, another spy in the Lennox household, now gave statements to the Council, listing a long series of potentially treasonable activities by Margaret, including witchcraft (apparently, the striking of St Paul's by lightening was her doing!) hearing Mass and conspiring to overthrow the Queen.

Margaret, unaware of these damning charges (whether or not they were true) began to write importunate letters to Cecil, on her husband's behalf, begging the Queen to either release him from the Tower, or at least give him more liberty within it – it seems Lennox struggled with some sort of sleeping disorder or fear of being left alone that made prison particularly hard for him. No response was made to these pleas.

In late May, the Council came to Sheen to interrogate Margaret. She steadfastly rejected all that Bishop and Forbes had deposed, asking them to be brought to face her, and requesting permission to see Elizabeth. She was particularly hot under the ruff about the accusation that she was illegitimate. Questioning of other Lennox servants only gave the information that the correspondence with the Scottish Queen had been about the restitution of the Lennox estates, not a marriage with Darnley.

Lennox continued to be held in the Tower, and Margaret at Sheen. Elizabeth does not seem to have believed they had any entanglement in de Quadra's scheme. Lennox, still badgered with questions, eventually pointed out that he had freely come to England to serve Henry VIII, and received his lands as a marriage settlement. If the Queen wanted rid of him, she could take back the lands, and send him on his way. This response lacked charm in the eyes of the Council and Elizabeth.

Over the summer, Margaret continued to protest her innocence, admitting only that Darnley's tutor had gone to Scotland, without permission, for which she and Lennox apologised, but no relaxation in their imprisonment was forthcoming. Margaret also began to worry about her finances and that the Lennox estates were not being properly managed.

Then, in autumn of 1562, Elizabeth fell ill with small-pox. She still refused to name a successor, but some of her lords supported the claims of Margaret and Darnley and Lord Robert Dudley suggested that Margaret be freed. Elizabeth recovered, and, after a further deluge of letters from Margaret, agreed to Lennox being released to join his wife at Sheen and then at Syon, but still under house arrest.

Eventually, Elizabeth relented – probably to keep the balance between the various possible successors – Margaret, Queen Mary, or Lady Katherine Grey. It was the Queen's policy to keep them all in suspense. Margaret was required to swear that Darnley would not marry without Elizabeth's consent.

In due course, Elizabeth agreed to promote Lennox's claims to his lands again. For some reason, the Lennoxes seem to have been in poor financial straits, although the vast value of their lands makes this difficult to understand.

Chapter 156: Success

It soon became apparent to Elizabeth's government that a marriage between Mary and Darnley might be the lesser of two evils. Queen Mary was still hoping to marry Don Carlos, the son of Philip of Spain - a far more worrying prospect than marriage with Darnley. Nevertheless, Elizabeth came up with a third option – that Mary should marry Lord Robert Dudley, whom she could rely on to protect her own interests. He was very much against the idea, and Mary was frankly disgusted at the idea she might marry Elizabeth's cast-offs. It is hard to believe that Elizabeth could seriously have thought Mary might agree, even if the pill were sweetened with a promise of the succession to the English Crown.

Darnley was now being paraded at the English court, to encourage Mary to keep in Elizabeth's good books. But Margaret was still hoping that Darnley would be married to Mary, and succeed to Elizabeth's Crown later. This would tend to suggest that she was not looking to overthrow Elizabeth, or she might have preferred Darnley to stay in England. Whilst Elizabeth was still canvassing Dudley as a husband for Mary, the Lennoxes sent their servant, Thomas Fowler, to Scotland to continue negotiations for a match with Darnley. As Don Carlos' mental incapacity was now becoming apparent, it appeared that Mary would not be able to marry him.

Fowler claimed his mission was merely to treat with the Scottish government about Lennox' restoration – to which Queen Mary had finally agreed, supported by her half-brother, the Earl of Moray, who wanted to keep Chatelherault and Arran out of power.

Elizabeth now, for some inexplicable reason, allowed Lennox to travel to Scotland. At first, she refused consent for Darnley to accompany him, but then relented. Meanwhile, Dudley, desperate to avoid being forced to marry Mary himself, was happy to work with Margaret to advance Darnley's hopes.

On 23rd September, 1564, Lennox was received in the Scots Parliament, and the sentence of forfeiture that had hung over him for twenty years was rescinded. Over the next couple of months he was reconciled to his old enemies and had his lands restored. Elizabeth continued to show favour to Darnley – he was permitted, as her nearest male relative, to carry the sword of state in front of her. Elizabeth discussed his merits with Mary's ambassador, and suggested that she was considering putting him forward to Mary as a suitor.

After much vacillation, Elizabeth allowed Darnley to join Lennox in Scotland. She must have known how it would end – was she tired of being badgered on the subject, or had she seen enough of Darnley now to know that Mary would regret marrying him within a very short space of time? The excuse the Lennoxes gave, that Elizabeth professed to accept, was that Darnley was needed about legal matters. He arrived in Scotland in February 1565.

When Mary saw Darnley, now aged twenty, she appears to have liked what she saw, but did not rush into anything. The young man then fell sick, and Mary insisted on visiting him. She was not the first, nor the last, young woman to fall in love with a man lying vulnerable on his sickbed.

In April, Mary wrote to Elizabeth, wishing her to approve a marriage with Darnley, and appoint her as her heir. Elizabeth received the request coldly, and turned on Margaret, ordering her to keep to her rooms. Again the Queen issued conflicting orders, seeming on the one had to encourage the match, and on the other to forbid it.

The Scottish Lords were not thrilled at Mary's choice – the Protestants disliked Darnley as a Catholic, the Hamiltons hated the Lennoxes, and the Douglases wanted to keep Margaret out of the Earldom of Angus. Neither Lennox nor Darnley were endearing themselves – behaving arrogantly and being *saucier than ever*. To buy favour from Moray and the Douglas faction, Margaret agreed to give up her claims to Angus.

On hearing that Darnley had accepted the Earldom of Ross (commonly a title given to the sovereign's younger brother) and for which he swore allegiance to Mary, Elizabeth ordered Lennox and Darnley to return to England immediately. They failed to do so and Margaret was sent to the Tower of London.

Chapter 157: The Tower

Margaret was lodged in an upper room, in the Lord Lieutenant's Lodgings, adjacent to the Bell Tower. She had two women and three men servants to attend to her wants and her room was furnished appropriately to her rank. Her younger son, Charles, who was eight, was taken into the household of the Archbishop of York, but not long after returned to his home at Settrington. Temple Newsam and other estates were sequestered – that is, their rents diverted to the Crown, even though they were not formally forfeited.

Margaret continued her interminable letters to Cecil, and also found means to communicate with the French and Spanish Ambassadors, which incensed Elizabeth when she heard of it.

Before long, news reached Elizabeth that Mary and Darnley were married. Darnley, in probably the last circumspect action of his life, forebore attending the nuptial Mass – indicating that he would be sympathetic to the Protestants in Scotland.

Mary and Darnley, now entitled King of Scots, although not invested with the Crown Matrimonial as her first husband had been, requested Elizabeth to release Margaret, promising they had no intention of interfering in England, other than wishing her to have an Act of Parliament passed, investing the succession in them and their heirs, or failing heirs, Margaret's other descendants. In return, they would promise not to change the religion of the country.

Elizabeth, requested by the Kings of France and Spain, as well as Queen Mary, to show mercy to Margaret, refused to sanction her release, but allowed her to be well attended and comfortable in captivity.

Meanwhile, all was not well in the new royal marriage. Darnley was a spoilt, arrogant fool. Mary refused to allow him complete equality with her, and she was also tired of Lennox, who was seeking vengeance on his old enemies. The only thing for which Darnley had proved useful, was his conjugal duty – the Queen was pregnant within a few months of their marriage.

Margaret, presumably, was thrilled. She was also sent a loving letter from her husband, in which he addressed her as his *'sweet Madge'* and told her how much he missed her. Unfortunately, she never received it, as their servant, Fowler, was captured, and the letter confiscated. Fowler was sentenced to death, but released on Queen Mary's request. Her pleas for Margaret, however, were refused.

In Scotland, Mary and Darnley's relationship was going from bad to worse. Concerned over Mary's reliance on her secretary, David Rizzio, Darnley and others of the Scottish Lords (amongst whom Margaret's biographer, Alison Weir includes Lennox, but Darnley's biographer, Caroline Bingham, does not) plotted his murder.

For the first time, so far as is known, Darnley wrote to Elizabeth, asking her to release his mother, saying she had not been party to his marriage to Mary but this too, fell on deaf ears. It was said that, had Margaret been allowed to travel to Scotland, the problems of Darnley's behaviour would not have arisen. According to the Spanish Ambassador, da Silva, *'she is prudent and brave, and the son respects her more than he does his father.'* Perhaps that was the reason for Elizabeth keeping Margaret under lock and key.

Mary and Darnley had patched up their relationship for public consumption after the Rizzio murder, but, once her son was born, Mary had no further use for him, and nor had any of the nobles of Scotland, except his father. Darnley was murdered in February 1567, certainly with the knowledge of many of the Scots lords and the active involvement of some. Mary's level of complicity, if any, continues to be disputed.

Chapter 158: Grief

When the news reached London of Darnley's death, Elizabeth was sufficiently moved by compassion for Margaret to send Mildred, Lady Cecil, and Margaret, Lady William Howard, (sister-in-law to the Lord Thomas who had been Margaret's first love) to break the news to her. At the time, it was thought that Lennox, too, had been killed, and Margaret was prostrate with grief. Sir William Cecil visited her in person to reassure as to Lennox still being alive, but Margaret was in such a state that Elizabeth was recommended to release her.

Although Margaret and Elizabeth had never been close, the Queen felt genuine compassion, and had Margaret conveyed to Sheen again, where she was reunited with her son, Charles.

Lennox and Margaret were both anxious their son should be avenged, and they believed that the less-than-enthusiastic prosecution of enquiries by Queen Mary indicated her complicity. Lennox harangued Queen Mary, and, with her permission, brought a private prosecution against the Earl of Bothwell, who was acquitted. This was fuel on the fire of the Lennoxes' suspicions.

In April 1567, Lennox returned to England, to try to comfort the grieving Margaret. Many of Elizabeth's courtiers were moved by their sorrow, and suggested that she should ameliorate Margaret's punishment. Eventually, the couple were allowed to live at Coldharbour, one of the lesser London palaces, but the incomes from their estates were still kept in the hands of the Crown.

Despite being strapped for cash, Margaret and Lennox commissioned a painting, known as the *Memorial of Lord Darnley* – of which both the original and an adapted copy survives. Aged 49 and 50, although they were not old, even by Elizabethan standards, the couple were certainly on the cusp of old age, and were concerned they might not live long enough to remind their grandson, James, of the need for vengeance. The painting makes it abundantly clear that they believed Queen Mary to be involved, if not actually the prime mover in the murder.

Margaret and Lennox were not the only people who believed Mary to be guilty, and her marriage, whether willing or not, to Bothwell sealed her fate. She was forced to abdicate in favour of her son, James, Margaret's grandson, and was finally overthrown at the Battle of Langside in 1568. Escaping to England, Mary threw herself on Elizabeth's mercy. Margaret and Lennox were appalled – fearful lest Mary be returned to her throne at the head of an English army. They raced to court and begged Elizabeth for justice. Margaret is described as having a face *'swelled and stained with tears.'*

Initially sympathetic, Elizabeth eventually became fed up with their grief and sent them away, saying they should not believe so great a crime of a Queen without more proof. Mary wrote indignantly to the Queen, complaining that she would see those who accused her of the crime, but would not meet Margaret herself. In Scotland, the baby James was crowned, and his uncle, Mary's illegitimate half-brother, the Earl of Moray, ruled as Regent, bringing James up in the Protestant faith.

Over the next two years Margaret and Lennox continued to proclaim Mary's guilt, but the matter was never resolved. Elizabeth would not take punitive action against an anointed Queen, but nor would she permit Mary to leave captivity. In 1570, the Regent Moray was assassinated. With Scotland in turmoil again, both Margaret and Queen Mary were terrified that something would happen to James. Margaret begged that Elizabeth should have James brought to England, preferably to be brought up by herself. Elizabeth would never have permitted Margaret to have James in her care – first, she would probably have tried to bring him up as a Catholic, and second, with the Queen's nearest male heir in her hands, she might present a danger.

At the same time, Mary wrote to Margaret, saying she had not previously been in correspondence with her, because she was knew that Margaret had been accusing her '*against [her] innocency.*' She asked Margaret's advice on whether James should be sent to England, although she would have preferred him to be sent further afield. Margaret did not (so far as is known) reply, but reiterated her belief in Mary's guilt in a letter to Sir William Cecil.

With Moray dead, there was confusion in Scotland, and a new regent was needed. After some humming and hawing, Elizabeth agreed that Lennox should be sent to Scotland to take over the government – obviously on the proviso that he carried out her instructions to the letter. Margaret and Charles were to stay behind, in London. Whilst no-one would have mentioned the word '*hostage*' there cannot have been any doubt that that was Margaret's role.

Chapter 159: Widowed

Lennox, protesting that he had never thought of being Regent, but was only eager to do Elizabeth's bidding, either as Regent himself, or working with whomever she might appoint, travelled north. He spent as much time as he could with the little king, who was now four years old, and the majority of his correspondence with Elizabeth was via Margaret, the only person he trusted. Unfortunately, the old rivalry with the Hamiltons was not extinguished, and in further feuding, Lennox had some dozen hostages of the Hamiltons hanged. From that moment, he was a marked man. He was on increasingly bad terms with the Earl of

Morton – Margaret's first cousin, and the prime mover behind the murder of Secretary Rizzio, back in 1566.

In September of 1571, on the day after Lennox opened the Scots Parliament with his grandson, an armed confrontation took place in the streets of Edinburgh led by the Queen's Party (ie, those favouring the restoration of Mary, which included the Hamiltons). Lennox was killed by a gunshot – possibly by the enemy, but possibly by one of his own ostensible allies – he was not popular even in the King's Party, as, although the Scots Protestants sought English protection, they did not wish to be ruled at second hand by Elizabeth. Two of his last utterances were recorded as – *'if the bairn's (*meaning King James*) well, all's well'*, and a message of love for his *'Sweet Madge'*.

Cecil informed the Queen of Lennox' death, but it was agreed that the matter should be kept quiet until it could be broken to Margaret by Elizabeth herself. Margaret was devastated – she and Lennox had been devoted to each other since their marriage, twenty-six years before.

But Margaret's nature was essentially optimistic and, to use a modern term, pro-active. She never waited for events, but took control where she could. She turned her attention to her remaining child, Lord Charles. He was now about fourteen, and, in her view, lacking a father's discipline. She also had an eye to his promotion. She therefore asked Cecil (now Lord Burghley) to take him into his household, a frequent way of training young people, and extending their connections.

Burghley refused, but appointed a Protestant tutor for Charles, whom she accepted. Margaret, all the records suggest, remained a Catholic, although many of her friends in her youth – Katherine Suffolk, Mary Richmond and Katherine Parr were Protestant. Lennox had conformed to Protestantism whilst Regent, and Darnley had shown that he could be flexible. It may be that Margaret was that rare creature in sixteenth century Europe, someone tolerant of other religious views.

During this period, Margaret was in close touch with the new regent, the Earl of Mar (who persuaded the Scots Parliament to re-grant the Earldom of Lennox, which had devolved on King James, to her son, Charles). Mar, too, had a short stint in office, although he died of natural causes, and was followed by the Earl of Morton. Morton was later executed for involvement in the death of Darnley, but Margaret either did not know he was involved, or dissembled well – their dealings were always courteous.

A most surprising change in Margaret's views came about in around 1573. In some way, she became (or said she was) convinced that the Queen of Scots was, in fact, innocent of the murder of Lord Darnley. How she was persuaded of this is a mystery. There is no record of the two women meeting, and the extremity of Margaret's earlier accusations make it difficult to imagine what could have passed to change her mind. Nevertheless, the very vehemence of her earlier condemnation also makes it hard to contemplate that she could have pretended to believe in Mary's innocence, if she were not convinced.

Chapter 160: The Last Intrigue

In the late summer of 1573, Margaret requested leave to return to her old home of Settrington. By now, Elizabeth knew that she had been reconciled with Queen Mary, so, although permission was granted, she was told not to go anywhere near Chatsworth, where Mary was being held in the custody of the Earl and Countess of Shrewsbury. The Countess, known to posterity as Bess of Hardwick, had been a friend of Margaret's for at least thirty years. Elizabeth informed Margaret that any visit to Queen Mary might lead people to think they were plotting together. Margaret laughed at such a notion, saying she could never forget the murder of her own child. Whatever the reasons for her change in views on Mary's guilt, she clearly did not intend to share them with Elizabeth.

The following year, Margaret visited travelled north again, to Temple Newsam, this time with Charles, now about nineteen. Not daring to visit Chatsworth, Margaret found an excuse to meet Countess Bess at her home at Rufford Abbey. Conveniently, Bess' daughter, Elizabeth Cavendish, was one of the party. The indulgent and romantic countesses saw that their children had fallen deeply in love, and permitted them to marry. Apparently, any other course would have ended in dishonour (the implication being that Charles and Elizabeth Cavendish had slept together.)

Naturally, there had been no thought of anything more than family joy, despite the fact that Charles was close enough to the throne to require royal permission before marrying. Margaret failed to mention that she had been discussing the marriage with Countess Bess, and her old friend Katherine Willoughby, Duchess of Suffolk, for at least a year. Queen Elizabeth, feeling she had been outwitted once again, sent Margaret back to the Tower.

Margaret must have seen its grey walls almost with a sense of homecoming. She whiled away her time embroidering a handkerchief for Queen Mary with her own hair. Despite diligent searching, Elizabeth's government could not find any evidence of actual treason, other than a marriage without royal consent. There was nothing to suggest a plan to free Mary, or replace Elizabeth, so, eventually, probably by the end of 1575, Margaret was released.

The new Earl and Countess of Lennox were separated, but Lady Lennox gave birth to a daughter, Lady Arbella Stuart.

Unable to influence her grandson's upbringing, Margaret concentrated on Arbella. As further evidence of the rapprochement with

Mary, the latter, on drawing up her will in 1577, restored to Margaret her long-lost Earldom of Angus. A futile gesture, as Queen Mary had absolutely no power to put her wishes into effect in Scotland. Margaret, her son, daughter-in-law and grand-daughter, lived quietly in Hackney. Charles had the remittance of the income from the Earldom of Lennox to finance the household, but Margaret had almost nothing of her own.

In 1577, Margaret had the grief of seeing the last of her eight children pre-decease her. She planned a grand tomb for him in Westminster, having him interred at St Augustine, Hackney in the meantime, but was not too busy to correspond with James in Scotland, and oversee the baby Arbella's care until the little girl moved to the home of her other grandmother in 1578. Nevertheless, Margaret still fought on her behalf, requesting the Scots government to recognise Arbella as Countess of Lennox, a plea which was refused. Queen Mary also added a new clause to her aforementioned will, granting the Lennox inheritance to Arbella, but it was of no more value than her grant of Angus to Margaret.

Once again, Margaret succeeded in persuading Elizabeth to help her. The Queen sent a stern letter to the Regent Morton, demanding that Arbella's rights should be recognised – although that might have been to save herself the cost of maintaining Margaret and Arbella – Elizabeth was notably parsimonious.

Margaret made her will in February 1578, presumably feeling her age. She died on either 9th or 10th March, 1578.

Elizabeth footed the bill for the funeral, and permitted it to take place in Westminster Abbey, where she lies still.

Letter from Margaret to Cromwell

Transcribed in 'Women's Works; 900 – 1550'

Footer, Donald W, and Donald W Foster, *Women's Works: 900 - 1550*, 1st edn (New York: Wicked Good Books, 2013) Published by Wicked Words, Editor

My Lord,

What cause have I to give you thanks, and how much bound am I unto you, that by your means hath gotten me, as I trust, the King's Grace's favour again, and besides that, that it pleased you to write and to give me knowledge wherein I might have his Grace's displeasure again (which I pray our Lord sooner to send me death, than that.) I assure you, my Lord, I will never do that thing willingly that should offend his Grace.

And my Lord, whereas it is informed you that I do charge the house (Syon Abbey) with a greater number than is convenient, I assure you I have but two more than I had in the Court, which indeed were Lord Thomas' servants; and the cause that I took them for was for the poverty that I saw them in, and for no other cause else. But seeing, my Lord that it is your pleasure that I shall keep none that did belong unto my Lord Thomas, I will put them from me.

And I beseech you not think that any fancy doth remain in me touching him, but that all my study and care I how to please the King's Grace and to continue in his favour. And my Lord, where it is your pleasure that I shall keep but a few here with me, I trust ye will think that I can have no fewer than I have; for I have but a gentleman and a groom that keeps my apparel, and another that keeps my chamber, and a chaplain that was with me always in the Court.

Now my lord, I beseech you that I may know your pleasure if you would that I should keep any fewer. Howbeit my lord, my servants hath put the house to small charge, fort hey have nothing but the reversion of my board; nor do I call for nothing but that that is given me, howbeit I am very well intreated. And my lord, as for 'resort'. I promise you I have none, except it be gentlewomen that comes to see me, nor never had since I came hither, for if any 'resort' of men had come, it should neither have become me to have seen them, nor yet to have kept them company, being a maid as I am. Now my Lord, I beseech you to be so good as to get my poor servants their wages; and thus I pray our Lord to preserve you, both soul and body.

Letter from Margaret to Angus 15 March 1549

My Lorde, after my humble commendacions and desiring of your blessing, this shalbe to signeffye unto you the gret unnaturalnes wiche ye showe me daylye, being to longe to reherse in all poyntes, butt in some I wyll declare nowe laste of all, my Lorde, being nere you, and so desirows to have spoken with you, yet ye refused it and wolde not, where in ye showed your selfe not to be so loving as ye ought to be, or elles so unstable that every body maye turne you, for diverse tymes ye have said you wolde be glad to speyke with your sonne my lorde.

Remember he bathe maryd your owne doughter, and the best chylde to you that ever ye had, if ye call to remembrance your being here in Englande. How be hit, your dedys showethe the forgetfulnes thereof, in so myche as ye ar so contraryto the Kynges majesties affayres, that nowe ys, hys father being so goode and so lyberall a prynce to you, wyche ought neyer to be forgotton ; butt nowe, my lorde, I here saye that ye have professed never to agree with Englande, for so myche as the moost parte of your frendes are slayne. Butt whome can you blame for that butt only youre selfewylles (selfwill), for if ye wolde agre to this godly maryage, *(between Mary Queen of Scots and King Edward VI)* there nedyd no Crjsten blode to be shed.

For Godes sake remember your selfe nowe in your olde age, and seke to have an honorable pease, wiche can not be withowte this marjiage. And what a memoryall shulde that be to you for ever, if ye colde be an instrument for that. If I should wryte so longe a letter as I colde fynde matter with the wrong of your part and the right of myne, hit were to tedyowse for you to rede ; butt for as myche as I purpose, God wylling, to comme to Carlyll shortly after Ester, I wyll kepe it in store to tell you my selfe, for I am sure ye wyll nott refuse commyng to me, all thow my uncle George and the Laideof Dromlaneryk speyke agaynst it, whome I knowe wolde be glad to se you inyour grave, all thowe they flatter you to your face.

My uncle George hathe seid, as dyverse Skottesmen have tolde me, that thowe you had sones he wolde be eyre, and make them all bastardis ; butt, my Lorde, if God sende you no moo sons, and I lyffe after you, he shall have leste parte thereof, or elles many a man shall smarte for it. This leyvinge to declare forther of my mynde tell I maye speyke with you my selfe, I commytte you to the kepinge off All myghty God. whoo sende you longe liffe withe myche honour.

Frome the Kynges magestyes castell of Wreyssell, the xvth daye of Marche,

Be your humble doughter,

Margrett Lennox.

Aspects of Lady Margaret Douglas' Life

Chapter 161: The Devonshire Manuscript

In Henry VIII's youth, his romantic streak had been given expression with jousts and tournaments, at which his immense physical prowess had let him excel, but by the time Lady Margaret Douglas came to court to serve Queen Anne Boleyn, the King was in his mid-forties and there were fewer jousts. The young men of the court, rather than wooing their ladies with feats of arms, took to writing music and extravagant verse.

The conventions of the game were clearly laid down in Baldassare Castiglione's *'The Book of the Courtier'*, an Italian work, published in the early sixteenth century, and known in the courts of Italy and France, which heavily influenced England – although an English edition was not published until 1561. Gentlemen sighed over unattainable ladies, who treated them with disdain, or flirted with them, with no intention of delivering on the promise.

Chief amongst the poets of the court were the Queen's brother, George Boleyn, Viscount Rochford; her cousin, Henry Howard, Earl of Surrey, (brother of Lady Margaret's friend Mary Howard, Duchess of Richmond) and Sir Thomas Wyatt, a childhood friend of Anne and George, and once Anne's suitor. Many of the other ladies and gentlemen, including the King himself, wrote verse too, varying in skill from the completely dreadful, to the barely adequate.

One of the fashionable styles was the *'verse conversation'*. A poem would be written down and shared amongst friends, with each adding an answer to the previous poem. A large group of verses is contained in a manuscript, now known as the Devonshire Manuscript, a collection of 185 poems plus a further eleven fragments of writing or anagrams. The manuscript itself is quarto sized – that is, a single sheet folded to make four pages, and then bound. In all, the book has 114 leaves. It seems likely the book was originally owned by Mary Howard (her married initials, MF for Mary FitzRoy, are on it).

Of these verses, the vast majority have been attributed to Sir Thomas Wyatt, with other items by the Earl of Surrey, Mary Shelton, Sir Edmund Knyvett and other members of the court, and a later one, to Henry, Lord Darnley, Margaret's son. A group have been attributed to Lord Thomas Howard and Lady Margaret Douglas.

The number of poems ascribed to Lord Thomas and to Margaret differs between scholars. As many as thirteen, and as few as three, have been attributed to him, and nine and two respectively to her. She appears to have transcribed 16 of them and annotated at least 50 of the pages, with comments such as *'and this'* or *'learn but to sing it'*. The other main transcriber appears to be Mary Shelton, whose name appears in an acrostic verse. Occasionally Margaret and Mary differ on their view of the worthiness of poems – Margaret writes on one *'forget this'* and Mary replies *'it is worthy.'*

The difficulty, of course, is knowing which of the poems Howard and Margaret actually composed, and which they merely transcribed. There is a group that appear to relate to the period when the couple were in the Tower of London, sent there as punishment for their unsanctioned betrothal. We must assume, if they were contemporaneous with that, that they sent poems back and forth between them (the individual poems were not entered sequentially). This is not impossible, as imprisonment for nobility, although onerous as a loss of freedom, was not usually repressive in itself.

In one poem he writes:

'There is no care for cure of mind

But to forget (which cannot be!)

I cannot sail against the wind,

Nor help the thing past remedy.'

In a later (probably) verse, the first and last stanzas of six are:

'Thy promise was to love me best

And that thy heart with mine should rest

And not to break this, thy behest –

Thy promise was, thy promise was.

…

But since to change thou dost delight

And that thy faith has ta'en his flight

As thou deservest, I shall the 'quite [requite]

I promise thee, I promise thee.'

Margaret's compositions include:

'…And though that I be banished him fro'

His speech, his sight and company,

Yet will I, in spite of his foe,

Him love and keep my fantasy

Do what they will, and do their worst

(for all they do is vanity)

For asunder my heart shall burst

Surer than change my fantasy'

The poems attributed to Howard bespeak his own faithfulness, and his depression when he discovers that Margaret has given up all thought of him. As she said to Cromwell, she no longer had '*any fancy thereunto.*' Whether her renunciation is genuine, is another question. The shadow of the axe is not conducive to romance.

One poem ascribed to her, suggests that, far from forgetting Lord Thomas, she grieved sincerely over his death, to the point of feeling suicidal:

'Wherefore, sweet father, I you pray,

Bear this my death with patience

And torment not your hairs grey

But freely pardon mine offence

Sith't [since it] proceeded of love's fervency

And of my heart's constancy

Lett me not [do not keep me from] from the sweet presence

Of him that I have caused to die.'

We need to be careful about inferring the actual feelings of Thomas Howard and Margaret Douglas from the poems, which reflect the conventions of courtly love, yet the Devonshire Manuscript gives a rare glimpse into the amusements and tastes of the young men and women of the 1530s.

Mary Howard would remain Margaret's friend until her own death in 1557, despite the widening gap in religion between them. Mary Shelton married Sir Anthony Heveningham in about 1540, and, later, Sir Philip Appleyard, dying in 1571.

Chapter 162: The Will of Lady Margaret Douglas

Lady Margaret Douglas' will makes interesting reading, and tells us a bit about Margaret, her relationships with her servants and also with two of the most important figures at Elizabeth's court, Sir William Cecil, Lord Burghley, and Robert Dudley, Earl of Leicester.

Margaret made the will in the spring of 1578 (although she dated it 1577, as old style dating was still in use). By this time, all her children had died, and she had only two grand-children, James VI, King of Scots, and Lady Arbella Stuart. She had urged the Scots government to recognise Lady Arbella as Countess of Lennox, but the Regent of Scotland, the Earl of Morton, had refused, and the lands and revenues of the earldom had reverted to King James.

At the time of her death, Margaret was living in Hackney, a country suburb on the edge of the City of London. Although the extensive lands that had been settled on Margaret and her husband, Matthew Stuart, Earl of Lennox, had not formally been confiscated, as despite various periods of imprisonment, no actual charges had been brought against them, the income and control had been sequestered by the government. Only her lands at Settrington in Yorkshire were in her hands, or those of her appointees.

For a woman who was the daughter of a queen-consort, half-sister of a king, and close friend of a sovereign Queen, as well as mistress of an estate third only to that of the Crown in the north of England, Margaret had surprisingly little to leave.

As was customary, she began by bequeathing her soul to Almighty God. She chose to be buried in Westminster Abbey – this is, in itself, Margaret's clearest statement of her belief in her royal lineage and the claim to the throne of England that she passed on to her descendants. Her beloved husband, Matthew, Earl of Lennox, had been buried in Scotland, following his assassination, but she chose to lie with her mother's family – the Tudors.

Westminster Abbey was the burial place of her grand-parents, Henry VII and Elizabeth of York, her cousin, Mary I, and her other cousin, Frances Brandon, Duchess of Suffolk. In due course, Elizabeth I, James VI & I and Mary, Queen of Scots (Margaret's niece) would all lie there. It seems that Elizabeth had no objection to Margaret being interred in the royal chapel, and in fact, ended up paying for the ceremony, as Margaret's possessions could not cover her debts and funeral expenses.

Margaret's grandson, James VI, received her new black velvet bed. This seems rather a bizarre bequest, but beds and their furnishings were extremely expensive, and a status symbol. Bed chambers were more public than they are now, and it was perfectly normal for guests to be received there. A smart set of hangings for the bed was important. Black velvet, too, was very pricey.

Her next major bequest is that of her sheep to Thomas Fowler – again, somewhat surprising to think of a Countess noting her sheep, but they were probably the next most valuable thing she owned, and great ladies in the sixteenth century were closer to estate management than their Victorian counterparts. Margaret clearly trusted Thomas Fowler, although there are indications in other records that he was actually reporting on her activities to both Burghley and Leicester – it is difficult to be sure, as factors, stewards and other senior servants often worked for several people – employment not being so fixed as it now is. He had certainly been instrumental in organising the match between Darnley and Mary.

Margaret also left Fowler her collection of clocks, watches and dials. Clocks, too were extremely valuable and fashionable items, only becoming indoor, table-top pieces, such as we now have, in the final quarter of the fifteenth century, when the spring mechanism was invented. They were often owned by kings or nobles as manifestations of wealth and sophistication. This mention of a collection of time-pieces, together with a comment on Margaret in the 1550s, that she had amassed many relics and icons, suggests that she had the nature of a collector.

Leaving items of such value to Fowler, implies a warmer relationship beyond the fact that she owed him money. Her trust in him is indicated by his appointment as her executor.

As well as executors, it was usual to name overseers of a will. Margaret chose the two most powerful men in Elizabethan England – William Cecil, Lord Burghley, Elizabeth's closest counsellor and Lord Treasurer, and Robert Dudley, Earl of Leicester, the Queen's closest male friend. These two men had been the recipients of many letters from Margaret, usually relating to requests from her to speak favourably of her to the Queen, but we can probably infer that they were also her friends. Burghley's wife, Mildred Cecil, had been one of the ladies sent to break the news of Darnley's death.

Leicester had promoted Margaret as a possible successor to Elizabeth in the early 1560s, rather than the more Protestant candidate, Lady Katherine Grey, and it was with Leicester (amongst others) that Margaret had dined three days before her death. Her bequest to him of her pomander beads, as well as of her *tablet* of Henry VIII, suggests a personal affection. A tablet might be a small book, or a picture.

Finally, her jewels were to be given to her grand-daughter, the Lady Arbella, on her marriage, or when she attained the age of fourteen. So far as is known, these jewels did not include the famous Lennox Jewel, although there is no inventory, so we cannot be sure.

It seems that Arbella did not receive her bequest. In 1590, there was a request to King James to release goods seized from the estate of Thomas Fowler, in satisfaction of a debt to the Earl of Lennox.

'Sundrie tymes I have moved the King and Lord Chancelour that the jewelles late in the handes of Thomas Fowler, deceased, and appertayning to the Lady Arbell, might be restored to her.'

Margaret's most important legacy, however, was her royal blood – it was a positive legacy for James, but caused Lady Arbella to live a sad and constrained life.

An Excerpt from the Will of Margaret, Countess of Lennox.

This transcript is taken from North Country Wills, published by the Surtees Society

I, Margaret, Countesse of Lennox, widowe, late wife of Mathewe, Erle of Lennox, Regent of Scotlande, deceased, the six and twentieth daye of Februarie, 1577.

My bodie to be buried in the greate churche of Westminster, in the monument sepulture or tombe alreadie bargeyned for, and appointed to be made and sett uppe in the saide churche.

Also I will that the bodie of my sonne Charles shalbe removed from the churche of Hackney, and laide with myne both in one vawte or tombe in the saide churche of Westminster. And I give for my buriall the somme of twelve hundred poundes alias one thowsande twoo hundred poundes to be made and furnished of my plate, howshouldstuffe, and move ables to be soulde therefore And I will that fourtie poundes of the saide twelve hundred poundes shalbe given to the poore people at the daie of my buriall, and that there be one hundred gownes furnished to a hundred poore women.

Also I give to the Kinge of Skottes for a remembraunce of me, his grandmother, my newe fielde bed of blacke velvet imbrodered with flowers of neadle worke with the furniture thereunto belonginge, as curteins, quilte, and bedsteed, but not aine other beddinge there unto.

Also I give to Margaret Wilton my woman fiftie poundes, and to everie other servant one yeares wages.

To Thomas Fowler my servaunte all my stocke of sheepe in the custodie of Lawrence Nessebett, Symonde Doddesworthe, and Rowland Fothergyll, within my lordshippe of Settrington, in the countie of Yorke, beinge in numbre eight hundred, at six scoare to the hundred.

And where I owe unto the saide Thomas Fowler seaven hundred threscore eightene poundes and fiftene shillings uppon the determinacon of his last aecompte, I will the same somme be paide of my goodes, chattells, plate, and jewells.

Also I give to the saide Thomas Fowler all my clockes, watches, dials.

And I make John Kaye, of Hackney, esquire, and the saide Thomas Fowler my executors.

And I give the saide John Kaye fourtie powndes, and I will my verie good lordes, William, Lorde Burghley, Lord Treasawrer of Englande, and Roberte, Earle of Leicester my overseers.

And I give to them for theire paines, viz. to the Lord Treasurer my ringe with fowre diamondes sett square therein, blacke enamiled, and to the Earle of Leycester

my chaine of pommaunder beades netted over with golde, and my tablett with the picture of Kinge Henrye the eighte therein.

All the reste of my jewells, goodes, I give to the Ladye Arabell, daughter of my sonne Charles, deceased.

Lady Margaret's Will in Modern English

Tudor Times translation with our notes in brackets.

I, Margaret, Countess of Lennox, widow, late wife of Matthew, Earl of Lennox, Regent of Scotland, deceased the six and twentieth day of February, 1577 (*old style, 1578 in modern dating*) My body to be buried in the great church of Westminster, (*Westminster Abbey*) in the monument, sepulchre or tomb already bargained for and appointed to be made and set up in the said church.

Also I will that the body of my son Charles (Lord Charles Stuart, 1st (*sometimes notated as 5th*)Earl of Lennox shall be removed from the church of Hackney, and laid with mine both in one vault or tomb in the said church of Westminster.

And I give for my burial the sum of twelve hundred pounds, alias one thousand two hundred pounds to be made and furnished of my plate, household stuff, and movables to be sold therefore. And I will that forty pounds of the said twelve hundred pounds shall be given to the poor people at the day of my burial, and that there be one hundred gowns furnished to a hundred poor women.

Also I give to the King of Scots (*James VI*) for a remembrance of me, his grandmother, my new field bed of black velvet, embroidered with flowers of needle work with the furniture thereunto belonging, as (*that is*) curtains, quilt, and bedstead, but not any other bedding there unto.

Also I give to Margaret Wilton my woman fifty pounds, and to every other servant one year's wages.

To Thomas Fowler my servant all my stock of sheep in the custody of Lawrence Nisbet, Simon Doddsworth and Rowland Fothergill, my lordship of Settrington, in the county of York, being in number eight hundred, at six score to the hundred (*ie 1000 sheep in total*).

And where I owe unto the said Thomas Fowler seven hundred threescore eighteen pounds and fifteen shillings (*£778 15s.*) upon the determination of his last account, I will the same sum be paid of my goods, chattels, plate, and jewels.

Also I give to the said Thomas Fowler all my clocks, watches, dials.

And I make John Kaye, of Hackney, esquire, and the said Thomas Fowler my executors.

And I give the said John Kaye forty pounds, and I will my very good lords, William (*Cecil*), Lord Burghley, Lord Treasurer of England, and Robert (*Dudley*) Earl of Leicester my overseers. And I give to them for their pains (trouble), viz. to the Lord Treasurer my ring with four diamonds set square therein, black enamelled, and to the Earl of Leicester my chain of pomander beads netted over with gold, and my tablet (possibly a book or a small picture) with the picture of King Henry the eighth (Margaret's uncle) therein.

All the rest of my jewels, goods, I give to the Lady Arabell (*Lady Arbella Stuart*), daughter of my son Charles, deceased.

The will was proved on 27th March 1578 (*New style dating*) by Thomas Fowler. The other executor renounced his role.

Chapter 163: Following the Footsteps of Margaret Douglas

Lady Margaret spent her childhood in Scotland and the borders before being housed in the palaces of the English court. During her married life, she spent the majority of her time in the great houses that Henry VIII had granted her – that is, when she was not in the Tower of London.

The numbers in the text below correspond to those on the map which follows.

*

Margaret was born in the English border castle of Harbottle (1), Northumberland. Today, Harbottle is quiet and isolated, it seems that nothing more exciting than lambing and shearing the hardy upland sheep could ever have happened here, but in 1515 things were very different.

The Anglo-Scots border was the scene of conflict for hundreds of years, between the kings, the kings and their rebellious subjects and between the border families who preyed on each other and on passing travellers. Reivers, they were called, and a spot of sheep or cattle rustling seems rather romantic in retrospect, but, for the people of the time, the screams in the night, the smoke from burn-out villages and farmsteads and the constant fear of blackmail (protection money, rather than the modern form) were a depressing fact of life. Loyalty was to clan, rather than king, and some of the most notorious families, such as the Armstrongs, refused to heed the laws of either country.

Because violence was endemic and insoluble, when the countries were not formally at war, there was a system of regular meeting days to resolve issues and offer redress where possible. These days were managed by the Wardens of the West, East and Middle marches for both countries. There are copious letters from the various wardens complaining that the other side had not turned up, or had refused redress, or wouldn't hand over stolen goods, or hostages as agreed, but generally, unless either king were seeking an excuse for war, the matters were managed locally.

So far as can be inferred from the letters, it seems that, whilst the Scots did more raiding over the border into England, the English Kings and their wardens spent more time and money deliberately undermining the Scottish government and suborning loyalties. Neither side comes out with any credit. For the Scots Kings, to be seen to dispense justice in the borders was an important part of their role, and James IV and V and Mary all presided over *'Justices in Eyre'* personally.

Such was the situation when Margaret, Dowager Queen of Scots, dashed over the border to Harbottle, where she and her baby stayed for some months before heading, via Morpeth, Durham and Newcastle for London. On arrival in the English capital, Lady Margaret, too young to know where she was, spent time at Barnard's castle, Greenwich Palace and Scotland Yard (where during the mediaeval period, the Scottish kings visiting or held hostage in England, were housed).

Returning to Scotland, aged eighteen months, Margaret spent her childhood in the royal palaces of Stirling (2), Edinburgh Castle and Holyrood Palace. She would also have spent significant amounts of time at Tantallon Castle (3).

Tantallon, one of the most impressive castles in the Scottish Lowlands, clings to the cliffs opposite the notorious Bass Rock. On a sunny day, it is an impressive sight; on a stormy day, it is a fearful one. Tantallon was almost impregnable, and James V failed to subdue it when he was attempting to capture Margaret's father, Archibald Douglas, 6th

Earl of Angus in 1528. Margaret may have been there at the time, but was more likely to have been at Coldingham Priory.

At some point Margaret was sent into England for safety, and perhaps for her value as a hold over her half-brother, King James, and her mother, the Dowager Queen. She went first to Norham Castle (4), another border fortress, actually on the River Tweed, where she could see out to Scotland, and later at Berwick Castle, England's outpost on the north side of the Tweed. After some months there, Margaret was sent south. She may have gone to her aunt, Mary, the French Queen, at Westhorpe in Suffolk, or straight to the English court, and the household of her cousin, the Princess Mary. The English court spent most of its time during the late 1520s at Greenwich and Richmond, with the Princess at Beaulieu and Hunsdon.

In the 1530s, Margaret was in the retinue of Anne Boleyn, often at Hampton Court and at the new palace of Whitehall (5), being constructed from the old palace of the Archbishops of York. It was at Whitehall that she agreed to marry Lord Thomas Howard. For this misdemeanour of engaging herself without royal consent, she was dispatched to the Tower of London (6) where she spent anything between six and fifteen months in the period from July 1536. This was followed by a period at Syon Abbey (8), which was not dissolved until 1539.

She had left Syon by June 1538, returning probably to the house of the Princess, now demoted to '*Lady*', Mary. In 1539, Margaret was named as one of the great ladies in attendance on Anne of Cleves, and she was present at the new Queen's entry to the capital at Blackheath. For the next few months, she was with the court at Hampton Court, Greenwich, Whitehall and Westminster. When Henry divorced Queen Anne to marry Katheryn Howard, (an event which took place at Oatlands Palace) Margaret remained in the royal household, probably in the same position as first of the Great Ladies. When Katheryn Howard's star crashed miserably to earth, Margaret was also reprimanded for *'lightness'* of behaviour – she had been conducting a flirtation with Charles Howard, the Queen's brother.

With no Queen, there was no role for ladies at court so Margaret spent the period between November 1541 and July 1542 largely at Kenninghall (9) in Norfolk, not far from where her lover, Lord Thomas Howard, who had not survived his sojourn in the Tower, was buried at Thetford. The palace of Kenninghall has long disappeared but in Margaret's day was a splendid late mediaeval structure, built in the period 1505-1525, and owned by the Duke of Norfolk. Margaret may well have been happy there, in the company of her friend, Mary, Duchess of Richmond.

In July 1543, she was back at Hampton Court where she witnessed the marriage of Henry VIII to his sixth wife, Katherine Parr. For the next year, she was in attendance on the Queen, then eleven months later, Margaret herself was married.

Her husband, Matthew Stuart, 4th Earl of Lennox, and she were granted huge estates in the north of England. Her first child was born in London, at Stepney Palace, but her second at Temple Newsam (10), near Leeds. Temple Newsam, originally owned by the Knights Templar, had been confiscated from Thomas, Lord Darcy, for his part in the Pilgrimage of Grace. Today, it is an extremely imposing Jacobean mansion, built in red brick in the traditional 'U' shape around a courtyard – it is so imposing, it has been called the *'Hampton Court of the North'*. The majority of the current building post-dates Margaret's residence, but part of the main block is still the original Tudor house she knew. Her son, the ill-fated Lord Darnley, was born here on 7th December 1545. It is now owned by Leeds City Council and contains an extensive art collection.

Temple Newsam wasn't the only great house the Lennoxes owned. They were granted the lands of Jervaulx Abbey (11) and built an extremely impressive mansion there, within the Abbey walls. They also had a manor at Settrington (12), in North Yorkshire, also confiscated from one of the rebels of the Pilgrimage of Grace, Sir Francis Bigod. Margaret spent much of her time here during Elizabeth's reign, as far away from court and as close to the coast as possible, to allow her to send messages and letters to France, Spain and Scotland with minimum chance of interception.

Wressle Castle, once the property of the Percy Earls of Northumberland, was another of the Lennoxes' properties. Now an impressive ruin, it was from Wressle that Margaret dated a letter to her father, the Earl of Angus, in which she tells him how angry she is that he has disinherited her. Wressle is close to the Humber, and, at that time, passage to London or Edinburgh from there would have been as easy by ship as by road, although we don't know if Margaret ever travelled by ship herself.

Margaret's life was devoted to the promotion of her two sons, and she went to extreme lengths to promote Lord Darnley's marriage to Mary, Queen of Scots, even suffering a long imprisonment in the Tower, when Elizabeth found out.

Not chastened by this experience, nor by Darnley's death, she continued to try to promote her family, even without royal consent. In 1574 she visited an old friend, Elizabeth (Bess) Hardwick, Countess of Shrewsbury. Elizabeth Shrewsbury was enormously rich, with a daughter, and Margaret had a second son whose veins were rich in royal blood.

Lady Shrewsbury and her husband were also the gaolers of Margaret's niece and daughter-in-law, Mary, Queen of Scots. Whilst Margaret did not dare so far to defy the Queen as to visit Queen Mary, she did visit Lady Shrewsbury at Rufford Abbey (13), and it was here that the two ladies were amazed to discover that their children had fallen so far in love, that the only honourable thing to do was to let them marry at once, even without royal permission. Rufford is currently in the care of English Heritage, and there is quite an extensive range of buildings to see, although they are not habitable. Margaret had another taste of the Tower for this unapproved marriage.

Towards the end of her life, Margaret spent most of her time in Hackney (14) a fashionable area of east London, and it was there that she died on 9th March, 1578. There is no trace now of Margaret's house, although the church tower of St Augustine remains, and can be visited on the first Sunday of each month. Hackney was a particularly popular area with Catholic recusants, and that might have influenced Margaret's choice of location.

Margaret was buried in Westminster Abbey (15), in the Lady Chapel built by her grandfather, Henry VII. On the accession to the English Crown of her grandson, James VI of Scotland, he had an impressive new monument built for her.

Key to Map

1. Harbottle Castle, Northumberland
2. Stirling Castle, Stirling, Scotland
3. Tantallon Castle, North Berwick, Scotland
4. Norham Castle, Northumberland
5. Berwick Castle, Northumberland
6. Whitehall, London
7. Tower of London
8. Syon Abbey, Greater London
9. Kenninghall, Norfolk
10. Temple Newsam, Leeds
11. Jervaulx Abbey, Yorkshire
12. Settrington, Yorkshire

13. Rufford Abbey, Nottinghamshire
14. Hackney, London
15. Westminster Abbey, London

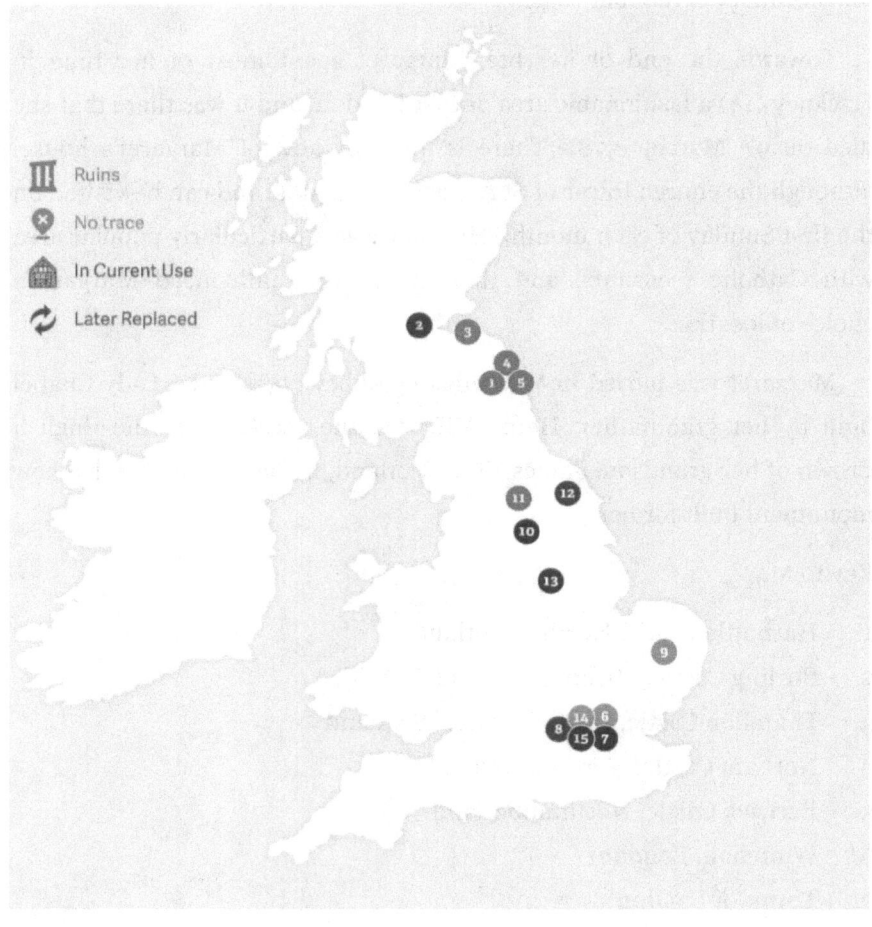

Chapter 164: Book Review

Lady Margaret Douglas has been largely neglected in Tudor historiography. She does, however, play an important part in Leanda de Lisle's *'Tudor: The Family Story'* as the link between the Tudors and Stuarts.

Tudor: The Family Story

Author: Leanda de Lisle

Publisher: Chatton & Winus

In a nutshell An ambitious panorama across the wider Tudor family, introducing the reader to some figures less well-known than Henry VIII and his wives.

Many histories of the Tudor period start with Henry Tudor, erstwhile Earl of Richmond, springing into life as he lands at Milford in South Wales, ready to capture the Crown. This book begins sixty years before and shows the progress of the Tudors from dispossessed gentry of Wales after the failure of Owain Glyndwr's attempts to throw off English control, to half-brothers of the King, and finally to the Crown. This was achieved first through the clandestine marriage of Owen Tudor to the widowed Queen, Catherine de Valois, then the marriage of their son, Edmund, into a junior member of the Lancastrian branch of the royal family – Margaret Beaufort.

Margaret Beaufort is only the first of the dominating female figures of the Tudor family whom Ms de Lisle shows as using all the weapons available to women when direct power for a female was rare: money, connections, intrigue and the sheer inability of men to contemplate that women might have more complex lives than their outward show of wifely obedience might suggest.

One of the curses of the Tudor family was the tendency of the men to die young: Prince Arthur; Henry Fitzroy; Edward VI; Henry, Earl of Lincoln and Charles, Earl of Lennox all died as young men, and many others in infancy. This left a plethora of female heirs in an era uncomfortable with feminine rule. De Lisle traces some of these young women, the Grey sisters, Lady Margaret Clifford, and Lady Arbella Stuart, through lives often made more dangerous, but never happier, through their proximity to the throne. Ms de Lisle skilfully weaves these characters in and out of the main narrative which follows the five (or six, if Lady Jane Grey is counted) monarchs as they quarrelled amongst themselves, and tried to isolate their heirs.

One of the most interesting facets of Ms de Lisle's writing, is her challenge to perceptions of history that have been conditioned by propaganda developed by later generations – good examples are the view of Frances Brandon, Duchess of Suffolk and mother of Lady Jane Grey as little better than a child-abuser, which has no basis in contemporary records; the inclination of Mary I to spare Lady Jane, shown here as a clever political ploy, in the wider context of religious turmoil, only foiled by the intriguing of Lady Jane's father; and the re-evaluation of Lady Margaret Douglas' relationship with Henry VIII, freed from the 'spin' of her enemies.

Necessarily, in a work of this vast scope, not everything can be covered, and there are some tantalising glimpses of other characters whom it would be interesting to learn more about, such as the elusive Lady Eleanor Brandon and her daughter, Lady Margaret Clifford, and Lord Strange and his siblings and children.

An elegantly written narrative which gives context to the Tudor century – highly recommended.

Part 12: Sir James Melville: Scottish Ambassador

Introduction

James Melville was one of many ambassadors employed by the Scottish Crown to manage relations with England. He knew everyone with influence at both courts. James began his career in the household of Mary, Queen of Scots in France. After a brief military excursion, he became a diplomat and travelled widely until returning to Scotland in 1564.

While there is little known about Melville's private life, he was at the heart of a network of family and co-religionists who were at the centre of affairs in both England and Scotland. Like others of his generation, he believed in witchcraft, and became embroiled in one of the more bizarre incidents of James VI's reign.

In his domestic life, Melville did not move far from his birthplace in Fife, but in his public career he travelled extensively on the continent, as well as frequently journeying between Edinburgh and London.

Part 12 contains Sir James Melville's Life Story and additional information about him, looking at different aspects of his life. On excellent terms with most of the leading figures of the day, he left a fascinating memoir of his life – although, reading between the lines, he wasn't always as straightforward as he seems. Was he a diplomat, or a spy?

SIR JAMES MELVILLE

Family Tree

Sir James MELVILLE of Halhill

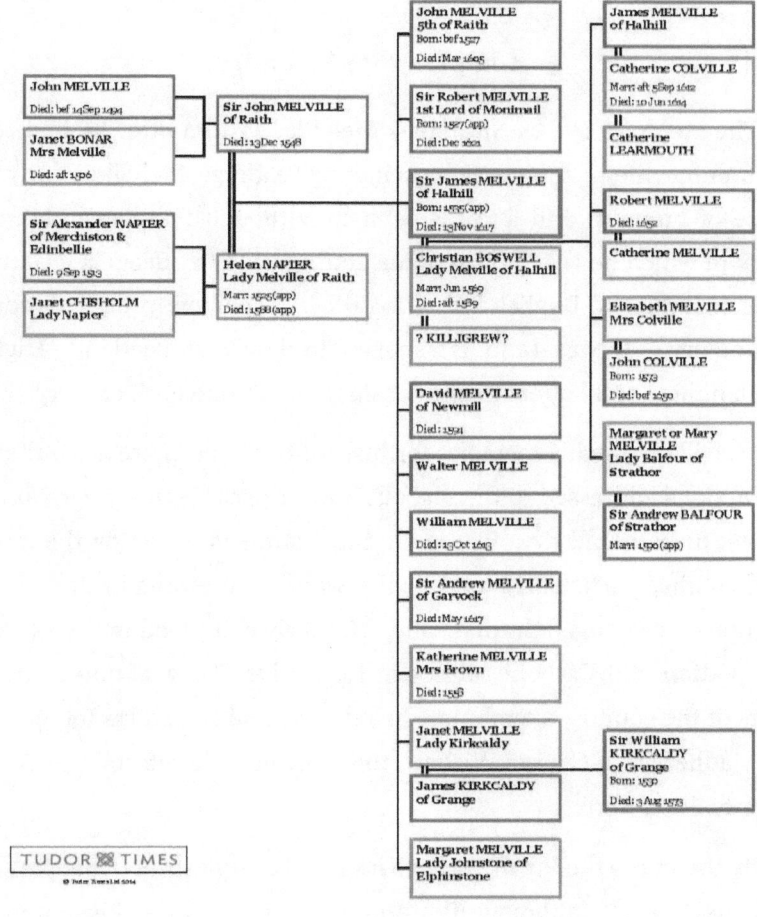

Sir James Melville's Life Story

Chapter 165: Memoirs

The memoirs left by Sir James Melville, written after he had retired from public life in 1603 make fascinating reading. Melville clearly has a sense of humour, and a readable style, although the sixteenth century Scots in which he wrote takes some getting used to. Scots is a Germanic dialect, similar to English but with different spelling, pronunciation and vocabulary. It was (and is) spoken in Lowland Scotland. Highland Scotland was still largely Gaelic speaking in the sixteenth century.

Melville wrote his memoirs for his children, and there are quite a few discursions addressed to them about how princes should govern and how honest men should live. These are interesting as reflecting the morality of the time, particularly as Melville was a Protestant in an era when religious life changed dramatically. His early childhood in the 1530s was in a nation still Catholic, although his native Fife was one of the first parts of the country to embrace the reformed faith, and his father was an early adherent of George Wishart, the most notable reformer in Scotland prior to John Knox.

By the 1580s the Presbyterian Kirk ruled every aspect of people's lives. Melville himself, although Protestant, seems to have been unusually tolerant in the matter of other people's religion, and, although he comments occasionally that someone is a *'Papist'* he does not seem to hold it against anyone. Like most of his contemporaries, most notably his king, James VI, he believed in witches and witchcraft.

Much of what we know of relations between Mary, Queen of Scots and her cousin, Elizabeth of England, has been derived from Melville's anecdotes, and his proximity to both people and events give a rich store of information about the complex political manoeuvrings of the time.

On the surface, Melville's memoirs appear to be frank and straightforward. He was a warm supporter of Mary, Queen of Scots, until, at her deposition, he accepted reality and transferred his allegiance to her baby son, always with the caveat that, should Mary be freed from her captivity in England, he would wish her to be returned to her throne. However, continued reading, and comparison of names and events with surviving correspondence from Melville and others suggest that he may not, in fact, have been quite such a devoted follower of the Queen's as he claimed.

Whilst it is not possible to deduce anything with certainty (so far as our current research has gone) the possibility that he was working with Mary's half-brother, the Earl of Moray, and Sir William Cecil in England, to destabilise Mary's government cannot be ignored.

The following life story therefore, whilst based on his memoirs, identifies some incidents where he may not have been entirely honest (although, it is possible, of course, that forty years after the events he was describing, he may have genuinely forgotten or misremembered facts).

Disappointingly, Melville gives absolutely no information about his personal life, other than references to his brothers.

Chapter 166: Youth

The Melville family was settled in Fife, a reasonably prosperous part of the Kingdom of Scotland, to the north-east of Edinburgh.

Melville's father, Sir John Melville of Raith, Captain of Dunbar Castle, was an early Scottish convert to Protestantism and supported the pro-

English party in Scotland that sought to unite Britain through a marriage between the Queen, Mary, and Prince Edward of England. One of the obstacles to this plan was Cardinal Beaton. Beaton was assassinated, with covert encouragement from the English, in 1546, but, although Sir John was associated with some of the assassins, he was not directly involved, and after the disastrous battle of Pinkie Cleugh in 1547, was dispatched to England to make terms. Whilst there, he shared information with the English government about Scottish and French military dispositions. For this treason, he was executed and his lands forfeited in December 1548.

One of the other men associated with the assassination of Beaton, and the pro-English faction, because of his strong religious affiliation with the Reformers, was Henry Balnaves of Halhill, near Kirkcaldy in Fife. Kircaldy was close to Raith, and according to John Knox, Sir John Melville was an early patron of Balnaves. This support was returned when Balnaves at some unknown time, but before 1569, adopted James Melville.

It is unknown what Melville's early education consisted of, but we can probably assume he learnt to read and write in Scots, Latin and French, and that he was brought up in the Reformed Faith, as it was being preached by the Scots Reformer George Wishart, and later, John Knox.

Despite the association of the Melvilles with the pro-English party, in late 1549, when Jehan de Monluc, Bishop of Vallance who had been sent to Scotland as Ambassador from the French King was returning home, thirteen year old James Melville was chosen to accompany him. He was to join the household of the young Mary, Queen of Scots who had been sent to France for safe-keeping, and with the intention of marrying her to the Dauphin François.

The journey to France was made via the west coast, with the objective of Vallance meeting the Irish lords who were trying to throw off English overlordship, preferring to be subject to Catholic France. The voyage was beset by storms, and the ship was obliged to shelter from the storm on a small island for thirteen days. By *'Fastrons Eve'* – that is, Shrove Tuesday, they reached Loch Foyle and were welcomed by the clan chief O'Dochartaigh.

The trip to Ireland obviously amused Melville. He recorded that the Bishop had been making eyes at O'Dochartaigh's daughter, so a *'harlot'* was brought to him secretly. Whilst she was waiting for him in his room, she found a small box of liquid, sitting on the window ledge, drying out after being soaked during the storm. She consumed it, licking the entire contents out of the box. Vallance, when he came in, let out a cry of annoyance, and so his plan to break his vows of celibacy was discovered. He was angry because the liquid was some rare and precious balm of Egypt, that had been given to him as a gift by the Sultan of Turkey, following an embassy there.

Meanwhile, the daughter of O'Dochartaigh who had been running away from Vallance, was running after Melville. She offered to marry him and go away with him anywhere he chose. He fended her off, thanking her for her kind offer, but telling her he was too young, and had no income, and, in any event was en route to France in his Queen's service.

After about three weeks of negotiations in Ireland, the party returned to Dumbarton. Following a short digression to Stirling to take leave again of the Dowager Queen, Marie of Guise, the party sailed from Dumbarton for France, via the Isle of Man, in two French ships. These vessels were returning to France after delivering money to pay the soldiers defending Scotland against the English in the War of the Rough Wooing.

After eight days at sea, Melville and the rest arrived at Le Conquet, in Brittany. Vallance hurried ahead to Paris, leaving Melville to travel in more comfort, furnishing him with enough money to buy horses and pay expenses for himself and two Scottish gentleman, his companions.

The trio fell in with two Frenchman and a Spaniard and decided to travel together in a journey that is reminiscent of every young traveller's experience over the centuries. On the first night, the six shared a room in an inn, two to a bed. Melville sharing with the Spaniard. In the middle of the night he heard the two Scotsmen plotting to tell Vallance that the journey had cost twice as much as it did, to cover their own expenses. Then he heard the Frenchmen planning to take advantage of the others not speaking French to bamboozle them over the prices. Narrowly missing being mugged by a couple of cronies of the two Frenchmen, Melville finally made it to Paris just after Easter 1550.

Melville expected Vallance to introduce him to the Queen of Scots immediately, but, after a month, he still had not been taken to her, although Vallance made arrangements for him to improve his French and learn to play the lute. The Bishop even talked of adopting Melville, but nothing came of the idea.

Before being introduced to the Queen of Scots, Melville came to the attention of the Constable of France, the strangely named Anne de Montmorency, who, together with his ally Diane de Poitiers, strongly influenced Henri II. The Constable requested Melville to join his service, which Melville agreed to, provided the Bishop would let him go. Bishop Vallance agreed, and Melville became a servant of the Constable in May 1553.

Chapter 167: Life in France

War was almost continuous between France and the Empire – sometimes in Italy, and sometimes in the area of Franco-Burgundian border. Melville accompanied the army led into Picardy by the Constable in 1553. The results of the various battles were inconclusive, and both armies fell back into winter quarters, with Melville returning to Chantilly with the Constable.

Attempts by Cardinal Reginald Pole (cousin to Mary I of England, soon to be Archbishop of Canterbury) to mediate between France and the Empire were unsuccessful. In 1554 Henri II again advanced, and Melville, although still in the Constable's retinue, was granted a pension by the King. After a season of war and sieges, both sides claimed victory. A five year truce was then signed, to facilitate the Emperor Charles' decision to retire – handing over his Spanish, Burgundian and New World lands to his son, Philip II, and persuading the Imperial Electors to select his brother, Ferdinand, as the new Emperor.

Before the five years of truce were completed, the Pope, Paul IV, tried to persuade Henri II to break it, to support his campaign against Spain in Naples. This idea was taken up by the Guise brothers – François, Duke of Guise and Cardinal Charles of Lorraine, the uncles of the Queen of Scots. The Constable opposed the breaking of the truce but his advice was overridden and France advanced into both Naples and Picardy. The Guise brothers were then horrified to discover that the Pope had made a separate truce.

An angry Philip II prepared for war, persuading his wife, Mary I of England, to support him. The Anglo-Spanish and French armies, the latter including Melville, met at St Quentin where the Anglo-Spanish, under the Duke of Savoy achieved a resounding victory. Melville was wounded by a severe blow to the head, but managed to escape the field.

He mentions being helped by a man he names as Henry Killigrew, describing him as an old friend. Killigrew, a Protestant, had been in exile in France since 1556. It is not clear which side Killigrew was fighting on, but, presumably, the French side.

Failing to follow up their victory, the tables were turned on the Anglo-Spanish when Henri II made a lightening swoop on Calais, capturing the town from the English garrison. Despite this victory, France was at a disadvantage, and was forced to make peace in the Treaty of Cateau-Cambresis.

Melville was present at proceedings, still serving the Constable, who had been captured at St Quentin. The French were divided amongst themselves – the Constable in favour of peace, which would release him from bondage, and the Guise party reluctant to have him back at court where they were increasing their influence. On this occasion, the Constable had the upper hand, but, at the urging of the Guise faction, the treaty encompassed oaths for France and Spain to try to restore the Catholic faith in parts of Europe where the Reformation had taken hold.

The English hoped to retain Calais, but, with Queen Mary now dead, Philip had less interest in England, and did not make restoration of the town a condition of peace. England received a sop in that Calais was to be restored after eight years, or a sum of 450,000 crowns paid for, it although it was apparent to all present that this would never happen. Scotland, whose Queen was married to the heir to the French throne, was encompassed in the peace.

With Queen Mary of England dead, there were many who thought that Mary, Queen of Scots was her legal heir, rather than Elizabeth, who had already been proclaimed queen and crowned. New silverware was ordered for the young Queen of Scots and her husband, the Dauphin, which was engraved with the arms of England. According to Melville, this was the idea of the Queen's uncle, the Cardinal of Lorraine. It proved to be one of the greatest mistakes the Queen (only sixteen at the time) ever made. The English were angry and protested but were put off with lame excuses.

The Scottish oath to observe the Treaty was to be sworn by the Regent, Marie of Guise. Originally, it was planned that Melville should return home to administer the oath, but it was decided to send a more influential figure who could persuade Queen Marie to step up persecution against Protestants – an action she had been unwilling to take. This undermining of Marie's policy of tolerance in return for support for her rule and for her absent daughter led to dissension, and revolt in Scotland, under the leadership of the Lords of the Congregation. The Lords, led by Mary's illegitimate half-brother, Lord James Stewart, had converted to Protestantism.

Henri II and the Constable agreed that Melville should return to Scotland to report on affairs. Melville was strictly charged by the Constable to determine whether it would be necessary for Henri II to send troops to support Queen Marie. Melville was to investigate whether the rebellion of the Lords of the Congregation was an attempt to overthrow the Queen and replace her with Lord James Stewart, or to protect the Protestant religion. If the latter, the Constable believed that France should not interfere.

So Melville returned to Scotland, via England. Once in Scotland, Melville hurried to Falkland Palace, to see Queen Marie. He was the introduced by Henry Balnaves (who had had his lands restored in 1556) to Lord James Stewart. The twenty-four year old Melville appears to have struck up a good relationship with Lord James, some four years his senior. Lord James assured Melville that he had no designs on the crown, and would be willing to live abroad to show that he was quite innocent of any improper ambitions. Melville, convinced by his sincerity, set out once again for France.

On his return to France, Melville passed through Newcastle in England, and recounts a strange tale that he picked up there. He met a man who claimed that Henry VIII, on being told that his son would die without children, tried to poison both his daughters, with the effect that, although neither died, they would both be barren. The tale seems quite extraordinary, but Melville appears to have believed it, and interprets other events on the assumption that it was true.

Chapter 168: Travelling in Europe

On arrival in France, Melville found the political situation quite altered. Henri II was dead, and his son, the fifteen year old François, was now King, with Mary, Queen of Scots as his consort. The young couple were dominated by her Guise uncles, who were determined both to pursue their Catholic mission and to push forward their niece as the rightful Queen of England. Melville's master, the Constable, with his more conciliatory approach, had been banished from court.

With Mary of Scotland now being proclaimed as Queen of England, and the mustering of French troops to support Marie of Guise in Scotland, the Lords of the Congregation sought help from Elizabeth of England. Elizabeth was never inclined to help rebels, even if they were apparently her co-religionists, but she could not afford to tolerate Mary's impertinent use of her titles. The situation in Scotland deteriorated, and was close to open war when Queen Marie died. The Lords of the Congregation having gained the upper hand, the Scots in France came under suspicion. Melville decided to leave France and travel around Europe.

His first port of call was the court of the Elector Palatine. The Elector, Frederick III, was a staunch Calvinist and Melville found favour with him. It was not long, however, before Melville was back in France. François II had died of an ear infection, leaving the Queen of Scots widowed at seventeen. The Guises were immediately dismissed from favour as the new king, Charles IX's, mother, Catherine de Medici became Regent of France. Constable Montmorency was back in favour.

Queen Mary, unloved by her mother-in-law, retired from court, and Melville returned to the Palatinate with messages from Queen Catherine to the Elector. Catherine was toying with the idea of joining a league with the Protestant princes of Europe, including Elizabeth of England, and the Elector, to counterbalance the faction of the Guises, and their ally, Philip of Spain.

With no place for her in France, Mary decided to return to Scotland where she took up personal rule, supported by her half-brother, Lord James, to whom she granted the Earldom of Moray, and Sir William Maitland of Lethington, who was a friend of Sir William Cecil, Secretary of State to Queen Elizabeth. The queens professed friendship and alliance and all seemed set fair.

Melville had journeyed from the Palatinate to France to swear allegiance to Mary before her departure. She told him he would be welcome in her service, should he wish to leave the Elector, but he returned to the Palatinate for the time being and continued to carry out diplomatic missions on the Elector's behalf.

The Elector was negotiating to marry his son, Prince Casimir, either to the sister of the Duke of Lorraine, or, failing that, to Queen Elizabeth. Melville recounted that he refused to negotiate a match with Elizabeth, as he knew she intended to remain single because of the poison he believed she had been given on her father's orders.

Melville then received orders to travel to the court of the Emperor Ferdinand to enquire into a marriage between Queen Mary and the Archduke Charles, Ferdinand's younger son. Ferdinand left much of the management of his affairs to his older son, Maximilian, King of the Romans. Maximilian was rumoured to be a Protestant, and was courting both the three Catholic Imperial Electors and the three Protestant ones (including the Elector Palatine) all of whom thought he was on their side of the religious fence. It was thus believed by the Scottish court that Melville, as a servant of the Protestant Elector Palatine, would be warmly received by Maximilian.

Maximilian talked to Melville pressing him for every particular about the state of affairs in Scotland and whether the Scots would really wish to press Queen Mary's claim to England. He remained with the King of the Romans for fifteen days.

Melville was not initially clear in his own mind what Maximilian thought about a marriage between his brother, Archduke Charles, and Queen Mary, but eventually concluded that Maximilian would prefer Charles to remain single, as, if he became King of Scots, and perhaps England, in right of his wife, Charles might be in a position to take Burgundy should Philip of Spain have no heirs, whilst currently, Maximilian, as the husband of Philip's sister, was likely to inherit.

On seeing that his embassy was likely to prove fruitless, Melville left Maximilian, and travelled to Venice and Rome before returning to the Elector's court at Heidelburg.

Chapter 169: Back to France

Melville's next embassy was back to France. Catherine de Medici was considering the Elector's daughter as a wife for Charles IX and Melville was despatched to deliver her picture and describe her charms to the

French court. He arrived at a court riven with faction. The Constable was back in his old place, but he and Catherine de Medici were not on good terms, and nor was she on particularly good terms with Admiral Coligny, leader of the Huguenot faction and the Constable's brother-in-law.

Melville was reprimanded for revealing his commission from the Elector to the Constable before informing Catherine and King Charles of the details, but was forgiven, and offered a place in the King's Privy Chamber. Whilst he was contemplating accepting the job, news came of a plot on Coligny's life – discovered by the Huguenot Duchess Renee of Ferrara (daughter of Louis XII of France and thus great-aunt to Charles IX, as well as mother to the now-widowed Duchess of Guise). The would-be assassin was himself found dead, and suspicion fell on the Constable and Coligny. At this point, Melville was relieved to receive a summons to return to Scotland to undertake commissions for Queen Mary.

He returned to the Elector before setting out for Scotland in 1564, and agreed to carry pictures of the young Prince Casimir to England. Casimir was still hoping Elizabeth would marry him, and Melville was still certain that she would not. Nevertheless, he was prepared to visit Elizabeth on Casimir's behalf, provided he was furnished with pictures of the whole family, not just Casimir, so that he could introduce the matter in a roundabout way.

As well as offering a husband she didn't want, Melville was also obliged to tell Elizabeth that the Protestant Electors, having agreed with Maximilian that he would declare himself a Protestant on the death of Ferdinand, had promised not to ally with any other monarchs. Should Maximilian go back on his word, they would be delighted to ally with Queen Elizabeth.

Elizabeth promised Melville that she wouldn't breathe a word of this to her Council, and they discussed the virtues of the Elector – this gave Melville the opportunity to show Elizabeth the picture of Casimir. She kept it overnight, but said that Lord Robert Dudley (the man half Europe believed she planned to marry) should be the judge of Casimir's suitability. Melville was confirmed in his opinion that Elizabeth would not marry Casimir, which he repeated by letter to the Elector.

Whilst he was at the English Court, Elizabeth talked much of her friendship for Queen Mary, and her desire to be treated as an older sister by the younger queen, saying that she would write on the topic to Melville with her own hand when he had returned to Scotland. In the meantime, Mary had written to Elizabeth, asking her opinion on a match between Mary and Archduke Charles.

Elizabeth, rather than writing to Melville, sent her thoughts on Mary's marriage by her own ambassador, Sir Thomas Randolph. She was quite clear that she would feel that the amity between the two queens would be undermined if Mary married Charles. Instead, she suggested that Mary should marry one of Elizabeth's own nobles. To make certain that the match with Charles would not take place, Elizabeth dispatched the Earl of Sussex to the Emperor's court (Maximilian was now Emperor) to hint that she herself might still be available – a far superior choice, as England was a good deal more prosperous than Scotland.

Elizabeth then made a proposition of another possible husband for Queen Mary who would please Elizabeth, and encourage her to nominate Mary as her successor. Her candidate was none other than Lord Robert Dudley, the mysterious death of whose first wife, Amy Robsart, had led Queen Mary to comment a couple of years before that

'The Queen of England [was] going to marry her horsemaster, who [had] murdered his wife to make room for her.'

Mary was angry and insulted – first, that Elizabeth was undermining her possible marriage to the Archduke, and, second, that she should think her own cast-off suitable for Mary.

Further distrust entered into the relationship when Matthew Stuart, Earl of Lennox, a Scot who had been exiled for many years in England was given leave to return home, much to the disquiet of the Lennox' hereditary enemies, the Hamiltons. Elizabeth advised Mary to beware of situations where rivalry between the factions could arise, but Mary, convinced that everything Elizabeth said had some ulterior, and damaging, motive, was chary of trusting her and wrote a letter that Elizabeth claimed to find offensive. It is easy to imagine the occasionally impetuous Mary dashing off a letter in the heat of her annoyance, and it appearing rude and ungrateful to Elizabeth, who rather fancied herself in the role of mentor to the younger woman.

Up until this point, Mary and Elizabeth had been corresponding in their own hands, with some regularity, but this now ceased, and there were no messages for a couple of months, until Mary decided to send Melville back to England to try to patch matters up, at least to outward appearance.

Chapter 170: Embassy to England

Melville had intended to return either to the Palatinate or to France, to pursue his career there, as he was unimpressed by the factious state of Scotland. However, he was so charmed by Queen Mary, and so impressed with her *'princely virtues'* that he felt it his duty to remain in her service, believing her to be *'more worthy to be served for little profit than any other prince in Europe for great commodity'*. He thus accepted her commission, including a pension of 1,000 marks.

In late September of 1564 Mary sent Melville to England to treat with Elizabeth, to send messages to Lady Margaret Douglas (wife of the aforementioned Earl of Lennox) who was her father's half-sister, and to meet the Spanish Ambassador and Mary's other supporters.

The main purport of Mary's letters to Elizabeth was to try to smooth over the dispute that seemed to have arisen between them over the matter of Lennox. Melville was to tell Elizabeth that Mary had been grateful for her advice, and that if she had written anything that could be misinterpreted, he was to assure Elizabeth that only the most positive messages should be taken from Mary's letters. Mary could not actually remember what she had written – she didn't think it necessary to copy any '*familiar letters*' she wrote with her own hand.

The next matter was to agree a meeting between trusted councillors of both queens who would be able to resolve any disputes there might be.

Melville was then to tread carefully, and try to find out what was to be discussed in the forthcoming English Parliament. Mary was aware that Parliament was pressing Elizabeth to name a successor. Elizabeth had refused to do so, but perhaps Parliament would force her hand. In so far as Elizabeth was willing to opine on the succession, she had observed that she knew of no-one with a better right than Mary, but that was not exactly a ringing endorsement. Melville was to hint to Elizabeth that a failure to confirm Mary as her successor might lead people to believe that her protestations of friendship were mere words.

Melville arrived in London and took lodgings at Westminster. As soon as she heard of his arrival Elizabeth sent a message to say she would see him the next morning at 8 o'clock as she was walking in her garden. That evening, Sir Nicholas Throckmorton paid a visit. The Throckmortons were a large clan, based at Coughton Court in Warwickshire, and pretty equally divided between committed Catholics and steadfast Protestants.

Sir Nicholas was in the latter camp. Melville had first become acquainted with him when Throckmorton was Elizabeth's Ambassador to France during the reigns of Henri II and François II. The two were good friends, and Throckmorton had even chiselled a pension out of the notoriously parsimonious Elizabeth for Melville, during his time in Germany. It may seem quite extraordinary to us that Melville could receive a pension from Elizabeth whilst working for Mary, but no-one thought it at all strange at the time.

Throckmorton, although a Protestant, and highly favoured by Elizabeth, was one of her courtiers who supported Mary as her successor. Throckmorton's advice was that, should Elizabeth prove recalcitrant in the matter of naming Mary her heir, the sight of Melville cosying up to the Spanish Ambassador would concentrate her mind.

The next morning, Elizabeth sent a servant, a horse harnessed with velvet and two gentlemen, including Sir Thomas Randolph, who had been her Ambassador to Mary the previous year, to fetch Melville from his lodgings.

He met the Queen pacing up and down, as was her custom, in one of the alleys in the Palace gardens. They conversed in French, Melville being more comfortable in that than in his native Scots after so long away, and the Queen, although she might have understood Scots which was similar to English, was fluent in French. The first matter was Queen Mary's allegedly offensive letter.

Elizabeth brandished a response she had drafted – equally blunt and '*despiteful*'. Melville, saying that Queen Mary could not remember what she had written, asked to see the original letter. Elizabeth let him read it. It was written in French, and Melville told Elizabeth that, although she spoke beautiful French, she could not be familiar with the everyday French that Mary wrote and spoke, which was rather less flowery between friends (such as he supposed the two queens to be) than Elizabeth might be used to.

Elizabeth allowed herself to be mollified, especially as Mary had made the first move in patching things up by sending Melville. She destroyed her draft letter, and promised to continue in loving friendship with Mary, interpreting anything the latter might do in the best possible light.

Elizabeth then moved on to talk of Mary's marriage. Had she come to any conclusion following Elizabeth's suggestion that she marry an English noble?

Melville answered that Mary had not given the matter any thought – waiting for a conference to be arranged to discuss the matter with all of the other business between the two countries. Mary would send Moray and Lethington, and hoped that Elizabeth would send the Earl of Bedford and Lord Robert Dudley.

Elizabeth pounced on Dudley's name, saying that Melville obviously held him of small account, as he had mentioned him second – but Elizabeth was going to ennoble him, in front of Melville's very eyes. Lord Robert, she added, was as dear as a brother and her best friend. She would have married him herself, if she felt inclined to marriage, but as it was, she thought him the best possible husband for Mary. If Mary did marry Dudley, Elizabeth would be very likely to name her as successor as she would then be free of all thought of being hurried to her end.

Chapter 171: Fencing with Elizabeth I

Elizabeth was as good as her word in regard to Dudley, and Melville and the French Ambassador were invited to stand next to the queen and watch the ceremony in which he was promoted to Earl of Leicester and Baron Denbigh. Melville observed that, wrapping the peer's robe around him, Elizabeth could not resist tickling Dudley's neck. Not necessarily the way to promote his suitability as the husband of another woman.

After the ceremony, Elizabeth asked what Melville thought of Dudley, or Leicester, as he now was. Melville answered that the new earl was lucky to have a mistress who appreciated his talents. Elizabeth then went for the jugular.

'*Yet,*' she said, '*you like better of yonder long lad,*' pointing at Henry, Lord Darnley. Darnley was the son of the Earl of Lennox and his countess, Lady Margaret Douglas. Leaving aside Henry VIII's machinations with the succession in his will, Darnley was Elizabeth's nearest male heir and second after Queen Mary in a traditional pattern of inheritance.

Melville brushed off the accusation, saying that Darnley was a mere boy, even though he had a commission burning a hole in his pocket to treat with the Countess of Lennox about sending Darnley to Scotland to undertake some legal business with his father – and perhaps for Mary to look him over. The Countess had been intriguing for some time for Mary to marry her son.

Elizabeth was determined to pursue the idea of Mary marrying Leicester, so, as she said she could not talk to Mary directly, she would talk to Melville as familiarly. He remained at Westminster for nine days, and met the Queen at least once, and sometimes as frequently as three times, each day.

The two fenced verbally – Elizabeth pushing Leicester, and Melville indicating that Mary had not even heard the suggestion, and that it might all be discussed as part of a commission, when she had been named as Elizabeth's heir. Elizabeth countered with the impossibility of naming Mary unless she had shown herself willing to take Elizabeth's advice.

Elizabeth had, however, commissioned lawyers to identify her legal successor – she did hope they would tell her it was Mary!

Melville brandished the fact that before the birth of his younger children, Henry VIII had contemplated leaving his throne to his nephew, James V (Mary's father) in default of male heirs (actually, Henry had stoutly resisted any such idea).

Elizabeth then told him that, if Mary did not co-operate, she would have to marry and have children herself. Melville, in an astonishing piece of plain speaking to a queen replied:

'Madam, you need not tell me that. I know your stately stomach (disposition). You think if you were married, you would be but Queen of England. Now you are King and Queen both. You may not suffer (will not tolerate) a commander.'

Elizabeth then showed Melville her miniature of Queen Mary – 'accidentally' letting him see she also had one of Leicester. Melville asked for the latter to show Mary, on the grounds that Elizabeth had the original, but Elizabeth refused. He then asked for a large ruby that Elizabeth had been flaunting, to be sent as a token. The Queen again denied the request but added that one day Mary would have everything, if she followed Elizabeth's advice. She would, however, send a diamond.

It now being late, Melville was sent away to have his supper with a request to return to the gardens in the morning. At supper, he sat with Lady Stafford, one of the Queen's ladies-in-waiting, and a close friend as well as a relative of Elizabeth. Dorothy Stafford, paternal grand-daughter of Edward, Duke of Buckingham and maternal grand-daughter of Margaret Plantagenet, Countess of Salisbury, had married her cousin, Sir William Stafford, the widower of Elizabeth's aunt, Mary Boleyn, and been exiled in Geneva with other Protestants during Mary's reign.

Melville had known Lady Stafford and her daughter, Elizabeth, at the court of France, as they passed through en route to Geneva, and had struck up a warm friendship with the daughter. Both ladies were a source of information as to happenings at the English court.

Mary had instructed Melville to entertain Queen Elizabeth, so he told her stories of the countries he had visited, and about the clothes that the women wore – Elizabeth was well aware of the power of clothes to demonstrate power, and political allegiance, and wore clothes in French, Italian and English styles. Melville was asked which he liked best and responded that the Italian style was the most attractive – this was a play on the Queen's vanity, as Italian ladies showed their hair, and Elizabeth was proud of her curly red-gold locks.

Having begun a quasi-flirtation, Elizabeth then wanted to know who was the prettier, herself or Mary. The silver-tongued Melville replied that the one was the prettiest queen in England, the other, the prettiest queen in Scotland. Elizabeth pursued the matter and he told her she was the fairer-skinned, but Mary was *'lusome'* (attractive or desirable). He was now backed into a corner with Elizabeth wanting to know who was the taller, what Mary did for exercise, and how well she played the virginals. Mary's virtuosity, was *'reasonable, for a Queen,'* he replied.

Later that day, after his audience with the Queen was over, Melville was invited by her cousin, Lord Hunsdon, to take a walk in a gallery, into which the sounds of expertly played virginals were wafting. He drew back a curtain to see the Queen, who, with her back to him, continued playing until she could no longer keep up the pretence of being unaware of his presence. She took her hands from the keys and protested that she never played in front of gentlemen.

He excused his bad manners in intruding on her, and asked for punishment. Elizabeth sat, and placing a cushion for him on the floor, and summoning Lady Stafford as chaperone, proceeded to quiz him on the relative charms of herself and Mary. He had to admit that Elizabeth was the better musician. Elizabeth then showed off her Italian (good, in his opinion) and German (not so good.)

Chapter 172: Return to Scotland

By now, Melville was keen to return to Scotland. Elizabeth complained that he had tired of her company, sooner than she had of his. Protesting that it was business that called him away, he was commanded to stay another two days to see the Queen dance. Melville was obliged to admit that Elizabeth was a more talented dancer than Mary.

Delighted with the praise, Elizabeth sighed again that she wished to meet Mary, if only she could find the time. Melville offered to carry her secretly to Scotland, disguised as a page.

Whilst Melville was waiting for the Queen's official response to his embassy to be drafted by Cecil, he was invited by Leicester to sail back up to London from Hampton Court, in his barge. During the trip, Leicester asked what Mary thought of the proposed marriage. Melville, as instructed by his Queen, answered '*coldly*'. Leicester then hastily assured Melville that he, personally, would never be so presumptuous as to consider himself a suitable husband for Queen Mary. According to Leicester, it was all Cecil's idea, to make Leicester look grasping and ambitious, and disgrace him in the eyes of both queens.

Melville and Leicester dined with the Earl of Pembroke, another Protestant, and brother-in-law to the late Katherine Parr. Pembroke was also a supporter of Mary's rights to the succession. After dinner, Melville took leave of the French and Spanish Ambassadors.

The following day, he received the dispatches from Cecil, together with letters from Cecil to Moray and Lethington. Cecil himself gave Melville a gold chain.

As well as messages from Elizabeth and Cecil, Melville was commissioned to carry other presents. Lady Lennox gave him several items to take as gifts: a diamond ring for Queen Mary; an emerald for own husband; a diamond for Moray; a watch with diamonds and rubies for Lethington and a ruby ring for Melville's brother, Sir Robert Melville. Lady Lennox was courting favour for the idea of marriage of her son, Darnley, to Queen Mary.

Melville arrived back in Edinburgh to report to Mary. In summary, Elizabeth's responses were that she was glad the misunderstanding over the letters was cleared up and that Mary need not fear any action being taken by Parliament to damage her rights without warning.

He could then turn to the messages from others in London. The Spanish Ambassador conveyed the warm wishes of both Philip II, and Philip's son, Don Carlos. Don Carlos was another possible suitor for Mary, but although it was not openly said, Philip did not want him to marry anyone, as he appeared to be mentally unstable.

Mary was pleased that relations with Elizabeth appeared to be mended, but asked Melville if he thought Elizabeth sincere. He replied that he believed not. There had been no '*plain meaning*' or '*upright dealing*' from Elizabeth but only '*dissimulation*'. Melville feared that Elizabeth's intent was to chase Mary out of her own kingdom, as evidenced by the interference in the marriage scheme with Archduke Charles, and the insulting offer of Leicester.

Mary promised Melville she had no intention of marrying Leicester, but sent Moray to meet the Earl of Bedford to talk terms at Berwick – not surprisingly, the English side was not so forthcoming once the match looked like it might take place. Leicester, in the meantime, wrote to Mary, protesting his innocence of any desire to advance himself by marrying her. Mary warmed to Leicester, frightening Elizabeth into thinking the marriage might occur.

It is for this reason, in Melville's view, that Elizabeth allowed Darnley to travel to Scotland – hoping Mary would fall for him. According to Melville, Cecil and Elizabeth did not believe Darnley would disobey Elizabeth's direct orders, for fear of loss of all his lands and titles in England, and the presence of his mother there. They just hoped to muddy the waters and delay Mary marrying anyone.

Chapter 173: Queen Mary's Friend

Melville was deeply impressed with Mary. He admired her both personally, and as a monarch. On her return from France, she was determined to conduct herself and her kingdom so *'honourably'* and *'discreetly'*, that her good reputation would spread around Europe. She enjoined Melville to advise her, should she make a wrong step. He refused, saying that she had plenty of advisors, including Moray and Lethington. Mary answered that the court was full of flatterers, and she needed someone she could trust to give her honest counsel.

Fearing to trust entirely in princes, Melville was somewhat hesitant, but accepted the Queen's command. From autumn of 1564, he became her chief advisor on foreign affairs – writing most of her letters, and reading everything she received from foreign rulers. He presents the Queen as intelligent and quick-witted, as well as somewhat lonely at the Scottish court, which was smaller and less sophisticated than that of France. Nevertheless, Mary was winning friends both at home and abroad.

Into this happy situation crept the seeds of disaster in the shape of David Rizzio. Rizzio, a Savoyard, became one of Mary's musicians, then her French secretary. His familiarity with the Queen, his Catholic faith, his elegant, foreign ways, and most of all, his contempt for Mary's nobles, created rivalry and animosity. The courtiers would shove him as they passed him in corridors, complaining he was always with the Queen and that he meddled with all of the country's business, rather than just writing letters in French. Instead of keeping out of politics, Rizzio became embroiled as suitors paid him to put forward their pleas to the Queen – this was perfectly normal and not seen as corruption, but there was a limit, and Rizzio, in the view of the Scottish court, overstepped it.

Rizzio, seeing the growing animosity against him, asked Melville's advice. He recommended that Rizzio stand back when the nobles were present, and show them more deference. He then decided that Mary, having asked him to give her advice when she went wrong, would now hear it plain and simple: she should cease favouring Rizzio, and not permit him to be insolent to her Lords.

Mary denied that Rizzio was involved in her business, beyond her French correspondence, but promised to think on Melville's words.

Meanwhile, Lord Darnley was pressing his suit, supported by Melville. Mary turned him down initially, but Darnley persuaded Rizzio to speak in his favour, too. Mary was keen to marry to have an heir, and she was attracted to Darnley. On paper, it was a good match. Darnley was attractive, healthy, well-educated and had a strong claim to the English throne, as well as a moderate claim to the Scottish one. Darnley was widely believed to be a Catholic, although in England he had conformed to the Reformed church established by Elizabeth – again, this should have made him a good choice – Catholic enough for Mary, Protestant enough for her nobles, who were largely of the reformed faith. Eventually, Mary decided to proceed.

Elizabeth sent frantic messages via Sir Nicholas Throckmorton for Darnley to return – or for Mary's nobles to hold out against it until Darnley could be persuaded to confirm allegiance to the Protestant faith.

Mary, angry at further interference in her kingdom, and seeing Elizabeth did not want her to marry at all, ignored the demands to send Darnley back and married him on 29th July, 1565. Her Lords, however, took Elizabeth's money, and broke out into open rebellion – Mary's half-brother, the Earl of Moray, angry at losing his place as her chief advisor; the Duke of Chatelherault, who had been Governor during her childhood, and the Earls of Argyll, Glenrothes and Glencairn concocted a plot to capture Darnley.

Queen Mary dressed herself in armour, and, together with Darnley, now proclaimed as Henry, King of Scots, led her troops in what became known as the *'Chaseabout Raid'*, as the royal army pursued the rebels hither and yon. The rebels escaped over the border into England, where their failure was greeted by Elizabeth with a refusal to acknowledge any involvement, and a public dressing-down for Moray, in front of the French and Spanish ambassadors. Moray was forced to confirm Elizabeth's denials, to satisfy France and Spain, who had both accused her of interfering in other kingdoms.

The Scots Lords were concerned that with Mary, Darnley and Rizzio, all Catholics (although, as noted, Darnley (as we will continue to call him that here) was rather flexible in religion) that they would attempt to reconcile Scotland to Rome. Abroad, the Pope and the Catholic monarchs of Europe had similar ambitions, although Mary had consistently kept her word not to try to overturn the Scottish Reformation. Pope Pius IV sent Mary 8,000 crowns in furtherance of his hopes, which she never received, as the ship containing it was wrecked on the coast of Northumberland. Melville was sent to the Earl of Northumberland to ask him to return it, but, despite the Earl (Henry Percy) being a Catholic and, in theory, a supporter of Mary, he hung onto the cash.

Chapter 174: Marry in Haste

After Mary's marriage, Melville, less needed by the Queen, busy with her new husband, and not liking the growing strife at the Scottish court, requested leave to return to France. Mary, however, wanted him to stay. She told him that she knew Darnley believed Melville to be a supporter of Moray's but that she herself believed, that, although Melville liked Moray, he was true to her. She also suggested that he make an effort to get on with Darnley and to continue his friendship with Rizzio.

Melville now advised Mary to forgive Moray and his supporters – they had been badly let down by Elizabeth, and a reconciliation with them would strengthen Mary, as showing herself both powerful enough to defeat rebels, and magnanimous enough to forgive them. Whilst Mary would no doubt have liked to hang them all, there was little she could do, since they were out of her reach in Newcastle, and their families were beginning to talk treason.

This advice was seconded by Sir Nicholas Throckmorton, who suggested that treating Moray and his cohorts mercifully, would encourage English Protestants to look kindly on Mary's claims to the throne, if they saw she could work with their co-religionists. It might persuade those who favoured Lady Katherine Grey as the Protestant heir to change their allegiance to Mary. The Queen, who had shown herself generally as inclined to compromise, listened to their advice, and sent Melville's brother, Sir Robert Melville, to England as her Ambassador, with orders to keep her abreast of any discussions in the English Parliament.

Whilst Melville was encouraging reconciliation, Mary received a letter from her brother-in-law, Charles IX, urging her, on the advice of her uncle, the Cardinal of Lorraine, to have nothing to do with her Protestant rebels. The Cardinal was fresh from the Council of Trent, where the Catholic powers of Europe had pledged themselves to root out Protestantism. Mary was in a quandary – she did not wish to offend her family, or the powerful kings of France or Spain, but she had accepted the wisdom of Throckmorton and Melville's advice, and they both knew more of events in England than Charles or Philip.

After some deliberation, Mary continued with the Parliament that had been originally called to forfeit the goods and titles of Moray and his colleagues. Meanwhile, another plot was brewing.

James Douglas, Earl of Morton; his cousin Sir George Douglas, who was Darnley's illegitimate uncle; Patrick, Lord Ruthven (Douglas' brother-in-law) and Patrick, Lord Lindsay (Moray's brother-in-law) now banded together to dispose of the hated David Rizzio. They persuaded Darnley to join with them, playing on the fact that, within a very short space of time after their marriage, Mary had lost all respect for him, and refused to grant him the Crown Matrimonial (ie, the right to remain king should she die with an underage heir, or, if she had no heir, for the crown to pass to him). Darnley was jealous of Rizzio, suspecting he had undermined him to Mary. There is also a theory that Rizzio and Darnley had been lovers.

The plotters burst into Mary's supper chamber at Holyrood Palace, held her fast (although she was six months' pregnant) and stabbed Rizzio to death. Mary was then locked into her room.

Melville claims that, the next day, he came into the gates of the Palace, and Mary called to him from a window for help, telling him to fetch the

Provost of Edinburgh, and raise troops to rescue her. As he tried to leave the Palace, he encountered James Nesbit, one of the Earl of Lennox' men, and persuaded him that he, Melville, was only going to hear the preaching in St Giles Kirk, it being a Sunday. Instead, he hurried to the Provost, but the citizens of Edinburgh declined to involve themselves.

Mary smuggled out another message to Melville to give to Moray, guessing that her half-brother would return immediately. She was right, for he appeared in Edinburgh on the Monday - which suggests he was aware of the plot, as he had been in Newcastle - a distance of 120 miles, which could hardly be done in less than a day. Her message to Moray was that she knew she would not have been so badly treated, had he been there, and that, if he helped her now, she would forgive his previous rebellion.

The Queen turned her undoubted charm on her husband, and, in a show of quick thinking and resolution it is hard not to admire, persuaded him that he should abandon his co-conspirators, who only meant to harm them both.

He realised she was right, and the pair of them came up with a scheme to enable them to escape from Edinburgh and ride as hard as they could for Dunbar Castle. Messages were left with Melville for Moray, and further messengers sent from Dunbar to the lords in exile in Newcastle to return. Their doings were as nothing in Mary's eyes, compared with the slaughter of her servant in her presence – a proceeding that was surely intended to cause her to miscarry, and perhaps die. If murdering Rizzio were their only goal, Morton and his allies could have done it anywhere.

Moray, who was not, perhaps, as ruthless as some of his fellow nobles, was overcome with remorse when he saw Mary, who kissed and hugged him. He promised to have nothing to do with Morton and his crew.

Chapter 175: Reconciliation?

Melville was delighted that Mary and Moray were reconciled, and tried to persuade her to forgive Darnley, casting the blame on George Douglas for leading him astray – but his words fell on deaf ears. The Queen had nothing but a '*great grudge*' in her heart against her husband. Darnley, failing to understand that he was now in a dangerous position, then worked himself up, complaining to Melville because Moray had written only to Mary, not recognising him as king.

Darnley enquired as to the whereabouts of Morton and the rest, to which Melville replied that he had no idea. The King's answer was brusque – '*as they have brewed, so let them drink,*' but Melville believed that Darnley regretted abandoning them. Her purpose won, Mary was being extremely cold. Hardly surprising, one might think, when her husband conspired against her, killed her friend in her presence, and allowed men to mishandle her – Ruthven even pointing a gun at her pregnant belly.

Melville tried to patch things up – he seems to have thought better of Darnley than did most others of his acquaintance – saying his folly was due to poor advice, and inexperience rather than ill-will. Mary became so fed up with Melville's support of Darnley that Moray was dispatched to tell him to cease his interference.

A new character now enters centre-stage in the Scottish court, James Hepburn, Earl of Bothwell. Bothwell was one of the few Scots lords who had never been paid by either France or England, and it appeared that, together with his confederates, the Earl of Huntly, and the Bishop of Ross, he was unhappy that Moray had been received back into favour. Mary was reverting to the advice that Melville and Throckmorton had given – to court Moray to appease the Protestant faction in England, but Bothwell suggested that Moray should be held under house arrest while

Mary was in childbed, to prevent him inviting Morton and the other banished lords back home.

Melville claims to have dissuaded her from this notion, but his own position was awkward. His brother, Sir Robert, who was now Ambassador to Elizabeth, had been asking the English government to send Morton out of England. At the same time, Melville's sister, Margaret, who was married to Morton's relative, Sir John Johnstone of Elphinstone, asked her brother to write to the Elector Palatine, to give Morton refuge. Melville showed the letters to the Queen, and discussed both Moray and Morton with her. She decided not to put Moray under arrest, but Melville was forbidden to do anything to help Morton.

A new Ambassador came from England, none other than the Henry Killigrew who had helped Melville following the Battle of St Quentin. At this point in his memoirs, Melville only mentions that Killigrew was an old friend, who had been known to him in France. He does not mention a warmer relationship, however, a couple of letters from both Melville and his brother Robert, suggest that the acquaintanceship was in fact, very close. Killigrew's wife, Katherine Cooke, was the sister of Mildred Cooke, who was wife to Sir William Cecil, Elizabeth's Secretary of State. Killigrew had been at the heart of English diplomacy since Elizabeth's accession.

Killigrew was to confirm to Mary that Morton and the others had been sent publicly out of England (although, in fact, they were there in hiding, to the English government's knowledge). He was also to congratulate Mary on her escape from the rebels, but was to question her about her dealings with the Irish chieftain, O'Neill.

The English government had also sent a spy, one Rokeby, who claimed to be a Catholic and a supporter of Mary's right to the English succession. The plan was for him to worm his way into Mary's confidence and report back to Cecil on her plans. Melville's brother got wind of the plot and warned Melville and Mary, so that when Ambassador Killigrew huffed and puffed about Mary entertaining Rokeby, a rebellious English subject, Mary immediately had the spy arrested and all his papers taken, amongst which were found letters from Cecil.

Rokeby was clapped into prison, and Mary, continuing to hide her knowledge that he was a spy, told Killigrew that he had been apprehended to please Elizabeth, who could have him delivered to her custody as soon as she liked.

Anticipating the birth of her child, Mary again prepared to send Melville to England, drafting letters lacking only the information on the child's gender, and requesting Elizabeth to send suitable god-parents, to promote friendship between them.

Chapter 176: England Again

Melville waited in Edinburgh Castle, praying for Mary to bear a healthy son. Between ten and eleven in the morning of 19th June, 1566, the Queen's lady-in-waiting, Lady Boyd, came with the good news that mother and son were doing well. Melville set out for London, reaching Berwick by nightfall, and London on the fourth day. He went first to his brother, then to Cecil, but asked them to keep it secret until he was in Elizabeth's presence. He travelled with Cecil to Greenwich, where Elizabeth was dancing after supper. Cecil whispered in her ear. Silence fell. The Queen put her hands to her head and sank onto a cushion, saying:

'the Queen of Scots [was] lighter of a fair son, whilst [she was] but a barren stock.'

The next morning, the Melville brothers were sent for. They were privately told that Elizabeth was deeply depressed by the news, but had been advised to put a good face on it, which she immediately proceeded to do, telling them the news had cheered her immensely, after a fortnight of illness.

Melville told Elizabeth that the news had been sent first to her, as Mary knew she would rejoice. He added, off his own bat, that although she was delighted to have a son, Mary had been so badly treated, that she wished she had never married. Elizabeth was once again toying with the idea of matrimony, so Melville was keen to discourage her.

Elizabeth accepted the invitation to stand godmother. It would be a good opportunity, he said, for the queens to meet. Alas, however, although Elizabeth was eager to meet her '*dear sister*', affairs would not permit her to travel. She would send proxies.

Melville then reported on Killigrew, explaining his long stay in Scotland by his waiting for Mary to give birth. He thanked the Queen on Mary's behalf for sending Morton and the others out of the country – he did not believe the rumours that they were being hidden – surely none of her subjects could be so disobedient! Indeed not, returned Elizabeth. If such a thing transpired to be true, severe punishment would follow. He also offered to send the alleged criminal Rokeby back, but Elizabeth seemingly forgot to ask him to arrange it.

It appeared to Melville that Leicester, Pembroke and the Duke of Norfolk were even more supportive of Mary being named heir, now that she had a son. Only Cecil seemed to have doubts. Melville assured Elizabeth that Mary would not dream of pushing herself forward into Elizabeth's shoes, she only wished to be named as successor.

The birth of the Prince, the Queen returned smoothly, just made it more urgent for the English lawyers to determine the legal position.

When Melville pointed out that she had made the same point a year before, she told him that the proxies she would send for the christening would tell Mary more. He clearly was not going to receive confirmation of Mary's position, so Melville returned to Scotland, leaving his brother behind, but the richer by a chain from the Queen.

He found Mary depressed and with a poor appetite – not recovered from the events surrounding the murder of Rizzio, and the threat to her life. Melville tried to cheer her, assuring her of many friends in both Scotland and England. He also suggested that forgiving Morton and the others would be a good move. Mary promised to think on the matter, and began to talk of allowing the rebels to be restored. Bothwell, getting wind of this, began to commune with them secretly.

The Earl of Bedford and the French and Spanish Ambassadors were to come to Stirling for the christening and Melville was sent to meet the Earl at Coldingham. Bedford was accompanied by a large group of English lords and gentlemen, including Master Carey, son of Elizabeth's cousin, Lord Hunsdon, and Sir Christopher Hatton, who, although a great friend of Elizabeth, was widely believed to be a Catholic, and a supporter of Mary's.

The English representatives were well treated, but were somewhat shocked at the little account paid to Darnley. They told Melville to advise Mary to treat him more respectfully, as it reflected badly on her to be at odds with her husband.

Mary began to recover her spirits, and rode to the Border to give justice in person, as her father, James V, and grandfather, James IV, had done. Bothwell and Huntly were both with her, and, according to Melville, tried to plot the death of Moray, but were prevented by Lord Home.

The Queen rode as far as Berwick, now in English hands, and was greeted with an artillery display. The Warden of Berwick, Sir John

Foster, came to meet her, to discuss peace-keeping. Whether his horse was frightened by the noise or for some other reason, it reared up, and tried to bite the Queen's horse in the neck, before striking Mary a severe blow on the thigh with a front hoof. The mortified Sir John leapt off his horse and fell to the ground, begging pardon. Mary graciously told him that she was not hurt, but was obliged to stay at Castle Home for two days.

Bothwell was riding high – he persuaded Mary to allow Morton to return. Mary then set about trying to reconcile Bothwell, Huntly, Argyll and Moray, and was successful, at least on the surface.

Chapter 177: The Murder of Darnley

Whilst Mary was in the Borders, Darnley followed her about miserably, but received short shrift. He retired to Glasgow, where he fell ill. On partial recovery, he moved to a house at Kirk O'Fields, where Mary visited him, and the two appeared to be moving towards a reconciliation.

According to Melville himself, although he was writing with hindsight and we should be careful of being wise after the event, there were rumours current in Edinburgh that Bothwell meant to harm Darnley. So when the King was found dead in the garden of his house, following an explosion, the finger of suspicion was immediately pointed at the Earl.

Melville went to the Queen, but was told by Bothwell that she was too upset to see anyone. In the meantime, Melville could look at Darnley's body, which had not suffered a mark – he had actually escaped from the house before the explosion, and, it was presumed, had been suffocated. Melville reports that he could not actually get a sight of the corpse, which was being guarded by one Alexander Durem.

Then an even more damaging rumour began to circulate – that Bothwell (a Protestant), recently married to the Catholic Lady Jean Gordon, sister of the Earl of Huntley, would divorce Lady Jean to marry the Queen. Mary's nobles were shocked and appalled at the dishonour this would bring on their Queen. One of them, Sir John Maxwell, 4th Lord Herries, and a Protestant himself, went on his knees to Mary to beg her to put any idea of marrying Bothwell out of her mind. Mary assured Herries that she had no such intent.

Melville, planning to second Herries' plea, received a letter from a man named Thomas Bishop. Bishop was a Scot, and had been for a long time in the service of the Earl of Lennox, with whose wife he quarrelled bitterly. From information that Melville could not have known, it seems likely that Bishop was also in the pay of Sir William Cecil, and Leicester at different times.

Bishop's story is so convoluted that it is hard to know whose side he was on, but Melville obviously took him at face value. Bishop wrote that England was full of rumours that Mary was to marry Bothwell, believed to be Darnley's murderer, and advised Melville to warn her strongly that such an action would lead to her downfall.

Melville took the letter to the Queen, who read it, and returned it. She then called Lethington over to read it, and told him that the letter was a ploy of Melville's own, to ruin Bothwell. Lethington took Melville aside, and, having read the letter, warned him to leave Edinburgh, as Bothwell would kill him.

When Bothwell returned, Mary informed him of the letter, asking him to leave Melville alone, but Melville, fearing Lethington was true in his estimate of Bothwell's character, went into hiding until Mary was able to persuade Bothwell to cease threatening him. Apparently, the Queen told Bothwell that he would leave her with no friends at all. Melville then returned to her side, telling her the letter truly had come from Bishop, but even if he had made it up, she should still listen to advice from those who wished her well. Mary again denied planning to marry Bothwell, but would not be drawn far into the topic.

A few days later, Mary travelled to Stirling to see her baby, Prince James, and on her return journey, she, together with Melville, the Earl of Huntly and Lethington, were abducted by Bothwell and his henchman, Captain Blackater, and carried off to Dunbar. Blackater told Melville that the Queen was party to the abduction, but that has been disputed.

Melville was allowed to leave Dunbar – presumably Bothwell did not want anyone stiffening any resolve Mary might have to resist him. During this period Bothwell and Mary slept together – whether he forced her has been a bone of contention for 450 years.

Bothwell persuaded a portion of the nobility to petition Mary to marry him. He divorced his wife and the pair were married on 15th May 1567. Mary was still only 24 years old – she had lost two husbands, been abducted and perhaps raped. Nowadays, we might think that she had fallen into the common syndrome of putting all her trust in the man who was abusing her. For her subjects, however, her actions were seen as adulterous, dishonourable and demeaning to her position.

Melville had avoided the court since he had been released from Dunbar, but was present at the marriage. Here, we find a small slice of the man's own appearance and personality. Bothwell said that Melville had been quite the stranger – he should sit down and dine with him. Melville replied shortly that he had already eaten. Well, then they should drink together, came the reply, as Bothwell thrust a cup of wine on Melville for them to toast each other, like, as Melville says contemptuously, '*Dutchmen*'. Melville merely sipped at the wine. Bothwell told him to drink up, until he put some weight on, for '*the zeal of the common weal has eaten you up and made you so lean.*' Melville replied that, whilst he should try to be useful, it was up to Bothwell and the nobles to consider the public good. Bothwell then started to talk of women, '*speaking such filthy language*' that Melville hurried away, a small outpost of sober dutifulness amidst a sea of self-serving brutes.

He went to the Queen, who was, unsurprisingly, glad to see him. Ever since she had returned to Scotland, she had tried to inculcate a more cultured and sophisticated court, but all her work was undone.

Chapter 178: Queen Mary's Downfall

Melville now became concerned as to the fate of Mary's son, Prince James. The child was in the keeping of the Earl of Mar, at Stirling, but Bothwell, apparently, was trying to get the child into his own hands and Mar was worried that once the Prince was in Bothwell's power, he would not make old bones.

Melville was unable to help directly, but aware that Sir James Balfour, who was the Keeper of Edinburgh Castle, and a former crony of Bothwell's, had quarrelled with him and refused to take part in the murder of Darnley, Melville went to Balfour, and told him to hold on to the castle. By so doing he might be able to help both Prince James and Queen Mary, who was now in such a state of despair that she was threatening to harm herself. If Balfour handed over the castle, he would be pursued with Bothwell for the murder of the late King.

For that faction of the nobility who were not supporters of Bothwell, were now hoping to pursue him for the murder, and planned to crown James as King. Bothwell was warned that a march on Holyrood was planned, so he left abruptly, taking Mary with him, and raced for Dunbar.

Melville had been a faithful supporter of Mary during her active reign, but once Bothwell was in the picture, his allegiance to Moray came to the fore. Moray and the Lords raised an army, and so did Bothwell and the Queen. The forces met at Carberry Hill on 15th June 1567. Many in Bothwell's army believed that Mary was secretly in league with Lords, because he had treated her so badly. From the events, this appears to be true. No battle was fought, but negotiations resulted in Mary leaving her army and returning to Edinburgh with the Lords.

This should have been a liberation for her, but she had been double-crossed again, the Lords had no intention of allowing her to resume power. She was shouted at and insulted in the streets as a whore and a murderer.

It has been pointed out, by Robert Stedall in his *'The Challenge to the Crown: The Struggle for Supremacy in the Reign of Mary, Queen of Scots'* that one of the reasons the Lords were eager to replace Mary with another minor was financial. Under Scots law, when a sovereign reached the age of twenty-five, he or she could resume all lands that had been granted away during his or her minority. Mary would be twenty-five in the forthcoming December, and, as the Crown was in a poor financial state would be very likely to do so. Another long minority would allow the nobility to continue to help themselves to Crown lands.

Whether their reasons were financial, religious or political, Mary was imprisoned at Lochleven. Whilst there, she was bullied into abdicating, having been assured, by Melville's brother, who remained one of her staunchest supporters, that anything done under duress could not be binding. Still trusting her brother, Moray, most of all the lords, she requested he be appointed as Regent.

There were now two parties in Scotland – the Queen's Party, that believed she had abdicated under duress, and the King's Party, who wished for a Regency. Melville seems to have equivocated somewhat. Initially, there was no open rupture, and Melville was sent to Berwick to meet Moray (who had been in France, avoiding both the death of Darnley, and its aftermath). Melville also had a commission from those in the King's Party who had only wished for the overthrow of Bothwell, and not for the deposition of Mary, to encourage Moray to make terms with the Queen that would bring her back to power, guided by him.

Moray, after some pressing, accepted the Regency, but when he went to Mary in Lochleven they quarrelled so bitterly (because, according to Melville he used *'language to break her heart')* that *'it cut the thread of credit and love between the Queen and [Moray] for ever.'*

In the meantime, as Melville notes, the English did all they could to *'kindle the fire'*, promising support to both sides, sending embassies under Throckmorton, Drury, Randolph, Davison and others. Apparently Throckmorton was so disgusted by the double-dealing of his own colleagues that he leaked information to Melville.

Mary then escaped from Lochleven Castle and supported by a good number of the nobles, took up arms. According to Melville, this all happened too soon – that Moray, over time, would have softened his stance and restored her. The Queen however, was pushed into giving battle early – she would have preferred to make a base at Dumbarton Castle and gather support gradually, but the Hamiltons, who were her chief supporters, were keen for battle.

At Langside on 13th May 1568, the Queen's forces were defeated, and she lost courage, which, Melville comments, she had never done before. Mary fled to England, and was never permitted her freedom again.

Chapter 179: Melville's Marriage

A commission was convened by Queen Elizabeth at York in October 1568 to look into whether Mary had been involved in the death of

Darnley. Moray and others of the King's Party were present, including Melville and his adoptive father, Henry Balnaves. The Commission was then moved to Hampton Court. The results were inconclusive, as Elizabeth had no intention of allowing Mary to be either convicted or cleared.

On his return to Scotland following the Commission, Melville got married for the first time, or so it appears. On 29th June 1569, a deed was presented before the Lords of Session, of whom Balnaves was one, to be registered. Dated both Balmuto and Edinburgh, the deed provided for the marriage of James Melville, adopted son of Balnaves, to marry Christian Boswell, daughter of Sir David Boswell of Balmuto.

It seems likely that the Boswells were connections of Balnaves' wife, who left £12 for the dowry of Helen Boswell in her will, although the relationship between Helen and Christian is unknown. There is no information as to whether Melville and Christian had any say in the matter of their marriage. They went on to have four children, two boys and two girls. In February of the following year, Balnaves died, and Melville inherited his lands at Halhill.

No mention is made of any other wife, before or after, however, a letter in the Cecil Papers at Hatfield gives a startling idea that Melville was at some point married to the sister of Henry Killigrew.

In June 1560, there is a letter addressed from Melville to Killigrew, in which he refers to him as *'his gentle brother'*. It is possible that the two men were so close they called each other brother (although that doesn't seem to have been a common practice) or, that Melville was married to Killigrew's sister, but that she died before he married Christian Boswell. However, there is a later letter of Melville's dated 7th December, 1583, also addressing Killigrew as *'brother'*, and, in the post-script, adding,

'*Your sister my wyf [wife] has hir hartly recommendit unto zow [you]*' that is, your sister, my wife, sends her hearty recommendations to you.

There are also letters in which Melville's brother, Robert, refers to Killigrew as brother.

So, it is a mystery – was Melville married twice? If so, which was the first wife? Or did the marriage to Christian never take place? But, if Melville were already married, why would Balnaves try to arrange a marriage to Christian? Further, if Melville had kept a marriage to Miss Killigrew secret, he would have had to confess it rather than commit bigamy with Christian. It would be surprising if such a confession resulted in a bequest to Melville's wife in the will Balnaves made less than six months after the bond to marry Christian.

It is a mystery, which our research has not yet solved!

Chapter 180: Regencies of Moray and Lennox.

Moray's Regency began to degenerate into faction, and quarrels. Melville, a firm supporter of Moray, tried to advise him, but his opinion of the Regent was that he was '*good with good company, wise with wise company, stout with stout company, and contrariwise with others of contrary qualities.*'

The Regent was assassinated by a member of the Hamilton family (who were of the Queen's Party) in January 1570. In his stead, the Earl of Lennox, grandfather to King James, was suggested as Regent. At the same time, the Earl of Sussex was approaching the border with a large army. Melville was sent by a group who, whilst part of the King's Party, were sympathetic to the Queen, to see what Sussex' intentions were.

Melville was greeted courteously and even lent the Earl's own furred nightgown (not a sleeping garment, more like an informal evening coat) as a token of how welcome he was. Sussex was full of gracious words – he respected the Queen of Scots, and her son, whom he took to be his own Queen's next heirs; he was not planning to assist either side or involve himself in Scotland's internal affairs. He was, in fact, just following orders.

Melville left the English camp, convinced that Sussex was, in truth, there to support the installation of Lennox as Regent and to promise assistance to the King's Party, whilst also sending messages of support to the Queen's Party, thus to foment further strife in Scotland. The Lennox and Hamilton families had been enemies for generations, so the appointment of Lennox as Regent would certainly limit any chance of reconciliation between the two sides.

Sussex crossed the border and took two castles, one of which was Home, driving Lord Home into the Queen's Party.

Melville, who had been a supporter of the Darnley marriage, was on good terms with Lennox, and went to visit him. Lennox told Melville that Lady Lennox had recommended that he listen to advice from both Melville and his brother. The best advice that Melville could give was for Lennox to refuse the Regency, as it would probably cost him his life. He warned Lennox that he would have enemies (including a small group, originally in the King's Party, but alienated by Moray, who were now holding Edinburgh Castle for the Queen). Melville promised to serve Lennox as Regent.

One of Lennox' first actions was to capture a castle in the hands of the Queen's Party. Melville had planned to ride with him, in part because he had been promised lands at Monimail, formerly in the possession of the Bishop of St Andrews, and then owned by Henry Balnaves. He was persuaded to stay in Edinburgh by the English ambassador, Sir Thomas Randolph, to try to broker a peace with the members of the Queen's Party, still holding out in Edinburgh Castle. Randolph said he would speak to Lennox about the lands, making sure they were given to Melville.

Melville now claims to have been hoodwinked by Randolph. He believed Randolph to be his friend, as he had helped him during Randolph's exile in France during the reign of Mary I of England. Randolph told Melville that he himself believed (in his personal capacity, not as Ambassador) that the only true authority in Scotland was Mary, and so Melville became a go-between Randolph and Sir William Kirkcaldy of Grange, who was holding the castle.

Kirkcaldy had originally been one of the King's Party, but was increasingly disaffected, and after Moray's death, had changed sides. Kirkcaldy and Melville had been friends for many years. In Melville's view, Kirkcaldy was still open to reconciliation with Lennox, as he believed that internal strife in Scotland was just giving more opportunity to England to stir up trouble.

Randolph suggested that Kirkcaldy surrender the castle to an English appointee, at which point Kirkcaldy refused to have any further discussions. His position hardened, and he refused to give up the castle to the King's Party.

Melville quarrelled with Randolph, probably because he failed to obtain the promised lands for him – even supporting their grant elsewhere. He now saw, or so he says, that Randolph had only meant to sow dissension.

There are two letters, written a fortnight apart in March 1572 from Melville to Randolph. In the first he talks of their old friendship and says he prefers to stay quietly in the country and not involve himself in affairs. In the second, he addresses him in very stiff language, requesting him to desist from harrying Melville's widowed mother, who feared that Randolph would burn her property in revenge for attacks upon Morton.

Chapter 181: Regencies of Mar and Morton

Lennox had a rival for the Regency, in the Earl of Morton, and within the King's Party there were supporters of both. Melville, continuing in his support for Lennox, because, he says, there was no point in hoping for the Queen to be freed, was taken into custody by the Earl of Buchan, with a threat to try him for some unspecified crime. The purpose, apparently, was to use him as a hostage to persuade Kirkcaldy to surrender Edinburgh Castle. Melville pointed out that the Castle group were so angry with him, that this plan could never work.

Nevertheless, Kirkcaldy obviously did retain some affection for him as he sent a secret message to Melville with an escape plan. Melville rejected the offer, saying he knew Buchan would not harm him, and he was eventually freed.

Melville gives his reasons for supporting the King's Party, as that he could see no hope for Mary to ever be freed – the English government would never let her go, and although the French might complain, they would not help. Catherine de Medici did not like her former daughter-in-law and, from the French perspective, the uniting of England and Scotland under a single monarch would be a poor proposition. Mary's relatives, the Guises, had never done more than use her for their own advantage. Spain too, would not help Mary, as it had enough to do with its problems in controlling Flanders.

Kirkcaldy now came up with a plan that, he hoped, would reconcile the two parties. The King's Party were planning to hold a Parliament at Stirling, so Kirkcaldy sent for as many as possible of the Queen's Party to surprise the others at Stirling, and take control of the Regent and his government, so an agreement could be worked out. Inevitably, matters went awry, and Lennox was shot, despite it having been agreed beforehand that there would be no violence. Kirkcaldy was beside himself as any hope of concord now disappeared.

Randolph pushed forward the Earl of Morton as Regent – Morton being decidedly pro-English, but the King's Party preferred the Earl of Mar. Whilst there was not open warfare, there were endless skirmishes between the groups.

Mar retired to Stirling, and Randolph, now hated by both sides, returned to England. Henry Killigrew, who had been on previous embassies, and had once been Melville's friend, now returned as ambassador. He was charged, he told Melville, with promoting peace – although the Queen of England favoured the Queen's Party. Melville then rounded on his former friend, saying that he knew that Killigrew was only in Scotland to make more trouble, and that as fellow-Protestants the English ministers should be ashamed of themselves for encouraging discord. Killigrew had to admit that his real intention was to see Morton installed as Regent.

Regent Mar sent for Melville to act yet again as go-between with the Queen's Party. Mar seems to have been an honest man, desperate for peace and reconciliation in Scotland. Melville was to ask Kirkcaldy for terms for surrender of the Castle. Kirkcaldy said that he would not sell himself for profit, but that his party would come to terms and support the Regent for so long as the Queen was detained in England, and that, should she be freed, he was sure she and her son could be reconciled.

Mar and Kirkcaldy came to terms, but, before their agreement could be shared with the rest of the King's Party, Mar died. He had recently dined with Morton, and there were suggestions of poison, but it was probably natural.

Morton then summoned Melville and persuaded him that he would fulfil the agreement made by Mar, to finally bring an end to the civil strife. He wanted to make peace with all of the Queen's Party, he said, and Kircaldy would be suitably rewarded. So Melville went back to Kirkcaldy, and persuaded him that he should surrender. Kirkcaldy agreed, on the proviso that Huntly and the Hamiltons, who were Mary's strongest adherents, but not involved in the holding of the Castle, should be included in the general peace. He refused to receive any sweeteners himself.

Morton did not like this – he had no intention of coming to terms with the rich Huntly and Hamilton families – there would be no profit in that! He just wanted reconciliation with the relatively poor Kirkcaldy.

Kirkcaldy was shocked, telling Melville it would disgrace him to abandon Huntly and the Hamiltons (who all along would have been happy to be reconciled with the King's Party.) He would prefer that they should betray him, than that he himself should act dishonourably. Nevertheless, he would surrender the Castle if the rest of the Queen's Party were included in discussion.

Melville carried this message back and agreed with Morton that the Castle would be surrendered in six months' time, once Morton had shown he intended to keep faith. This was agreed to and Morton then sent messages to Huntly and the Hamiltons who agreed terms.

Immediately he had half of the Queen's Party on side Morton proclaimed that Kirkcaldy and the others in the Castle were traitors and had refused to come to reasonable terms. Morton collected English troops to besiege the Castle, and, owing to the dry summer, Kirkcaldy was obliged to surrender as the wells ran dry. Among the men in the castle were two of Melville's brothers.

It was agreed with Kirkcaldy that he and his colleagues would be brought into the King's Peace, and their lands restored, but after three days of liberty, during which time they stayed with the English Warden of Berwick, a letter was received from Queen Elizabeth, ordering the Warden to hand over the men to Morton. Melville's brother's life was spared, on petition from Killigrew. Lord Home was spared but died soon after, but Kirkcaldy, who could claim to be the only honourable man in Scotland, was hanged on 3rd August 1573.

Morton, having disposed of all of his rivals, and supported by the English, proved an effective Regent, although there were many who disliked him, and believed him to be an extortioner.

Chapter 182: Childhood of James VI

Melville seems to have taken a step back from public affairs at this point, although where he was, and how he passed is time, is unknown. Presumably, he was at Halhill with his wife, bringing up a young family.

He recounts how the young King, James, was brought up at Stirling by Lady Mar, and the Lord Erskine, neither of whom were friends to Morton. Morton was forced to resign in 1578 when James was twelve, but attempted to regain power in 1579. In 1580, he was publicly accused of murdering Darnley, and arrested. The English, displeased by the overthrow of their preferred Regent, made warlike noises, but James and his advisors (his cousin, Esme Stuart, Duke of Lennox, who was nephew of the assassinated Regent Lennox, and Lord James Stewart, Earl of Arran) raised taxation for an army, and the English retreated – not so enamoured of Morton that they wished to go to war.

The young King's favouring of Lennox and Arran was not popular with his other lords, and a scheme was hatched to deal with them.

Lennox had converted to the Presbyterian faith that was now the official religion of Scotland, but his conversion was considered suspect.

In 1582, Melville reappears at the forefront of affairs. He had been appointed a Justice in Ayre in West Lothian. One morning, an unknown man came into his bedroom with a story of a plot against Lennox, Arran and the King. Melville warned Lennox, but it was too late. James had been captured and was being held at Stirling Castle by a group who became known as the Lords Enterprisers.

Both Queen Elizabeth and King Henri III of France sent messages to James, assuring him they would help him escape, but James, aged sixteen, was too wise to fall into the trap of accepting foreign aid. He was very happy in the care of his subjects, he said, who had mistakenly thought ill of the Duke of Lennox and Earl of Arran.

James, however, was just biding his time. He called a meeting of his nobles at St Andrew's, ostensibly to hear the report of two ambassadors he had sent to England. He summoned to it all of the Lords who had not been involved in his detention, including Melville. Melville was loath to attend – he was tired of public life, and the strife and factions he had seen in his many years of service, and had hoped to continue a quiet life in retirement. He was now in his late forties – not considered very old by the standards of the day, but certainly not young.

However, duty called, and he trundled off to James at Falkland, where he listened to James complaining about how badly he had been treated. Melville pointed out that minorities were always difficult times, with factions and self-seeking abounding but that the best thing for a King to do on attaining his majority, was to forget the past. James, not entirely taking Melville's advice, rode on to St Andrew's having made a proclamation that only such lords as he had sent for should meet him there. Melville was angry, believing that the Lords Enterprisers would ignore the orders and come to St Andrew's quicker than the ones sent for. His misgivings were proven correct as uninvited lords and their retinues turned up.

James however, persuaded them that he would let bygones be bygones, and that he bore no grudge for his imprisonment. He then called Melville up before the whole court, and praised him for his good advice —much to Melville's embarrassment, and also annoyance, as he was already disliked for having given the King warning of the plot against him.

In due course, James' friend, the Earl of Arran, petitioned to be allowed back to court. James asked Melville's advice and received the answer that for him to hide the truth would imperil James, but to tell it would imperil Melville. On being asked to explain, Melville told James that Arran was a trouble maker, and that if he were returned to favour, factions would break out again. If Arran found out that he had advised James against returning him to favour, Melville's life would be endangered.

James decided that Arran should be allowed back to court once, so that his other lords could see that Arran should be well-treated, but that Arran should then retire. Arran, however, refused to leave and soon regained the King's ear. In Melville's opinion, things went from bad to worse as Arran prevented the King from hearing other advice.

Melville was not the only one to advise James to be rid of Arran. Elizabeth wrote, reprimanding him for going back on his promise to treat all his lords equally. Melville was deputed to draft an answer, which was along the lines of telling Elizabeth to mind her own business.

Arran now had considerable influence, and, as Melville had predicted, wanted to get him out of the way. He suggested that Melville be sent on an embassy to England. Melville was summoned to Stirling, where he handed the King a long letter, full of advice on good governance. On being told of the plan to send him to England, Melville told the King that the English would never respect James and consider him as the heir to the English Crown until he had got his own house in order, and that it was not the right time for an embassy. James accepted the advice and allowed Melville to return home.

Chapter 183: Breach with Arran

Elizabeth had followed up her letter of admonition with an ambassador who proved to be none other than that Puritan enemy of Mary, Queen of Scots, Sir Francis Walsingham. Melville, who had known Walsingham for many years, was sent to meet him and bring him to James.

Walsingham met the King, and claimed to be very impressed with him, but refused to have anything to do with Arran, who got his revenge by substituting a diamond ring sent to Walsingham from the King with a glass one.

James suggested that Melville might become his Secretary, but Melville refused. Melville and Arran quarrelled in Council, when Arran shouted that Melville's love for the Lords Enterprisers would ruin the King. Melville replied smartly that Arran's love for their lands would do the job. This open breach eventuated in Melville being removed from the Council, with the excuse from James that it would be unsuitable to have two brothers on the Council (Sir Robert Melville had been a Councillor for many years). Nevertheless, James added, when he married, Melville would be appointed as Councillor to his Queen.

Glad to be relieved of involvement in a government he feared was heading for disaster, Melville consented to go to England again, and an obsequious letter to Elizabeth was penned. Before he could depart,

Melville again took James to task about favouring the Earl of Arran, who, he said was undermining James' promise to forgive the Lords Enterprisers. Arran demanded to know why Melville was undermining him, and asked who he thought should be around the King instead?

The two men lost their tempers, and Arran swore that he would kill Melville if he *'fished in his waters'* again. Melville shouted back that he would find more honest men to protect him than Arran would find throat-cutters to kill him.

James, angry at such a scene, sent a rebuke to Arran, who retired in a sulk to Edinburgh Castle, not returning until Melville left the court, believing the King did not want him to remain. The mission to England was dropped.

So James' reign continued, with continual strife between Arran and the other lords, culminating in the execution of the Earl of Gowrie, Arran's particular bete noir.

Another embassy arrived from London, led by William Davison, which had orders this time to deal with Arran. Melville again believed that the English were just plotting to keep the factions alive in Scotland, especially as Arran was persuaded to prevent James marrying for at least three years.

The English Council had yet another trick up its sleeve. They sent a new Ambassador, named Wootton, who was to be the King's friend and to spend time with him hunting and in other pastimes. Melville had met Wootton thirty years before, at the French Court, when he had tried to trick the Constable, Montmorency, into breaking the peace with England. Melville did not trust him and warned James to beware. James however, took to Wootton.

Melville was proved right. It was time for James to look for a wife, and a Danish Embassy arrived to begin negotiations. According to

Melville, Arran and Wootton between them did everything they could to undermine negotiations and the Danish ambassadors were mistreated and insulted.

Melville explained to the offended Danes that, although the Queen of England was a *'wise princess'* there were many about her who did not wish James to be her successor, and so were making every effort to prevent James forming alliances or marrying. He then informed James of the insults that the Danes were receiving and persuaded him to treat them well.

Arran was about to get his come-uppance. A disturbance on the Border resulted in a murder, for which he was held responsible, and imprisoned. After a few days he was released, but commanded to return to his own lands.

Chapter 184: Last Years of Service

Further uprisings and plots occurred in the 1580s, and eventually Arran was completely dismissed, as James took more power into his own hands. Melville remained a member of the Privy Council but began to withdraw from affairs. Several embassies were proposed for Melville – to England, to Spain, to Denmark and even to Navarre but he refused them all, preferring to retire to his lands at Halhill. Nevertheless, he continued to correspond with both Scottish and English lords, including Archibald Douglas, 8th Earl of Angus, whom he thanked in 1588 for sending a pair of virginals as a gift for Melville's daughter.

He even refused a final embassy to Denmark, to treat of the King's marriage to Anne of Denmark – suggesting his brother be sent instead.

On the arrival of the Queen Anne, Melville was summoned back to court to meet her. He was knighted at her coronation on 17th May, 1590 and was appointed to her Council, where he served for some years. Initially, the Queen did not like him, but she warmed to him over time.

During the 1590s more plots and attempts to control James were discovered, and it is with an air of weariness that Melville recounts the endless shufflings for favour, raids in the night, and private quarrels that spilled over into the court. In particular, there was the strange case of the Earl of Bothwell (not Queen Mary's husband) who was accused of witchcraft and then attempted to abduct the King.

As often as he could, he returned to his own home at HalHill. On the birth of James and Anne's first son, Melville was detailed to entertain various ambassadors. The King of France failed to send an Ambassador, and Queen Elizabeth was so late in doing so, that the baptism was postponed, and Melville was ordered to keep the other ambassadors happy whilst James waited to hear from Elizabeth. He was then at the Queen's side as she graciously received the gifts from other countries.

In 1603, Elizabeth died, and James was proclaimed as James I of England. The majority of the court moved south, but Melville declined to go, finally retiring to Halhill, where he spent his time writings his memoirs, dying on 13th November 1617. The birth and death dates of his children are unknown, with the exception of his son Robert, who died in 1562.

Aspects of Sir James Melville's Life

Chapter 185: Links in a Chain

The word *'networking'* in the modern sense of expanding your influence by building relationships with a range of people who can support you, was not used in the sixteenth century. The concept, however, was at the heart of all political and family life.

No matter what stratum of society you were born into, the links of kinship and mutual obligation were cherished and reinforced, where possible, by marriage. It was expected that you would do a good turn for a family member, or someone recommended to you, and the recipient of your help, would, in turn, help you, or your family.

Similarly, if you quarrelled with someone, your *'affinity'* would be expected to quarrel too, leading to feuds lasting for generations.

In a small society, such as that of the Scottish Court, repeated intermarriages created a web of complex familial and patronage links. Without understanding these kinships, it can be very difficult to understand why certain factions coalesced or fought. Matters became even more complex in the mid-sixteenth century with the advent of the Reformation, which added a layer of religious agreement or dissent over old connections.

James Melville was no exception to the rule, and he was linked to many of the central players involved in the politics of the English and Scottish courts.

Starting with his family of birth, Melville had five brothers who survived to adulthood: John, Robert, David, William and Andrew, as well as three sisters. All six of the brothers had royal appointments. Robert and Andrew were both Masters of the Household to Queen Mary and James VI, William served the Prince of Orange, and Robert was also a long-serving ambassador at the English court. Andrew's first wife, Lady Jane Kennedy, was drowned in the storms that prevented the arrival of Anne of Denmark, and gave rise to the witchcraft trial of North Berwick. Lady Jane was probably the same Lady Jane Kennedy who attended Mary, Queen of Scots to her execution.

Both Robert and Andrew remained faithful to Queen Mary. Robert was besieged with other members of the Queen's Party in Edinburgh Castle, as Sir William Kirkcaldy of Grange held out against the Regents Moray, Lennox, Mar and Morton. It is likely that Kirkcaldy was, in fact, the Melvilles' brother-in-law, married to their sister Janet.

It seems straightforward, therefore, to assume that the Melvilles all supported the Queen's Party, but there were complications. Another sister, Margaret, was married to Lord Elphinstone, and he was a supporter of the Earl of Morton. When Morton was banished, following the murder of David Rizzio, in which he played a prominent part, Margaret asked Melville to plead for him.

More difficult to define were the relationships that Melville had with members of the English court. During his youth in France, a cohort of young, Protestant, Englishmen was also there, having gone into voluntary exile when Mary I came to the throne. Henri II of France, although quite as Catholic as Mary I, could not resist the opportunity to undermine the Queen of England by harbouring her enemies.

Amongst these young men who became friends of Melville were Nicholas Throckmorton of Coughton, and Henry Killigrew of Arwenack. Both Melville and his brother Robert became very close to Killigrew, and it is possible that Melville was married to one of his sisters. Killigrew himself was married to Katherine Cooke, whose sister, Mildred, was the wife of Sir William Cecil, Lord Burghley. Melville therefore had close contact, if not a family connection, with Queen Mary's most implacable enemy. Killigrew was so close to Cecil and Elizabeth, that he was the only one entrusted with their plan to hand Mary back to her Lords with a view to her being tried (and almost certainly executed) in Scotland.

Nicholas Throckmorton, senior to Killigrew in France, also played a role in Scottish politics. A cousin of Queen Katherine Parr, he was a strong adherent of the Reformed faith, yet he favoured Mary, Queen of Scot' right to succeed Elizabeth. Perhaps changing his mind, when Mary was deposed, he recommended Elizabeth support the rebel lords, but was later implicated in the Duke of Norfolk's plan to marry Mary.

Thomas Randolph was another friend of Melville's from the time Melville spent on the continent – they probably met in Germany, when Melville was in the service of the Elector Palatine, and Randolph was an English envoy. Randolph was trusted by the Protestant party in Scotland and had good relations with the Queen's half-brother, the Earl of Moray, who, although relied on by the Queen initially was certainly plotting behind her back, involved in both the murder of Rizzio, and the planning behind the death of Darnley. Melville and Randolph quarrelled when it appeared that Randolph was threatening to burn Melville's mother's land, in retaliation for attacks on the Regent Morton.

Another layer of obfuscation about motives and connections is added when the relationships between the various Regents of Scotland are considered. James Hamilton, Duke of Chatelherault (formerly the Earl of Arran) was considered to be the Queen's heir before the birth of her son. He was hated by his distant cousin, Lennox, who considered he had a greater right to the throne. When Lennox' son, Darnley, married the Queen, the Lennox star appeared to be rising.

On Darnley's death, Mary married the Earl of Bothwell, who was formerly brother-in-law to George Gordon, Earl of Huntly. Huntly and Moray were at daggers drawn, even though Huntly's wife was the aunt of Moray's wife.

Moray was half-brother to Morton's wife, who was Chatelherault's sister-in-law. Moray was also nephew to John Erskine, Earl of Mar, who succeeded Lennox as Regent. Lennox' wife, Lady Margaret Douglas, hated Morton, her first cousin, because her father's earldom of Angus had been bequeathed to his branch of the family...

These entangled relationships are just the tip of the iceberg – but it is quite impossible to understand what was going on in the politics of England and Scotland without knowing about these convoluted links. There were as well, all the usual human factors of affection, dislike, distrust and greed to mystify matters further.

Chapter 186: Melville's Inheritance

On 9th February, 1570 Henry Balnaves died. Balnaves was a *'Senator of Our Sovereign Lord's College of Justice'*, otherwise known as a Lord of Session. A native of Fife, Balnaves was born around 1502 but does not seem to have been of a particularly illustrious background. In 1526 he was enrolled in St Salvator's College, at the University of St Andrew's, suggesting that he was planning at one point to join the priesthood, as most university students did. Balnaves, however, specialised in law. After a period in the Low Countries and Cologne, during which he was converted to Protestantism, he returned to Scotland.

Back in Fife, he either became acquainted with, or renewed a friendship with Sir John Melville of Raith. Balnaves was employed as a treasurer by Sir James Kirkcaldy of Grange, whose wife was Sir John Melville's daughter, Janet. By 1537, he was an Advocate in front of the Court of Session, becoming a Lord of Session on 31st July 1538. On 8th August 1539 he and his wife, Christian Scheves, acquired lands at Halhill, East Colessie, in Fife from Sir Alexander Cumming of Inverlochy, with an entail to their lawful children.

It does not appear that Balnaves had any children, and when he made his will on 3rd January 1570, he named his adopted son, James Melville, as his heir and executor. The estate that Melville inherited included:

Lands at Halhill, with barns and barnyard

16 drawing oxen, worth £5 6s 4d each

4 cows, two with calves worth £4 per head

2 unknown animals, perhaps stirks, worth 40s each

23 ewes at 15s each

34 pigs at 10s each

70 bolls of oats at 13s 4d (a boll was a Scots measure equal to 5 bushels 3 pecks in English measure or about 600kg in metric)

13 bolls of wheat at 30s each (c. 108kg)

10 bolls of peas at 20s (c. 75 kg)

27 bolls of beer at 26s 4d each (possibly around 35 barrels in modern measurements of 36 gallons to the barrel)

Household goods and utensils to the value of £26 13s 8d.

Outstanding debts owed to the estate, for rent and crops £147 8s.

The whole estate was worth £421 6s 8d Scots (about £105 English) from which Melville was to pay various bequests, including £10 to the poor of Edinburgh.

Balnaves' best damask gown, lined with velvet, was left to Melville's wife, Christian Boswell, who was, perhaps, a relative of Mrs Balnaves. We can infer this because Mrs Balnaves left £12 to a lady named Helen Boswell. The remainder of Balnaves' silk clothes were left to Melville, and various other small bequests of money and clothes to family and friends.

To give an idea of the purchasing power of the money in 2015, a farm and buildings in Fife today would cost in the region of £600,000 – 700,000.

On the death of Melville in 1617, the lands passed to his eldest son, another James, but his direct descendants had died out by the early 18th century.

Chapter 187: Following the Footsteps of James Melville

Melville spent much of his youth in France, before journeying to the courts of European rulers, on behalf of the various men and women he served. Once back in Scotland, he travelled around Lowland Scotland with the Scottish Court as well as making several journeys south to the court of Elizabeth I.

The numbers in the article below correspond to those on the map which follows.

*

Melville was born in Raith (1), in Fife. Raith today is a suburb of Kirkcaldy, a pretty sea-side town with an unusually long sea-front. Fife was one of the first areas of Scotland to follow the Reformed faith, and the legacy has lasted through the centuries. Former British Prime Minister, Gordon Brown, son of the Presbyterian Minister of Kirkcaldy, sat for the Parliamentary seat from 1983 – 2015.

Melville's father, Sir John, was Captain of Dunbar Castle, but it is unlikely Melville went there during early childhood, although he knew it later. Together with his six brothers and three sisters, he probably remained at home.

In 1548, Sir John was executed for treason and his lands forfeit. It is not apparent exactly what provision was made for his children, but James and his older brother, Robert, were soon found court appointments. Marie of Guise, mother of the young Mary, Queen of Scots and later Regent, sent Robert to France with the Queen in 1548, and the following year, James, too, was sent there.

He travelled in the train of the Bishop of Vallance, and their first port of call was Ireland, which they reached after considerable time at sea, tossed by storms. They spent three weeks there, then returned to Dumbarton Castle (2). Dumbarton, one of the strongest forts in Scotland, is on the mouth of the River Clyde, and the usual sailing point for France by the western route. Dumbarton today is largely an 18th and 19th century structure, but its origins are a thousand years older, it having been the capital of the old Celtic kingdom of Strathclyde.

Following a brief visit to Stirling Castle (3) (well worth a visit to see the royal apartments) to report to Queen Marie on affairs in Ireland, the party set sail again, landing in France some three weeks later, battered again by storms.

Whilst in France, Melville fought at the Battle of St Quentin, now in the department of Aisne in Picardy, not far from the Belgian border. He was present at the negotiation of the peace treaty agreed after the battle at Le Cateau-Cambresis, near Bordeaux.

In the next couple of years Melville made a number of journeys around Europe. His first trip was a return home in 1559. It appears that, whenever possible, Melville travelled by land, and so on this occasion, he travelled via England. Probably the initial awful journey to France put him off sailing. He attended Queen Marie at Falkland Palace (4) in his native Fife. Falkland today is an extremely well preserved palace, open to the public and with many traces of the occupation of Marie of Guise, and James V.

Travelling back to France, Melville would have travelled down what is now the A1 – The Great North Road from London to Edinburgh. He stopped en route in Newcastle (5), whose Norman Castle overshadowed the small town at its foot. The Castle is open to the public, and gives a good idea of what life in the Borders was like, when Scotland and England were frequently at war.

Back on the continent, Melville travelled to the court of the Frederick III, Elector Palatine, in Heidelburg, and then on various embassies for Frederick, including to the court of Maximillian, King of the Romans, and soon to be Emperor, at Innsbruck. He also visited Venice and Rome, but left no information about his opinion of those cities.

He left the service of the Elector, to join that of Mary, Queen of Scots, who had returned to Scotland in 1561. On Mary's behalf, he undertook a couple of embassies to the court of Elizabeth I, attending Elizabeth at Hampton Court (6) on the first occasion. Hampton Court is open to the public and is one of the greatest palaces in England – don't miss an opportunity to see it!

On a subsequent visit he went to Westminster Palace (9). The only fragment of the original Westminster Palace to remain is Westminster Hall, whose great hammer-beam roof dates from the reign of Richard II. The palace Melville would have known burnt down in the Great Fire of

1834. The current Houses of Parliament stand more-or-less where the Palace was. Westminster Hall may be visited as part of a booked tour.

Mary's court moved around Scotland, and Melville attended her at St Johnstone, near Perth (7), where the castle had been in royal hands since the time of Robert the Bruce. Although there are other castles nearby, nothing remains of Perth Castle.

The Queen's favourite palace in Edinburgh was Holyroodhouse, largely built by her grandfather, James IV, and father, James V. It was the burial location of James V, and Mary's two elder brothers, who had died as infants. It was here that she married Lord Darnley on 29th July, 1565, a match approved of by Melville.

Holyroodhouse, the current Queen's official residence in Scotland, is delightfully situated in Edinburgh, surrounded by gardens, and with views to Arthur's Seat, the crag overlooking the city. It was here that the shocking murder of David Rizzio, Mary's secretary took place, in front of the pregnant Queen.

Mary retreated to Dunbar in East Lothian, where Melville's father had been Captain of the Castle, but then emerged and spent a short period at Haddington (11), where she instructed Melville to write letters summoning her estranged half-brother, Moray, home.

Mary, fearful for her own safety and that of her unborn child, chose the great fortress of Edinburgh Castle (9) to give birth to Prince James in 1566. Melville waited outside her apartments to hear of her delivery, before setting off for London to inform Elizabeth I. He reached Berwick (12) the same day. Berwick-upon-Tweed, now a small, pretty town, on the north side of the Tweed is one of the most fought over locations in British history. By the sixteenth century, it had settled into English hands, and was the location where many conferences and meetings took place between diplomats of both sides. Nevertheless, the border was not secure and a new encircling wall was built by the English, which may be seen today.

Four days after setting out with his good news, Melville arrived in London, and travelled down the river to make his announcement to Elizabeth at Greenwich (13). The site of the palace at Greenwich, called Placentia, is now covered by what were once the Royal Naval College buildings and is now the University of Greenwich.

Melville's last known trip out of Scotland was in 1568. Mary had been defeated at the Battle of Langside, and had escaped (or so she thought) into England. Alas, she was now trapped. Elizabeth, wishing neither to free her, nor condemn her, set up a Commission to investigate the murder of Darnley. Melville was present at its deliberations in both York and Hampton Court.

Following this last journey, although Melville travelled extensively between the royal palaces and castles in Scotland, he refused all commissions to travel further than Berwick. He spent as much time as he could at his home of Halhill, near Collessie, in Fife, where he was buried in 1617 in a Church where his vault, built by him in 1609, may still be seen, following extensive restoration. The inscription on the tomb reads (with a couple of interpolations where the text is unclear)

> *Ye loadin pilgrims passing langs this way*
>
> *Pans [think] on your fall your offences past*
>
> *How your frail flesh first formit of the clay*
>
> *In dust mon [must] be desovit at the last*
>
> *Repent amen on Christ the burden cast*
>
> *Of your sad sinnes who can your sauls [souls] refresh*
>
> *Syne [since] rais from grave to gloir your grislie flesh*

Defyle not Christs kirk with your carrion

A solemn seat for Gods service prepared

For prayer preaching and communion

Your burial should be in the kirkyard

On your uprising set your great regard

When saul and body ioynes [joins] with joy to ring

In heave for ay [ever] with Christ over head and king.'

The question of whether burial should take place in the Church (Catholic practice) or the Churchyard (Protestant practice) was a vexed one at the time, and Melville is confirming his Protestant views.

Key to Map

1. Raith, Fife, Scotland
2. Dumbarton Castle, Clyde & Ayrshire, Scotland
3. Stirling Castle, Stirling, Scotland
4. Falkland Palace, Fife, Scotland
5. Newcastle, Tyne & Wear, England
6. Hampton Court, nr Kingston, England
7. St Johnston, nr Perth, Perthshire, Scotland
8. Edinburgh Castle, Edinburgh, Scotland
9. Westminster Palace, London, England
10. Holyrood Palace, Edinburgh, Scotland
11. Haddington, East Lothian, Scotland
12. Berwick-upon-Tweed, Northumberland, England
13. Greenwich, London, England
14. York, North Yorkshire, England
15. Halhill, Collessie, Fife, Scotland

Chapter 188: Book Review

There are no biographies about James Melville himself, so we have chosen a third account of the reign of Mary, Queen of Scots to compare with the other two, previously reviewed ('*My Heart is My Own*' by John Guy on page 253 and '*Crown of Thistles*' by Linda Porter on page 384). In '*The Challenge to the Crown*', Robert Stedall brings a different perspective to events.

The Challenge to the Crown: The Struggle for Influence in the Reign of Mary, Queen of Scots 1542 – 1567

Author: Robert Stedall

Publisher: The Book Guild Ltd

In a nutshell A detailed analysis of the plots, and counterplots that characterised the reign of Mary, Queen of Scots, with credible insight into the complex motivations of those involved.

Mr Stedall did not begin his career as a professional historian, but that does not handicap his ability to pick his way through the complex politics at the court of Mary, Queen of Scots. He begins the narrative with a description of the situation in Scotland in the early 1540s – the King dead, the struggle for the Regency, and the looming threat of England. He then carries us into France with the little Queen, sent there for safety, aged 5. Stedall covers Mary's childhood and education in some detail. There is useful information about the politics of France, peppered with some of the more scandalous details of the French courts' love affairs, and background about Catherine de Medici.

He examines the political implications of the marriage of Mary to the Dauphin of Scotland, and that the ceding of the Crown Matrimonial to François meant that Mary's natural heir, the Duke of Chatelherault, and his son the Earl of Arran were given a reason to join the Lords of the Congregation in their opposition to the Regency of Mary's mother. As Mary grew to adulthood in France, Scotland's elite, with the exception of her mother, the Queen-Regent, were turning away from the Auld Alliance with Catholic France, and seeking to join in common cause with Protestant England.

Stedwall gives an excellent summary of the position in Scotland and the alignment of the various factions on Mary's return as a widow from France. He makes it clear that combination in factions was not just a religious matter. The Catholic Huntly and the Protestant Bothwell were both opposed to the Protestant Moray, who was pro an alliance with England. Stedall, unlike many other writers, believes that Moray always entertained ambitions to snatch his half-sister's throne, but was willing to content himself with being her chief advisor, until the advent of her second husband, Lord Darnley.

In describing her reign, Stedall concludes that Mary, whilst clever and astute in many ways, and adept at gathering personal support '*showed political naivety and a misjudgement of people*'. He also convincingly demonstrates that her marriage to Darnley was a headstrong act, undertaken almost entirely without support from any of her nobles and saddled her with a fatal liability.

Stedall takes a different approach to the murder of Rizzio, from that espoused by John Guy in '*My Heart is My Own*'. (see page 253). It is Stedall's contention that Darnley intended Mary and their unborn child to die after the shock of witnessing the murder, with the goal of claiming the Crown himself, through his own Stewart blood (although the Duke of Chatelherault was widely accepted as the next heir).

The narrative of Darnley's death is complex, as the subject itself is complex. Stedall's view is that Mary was innocent of the murder, and the whole plot was masterminded by Moray from start to finish, with Bothwell being manipulated into thinking it his own idea, and actually arranging it. Mary is shown as walking into the trap of appearing to be complicit in the murder of Darnley and her apparent abduction, by being too shamed by having slept with Bothwell (whether willingly or not) to refuse to marry him. Stedall concludes, however, that Mary's own failure to listen to sensible advice, and her stupidity in marrying Bothwell, despite it being evident that he had been involved in Darnley's murder, were the ultimate causes of her downfall.

This first volume in a two-volume work ends with Mary's deposition and Moray's acceptance as Regent.

Stendall's style is readable, and I received the impression that he knew the details of his subject well. Where the writer's inexperience perhaps shows is in a few places where the narrative becomes confused. Occasionally, lots of pronouns rather than names mean it is unclear exactly who was doing what to whom – the tendency of all the participants in the politics of the 1550s and 1560s to change sides and betray each other making it difficult to infer the identities from the context.

Annoyingly, the Kindle version of the book has jumbled footnotes that merge into the text.

General Bibliography

The works listed below were consulted for several of the Profiles with more specific works related to the individuals listed under their names.

Accounts of the Treasurer of Scotland: v. 5-8:. Edinburgh: H.M. General Register House, 1877

Calendar of State Papers: Domestic Series: Edward VI, 1547-1553. United Kingdom: Stationery Office Books.

Calendar of State Papers: Domestic: Mary I 1553-1558. London: Public Record Office.

Calendar of State Papers Simancas, British History Online (HMSO, 1892) Hume, Martin A S, ed.,

Calendar of State Papers: Venice <http://www.british-history.ac.uk/cal-state-papers/venice/vol2/vii-lxi> [accessed 7 October 2015]

Cecil Papers, http://www.british-history.ac.uk/cal-cecil-papers (Accessed: 7 September 2015)

Letters and Papers, Foreign and Domestic, of the Reign of Henry VIII: Preserved in the Public Record Office, the British Museum, and Elsewhere in England (United Kingdom: British History Online, 2014) https://www.british-history.ac.uk/letters-papers-hen8/ Brewer, John Sherren, and James Gairdner,

Childs, Jessie, *God's Traitors: Terror and Faith in Elizabethan England* (United States: Oxford University Press, USA, 2014)

De Lisle, Leanda, *Tudor: The Family Story* (United Kingdom: Chatto & Windus, 2013)

De Lisle, Leanda, *The Sisters Who Would Be Queen the Tragedy of Mary, Katherine, & Lady Jane Grey* (Glasgow: HarperCollins e-books, 2008)

Drummond, William, ed., *The History of Scotland from the Year 1423 until the Year 1542, Containing the Lives and Reigns of James I, II, III, IV and V* (London: H Hills for R Tomlins and himself, 1655)

Ellis, Henry, *Original Letters, Illustrative of English History: Including Numerous Royal Letters: From Autographs in the British Museum, the State Paper Office, and One or Two Other Collections.*, 1st edn (New York: Printed for Harding, Triphook, & Lepard, 1824)

Foxe, John, *The Acts and Monuments of John Foxe: A New and Complete Edition: With a Preliminary Dissertation by the Rev. George Townsend* (London: R.R. Seeley and W. Burnside, 1837)

Fraser, Antonia, *Mary Queen of Scots* (London: HarperCollins Publishers, 1970)

Hall, Edward, *Hall's Chronicle.* (S.l.: Ams Press, 1909)

Hayward, Maria, ed., *The Great Wardrobe Accounts of Henry VII and Henry VIII* (United Kingdom: London Record Society, 2012)

Holinshed, Raphael, *Holinshed's Chronicles of England, Scotland & Ireland* (United Kingdom: AMS Press, 1997)

Ives, Eric, *Lady Jane Grey: A Tudor Mystery*, 1st edn (United Kingdom: Wiley-Blackwell (an imprint of John Wiley & Sons Ltd), 2012)

Jerdan, William, ed., *Rutland Papers. Original Documents Illustrative of the Courts and Times of Henry VII. and Henry VIII. Selected from the Private Archives of His Grace the Duke of Rutland* (Leopold Classic Library, 2015)

Lemon, Robert, ed., *Calendar of State Papers: Domestic Series: Edward, Mary and Elizabeth*, British History Online (London: HMSO, 1856)

Marshall, R. K. (2003) *Scottish Queens 1034 - 1714*. United Kingdom: Tuckwell Press.

Marshall, Rosalind Kay, *Queen Mary's Women: Female Relatives, Servants, Friends and Enemies of Mary, Queen of Scots* (Edinburgh: John Donald Publishers, 2006)

Morse H., *Select Documents Of English Constitutional History*, ed. by George Burton Adams and Morse H Stephens (United States: Kessinger Publishing, 2007)

Oliver, Neil: *A History of Scotland* (Phoenix PR, 2011)

Pitcairn, Robert: *Criminal Trials in Scotland from AD 1488 to AD 1624* (Edinburgh: William Tait, 1833)

Records of the Parliaments of Scotland <http://www.rps.ac.uk/> [accessed 17 September 2015]

Porter, Linda, *Crown of Thistles: The Fatal Inheritance of Mary Queen of Scots* (United Kingdom: Macmillan, 2013)

Strickland, Agnes: *Lives Of The Queens Of Scotland And English Princesses: Connected With The Regal Succession Of Great Britain* (Harper & Brothers, 1859), i & ii

Strype, John, Annals of the Reformation and Establishment of Religion and Other Various Occurrences in the Church of England Etc. (Oxford: Clarendon Press, 1824),

Vergil, Polydore, *Anglica Historia AD 1485-1637* (Royal Historical, 1950)

Weir, Alison, *Henry VIII: King and Court* (London: Jonathan Cape, 2001)

Williams, Neville, *Henry VIII and His Court*. (London: Littlehampton Book Services, 1971)

Williams, Neville, *The Cardinal and the Secretary: Thomas Wolsey and Thomas Cromwell* (United States: Macmillan, 1976)

Katherine Parr

Fraser, Antonia, *The Six Wives of Henry VIII*, First (London: Weidenfeld & Nicolson, 1992)

James, Susan E., *Catherine Parr: Henry VIII's Last Love* (United Kingdom: Tempus Publishing, 2008)

Norton, Elizabeth, *Catherine Parr* (United Kingdom: Casemate Pub & Book Dist, 2010)

Porter, Linda, *Katherine the Queen: The Remarkable Life of Katherine Parr*, Kindle (Macmillan, 2010)

Starkey, David, *Six Wives of Henry VIII* (London: Vintage, 2004)

Thornton, Tim, 'Henry VIII's Progress Through Yorkshire in 1541 and Its Implications for Northern Identities', *Northern History*, 46 (2009), 231–44 http://dx.doi.org/10.1179/174587009x452323

Weir, Alison, *The Six Wives of Henry VIII*, 1st edn (London: Random House UK Distribution, 1991)

James IV

Charters and Documents Relating to the City of Glasgow 1175 - 1649, *British History Online* <http://www.british-history.ac.uk/glasgow-charters/1175-1649/no2/pp79-87> [accessed 17 September 2015]

http://www.nas.gov.uk/downloads/jamesIIIDeath.pdf [accessed 17 September 2015]

Goodwin, George, *Fatal Rivalry, Flodden 1513: Henry VIII, James IV and the Battle for Renaissance Britain,* ebook (London: Weidenfeld & Nicolson)

Harris, George, *James IV: Scotland's Renaissance King* (Lectures in Scottish History Book 4), Kindle, 2013

Lang, Andrew, *The History of Scotland from the Roman Occupation: Vol III C. 79 - 1545*, 3rd edn (New York: Dodd, Mead & Co., 1903)

Lindsay of Pitscottie, Robert, *Pitscottie's Chronicles of Scotland*, ed. by Ae. J. G Mackay (Edinburgh: Blackwood for the Society, 1911)

Marshall, Rosalind Kay, *Scottish Queens 1034 - 1714* (United Kingdom: Tuckwell Press, 2003)

Perry, Maria, *Sisters to the King*, 2nd edn (Andre Deutsch, 2002)

Pitcairn, Robert, *Criminal Trials in Scotland from AD 1488 to AD 1624* (Edinburgh: William Tait, 1833)

Reese, Peter, *Flodden: A Scottish Tragedy (Birlinn)* (Edinburgh: Birlinn Publishers, 2003)

Reid, Stuart, *Battles of the Scottish Lowlands* (Barnsley: Pen & Sword Military, 2004)

Strickland, Agnes, Lives Of The Queens Of Scotland And English Princesses V2: Connected With The Regal Succession Of Great Britain (Harper & Brothers, 1859), i & ii

Treasurer, Scotland. Scottish Record Office, and Thomas Dickson, *Accounts of the Lord High Treasurer of Scotland: Compota Thesaurariorum Regum Scotorum* (Edinburgh: H.M. General Register House, 1877)

Lady Margaret Pole

Dodds, M. H. and Dodds, R. (1971) *The Pilgrimage of Grace, 1536-1537 and the Exeter Conspiracy, 1538*. London: Frank Cass Publishers.

Fletcher, A. and Vernon, L. (1973) *Tudor Rebellions (Seminar Studies in History)*. 2nd edn. Harlow: Longman.

Jones, D. (2014) *The Hollow Crown: The Wars of the Roses and the Rise of The Tudors*. 1st edn. United Kingdom: Faber & Faber Non-Fiction.

Pierce, H. (2009) *Margaret Pole, Countess of Salisbury: 1473 - 1541: loyalty, lineage and leadership*. Cardiff: University of Wales Press.

Strickland, A. and Strickland, E. (2011) *Lives of the Queens of England from the Norman Conquest: Volume 3 & 4*. United Kingdom: Cambridge University Press (Virtual Publishing).

Tremlett, G. (2010) *Catherine of Aragon: Henry's Spanish Queen*. London: Faber and Faber.

Whitelock, A. (2010) *Mary Tudor: princess, bastard, queen*. 1st edn. New York: Random House Publishing Group.

Thomas Wolsey

Cavendish, George, *Life of Cardinal Wolsey* (Forgotten Books 2009)

Creighton, Mandell, *Cardinal Wolsey* (Bibliolife 28 Jan 2009)

Gwyn, Peter, *The King's Cardinal: The Rise and Fall of Thomas Wolsey* (Pimlico 1992)

Matusiak, John, *Wolsey: The Life of King Henry VIII's Cardinal* (United Kingdom: The History Press Ltd, 2015)

Ridley, Jasper, *Statesman and the Fanatic: Thomas Wolsey and Thomas More* London Constable 1982

Scarisbrick, J. J., *Henry VIII (Yale English Monarchs Series)* (Yale University Press 2 April 1997)

Starkey, David, *The Reign of Henry VIII: Personalities and Politics* (Vintage 3 October 2002)

Marie of Guise

Guy, J. (2004) *My Heart is My Own: the Life of Mary Queen of Scots*. London: Harper Perennial.

Porter, L. (2013) *Crown of Thistles: The Fatal Inheritance of Mary Queen of Scots*. United Kingdom: Macmillan.

Ritchie, P. E. (2002) *Mary of Guise in Scotland, 1548-1560: A Political Study*. United Kingdom: Tuckwell Press.

Thornton, T. (2009) *Henry VIII's Progress Through Yorkshire in 1541 and its Implications for Northern Identities, Northern History*, 46(2), pp. 231–244. doi: 10.1179/174587009x452323.

Thomas Cromwell

Select Documents Of English Constitutional History, ed. by George Burton Adams and Morse H Stephens (United States: Kessinger Publishing, 2007)

Borman, Tracy, *Thomas Cromwell: The Untold Story of Henry VIII's Most Faithful Servant* (United Kingdom: Hodder & Stoughton, 2014)

Cavendish, George, *Life of Cardinal Wolsey* (George Routledge & Sons, 1890)

Creighton, Mandell, *Cardinal Wolsey* (Barnes & Noble Digital Library) (United States: Barnes & Noble)

Everett, Michael, *The Rise of Thomas Cromwell: Power and Politics in the Reign of Henry VIII 1485 - 1534,* Kindle (New Haven and London: Yale University Press, 2015)

Gwyn, Peter, *The King's Cardinal: The Rise and Fall of Thomas Wolsey* (United Kingdom: Barrie & Jenkins, 1990)

Hutchinson, Robert, *Thomas Cromwell: The Rise and Fall of Henry VIII's Most Notorious Minister* (London: Weidenfeld & Nicolson, 2007)

Merriman, Roger Bigelow, *Life and Letters of Thomas Cromwell: 2 Volumes* (Oxford Scholarly Classics) (Oxford: Oxford University Press, USA, 1901)

Starkey, David, *The Reign of Henry VIII: Personalities and Politics* (United Kingdom: Trafalgar Square, 1991)

Williams, Neville, The Cardinal and the Secretary: Thomas Wolsey and Thomas Cromwell (United States: Macmillan, 1975)

Lady Penelope Devereux

Butler, M. *The Court Masque*, The Cambridge Edition of the Works of Ben Johnson - Online Edition (2015)

Doran, S. *The Tudor Chronicles*. (London: Quercus Publishing Plc, 2008)

Doran, S. *Elizabeth I and her Circle* 1st edn. (Oxford: OUP, 2015)

Varlow, S. *The Lady Penelope: The Lost Tale of Love and Politics in the Court of Elizabeth I* (London: Andre Deutsch. 2008)

Warnicke, R. M. *Wicked Women of Tudor England: Queens, Aristocrats, Commoners* (New York, NY: Palgrave Macmillan, 2012)

Woudhuysen, H. R. *Philip Sidney and the Circulation of Manuscripts, 1558-1640* (New York: Oxford University Press, 1996)

James V

Coltman, Dayle, and Gordon Donaldso:, *The Edinburgh History of Scotland: James V-James VII v. 3* (The Edinburgh History of Scotland) (Edinburgh: Hyperion Books, 1998)

De Nicolay, Nicolas: *The Navigation of James V Round Scotland, the Orkney Isles and the Hebrides or Western Isles*

Eaves, Richard Glen: *Henry VIII and James V's Regency, 1524-1528: A Study in Anglo-Scottish Diplomacy* (Lanham: University Press of America, 1987)

Gibb, George Duncan: *The Life and Times of Robert Gib. Lord of Caribber, Famililar Servitor and Master of the Stable to King James V of Scotland* (London: Longmans, Green & Co., 1874)

Hotle, Patrick C.: *Thorns and Thistles: Diplomacy between Henry VIII and James V, 1528-1542* (Lanham, MD: University Press of America, 1996)

Keith, Robert: *History of the Affairs of Church and State in Scotland from the Beginning of the Reformation to the Year 1568* (Edinburgh: Spottiswoode, 1844),

Perry, Maria: *Sisters to the King*, 2nd edn (Andre Deutsch, 2002)

Lady Katherine Grey

Borman, Tracy, *Elizabeth's Women: The Hidden Story of the Virgin Queen*, Kindle (London: Jonathan Cape, 2009)

De Lisle, Leanda, *The Sisters Who Would Be Queen: the Tragedy of Mary, Katherine, & Lady Jane Grey* (Glasgow: HarperCollins e-books, 2008)

Durant, David N. *Bess of Hardwick: Portrait of an Elizabethan Dynast*, 1st edn (London: Weidenfield and Nicolson, 1977).

Hoby, Sir Thomas, *The Travels and Life of Sir Thomas Hoby Kt of Bisham Abbey, Written by Himself 1547 - 1564*, ed. by Edgar Powell (London: Royal Historical Society, 1902)

Ives, Eric, *Lady Jane Grey: A Tudor Mystery*, 1st edn (United Kingdom: Wiley-Blackwell (an imprint of John Wiley & Sons Ltd), 2012)

Sidney, Philip, *'Jane the Quene': Being Some Account of the Life and Literary Remains of Lady Jane Dudley, Commonly Called Lady Jane Grey* (London: Swann, Sonneschein and Co., 1900)

Weir, Alison, *Elizabeth, the Queen,* Kindle (London: Random House UK, 2009)

Whitelock, Anna, *Elizabeth's Bedfellows*, Kindle (London: Bloomsbury Publishing plc, 2013)

Whitelock, Anna, *Mary Tudor: England's First Queen*, Kindle (London: Bloomsbury Publishing plc, 2010)

Sir William Cecil

Alford, Stephen, *Burghley: William Cecil at the Court of Elizabeth I* (London: Yale University Press, 2008)

Charlton, W B, *Burghley* (Stamford, Lincs: W. Langley, 1847)

Danner, Bruce, *Edmund Spenser's War on Lord Burghley* (Houndmills, Basingstoke, Hampshire: Palgrave Macmillan, 2011)

Guy, John, *Elizabeth and Cecil*, <http://www.tudors.org/undergraduate/elizabeth-and-cecil/> [accessed 6 September 2015]

Higham, C S S, *Wimbledon Manor House under the Cecils* (Longmans Green & Co. Ltd, 1962)

Lettenhove, Kervyn de, ed., *Relations Politiques Des Pays-Bas et d'Angleterre* (Brussels: L'Academie Royale de Belgique, 1882)

Marshall, Rosalind K, *John Knox* (Edinburgh: Birlinn, 2008)

Ross, Josephine, *Suitors to the Queen: The Men in the Life of Elizabeth I of England*, 1st edn (New York: Coward, McCann & Geoghegan, 1975)

Simms, Brendan, Europe: The Struggle for Supremacy, from 1453 to the Present (United States: Basic Books, 2014)

Skelton, R A, and John Summerson, A Description of Maps and Architectural Drawings in the Collection Made by William Cecil, First Baron Burghley, Now at Hatfield House (Oxford: Oxford Press, 1971)

Whitelock, Anna, *Elizabeth's Bedfellows*, Kindle (London: Bloomsbury Publishing PLC, 2013)

Williams, Neville, *The Life and Times of Elizabeth I* (New York: Welcome Rain Publishers, 1998)

Wimbledon Common Committee, ed., *Extracts from the Court Rolls of the Manor of Wimbledon from Edward IV to AD 1864* (London: Wyman and Sons, 1866)

Lady Margaret Douglas

Ambassdes de Messieurs de Noailles En Anglettere, 5 vols., 1783

Bingham, Caroline, *Darnley: A Life of Henry Stuart, Lord Darnley, Consort of Mary Queen of Scots* (London: Constable, 1995)

Brigden, Susan, *Thomas Wyatt: The Heart's Forest*, 1st edn (London: Faber and Faber, 2012)

Cotton. MS Caligula, B III. Fol 273. (n.d.).

Cotton MS Caligula B II Fol. 283. (n.d.).

Cotton MS Caligula B VI Fol 119b'

Cotton MS Vesp F XIII Fol. 138 (n.d)

Durant, David N. *Bess of Hardwick: Portrait of an Elizabethan Dynast*, 1st edn (London: Distributed in the USA by Dufour Editions, 1999)

Footer, Donald *Women's Works: 900 - 1550*, 1st edn (New York: Wicked Good Books, 2013)

Fraser, William, *The Douglas Book*, 4 vols. (Edinburgh, 1885)

Leslie, John, The History of Scotland: From the Death of King James I, in the Year 1436 to 1561 (United States: Kessinger Publishing, 2007)

Shulman, Nicola, *Graven with Diamonds: The Many Lives of Thomas Wyatt: Courtier, Poet, Assassin, Spy* (London: Short Books, 2011)

Weir, Alison, *The Lost Tudor Princess* (London: Jonathan Cape 2015)

Sir James Melville

http://www.scottishgraveyards.org.uk/downloads/16Collessie.pdf> [accessed 9 November 2015]

Calendar of Border Papers: Volume 1, 1560-95 <http://www.british-history.ac.uk/cal-border-papers/vol1/> [accessed 12 November 2015]

Calendar of State Papers: Scotland <http://www.british-history.ac.uk/cal-state-papers/scotland> [accessed 10 November 2015]

Knox, John, *The Works of John Knox* Vols 1 - 6, ed. by David Laing (United Kingdom: James Thin, 1895)

MacDonald, Stuart, *The Witches of Fife: Witch-Hunting in a Scottish Shire 1560 - 1710*, Kindle (Edinburgh: John Donald Publishers, 2002)

Melville, James Sir and Donaldson, Gordon (ed), *The Memoirs of Sir James Melville of Halhill, Containing an Impartial Account of the Most Remarkable Affairs of State during the Sixteenth Century Not*

Mentioned by Other Historians, More Particularly Relating to the Kingdoms of England and Scotland under the reigns of Queen Elizabeth, Mary Queen of Scots and King James (London: Folio Society, 1969)

Sadler, Sir Ralph, *The State Papers and Letters of Sir Ralph Sadler in 3 Volumes*, ed. by Arthur Clifford (Edinburgh: Archibald Constable & Co., 1809)

Stedall, Robert, *The Challenge to the Crown: The Struggle for Influence in the Reign of Mary, Queen of Scots 1542 - 1567*, 1st edn (Sussex, England: Book Guild Publishing, 2012)

Thomson, John Maitland, ed., *The Register of the Great Seal of Scotland* (Edinburgh: HM General Register House, 1894)

www.tudortimes.co.uk

www.ingramcontent.com/pod-product-compliance
Lightning Source LLC
Chambersburg PA
CBHW021822220426
43663CB00005B/98